The Smalltalk Developer's Guide to VisualWorks

ADVANCES IN OBJECT TECHNOLOGY SERIES

Dr. Richard S. Wiener
Series Editor

Editor
Journal of Object-Oriented Programming
Report on Object Analysis and Design
SIGS Publications, Inc.
New York, New York

and

Department of Computer Science
University of Colorado
Colorado Springs, Colorado

Additional Volumes in Preparation

The Smalltalk Developer's Guide to VisualWorks

Tim Howard

Independent Consultant
Dallas, Texas

SIGS
BOOKS

New York

Library of Congress Cataloging-in-Publication Data

Howard, Tim, 1962–
    The Smalltalk developer's guide to VisualWorks / Tim Howard.
      p. cm. -- (Advances in object technology ; 9)
    Includes index.
    ISBN 1-884842-11-9 (ppbk. : alk. paper)
    1. Object-oriented programming (Computer science) 2. Smalltalk
(Computer program language) 3. VisualWorks.   I. Title.
II. Series.
    QA76.64.H68 1995
    005.13'3--dc20
                                                        95-16526
                                                           CIP

PUBLISHED BY
SIGS Books
71 W. 23rd Street, Third Floor
New York, New York 10010

Design and composition by Susan Culligan, Pilgrim Road, Ltd. Set in Bembo.
Cover design by Jean Cohn.
Printed on acid-free paper.

SIGS Books ISBN 1–884842–11–9
Prentice Hall ISBN 0-13-442526-X

Printed in the United States of America
99 98 97 96 95   10 9 8 7 6 5 4 3 2 1
First Printing August 1995

About the Author

Tᴵᴹ Hᴏᴡᴀʀᴅ is president and cofounder of FH Protocol, Inc., Dallas, Texas, a Smalltalk training and consulting company. He has been developing software applications for eight years and has been working with *VisualWorks* since its initial beta release. He focuses primarily on extending and enhancing *VisualWorks* and on creating frameworks to facilitate the development of robust applications. Over the years, Howard has acted as Smalltalk consultant, mentor, and program developer for companies such as Advanced Micro Devices, Hewlett-Packard, Northern Telecom, Sprint, and Texaco.

Howard holds master's degrees in industrial engineering (1990) and in business administration (1989) from Texas A&M University, College Station, Texas. He has lectured on topics such as forecasting, inventory control, quality control, mathematical modeling, nonlinear optimization, probability and statistics, and distribution management. He has developed introductory courses and seminars for both Smalltalk and *VisualWorks,* and he mentors other programmers in application development. He has been published in the *Journal of Object-Oriented Programming* and is a columnist for the *Smalltalk Report* (SIGS Publications).

Foreword

THE PARCPLACE *VisualWorks* system was designed for the professional Smalltalk programmer. It consists of a "layered architecture," layered by the roles played by the objects that comprise the system. The particular roles were chosen to support the everyday needs of programmers who wish to build graphical interactive applications, alone or with their friends and colleagues. As such, roles range from representing data elements expected of a software programming system, to accessing and creating software elements, to providing the initial framework of a use interface or business application. A large part of the effort in designing *VisualWorks* involved decisions as to how to assign roles to specific Smalltalk objects so that these roles could be reused by programmers easily and effectively. An even larger part of this effort was to define the roles so that they were beginnings rather than endings; that is, so that they provided a general set of capabilities that could be combined and refined by the programmer in solving a systems building problem.

In the beginning of the invention of Smalltalk, the roles and therefore objects of interest provided support for basic data structures, number systems, lines and text and bitmapped images to be drawn on a computer display, and storage of commands for making use of objects—that is, class descriptions, methods, and non-sequential processing. A critical decision was made to factor the roles for presentation and interaction with displayed information, from the roles for the purpose of describing the underlying application semantics. The purpose of such factoring was to allow reuse of the application semantics with different forms of textual, numeric, and graphical presentation, and to allow reuse of these various presentations with different techniques for interaction by which the user could query and modify the content and form of the presentation. This particular factoring idea was called model–view–controller (or MVC), naming the three kinds of objects that the programmer combines to create an application. MVC relied on a simple mechanism for dependency by which changes in a model would be broadcast to interested other objects, notably so that the changes would be reflected in multiple views of the model.

Interest in Smalltalk programming grew with the growing availability of and access to personal client workstations with high-resolution graphical capability. Smalltalk became of greater interest as programmers started to tackle more complex systems, building problems, and came to realize that objects offered assistance in organizing the inherent complexity of the resultant solutions. Smalltalk's pure object model, along with its tools supporting the re-use of customizable sets of objects, offered a programming context that proved easier to learn for the highly skilled business programmer familiar with COBOL or Basic and more likely to create maintainable results than possible with other object-based or object-oriented offerings. The original Smalltalk development environment evolved with the changing needs of these new programmers, notably to provide a framework for porting applications across hardware/operating system/windowing system platforms, and to provide a framework for creating graphical interfaces to applications without a deep understanding of MVC.

These software frameworks were designed based on several ideas. First, create an applications programming interface (API) specification, supported by a general set of objects that worked together to create a general solution but that could be customized to deal with differences in hardware platforms, operating systems, windowing systems, graphical widgetry for visualization and interaction, and database storage. Second, focus the developer on specifying how the software should work and then, where possible, generate the customization of the APIs. In this way, the professional developers can focus on creating the less generic aspect of their systems—the objects representing business semantics. And third, allow the developer to programmatically customize any of the objects that represent the generic application-support solutions, such as how the business objects give and get information from objects representing views and controllers, and which visual techniques must appear in every application. To meet these requirements, *VisualWorks* introduced some general mechanisms, for linking aspects of a business model to the logic that determines what use the application should make of these aspects of the model, and for creating dependencies among applications parts. The first mechanism is supported by Application Models, and the second is embodied in a set of objects called Value Models and another called Aspect Adaptors.

VisualWorks contains a painter by which the developer draws the layout of an application's user interface—literally, the developer takes visual widgets from a palette of reusable objects and paints a canvas. A set of canvases provides the specification of an application's graphical user interface, which is then linked via Application Models, Value Models, and Aspect Adaptors to a model of the business semantics and business data underlying the application. Objects that play the roles of business objects, application logic, dependency relations, visual techniques, and so on, are important contributors to the Smalltalk developer's ability to create software quickly and robustly. Understanding the *VisualWorks* architecture, and how these objects work together, enhances the developer's ability to use *VisualWorks*. Tim Howard's intent in writing *The Smalltalk Developer's Guide to VisualWorks* is to take the reader on a whirlwind tour of the details behind the scenes in order to make developing with *VisualWorks* more effective and more enjoyable.

—Adele Goldberg

Preface

IF YOU WANT to fully master a topic, you must continually revisit the fundamentals. An expert is not necessarily one who is well versed in the most complex aspects of a subject, but one who genuinely understands the fundamentals upon which the more complex parts are founded. It is only with such an understanding that one can offer creative and original solutions to difficult problems. It is with this perspective that I originally endeavored to write this book. The major premise of this book is that an investment in analyzing *VisualWorks* in terms of fundamental Smalltalk concepts will pay tremendous dividends in terms of better application development and a generally more powerful tool.

I have to admit that this is somewhat a contrarian approach. One of the intended purposes of a tool such as *VisualWorks* is to remove the developer from having to be concerned with the lower level details of application development. This book takes the position that having minimal concern for such details is one thing, and being ignorant of them is something else. Developers who use *VisualWorks* should have a good appreciation for how the tool works in terms of fundamental Smalltalk concepts. Just as people who use calculators should never forget how to do arithmetic!

It is intended that this book appeal to readers on many levels. First, as stated above, this book is meant to be a thorough description of the *VisualWorks* environment in terms of fundamental Smalltalk concepts with the intention of exploiting such knowledge to customize the tool and enhance application development. Second, this book can be used as a guide to practical solutions to very common and general *VisualWorks* problems. Third, there are plenty of tutorials which demonstrate how to go about solving problems in *VisualWorks* and which set good examples for Smalltalk development in general. Fourth, this book can serve as a reference for *VisualWorks* terms and concepts which might not otherwise be adequately explained. Finally, this book is a source of enhancements to the *VisualWorks* environment that can be filed in and used without even reading much of the book at all!

This book has a somewhat hidden agenda as well. There is a very sincere effort to introduce a certain amount of rigor and consistency in the terminology used in Smalltalk and *VisualWorks*. Much of the existing literature is both sloppy and inconsistent. Following this introduction is a section dedicated to a thorough discussion of conventions and terminology. This having been said, it should be mentioned that from time to time, certain liberties are taken with respect to both conventions and technical accuracy in the greater interests of simplicity and readability.

This is an intermediate book and is not intended for beginning Smalltalk developers. As a minimum, the reader should be comfortable with using the system tools such as the Browser and Inspector, and be able to create simple *VisualWorks* applications. The reader is expected to already have an appreciation for what *VisualWorks* is about and to have a working knowledge of most of its tools and features. In addition, the reader is also expected to be familiar with certain terms and phrases specific to OOP and Smalltalk, such as hierarchy, class, superclass, subclass, instance, method, and message.

This book comes with an accompanying diskette which provides a great deal of source code and examples to be worked by the reader using a special browser called the Examples Browser. These examples are designed to reinforce the concepts covered in the book. The examples are provided in a browser instead of directly in the text of the book for two reasons. First, including the examples in the book text would add some two hundred pages to the content. Second, by providing the examples in a browser, the reader does not have to waste time typing—merely read the example text and inspect on, or evaluate the Smalltalk code already provided in the example. Appendix A discusses loading the disk onto the host machine and installing the Examples Browser and the other source code.

The book is divided into two parts. Part I is the description of how *VisualWorks* is implemented in Smalltalk and Part II is a demonstration of the value that such an education affords the developer. Part I consists of Chapters 1 through 8. Chapter 1 begins with the fundamental concepts of MVC upon which the implementation of *VisualWorks* is founded. The intention here is that a thorough understanding of MVC is a prerequisite for any real understanding of *VisualWorks*. Chapter 2 uses the concepts of MVC in describing the *VisualWorks* components which are the fundamental building blocks of a *VisualWorks* interface. Chapter 3 talks about the very special object called the builder and how it builds an interface from a set of specifications describing the intended interface. In Chapter 4, the application model is introduced. This chapter explains how an application model employs a builder to build an interface and it also covers the issue of modal dialogs. Chapter 5 introduces the concept of subcanvases and describes this feature in terms of the material covered in the previous chapters. Chapter 6 is a discussion of windows and all of their special state and behavior. Chapters 7 and 8 look at the tools of *VisualWorks* as applications. That is, these chapters are not a discussion on how to use the tools but how the tools themselves are designed and implemented as *VisualWorks* applications.

Part II is more or less the payoff for having worked through Part I. It demonstrates what can be accomplished when one has a thorough understanding of the implementation of *VisualWorks*. There is no real logical flow to the information presented in Part II and the chapters can be covered out of sequence. The one exception to this is that the material in Chapter 11 depends on the material presented in Chapter 10 and therefore Chapter 11 must necessarily follow Chapter 10. While Part II assumes that the reader has covered Part I, it is written with the understanding that some readers may skip ahead. Therefore, the reader who is not sufficiently motivated to work through Part I may very well start with Part II; however, the intended benefits will be somewhat diluted. Part II begins with Chapter 9 which is mostly a mixed bag of tips, tricks, and techniques which may be of interest to most *VisualWorks* developers. Chapter 10 enhances application development by creating an abstract subclass of ApplicationModel which adds several features to facilitate application model development. Chapter 11 continues with this idea by creating yet another abstract subclass which provides an easy mechanism for developing application models which act as the interface for purely domain objects. Chapter 12 provides a generalized and rigorous approach to adding new components to the palette. It is also the first chapter to include a tutorial which the reader is expected to work. Chapters 13 and 14 are demonstrations of how easy it is to extend the tools of *VisualWorks* to fit the needs of the developer and further facilitate application development. Both of these chapters are tutorial in nature. Chapter 15 presents a high level discussion of some additional tools which have been developed using *VisualWorks* and the full source is available on the accompanying disk.

I would like to mention that I believe Chapters 10 and 11 are by far the most valuable chapters in the book. The material covered in these chapters will be of tremendous benefit to anyone developing applications in *VisualWorks*. If the reader does nothing else, he or she should at least cover these two chapters.

While it is important to know what this book is about, it is equally important to know what it is not about! This book is not meant to be a discourse on application development. It is not the intention of this book to discuss strategies of application development using *VisualWorks* or to demonstrate how to take a design and implement it using *VisualWorks*. However, after mastering the material in this book, the reader should be much better prepared to attack such problems and more proficient at generating creative solutions. This book does not cover the database related tools of *VisualWorks* because the original charter of this book intended to remain neutral on matters of persistent store. Finally this book is not meant to interfere with or replace the *Visual-*

Works manuals provided by ParcPlace. Instead, this book tries to augment the material provided in the manuals and at the same time minimize any redundancies.

I would like to thank Adele Goldberg, of ParcPlace Systems; Wilf LaLonde, of the Object People; Howard Fultz, of FH Protocol, Inc.; Marni Holcomb, of Northern Telecom; Paul Johnson, of Rothwell International; John Keenan, of Set Point; and Bill Kohl, of Rothwell International for their input and technical review of the material.

Conventions and Terminology

IN A BOOK such as this, it is necessary to provide certain conventions in terminology and type set. This is especially true for Smalltalk which is still a non-standard computing language/environment. What follows are the conventions adopted by this book to provide consistency and readability. Whenever possible, the chosen conventions have been extracted from the *VisualWorks* manuals for consistency. Other conventions are used because of their historical significance or for reasons of convenience.

Throughout the book there will be a few exceptions to some of these conventions. Typically these exceptions are made in the interest of readability. A strict adherence to the conventions can sometimes lead to a somewhat convoluted statement. In such cases, liberties are taken which may sacrifice a small amount of technical accuracy in favor of a more readable sentence.

Text Formatting

This book uses the following formatting conventions.

Format	Indicates	Example
Serif Regular	regular text	In the next chapter we will...
Serif Italic	proper names, emphasis, and loose definitions	*VisualWorks, ParcPlace* the term *model* can be used...
Serif Bold	rigorous term definition	a **model** is an object which...

Sans Serif Regular	Smalltalk classes, methods, messages, and variables which are embedded in text or appear as a single line of text	the window is an instance of ScheduledWindow and is opened… self changed: #height
Sans Serif Bold	menu options and label names of interface components	select **copy** from the \<operate\> menu press the **OK** button
Sans Serif Small	Smalltalk method or large sample of code	| builder | builder := UIBuilder new. builder add: self getSpec. builder open
Enclosed in \<\>	mouse keys and keyboard keys	\<operate\> \<Ctrl\> \<Shift\>
Double Right Angle Brackets \>\>	a class specific implementation of a method	Object\>\>update: View\>\>update:
Right Arrow →	a link between a menu selection and a sub menu selection	**File→Open…** **Edit→Paste**
Serif Regular in Single Quotes	method protocols and class categories	'accessing' 'Interface-Models'
Sans Serif Character Preceded by a $	a Character object	$g $H

General Smalltalk Terminology

The terminology of Smalltalk is very much a mixed bag. Several terms have no standard or commonly accepted definition. Many terms suffer from definition overload in that they have several loose definitions. In a book such as this however, it is absolutely essential that the terms introduced are accompanied by a rigorous definition and that all subsequent uses of the term are consistent with that definition. It is equally important that this book not over step its bounds and try to decide for the Smalltalk community at large how a certain term should be defined. Therefore, when a term needs to be defined, and that term currently has no rigid, commonly accepted definition, it is offered with a qualification such as "For the purposes of this book, we will define a _____ to be a...". This allows this book to be consistent with respect to its use of a term without misleading the reader into believing that the definition offered is an industry standard definition. In addition, several new terms are introduced. These terms do not appear in any current literature and are mostly specific to the implementation of *VisualWorks*. It is not intended that they be adopted as standard terms and they are not offered as such. They are merely convenient definitions meant to serve a purpose within the context of this book.

The Smalltalk Environment

The term *Smalltalk* without any emphasis or formatting is used when referring to the general Smalltalk language independent of vendor. The term *ParcPlace\Smalltalk* is used to indicate the *ParcPlace* specific implementation of Smalltalk. The term *VisualWorks* is used to refer to the *VisualWorks* v2.0 environment. *VisualWorks* v1.0 is always mentioned with the version number as a qualifier. The term *Objectworks\Smalltalk* refers to the *ParcPlace* implementation of the Smalltalk language which is the predecessor of *ParcPlace\Smalltalk* and *VisualWorks*.

The exact relationship between *ParcPlace\Smalltalk*, *VisualWorks*, and *Objectworks\Smalltalk* is a murky one at best, and this book does little to mitigate the confusion. This book takes the position that *Objectworks\Smalltalk* is the predecessor of *ParcPlace\Smalltalk* and that neither includes *VisualWorks* functionality. In this book, *VisualWorks* is sometimes viewed as an addition to *ParcPlace\Smalltalk* and *VisualWorks* functionality is distinguished from other *ParcPlace\Smalltalk* functionality. Other times however, it is viewed as a superset which includes all of *ParcPlace\Smalltalk* since *VisualWorks* ultimately depends on most everything in *ParcPlace\Smalltalk*. Unfortunately, this is a necessary ambiguity.

The term *virtual image* is used to describe the file, or local memory, which contains all the objects used in the Smalltalk environment. In some literature this is merely referred to as the *image* but this is too easily confused with a bitmap object which is also referred to as an image. The term *virtual machine* is historically the term used to refer to the host application program running the Smalltalk virtual image. *VisualWorks* 2.0 also refers to the virtual machine as the *object engine*. This book prefers the term *virtual machine* which is sometimes abbreviated as VM.

Objects

Sometimes this book refers to an object by its type or class name such as

> a ValueHolder

where the class name appears in a sans serif font. Many times an s is appended to the class name to indicate a group of instances of that class such as

> ValueHolders use value model protocol...

In such cases, the class name ValueHolder is in a sans serif font, but the s is a normal serif font. This is a subtle distinction, but technically correct. Sometimes the qualifying term *object* is used to further emphasize that we are talking about an instance of the class and not the class. For example, the phrases

> a ValueHolder

and

> a ValueHolder object

mean exactly the same thing—the second version however, leaves no room for interpretation.

Sometimes this book refers to a group of objects which share a common ancestry or common functionality but are not all necessarily instances of the same class. Examples of this are visual components, views, models, application models, collections, windows, controllers, wrappers, and composites. The singular forms are used as well when referring to a single object which is a member of such a group—a model, a window, a collection—for example.

Most references to objects which represent traditional data types will appear in lower case unformated text and without class affiliation such as string, text, number, integer, float, character, boolean, file, and date. For convenience, this list is extended to include block, cursor, and image. When necessary however, such an object will be referred to as a Text object or a Date object when discussing specific implementations of the class.

Several other types of objects appear in lower case unformatted text and without class affiliation even if it is obvious that there is only one class to which it could possibly belong. Examples of this are builder for UIBuilder and full spec for FullSpec. This is done mostly in the interest of readability; however, it does have the added benefit that a type of object can be described and discussed prior to mentioning its implementation class.

The unique objects true, false, and nil appear in a sans serif font to refer to the single instances of True, False, and UndefinedObject respectively. The standard English terms *true* and *false* are also used and should not be confused with the objects true and false. For example, true   is an object which is the sole instance of the True class.

true   is a standard English term indicating a boolean condition and not necessarily related to Smalltalk.

Object Types and Classes

For the most part, this book takes a very simplistic view of classes and instances. A class is the description of a set of objects and an instance is a member of that set. In addition, the terms *type* and *class* are used synonymously.

Sometimes when referring to a class' implementation, it is necessary to refer to that class' *instance side* or *class side*. The reader should already be aware of the fact that each class description has two parts: one describing the instances and one describing the class as an object. This book offers no explanation as to what this actually means other than to say that the *instance side* means that the **instance** radio button is selected in the System Browser and the *class side* means the **class** radio button is selected.

It is not the purpose of this book to cover class, metaclass, the fact that all classes are objects, or any of the paradoxes and singularities which arise in the hierarchy as a result. Nor is it assumed that the reader has a clear understanding of these issues for it is not absolutely essential for the purposes of this book.

While this book tries to maintain the simple perspective that a class is just a description of an object, sometimes it is necessary to perceive the class itself as an object—which of course it is. A class often times contains instances, default values, and other necessary information it makes publicly available. Many classes implement class methods providing special functions and services. And, of course, objects are created by sending instance creation messages to their class. It is in these cases that it becomes necessary to depart from the limited perspective of a class as described above and treat a class as an object and a receiver of messages.

Inheritance

The term *subclass* is used to mean that class B inherits state and behavior from class A. In such a case, class A is referred to as the *superclass* of class B. However, there should be no assumption that class B immediately follows class A in the class hierarchy. For example, Object is considered to be a superclass of View but only DependentPart is the *immediate* superclass of View. Likewise, View is a subclass of Object and it is the *immediate* subclass of DependentPart. Using this terminology, each class can have several superclasses but only one immediate superclass. Each class can have several immediate subclasses however.

The phrase *is a kind of* describes a relationship between an object and a class. The *is a kind of* relationship says that the object is an instance of that class or one of its subclasses. The main point is that the object has state and behavior described in that class. For example, an instance of ValueHolder is a kind of Model. It is incorrect to say however that the class ValueHolder is a kind of Model. Do not confuse *subclass* and *is a kind of*. Class B is a subclass of class A, while an instance of class B is a kind of class A.

References

There are several ways to describe how one object references another such that the first object can send messages to the second. Some examples are: *points to, holds on to, references,* and *contains.* While certain perspectives can be implied based on which phrase is used, technically they are all identical. For instance, saying a view *references* its model is certainly preferable to saying that it *contains* its model. In either case however, we are talking about an instance variable with a handle to an object.

Messages and Methods

Messages are sent or dispatched to objects. Methods are defined or implemented by classes and executed during a program. There is a correspondence between messages and methods in that each message has at least one corresponding method definition. In this book, both messages and methods are written in a sans serif font for example

> the button view sends the message value: true to its model...

and

> the method changed: aSymbol as defined in the class...

Arguments belong to messages and parameters belong to methods. In the two examples above, true is an argument of the message value: true and aSymbol a parameter of the method changed: aSymbol. The difference between arguments and parameters is largely a matter of perspective. The sending object sends arguments and the receiving object receives parameters. In this book, messages may or may not appear with arguments depending on the context. Likewise, methods may or may not appear with parameters depending on the context.

Three terms related to the topic of methods and messages are *selector*, *protocol*, and *method category*. A selector is a Symbol object which is the identifying signature, or name, of a method. For example, #update:with:from: and #onChangeSend:to: are selectors. A protocol is nothing more than a group of messages or methods. For example, the instance creation protocol of a class would be the set of messages which can be sent to the class to create instances of that class. For the most part *method category* is used synonymously with *protocol*. There is a subtle distinction however. Method categories describe how the methods are organized within a class definition. Protocols on the other hand organize methods or messages according to common functions and features. While protocols and method categories are well correlated, the mapping is not exact.

In this book, shorter messages and method names are embedded in the main text. Longer messages and method names are offset from the main body of text with blank lines above

onChangeSend: aSymbol to: aReceiver

and below, and indented as is done in this example. Methods that appear with source code—that is, method implementations—are written in a small sans serif font, indented, and offset from the main body of text with blank lines, and the method header is in bold as shown below.

setModel: aModel
    "Set the receiver's model to be aModel. Also set the receiver's
    controllers model."

    super setModel: aModel.
    controller == nil
        ifFalse: [controller model: aModel]

Sometimes a method is qualified by the class in which it is implemented by using the >> operator. For example, ApplicationModel>>postBuildWith: indicates the particular implementation of postBuildWith: found in ApplicationModel that is different from the implementation of MyAppModel>>postBuildWith:.

The term *accessing methods* refers to those methods that retrieve and replace an object's instance variable references. An accessing method that retrieves an instance variable reference is referred to as a *get method* or an *accessor method*. An accessing method that replaces an instance variable reference is referred to as a *put method* or a *mutator method*. Depending on the context, either the get/put convention is used or the accessor/mutator convention.

Tools

In this book, the various tools are referenced using their formal names such as Workspace, System Browser, and Menu Editor. This is consistent with the *ParcPlace* literature which also uses the formal names. The one major exception to this is that a canvas is referred to informally even though it is implemented by *VisualWorks* classes. Also, the *VisualWorks* Main Window is historically referred to as the Launcher. This book prefers this latter term.

Sometimes the tools are referred to by the class that implements them; for example, UIMaskEditor for the Image Editor and UIPalette for the Palette. This is usually done when discussing some implementation detail of the tool.

Mouse Buttons

Smalltalk was designed to use a three button pointing device, or mouse. There are three different conventions used to refer to a mouse button—by position, by name, and by color—as shown below.

Position	left	middle	right
Color	red	yellow	blue
Name	<select>	<operate>	<window>

Each convention has something to recommend it. The position convention is obviously the most intuitive; however, not every mouse has three buttons. The color convention is what is used in the actual source code for controllers and sensors. The current *ParcPlace* literature, however, favors using the button name convention. This book will use the button name convention in order to maintain consistency with the *VisualWorks* manuals; however, the color references will be appended with a | character when necessary. For example, there may be a reference to the <select>|<red> button or the <operate>|<yellow> button. This occurs usually when discussing mouse handling source code which uses the color convention.

The *VisualWorks* manuals capitalize the names of the mouse buttons, such as <Select>, which is a departure from the historical convention which does not capitalize the name such as <select>. This book uses the later convention.

Keyboard Keys

Keyboard keys are represented by the key's name inside of angle brackets, such as <Tab> and <R>. In this book, the key name is the exact lettering usually found on the key such as <Enter>, <Ctrl>, and <Esc>, or sometimes a convenient abbreviation such as <PgUp>. This varies slightly from the current *ParcPlace* literature which tends to use full names such as <Return>, <Control>, <Escape>, and <Page Up>. Key combinations pressed simultaneously are concatenated with a hyphen such as <Alt>-<H> and those pressed sequentially are expressed without a hyphen such as <Esc> <g>. Do not confuse <g> with $g. The former is a keyboard key and the latter is a Character object.

Menus

In Smalltalk, many views have their own pop up menu that is invoked with the <operate> mouse button. In keeping with tradition, this book refers to such a menu as an <operate> menu. Likewise, each window has its own pop up menu invoked with a <window> mouse button and it is referred to as a <window> menu.

In addition to the <window> pop up style menu, many windows have a main menu which is a menu bar at the top of the window. This type of menu is referred to as either the *main menu* or *menu bar*.

Menu selections appear in a bold sans serif font such as **File** and **Edit**. When one or more subselections are required, they are linked with an arrow such as

    File→Open... and Edit→Paste.

Contents

VisualWorks Principles

PART I IS meant to be a very rigorous analysis of *VisualWorks* in terms of fundamental Smalltalk concepts. It is fully expected that most readers will not have the motivation to complete all of the material. In fact, much of it is intended to be used as a reference. As a minimum, however, I recommend the following outline.

Chapter 1, Sections 1.1 and 1.2

Chapter 2, Sections 2.1, 2.3, and 2.5

Chapter 3

Chapter 4

This will give a general understanding of *VisualWorks* concepts and provide good support to Chapters 10 and 11 in Part II, which I consider to be of the chapters of greatest value.

If you are interested in fully understanding subcanvases, then you should include Chapter 5. If you are interested in how the various visual components actually work and in implementing your own components, then I would add the following to the outline above.

Chapter 1, Sections 1.3 and 1.4

Chapter 2, Sections 2.2 and 2.4

Chapter 6, Sections 6.2, 6.3, and 6.4

This will give good support to most of Chapter 9 and especially to Chapter 12. If you are interested in the implementation of the *VisualWorks* tools, then you should add Chapters 7 and 8. This will make the tutorials of Chapters 13 and 14 much more meaningful. Finally, if you are interested in how applications were put together prior to *VisualWorks,* then Chapter 1, Section 5 should be of some benefit.

Review of MVC

IN THE BEGINNING, there was MVC. Prior to *VisualWorks*, all application interface building required a thorough understanding of this topic. MVC, or Model-View-Controller, represents the factoring of an application's interface (or a piece of that interface) into: (1) what the application does logically—the model, (2) how it displays itself visually—the view, and (3) how it handles input from the user—the controller. In order to get a window up and running, the budding Smalltalk developer had to first agonize over this somewhat unique way of looking at an application. The mastering of MVC required patience and fortitude; however, it forced an understanding that is absolutely critical to successful programming in Smalltalk—*VisualWorks* notwithstanding!

The introduction of *VisualWorks* has changed the MVC landscape in many ways, one of which provides the justification for this chapter. That is, *VisualWorks* allows the developer to get at least a shell of an application up and running without any concern for MVC architecture, tending to foster a misconception that an understanding of MVC is no longer a prerequisite for successful Smalltalk development. This is terribly unfortunate, since any application of merit requires far more functionality than can be had simply by drawing the screen and generating stub methods. Furthermore, the real power of *VisualWorks* lies in understanding, modifying, and extending the tool beyond the original intentions of its designers. But in order to accomplish any of this, the developer must have a firm grasp of MVC, for it is the lever that transforms *VisualWorks* from just another GUI builder into the most dynamic, flexible, and extendible application development system available today. For this reason it is necessary to dedicate this first chapter to an introduction/review of fundamental MVC concepts.

This chapter is not intended to be an exhaustive treatment of MVC. Instead, it is meant to provide a general understanding of the topic and a practical approach to building models, views, and controllers. Furthermore, this discussion of MVC does not depend on any topics specific to *VisualWorks* since this material is fundamental to *ParcPlace\Smalltalk* and predates the advent of *VisualWorks* altogether. In fact, *VisualWorks* was developed on top of these fundamental concepts. This chapter describes MVC in general and provides a strong foundation for the remaining chapters that do concern *VisualWorks*.

In the first section of this chapter, we will take a high-level look at MVC and its basic concepts. The three subsequent sections provide an in-depth look at each of the three components: model, view, and controller. The last section covers a full example of a traditional MVC application and provides a springboard into the discussion of *Visual-Works* proper beginning in Chapter 2. Throughout this chapter, terms and concepts will be introduced that will serve us well for the remainder of the book.

1.1 Overview of MVC

The MVC perspective is a way of breaking an application, or even just a piece of an application's interface, into three parts: the model, the view, and the controller. In this section, we will discuss the general roles of these three parts of an application and see how they relate to one another.

1.1.1 Application

The MVC architecture was developed for the production of application software and takes into account the human element introduced by the user. MVC is not necessarily applicable to system software such as operating system services and device drivers, which typically interface only with hardware and other programs.

For the purposes of this book, I will use the term **application** to mean one or more windows working in a coordinated and related effort to provide a service to a user community. A word processor is an example of an application—its printer driver is not. *VisualWorks* itself is an application serving the community of Smalltalk programmers. We can even consider an application to be a confederation of smaller applications. In this vein, the graphical drawing utility that comes with your word processor can be considered an application. So can a System Browser or the *VisualWorks* Image Editor.

1.1.2 Model

A **model** is an object that manages information. It calculates, sorts, stores, retrieves, simulates, emulates, converts, and does just about anything else you can think of doing to information. As MVC architecture has matured, it has become apparent that the model's information can be divided into two categories: domain information and application information. A model's **domain information** includes that information concerned with the problem domain. For example, if we have an airline reservation application, then flight schedules, prices, seating arrangements, and credit card numbers would all be domain information. Each identifiable piece or subset of the model's domain information is called an **aspect**. An aspect can be as simple as a single string or number or as complex as a subsystem of other interrelated objects. A model's **application information** is any information that is used by the application but is not part of the problem domain. In the airline reservation example, error messages, icons, and menus would be part of the application information.

The model by itself has no visual representation. It does not know how to display the information it contains. Nor does a model interact with the user or receive any user input.

1.1.3 View

The **view** provides a visual representation of the information contained in the model. The view knows how to draw itself in a window and uses information in the model to determine its exact appearance. As the information in the model changes, the view should automatically redraw itself to reflect those changes. A view depends on the information contained within its model in order to fulfill its duties. A good example of a view is a pie chart view. A pie chart view knows how to draw legends, place labels, and construct the wedges. But the actual number of wedges, their size, color, and label, will be contained in the model. A pie chart view will have to send messages to the model to acquire this information in order to draw itself appropriately. As this information in the model changes, the view is expected to update immediately and redraw the pie wedges to reflect the new distribution of values. Other examples of views are input fields, text editors, and even entire windows.

A view provides a visual *interpretation* of model information, which suggests that there can be more than one view for any given model. The model that contains the information for the pie chart view example can also be represented by a bar chart view, a table view, or even a view that is just a list of text lines.

1.1.4 Controller

A **controller** is the means by which the user makes changes to the application by changing the information in the model or by changing the appearance of a view. A controller accepts input from the user and sends messages to the view and model based on that input. The input is usually in the form of a keystroke or mouse activity. The controller also has the added responsibility of displaying pop-up menus and processing

Table 1.1. Controller Input Handling.

User input	Typical controller response
Left mouse button down	Tell the view to draw itself with a highlighted background
Middle mouse button down	Pop up a menu and send a message to the model based on the user's selection
Character keystroke	Send the character to the view for insertion into text
Tab	Give up control to the next controller

the selected menu item as just another form of user input. Some examples of how a controller might handle various types of user input are shown in Table 1.1.

1.1.5 Connecting the Model, View, and Controller

As we can see from the three definitions, the model, view, and controller are in very intimate contact with each other. Since they send messages back and forth, they must reference each other in some way.

1.1.5.1 Basic MVC Connections

Figure 1.1 shows the basic (albeit not entirely accurate, as will be explained later) lines of communications among the model, view, and controller. In this figure we can see that the model points to the view, which means it can send the view messages. The view points back to the model and also to the controller. The controller points to the view and the model. Notice that the model does not reference the controller.

1.1.5.2 Dependents

So far, we have talked about an arrangement of one model, one view, and one controller. If our model is a factory scheduling program, then we will need much more than a

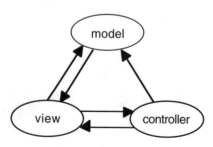

Figure 1.1. Basic Model-View-Controller Relationship.

single view and a single controller in order to provide an adequate user interface. It's hard to think of any interface that consists of just a single list or a single text editor! Fortunately a model can reference an arbitrary number of views.

In Smalltalk an object uses its instance variables to reference other objects. Any object that references a second object can send that second object a message. Does this mean that each time we add a new view to the application's interface, we have to add an instance variable to the model so it can reference the new view? The answer is *no*, of course, and the reason lies in how the model points to, or references, its views. A model keeps all of its views in a single collection called its **dependents collection**. It is called the dependents collection because the objects in the collection *depend on* the information in the model in order to perform their function. The objects in this collection are referred to as *dependents* (defined formally in Section 1.2.2). Other types of objects can be dependents, but for now we will restrict the discussion to views.

The dependents collection solves the problem of having an instance variable for each view. Figure 1.2 shows a more accurate representation of how a model references its views. Through its dependents collection, a model can reference an arbitrary number of views. While the diagram in Figure 1.2 is technically accurate, most object diagrams show the model referencing the views directly, as is done in Figure 1.1.

1.1.5.3 View/Controller Pair

The relationship between the view and controller is especially close. For each type of view, there is usually a unique type of controller. That is, action button views have action button controllers, list views have list controllers, text editor views have text editor controllers, etc. Also, each view points to only one controller, and that controller points back to that view and only that view. Contrast this with a model that may reference several views (albeit indirectly through its dependents collection). For these reasons, the

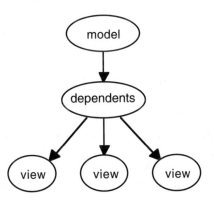

Figure 1.2. How a Model References Its Views.

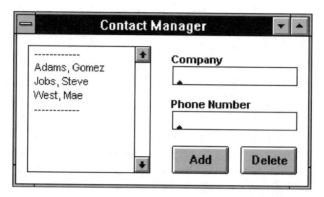

Figure 1.3. Contact Manager Application Window.

term view/controller pair has come into common usage. A **view/controller pair** is a view and a controller that work in tandem as a single piece of user interface, for example, an action button, a list, or a text editor. Sometimes, it is convenient to think of the view/controller pair as the dependent of the model instead of just the view.

1.1.5.4 MVC Application

As an illustration of what we have covered so far, consider a simple application that manages a list of business contacts. Each contact consists of a person's name, the company with which the person is affiliated, and the person's phone number. We will refer to this application as the Contact Manager application. Figure 1.3 shows a user interface suitable for this application. There are several other interface designs that could work just as well.

Figure 1.4 shows the object diagram for such an application. The model in this case is loosely referred to as contact manager. It has five view/controller pairs as dependents: names list, phone field, company field, add button, and delete button. For technical accuracy, it should be mentioned that there is usually an intermediary model between a button view and its model, and these intermediaries are not shown for the two buttons. The notion of intermediary models are covered in Chapter 2.

The model, in this case contact manager, has an instance variable for each of the pieces of information it manages: contacts, contact names, current name, current company, and current phone number. These pieces of information comprise the domain information, and each single piece is considered to be an aspect of the model. The names list view is responsible for displaying both the contact names aspect and current name aspect. The phone field view is responsible for displaying the current phone aspect and accepting new values for this aspect. The company field view is responsible for displaying the current company aspect and for accepting new values for this aspect.

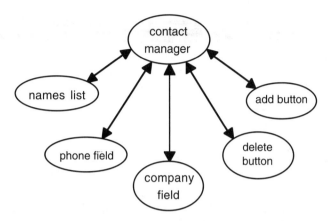

Figure 1.4. Object Diagram for Contact Manager Application.

The button views add a little bit of a wrinkle to the simple perspective of MVC covered so far. The button views do not represent an aspect of the model. Instead, they initiate an action of some kind. They are views however and do have models (intermediary models not represented in the object diagram in Figure 1.4) and controllers. The contact manager model and its interface components constitute an entire application. This cannot be said for all implementations of MVC, some of which are just smaller pieces of a larger application. In Section 1.5 we will revisit this application and study it in detail.

1.2 Models and Their Dependents

In this section we will look at models and what it takes to be a model. Most of the discussion concerns the model's dependents collection since it is this attribute that qualifies an object to be a model.

1.2.1 Who Can Be a Model?

What does it take to be a model? Any object can be a model. All of the behavior we associate with models—managing information and maintaining a collection of dependents—is defined in the class Object. Most of the time, however, a model is an instance of some subclass of Model. The Model class adds state and behavior to better support a dependents collection and therefore is the preferred superclass of all model types (see Section

1.2.4.8). For the purposes of this book, I will narrow the definition of model somewhat and consider a model to be any object that is an instance of some subclass of Model. It is important to remember, however, that *any* object can behave as a model and have dependents.

1.2.2 Who Can Be a Dependent?

As we saw in Section 1.1, a model references its views by keeping them in its dependents collection. If you browse the class definition of Model, you will see that it defines one instance variable, dependents. Why isn't this collection called the *views* collection? The obvious answer is that other objects besides views can be dependents of a model. In fact, any object can be a dependent; however, you typically find only views, windows, and other models as dependents. For the purposes of this book, I will use the following definition of dependent. A **dependent** is an object—usually a view, a window, or another model—that is contained in the dependents collection of a model and relies on information residing in that model. Disk Example 1.1 uses a System Browser as an example of a model that has several dependents.

1.2.3 The Model/Dependents Relationship

One of the original objectives of the MVC architecture was to allow the model to be completely independent of the objects that depended on it. That is, the model should not be required to know anything about its dependents. The dependents are interested in the model; the model is not at all interested in its dependents. The model should behave the same regardless of what kind of dependents it has, how many it has, or if it has any at all. The dependents, on the other hand, are very interested in the model and the information it contains. The dependents are especially interested in any changes in that information. The dependents expect to be notified immediately of any changes in the model that may be of interest. Therefore, it is the model's responsibility to notify all of its dependents of such internal changes in its state. Also, even though a model can have several dependents, a dependent usually depends on only one model.

1.2.4 Changed/Update Mechanism

Several objects can depend on a model. Each of these dependents can be interested in a different aspect of the model. Furthermore, when one of these aspects changes, the dependents that are interested in that aspect of the model expect to be notified of this

change so that they can update appropriately. But since the model wants to remain independent of the objects that depend on it, it cannot pick and choose among its dependents
to decide which ones will receive a certain notification of a change and which ones will
not. Therefore, whenever a model changes in any way that may be of interest to at least
one dependent, it must broadcast a notification of this change to *all* of its dependents. It is
then up to each dependent to decide if it is interested in that particular change or not.
The **changed/update mechanism** is the mechanism by which a model broadcasts a
notification of change to all of its dependents. See Disk Example 1.2 for a good exercise
on the changed/update mechanism covered in this section.

1.2.4.1 Notification of Change

When a model has changed in some way, its immediate response is to first notify itself
of this change. It does this by sending itself one of the following messages.

> changed
>
> changed: anAspectSymbol
>
> changed: anAspectSymbol with: aParameter

These are the change messages, and they are implemented in the class Object. So all objects, not just those that are a kind of Model, know how to broadcast changes to dependents. The argument anAspectSymbol is a Symbol that describes what aspect of the model
has changed and is usually the message selector used to access the changed information
from the model. Some typical examples of the argument anAspectSymbol might be
#billingAddress, #annualProduction, or #velocity depending on what type of information
that particular model happens to manage. The argument aParameter is any other arbitrary object that may be pertinent to the change.

1.2.4.2 The Change Messages

As is often the case in Smalltalk, the implementation of the various change methods is
to dispatch the next more general form of change message as shown below.

> **changed**
> "Receiver changed in a general way; inform all the dependents by sending
> each dependent an update: message."
>
> self changed: nil

> **changed: anAspectSymbol**
> "Receiver changed. The change is denoted by the argument anAspectSymbol.
> Usually the argument is a Symbol that is part of the dependent's change protocol,
> that is, some aspect of the object's behavior. Inform all of the dependents."

self changed: anAspectSymbol with: nil

> **changed: anAspectSymbol with: aParameter**
> "The receiver changed. The change is denoted by the argument
> anAspectSymbol. Usually the argument is a Symbol that is part of the
> dependent's change protocol, that is, some aspect of the object's behavior,
> and aParameter is additional information. Inform all of the dependents."
>
> self myDependents update: anAspectSymbol with: aParameter from: self

The changed message is promoted to a changed: anAspectSymbol message, where nil is used as the default for anAspectSymbol. The changed: anAspectSymbol message is promoted to the changed: anAspectSymbol with: aParameter message, where nil is used as the default for aParameter. Therefore, regardless of the original form of the change message, the method changed: anAspectSymbol with: aParameter is always executed. It is the implementation of this method that notifies the dependents of the internal change of state in the model.

1.2.4.3 Updating the Dependents

The implementation of the method changed: aSymbol with: anObject, shown above, is to send each of the model's dependents the update message

> update: anAspectSymbol with: aParameter from: self

where anAspectSymbol and aParameter are the same arguments used in the change messages described above and self is, of course, the model sending the update.

The model's dependents are accessed with the myDependents message. Both the classes Object and Model implement the myDependents method, but these classes vary in how they implement it (see Section 1.2.4.6).

1.2.4.4 Update Messages

As with the change messages, there are three forms of update message:

> update: anAspectSymbol with: aParameter from: self
>
> update: anAspectSymbol with: aParameter
>
> update: anAspectSymbol

The methods corresponding to these messages are defined in the class Object so that each of the model's dependents, regardless of its type, knows how to respond to these update messages. The default behavior for each of these methods is to forward the next less general form of the message. At the bottom of this chain is update:, whose default implementation, as defined in Object, is to do nothing. Therefore, each type of dependent should override one of the above update methods if it intends to respond to updates from its model.

1.2.4.5 The Condensed Version

Very often it is the case that when a model changes, it uses the intermediary form of the change message, changed: anAspectSymbol. Also, most types of dependents prefer to implement the simplest form of the update method, update: anAspectSymbol. In both cases, the argument anAspectSymbol describes what aspect of the model has changed. For instance, if the model has an address variable that changes in some way, then the model will send changed: #address to self. This in turn results in each of its dependents receiving the message update: #address.

1.2.4.6 Accessing the Dependents Collection

The classes Object and Model describe two different approaches to maintaining the dependents collection. This is the primary difference between models that are a kind of Model and those that are not. Objects that are not a kind of Model get all their model behavior, including dependents maintenance, from the Object class (there are a few exceptions to this such as List and ScrollWrapper, which implement their own dependency mechanism). The Object class keeps the dependents for all such objects in the DependentsField class variable. DependentsField is an IdentityDictionary where keys are the objects themselves and the values are the collections of dependents for the corresponding objects.

Recall from Section 1.2.4.3 that a model accesses its dependents by sending the message myDependents to self. Object implements the myDependents instance method as follows.

> **myDependents**
> "Answer the receiver's dependents or nil."
>
> ^DependentsFields at: self ifAbsent: [nil]

Objects that are a kind of Model inherit their change message protocol from Object but get their dependents maintenance behavior from the Model class. The Model class defines an instance variable, dependents, to hold on to the dependents collection, and therefore, it implements the myDependents instance method as follows.

> **myDependents**
> "Answer the receiver's dependents or nil."
>
> ^dependents

This is much more efficient than looking up the dependents in a class variable such as DependentsField.

1.2.4.7 Adding and Releasing Dependents

So how does a model acquire a dependent? Actually, the correct perspective is not that a model acquires a dependent, but that an object chooses to depend on a model. When

Pablish / Subscribe

an object wants to depend on a model, it sends the message addDependent: self to that model. This method adds the argument (the dependent) to the receiver's (the model's) dependents collection.

A model can also rid itself of all of its dependents by sending the message release to self. The release method replaces the model's dependents collection with nil so that the model no longer references any of its dependents (the dependents may still reference the model, however).

1.2.4.8 Benefits the Model Class

In Section 1.2.1 it was stated that most models in Smalltalk are instances of some sub-class of Model (i.e., are a kind of Model) because Model implements a better dependency handling mechanism than does Object. So why is it better? First, the instance variable dependents provides a much more efficient access to the dependents collection than does the look-up in the DependentsField class variable defined in Object. A much more impor-tant reason, however, is that the dependents of a model that is a kind of Model do not have to be explicitly released in order to be garbage collected—provided, of course, that they and the model are no longer accessible from the root object. The root object is the Smalltalk dictionary, and it is the single access point for all objects in the virtual image.

A model that is no longer accessible from the root object can be garbage collected. If its dependents are also not accessible from the root, then they are available for garbage collection as well. Unfortunately, all class variables, which includes DependentsField, and any objects they reference are accessible from the root object and therefore will never be garbage collected. This means that for models that are not a kind of Model, if the dependents are not explicitly released, they will persist in the virtual image. Further-more, since most dependents reference their model, the model and everything it refer-ences will not be collected either and will continue to persist in the virtual image. This can have detrimental repercussions since most models are used in an interface, all of whose parts (windows, controllers, other models, etc.) can be accessed by that one model and its dependents. This places a huge responsibility on the developer who uses models that are not a kind of Model to make sure that the dependents are explicitly re-leased once the model is no longer being used. It only takes a few slip-ups to bloat the virtual image to where it is carrying the unnecessary baggage of a few megabytes. It is for this reason that most models in Smalltalk are a kind of Model.

It should be mentioned that there are a few other classes that are not subclasses of Model but do define the same dependency mechanism as is found in the Model class. In order to do this, each of these classes must define a dependents variable and the corre-sponding methods as is done in the Model class. Some examples of such classes are List, TwoDList, and WidgetWrapper. If you browse all implementors of myDependents, you will get the complete list. These are redundant implementations of model behavior since there is no multiple inheritance in the current implementation of *ParcPlace\Smalltalk*.

1.2.5 Building a Model

The state and behavior for managing dependents and broadcasting update messages to those dependents is inherited from Model and Object. All you really have to remember is that any time the model changes, changed: anAspectSymbol should be sent to self where anAspectSymbol is usually the name of the aspect of information that has just changed. For example, suppose a model has a variable called companyName. Most likely, there will be a get method, which returns companyName, and a corresponding put method, which assigns a new value to companyName. Since the put method changes the state of the model, it should also notify the dependents of this change. In just such a model, the companyName: method would look something like the following.

```
companyName: aString
    "Change the receiver's companyName to aString and update
    the dependents."

    companyName := aString.
    self changed: #companyName
```

As another example, consider a ValueHolder. As you are probably well aware, ValueHolder objects are used quite extensively in *VisualWorks*. A ValueHolder is just a very simple, generic model. Its one aspect of information is referenced by its value instance variable. Whenever a ValueHolder receives the value: message, it sends changed: #value to self. This results in all of its dependents receiving the update: #value message. We will cover Value-Holder more thoroughly in Chapter 2.

There are other ways a model can change besides put methods, but the general technique is always the same. Whenever the model changes, it should notify its dependents by sending the message changed: anAspectSymbol to self. Disk Example 1.3 illustrates how a model is built.

1.2.6 Building a Dependent

Any object can be a dependent. All that is required is that it have an implementation for one of the update messages. For example, an object that intends to depend on a model might have the following update: method.

update: anAspectSymbol
　　"If anAspectSymbol equals the receiver's aspect variable,
　　then turn on the receiver. Otherwise, ignore the update."

　　anAspectSymbol == self aspectOfInterest
　　　　ifTrue: [self turnOn]

In this example, our fictitious dependent object has an instance variable called aspectOf-Interest which is a Symbol. Each time the dependent gets an update from its model, it checks the argument anAspectSymbol against its own instance variable aspectOfInterest to see if it should be interested in that particular change in the model. If the two match, then our dependent takes appropriate action (in this case, turns itself on, whatever that means!). Otherwise, it ignores the update.

1.2.7 Summary

We have seen that the generic functionality of a model is defined in the classes Object and Model. The generic functionality of a dependent is defined in Object. To summarize the more important parts of this section:

- Any object can be a model, but usually models are instances of a subclass of Model.

- Any object can be a dependent, but the vast majority of dependents are views, windows, or other models.

- A dependent relies on information in its model in order to fulfill its duties and, therefore, needs to be alerted any time the information contained within the model changes.

- A model is not at all interested in its dependents, and its behavior is not at all affected by the number of dependents it has or their type.

- When the model changes in some way, it sends changed: anAspectSymbol to self, which results in update: anAspectSymbol being sent to each of its dependents.

- The argument anAspectSymbol indicates what aspect of the model has changed. Each dependent checks anAspectSymbol to see if it is interested in this particular change in the model and needs to take appropriate action.

In the next section, we will see more meaningful uses of the dependency mechanism as we look at views as dependents.

1.3 Views

In Section 1.1.3, it was stated that a view provides a visual representation of the information in its model. This definition is somewhat vague and can be interpreted in more than one way. Sometimes it is taken to mean that a view is a specific kind of object, an input field, for example, which draws itself in a window and represents one or more aspects of its model's information. Other times, it is taken to mean all the windows and visual objects that constitute the entire visual representation of a model. For the purposes of this book, we will use the former interpretation, which gives us the following, more concrete, definition of view: a specific object that draws itself in a window, has both a model and controller, and usually represents one or more aspects of its model's information.

In this section we will look at what is required of a view with respect to communicating with its model as well as drawing itself in a window. The general approach is to take a look at the methods all views must implement or know about, such as update:, invalidate, displayOn:, bounds, preferredBounds, container, component, and defaultControllerClass. Other pertinent information related to this topic is mentioned as well, such as the relationship between views and their window, the process of drawing in a window, containers, components, and wrappers. Finally, we will talk about what is required to build a view.

1.3.1 Who Can Be a View?

Not all objects that draw themselves in a window are views. There are two broader categories of such objects: visual components and visual parts. These concepts are introduced here to help explain views, and they will serve us well for the remainder of the book. The answer to the question *Who can be a view?* will be revealed in Section 1.3.1.3.

1.3.1.1 Visual Components

A **visual component** is the most general type of object that can draw itself in a window. A visual component responds to **visual component protocol**, which includes the messages displayOn: and preferredBounds. All the behavior describing visual components is implemented by the abstract class VisualComponent, which is a subclass of Object (see Figure 1.5). All views are visual components. There are other types of objects, such as images and labels, which are visual components as well but not necessarily views.

1.3.1.2 Visual Parts

A **visual part** is a kind of visual component that references its container in a container/ component relationship. A visual part has an instance variable, container, which points

back to a containing visual part. This container/component relationship is described in
Section 1.3.4. A visual part's state and behavior is implemented in the abstract class
VisualPart, a subclass of VisualComponent (see Figure 1.5). All views are visual parts. Some
objects, however, such as labels and wrappers (Section 1.3.4.3 covers wrappers), are visual parts but not necessarily views.

The *VisualWorks User's Guide* defines an *active component* as a visual component that
is also a visual part. It defines a *passive component* as a visual component that is not a
visual part, the main difference being that an active component has a container and a
passive component does not. For this chapter only, we will adopt these definitions. Beware, however, that in Chapter 2, active component and passive component will be redefined and the new definitions will be used for the remainder of this book.

1.3.1.3 Views

The abstract class DependentPart is a subclass of VisualPart and adds the state and behavior
necessary for depending on a model. DependentPart has only one subclass, the abstract
class View, which adds the remaining behavior necessary for a view—working with a
controller. It is even convenient to think of DependentPart and View as a single class
spread out over two class definitions.

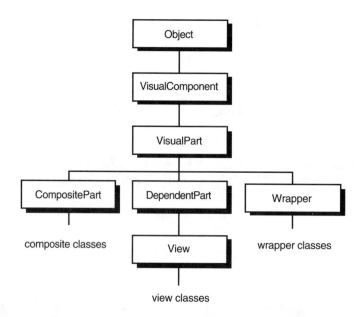

Figure 1.5. Visual Component Hierarchy.

So, to answer the question *Who can be a view?*, a view is any instance of a subclass of View. Because of the inheritance relationship, all views are visual parts, and all visual parts are visual components. Much of what is covered in this section about views is generalized to include all visual parts or all visual components whenever possible. Be careful to notice which statements apply to which type—visual components, visual parts, or views.

1.3.2 Updating Views

Views are dependents of some model and usually display information contained in the model (but not always as in the case of action buttons). Since views are dependents, they should implement one of the update methods, such as update: aSymbol. The proto-typical implementation of this method for a view is shown below.

```
update: anAspectSymbol
    "Check anAspectSymbol to see if it equals some aspect of interest and if
    it does, then send invalidate to self so that the window manager knows to
    redraw the receiver."

    anAspectSymbol == anAspectOfInterest
        ifTrue: [self invalidate]
```

This looks very much like the update: method implementation from Section 1.2.6 except for the statement self invalidate. In general, when something in the model changes that is of interest to the view, the view responds by redrawing itself based on this new information. From this you can surmise that the invalidate message is what initiates a view's redrawing process. Keep in mind that a view's implementation of the update: method is usually much more elaborate than this, but the underlying principal is the same—test the argument anAspectSymbol, and if its something of interest, then update by redrawing.

1.3.3 Visual Structure

A window contains only one visual component, which it simply refers to as its component. How can this be so? We know that several visual components can inhabit a window. Besides, a window with only one input field or one check box makes for a very dull and limited user interface. Most windows have several input fields, check boxes, buttons, lists, and other assorted visual components. The resolution of this dilemma lies in the fact that certain types of visual components can contain other visual components. Recall that a visual component is anything that can draw itself in a window, and a visual part is a special kind of visual component—one that references a containing visual part.

Some of these contained visual parts can themselves contain still more visual components. This containing relationship can continue ad infinitum. All of the visual components that inhabit a window fit into such a structure called the visual structure (see Figure 1.6). The **visual structure** of a window is a tree structure where the root node is the window itself and all the subnodes are visual components. The visual structure also goes by the name of the **visual component tree** since the structure is a branching tree so familiar to most computer programmers. In this tree, certain kinds of visual components behave as branch nodes and other kinds behave as leaf nodes. We will now take a look at the various categories of visual components that make up the visual structure. Most of the discussion deals in the abstract so it can be quite confusing at times, but the concepts are brought together with a real example at the end. In addition, Disk Example 1.4 gives a good working example of the material covered in this section.

1.3.3.1 Containers and Components

In order to have a visual structure, we must have containers and components. A **container** is a visual part (or the window) that contains one or more other visual components. Such a visual component is referred to as the container's **component**. Certain axioms can be stated about the container/component relationship:

‣ Every visual component has exactly one container (the visual part or window that contains it).

‣ Any visual part can access its container by sending the message container to self.

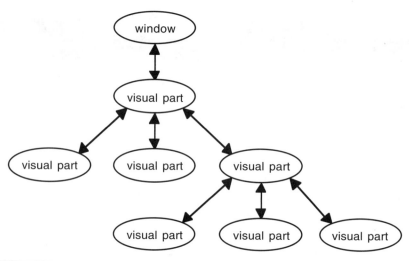

Figure 1.6. A General Visual Structure.

▶ Visual components that are not visual parts do not reference their container and cannot access their container.

There are two general categories of containers: *wrappers* and *composites.* Wrappers typically have just one component, while composites have a collection of components. Wrappers and composites are discussed further in Sections 1.3.3.3 and 1.3.3.4, respectively. A container accesses its component or components by sending the message component or components to self. All visual parts play the role of a component and therefore have a container (the class VisualPart defines an instance variable called container). Not all visual parts are containers and, therefore, may or may not have a component (or components). Containers act as branching nodes in the visual component tree.

To say that one visual part contains another is to express two different types of relationships: one of object reference and one of topographical layout. First, when a container contains a component, it references its component with an instance variable and, therefore, contains it as part of its object structure. Second, when a container contains a component, the area of the window occupied by the component resides completely within the area of the window occupied by the container.

1.3.3.2 The Window

At the top of the visual component tree is the window that serves as the root node. Sometimes the window is referred to as the **top component** of the visual component tree. The window contains and knows about only one visual component, which it refers to as its component. The window's component is responsible for filling the window's entire display surface. The window's component is usually a composite containing several other visual components. Any visual part, no matter how deeply nested it may be in the visual structure, can access the window by sending the message topComponent to self.

1.3.3.3 Composites

A **composite** is a kind of visual part that contains an arbitrary number of components. A composite is a branching node in the visual component tree. A composite allows several visual parts to be treated as a single unit. A composite's components are always wrappers. A composite has no visual representation unique to itself and depends entirely on its components for visual representation. A composite merely defines a common bounding box within which all of its components reside. Certain composites, **composite views**, have their own model and controller. The class CompositePart defines the general state and behavior for all composite types (see Figure 1.5) and is itself a concrete class.

1.3.3.4 Wrappers

A **wrapper** is a container with a single component that provides certain services to this component. These services include translation of coordinates, a bounding box, a border, and scrollbar facilities. All wrappers are subclasses of the abstract class Wrapper, which is a subclass of VisualPart (see Figure 1.5). As visual parts, wrappers can draw themselves in a window, but not all wrappers have a visual representation. For example, a Bordered-Wrapper draws a border around its component, while a BoundedWrapper has no visual representation whatsoever. Wrappers are used quite extensively in *VisualWorks,* so it is best to become comfortable with them. It is not uncommon to see wrappers within other wrappers, each one providing a different service to the ultimate component. While wrappers are very much a part of the visual structure, for the most part they are transparent. A wrapper acts as a branching node in the visual component tree since it references one additional visual component.

1.3.3.5 Visual Component Tree Correspondence

There is quite a bit of communication among the window and the visual components that constitute the visual component tree. Messages are constantly being passed up and down the tree structure. Containers send certain messages down to their components, and components send certain messages back up to their container. The three most common messages a container sends its component(s) are:

displayOn:	The refresh or redraw process starts with the window, since it is the window that keeps track of the damaged areas which need to be redrawn. The window instantiates a ScreenGraphicsContext object and, using it as an argument, sends the displayOn: message to its component. This component either draws on the window using the ScreenGraphicsContext or forwards the displayOn: message on down the visual structure—or both.
objectWantingControl	A container wants to take control (see Section 1.4.2) only if one of its components wants to take control. So whenever a container receives this message, it merely forwards it to each of its components.
downcastEvent: with: from:	An event is being passed down the visual structure so that all the various component parts have the opportunity to respond to it.

The messages a component is most likely to send its container are:

invalidateRectangle: repairNow:	When a view becomes invalid, it notifies its container, which then notifies its container, and so on until the

forComponents:	window is finally reached. The window then records the bounds (area) of the invalid view as damaged.
compositionBoundsFor:	The container is responsible for determining its component's bounds so if a component wants to know its bounds, it asks its container using this message.
topComponent	The top component is always the window. When a component sends this message to its container, the container then forwards the message to its container. This recursion continues until the window is reached. The window merely returns self.

1.3.3.6 A Simple Example

As you have no doubt noticed by now, the study of the visual structure can be quite confusing. To mitigate some of the confusion, consider an example of a window that consists of a label, an input field, and a button (see Figure 1.7).

The corresponding visual structure for this simple window is shown in Figure 1.8. For simplicity, the composite is shown referencing its components directly. In reality, however, a composite references an OrderedCollection, which then references the components as shown in Figure 1.9.

From the object diagram in Figure 1.8, we can make certain statements.

● window's component is composite.

● composite's container is window.

● composite has three components: wrapper 1, wrapper 2, and wrapper 3.

● wrapper 1's container is composite (same for wrapper 2 and 3).

● wrapper 1's component is label visual component.

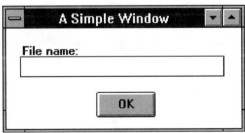

Figure 1.7. A Simple Window.

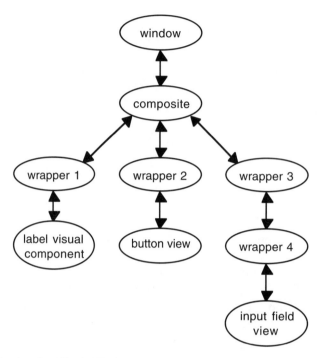

Figure 1.8. Visual Structure for a Simple Window.

- wrapper 2's component is button view.
- wrapper 3's component is another wrapper, wrapper 4.
- wrapper 4's component is input field view.

In the object diagram of Figure 1.8, wrapper 3 contains another wrapper, wrapper 4. This is not at all uncommon. There may be several layers of wrappers, each one providing a different service to the ultimate component. In this example, both wrappers service the input field object. wrapper 3 provides a border and coordinate translation, and wrapper 4 provides the horizontal scrolling of text within the input field.

1.3.4 The Drawing Process

Each window is responsible for keeping itself displayed. For example, if a window is temporarily covered by another window, which is then removed, the newly exposed window must redisplay itself. Otherwise, the user will be left looking at a big blank

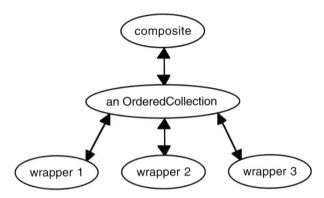

Figure 1.9. A Composite Referencing Many Components.

space in the window! This section covers the visual structure's role in keeping the window displayed properly. For now, the role played by the window is described only to the extent necessary for our discussion on views and the visual structure. Chapter 6 covers in depth the role played by the window.

1.3.4.1 Window Damage

Each window in *VisualWorks* knows how to redraw itself or any part of itself. It does so by telling its component to redraw itself. This component in turn tells its component parts to redraw themselves. This request for redrawing continues on down to the leaf nodes of the visual component tree. The parts of a window that are in need of being redrawn are marked as **damaged**. The window keeps track of its damaged areas and, when given the opportunity, has the appropriate visual components redraw those areas. A window records damage if it is temporarily obscured by another window. A window also records damage when one its views becomes invalid (see Section 1.3.4.2). The actual mechanics of how a window records damage and initiates a redraw is discussed in Chapter 6, Section 6.4.5.

1.3.4.2 Invalid Views

When a view no longer accurately reflects the information contained within its model, it is said to be **invalid**. The view notifies its window of this condition by sending invalidate to self. This message (actually a more general form of the message) travels up the component tree eventually reaching the window. As a result of receiving this message, the window records the area occupied by the view as damaged. As soon as the window gets the opportunity to do so, it initiates the process of redrawing those areas that it has recorded as being damaged. It does this by dispatching the message displayOn: aGraphics-Context back down the visual component tree.

There are times when a view only wants to redraw a part of its area and therefore only wants to invalidate this portion. In such cases, the view uses the invalidateRectangle: aRectangle message, which invalidates only that area of the view defined by aRectangle. A good example of this is the selected item within a list view. When an item in a list view becomes selected or unselected, there is no need to redraw the entire list view. Only the area occupied by that particular selection needs to be redrawn.

A third invalidation message is the invalidateRectangle:repairNow: message. This message takes an additional argument, which is a boolean. If this boolean is true, the window does not record the area as damaged but instead redraws the area immediately. This eliminates any delay between notification of an invalid state and the redraw process.

1.3.4.3 The displayOn: Method

Each visual component should have a displayOn: method. It is this method that actually draws the visual component on the window's display surface. The argument of this method is an instance of ScreenGraphicsContext, which is a special kind of graphics context object. A graphics context object contains certain drawing parameters describing how graphics and text will appear. A ScreenGraphicsContext applies in the case of screen-related graphics (other kinds of graphics context objects do the same thing for printer-related graphics). These parameters include such things as color, line thickness, and font. The following lines of code are examples of what might be found in a typical displayOn: method.

```
aGraphicsContext displayRectangle: (0@0 extent: 100@100).
(Circle center: 10@10 radius: 50) displayFilledOn: aGraphicsContext.
'Hello, World!' displayOn: aGraphicsContext at: 50@50.
```

The ScreenGraphicsContext object is provided by the window. Each time the window redraws itself, it first creates a new instance of ScreenGraphicsContext and then broadcasts the displayOn: aGraphicsContext message down the visual component tree (how this actually happens is discussed shortly). The argument aGraphicsContext is the new instance of ScreenGraphicsContext.

1.3.4.4 Direct Redraw

Though the window provides the ScreenGraphicsContext to the components in the visual structure when it wants to redraw itself, any visual part can retrieve a ScreenGraphicsContext object from its window at any time by sending the message graphicsContext to self. This technique of accessing a graphics context directly for immediate display is sometimes referred to as a **direct redraw**. The benefits of using this technique are that the visual part does not have to wait for the window to start the redraw process, which can sometimes be quite a noticeable amount of time. The invalidateRectangle:repairNow:

message mentioned in Section 1.3.3.2 also has this advantage. The direct redraw technique has an additional advantage. A redraw initiated by any of the invalidation messages starts with the window completely blanking out the damaged area with its own background color. Only then do the visual components redraw themselves. In the case where the window and the visual component have different background colors, this can have an unacceptable visual effect. This does not occur with a direct redraw.

Despite the benefits of a direct redraw, the invalidation process is preferred. When the invalidation process is used, the window keeps track of those areas that have been marked as damaged. Even if a single area is marked as damaged more than once, the window will only redraw it once. Since a direct redraw circumvents this process, a single visual component may end up being redrawn more than once in rapid succession.

1.3.4.5 Displaying Model Information

Since most views are a visual interpretation of one or more aspects of information contained within their model, the redraw process usually involves one or more messages being sent to the model to access that information. A view uses its model instance variable to reference its model.

1.3.4.6 Bounds and Preferred Bounds

When a visual component draws itself, it needs to be aware of its size so that it knows how to scale things and how much of the window it must fill. A visual component has two different notions of how big it is: bounds and preferred bounds. **Preferred bounds** is defined by the visual component itself and indicates how much real estate it requires in order to adequately draw itself. **Bounds** is the actual amount of real estate allocated to the visual component by the window (actually allocated by the container). Both of these methods return a Rectangle object.

All visual components must implement the preferredBounds method, which returns a Rectangle describing that visual component's preferred bounds. The preferredBounds method is part of the visual component protocol. The default implementation for preferredBounds is found in VisualComponent, and it returns a Rectangle that describes the entire area of the screen. The bounds method is implemented in the abstract classes so you as a developer do not have to worry about it.

1.3.4.7 Simple Example Revisited

Now let's see how messages are passed up and down the visual structure to initiate and conduct the redrawing process. For this we will use the simple example provided in Section 1.3.3.6 and Figures 1.7 and 1.8. Below is the sequence of events describing a typical redraw process.

1. The model for input field view changes and sends an update message to its dependent, input field view.

2. input field view invalidates itself by sending invalidate to self, the result being that input field view notifies its container, wrapper 4, that its area is invalid.

3. wrapper 4 then notifies its container, wrapper 3, of the invalid area.

4. wrapper 3 notifies its container, composite, of the invalid area.

5. composite notifies its container, window, of the invalid area, and window records this area as damaged.

6. window refreshes or redraws this damaged area by creating a ScreenGraphicsContext and sending the message displayOn: aGraphicsContext to its component, composite.

7. composite forwards the displayOn: message to only those of its components whose bounds overlap the invalid area. Only wrapper 3 qualifies and, therefore, only wrapper 3 is sent the displayOn: message.

8. When wrapper 3 receives the displayOn: message, it draws a border and forwards the message to its component, wrapper 4.

9. When wrapper 4 receives the displayOn: message, it forwards it to its component, input field view.

10. When input field view receives the displayOn: message, it draws itself in its bounds using the new information in its model.

In the scenario above, wrapper 1 and wrapper 2 never receive the displayOn: message because they lie outside the invalidated area. Disk Example 1.4 provides another concrete example of a window and its visual structure, including composites, wrappers, and other visual components.

1.3.5 Default Controller

As mentioned in Section 1.1.5.3, each type of view usually has its own preferred type of controller. Each view is responsible for instantiating and connecting to its **default controller**, which is an instance of this preferred controller class. All the behavior for doing this is defined in the View class. The only thing that changes from one view class to the next is the type of controller it instantiates. Each view class usually implements a method called defaultControllerClass, which does nothing more than return the class of the controller that the view expects to instantiate and use as its default controller. For example, a ComposedTextView uses an instance of ParagraphEditor as its controller. If you browse ComposedTextView, you will see that it implements the method shown below.

defaultControllerClass
   "Answer the default controller class for the receiver."
   ^ParagraphEditor

1.3.6 Building a View

Building a view is not very difficult in general. All that is required is that the view class implement the following methods (or inherit meaningful implementations): update:, displayOn:, preferredBounds, and defaultControllerClass. Most views will also include several other methods specific to their task. It is the elaboration of the drawing and the coordination with the controller that can sometimes make building a view somewhat difficult. Disk Example 1.5 covers building a view, which is then connected to the model built in Disk Example 1.3.

1.3.7 Summary

In this section we have seen how a view behaves as a dependent of a model. We have also seen how a view relates to the window and how it redraws itself. The major points of this section are as follows.

* A visual component is the simplest kind of object that displays itself in a window.

* A visual part is a kind of visual component that has a reference back to its containing visual part.

* A view is a kind of visual part that depends on a model and knows how to work with a controller.

* The window and all the visual components inside it form a tree structure—called the visual component tree or visual structure—where the window is the root node, wrappers and composites are branching nodes, and other visual components are the leaf nodes.

* When a view wants to redraw itself, it notifies the window that it is invalid by sending an invalidation message to self.

* The window is responsible for redrawing itself and does so by propagating the message displayOn: down the visual component tree eventually reaching all of the visual components that need to be redrawn.

- The displayOn: method is what actually draws a visual component on the window's display surface. The argument for this message is an instance of Screen-GraphicsContext that determines drawing parameters such as color and font.

- A visual component knows its own size by sending the message bounds to self.

- A view is responsible for instantiating its own controller, and the type of controller it uses is determined by sending the message defaultControllerClass to self.

- When creating a new view class, the minimal amount of work will typically include implementing the following methods: update:, displayOn:, preferred-Bounds, and defaultControllerClass.

1.4 Controllers

Controllers can be very mysterious and prove to be a somewhat difficult study at first. At least part of the reason for this lies in the fact that the controller classes define methods whose names all seem to sound the same! While we cannot adequately cover the labyrinth of Smalltalk controllers within the confines of a few pages, we can cover the basic minimum required to get started with the topic. There is more material on controllers throughout the remainder of the book—primarily in Chapters 2 and 6.

It should be mentioned here that both view objects and window objects have controllers and that these controllers operate in very much the same way. In Section 1.3 we narrowed the definition of *view* to include only those objects that are a kind of View. While windows are not considered views under this strict definition, they are similar to views in many ways—the use of a controller is one of them.

In this section we will talk about what qualifies an object as a controller and cover the basic behavior of a controller. Part of the realm of controllers includes sensors, which are covered as well. Finally we will talk about what is involved in building a new controller class.

1.4.1 Who Can Be a Controller?

A controller is any object that is an instance of some subclass of Controller. Actually, there are two primary superclasses of controllers: Controller and ControllerWithMenu. The Controller class provides all the basic behavior necessary for any controller. ControllerWith-Menu is a subclass of Controller and goes a step further by providing menu handling mechanisms and hooks for certain mouse input. All controllers are a kind of Controller, but many of those are also a kind of ControllerWithMenu.

1.4.1.1 Controller

The Controller class is an abstract class and a subclass of Object. The Controller class defines the basic behavior for all controllers. This includes the ability to acquire, maintain, and relinquish control (Section 1.4.2) and the ability to execute a control loop (Section 1.4.3).

The Controller class defines an instance variable, sensor, which references a Translating-Sensor. A **sensor** provides a controller with access to the stream of keyboard events and current mouse state. The Controller class defines two additional variables, view and model, so it can reference its view and model, respectively (see Figure 1.1).

1.4.1.2 ControllerWithMenu

Since many view/controller pairs employ a pop-up menu, the abstract class Controller-WithMenu was created. ControllerWithMenu is a subclass of Controller and defines two additional variables: menuHolder and performer. The menuHolder variable is a ValueHolder whose value is a Menu (ValueHolder is covered in Chapter 2, Section 2.3.2). The performer variable references the controller's performer. The **performer** is the object that is to receive the message resulting from a menu selection. The performer variable is initialized to be the controller itself, but many types of controllers establish the model as the performer. ControllerWithMenu also defines hooks for the <select>|<red> and <operate>|<yellow> button activity (the <window>|<blue> button is, by Smalltalk conventions, fielded by the window controller). The pop-up menu displayed by the <operate>|<yellow> button is often referred to as the <operate> menu.

1.4.2 Active Controller

In the Smalltalk virtual image, there may be several windows open at one time. Each of these windows has its own controller. Each of these windows most likely also contains one or more views. Since each view has its own controller, there are several controllers for a given window. So which controller processes the user's input? Even though there are several controllers, only one controller, the **active controller**, has control at any given time. The term **control** means to process the current user input. Therefore, it is the active controller that processes the current keystrokes and mouse state. The next logical question is, *How does a controller become the active controller?*

There is quite an involved process in determining the active controller. A greatly simplified version will be given here. Of all the open windows, only one is the active window in that it is the window currently receiving user events from the window manager. The active window's controller begins asking each of the window's views if it wants control. It does this by sending each view the message objectWantingControl, which returns a boolean. The first view to respond true is sent the startup message. The view's startup method in turn sends startup to its controller making it the active controller. The active controller will maintain control until it decides to relinquish control back to the window's controller and the search for an active controller starts all over again.

1.4.3 The Control Loop

When a controller becomes active, it starts a loop called the **control loop**. The control loop is implemented in the controller's method controlLoop. With each pass through the loop, the controller executes a three-step process:

1. Temporarily give control to the window controller so that it can see if it needs to perform any window activities such as closing or redrawing the display surface.

2. Check to see if it wants to maintain control (i.e., remain the active controller).

3. Check for user input and processes it accordingly.

The method controlLoop is implemented in the Controller class and is shown below.

```
controlLoop
    "Sent by Controller|startUp as part of the standard control sequence.
    Controller|controlLoop sends the message Controller|isControlActive to test
    for loop termination. As long as true is returned, the loop continues. When
    false is returned, the loop ends. Each time through the loop, the message
    Controller|controlActivity is sent."

    [self poll.
    self isControlActive]
        whileTrue:
            [self controlActivity]
```

The three steps of the control loop as implemented in the above method are described below.

1.4.3.1 Step 1: Polling

In the first statement in the controlLoop method, self poll, the controller is temporarily yielding to the window's controller, which is the first step of the three-step process. This gives the window controller the opportunity to field any recent window events like closing, resizing, or displaying the <window> menu.

1.4.3.2 Step 2: Maintaining Control

In the second statement in the controlLoop method, self isControlActive, the controller is checking to see if it wants to maintain control. As long as the message isControlActive returns true, the controller will remain the active controller. Each controller implements isControlActive and therefore decides for itself if and when it wants to relinquish control. For example, many controllers want to maintain control as long as the mouse is within the bounds of its view. Such controllers will implement the isControlActive method as follows.

> **isControlActive**
> "Maintain control as long as the view has the cursor."
>
> ^self viewHasCursor

1.4.3.3 Step 3: Control Activity

The last statement, self controlActivity, is the third and last step in the loop. The controlActivity method is where the controller processes user input. It is at this point that the various controller types begin to differ. When the controller is done with its control activity, the loop is started over again.

1.4.4 Processing User Input

Each controller has an instance variable called sensor, which is an instance of TranslatingSensor (a window controller's sensor is an instance of WindowSensor or ApplicationWindowSensor). A sensor provides access to the keystrokes and mouse information originating from the host window environment. The controller accesses keyboard and mouse information from its sensor by sending it a variety of messages. A small sample of these messages and the information or function they provide is shown in Table 1.2.

Table 1.2. Sample of InputSensor Services.

Sensor message	Function performed
redButtonPressed	Returns true if the \<select\>|\<red\> mouse button is down, false otherwise
noButtonPressed	Returns true if no mouse buttons are down, false otherwise
waitButton	Delay execution until a mouse button is pressed
cursorPoint	Returns location of cursor
keyboardEvent	Returns most recent keystroke

1.4.5 Building a Controller

There are three choices when choosing a superclass for a new kind of controller: Controller, ControllerWithMenu, or some other controller class that already contains much of the state and behavior you require. Disk Examples 1.6, 1.7, and 1.8 cover building a controller that can be used with the view built in Disk Example 1.5. Disk Example 1.6 creates a new controller class and implements mouse functionality. Disk Example 1.7 adds a menu and Disk Example 1.8 adds keyboard handling.

1.4.5.1 Subclassing Controller

When subclassing from Controller, you should implement the controlActivity method. It is this method that starts the process of handling user input. More than likely, this process requires several other support methods specific to your type of controller.

1.4.5.2 Subclassing ControllerWithMenu

If ControllerWithMenu is the superclass, then two hooks are provided for dealing with mouse input: redButtonActivity and yellowButtonActivity. You may also want to initialize the menu performer. The default performer is the controller itself. In many cases, however, the performer is initialized to be the model.

1.4.5.3 Subclassing Another Controller Class

When subclassing from some other controller class, the intention is usually just to modify certain existing behaviors or add a few new ones. A good example would be to enhance SequenceController, whose instances control list views, in such a way that the user can drag the mouse for multiple selections—a behavior not currently supported.

1.5 A Traditional MVC Application

History is always important. If you want to understand where you are at and where you are going, then look at where you've been. This applies even in Smalltalk. Much of what constitutes *VisualWorks* is a direct consequence of traditional application development. I refer to **traditional application development** as the approach to application development used by developers prior to *VisualWorks*. In this section, we will take a look at an application developed with just such an approach. The obvious difference between this approach and that of *VisualWorks* is that the traditional approach required the developer to hard-code the interface—not providing him or her with the luxury of building and modifying interfaces using the Palettes, canvases, and Properties Tools provided in *VisualWorks*. The differences, however, go far beyond these labor-saving devices and can be divided into two broad categories: the MVC architecture and the variety and flexibility of the user interfaces. Traditional application development employs what I will refer to as **classical MVC architecture**. Traditional applications also have a somewhat limited user interface compared to *VisualWorks* applications.

There is an additional benefit of this section. *VisualWorks* tools, such as the Palette, canvas, and Properties Tool, are themselves *VisualWorks* applications, but the traditional Smalltalk programming tools—such as the System Browser, the Inspector, and the Debugger—are written with the traditional approach and use the classical MVC architecture. As it turns out, this is both a blessing and a curse. You can tamper with the fundamental mechanics of *VisualWorks* and still be confident that your programming tools are available to bail you out. On the other hand, if you would like to change the functionality of the programming tools, *VisualWorks* will be of little help. This requires a familiarity with traditional application development and the classical MVC architecture. This section can provide some insights into how these tools work, at least from a user interface perspective.

The first three parts of this section deal with developing an application using the traditional approach. The last part focuses on some of the problems plaguing the traditional approach. This discussion is used as a springboard into Chapter 2, which begins the discussion of *VisualWorks* proper.

1.5.1 Application Description

The application of interest was first mentioned in Section 1.1.5.4, the Contact Manager application. This application manages a set of business contacts. Its interface looks like the window shown in Figure 1.3. When the user selects a contact name in the list, that contact's company and phone number is displayed in the fields and are available for editing. The currently selected contact can be deleted from the list by pushing the **Delete** button. A new contact can be added by pushing the **Add** button and typing the new contact's name in the resulting dialog box. In a Workspace, evaluate the statement below, which will start this application (see Appendix A for installing the source code which accompanies this book).

    ContactManager open

Experiment with the fields and buttons to get a feel for what they do. If you change a field value, you must select the **accept** command in that field's <operate> menu for the change to take effect.

1.5.2 The Model

In *VisualWorks,* the development of an application usually starts with painting the window. In the traditional approach, the beginning of an application always starts with developing the model. The type of model for this application is ContactManager, which is a subclass of Model. This model is rather simple and requires no other special classes to be built in order to function properly.

1.5.2.1 Class Definition

If you browse the class ContactManager, you will find that it has the following definition.

```
Model subclass: #ContactManager
    instanceVariableNames: 'contacts names name company phone'
    classVariableNames: ''
    poolDictionaries: ''
    category: 'SDGVW-Chapter 1'
```

Notice that it is a subclass of Model and defines five instance variables. You may want to browse the class comments to get a better feel for each of these variables.

1.5.2.2 Accessing Methods

Two of the instance methods, names: and currentName:, include the changed: message to notify the views that the model has changed.

```
names: aCollection
    "Set the names variable to aCollection and notify
    the dependents that the names list has changed."

    names := aCollection.
    self changed: #names
```

Whenever the names instance variable is changed, the dependents are notified by way of the self changed: #names statement. We expect that only the list view will be interested in this change and redraw itself with the new collection as its contents. Now consider the **currentName:** method.

```
currentName: aString
    "When the currently selected name changes, set company
    and phone to their new values and update the views."

    | array |
    currentName := aString.
    array := self contacts at: aString ifAbsent: [Array new: 2].
    self company: (array at: 1).
    self changed: #company.
```

```
self phone: (array at: 2).
self changed: #phone
```

Whenever the user selects a new name in the list view, the list view notifies the model by sending it the currentName: message with the new selection as the argument. In the current-Name: method, the model then sets its company and phone instance variables to those values corresponding to the new value of currentName. It is also necessary to let the views know of the changes in company and phone so the two input fields can update themselves with their respective new values.

The question arises, *Why not let the company: and phone: methods implement the notification of change?* The reason is that the input fields themselves will be sending these messages but do not need to be notified of the change since they are the reason for the change to begin with. Keeping track of who has changed, who needs to be notified, and from where the notification should take place is one of the drawbacks of classic MVC architecture.

1.5.2.3 Action Methods

In the ContactManager class, there are two instance methods, add and delete, in the 'action' protocol. These methods are triggered when the user pushes the **Add** or **Delete** button, respectively. Such methods are referred to as *action methods*.

1.5.3 View Creation

You may already know that in *VisualWorks,* an interface description (in the form of an array) is kept in a class method of the application model. The notion of having a model's interface reside in one of the its class methods is a legacy from traditional application development. The ContactManager class is a good example of this legacy. Before *VisualWorks,* all the code for creating a user interface for a model was usually located in one or more of that model's class methods, primarily because there was no where else to put it!

In ContactManager, all the code for creating the interface is located in a single, very large class method, openOn:. This method takes one argument, which is an instance of ContactManager, the model for which it is opening. This is a very long method of mostly procedural and redundant code. It should be pointed out that often the view creation behavior was factored into several private class methods that supported the openOn: method. This is not done in our example.

1.5.3.1 The Window

The first few lines of the openOn: class method recreated below instantiate the window and its component. Since the window's component will hold onto several views (i.e., a list, buttons, input fields) it is created as a CompositePart, which can hold onto an arbitrary number of visual parts as its components.

> **openOn: aContactManager**
>   "Open a user interface for the model aContactManager."
>
> | window component view layout wrapper |
>   window := ScheduledWindow new
>   model: aContactManager;
>   label: 'Contact Manager';
>   minimumSize: 300@150.
>   component := CompositePart new.
>   ...

What follows is a rather repetitive series of events. A view is created, its layout is created, and the view is wrapped and added to the component variable using the specified layout.

1.5.3.2 Adding the List View

The code for adding the list view is shown below. Notice that the list view must be told several things about the model, such as its aspect and the methods for accessing the collection and current selection. Also notice that this code follows the process described above: the view is created, its layout is created, the view is placed inside of a wrapper, and the wrapper is added to the component variable with the given layout.

> **openOn: aContactManager (excerpt)**
>
>   ...
>   view := SelectionInListView
>   on: aContactManger
>   aspect: #names
>   change: #currentName:
>   list: #names
>   menu: nil
>   initialSelection: #currentName
>   layout := LayoutFrame
>   leftFraction: 0.0
>   offset: 10
>   rightFraction: 0.5
>   offset: -10
>   topFraction: 0.0
>   offset: 10
>   bottomFraction: 1.0
>   offset: -10.
>   wrapper := LookPreferences edgeDecorator on: view.
>   component add: wrapper in: layout.
>   ...

1.5.3.3 Adding a Label

Each of the two input fields has an accompanying label. A label is not a view so it has neither a model nor a controller; however, it is a visual part and does show up in the window. The code for adding the **Company** label to the interface is shown below. Notice that it has a layout and is added to component just as if it were a view. Also notice that no wrapper is created explicitly. The component variable is a CompositePart. If a CompositePart receives a visual part that does not have a wrapper, then it supplies one itself. Remember, a composite's components are always wrappers, and the composite will enforce this rule if it has to by creating a wrapper for the component.

openOn: aContactManager (excerpt)

```
...
view := 'Company' asText allBold asComposedText.
layout := LayoutFrame
        leftFraction: 0.5
        offset: 10
        rightFraction: 1.0
        offset: -10
        topFraction: 0.0
        offset: 15
        bottomFraction: 0.0
        offset: 36.
component add: view in: layout.
...
```

1.5.3.4 Adding an Input Field

Prior to *VisualWorks,* there really was no class dedicated exclusively to input field editing. Therefore, the input fields in our example are implemented as TextView objects, which are limited to a single line of text. Each of the text views is constructed in much the same way as the list view. As an example, the excerpt below shows how the **Company** field is created. Like the list view, it too needs very specific information about its model in order to function.

openOn: aContactManager (excerpt)

```
...
view := TextView
        on: aContactManager
        aspect: #company
        change: #company:
        menu: nil.
view controller initializeMenuForText.
layout := LayoutFrame
        leftFraction: 0.5
```

```
                    offset: 10
                    rightFraction: 1.0
                    offset: -10
                    topFraction: 0.0
                    offset: 30
                    bottomFraction: 0.0
                    offset: 51.
            wrapper := (LookPreferences edgeDecorator on: view)
                    noVerticalScrollBar.
            component add: wrapper in: layout.
            ...
```

1.5.3.5 Adding an Action Button

The buttons provide a bit of a twist in that their model is not aContactManager but a PluggableAdaptor (PluggableAdaptor is covered in Chapter 2). It is the PluggableAdaptor that knows which action message to send to aContactManager when the user pushes a button. The excerpt for creating the **Delete** button is shown below.

openOn: aContactManager (excerpt)

```
            ...
            view := Button trigger
                    model: ((PluggableAdaptor on: aContactManager)
                        performAction: #delete);
                    label: 'Delete'.
            layout := LayoutFrame
                    leftFraction: 1.0
                    offset: -70
                    rightFraction: 1.0
                    offset: -10
                    topFraction: 1.0
                    offset: -40
                    bottomFraction: 1.0
                    offset: -10.
            wrapper := BoundedWrapper on: view.
            component add: wrapper in: layout.
            ...
```

1.5.3.6 Opening the Interface

Once all the visual parts have been added to the component variable, it then must be installed as the component of the window (remember, the window only references one visual component, called its component, which invariably is a composite containing many more visual components). Finally the window is told to open. These last two lines of the openOn: method are shown below.

openOn: aContactManager (excerpt)

```
...
window component: component.
window open
```

The model, aContactManager, can now be viewed and edited by way of the interface just created.

1.5.4 Analysis of Traditional Application Development

There are some fundamental problems with the traditional approach to application development: (1) interface construction, (2) classical MVC architecture, and (3) variety and flexibility of user interface. Each of these is discussed below.

1.5.4.1 Interface Construction

In the Contact Manager example, all of the view creation code had to be written by the developer. Using this technique, the developer is never really sure what the interface will look like, and several iterations of tweaking values and then opening the interface to see the effect are required before he or she gets it right. It is much easier and faster to "draw" an interface than it is to write the code for the interface.

1.5.4.2 Classical MVC Architecture

The traditional approach to application development employs what is known as the classical MVC architecture. From the example application, we can see that the following areas of this architecture could use some improvement.

- A single, overloaded model manages all the information, runs the window, and runs all of the views that inhabit the window.

- The model has several dependents and must broadcast the message update: to each of its dependents, even though only one may actually be interested in the change.

- Many times a view must know specific information about its model, such as the name of the aspect and the get and put selectors used for accessing the aspect value.

- Some views require the developer to include an intermediary model such as a PluggableAdaptor in order to communicate with its model.

- Interface opening requires a great deal of cumbersome, mostly procedural, and somewhat redundant code.

- The interface opening code is quite often located on the class side of the model. View creation is not necessarily appropriate behavior for a model class.

- The model contains information that is germane to the problem domain (domain information) as well as information required by the interface (application information).

- Objects interested in an aspect of a model must register directly as a dependent of that model and implement an update: method.

- Each change in the model must include a changed: message in order to update the dependents.

1.5.4.3 Variety and Flexibility of the User Interface

The areas of the user interface that could use some improvement are as follows.

- There is no explicit support for allowing input fields to edit data types other than text (i.e., cannot edit dates, numbers, etc.).

- There is no explicit mechanism for implementing cooperation among views such as that required by a bank of radio buttons or a tab sequence.

- There is no explicit support for a window menu bar, an integral part of any standard window environment.

- There is not a clear and easy way to apply runtime changes to the interface such as disabling views and making components invisible.

- There is no special support for multiwindow applications.

- It is difficult to reuse specific interfaces (other than cut and paste the code).

- Custom dialogs can be difficult to implement.

- There is a lack of support for some very standard interface components such as input fields, combo boxes, and drop down menus.

1.5.4.4 VISUALWORKS to the Rescue

VisualWorks addresses each and every one of the issues raised above. It is important to note that *VisualWorks* has done much more than just automate the creation of user interfaces. If this is all *VisualWorks* accomplished, then we would still have all of the problems listed in Sections 1.5.4.2 and 1.5.4.3. The additional contributions of *VisualWorks* are that it has greatly enhanced the MVC architecture and brought more variety and flexibility to the user interface. The GUI builder feature of *VisualWorks* is convenient; these other two contributions—MVC architectural changes and more powerful user interface classes—are fundamental!

1.6 Summary

This chapter covered the most crucial topic of model-view-controller, or MVC. A model is an object that manages information. This information can be divided into two categories: domain information, which concerns the problem domain, and application information, which includes information specific to the user interface such as menus and error messages. Each identifiable piece of a model's information is called an aspect. A model can have one or more different views for a given aspect of information. Each of these views is capable of displaying that aspect of information in a different way. Each view has a controller, which processes user input such as current mouse state and keyboard events. A view and its corresponding controller are sometimes referred to as a view/controller pair.

Any object can be a model, but usually models are an instance of some subclass of the Model class. The model's views are called dependents because they depend on information in the model. Any object can be a dependent of a model, but usually dependents are views, windows, or other models. When a model changes, it sends the message changed: anAspectSymbol to itself, which results in update: anAspectSymbol being sent to each of its dependents. The argument anAspectSymbol identifies the aspect of the model that has changed.

A visual component is the simplest object that can display itself in a window. A visual part is a kind of visual component that references its containing visual part. A view is a visual part that has a model and a controller. A window and its visual components are connected in a treelike structure called the visual structure or visual component tree. The root node is the window, wrappers and composites are branch nodes, and the remaining visual components are the leaf nodes. Containers are visual parts that contain other visual components. Components are visual components contained by wrappers and composites. A wrapper is a container providing services to its component such as edge decoration and coordinate translation. A composite is a container that references several other visual parts, which are almost always wrappers. All views must implement or know about certain methods: update:, invalidate, displayOn:, preferredBounds, container, and component. The displayOn: method is what draws a visual component in the window and takes a ScreenGraphicsContext as its argument. The ScreenGraphicsContext indicates certain drawing parameters such as font and line thickness.

Each window has several controllers, but only one controller can process user input at any given moment. The controller currently processing user input is the active controller and is said to have control. While a controller has control, it repeats a loop implemented in the method controlLoop. Each time through the loop, the controller does three things: yields to the window controller for processing of window events, checks to see if it wants to maintain control, and processes user input. The method controlActivity is where the controller processes the user input.

The enhancements to *ParcPlace\Smalltalk* provided by *VisualWorks* go far beyond the labor-saving devices of a typical GUI builder to include a much more sophisticated MVC architecture and more variety and flexibility in user interfaces.

CHAPTER 2

Components

PRIOR TO VISUAL WORKS, there were only a few stock interface classes such as TextView and SelectionInListView with which to build user interfaces. These views expected to depend on models that managed several pieces of information and therefore had several aspects. Connecting the view/controller pairs to this type of model was a somewhat laborious endeavor. Other interface components, such as action buttons, required the developer to add an intermediary model such as a PluggableAdaptor. And implementing radio buttons required a degree in rocket science!

VisualWorks started from scratch with new visual classes and controller classes opting to reuse very little of the preexisting user interface classes. *VisualWorks* also introduced several new models and reworked the existing model classes as well. This start from scratch allowed *VisualWorks* to standardize and simplify the way interfaces are built while adding a great deal of variety and flexibility to those interfaces. Now, all views and models use the same means of communication called *value model protocol*. Also, the various parts of the interface inherently know how to work in cooperation with each other.

A *VisualWorks* window is built by assembling various self-contained pieces of user interface. These pieces are called *VisualWorks* components, and they are the fundamental building blocks of a user interface. Lists, buttons, and labels are examples of such components. Some *VisualWorks* components are rather passive in nature, such as labels and regions. Others, such as input fields and sliders, are constantly changing during runtime and interact with the user. Some *VisualWorks* components are merely a collection of other components treated as a whole. A window interface in *VisualWorks* can be viewed as nothing more than an assembly of *VisualWorks* components inside of a window.

In this chapter, we will look at these fundamental building blocks of a *VisualWorks* interface and at all the types of objects that comprise them. The first section gives a high-level overview of *VisualWorks* components in general. The next section covers the widget classes, which give the components their visual appearance. Section 3 is about the various model classes available for *VisualWorks* components and for other uses as well. Section 4 discusses the controller classes, which allow the components to interact with the user. Section 5 covers the notion of creating blueprints for *VisualWorks* components called specification objects.

This chapter leans heavily on the topics covered in Chapter 1. You should be comfortable with MVC and how visual components relate to one another in the visual structure before continuing with this chapter.

2.1 VisualWorks Components

The term *component* suffers considerably from definition overload. The most general definition was given in Chapter 1: a visual component that is contained by a visual part or a window and draws itself on a window's display surface. Forming a subset of this group are what I refer to as *VisualWorks* components. A *VisualWorks component* is a spec wrapper. A *spec wrapper* is a special type of wrapper developed explicitly for *VisualWorks* componentry (the formal definition is provided in Section 2.1.3). The spec wrapper contains a widget. A *widget* is a visual part that gives the *VisualWorks* component its specific appearance and functionality (the formal definition is provided in Section 2.1.2.3). All *VisualWorks* components are spec wrappers, and it is the widget that distinguishes one type of *VisualWorks* component from the next. For example, the widget for a list component is a SequenceView and the widget for an input field is an InputFieldView.

All *VisualWorks* components respond to a set of messages I refer to as *VisualWorks component protocol*. All widgets should respond to a certain set of messages I refer to as *widget protocol*.

This section covers the basics of all *VisualWorks* components. First we will look at dividing the *VisualWorks* components into logical categories. Next we will discuss widget fundamentals and widget protocol. Then we will look at spec wrappers and *VisualWorks* component protocol.

2.1.1 Component Categories

The group of components referred to as *VisualWorks* components can be divided into five categories: active components, passive components, arbitrary components, composites, and subcanvases. The first four are covered in this chapter. The topic of subcanvases requires information not yet covered, so its treatment is deferred until Chapter 5.

2.1.1.1 Active Components

For the purposes of this book, an **active component** is a *VisualWorks* component whose widget is some type of view. (You should be aware that the *VisualWorks User's Guide* has an alternative definition for *active component:* a visual component that references its container.) Since a view has a model and a controller, active components can interact with the user. Table 2.1 shows the active components available in *VisualWorks*. The first column is the given name of the component. The second column indicates the default model used by the widget. Most of these models can be replaced by models with similar behavior. Also, these models are not necessarily the models returned by the component's corresponding aspect method as is the case with list and table components. The third column lists the widget's class. The type of widget for a given active component is either the class indicated or one of its subclasses. The last column indicates the default controller used by the widget. Disk Example 2.1 gives examples for most of the active components.

[a]The ComboBoxView is actually a composite containing a special type of input field (an instance of ComboBoxInputFieldView) and a special type of action button (an instance of ComboBoxButtonView). This input field is the active part of the combo box in that it has a model, the ValueHolder listed in the table, and a controller, which is an instance of ComboBoxInputBoxController. The ComboBoxView itself however, has neither a model nor a controller, but it is the widget for a combo box component.

Table 2.1. *VisualWorks* Active Components.

Component	Model type	Widget type	Controller type
Action Button	PluggableAdaptor	ActionButtonView	TriggerButtonController
Radio Button	PluggableAdaptor	RadioButtonView	ToggleButtonController
Check Box	ValueHolder	CheckButtonView	ToggleButtonController
Menu Button	ValueHolder	MenuButtonView	MenuButtonController
Combo Box	ValueHolder	ComboBoxView	a
List	ValueHolder	SequenceView	SequenceController
Table	ValueHolder	GeneralSelectionTableView	SequenceController
Input Field	ValueHolder	InputFieldView	InputBoxController
Text Editor	ValueHolder	TextEditorView	TextEditorController
Slider	ValueHolder	SliderView	SliderController
Data Set	ValueHolder	DataSetView	DataSetController
Linked Detail	PluggableAdaptor	ActionButtonView	TriggerButtonController

2.1.1.2 Passive Components

VisualWorks has four types of passive components: labels, regions, dividers, and group boxes. A **passive component** is a *VisualWorks* component whose widget does not depend on a model, does not have a controller, and is quite passive in nature. (You should be aware that the *VisualWorks User's Guide* has an alternative definition for the term *passive component:* a visual component that does not reference its container.) Table 2.2 lists each of these components and its widget's class. All four of these classes are direct subclasses of SimpleComponent, which is a subclass of VisualPart. See Disk Example 2.2 for examples of each of these passive components.

2.1.1.3 Arbitrary Components

An **arbitrary component** is special type of *VisualWorks* component whose widget can be any arbitrary visual part, and not necessarily one specifically constructed to be a *VisualWorks* widget (see Disk Example 2.3 for a good example). An arbitrary component can also go by the name of **view holder** (this term is used by the Palette but is somewhat misleading since there is no restriction on the widget being a view). An arbitrary component is the *VisualWorks* equivalent of a wild card. The widget for an arbitrary component can be a view, a composite, or any other type of visual part.

There are two real advantages to arbitrary components. First, they provide a mechanism for legacy interface objects to be included in *VisualWorks*. This is the *VisualWorks* form of backward compatibility. Any visual part constructed prior to *VisualWorks,* and without any knowledge of *VisualWorks*, can be placed in a *VisualWorks* interface using an arbitrary component. Second, arbitrary components provide an easy route to extending the list of available *VisualWorks* components. The alternative to using an arbitrary component is to create a first class *VisualWorks* component, which involves a considerable amount of work. The tradeoffs between using arbitrary components and developing new, first-class *VisualWorks* components is explored in Chapter 12.

2.1.1.4 Composite Components

A **composite component** is another special type of *VisualWorks* component. Its widget is a composite of several other *VisualWorks* components. A composite component

Table 2.2. *VisualWorks* Passive Components.

Component	Widget type
Label	PassiveLabel
Region	VisualRegion
Divider	VisualDivider
Box	GroupBox

allows a collection of *VisualWorks* components to be treated as a single component. Its widget is implemented by a CompositePart. Composite components are distinguished by the fact that they are not available from the Palette. Instead, they are manufactured directly by the canvas by grouping a multiple selection of components (they can also be manufactured programmatically during runtime). Disk Example 2.4 gives a brief illustration of composite components.

2.1.2 The Widget

A **widget** is a visual part responsible for the visual representation of a *VisualWorks* component. Each widget in *VisualWorks* is expected to maintain certain state information and respond to certain messages referred to as **widget protocol**. The state information includes visual properties (i.e., look preferences or a color scheme), text properties, and a bookkeeping device for tracking the current status of the widget, such as if it is disabled or visible. The widget protocol involves such behaviors as becoming enabled or disabled, taking keyboard focus, and propagating changes down the visual structure. Not all widgets respond to the entire set of widget protocol.

Unfortunately, there is no single abstract class for widgets, as you will see in Section 2.2. In fact, the characteristics of a widget are redundantly implemented in several locations throughout the hierarchy. However, for a good reference for this section, see the class SimpleView, which is the quintessential implementation of the abstract widget state and behavior discussed below.

2.1.2.1 The Widget's State

Each widget in *VisualWorks* is required to keep track of its own state (usually the term *state* applies to all of an object's attributes, but in this context *state* applies only to those attributes mentioned here). A widget's state is its current condition with respect to such things as color, visibility, and keyboard focus. A widget monitors its current state with an instance of WidgetState held in its state instance variable. A widget's state variable is accessed using the widgetState and widgetState: messages. Each widget knows how to create and initialize its own instance of WidgetState.

A WidgetState is sort of an accounting object—it keeps track of information for its widget. The kind of information it tracks can be divided into four categories: boolean conditions, look preferences, text attributes, and label information. A WidgetState's ability to track text attributes and label information is currently unused by *VisualWorks*.

A WidgetState keeps track of 11 boolean attributes describing its widget. These are listed in Table 2.3. The first column lists the messages for accessing and changing the boolean. The second column describes the condition being monitored.

WidgetState implements these boolean conditions with a single instance variable called bits. This is a SmallInteger used as a bit mask where each bit is responsible for one of the boolean conditions. This is much more efficient than allocating 11 boolean instance variables.

As can be seen in Table 2.3, not all widgets track all of the boolean conditions. Some state conditions only apply to a subset of the widgets.

A WidgetState keeps track of its widget's current color scheme using a LookPreferences object, which it references with its colors instance variable. A LookPreferences describes the colors to be used for various colors roles such as foreground, background, selection foreground, and selection background. The lookPreferences instance variable is accessed with the colors message and replaced with the colors: message.

2.1.2.2 Text Properties

Since most widgets use text or have a label, each widget is expected to maintain its own default text properties. The message getTextStyle returns a widget's default text attributes. The message setTextStyle: aTextAttributes sets the widget's text attributes. Also, all widgets, except those used for text editors and input fields, know how to make a Label object. This is a handy service provided by the method makeTextLabelFor: aStringOrText. This method creates a Label object based on aStringOrText and the widget's own text attributes.

Table 2.3. Widget State Boolean Conditions.

Accessors	Description
canTakeFocus canTakeFocus:	Indicates if the widget can take focus. Applies to all active components except sliders and menu buttons.
hasBackgroundColor hasBackgroundColor:	Indicates if the widget has its own background color.
hasBorder hasBorder:	Indicates if the component has a border.
hasKeyboardFocus hasKeyboardFocus:	Set to true when the widget takes focus and set to false when it gives up focus. Applies to all active components except sliders and menu buttons.
isDefaultAction isDefaultAction	Set to true if the widget is expected to be the default action for an <Enter> keystroke. Applies only to action buttons.
isDefaultSized isDefaultSized	Indicates if the widget should be drawn with the default size or with the regular size. Applies only to action buttons.
isEnabled isEnabled:	Indicates if the widget is currently enabled.
isOccluded isOccluded:	Indicates if part or all of the component is covered by another component.
isOpaque isOpaque:	Indicates if the background of the widget can occlude other components.
isTabStop isTabStop:	Currently used by only DataSetView.
isVisible isVisible:	Indicates if the widget is currently visible.

2.1.2.3 Broadcast Protocol

Whenever a composite component becomes invisible, it must notify its component parts of this change in state so that they can become invisible as well. In fact, each visual part in the visual structure is expected to propagate any changes in its visual state down to any components it may contain. The message it uses to notify its component(s) of a change in state is

> downcastEvent: aKey with: aParameter from: anInitiator.

The arguments for this message are

aKey	A Symbol describing the type of event or change in visual state.
aParameter	Any arbitrary object containing information about the change, usually a boolean.
anInitiator	The object from which the message originated, usually the window.

A related message is

> downcastLocalEvent: aKey with: aParameter at: aPoint from: anInitiator

This message is used to pass an event that is targeted to a specific widget. The additional argument, aPoint, is a Point object that indicates the location of the event, which is usually a mouse event. The event is passed down the visual structure until it is handled by the appropriate component. The appropriate component is the component whose bounds contains the Point argument, and the event is usually handled by that widget's controller.

The two messages downcastEvent:with:at: and downcastLocalEvent:with:at:from: constitute the widget's broadcast protocol.

2.1.2.4 Widget State Protocol

In order to adequately propagate and record changes in state and perform other services as well, each widget is expected to respond to the messages listed in Table 2.4.

Table 2.4. Widget State Protocol.

Message	Behavior
isEnabled	Return a boolean indicating if the widget is enabled.
isEnabled: aBoolean	Set the widget's enabled state to aBoolean.
isVisible	Return a boolean indicating if the widget is visible.
isVisible: aBoolean	Set the widget's visibility, maintained in its state variable, to aBoolean
widgetState	Return the widget's instance of WidgetState.
widgetState: aWidgetState	Set the widget's state to a aWidgetState

Do not confuse the messages in Table 2.4, which are sent to the widget directly, with those in Table 2.3, which are sent to the WidgetState object contained by the widget.

2.1.2.5 Visual Properties Protocol

Each widget is expected to know the colors in which it should be rendered in a window. The group of methods that access these colors from the widget are defined in the 'visual properties' protocol. A widget does not specify these colors directly but rather symbolically using a SymbolicPaint object. That is, the visual properties protocol messages do not return ColorValue objects but SymbolicPaint objects. A SymbolicPaint specifies a color role such as background color or foreground color. The exact color for each of these roles is determined at runtime. This mechanism ensures that at runtime, the background portions of the widget will be drawn in the current background color and foreground portions of the widget will be drawn in the current foreground color. The exact colors used for each role are specified in the widget's WidgetState variable (see Section 2.1.2.1) or inherited from the widget's container. These colors also vary based on whether the widget is enabled or disabled.

2.1.2.6 Widget Protocol

The broadcast protocol, widget state protocol, and visual properties protocol together constitute the widget protocol. The widget protocol is the set of messages that all widgets are expected to understand.

2.1.3 Spec Wrapper

All *VisualWorks* components are actually spec wrappers. A **spec wrapper** is a wrapper that contains a widget, decoration for the widget, a copy of that widget's state, and a blueprint for describing itself called a component spec (see Figure 2.1). A spec wrapper is implemented by the class SpecWrapper, which is a subclass of the abstract class Widget-Wrapper. WidgetWrapper, in turn, is a subclass of Wrapper. Much of what distinguishes a SpecWrapper from other types of wrappers is actually implemented in its immediate superclass, WidgetWrapper. The spec wrapper behaviors described in this section constitute the *VisualWorks* component protocol. The **VisualWorks component protocol** is the set of messages to which all *VisualWorks* components should respond.

2.1.3.1 Container, Component, and Decoration

Since a SpecWrapper is a kind of Wrapper, it has a container and a component. It should be noted that a SpecWrapper object's component is not the widget. Its component is always some other kind of wrapper, which contains either the widget or yet another wrapper. In fact, there may be several layers of wrappers between the spec wrapper and its widget. Figure

2.1 uses a list component as an example. The spec wrapper's component is a bounded wrapper. And the bounded wrapper's component is a border decorator, and so on. The widget in this case, a SequenceView, is actually four times removed from the spec wrapper.

A SpecWrapper object can also hold on to a decoration object with its decorator instance variable. This is usually a BorderDecorator and is used to provide scrolling facilities. If the *VisualWorks* component does not scroll, then the decorator instance variable is nil.

2.1.3.2 Accessing the Widget

Because of the varying number of wrappers between a spec wrapper and its widget, a SpecWrapper also maintains a direct pointer to its widget with its widget instance variable (see Figure 2.1). This avoids the need to use a succession of component messages in order to access the underlying widget. Instead, the widget message will return the widget directly regardless of how many wrappers there are.

2.1.3.3 Accessing the Widget State

A SpecWrapper also keeps track of its widget's state. It does this with its widgetState instance variable. When a runtime *VisualWorks* component is created, the SpecWrapper's widgetState variable is set to the widget's state variable. That is, the SpecWrapper and its widget both reference the same instance of WidgetState.

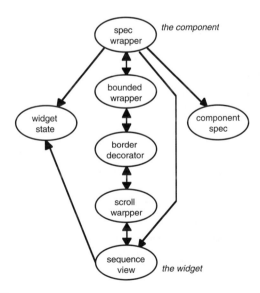

Figure 2.1. A SpecWrapper.

2.1.3.4 Spec Object

A spec wrapper holds on to a spec object that describes the component. It is this feature that gives the SpecWrapper class its name. A spec object is a description, or blueprint, for constructing a piece of interface (spec objects are discussed in Section 2.5 and again in Chapter 3). An instance of SpecWrapper holds on to this spec object with its spec instance variable. Because of this attribute of SpecWrapper, each *VisualWorks* component contains complete instructions for duplicating itself.

2.1.3.5 Widget Control Protocol

SpecWrapper inherits certain widget control methods from its superclass WidgetWrapper. WidgetWrapper defines these methods in its instance protocol 'widget control.' These methods affect how the widget will behave, and they are described below.

beInvisible	Make the widget invisible.
beVisible	Make the widget visible.
disable	Downcast a disable change to the widget and redraw if necessary.
enable	Downcast an enable change to the widget and redraw if necessary.
takeKeyboardFocus	If the widget is visible, enabled, and allowed to take keyboard focus, then give it the keyboard focus.
setDispatcher:	For active components, set the widget's controller's dispatcher (see Section 2.4.2.3).

SpecWrapper also adds conditions to the objectWantingControl method. When a SpecWrapper receives the message objectWantingControl, it checks to see if its widget is both enabled and visible. If either of these conditions is false, it will not allow the widget's controller to become the active controller.

2.1.3.6 Positioning Protocol

SpecWrapper also inherits positioning methods from its superclass WidgetWrapper. WidgetWrapper defines these methods in it, instance protocol 'positioning.' These methods are described below.

moveBy: aPoint	Move the *VisualWorks* component by aPoint within the container's bounds.
moveTo: aPoint	Move the *VisualWorks* component so that its origin is at aPoint relative to its container's bounds.
newBounds: aRectangle	Lay out the *VisualWorks* component within aRectangle.

Thus, all *VisualWorks* components can be moved or resized within their container.

2.1.3.7 Displaying and Visual Properties Protocol

Each *VisualWorks* component can have its own color scheme or look preferences. This look preferences is kept by the WidgetState object. When a SpecWrapper receives a displayOn: message, it merges its look preferences object with that already contained within the graphics context object before forwarding the displayOn: message on down to the widget. This ensures that the widget will draw itself in the appropriate color scheme.

Also, a SpecWrapper will prevent a displayOn: message from being propagated down to its widget if the widget's state is currently invisible. If something is meant to be invisible, you certainly do not want it drawing itself in a window!

2.1.3.8 VISUALWORKS Component Protocol

The positioning protocol, widget control protocol, displaying protocol, and visual properties protocol all constitute *VisualWorks* component protocol. All *VisualWorks* components can respond to these messages.

2.1.4 Summary

In Chapter 1 we defined the term *component* to be a visual component contained within a window or visual part. The components used in *VisualWorks* are a subset of these components. A *VisualWorks* component is a spec wrapper that contains a visual part, called its widget. *VisualWorks* components can be further divided into five categories: active components, passive components, arbitrary components, composites, and subcanvases.

All widgets in *VisualWorks* are expected to maintain certain state information and respond to certain protocol, which is loosely referred to as widget protocol. The state information is maintained in a WidgetState object. A WidgetState keeps track of such things as look preferences (color scheme), visibility, enablement, and keyboard focus. A widget is required to propagate certain changes in its state down to any components it may have. A widget is also required to maintain its own state information and visual properties.

A spec wrapper's component is not the widget but another wrapper. While there may be an arbitrary number of wrappers between the spec wrapper and its widget, the spec wrapper also maintains a direct reference to its widget. A spec wrapper also maintains a direct reference to its widget's state variable. A spec wrapper contains a blueprint for replicating itself, and this blueprint, called a spec object, is referenced via the spec instance variable. The public methods implemented specifically in WidgetWrapper and SpecWrapper constitute what is loosely referred to as *VisualWorks* component protocol.

2.2 Widgets

All *VisualWorks* components have widgets. This section covers the classes that implement those widgets. In the case of active components, the widgets are views and have models and controllers. For passive components and composite components, however, the widgets are not views and have neither models nor controllers. Arbitrary components, by their very nature, have widgets that can fit into either category.

For the purposes of this book, the widget classes have been divided into four groups based on similarities of both type and function. These categories are button and slider widgets, text widgets, selection widgets, and passive widgets. This section begins with a discussion on the hierarchy of the visual classes and what they all have in common. Then each of the four categories is discussed in turn along with the concrete classes comprising that category.

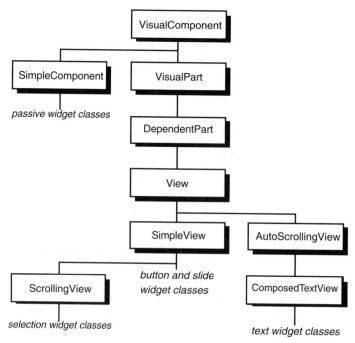

Figure 2.2. Four Branches of *VisualWorks* Widgets.

2.2.1 Hierarchy of Widget Classes

Figure 2.2 shows the four main branches of the widget hierarchy for *VisualWorks* components: button and slider widgets, text widgets, selection widgets, and passive widgets. Although table widgets are considered selection widgets, the table widget classes are actually subclassed from AutoScrollingView and not ScrollingView.

2.2.2 Button and Slider Widgets

There are six *VisualWorks* components that either have buttons as their widgets or include buttons in some way: action button, radio button, check box, menu button, combo box, and linked detail button. The button and slider branch of the widget hierarchy of Figure 2.2 is shown in Figure 2.3. The class SimpleView is a subclass of View that adds the state and behavior required by all *VisualWorks* widgets. Primarily, it defines an instance variable, state, which references a WidgetState object. It also implements all the necessary widget protocol described in Section 2.1.2. SimpleView is the superclass for all sliders and buttons. BasicButtonView is a subclass of SimpleView and the abstract superclass of all button view types. It defines the state and behavior for keeping track of a current value and knowing if that current value is in the process of changing (a BasicButtonView refers to this as being in

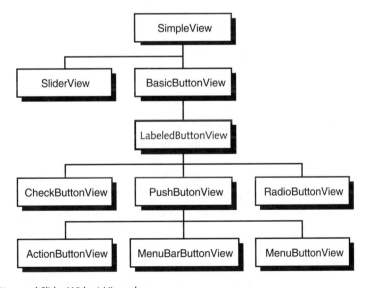

Figure 2.3. Button and Slider Widget Hierarchy.

transition). LabeledButtonView is an abstract subclass of BasicButtonView, and it adds the capability of a providing a label for the button. It has instance variables to reference both its label (label variable) and the text attributes (textStyle) used to display the label.

Below are brief descriptions of the widget classes implementing the button and slider widgets.

2.2.2.1 ActionButtonView

An ActionButtonView is the widget for an action button component. It is also the widget for a linked detail component used for database access. Its model is usually a PluggableAdaptor whose put block has been defined to send a certain action method to an application model. When an ActionButtonView is pressed, it sends the message value: to its model, the PluggableAdaptor. The PluggableAdaptor responds by evaluating its put block, which sends the action message to the application model. ActionButtonView is the concrete implementation for the Default look policy (look policy is covered in Chapter 3, Section 3.4). There are four subclasses, however, for each of the remaining four look policies: CUAActionButtonView, MacActionButtonView, MotifActionButtonView, and Win3-ActionButtonView. An additional subclass, UndecoratedActionButtonView, is used for all look policies when the button is not to display its borders. Such a button appears in the window to be invisible but still responds to mouse input just as if it were visible.

2.2.2.2 RadioButtonView

A RadioButtonView is the widget for a radio button component and a subclass of LabeledButtonView. Its model is a PluggableAdaptor, which is coupled to a ValueHolder whose value is a Symbol. Its controller is a ToggleButtonController. RadioButtonView is actually an abstract class. Its five subclasses are the concrete implementations for each of the five look policies. These classes are CUARadioButtonView, DefaultLookRadioButtonView, MacRadioButtonView, MotifRadioButtonView, and Win3RadioButtonView.

2.2.2.3 CheckButtonView

A CheckButtonView is the widget for a check box component and a subclass of LabeledButtonView. Its model is a ValueHolder whose value is a boolean and its controller is a ToggleButtonController. CheckButtonView is actually an abstract class. Its five subclasses are the concrete implementations for each of the five look policies. These classes are CUACheckButtonView, DefaultLookCheckButtonView, MacCheckButtonView, MotifCheckButtonView, and Win3CheckButtonView.

2.2.2.4 MenuButtonView

A MenuButtonView is the widget for a menu button component. Its model is a ValueHolder whose value is a number, string, or Symbol. Its controller is a MenuButtonController. A

MenuButtonView keeps a menu inside a ValueHolder, which it references with its menu instance variable. The MenuButtonView registers as a dependent of this ValueHolder.
MenuButtonView is the concrete implementation of the menu button widget for the Default look policy. It has four subclasses, which are the concrete implementations for the
remaining look policies. These classes are CUAMenuButtonView, MacMenuButtonView,
MotifMenuButtonView, and Win3MenuButtonView. It has an additional concrete subclass,
UndecoratedMenuButtonView, which is used, regardless of look policy, whenever the button is not to display its borders.

2.2.2.5 SliderView

A SliderView is the widget for a slider component. Its model is a value model whose
value is a number. Its controller is a SliderController. SliderView is the concrete implementation of the slider widget for the Default, *CUA,* and *Motif* look policies. Its two subclasses, MacSliderView and Win3SliderView, implement the *Macintosh* and *MS Windows*
sliders, respectively. A SliderView can orient itself in a horizontal or vertical fashion.

2.2.3 Text Widgets

There are four components that allow the user to edit text: text editor, input field,
combo box, and data set. Three concrete view classes allow text editing in *VisualWorks:*
TextEditorView, InputFieldView, and ComboBoxInputFieldView. These are arranged in a hierarchy shown in Figure 2.4, which is the text widget branch of Figure 2.2. Each of these is
discussed in turn below.

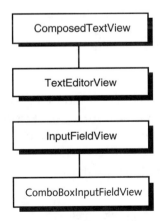

Figure 2.4. Text Widget Hierarchy.

2.2.3.1 TextEditorView

A TextEditorView is the widget for a text editor component. It is a subclass of Composed-TextView, the traditional text view of *ParcPlace\Smalltalk* (see Figure 2.2), which predates *VisualWorks* altogether. A ComposedTextView is used in all the familiar tools: workspace, browser, file list, and debugger. A ComposedTextView is practically a word processor in and of itself. TextEditorView adds to ComposedTextView the state variable (to reference a WidgetState object) and the necessary widget protocol (see Section 2.1.2). And unlike a ComposedTextView, a TextEditorView expects a value model (value models are covered in Section 2.3.1) as its model. TextEditorView is the concrete implementation of a text editor widget for all of the look policies, and there are no look policy specific subclasses of TextEditorView.

2.2.3.2 InputFieldView

The widget for an input field is InputFieldView, which is a subclass of TextEditorView. It adds the ability to have horizontal scrolling within the view instead of wrapping the text as is done in its superclass TextEditorView. An InputFieldView performs the necessary conversion of the model's value from a date or number to a text representation. That is, the model may contain a date, number, string, or Symbol. The InputFieldView, however, only works with text. Therefore, the InputFieldView must make the necessary conversion so that the model's value is editable. An InputFieldView also performs any necessary formatting of the text. The InputFieldView references a PrintConverter object with its converter instance variable, and it is this PrintConverter object that performs the necessary data conversions and formats the text (see Section 2.2.3.3). An InputFieldView is also the editor used by a data set component to edit the contents of its cells. The model for an InputFieldView is a value model, and the default controller is an InputBoxController. InputFieldView is the concrete implementation of an input field widget for all of the look policies, and there are no look policy specific subclasses of InputFieldView.

2.2.3.3 PrintConverter

Two special behaviors of the InputFieldView are to perform conversions between the input text and the data object stored in the model and to format the text which is displayed within the field. The input field uses a PrintConverter object to perform both of these functions. The first of these functions, data object/text object conversion, was performed by a TypeConverter in *VisualWorks* v1.0.

PrintConverter is a subclass of Object, and it defines the following variables, which are all blocks.

toPrint   Provides a text representation of the data object held in the model. This text is what is displayed to the user in the field.

toRead	Converts the string entered by the user to a data object for the model.
toFormat	Takes the text result of the toPrint block and formats it more fully.

The toFormat block may or may not be used based on if the user specified formating for the field.

PrintConverter has several initialization methods for defining the blocks for different data types and different format preferences. Much of the formating behavior is actually defined on the class side of PrintConverter. The PrintConverter does not format the user's input but only formats the result once the field has been accepted. Nor does PrintConverter provide emphasis options (i.e., bold and italic) for the displayed text.

2.2.3.4 ComboBoxInputFieldView

A combo box component has an input field. The view for this field is implemented by ComboBoxInputFieldView, a subclass of InputFieldView. It adds only one slight twist to its superclass. Normally, an input field indicates that it has focus by displaying the type-in point. This is the small triangular marker used to indicate the insertion point of any additional text entered by the user. A combo box input field, however, indicates focus by changing its background in addition to displaying an insertion point. The model for a ComboBoxInputFieldView is a value model, and the default controller is a ComboBoxInput-BoxController. ComboBoxInputFieldView is the concrete implementation of a combo box input field widget for all of the look policies, and there are no look policy specific subclasses of ComboBoxInputFieldView.

2.2.4 Selection Widgets

The selection widgets are the widgets for lists, tables, and data set components.

The selection widgets include SequenceView, MultiSelectionSequenceView, GeneralSelectionTableView, and DataSetView. What these widgets have in common is that they each display a one- or two-dimensional sequence of elements from which the user selects some subset. These widgets are arranged in a hierarchy shown in Figure 2.5, which is the selection widget branch of Figure 2.2.

The table widget classes are included in this discussion of selection widgets based on functionality, but they are not part of this branch of the widget hierarchy. Instead, the table widget classes are subclasses of AutoScrollingView as shown in Figure 2.6.

Each of the selection widget classes is discussed below.

2.2.4.1 SequenceView

A SequenceView is a subclass of SelectionView, and it is the widget responsible for displaying a single selection list component. Its model is a ValueHolder, whose value is a sequenceable collection (its model is *not* a SelectionInList), and its controller is a SequenceController. A SequenceView has many instance variables, but those of most importance to the developer are

grid	An integer that determines the height of each element in pixels
displayStringSelector	A Symbol that is the message sent to each element to obtain a text representation of that object
visualBlock	A block that describes how each element is to be displayed in the list
selectedVisualBlock	A block that describes how an element is to be displayed when it is selected.

The instance variables visualBlock and selectedVisualBlock are collectively referred to as the visual blocks and are used to determine how the objects in the sequenceable collection are rendered in the view. The objects in the collection can appear as formated text, an image, or any other visual component. For instance, a SortedCollection of Cursor objects can be displayed as a list of the cursor names or a list of the actual cursor images or a combination of the cursor name prefixed with the cursor image. SequenceView is the concrete implementation of a single selection list widget for all of the look policies, and there are no look policy specific subclasses of SequenceView.

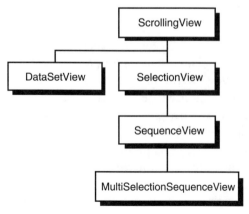

Figure 2.5. Selection Widget Hierarchy.

2.2.4.2 MultiSelectionSequenceView

This class is a subclass of SequenceView and is the widget for a list component that allows the user to make multiple selections. It is similar in every respect to its superclass (including the type of controller used) except that it can display more than one element as being selected. MultiSelectionSequenceView is the concrete implementation of a multiple selection list widget for all of the look policies, and there are no look policy specific subclasses of MultiSelectionSequenceView.

2.2.4.3 GeneralSelectionTableView

A table component presents the user with a two-dimensional list of elements from which the user can select a single element, a single row of elements, or a single column of elements. Most of the table widget behavior is implemented in the superclass TableView. The concrete class for a table widget is a GeneralSelectionTableView, which is a subclass of TableView. It is the GeneralSelectionTableView that adds the behavior for selecting a single cell, a row, or a column. The cells in a table can be rendered in the same way as the elements in a list component—as text, images, or any arbitrary visual component. The model for a GeneralSelectionTableView is a value model, and the default controller is a SequenceController. GeneralSelectionTableView is the concrete implementation of a table widget for all of the look policies, and there are no look policy specific subclasses of GeneralSelectionTableView.

TableView is worth mentioning in its own right, as it is much more than just the superclass of GeneralSelectionTableView. Instances of TableView are used as the scrolling row labels and column labels for a table component.

2.2.4.4 DataSetView

A DataSetView allows the user to actively edit the elements in a collection using either menu buttons, check boxes, combo boxes, or input fields. DataSetView is distinguished

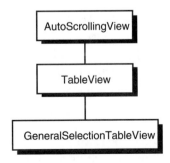

Figure 2.6. Table Widget Hierarchy.

by the fact that it is not used to represent the data set component in edit mode. Instead, its subclass PaintedDataSetView is used. This is so that the developer can have a limited amount of live interaction with the component while editing a canvas. DataSetView is the concrete implementation of a data set widget for all of the look policies, and there are no look policy specific subclasses of DataSetView.

2.2.5 Passive Component Widgets

There are four passive type components: label, divider, region, and group box. The widget classes for these are PassiveLabel, VisualDivider, VisualRegion, and GroupBox, respectively. Each of these is a subclass of the abstract class SimpleComponent, and together they constitute the passive widget branch of Figure 2.2. SimpleComponent is a subclass of VisualPart that adds the necessary state and behavior required by all *VisualWorks* widgets. That is, it defines a state instance variable to reference a WidgetState object and it implements all of the necessary widget protocol (see Section 2.1.2). The four passive widget classes are discussed below.

2.2.5.1 PassiveLabel

A PassiveLabel is a kind of SimpleComponent that displays text or an image (i.e., a bit map) in a window. It defines three instance variables: label, textStyle, and margin. The label variable holds onto a visual component, usually an instance of Label or an image. The textStyle variable holds onto a TextAttributes or a VariableSizeTextAttributes. The margin variable is an integer that describes the x and y offset for drawing the label. PassiveLabel is the concrete implementation of a label widget for all of the look policies, and there are no look policy specific subclasses of PassiveLabel.

2.2.5.2 VisualDivider

A VisualDivider is a kind of SimpleComponent and draws a line in a window, which is usually used to visually divide two sets of components. A VisualDivider can be horizontal or vertical and have a flat look or an etched look. VisualDivider defines two instance variables: orientation and lineWidth. The orientation variable is set to #horizontal or #vertical to indicate whether the line is drawn horizontally or vertically. The lineWidth variable is an integer and indicates the thickness of the line. VisualDivider is the concrete implementation of a divider widget for all of the look policies, and there are no look policy specific subclasses of VisualDivider.

2.2.5.3 VisualRegion

A VisualRegion is a kind of SimpleComponent that colors a given area of a window. This area can be a rectangle or an ellipse. VisualRegion defines three instance variables: extent, lineWidth, and isElliptical. The extent variable is a Point that defines the extent, or dimensions, of the region. The lineWidth variable is an integer and determines the thickness of the border—a zero value means no border. The variable isElliptical is a boolean and indicates the type of region—rectangle or ellipse. VisualRegion is the concrete implementation of a region widget for all of the look policies, and there are no look policy specific subclasses of VisualRegion.

2.2.5.4 GroupBox

A GroupBox is a kind of SimpleComponent that draws a rectangular border within its bounds. It includes an optional label in the upper lefthand corner. A GroupBox is hollow in nature, that is, a point within its bounds is not considered to be contained by the GroupBox object. Only those points on its border or its label are considered to be contained by the GroupBox. GroupBox defines three instance variables: label, textStyle, and border. The label variable is an instance of Label by default, but it could be any visual component. The text-Style variable holds onto a TextAttributes or a VariableSizeTextAttributes object and is also used only in the event that the GroupBox is labeled. The border variable holds onto one of the many types of border objects (see Chapter 9, Section 9.2.2 for a discussion on border types). GroupBox is the concrete implementation of a group box widget for all of the look policies, and there are no look policy specific subclasses of GroupBox.

2.3 Models

One of the major contributions *VisualWorks* brings to the topic of models is the factoring of models into several different types, each providing different specific behaviors. There are two broad categories, however: application models and aspect models. The differences between the two is a matter of granularity and developer implementation. An application model is responsible for managing several pieces of interface for a window, a group of windows, or a subcanvas. (A more complete definition of application model is forthcoming in Chapter 4, which deals explicitly with application models.) An **aspect model**, on the other hand, contains a single aspect of information and provides model behavior for a single *VisualWorks* component. Also, application model classes are designed by the developer for each specific application. Aspect model classes, however, are much more general in nature, and the developer rarely has need to design new ones. The relationship between an application model and an aspect model is that an application model contains one or more aspect models.

Completely orthogonal to the application/aspect classification of models is another classification of models called value models. Value models are the backbone of interface building in *VisualWorks* and are used for a variety of purposes as described in Section 2.3.1.

This section looks at the value models and aspect models. The topic of application model is reserved for Chapter 4. We will start by discussing the value model concept. We will follow this with the various concrete implementations, some of which are used as aspect models and some of which are not. Finally, we will look at remaining aspect model classes.

2.3.1 Value Models

A **value model** is a model that has one primary aspect of information, called its value; this aspect is accessed using the messages value and value:. Before *VisualWorks,* value models were used primarily to provide model behavior to nonmodel objects, such as strings and numbers. Since the advent of *VisualWorks,* the importance of value models has grown tremendously. All views in *VisualWorks* have value models as their model (this is not necessarily the case for *ParcPlace\Smalltalk* in general as was demonstrated in Chapter 1, Section 1.5). Value models are also used quite frequently as the common reference point for a changing value (the channel concept discussed in Section 2.3.1.2). *VisualWorks* has introduced several new types of value models as well, each with a slight variation of the basic theme. And with the advent of the DependencyTransformer to work with value models, the dependency mechanism is now much easier to use (see Sections 2.3.2.2 and 2.3.2.3).

2.3.1.1 Value Model Protocol

In traditional application development as discussed in Chapter 1, Section 1.5, the typical model developed for a specific application usually had several aspects, or pieces of information, which it managed. Each one of these aspects had a get and put selector. When a view registered with the model as a dependent, it had to be told the aspect on which it depended, as well as the get and put selectors for accessing that aspect (see Chapter 1, Section 1.5 for an example). For instance, consider a model that has an instance variable called notes. Most likely, this instance variable is accessed using the get and put selectors notes and notes:, respectively. In order to have a view display and edit this model's notes information, the developer would have to let the view know the names of the get and put selectors so it can do its job. The developer would also have to tell the view to look for the argument #notes in its update: method. This puts a burden on each view to have to learn internal details about the model on which it depends, not to mention the burden placed on the developer to set it all up!

The views in *VisualWorks* are relieved of having to know anything specific about their model. All *VisualWorks* views depend on a value model. A value model's primary aspect of information is called its value, and this value is accessed with the messages value and value:. These two messages are referred to as **value model protocol**. Each view in *VisualWorks* automatically knows to send value to access its model's information and to send value: to change its model's information. Value model protocol is the backbone of communication among objects in *VisualWorks*.

2.3.1.2 Channel

There is an additional benefit to value models. They provide a common access point for a changing value. In Figure 2.7a, object 1, object 2, and object 3 all reference the same value (or object), value 1. In order to replace this object with another, value 2 in this example, all three references must be updated (Figure 2.7b). That is, each of the three objects must be sent a message to replace value 1 with value 2. In Figure 2.7c however, object 1, object 2, and object 3 all reference a value model, which in turn references value 1. The value model's value can be replaced with another object, value 2 in this case, but the references of object 1, object 2, and object 3 do not have to be updated (Figure 2.7d). They stay fixed on the value model. When a value model is used in this way, it is referred to as a channel. A **channel** is a value model that is used as the common access point for a changing value.

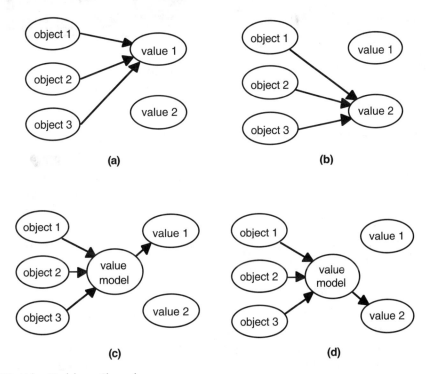

Figure 2.7. Value Model as a Channel.

I would like to make clear the fact that object 1, object 2, and object 3 are not *dependents* of the value model and do not receive any updates from the value model. They merely *reference* the value model as they might reference any other object.

2.3.1.3 Implementation

The state and behavior for value model protocol is defined in the abstract class Value-Model, which is a subclass of Model. Most types of value models, though not all, are a subclass of ValueModel. If you browse the class ValueModel, you will see that its implementation of the value: method is as shown below.

```
value: newValue
    "Set the currently stored value, and notify dependents."

    self setValue: newValue.
    self changed: #value
```

This is very much as we expect. Since the aspect is called #value, the argument for the changed: message is #value. This means that the *VisualWorks* views, which expect their model to be a value model, implement update: anAspectSymbol by testing anAspectSymbol to see if it is equal to #value. Therefore, any replacement of the value instance variable automatically updates the views or other dependents so they can reflect this change. Well, almost! It is possible to replace the value instance variable without updating any dependents. This is done using the setValue: method. The setValue: method assigns newValue to the instance variable value but does not notify the dependents. ValueModel defers implementation of the setValue: method to its subclasses.

2.3.1.4 Value Model Protocol Revisited

Value model protocol was defined in Section 2.3.1.1 as the messages value and value:. Several types of objects understand value model protocol but are not value models in the sense that they do not exhibit model type behavior. An excellent example is an Association. An Association object can receive the messages value and value:, but it is not meant to be used as a model, and therefore, it is not considered a value model. Since it understands the protocol, it can be used as a value model; however, it will not send any updates whenever it changes value.

2.3.1.5 Changes in the Value Model

When the value of a value model changes, it propagates a change message to all of its dependents just as any model would. The difference is that the argument of the change message is always #value. Dependents of a value model know to look for this Symbol for updates and, therefore, do not have to look for anything specific in the update message.

2.3.2 ValueHolder

A ValueHolder is a value model, and the ValueHolder class is a direct subclass of the class ValueModel. It is the model most used by a *VisualWorks* developer and the default model for several of the widgets (see Table 2.1). It is a concrete implementation of the basic value model concept. ValueHolder is appropriately named since it *holds* on to a single *value*. Since Smalltalk is typeless, a ValueHolder can hold onto any type of object from a string or number to a window or collection—or even another model.

2.3.2.1 Creating a ValueHolder

ValueHolder objects are usually created in one of three ways. First, a ValueHolder can be created by sending the with: message to the class as shown below.

ValueHolder with: anObject

The ValueHolder class also has three specific instance creation methods for creating and initializing ValueHolder objects for booleans, strings, and Fraction objects. For instance, to create a ValueHolder on a boolean, use the statement below.

ValueHolder newBoolean

Finally, any object will respond to the asValue message by returning a ValueHolder with itself as the value as shown below.

anObject asValue

The exceptions to this are the value models themselves, which respond by returning self.

2.3.2.2 Registering Interest in a Value Model

The topic of registering interest applies to all subclasses of ValueModel, but we will address it using ValueHolder. Any object can register interest in the value of a value model. As a consequence of **registering interest**, an object will automatically be notified of a change in a value model without having to be a dependent of that value model and without having to implement an update method. The object that registers interest in a value model is known as the **interested object**. The notification of change is in the form of a predetermined message, which is sent to the interested object whenever the value model changes its value (i.e., receives the value: message). The message that is sent to the interested object as a result of a change in a value model is known as a **change message**.

An interested object registers interest in a value model by using the onChangeSend: to: message demonstrated below.

aValueModel onChangeSend: aChangeMessage to: anInterestedObject

In this example, aValueModel is a value model that has a value of interest, aChangeMessage is the change message expressed as a Symbol, and anInterestedObject is the object that will receive the change message. Whenever the value in aValueModel is replaced using the value: message, the message defined by aChangeMessage is sent to the interested object anInterested-Object. Any number of objects can register interest in the same value model and each one can have its own unique change message. The message aChangeMessage must be a unary message, a single argument keyword message, or a double argument keyword message, and it must be understood by anInterestedObject. The reason for this restriction on the form of aChangeMessage will become evident in Section 2.3.2.3. The behavior for onChangeSend:to: is implemented in ValueModel so any object that is a kind of ValueModel can make use of this technique. Disk Example 2.5 covers the topic of registering interest in a value model.

2.3.2.3 DependencyTransformer

The exact mechanism behind an object registering interest in a value model is implemented in DependencyTransformer. It is important to point out at this time that this mechanism can apply to any aspect of any model and is in no way restricted to the #value aspect of a value model. Currently, however, this mechanism is used only with value models.

The DependencyTransformer has the sole mission of registering itself as the dependent of a model and translating the generic update message

> update: anAspectSymbol with: aParameter from: aModel

into a specific change message targeted at the interested object. Figure 2.8 shows the relationship between the model, its dependents collection, the DependencyTransformer, and the interested object.

To accomplish its task, DependencyTransformer defines four instance variables: receiver, selector, numArguments, and aspect.

receiver	Used to reference the interested object. This is the object that will receive the change message.
selector	A Symbol that is the name of the change message to be sent to the interested object, to notify it that a change of value has occurred.
numArguments	An integer of 0, 1, or 2 indicating the number of arguments required by the change message referenced by the selector instance variable above.
aspect	A Symbol that is the name of the aspect in which the receiver is interested. Its default is #value since DependencyTransformer objects are almost always used with value models.

When the model of interest (usually a value model but not necessarily so) changes, it notifies its dependents collection with the message

> changed: #value with: aParameter

the implementation of which broadcasts the message

>   update: #value with: aParameter from: self

to all of the dependents. Since the DependencyTransformer is a dependent of the model, it receives this update message. The DependencyTransformer implementation of the update: with:from: method is shown below.

>   **update: anAspect with: parameters from: anObject**
>
>   aspect == anAspect ifFalse: [^self].
>   numArguments == 0 ifTrue: [^receiver perform: selector].
>   numArguments == 1 ifTrue: [^receiver perform: selector with: parameters].
>   numArguments == 2 ifTrue: [^receiver perform: selector with: parameters with: anObject]

This method first tests to see if anAspect matches its aspect variable. (In update methods discussed previously in this book, the anAspect argument is called anAspectSymbol.) If it does, then it dispatches the message held in its selector variable to the interested object referenced by its receiver variable. If the message is a single keyword message, then parameters is used as the argument. (In update methods discussed previously in this book, the parameters argument is called aParameter.) If the message is a double keyword message, then parameters is the first argument and anObject is the second argument. This is the reason why the change message must be either a unary, single keyword, or double keyword message. While a DependencyTransformer can register as a dependent of any model, it is used almost exclusively with value models.

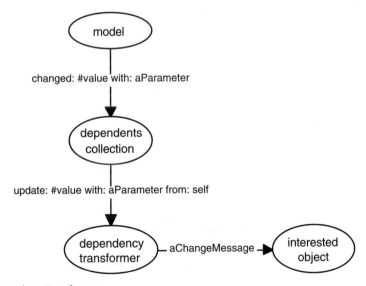

Figure 2.8. DependencyTransformer.

2.3.2.4 Overriding and Removing Interest

Sometimes it is desirable to replace the value in a value model without triggering any updates or sending any change messages to interested objects. There are two ways to do this. First, you can use setValue:, instead of value:, to replace the value of the value model. As was mentioned in Section 2.3.1.3, setValue: replaces the value instance variable without sending notification to the dependents.

The second technique involves removing the DependencyTransformer from the value model's list of dependents. The ValueModel class defines the following instance method for doing just this type of surgery.

> valueModel retractInterestsFor: anObject

This is done just prior to sending value: to the value model. Immediately afterwards, interest can be reinstated using the onChangeSend:to: message.

Using setValue: disallows any and all updates. Removing a DependencyTransformer only disallows a specific update, allowing all others to proceed. It also requires the additional work of reinstating the dependency. Disk Example 2.6 covers the topic of overriding and removing interests.

2.3.2.5 Registering Interest versus Registering as a Dependent

In *VisualWorks,* there are two approaches by which an object can take interest in the internal state of a model: registering interest and registering as a dependent. It is important that you be able to distinguish between the two. They both have the same ultimate goal: to notify an object whenever a model has changed a certain aspect. They both use the same basic mechanism: the changed/update mechanism. They differ, however, in four fundamental ways: who is actually the dependent, the aspect of interest, the update/notification message, and the setup.

To register interest, the interested object employs a DependencyTransformer to become the dependent of the model. When registering as a dependent, the interested object itself becomes the dependent. With respect to the aspect, the registering interest approach is only interested in the #value aspect (it is the implementation of the onChangeSend:to: method that imposes this restriction, not the DependencyTransformer). However, when registering directly as a dependent, the aspect is completely arbitrary. The notification message is arbitrary in the case of registering interest, but when registering as a dependent, the notification message is necessarily the update:with:from: or one of its two less general forms. Finally, both mechanisms are set up with a single line of code, but the registering interest setup is more informative. In addition, registering as a dependent may also require changes to the source code of one of the object's update methods. Table 2.5 summarizes these differences.

For the remainder of the book, I will use the terminology *register interest* to refer to an object that uses an onChangeSend:to: message to take interest in the value of a value

Table 2.5. Registering Interest versus Registering as a Dependent.

Difference	Registering interest	Registering as a dependent
Dependent	a DependencyTransformer	the interested object
Aspect	#value	arbitrary
Update Message	arbitrary with restrictions	update:with:from:
Setup	onChangeSend:to:	addDependent:

model. I will use the terminology *register as a dependent* or *become a dependent* or *depend on* to refer to an object that registers itself directly as a dependent of a model.

2.3.3 AspectAdaptor

The AspectAdaptor is one of the more challenging topics in *VisualWorks*. An AspectAdaptor is a value model whose value actually belongs to another object called the **subject**. The AspectAdaptor references its subject and also knows the accessors for getting and changing the value contained by its subject. It references these selectors with its getSelector and putSelector instance variables, respectively. It does not, however, reference the value directly as does a ValueHolder. In this respect, an AspectAdaptor is a value model once removed from its value. That is, it does not reference its value directly, but instead references its subject, which references the value (see Figure 2.9). The subject can be replaced with another subject at any time by sending the message subject: to the AspectAdaptor with the new subject as the argument. See Disk Example 2.7, which illustrates the basics of using AspectAdaptors.

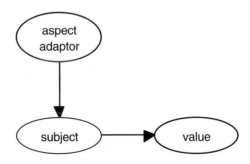

Figure 2.9. AspectAdaptor and Its Subject's Value.

2.3.3.1 Creating an AspectAdaptor

While an AspectAdaptor behaves just like a ValueHolder, it requires a little more work to set up. Instead of initializing an AspectAdaptor with a value, we must initialize it with a subject, which in turn contains the value. We must also provide the get and put selectors used to access the value contained within the subject. For example, suppose we want to bind an AspectAdaptor to an Address object's city variable. If the accessors for the city variable are city and city:, then the following code will create and initialize the appropriate AspectAdaptor.

```
aa := AspectAdaptor subject: Address new.
aa accessWith: #city assignWith: #city:.
```

Since the two accessors are the same except for the colon, we can also use a slightly abbreviated setup.

```
aa := AspectAdaptor subject: Address new.
aa forAspect: #city
```

At this point, if we were to send the message value: 'Paris' to our AspectAdaptor, we would actually be changing the city variable in the Address object.

2.3.3.2 Value Model Behavior

An AspectAdaptor appears to behave just like a ValueHolder in all respects and can be used wherever a ValueHolder is used. Internally, however, it redirects the value message by dispatching the get selector message to its subject. It also redirects the value: message by dispatching the put selector to its subject. Any object can register interest in an AspectAdaptor just as if it were a ValueHolder (see Disk Example 2.5 for registering interest in a value model).

2.3.3.3 The Subject Channel

You rarely find a single AspectAdaptor operating on behalf of a subject. Usually several AspectAdaptors reference the same subject, each one associating itself with a different instance variable within that subject. When several AspectAdaptor objects share the same subject, it becomes convenient to keep the subject in a ValueHolder. The ValueHolder containing the subject is referred to as the subject channel. A **subject channel** is a ValueHolder whose value is the subject for several AspectAdaptors. Each of the AspectAdaptors references the same subject channel as well as the subject it contains.

The benefit of using a subject channel is that regardless of how many AspectAdaptors are sharing the same subject, a change in subject only requires a change in the subject channel (this is a good example of the channel concept described in Section 2.3.1.2 and illustrated in Figure 2.7). That is, instead of sending the message subject: newSubject to each and every AspectAdaptor, it is only necessary to send value: newSubject to the single subject channel. Each AspectAdaptor is automatically associated with the new subject in the subject channel. This automatic update is possible because each AspectAdaptor is a dependent of the subject channel. Disk Example 2.8 gives a good example of how to use a subject channel.

2.3.3.4 The Target Object

Sometimes the value on which the AspectAdaptor operates is not immediately accessible from the subject. That is, the value is not one of the subject's instance variables that can be accessed with the access selectors held by the getSelector and putSelector variables. In such cases the value is contained by an object that is itself contained by the subject. This object is referred to as the target. The **target** is an object that is part of the subject's object structure and contains the value of interest. An AspectAdaptor accesses the target with a series of access selectors contained within its accessPath instance variable. These accessors are used to walk down the structure of the subject to obtain the target object. The accessors referenced by the getSelector and putSelector are then applied to this target object. If the accessPath instance variable is nil, then the target object defaults to the subject. See Disk Example 2.9 for more on the target object.

2.3.3.5 Lazy Updates

To add one more layer of complexity, the subject itself can be a model that issues updates (ordinarily, the subject is not a model). If the subject is a model that does issue updates and the AspectAdaptor has dependents of its own, then the AspectAdaptor will register as a dependent of the subject. Any updates the AspectAdaptor receives from its subject will be forwarded to its dependents. This allows the AspectAdaptor and its dependents to know about a change to its subject that occurred by way of some other agent. The notion that an AspectAdaptor will depend on its subject if and only if the AspectAdaptor has dependents and the subject sends updates is called **lazy dependency**. If the subject does send updates, the AspectAdaptor must be set up appropriately by sending it the message subjectSendsUpdates: true.

2.3.4 PluggableAdaptor

Prior to *VisualWorks*, PluggableAdaptors were quite prominent in user interface construction. The PluggableAdaptor was the all purpose value model. PluggableAdaptor objects are so flexible, in fact, they can be configured to behave just like any other type of value model mentioned in this chapter. Since *VisualWorks* has fully adopted the value model protocol, however, and added several specific value model types, the role of PluggableAdaptor has diminished somewhat and any remaining uses are very well hidden from the developer. Nevertheless, as you desire to give your applications more intricate behavior, an understanding of PluggableAdaptor will prove to be most beneficial.

The best description of a PluggableAdaptor is that it facilitates communication between two objects that otherwise would not be able to communicate. The gap in communication is usually because of a mismatch in protocol or in the type of argument being passed. More often than not, the two objects involved are a model and its dependent. The dependent communicates using value model protocol, but the model does not. The PluggableAdaptor is used as an intermediary between the two so that they can communicate.

PluggableAdaptor objects are extremely flexible, and their uses are quite limitless. Counted among the more common uses are an interpreter of messages, an interpreter of values, and an initiator of an action.

2.3.4.1 How It Works

The PluggableAdaptor typically inserts itself between a model and one of the model's dependents. That is, the PluggableAdaptor becomes a dependent of the model, and it becomes the new model for the dependent (see Figure 2.10). Let us begin by referring to the model in this case as the *original model* to distinguish it from the PluggableAdaptor, which is also a model. The dependent is no longer directly dependent on the original model, and all communication between the dependent and the original model goes through the PluggableAdaptor. This allows the PluggableAdaptor to intercept any message passing between the two and perform its translation.

2.3.4.2 Implementation

The PluggableAdaptor class defines four instance variables:

model	The original model, that is, the model the dependent would like to depend on but cannot for various reasons.
getBlock	A block that takes one argument. This block is evaluated whenever the dependent sends the value message to its model, the PluggableAdaptor. The argument is the original model.
putBlock	A block that takes two arguments. This block is evaluated whenever the dependent sends the message value: anObject to its model, the PluggableAdaptor. The two arguments are the original model and anObject.
updateBlock	A block that takes three arguments and must evaluate to a boolean. This block is evaluated whenever the original model updates its dependents, which includes the PluggableAdaptor. The three arguments are the original model, the aspect being updated, and any other arbitrary object included as a parameter of the update message. If the block evaluates to true, then the update is forwarded to the PluggableAdaptor object's dependents. If it evaluates to false, then nothing further happens.

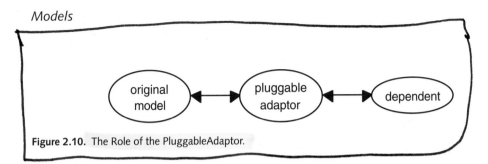

Figure 2.10. The Role of the PluggableAdaptor.

I will refer to the three block objects as get block, put block, and update block. When the dependent sends the value message to its model, the PluggableAdaptor evaluates its get block (remember, the PluggableAdaptor is the dependent's model). When the dependent sends the value: message to its model, the PluggableAdaptor evaluates its put block. When the original model broadcasts an update to its dependents, the PluggableAdaptor evaluates its update block (remember, the PluggableAdaptor is a dependent of the original model).

2.3.4.3 Creating a PluggableAdaptor

There are several things involved in creating a PluggableAdaptor. First, the Pluggable-Adaptor must be handed the original model. Second, its three blocks must be defined. These are what give the PluggableAdaptor its particular behavior (it is often convenient to think of a block as a way of defining behavior on a per instance basis). And finally, the PluggableAdaptor becomes the model for the dependent object. The most general way to set up a PluggableAdaptor is to use the getBlock:putBlock:updateBlock: message. The example below uses this method to interpret value and value: as address and address:.

```
pa := PluggableAdaptor on: anOriginalModel.
pa
    getBlock: [:m | m address]
    putBlock: [:m :v | m address: v]
    updateBlock: [:m :a :p | a == #value].
aView model: pa
```

The PluggableAdaptor class defines certain initialization instance methods to make it easier to define the blocks for specific tasks.

collectionIndex: anInteger	Interprets value to be at: anInteger and interprets value: anObject to be at: anInteger put: anObject.getSelector: aSymbol1 Interprets value to be the message named.
putSelector: aSymbol2	by aSymbol1 and value: to be a message named by aSymbol2.
performAction: aSymbol	When PluggableAdaptor receives value: message, the action message aSymbol is sent to the original model.
selectValue: aValue	The value message returns true if the original model's value is equal to aValue, false otherwise. The value: anObject message sets the original model's value to aValue if anObject is true and

sets it to nil if the value of the original model is already equal to aValue.

2.3.4.4 An Interpreter of Messages

One common function of a PluggableAdaptor is to interpret value and value: as something more meaningful to the original model. Suppose we have a model with an instance variable called annualSales, which references a float. This model has two methods, annualSales and annualSales:, to access and replace the annualSales variable. Now suppose we have a view that will draw some kind of visual representation of this float, but the view only knows how to access information using value and value:. A PluggableAdaptor can be used to stand in between the model and its view and interpret value as annualSales and value: as annualSales:. So when the view sends the message value to its model, the PluggableAdaptor responds by forwarding the message annualSales to the original model, returning that value to the view. Likewise when the model sends update: #annualSales to all of its dependents, the PluggableAdaptor forwards the message update: #value to the view. The model thinks it is talking to a view that understands update: #annualSales, and the view thinks it is talking to a model that understands value and value:. The initialize method getSelector:putSelector: is used to set up such a PluggableAdaptor in the example below.

```
pa := PluggableAdaptor on: anOriginalModel.
pa getSelector: #annualSales putSelector: #annualSales.
aView model: pa
```

Notice that in this example, the PluggableAdaptor is behaving very much like an Aspect-Adaptor. There is not much difference except that a PluggableAdaptor used in this way usually works with a model that sends updates while an AspectAdaptor's subject is typically not a model and does not send updates. Both PluggableAdaptor and AspectAdaptor, however, are equipped to deal with both models and nonmodels. The PluggableAdaptor can be used to interpret an update message as well. In this respect, it is behaving much like a DependencyTransformer. Disk Example 2.10 covers the use of a PluggableAdaptor as an interpreter of messages.

2.3.4.5 A Converter of Types

Sometimes it is the case that the model maintains a date or a number value but the view responsible for displaying this value only works with text. In such a case, a Pluggable-Adaptor can be used to convert the value from one type to another. For example, suppose an input field, which works with text only, is supposed to edit a model's Date value. When the view sends the value message to its model, the PluggableAdaptor evaluates its get block, which might look like the following.

```
[:model | model value printString asText]
```

This assures the view that it will receive a text representation of the Date value. Once the input field is done editing the text, it will try to put the new value back into the model by sending the value: message. The PluggableAdaptor intercepts this message and evaluates its put block, which might look something like the following.

[:model :value | model value: (Date readFromString: value string)]

A subclass of PluggableAdaptor, the class TypeConverter, discussed in Section 2.3.5, was designed specifically to provide this kind of behavior. Disk Example 2.11 covers how to use a PluggableAdaptor as a converter of value types.

2.3.4.6 Additional Uses

PluggableAdaptors are extremely flexible and can be used for a variety of purposes other than interpretation of messages and conversion of value types. For example, a Pluggable-Adaptor can also be used as an action button message trigger. In this case, the PluggableAdaptor is set up as the model of an action button view. When the action button is pressed, the view sends value: true to its model, the PluggableAdaptor. The Pluggable-Adaptor responds by evaluating its put block, which is defined to send an action message to the intended receiver of the action message. If the intended receiver of the action message is the original model, then the initialize message performAction: aSymbol can be used to set up the PluggableAdaptor's blocks. If the intended receiver of the action message is some other object (as is the case in *VisualWorks*), then each block must be defined appropriately. See Disk Example 2.12 for more on using a PluggableAdaptor as an action button message trigger.

In the past PluggableAdaptors were instrumental in providing the toggle behavior for a radio button. When the user selects a radio button, all the related radio buttons must be notified so that they can assure that they are not selected. It is the PluggableAdaptor that provides the mutually exclusive behavior among radio buttons (*VisualWorks* has since replaced this approach with another, more efficient one.)

2.3.5 TypeConverter

TypeConverter is a subclass of PluggableAdaptor, and it defines behavior for operating specifically as a converter of value types (see Section 2.3.4.5). More specifically, it converts a nontext object such as a date or number into a text object. The TypeConverter adds two main features to its superclass. First, it provides all the necessary instance creation and initialization methods for an easy setup. Second, it trims any trailing separator characters (such as blanks) from the Text object edited by the input field.

In *VisualWorks* v1.0, TypeConverter was used for type conversion between an input field and its aspect model. In *VisualWorks* v2.0, however, this responsibility is handled by a PrintConverter object. In *VisualWorks* v2.0, TypeConverter objects are still used by input fields in the Properties Tool and the Position Tool.

2.3.6 Selection Models

The selection models are used as aspect models for the selection widgets (see Section 2.2.4). They maintain a collection and a current selection of one or more elements in the collection. These models are aspect models, but they are not value models and do *not* serve as the model for the corresponding widget. They do, however, contain value models, which then serve as the models for the widgets. The three types of selection models are SelectionInList, MultiSelectionInList, and TableInterface.

2.3.6.1 SelectionInList

A SelectionInList keeps track of both a sequenceable collection and the currently selected element in the collection. A SelectionInList is the aspect model for a single selection list component. SelectionInList defines two instance variables:

listHolder	A value model containing the sequenceable collection. This ValueHolder serves as the model for the widget, a SequenceView.
selectionIndexHolder	A ValueHolder whose value is the index of the current selection.

Even though the SelectionInList is a kind of Model, it doesn't have any dependents of its own. Both of its instance variables, however, have the same two dependents: the SequenceView and the SelectionInList object itself.

It is important that the collection be a sequenceable collection because the SelectionInList object tracks the current selection using an integer index and not a direct reference to the selected object. Only elements in a sequenceable collection can be referenced using an integer index. This rules out Set, Bag, and Dictionary type collections.

While a SelectionInList only manages two pieces of information—a collection and an integer index of the currently selected item—this information can be accessed in a variety of ways. Table 2.6 lists the more common public protocol for SelectionInList.

2.3.6.2 List Class

VisualWorks has a special collection class that can be used with SelectionInList. It is the List class. A List object is very much like an OrderedCollection, but it has the added feature that it is a model and can manage a collection of dependents. The List object expects to have the SequenceView as its dependent and therefore behaves as a model. This allows the special behavior that whenever an element is added to, or removed from, the List object, the SequenceView is notified and redraws itself to reflect this change. This behavior only

Table 2.6. SelectionInList Protocol.

Message	Behavior
list	Returns the collection
list: aCollection	Puts a new collection into the listHolder
listHolder	Returns the ValueHolder on the collection
listHolder: aValueHolder	Replaces the listHolder with aValueHolder
selection	Returns the currently selected object
selection: anObject	Selects anObject in the collection
selectionIndex	Returns index of currently selected object
selectionIndex: anInteger	Selects object whose index is anInteger
selectionIndexHolder	Returns the ValueHolder on the selection index
selectionIndexHolder: aValueHolder	Replaces the ValueHolder on the selection index with aValueHolder

occurs when the collection contained in the SelectionInList object is a List. This will not work when the collection is an OrderedCollection or SortedCollection. The List class implements its own dependents collection handling mechanism similar to that of the Model class. This allows a List object to function successfully as a model.

2.3.6.3 MultiSelectionInList

MultiSelectionInList is a subclass of SelectionInList, and it is the aspect model for a list component with multiple selections. It distinguishes itself from its superclass in that its selectionIndexHolder holds onto a collection of indices of selected elements instead of just the index of a single element. This allows the user to select more than one element in the list.

2.3.6.4 SelectionInTable

A SelectionInTable is the information model for a TableInterface object. It defines two instance variables:

tableHolder	A ValueHolder that holds onto a TableAdaptor or a TwoDList. This ValueHolder serves as the model for the table widget, a GeneralSelectionTableView.
selectionIndexHolder	A ValueHolder that holds onto a Point. This Point indicates the currently selected row, column, or cell.

2.3.6.5 TwoDList

The information a table component displays can be contained within a TwoDList object. A TwoDList behaves as a two-dimensional array, and its elements are accessed with a Point. Entire rows and columns can be accessed as well. While the elements can be accessed in a two-dimensional fashion, the implementation is one dimensional in that all the elements are contained by a single sequenceable collection referenced by the collection instance variable. Internally, the row and column values are used to determine the proper offsets into the sequenceable collection.

2.3.7 Other Models

Several other interesting models are provided by *VisualWorks*. The four types discussed below are all value models and provide some variation on the basic value model theme.

2.3.7.1 ProtocolAdaptor

This is an abstract class and the superclass of AspectAdaptor. It defines the state and behavior behind the subject, subject channel, and access path. It also defines the lazy update behavior that determines who sends updates to dependents. ProtocolAdaptor has two other concrete subclasses—IndexedAdaptor and SlotAdaptor—both discussed below.

2.3.7.2 IndexedAdaptor

The IndexedAdaptor is similar to AspectAdaptor except that its subject is a sequenceable collection and value and value: are dispatched to the subject as at: and at:put:. The Indexed-Adaptor must be told initially the index of the element for which it is responsible. Put another way, an IndexedAdaptor operates on a *numbered* instance variable in its subject, whereas an AspectAdaptor operates on a *named* instance variable. An IndexedAdaptor is useful for providing model behavior for an individual element of a sequenceable collection.

Though the name IndexedAdaptor suggests that it operates only on sequenceable collections whose elements are accessed with an integer index, the IndexedAdaptor will work equally well on a Dictionary whose elements are accessed with an arbitrary object as a key. Disk Example 2.13 demonstrates how to use an IndexedAdaptor.

2.3.7.3 SlotAdaptor

A SlotAdaptor is just like an AspectAdaptor except that value and value: are sent to the subject as instVarAt: and instVarAt:put:. The SlotAdaptor must be initialized with the index of the subject's instance variable, for which it is responsible. SlotAdaptor is used for communicating with objects accessed from outside the image such as database queries.

2.3.7.4 BufferedValueHolder

A BufferedValueHolder is a value model that references another value model called its *subject*. It references yet another value model called its *trigger channel*. The purpose of the BufferedValueHolder is to buffer any changes to its subject until such time as the value of its trigger channel becomes true. When the BufferedValueHolder receives a value: message, it holds onto the new value but does not update its subject at that time. If its trigger-Channel changes to true, the BufferedValueHolder forwards the new value to its subject. If its triggerChannel changes to false, it refreshes its own value with the value in its subject and its subject remains unchanged. BufferedValueHolder can be used for dialog box editing or other such circumstances where it is necessary to roll back changes. Disk Example 2.14 gives an example of how to use a BufferedValueHolder.

2.4 Widget Controllers

Only widgets for active components will have controllers. This is because the widgets for active components are views and all views have models and controllers. I will refer to these controllers as *widget controllers* to distinguish them from window controllers. Formally, a **widget controller** is a controller for the widget of an active component. Since widgets (in this case, views only) and their controllers are very closely related, we can divide the widget controllers into the same categories as the widget views: button and slider widget controllers, text widget controllers, and selection widget controllers.

This section begins with a discussion of the widget controller hierarchy. Then we will look at the common characteristics of widget controllers that field keyboard events. Finally, the controller classes for each of the three categories—button and slider controllers, text controllers, and selection controllers—will be discussed in detail.

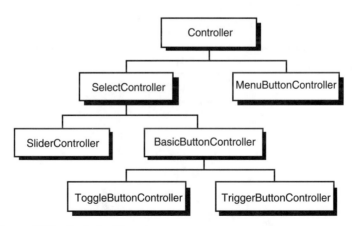

Figure 2.11. Button and Slider Controller Hierarchy.

2.4.1 Controller Hierarchy

As mentioned in Chapter 1, most controller types are some subclass of Controller or ControllerWithMenu. Since the button and slider components do not have <operate> menus, their branch of the controller hierarchy subclasses directly from Controller and not from ControllerWithMenu (see Figure 2.11).

The selection components and text components, however, do have <operate> menus, and, therefore, their widget controllers are part of the ControllerWithMenu branch (see Figure 2.12).

2.4.2 Keyboard Event-Handling Widget Controllers

All active components, except for the menu button and slider, handle keyboard events and therefore, are expected to be able to take keyboard focus. When a *VisualWorks* component has **keyboard focus**, it is the current recipient of all incoming keyboard events and is expected to handle those events. In order to do this, the widget controllers for such a component must know about the keyboard processor and provide a keyboard

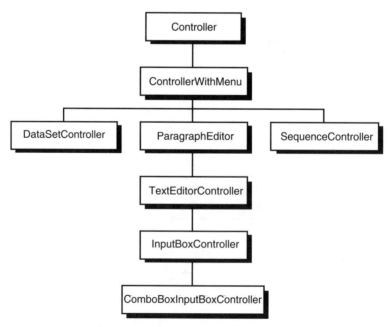

Figure 2.12. Selection and Text Controller Hierarchy.

hook for intercepting keystroke events before they are processed by the widget. Also, these components must be able to dispatch messages to the application model when focus is acquired or lost. Each of these behaviors is described below. While this section talks about how the *VisualWorks* components deal with keyboard events, Chapter 6, Section 6.3, discusses how the keyboard processor manages all keyboard activity for a given window and dispatches the keyboard events to the various components.

2.4.2.1 Keyboard Processor

A *VisualWorks* component that expects to take focus should know about the keyboard processor. The keyboard processor is responsible for dispatching keyboard activity to the component with keyboard focus and for maintaining the tab order of tabable components. The keyboard processor is an instance of KeyboardProcessor, and there is only one keyboard processor per window. Each *VisualWorks* widget controller that takes focus has an instance variable, keyboardProcessor, used to reference its window's keyboard processor. The keyboard processor is defined formally and covered in detail in Chapter 6, Section 6.3.

2.4.2.2 Keyboard Hook

Each *VisualWorks* component that expects to take keyboard focus should provide a hook for the developer to intercept all keyboard activity going to that component. Such a hook is referred to as a keyboard hook. A **keyboard hook** is a block that is evaluated just prior to the widget controller handling a keyboard event. It takes two arguments: the keyboard event and the widget controller. Each time the widget controller receives a keyboard event, it first checks to see if its keyboardHook variable is nil. If it is not, then it gives the keyboard hook first crack at handling the event. If the keyboard hook handles the event, then it should evaluate to nil and no further processing will occur to that event. If the keyboard hook does not handle the event, then it should simply return the event for further processing. Each *Visual-Works* component that can take focus has its own keyboard hook.

2.4.2.3 Dispatcher

Every widget controller has its own dispatcher. A **dispatcher** is an instance of UI-Dispatcher and can dispatch predefined messages the application model. The messages to be sent are defined by the developer using the Properties Tool. Each message is associated with a certain event: acquiring focus, loosing focus, changing value, or a double click. Whenever one of these events occurs, the dispatcher sends the corresponding message to the application model. These dispatch messages are divided into two categories: notification messages and validation messages. A **notification message** is used to notify the application model of the event. A **validation message** requests permission from the application model to proceed with event. Permission is granted if the message returns true. Permission is refused if the message returns false.

The dispatcher concept is implemented by the class UIDispatcher, which is a subclass of Object. UIDispatcher defines nine instance variables: the receiver variable and eight dispatch message variables. The receiver variable references the application model, that is, the object to receive the dispatched message. The eight dispatch message variables are listed in Table 2.7.

2.4.3 Button and Slider Controllers

There are three ways a button can respond to mouse clicks: trigger some action, toggle a value, or display a menu. It should come as no surprise then that there are three different types of button controllers—one for each of these behaviors. There are also two abstract button controller classes: SelectController and BasicButtonController (see Figure 2.11). Included in this discussion of button and slider controllers is the slider controller implemented by the class SliderController.

2.4.3.1 SelectController

This is an abstract class for all controller types (not just button controllers) that implement a simple response to a mouse click. It provides the state and behavior for dealing with the keyboard processor, a keyboard hook, and a dispatcher. It also provides methods for dealing with mouse state.

2.4.3.2 BasicButtonController

BasicButtonController is an abstract subclass of SelectController. It implements the common behavior for all button controller types. Its main behavior is called a *press action,* which is the action associated with the user pressing a mouse button. The press action is initiated on a <select> mouse button up condition. When the user first presses the <select> button down, the controller tells its view to change visual state (e.g., the button appears to

Table 2.7. UIDispatcher Message Variables.

Instance variable	Associated event	Type
focusIn	Component receives focus	notification
focusOut	Component looses focus	notification
valueChange	Value of model changes	notification
doubleClick	User double clicks	notification
requestFocusIn	Component receives focus	validation
requestFocusOut	Component looses focus	validation
requestValueChange	Value of model changes	validation
requestDoubleClick	User double clicks	validation

go in) but does not initiate its press action. Only when the button comes back up within the bounds of the button view will the press action be initiated. This explains why a user can press an action button, check box, or radio button and, with the mouse button still down, move the mouse outside of the button view and release the mouse button, and the button will not toggle its state.

BasicButtonController also implements a *simulated press action* used by the keyboard processor for the purposes default actions. For instance, when a dialog is open, the user usually has the option of hitting the <Enter> key to close the dialog instead of pressing the **OK** or **Cancel** button. The keyboard processor intercepts the <Enter> keyboard event and initiates a simulated press action for the default button. This causes the default button to behave just as if the user had pressed that button. In the dialog example, this typically closes the dialog. BasicButtonController implements responses to the following keyboard activity.

<Tab>	Give up focus
<Enter>	Do default action
<Space>	Press action

2.4.3.3 ToggleButtonController

ToggleButtonController is a subclass of BasicButtonController and is used by the radio button and check box components. Its press action merely toggles the model's value back and forth between true and false. When the <select> button is pressed down, the controller sets its view's *in transition* state to true. While the <select> button is down and the cursor is within the view's bounds, the view is in transition. If the button comes back up or the cursor leaves the bounds, the view's *in transition* state is set to false. The <select> button must come up with the cursor within the view's bounds in order for the press action to be initiated.

2.4.3.4 TriggerButtonController

TriggerButtonController is a subclass of BasicButtonController, and its instances are the widget controllers for the action button widgets. It has an implementation identical to that of ToggleButtonController except for one additional behavior. TriggerButtonController implements the method desiresToTakeAction, which indicates if its view is disabled or not. If the action button is the default action for a window, then the keyboard processor will send the desiresToTakeAction message to the TriggerButtonController first to make sure it is available to fulfill its role as the default action. Other than this simple behavior, TriggerButtonController and ToggleButtonController behave identically (although their implementations vary slightly). Like the ToggleButtonController, the TriggerButtonController requires that the <select> button come back up within the confines of the view's bounds in order for the press action to proceed. This allows a user to press the <select> button and, with the button still down, move the mouse outside of the view's bounds and release the mouse button without triggering an action.

2.4.3.5 MenuButtonController

MenuButtonController is a subclass of Controller. A MenuButtonController serves as the controller for the button view of the menu button component and combo box component. Unlike all the other *VisualWorks* widget controllers, it does not have the keyboardProcessor and keyboardHook instance variables. This is why menu button components cannot take focus. It is also unlike the other widget controllers in the button and slider category in that it is not a kind of SelectController. Furthermore, its behavior is much more complex than the other controllers in this category.

A MenuButtonController is responsible for displaying a menu whenever the user presses the <select> button. A MenuButtonController can display its menu in one of three ways: as a pop-up menu, as a pull-down menu, or as a combo list box (not a menu). The way in which it will behave is indicated by the value of the controlType instance variable, which can be nil, #pullDown, #popUp, or #comboBox. The value returned from the menu (or combo list box) is then given to the model as its new value. When the model changes, it notifies the input field so that it can update itself.

2.4.3.6 SliderController

SliderController is a subclass of SelectController. An instance of this class serves as the widget controller for a slider component's widget. SliderController overrides two of its superclass's mouse-handling methods: mouseMovedTo: and mouseDownAt:. These methods have identical implementations. The view is asked to map the current mouse location into the corresponding linear value between the two anchor values of the slider. This value is then given to the model. While a SliderController inherits all the functionality for interacting with the keyboard processor, it does not handle any keyboard events and does not take focus.

2.4.4 Selection Controllers

The selection components are the list, table, and data set. There are two selection controllers: SequenceController and DataSetController. Each of these is discussed below.

2.4.4.1 SequenceController

Both tables and lists share the same type of controller—SequenceController, which is a subclass of ControllerWithMenu. SequenceController defines the keyboardProcessor, keyboard-

Hook, and dispatcher instance variables. A SequenceController knows how to operate based on mouse input and keyboard input. Arrow keys can be used to make selections as well as mouse clicks. It will also conduct a keyboard driven search of its elements based on a character match. A SequenceController knows how to work in either one or two dimensions and with single or multiple selections.

2.4.4.2 DataSetController

A DataSetController is the controller for a DataSetView. It determines the selection, scrolling, and callback behavior for the current selection. DataSetController is a subclass of ControllerWithMenu and defines the keyboardProcessor and dispatcher instance variables to make it compliant with *VisualWorks* widget controllers.

2.4.5 Text Controllers

There are four *VisualWorks* components that include text editing: text editor, input field, combo box input field, and a data set. Their controller behavior is mostly defined in ParagraphEditor. Each has its own specialized controller class, however: TextEditorController for text editors, InputBoxController for input fields, and ComboBoxInputBoxController for combo boxes.

2.4.5.1 ParagraphEditor

ParagraphEditor was around long before *VisualWorks* and is possibly the most interesting class in the entire hierarchy. ParagraphEditor implements all of the text editing capabilities of all the text views, even those not used by *VisualWorks* applications such as those found in the System Browser and Workspace. ParagraphEditor was designed to operate on rather small pieces of text (fewer than 50,000 characters) and should not be confused with a word processor; although it does have most of the basic functionality of a commercial word processor.

A full discussion of ParagraphEditor would take several pages, so I will just make brief mention of some of its features. ParagraphEditor is responsible for the cut, copy, and paste operations. It also implements find and replace operations. It is ParagraphEditor that knows how to select a word, the entire text, or all text between matching end characters (i.e., single and double quotes, parentheses, blocks, and brackets). ParagraphEditor can accept, cancel, and undo changes to its text. It is ParagraphEditor that knows how to provide emphasis (i.e., boldness, italics, and character size) to the text. ParagraphEditor takes input from the mouse, the keyboard, and two different <operate> menus, which it also provides. ParagraphEditor has a class variable that acts as the paste buffer for all text operations in the entire system. It has another class variable that maps keystroke combinations to various functions.

ParagraphEditor is a very rich class and well worth any time you can dedicate to its study. For those who want to implement more sophisticated editing and word-processing features, or just come to understand text operations already available, all roads lead to ParagraphEditor.

2.4.5.2 TextEditorController

This is a subclass of ParagraphEditor and is the controller for text editor components. It extends ParagraphEditor to make it compliant with *VisualWorks* componentry by implementing the keyboard processor, keyboard hook, and dispatcher references. TextEditor-Controller also adds some new behavior. TextEditorController allows a text editor component to be *read only*. It can also be told to interpret a <Tab> as either a tab within the text or a change of focus to the next component in the window. A TextEditor-Controller can be set to accept changes in three ways. The first is inherited from ParagraphEditor and requires the user to explicitly accept the changes (i.e., select **accept** from the <operate> menu). TextEditorController also adds the capability of accepting changes automatically on each keystroke or all at once when it gives up focus to the next widget controller. This last is the default behavior.

2.4.5.3 InputBoxController

This is a subclass of TextEditorController and is used specifically for input field components. It inherits all the behavior of its superclass and adds a few new features specific to editing input fields. For example, an InputBoxController can limit the number of characters allowable for the input field.

2.4.5.4 ComboBoxInputBoxController

A ComboBoxInputBoxController is a subclass of InputBoxController. It adds the ability to work with a button that, when pressed, will display a list of options for the field.

2.4.6 Summary

All active components have widgets that require controllers. These controllers are referred to as widget controllers and can be divided into three broad categories based on similar behavior: button and slider controllers, selection controllers, and text editor controllers. All *VisualWorks* active components except for menu buttons and sliders handle keyboard events. Their widget controllers reference a keyboard processor and can take focus. They also have a dispatcher object, which can send notification and validation messages to the application model on a change of focus, change of value, or double click.

2.5 Component Specs

Perhaps the most interesting aspect of *VisualWorks* componentry is that the information describing a *VisualWorks* component can be stored in a special object called a component spec. A **component spec** describes what properties and features a given *VisualWorks* component should have. It contains information—such as layout, model, and colors—about a particular component such as a list, an action button, or text editor. Each *Visual-Works* component contains its own component spec (see Figure 2.1), which fully describes that component and can be used to create an exact replica of that component.

A component spec is but one category of a more general type of object called a spec object. It is by virtue of these spec objects that an interface can persist in the form of source code or in a text file. Spec objects in general are covered in detail in Chapter 3, Section 3.2.

2.5.1 Spec Hierarchy

Each different component has its own type of component spec. Regions have Region-Spec, action buttons have ActionButtonSpec, and so on. These spec classes are arranged in a moderately deep hierarchy. The top of this hierarchy is shown in Figure 2.13.

2.5.1.1 UISpecification

UISpecification is the abstract class for all spec object types, and it describes behavior common to all spec objects. Chief among these behaviors are the abilities to represent itself as a literal array and instantiate an exact duplicate of the original spec based on that literal array. Spec objects are covered more fully in Chapter 3.

2.5.1.2 ComponentSpec

This is an abstract class for all component spec classes. It includes state and behavior for describing a *VisualWorks* component's layout. Since each component has a layout describing its position inside of a window, it makes sense that all component specs should be able to describe a layout.

2.5.1.3 NamedSpec

NamedSpec, like its superclass ComponentSpec, is also an abstract class for all component spec types. It adds state and behavior for naming the component (i.e., assigning it a unique ID) and describing certain visual appearances such as color (or look preferences), opacity, and border decoration.

2.5.1.4 Component Specs for Passive, Composite, and Arbitrary Components

All of the component spec classes for passive components, composites, and arbitrary components are direct subclasses of NamedSpec. Each of these is a concrete class and has no subclasses. They each describe a corresponding *VisualWorks* component.

2.5.1.5 Component Specs for Active Components

WidgetSpec is an abstract class combining all state and behavior common to component specs that describe active components. This state and behavior includes describing the connection to a widget's model and describing how the widget should handle tab events. WidgetSpec has six subclasses: ButtonSpec, DataSetColumnSpec, MenuComponentSpec, MultiSpec, NoteBookSpec, and SliderSpec. ButtonSpec is an abstract class and defines state and behavior common to all component specs that describe button components. Menu-ComponentSpec is also abstract and defines state and behavior common to all component specs describing components that have menus. Examples of such components are input fields, lists, and text editors. SliderSpec is a concrete class and defines all the state and behavior for a component spec used to describe a slider component.

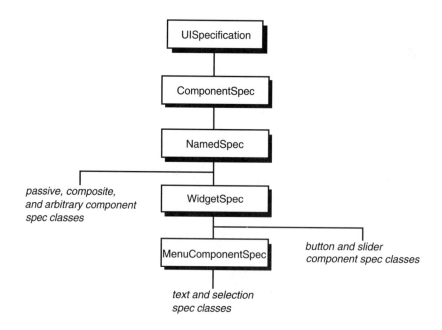

Figure 2.13. Component Spec Class Hierarchy.

ButtonSpec has four subclasses: ActionButtonSpec, CheckBoxSpec, MenuButtonSpec, and RadioButtonSpec. Each of these subclasses is a concrete class and describes a different kind of *VisualWorks* button component. MenuComponentSpec has four subclasses: DataSetSpec, SequenceViewSpec, TableViewSpec, and TextEditorSpec. Each of these is concrete and describes a *VisualWorks* component. TextEditorSpec has a concrete subclass, InputFieldSpec, which is used to describe an input field component. This too has a concrete subclass, ComboBoxSpec, which describes a combo box component.

2.5.2 Components and Their Specs

Components are built from their component specs (with the aid of several other objects). The component specs are extracted from their components. This relationship between components and their specs is described below.

2.5.2.1 Components from Component Specs

A component spec not only describes a *VisualWorks* component but also assumes some of the responsibility for creating the component. A component spec cannot, however, perform this function alone. There are several major players involved in converting a set of component specs into their corresponding user interface components. Some of the other objects involved in the process are a builder, the builder's source, and a look policy object. These objects and the process of building user interfaces from a set of specs is the topic of Chapter 3.

2.5.2.2 Component Specs from Components

Each *VisualWorks* component contains a copy of the spec from which it was built (see Figure 2.1). Therefore, each component contains the information for replicating itself. It is convenient to think of component specs as the DNA of *VisualWorks*.

2.5.2.3 Look Policy Independence

As you already know, components can be built in several different look and feel metaphors according to the current look policy. The component spec, however, describes the component independently of look policy. The component spec does not contain any look policy specific information. Look policy is discussed formally in Chapter 3, Section 3.4.

2.5.3 Summary

Component specs are objects that describe the characteristics of a particular *VisualWorks* component. Each kind of component has a corresponding type of component spec that describes it. These descriptions are independent of look policy, such as *Motif* and *MS Windows*. These descriptions also provide a means of making an interface persist. That is, instead of storing an interface, *VisualWorks* stores the description of the interface. Each *VisualWorks* component contains a component spec that fully describes that component and is sufficient to reconstruct an exact replica of the component. A component spec, when used in conjunction with other objects, such as a builder, its source, and its look policy, is all that is necessary to recreate the specified component.

2.6 Summary

A *VisualWorks* interface is nothing more than an assembly of components. A *VisualWorks* component is a spec wrapper containing a widget. A widget is a visual part that gives the *VisualWorks* component its visual representation. There are five types of components: active components, passive components, composite components, arbitrary components, and sub-canvases. Active components have life and interact with the user. Passive components do not interact with the user and can only be changed by some other agent such as the application model. A composite is collection of other *VisualWorks* components, which is then treated as a single component. Arbitrary components, also known as view holders, can contain any arbitrary visual part as a widget. Subcanvases are discussed in Chapter 6. *VisualWorks* component are expected to understand certain messages called *VisualWorks* component protocol and their widgets are expected to understand certain messages called widget protocol.

The widget classes describe the widgets that are responsible for giving the components their visual representation. There are four broad categories of widget classes: button and slider widgets, selection widgets, text widgets, and passive component widgets.

VisualWorks has a rich set of models from which to choose. Aspect models are models that manage a single aspect of information. Value models are models with a primary aspect called the value. This value is accessed using value model protocol. Not all aspect models are value models but instead, many contain value models.

All active components have widgets that need controllers. These are called widget controllers. Most *VisualWorks* widget controllers process keyboard events and have a keyboard hook and a dispatcher. The keyboard processor manages all keyboard activity for a window. A keyboard hook allows the developer to intercept events targeted for a particular component. A dispatcher sends messages to the application model based on certain events.

Each component in *VisualWorks* can be described by a corresponding object called a component spec. Each *VisualWorks* component keeps a component spec describing that component. The component spec, along with a builder, its source, and look policy object, can be used to create a replica of the component it describes.

CHAPTER 3

The Builder

YOU MAY RECALL from Chapter 1 that one of the more awkward things about interface construction in a traditional MVC application is that the model class assumes responsibility for creating the interface. To correct this, the authors of *VisualWorks* adopted the notion that some other independent object should assume this responsibility. You probably already know this object as the builder.

In this chapter we look at the builder and its role in *VisualWorks*. The first section covers the three roles of the builder. Section 2 takes an in-depth look at the process of building from specifications. The third section covers how the builder acquires the resources necessary to construct the interface. Section 4 discusses how *VisualWorks* accomplishes its chameleonlike behavior of providing interfaces that emulate various window environments. Section 5 covers the remainder of the builder's state. In section 6 we will see how the builder actually builds an interface.

3.1 The Role of the Builder

A **builder** is an instance of UIBuilder whose primary responsibility is to construct a user interface according to specifications. These specifications are in the form of spec objects. Most developers only think of the builder in terms of this primary responsibility, but the builder has two other responsibilities as well. The builder is responsible for helping create the user interface in the canvas editing process, and it also provides access to the interface for the running application after the interface is built.

3.1.1 Building a Runtime Interface

The builder's primary role is to build a runtime user interface according to some specification provided by a client object. It can be argued that the other two responsibilities of the builder should be delegated to other objects (there are those who would strongly argue for doing just this). Nevertheless, we would still need a builder to construct the runtime user interface.

In order to build the interface, the builder needs certain construction materials such as menus, aspect models, and images. Also, each builder can build only one window (or subcanvas), and each window is created by a separate builder.

3.1.2 Painting a Canvas

Instead of having to write the code to create a user interface, *VisualWorks* allows the developer to describe an interface graphically. You know this process as painting a canvas. The same kind of builder that creates a runtime user interface also creates the edit mode interface for canvas painting. The primary difference is that, in the first case, the interface is built all at once from a set of specifications and, in the second case, the interface is built in an incremental fashion under the direction of the developer.

The builder for a canvas window runs in edit mode. When the developer is through painting the canvas, each of the components in the canvas window contains the specifications for recreating itself. These specifications can then be extracted and stored for future use.

3.1.3 Providing Access to Runtime Interface

Once the builder is finished building a runtime interface, it retains certain information which is of great interest to the running application. This information includes such things as aspect models, named components, the keyboard processor, and the window. The application can access this information for the purpose of changing the interface during the interface building process or during runtime.

This particular role of the builder is somewhat removed from the previous two. Providing access to the various parts of the interface does not require much special behavior, just accessing methods. It could be argued that some other object should be responsible for holding onto this information for the benefit of the running application, allowing the builder to be garbage collected immediately after it has constructed the runtime interface. As it is, the builder persists long after it has done its job of interface construction, strictly for providing a means of access to the user interface objects.

3.2 Building According to Specifications

In Chapter 2 we learned that *VisualWorks* components have blueprints called component specs. A component spec contains all the necessary information for creating the component it describes. We saw that each different type of *VisualWorks* component has its own corresponding type of component spec. For example, input field components have InputFieldSpec and label components have LabelSpec. In this section we will further explore the general concept of using specifications to describe a user interface and look at how the builder uses these specifications to build an interface.

3.2.1 Spec Objects

Chapter 2 defined a component spec as an object that describes the properties and attributes of a *VisualWorks* component. A component spec is but one kind of spec object. A **spec object** is an object that describes the properties and attributes of a particular piece of interface—a component, a window, a collection of components, or a full window interface. All of the spec objects discussed in Chapter 2 are component specs. There are four more kinds of spec objects: window spec, spec collection, full spec, and sub spec. Each of these is discussed in turn below.

3.2.1.1 Window Spec

A **window spec** describes the window frame used to display a user interface. A window spec is an instance of WindowSpec. A WindowSpec has several instance variables that describe a window's maximum and minimum size, color, label, as well as other attributes. A builder always requires a window spec.

3.2.1.2 Spec Collection

A **spec collection** maintains a list of component specs for all of the components destined to populate a given window. A spec collection is an instance of SpecCollection and has one instance variable, collection, which holds onto an Array of component spec objects (Fig. 3.1).

3.2.1.3 Full Spec

A **full spec** is a combination of a window spec and a spec collection. A full spec, therefore, describes a window and all of its components and is sufficient to describe a complete window interface. A full spec is an instance of FullSpec and has two instance variables, window and component, which hold onto a WindowSpec and a SpecCollection, respectively. A full spec is often referred to as an interface spec since it describes a complete window interface. (See Fig. 3.1.)

3.2.1.4 Sub Spec

A **sub spec** is a special kind of spec, which is used as an instance variable of another spec for the purpose of holding onto additional spec information. The class SubSpec is an abstract class that describes this kind of recursive spec behavior. It has only one subclass, UIEventCallback-SubSpec, which describes the callback specifications for an active component.

3.2.2 Building from Specifications

The minimal requirements for building an interface in *VisualWorks* are a builder and an interface specification, or full spec. Create the builder, hand it a specification, and tell it to open its window. The code below demonstrates this minimalist's approach to interface construction.

```
builder := UIBuilder new.
builder add: aSpecObject.
builder open
```

Since all interfaces ultimately reside inside of a window, a window spec is always required by the builder. If aSpecObject in the code above is not a FullSpec, then it does not include a WindowSpec, and one must be provided as shown in the code below.

```
builder := UIBuilder new.
builder add: aWindowSpec.
builder add: aSpecObject.
builder open
```

Component specs can be handed in one at a time as shown below.

```
builder := UIBuilder new.
builder add: aWindowSpec.
builder add: anInputFieldSpec.
builder add: aLabelSpec.
builder add: aTextEditorSpec.
builder open
```

As each component spec is handed in, the builder immediately constructs the component described by the component spec. After the builder has built the last component, the interface is complete and ready to be opened.

The component specs can also be handed in all at the same time along with a window spec in the form of a full spec. Since a full spec describes a window and all of its components, the code below is all that is needed to create a fully developed user interface.

```
builder := UIBuilder new.
builder add: aFullSpec.
builder open
```

Disk Example 3.1 covers the topic of building interfaces from specifications.

3.2.3 Literal Arrays

Certain objects in *VisualWorks* can be represented by an Array called a literal array. A **literal array** is an Array containing information of a literal nature and is used to represent some object. A literal array can easily create an exact copy of the object it represents.

3.2.3.1 Literals

The elements of a literal array are literals. A **literal** is piece of Smalltalk code that the compiler converts immediately to an object. Table 3.1 lists the seven types of literal information used in a literal array and gives an example of each.

3.2.3.2 Literal Array Contents

The contents of a literal array represent the class, message names, and arguments necessary to instantiate a copy of the object represented by the literal array. The following example is a literal array for a Rectangle with origin 0@0 and corner 100@250.

> #(#Rectangle 0 0 100 250)

The next two examples are for a ColorValue of blue and a LabelSpec. The second of these two examples illustrates the nesting property of literal arrays.

> #(#ColorValue #blue)

> #(#LabelSpec #layout: #(#Point 5 9) #label: 'First Name')

Notice that each of the three examples so far is an Array and that the elements of the Array are all of the types specified in Table 3.1.

Table 3.1. Literal Information.

Literal type	Example
Number	35.6
Boolean	true
String	'Mary Jones'
Character	$G
Symbol	#lastName
UndefinedObject	nil
Array	#('fred' 123 nil)

3.2.3.3 Literal Array Decoding

A literal array can reconstruct the object it represents. Technically, it doesn't create the exact object, but just one of equivalent value, or a copy. The object is created by sending the message decodeAsLiteralArray to the literal array. The statement below instantiates a Rectangle based on the information contained within a literal array.

```
#( #Rectangle 0 0 100 250 ) decodeAsLiteralArray
```

3.2.3.4 Literal Array Encoding

Objects that can be represented in literal array format are responsible for creating their own literal array. This is done by sending the message literalArrayEncoding to the object. For example, the statement below creates an instance of Rectangle and then creates a literal array to represent or describe that Rectangle.

```
| rectangle |
rectangle := (Rectangle origin: 0@0 corner: 100@250).
rectangle literalArrayEncoding
```

3.2.3.5 Objects as Literal Arrays

Several kinds of objects can be represented in literal array format. Typically, these are the kinds of objects used in building a user interface, such as Rectangle, Point, ColorValue, LayoutFrame, and LookPreferences, to name a few.

3.2.3.6 Spec Objects as Literal Arrays

All of the spec objects can be represented in a literal array format. The literal array format is convenient for two reasons. First, it allows an entire interface to be described in a literal form and not as an instance of the interface. Second, the literal array is easily made persistent in a database, written out to a text file, or included as source code in a method. Disk Example 3.2 demonstrates the utility of literal arrays in building user interfaces.

3.2.3.7 Interface, Specification, and Literal Array Relationship

The approach to interface building adopted by *VisualWorks* is predicated on a very fundamental relationship between the interface, its specification, and the specification's literal array representation. When a developer paints a canvas, that canvas contains a user interface from which a full spec describing that interface can be extracted. A copy of this spec object can, at some later time, be used to recreate the interface intended by the developer. This same spec object can also be written as a literal array and stored in a text form as Smalltalk source code. This literal array, in turn, can be used to create a copy of the original spec object. This is a very fundamental relationship of *VisualWorks* and is illustrated in Figure 3.1.

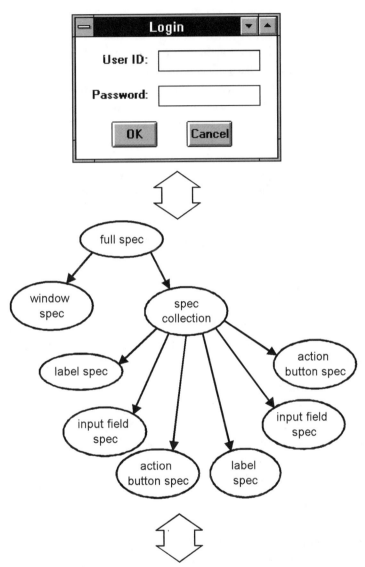

#(#FullSpec #window: #(#WindowSpec #label: 'Login' #bounds: #(#Rectangle 664 112 862 219))
#component: #(#SpecCollection #collection: #(#(#InputFieldSpec #layout: #(#Rectangle 70 14 184 35)
#model: #userID) #(#InputFieldSpec #layout: #(#Rectangle 70 42 184 63) #model: #password)
#(#ActionButtonSpec #layout: #(#Rectangle 28 77 82 102) #model: #accept #label: 'Ok' #defaultable: true)
#(#ActionButtonSpec #layout: #(#Rectangle 112 77 166 102) #model: #cancel #label: 'Cancel' #defaultable:
true) #(#LabelSpec #layout: #(#Point 18 14) #label: 'User ID:') #(#LabelSpec #layout: #(#Point 7 42) #label:
'Password:')))

Figure 3.1. Interface, Specification, and Literal Array Relationship.

3.2.3.8 Store String Alternative?

The literal array concept was introduced with *VisualWorks* and was not a part of *ParcPlace\Smalltalk* prior to *VisualWorks*. Furthermore, it applies only to those objects that can help describe an interface. A similar concept has always existed in Smalltalk and applies to all objects—the store string concept. Each object knows how to respond to the message storeString by returning its store string. A store string is a string of Smalltalk source code that, when compiled, returns a copy of the original object. This is exactly the behavior we require of spec objects and their literal array representation. So why not just store the specs using their store string representation instead of their literal array representation? Why was it necessary to implement the literal array mechanism when the store string mechanism already existed? There are two reasons. First, a store string can be up to twice as large as its literal array equivalent. Second, store string writes out all attributes of the object (although this can be overridden), and the literal array format is selective in that it only includes those attributes necessary for adequately replicating the original object.

3.2.4 Why Use Spec Objects?

You may wonder why *VisualWorks* bothers at all with this intermediate step of spec objects. Actually, there are three reasons for using spec objects: (1) interface persistence, (2) look and feel independence, and (3) interface design and construction.

3.2.4.1 Interface Persistence

When a developer paints an interface, he or she wants to be able to store that interface for later use in a runtime application. An interface cannot persist if it is currently on the screen. This is because the screen, the windows, and the various parts of the window are known to the virtual machine. Also, views point to a model that has dependents, and these dependencies are not necessary for describing or storing an interface.

3.2.4.2 Look and Feel Independence

The information contained within a spec for a component does not indicate whether that component will be drawn in the *Macintosh* style, the *Motif* style, or any other platform-specific look. This means that the same full spec can be opened in any one of the look policies.

3.2.4.3 Interface Design and Construction

The objective of painting a canvas is not to create an interface, but to create the blueprints from which the interface can be built. These blueprints can then be stored conveniently and used at some later time to construct the interface. In fact, the same blueprints can be used to construct an arbitrary number of copies of the interface. The spec objects are just such blueprints.

3.3 Building with Resources

The builder cannot build an interface from specifications alone. The builder requires materials for constructing an interface. These materials are called resources. A **resource** is an object that the builder requires in order to construct the interface according to specifications. Some typical resources are menus, labels, images, and aspect models. Resources come in two varieties: static and dynamic. A **static resource** is not expected to change during runtime. A **dynamic resource** is expected to change during runtime, is usually referenced by an instance variable, and is usually held inside of a value model (acting as a channel) to facilitate its dynamic behavior. Many of the concepts covered in this section are illustrated in Disk Example 3.3.

3.3.1 The Builder's Source

When the builder requires a resource, it looks internally first to see if it might already have that resource. If it does not, it then asks its source. The builder's **source** is a kind of ApplicationModel and provides the builder with the necessary resources for building an interface according to specifications. The ApplicationModel class defines the necessary protocol for responding to a builder's requests for resources (the ApplicationModel class is discussed in detail in Chapter 4). A UIBuilder references its source with its source instance variable. Having a source is not absolutely essential. As we saw in Section 3.2, interfaces can be built without a source. These types of interfaces, however, are next to trivial. If the builder is to build a meaningful interface, it usually has a source.

3.3.2 The Builder's Client

The builder builds an interface for its client. A **client** is an object that creates a builder for the purpose of having it build an interface. The client is usually the source as well. That is, the object that creates the builder usually acts as the builder's source for building materials. The code below demonstrates how a client object can also act as the builder's source. Assume that the code below is located in one of the client's instance methods, so self refers to the client object.

```
builder := UIBuilder new.
builder source: self.
builder add: someSpecObject.
builder open
```

In this code, the client object creates an instance of UIBuilder, registers itself as the source of that builder, hands the builder the specification for an interface, and tells the builder to open its window.

3.3.3 Caching Resources

As stated previously, when the builder requires a resource, it checks internally first. The builder has three variables it uses to cache certain resources: bindings, labels, and visuals. (A fourth such variable, subCanvasSpecs, is discussed in Chapter 5.) All three are Identity-Dictionary objects, which use Symbols as keys and the resources themselves as values. The keys are developer-defined Symbol objects and uniquely identify each resource within a given full spec. These Symbols are usually the names of the messages used to access the resources from the source.

The bindings variable caches aspect models required by active components. The labels variable caches text labels, and the visuals variable caches visual components. In keeping with the metaphor, these variables act as the builder's local warehouses.

The builder can elect not to cache resources. If its cacheWhileEditing variable is set to false, a UIBuilder will forgo caching any resources. The cacheWhileEditing variable is set to true for building a runtime interface and false for editing an interface.

3.3.4 The Client Populating the Resource Cache

The client object can populate the builder's resource caches prior to handing it any specs, thereby making any requests for these resources from a source object unnecessary. For instance, if a full spec describes an interface that requires an aspect model named #phoneNumber, then the client may do something like the following:

```
builder := UIBuilder new.
builder aspectAt: #phoneNumber put: '111-2222' asValue.
builder add: aFullSpec.
builder open
```

The code above is just like some of the previous examples, except that a ValueHolder containing the object '111-2222' is placed in the builder's bindings resource cache prior to handing it the specification for the interface. Presumably, this specification includes the description of a component that requires such a ValueHolder as a model and expects to access it by its name, #phoneNumber. There are several accessing messages that a client object can use to populate the builder's caches, as well as access those resources already in the builder's caches. These messages are listed in Table 3.2 (the accessors for subcanvas resources are purposely omitted and will be addressed in Chapter 5).

Table 3.2. Accessing the Builder's Resource Caches.

Accessors	Type of resource	Cache variable
actionAt: actionAt:put:	PluggableAdaptor	bindings
arbitraryComponentAt: arbitraryComponentAt:put:	A kind of VisualPart	bindings
aspectAt: aspectAt:put:	A kind of Model	bindings
clientAt: clientAt:put:	A kind of ApplicationModel	bindings
labelAt: labelAt:put:	String or Text	labels
menuAt: menuAt:put:	Menu or ValueHolder with Menu	bindings
visualAt: visualAt:put:	A kind of VisualComponent	visuals

Notice that several accessor pairs in Table 3.2 operate on the bindings variable. While this may seem redundant, there are two main reasons for this apparent duplication of efforts. First, having the various implementations improves readability. Take, for example, the accessors aspectAt:put: and arbitraryComponentAt:put:. While either can be used for populating the bindings variable, aspect models should be placed in the builder's bindings using aspectAt:put: and arbitrary components should be placed in the builder's bindings using arbitraryComponentAt:put:. The second reason for duplicating the bindings variable accessors is that the get method is not implemented the same in all cases. All the put methods, however, do have the same implementation.

3.3.5 Acquiring Resources

If the builder does not already have the required resource in one of its caches, then it asks its source object to provide it. Each type of resource has its own accessing message. Table 3.3 lists these messages and the type of resource requested. Since the source is a kind of ApplicationModel, each of these messages has a corresponding method implementation in the class ApplicationModel (see Chapter 4, Section 4.2 for more on the ApplicationModel implementation of source behavior).

Notice that all of the messages in Table 3.3 are keyword messages that take a single argument. In each case this argument is a Symbol, which uniquely identifies the requested resource. Typically, this Symbol is a selector for a unary message understood by the source object or its class. As an example, the spec object describing the interface to be built might

Table 3.3. Messages for Acquiring Resources.

Message	Type of resource
actionFor:	PluggableAdaptor
arbitraryComponentFor:	A kind of VisualPart
aspectFor:	A kind of Model
clientFor:	A kind of ApplicationModel
labelFor:	String or Text
menuFor:	Menu or ValueHolder with Menu
specificationFor:	A FullSpec
visualFor:	A kind of VisualComponent

specify that an aspect model named #zipCode is required for one of the interface's components. To acquire this model, the builder will solicit its source as shown below.

        source aspectFor: #zipCode

The aspectFor: method, which is defined in ApplicationModel, is shown below.

> **aspectFor: aSymbol**
>
> ^self perform: aSymbol

And for the process to conclude successfully, the source object's class must define the instance method zipCode, whose implementation probably looks something like:

> **zipCode**
>
> ^zipCode isNil
>   ifTrue: [zipCode := String new asValue]
>   ifFalse: [zipCode]

Notice that the messages in Table 3.3 very closely resemble the messages in Table 3.2. Do not confuse these, however. The messages in Table 3.2 are messages sent to the builder, and the corresponding methods are implemented in UIBuilder. The messages in Table 3.3 are messages the builder sends to its source, and the corresponding methods are implemented in the ApplicationModel class.

3.3.6 Safely Acquiring Resources

Suppose in the example above that the source does not understand the message zipCode. Under normal operations, this is sufficient to halt all execution and raise a notifier. For this reason, the builder acquires resources using the safelyPerform:key: message shown below.

```
safelyPerform: aSelector key: aKey

^source messageNotUnderstoodSignal
    handle: [:ex |
        | sel |
        sel := ex parameter selector.
        (sel := aKey or: [sel == aSelector])
            ifTrue: [ex returnWith: nil]
            ifFalse: [ex reject]]
    do: [source perform: aSelector with: aKey]
```

In this method, the first argument, aSelector, is one of the message selectors listed in Table 3.3 and the second argument, aKey, is the name of the resource. In the zip code example from Section 3.3.5, aSelector would be #aspectFor: and aKey would be #zipCode. The builder asks its source to perform the resource lookup inside of a signal handler so that if anything goes wrong, such as the source object not understanding the message named by aKey, a notifier will not be raised and nil is returned instead.

While it is the builder that performs a resource lookup by soliciting its source object, it usually does so on behalf of some other object such as a component spec or look policy object. It is the responsibility of the builder to safely perform the resource acquisition and to return nil if none is found. It is the responsibility of the object requesting the resource from the builder to decide if a nil value is sufficient to halt execution and to raise a notifier.

3.4 Building According to Policy

A *VisualWorks* application can emulate the look and feel of four different popular window environments. These environments are MS *Windows, Motif, Macintosh,* and *CUA-OS/2.* Before *VisualWorks, Objectworks\Smalltalk* had its own unique look and feel. In *VisualWorks,* this particular look and feel is referred to as Default. For the sake of generality, I will refer to Default as a window environment as well, bringing the total of *VisualWorks* look and feel emulations to five. This section gives a brief overview of how *VisualWorks* achieves this extraordinary behavior. The concepts covered in this section are illustrated in Disk Example 3.4.

3.4.1 Look Policy

The builder does not actually build the interface, it merely coordinates the construction activity. A *VisualWorks* component is actually built by either the component spec that represents it or by the builder's look policy object—of these two, it is most often the look policy object. A **look policy** object creates a *VisualWorks* component based on the specification for the component and conforming to a particular window environment's look and feel. To extend the metaphor, it could be said that the builder subcontracts component construction to the component specs and the look policy object.

There are six classes of look policy objects—one abstract and five concrete. There is one concrete look policy class for each of the window environments emulated by *VisualWorks*. These five concrete look policy classes are DefaultLookPolicy, MotifLookPolicy, MacLookPolicy, Win3LookPolicy, and CUALookPolicy. Each of these is a subclass of the abstract class UILookPolicy.

A UIBuilder has an instance variable, policy, which it uses to reference its look policy object. The look policy is set prior to any interface construction, but it can be changed at any time. The statement below gives an example of how to set the look policy for a builder.

> aBuilder policy: MacLookPolicy new

3.4.2 Component Building Methods

The UILookPolicy class is an abstract class and defines most of the behavior for its five subclasses. In its instance method protocol 'building,' it has several methods that I will refer to as component building methods. A **component building method** is a look policy instance method that constructs a component based on the description provided in a component spec and in the look and feel of that particular look policy. A component building method is also responsible for adding the new component to the interface under construction. For example, the UILookPolicy method

> actionButton: anActionButtonSpec into: aBuilder

creates an action button component based on the information in the argument anActionButtonSpec and adds that component to the interface under construction by aBuilder. Depending on the particular kind of look policy object that receives the message (i.e., MacLookPolicy, MotifLookPolicy, etc.), the button will be built with a particular look and feel.

Each of the component building methods has two arguments: the component spec and the builder that is requesting the component construction. It is necessary that the look policy have the component spec so it can build the component as it was originally described by the developer. It is necessary that the look policy receive the builder as an argument for two reasons. First, the builder provides the look policy object with certain resources so that it can complete the construction of the component. For instance, the component spec may specify that the component is to have a model or a menu. The look policy object looks to the builder to supply such resources. Second, it is the builder that contains the interface under construction, and part of the responsibility of a component building method is to add the new component to that interface.

Adding a new, look policy-specific component to *VisualWorks* requires adding a corresponding component building method in UILookPolicy to actually build the component according to a component spec (actually, this is not the case for all components, as we will see in Section 3.6). Adding new components to *VisualWorks* is covered in Chapter 12.

3.4.3 Look and Feel Emulation

Each type of look policy object builds the components in a manner consistent with the platform look and feel it is trying to emulate. I use the term *emulate* because no special libraries or tool kits are employed by *VisualWorks*. Most platform-specific GUI applications depend on the host window environment to provide high-level functions for such things as scroll bars, buttons, menus, and dialogs, relieving the programmer from having to work at such levels of minutiae. For instance, *MS Windows* has the Windows API and *Macintosh* has the Mac Toolkit. *VisualWorks* is completely portable and, therefore, not platform specific. In a *VisualWorks* application, all scroll bars, borders, buttons, dialogs, and menus are built from scratch. This makes all five look policies equally available to all platforms supported by *VisualWorks*.

3.4.4 Look Policy-Specific Classes

Each look policy has several of its own classes for constructing the *VisualWorks* components in its own particular idiom. For example, an action button for the *Motif* look policy is an instance of MotifActionButtonView. This factoring of the visual classes along the lines of look policy is quite obvious when you consider that the point of a look policy is to provide different component appearances and behaviors. Each set of look policy-specific classes has its own class category. For instance, the classes used in a *Macintosh* look policy are found in the class category 'UILooks-Mac.'

Each concrete look policy class, such as MacLookPolicy or CUALookPolicy, has several **implementation methods**, which return the class or instance of the class required for constructing a component according to policy. These can be classes or instances of widgets, menus, borders, composites, or wrappers. The implementation methods are found in the instance protocols 'private,' 'private-borders,' 'constants,' and 'implementation classes.' The component-building methods covered in Section 3.4.2 use the implementation methods to build the component according to policy. As an example, MotifLook-Policy defines the following implementation method:

checkBoxClass

    "Answer the appropriate class to implement Check Buttons for this LookPolicy."

    ^MotifCheckButtonView

This method is used by the corresponding component building method, checkBox:into:, which builds a check box component. It makes sure that a *Motif* looking check box is built and not some other kind of check box.

3.5 Other Building Attributes

So far in our discussion of UIBuilder, we have mentioned several variables: policy, source, bindings, labels, visuals, isEditing, and cacheWhileEditing. There are several more variables used by a builder in performing its duties: window, keyboardProcessor, namedComponents, and a group of variables I will refer to as the *construction variables*. Each of these additional UIBuilder instance variables is discussed in this section.

    The first three variables discussed—window, keyboardProcessor, and namedComponents—are made readily available to the running application after the interface has been constructed. Disk Example 3.5 covers the topic of runtime manipulation of interface objects.

3.5.1 Window

As mentioned earlier, the builder only builds an interface for a single window, and each *VisualWorks* window is built by a separate builder. This window is an ApplicationWindow, and the builder holds on to it with its window variable. This makes the window available to other objects that know about the builder, allowing modifications to the window during runtime.

    The window is one of the items of interest to the runtime application after the interface is built. Some of the more common reasons for accessing the window after interface construction are changing the label, setting an icon, collapsing or expanding the window, and moving the window. Chapter 6 is dedicated entirely to the topic of *VisualWorks* windows.

3.5.2 Keyboard Processor

A keyboard processor is an object that directs keyboard events to the current widget controller and maintains tab order among the tabable components (a formal definition is provided in Chapter 6, Section 6.3.2). The builder includes a keyboard processor with each window. It makes sure that each active component in the window (except menu buttons and sliders) is registered with the keyboard processor. A keyboard processor is an instance of KeyboardProcessor. The builder references this object with its keyboardProcessor variable. Other objects can access a builder's keyboard processor by sending the message keyboardProcessor.

The keyboard processor is one of the items of interest to the runtime application after the interface is built. Some of the reasons for accessing the keyboard processor after interface construction are to intercept keyboard events or to abort a change of control from one tabable component to the next. The topic of the keyboard processor is covered in depth in Chapter 6, Section 6.3.2.

3.5.3 Named Components

Each component placed inside of a window can have a unique, developer defined name associated with it. This name is typically referred to as the component's ID. A **component ID** is a Symbol that uniquely identifies a component within the set of components known to the builder. A component that has been assigned an ID is referred to as a **named component**. The builder places all named components in its namedComponents variable. This variable is an IdentityDictionary where the keys are the IDs and the values are the components.

The builder does not need this dictionary for the purpose of constructing a user interface. The builder maintains the namedComponents dictionary solely for the benefit of the runtime application. The dictionary provides a means for accessing the components during runtime. In this capacity, the builder is operating exclusively in the third of its three roles (see Section 3.1), providing access to the interface for the runtime application. There are several reasons why an application may want to access a component during runtime: to make it invisible, to disable it, or to change its color, to name a few.

3.5.4 Construction Variables

A UIBuilder has several variables, called construction variables, which it uses in facilitating the interface construction process. Most of the construction variables are constantly changing value as the interface construction process proceeds. Contrast this with such variables as window, source, and keyboardProcessor, which are set once and do not change throughout the interface construction process. The UIBuilder construction variables are spec, decorator, wrapper, composite, stack, windowSpec, and converterClass. Each of these is discussed below (this completes the list of UIBuilder instance variables except for subCanvasSpecs, which is covered in Chapter 5).

3.5.4.1 spec

When a UIBuilder is building a runtime interface, it needs a way to hold on to the specs that are handed in by the client. For this purpose, it uses an instance variable called spec. If spec objects are handed in one at a time, spec holds on to the most recent. Remember, as soon as a spec object is handed in, it is immediately used to construct the part of the interface it describes, so there is no reason for the builder to hold on to old specs. Also, each component already contains a copy of the spec used to create that component so maintaining separate specs would be redundant.

3.5.4.2 decorator and wrapper

All components constructed for an interface require a spec wrapper. A UIBuilder uses its wrapper variable to hold on to the SpecWrapper of the component currently under construction. Certain components need edge decoration such as a border or a scroll bar. The edge decoration for the component currently under construction is maintained in the UIBuilder's decorator variable.

3.5.4.3 composite and stack

When the builder builds a component, it adds the new component to a composite. The default composite is a CompositePart, which will serve as the window's component. For the purposes of this book, we will refer to this composite as the *top composite*. When the builder is building a composite component, however, it must create a new CompositePart to hold the components of the composite component. Therefore, the builder must keep track of the various levels of composites. It does this with a stack structure.

As an example, consider that we are handing a builder a series of component specs, which are currently being added to the top composite. Now suppose that one of these component specs describes a composite component. The builder pushes the top composite onto a stack and instantiates a new composite to be the current composite. It then creates each of the new composite's components, adding each one to the new current composite. If one of those components should also happen to be a composite component, this new current composite is pushed onto the stack as well and a third composite is created and populated with its own components. When the builder finishes with this third composite's components, it pops the previous composite off the stack and continues with its remaining components. When this composite is completed, it pops the original composite, the top composite, off of the stack and resumes populating it according to the original series of components specs.

A UIBuilder uses a variable called stack to hold on to the stack structure and a variable called composite to hold on to the current composite. This recursive process is covered in depth in Section 3.6.6.

3.5.4.4 windowSpec

The windowSpec variable holds on to the window spec until it is time to open. It then uses the information in this window spec to modify the window with the appropriate colors, size, label, etc.

3.5.4.5 converterClass

The converterClass instance variable references the class of print converter to be used by the input fields. Instances of InputFieldSpec are the users of this method.

3.6 The Building Process

This section covers the building process. We will look at what actually happens when a spec object is handed to the builder. First we look at the general case of handing any kind of spec object to the builder using the add: message. Then we will take a top–down approach in looking at the specific cases of handing the builder a full spec, a window spec, a spec collection, a component spec, and the special case of a composite spec.

3.6.1 Adding a Specification

The building process always starts by handing the builder a specification object using the add: message as shown below.

> builder add: aSpec

The argument aSpec can be a full spec, a window spec, a spec collection, or a component spec. Regardless of the type of spec, the process always starts out the same.

1. Hand the spec to the builder.

2. The builder initializes its construction variables.

3. The builder appeals to the spec object to create the part of the interface it describes—a window, a component, etc.

Sending the add: message to the builder is the first step. UIBuilder's implementation of the add: method is shown below.

> **add: aSpec**
>   "Reset current internal state and build within the current composite
>   according to aSpec."
>
>   self startNewComponent.
>   self addSpec: aSpec.
>   ^wrapper

The startNewComponent message is the second step of adding a spec object to the builder. The startNewComponent method just sets the builder's wrapper, component, and decorator variables to nil. The addSpec: message is the third step in adding a spec to a builder. The implementation for the addSpec: method is shown below.

> **addSpec: aSpec**
>   "Appeal to aSpec to add itself; it in turn will ordinarily appeal to the
>   receiver's policy"
>
>   spec := aSpec.
>   aSpec addTo: self withPolicy: policy

In this method, the builder sets its spec variable to aSpec and then appeals to aSpec to build the part of the interface it describes. Therefore, the builder does not actually do the building, but delegates this responsibility to the spec object. It does this by sending the message addTo:withPolicy: to aSpec. From here, the building process varies based on the type of spec object. This variation reveals itself in each spec class's implementation of the addTo:withPolicy: method.

3.6.2 Adding a Full Spec

Recall from Section 3.2.1.3 that a full spec is nothing more than a container for a window spec and a spec collection. A FullSpec uses its window instance variable to reference its WindowSpec and its component instance variable to reference its SpecCollection. When a FullSpec is handed to a builder, the builder will appeal to the full spec to create the interface it represents by sending it the message addTo:withPolicy:. The FullSpec implementation of this method is shown below.

> **addTo: builder withPolicy: policy**

```
builder add: window.
builder add: component
```

In the first statement, the FullSpec hands its window spec to the builder. In the second statement, the full spec hands its spec collection to the builder. So the FullSpec completes its responsibility of creating its interface by telling the builder to build a window from its window spec and to populate that window with the components described in its spec collection.

3.6.3 Adding a Window Spec

A builder always needs a window spec (unless it is building a subcanvas covered in Chapter 5). When a builder receives a window spec, it doesn't assume the responsibility of building the window, but instead delegates this task to the window spec. The builder does this by sending the message addTo:withPolicy: to the window spec. WindowSpec inherits its implementation of addTo:withPolicy: from its superclass UISpecification. This implementation is shown below.

addTo: builder withPolicy: policy

```
self dispatchTo: policy with: builder.
self finalizeComponentIn: builder
```

The WindowSpec implementation of dispatchTo: builder withPolicy: policy is shown below.

dispatchTo: policy with: builder

```
policy window: self into: builder
```

In this method, we can see that the window spec does not assume responsibility for building the window either. Instead, it appeals to the look policy object to actually build the window. The look policy object uses the information in the window spec to build the window. WindowSpec's implementation of finalizeComponentIn: merely sets the UIBuilder's windowSpec variable, as shown below.

finalizeComponentIn: builder

```
builder windowSpec: self
```

To summarize building a window from a specification,

1. Some object such as a full spec or the builder's client asks the builder to build a window according to a window spec.

2. The builder delegates this task to the window spec.

3. The window spec further delegates this task to the look policy object, which finally assumes the responsibility of building the window.

3.6.4 Adding a Spec Collection

Recall that a spec collection is nothing more than a collection of component specs. The spec collection is an instance of SpecCollection that has its own special implementation of addTo:withPolicy: shown below.

addTo: builder withPolicy: policy

```
1 to: collection size do:
    [:i |
    builder add: (collection at: i)]
```

So when a builder asks a spec collection to create the interface it represents, the spec collection merely adds each of its component specs to the builder.

3.6.5 Adding a Component Spec

When a component spec is handed to a builder, the builder will appeal to the component spec to create the component it describes by sending it the message addTo:withPolicy:. The component spec actually has two responsibilities: to construct the component and to add the component to the interface. Like WindowSpec, each component spec class inherits its implementation of addTo:withPolicy: from UISpecification. This implementation is shown below.

addTo: builder withPolicy: policy

```
self dispatchTo: builder withPolicy: aPolicy.
self finalizeComponentIn: builder
```

The first statement takes care of constructing the component, and the second statement takes care of making certain the newly constructed component is added to the rest of the interface. These two responsibilities of the component spec are discussed below

3.6.5.1 Building the Component

The first responsibility of the component spec is to build the component it describes. While most components are constructed according to a look policy, some components appear the same in all of the look policies. Those components that are look policy independent are arbitrary components, regions, composites, and subcanvases. Subcanvases are a special case discussed in Chapter 5. If a component is independent of look policy, such as a region, then the component spec assumes the responsibility of constructing the component in its dispatchTo:withPolicy: method. If a component is look policy dependent, however—a text editor, for example—then the component spec will appeal to the look policy object to construct the component in its own particular idiom. In such cases, the component spec's implementation of dispatchTo:withPolicy: is to dispatch a component building message (see Section 3.4.2) to the look policy object. For example, the ActionButtonSpec implementation looks like

> **dispatchTo: builder withPolicy: policy**
>
> policy actionButton: self into: builder

and the CheckBoxSpec implementation looks like

> **dispatchTo: builder withPolicy: policy**
>
> policy checkBox: self into: builder

Each component that is look policy dependent has its own component-building method, defined in UILookPolicy.

Regardless of whether the component is built by the spec object or the look policy object, the construction process usually involves the following steps.

1. Acquire the model if necessary.

2. Instantiate the widget.

3. Instantiate the controller if necessary.

4. Set any component specific attributes, such as tabability and read-only behavior.

5. Instantiate decoration object if necessary.

6. Apply layout.

3.6.5.2 Adding the Component to the Interface

The second responsibility of a component spec is to add the new component to the builder's current composite and named components list. It does this in the finalize-ComponentIn: builder method as implemented in NamedSpec and shown below.

> **finalizeComponentIn: builder**
>
> builder addComponent.
> name == nil
>   ifFalse: [builder componentAt: name put: builder wrapper]

In the first statement above, the builder adds the component to its current composite. The second statement adds the component to the builder's list of named components.

3.6.6 Adding a Composite Spec

When a newly constructed component is added to the builder's interface, it is actually added to the builder's current composite. Recall that the builder maintains a stack of composites and a pointer to the current composite (see Section 3.5.4.3). It uses this stack to keep track of the nesting of the composites within the interface.

The component spec for a composite component is a CompositeSpecCollection. This object consists of a CompositeSpec, which describes a CompositePart, and a collection of component specs, which describe the components to populate that CompositePart.

A composite component is look policy independent, so the CompositeSpecCollection assumes the responsibility of building the component it describes. While the composite component is look policy independent, its components may very well be look policy dependent. A CompositeSpecCollection creates the component it describes with a three-step process:

1. Tell the builder to push its current composite onto its stack and create a new CompositePart to become the new current composite.

2. Populate this new current composite with the components described in its collection of component specs.

3. Add the CompositeSpec, which completes the builder's current composite and pops the previous composite off of the stack.

CompositeSpecCollection implements this three-step process in its addTo:withPolicy: method, shown below.

```
addTo: builder withPolicy: policy

    builder newComposite.
    1 to: collection size do:
        [:i
        builder add: (collection at: i)].
    builder add: compositeSpec
```

In the first line above, which corresponds to the first step, the CompositeSpecCollection tells the builder to push its current composite onto the stack and to start a new composite. In the second statement, which corresponds to the second step, the CompositeSpecCollection iterates over the collection of component specs and adds each to the builder, thus populating the new composite with components. In the last statement, which corresponds to the third step in the process, the CompositeSpecCollection adds its CompositeSpec to the builder, which completes the current composite and pops the previous composite back off the stack.

3.7 Summary

The builder performs three functions in *VisualWorks:* builds the runtime user interface, incrementally builds the canvas as described by the developer, and provides access to the runtime interface for the running application after the interface is built.

The builder builds an interface according to specifications. These specifications are in the form of spec objects. A component spec describes a single *VisualWorks* component. A spec collection is a collection of component specs describing all the components for a single window. A window spec describes the window to be built. A full spec is a combination of a window spec and a spec collection and is sufficient to describe a complete window interface. The builder can receive specs one at a time or all at once. The only stipulation is that it must receive a window spec.

A spec object can be represented as a literal array. A literal array is an Array that contains only literal information. Literal information includes such objects as numbers, booleans, Characters, strings, Symbols, and arrays. An interface in *VisualWorks* contains all the information necessary for generating a spec object describing that interface. This spec object can be converted by the builder back into the intended interface. This same spec object can create its own literal array representation. This literal array, in turn, can be used to recreate the spec object (actually a copy).

The builder requires certain construction materials in order to build its interface according to specifications. These construction materials are called resources and are provided by a source object. Resources can be static, in which case they do not change during runtime, or dynamic, in which case they are expected to change during runtime. Resources are cached by the builder when building a runtime interface. A builder has a client, which is the object that creates the builder for the purpose of having the builder construct its interface. The builder's client and its source are usually the same object, and it is always a kind of ApplicationModel.

VisualWorks has the ability to emulate five different window environments. The window environment a builder chooses to emulate is set by its look policy. The look policy is the object that actually does most of the component construction, not the builder. UILookPolicy is an abstract class that defines most of the look policy state and behavior. It has five concrete subclasses, one for each of the emulated window environments. Each of the different look policy objects builds components in its own particular idiom, resulting in a window consistent with the look and feel of the window environment it is trying to emulate. It is important to realize that these are in fact *emulations* in that no platform-specific tool kits are used to build the interface.

The builder has several other attributes it uses in constructing a user interface. It holds on to the window and keyboard processor. Both of these are available to the application after interface construction. It also maintains a dictionary of named components also used by the runtime application. Unlike the window and keyboard processor however, which are required for interface construction, the named components dictionary plays no part in interface construction and exists merely for the benefit of the running application. The builder has several other variables used in interface construction: spec, decorator, wrapper, composite, stack, windowSpec, and converterClass.

While the builder is responsible for building an interface according to specifications, it delegates the actual construction to the spec objects. The window spec and most of the component specs further delegate this responsibility to the look policy object.

CHAPTER 4

Application Model

I N CHAPTER 1, we looked at the traditional approach to building a Smalltalk application, which employs the classical MVC architecture. As you may recall, this approach had several shortcomings. Most of these problems stemmed from the fact that the model running the application

> ◂ was responsible for constructing its own interface

> ◂ had to micromanage each of the interface components

> ◂ included a mixture of application and domain information

In this chapter we will take a look at how applications are designed and built in *Visual-Works*. The first section deals with the change in MVC architecture introduced by *VisualWorks*—what I will refer to as the application model architecture. The next section looks at the application model's role as the builder's source. Section 3 covers the interface opening behavior of the application model. The fourth section looks at a special subset of application models—those dealing explicitly with modal dialogs.

4.1 Application Model Architecture

VisualWorks has enhanced the MVC architecture in several ways. Chief among these is the realization that standard model behaviors (i.e., those described in the classes Object and Model) are insufficient for running applications. In order to manage an entire application, or at least an entire window, a specific type of model is required. I will loosely refer to the design of such a model as the application model architecture.

Formally defined, the **application model architecture** is the architecture for designing, building, and running applications in *VisualWorks*. The remainder of this section. Disk Example 4.1 uses the Contact Manager application from Chapter 1 to compare and contrast the classical MVC architecture from Chapter 1 and the application model architecture described in this section.

4.1.1 Application Model Concept

In Chapter 1, an application was defined as one or more windows working in a coordinated and related effort to provide a service to a user. The term *application model* describes a model designed specifically for running such an application. But more importantly, such a model should be designed to rectify the problems inherent in the classical MVC architecture mentioned at the start of this chapter and documented in Chapter 1, Section 1.5. Furthermore, in *VisualWorks*, an application model is usually responsible for just a single window so that an application is actually composed of several related and interconnected application models. Therefore, let's define an **application model** as a model that is responsible for creating and managing a runtime user interface, usually consisting of a single window, but delegates much of the detail work, such as the interface construction and aspect model behavior, to various support objects.

The object diagram for an application model is shown in Figure 4.1. The application model delegates interface construction to its builder. It delegates model behavior related

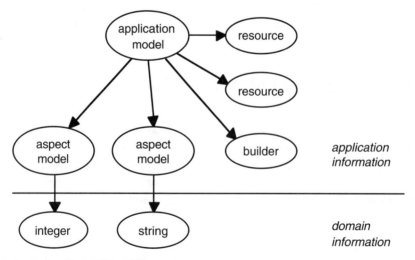

Figure 4.1. Application Model Object Diagram.

to the view/controller pairs to its aspect models. An application model only manages application information. It leaves the domain information to its aspect models. Chapter 11 is dedicated exclusively to the idea of segregating application and domain information.

4.1.2 Delegating Model Responsibilities

The application model manages several other smaller and simpler models called aspect models. Each aspect model manages a single aspect of information such as a string, an integer, or a collection of some type. Many aspect models, such as a ValueHolder, are value models and serve as the model for an active component's widget. Some aspect models, however, such as a SelectionInList, are not value models themselves and do not serve as the model for a widget but do contain a value model, which then serves as the model for a widget.

4.1.2.1 Segregation of Application and Domain

The domain information is contained entirely within the aspect models. This creates a tremendous amount of freedom in developing applications. Domain information can be created, changed, replaced, and stored without affecting the application model directly. The application model is only required to manage application information such as menus, labels, and aspect models. While the domain information is segregated from the application information in the application model architecture, this domain information is very loosely linked and is difficult to manage as a whole. Chapter 11 deals with this issue exclusively.

4.1.2.2 Dependents and Updates

An application model's only dependents are its windows, of which there is usually just one. Each of the other models in the application—the aspect models, value models, etc.—has dependents as well, usually just one or two. Thus, in the application model architecture, any updates that are sent from a model are specifically targeted to those objects that need to receive them. Within the application model architecture, there is usually no such scenario as a model broadcasting an update to several dependents in order to reach the one dependent that is actually interested in the change. This is in sharp contrast to the classical MVC architecture, where several objects can depend on the same model but only one or two of the dependents will ever be interested in any given update.

4.1.2.3 Value Model Protocol

In *VisualWorks,* all widgets that are views have a value model as their model and therefore do not need to know any specifics about their model such as message selectors and aspect names. They know to send the message value in order to obtain information and value: to change information. The view is only interested in receiving updates from its model, so it implements its update methods to look specifically for the #value aspect.

4.1.2.4 Registering Interest

If any object needs to be aware of a change in some aspect of information, it merely registers interest in the value model holding on to that aspect of information. The interested object does not have to register as a dependent of either the value model or the application model. Nor is the interested object required to implement an update method, but instead receives a predetermined message more germane to its task (see Chapter 2, Section 2.3.2.5, for a comparison between registering interest and registering as a dependent).

4.1.3 Delegating Interface Construction

An application model is responsible for creating its user interface, but it delegates this task to its builder. It is also responsible for providing its builder with a specification (or blueprint) for its interface and any required building materials such as menus and labels.

4.1.3.1 The Builder

An application model creates its own instance of UIBuilder. It commissions this builder to build the user interface. The application model maintains a reference to this builder, even after the interface is built. It does so in order to access certain parts of the interface such as the window, the keyboard processor, and the interface components.

Recall that each builder can build only one window. So if a single application model wants more than one window, it must create a new builder for each additional window. A HelpBrowser is a good example of an application model that builds and opens more than one window (see Chapter 7, Section 8.3.4). As was mentioned in Section 4.1.1, however, most application models only build and manage a single window (or subcanvas, as we will see in Chapter 5), and this window is built by the application model's single instance of UIBuilder.

4.1.3.2 Interface Specification

The application model is responsible for providing the interface spec that serves as the builder's blueprint in constructing the interface. The application model can actually have several interface specs, each describing different windows or different versions of the same window. The interface spec is stored in literal array format so the application model must convert this literal array to a FullSpec object before handing it to the builder.

4.1.3.3 Providing Resources

The application model is responsible for providing any resources required by the builder. These resources are the aspect models, labels, images, menus, and any other interface pieces. To put it another way, the application model acts as the builder's source of building materials (see Chapter 3, Section 3.3.1, and Section 4.2 of this chapter).

4.1.3.4 Action Method Support

Action buttons differ from their fellow active components in that they do not have a corresponding aspect model. Instead, an action button's model is a PluggableAdaptor, which must be initialized to send an action message to the application whenever the PluggableAdaptor receives the value: message. The ActionButtonSpec is responsible for creating this PluggableAdaptor. The application model, however, supplies a block that is defined to trigger the action message whenever it is evaluated. The ActionButtonSpec uses this block in initializing the PluggableAdaptor.

4.1.4 Implementation

The application model architecture is implemented on both the abstract level and the concrete level. The abstract implementation contains state and behavior common to all application models. The concrete implementations include only those things that vary from one specific kind of application model to the next.

4.1.4.1 Abstract Implementation

The abstract implementation of the application model architecture is provided by the class ApplicationModel. ApplicationModel is an abstract subclass of Model and defines one instance variable, builder, which of course references an instance of UIBuilder. The ApplicationModel class provides the following services.

- ▶ interface opening and closing behavior

- ▶ several hooks for subclasses to adjust the interface opening process

- ▶ automatic resource lookup for the builder

- ▶ access to the builder and the completed interface after the interface is built

- ▶ conversion of full spec literal arrays to FullSpec objects

These services are common to all application models.

4.1.4.2 Concrete Implementation

A concrete application model class is usually created for each separate application interface window. Such classes are typically created when the developer first installs a new canvas.

Each concrete application model class is a subclass of ApplicationModel and inherits all of its application model functionality. A concrete application model class provides state and behavior for

- aspect models

- actions

- resources

- full spec literal arrays

- interface opening hooks

- change, notification, and validation of values

- active component call backs

- other application specific behaviors

These are the things that vary from one type of application model to the next.

4.1.4.3 Other Implementations

One interesting implementation of application model is SimpleDialog. This class is an abstract subclass of ApplicationModel and defines all the state and behavior necessary for application model windows to behave like modal dialogs. Some other abstract subclasses of ApplicationModel are UIPainterWatcher, SpecModel, and LensApplicationModel. Each of these enhances ApplicationModel with state and behavior common to a specific group of application models. In Chapters 10 and 11, we will develop some additional abstract subclasses of ApplicationModel to enhance application model functionality and development.

4.2 Application Model as Source

As mentioned in Chapter 3, the client of the builder is usually its source. This makes the application model the source for all of its builder's needs. The builder will look to its source (the application model) to supply aspect models, menus, labels, images, action blocks, and widgets for arbitrary components. Disk Example 4.2 illustrates how a builder uses an application model as a source of building materials.

4.2.1 Aspect Models

All active components require a model. All of the active components, except for action buttons, display and edit domain information. When the look policy object is asked to construct an active component, it will ask the builder for the corresponding aspect model. The builder will then appeal to its source to provide that aspect model. Such aspect models are accessed by sending the message aspectFor: aSymbol to the application model. The argument aSymbol is the name of a message understood by the application model. This message returns an aspect model that either serves as the model for a widget or contains a value model, which then serves as the model for a widget.

4.2.2 Action Methods

An action button is the one type of active component that does not require an aspect model. Instead, its widget's model is a PluggableAdaptor constructed by the ActionButton-Spec, which describes the action button. In order to build this PluggableAdaptor, the ActionButtonSpec must first ask the builder to describe the action that is to take place when the button is pushed. The builder defers to the application model to describe this action by sending the message actionFor: aSymbol to the application model. The argument aSymbol is the name of the action method.

The actionFor: message, shown below, returns a block that, when evaluated, sends the action message to the application model.

```
actionFor: aKey
    "Return a block that will be sent the message value when the
    button is pressed."

    ^[self perform: aKey]
```

I will refer to this block as an action block. An **action block** is a block that, when evaluated, forwards an action message to an application model. The ActionButtonSpec then includes the action block inside of the put block of the PluggableAdaptor, which serves as the model for the action button widget. This PluggableAdaptor is created in the method ActionButtonSpec>>typeConvert: shown below.

```
typeConvert: aValue

    (aValue isKindOf: BlockClosure) ifFalse: [^aValue].
    ^(PluggableAdaptor on: ValueHolder new)
        getBlock: [:b | false]
        putBlock: [:b :v | aValue value]
        updateBlock: [:b :a :p | false].
```

The argument aValue is the action block created by the application model. The result of all this is that when the action button is pushed, the widget sends the message value: to its model, the PluggableAdaptor. The PluggableAdaptor responds by evaluating its put block, which evaluates the action block, which dispatches the appropriate action message to the application model.

4.2.3 Dynamic Resources

In Chapter 3 we learned that certain resources are dynamic in that they are expected to change during runtime. Such resources are provided by an instance method and are usually referenced by an instance variable. Some typical dynamic resources are aspect models, menus, and widgets for arbitrary components. The builder accesses such resources from the application model by sending the messages aspectFor:, menuFor:, and componentFor:, respectively. In each case the argument is a Symbol naming the application model instance method that returns the resource. When menus are expected to be dynamic, they are provided inside a ValueHolder, which serves as a channel (see Chapter 2, Section 2.3.1.2 for more on channels).

The application model should have an instance variable that references a dynamic resource so it can make changes to the resource during runtime. If the application model does not reference the resource, then that resource is static and should be provided by a class method (see Section 4.2.4 below). A possible exception to this is the widget for an arbitrary component. The application may choose to not reference the widget with an instance variable but, instead, reference that widget's model.

4.2.4 Static Resources

In Chapter 3 we learned that certain resources are static in that they are not expected to change during runtime. Such resources are provided by class methods. Some typical static resources are labels, images, menus, and even interface specs. The builder accesses such static resources from the application model by sending the messages labelFor:, visualFor:, menuFor:, and specificationFor:, respectively. The argument in each case is a Symbol naming the application model class method that returns the resource. The typical implementation of such a method is to create a new instance of the resource each time it is accessed. Such a resource is not referenced by either an instance or class variable. The exceptions to this are labels and visuals that can be cached in the class variables DefaultLabels and DefaultVisuals defined in ApplicationModel (see Section 4.2.5).

You may have noticed an inconsistency in the procedure described above. The static resources are defined on the *class* side of the application model class definition, yet the builder accesses them from the *instance* of the particular application model that serves as its source. The resource accessing messages such as labelFor: and visualFor: are defined on both the instance side and the class side of ApplicationModel. The instance implementation for purely static resources such as labels and visuals merely defer to the class to provide the resource.

Certain resources such as menus and widgets for arbitrary components can be either static or dynamic. There is no conflict here. For example, when the builder requests a menu using the menuFor: message, the lookup for that menu starts on the instance side of the application model. If it is not located there, then the lookup continues on the class side. If a menu resource is defined on both the instance and class side, then the instance side definition, or dynamic definition, is located first and returned to the builder.

4.2.5 Cached Resources

The ApplicationModel class has the capability to cache labels and images. It does this in its DefaultLabels and DefaultVisuals class variables, respectively. The caching can speed things along since most static resources are instantiated on each access, a potentially time-consuming process. Since these are class variables, the cached objects are available to all instances at any time, which means all instances of all application model types are drawing from this same pool of resources.

4.3 Building and Opening Interfaces

One of the important functions of an application model is that it knows how to build and open an interface. Most of this work, however, is done by its builder. An application model's interface consists of a single window (or subcanvas, as we will see in Chapter 5).

4.3.1 The General Opening Process

You may recall the discussion in Chapter 3 on using the builder to create and open an interface. The basic approach was to create a builder, hand it a spec object, and tell it to open its window. For convenience, this code is recreated below.

```
builder := UIBuilder new.
builder add: spec.
builder open
```

ApplicationModel uses this same basic technique, slightly enhanced and generalized.

4.3.1.1 openInterface: Method

The behavior for opening an application model's interface is defined in the openInterface: method. To understand how this method works, start with the basic interface opening procedure described above and enhance it in the following manner.

> **builder := UIBuilder new.**
> *Install application model as source of builder.*
> *Acquire full spec from class method.*
> *Perform any modifications to the builder before it builds the interface.*
> **builder add: spec.**
> *Perform any modifications to interface after it is built.*
> *Install the application model as the model for the window.*
> **builder openWithExtent: spec window bounds extent.**
> *Perform any modifications to the interface after the window is opened.*

The actual implementation is shown below.

```
openInterface: aSymbol
    "Open the ApplicationModel's user interface, using the specification
    named."

    | spec |
    builder := UIBuilder new.
    builder source: self.
    spec := self class interfaceSpecFor: aSymbol.
    self preBuildWith: builder.
    builder add: spec.
    self postBuildWith: builder.
    builder window model: self.
    builder openWithExtent: spec window bounds extent.
    self postOpenWith: builder.
    ^builder
```

The various steps of this method are discussed below.

4.3.1.2 Creating the Builder

First, the application model creates the builder for the purpose of building an interface and thus becomes the builder's client. It then installs itself as the builder's source as well. The application model can only open one window with this particular instance of UIBuilder.

4.3.1.3 Acquiring the Specification

ApplicationModel has a class method, interfaceSpecFor:, which takes the name of a class method as an argument and returns a full spec. The implementation of interfaceSpecFor: is shown below.

```
interfaceSpecFor: aSymbol
    "Return an actual specification object based on the named resource
    method."

    ^UISpecification from: (self application specificationFor: aSymbol)
```

The parenthetical expression

(self application specificationFor: aSymbol)

merely sends the argument aSymbol as a message to the application model class. This returns a full spec literal array. This literal array is then passed to UISpecification, which uses it to instantiate a full spec object represented by the literal array. This is the same process described in Chapter 3, Section 3.2.3. It is the standard technique for creating a full spec from its corresponding literal array.

4.3.1.4 Building the Interface

Building the interface is a three-step process. These steps are summarized in Table 4.1. The first step is the prebuild operation. The **prebuild operation** allows the developer to make adjustments to the builder prior to the actual building process. Typically it is used for preloading the builder with resources that will not be found in the source. The prebuild operation is implemented in the preBuildWith: aBuilder method, where the argument is the instance of UIBuilder that will be building the interface. The second step is the build operation, which occurs when the client hands a full spec to the builder using the add: message as discussed in Chapter 3. The third step is the postbuild operation. The **postbuild operation** allows the developer to make any lastminute changes to the interface built by the builder. The postbuild operation is implemented in the postBuildWith: aBuilder method, where the argument is the instance of UIBuilder that has just built the interface. There is a relevant distinction between the prebuild and postbuild operations. The prebuild operation affects the *builder* and the postbuild operation affects the *interface*. The methods preBuildWith: and postBuildWith: are sometimes referred to as hooks because the mechanism for dispatching these messages is already defined in ApplicationModel>>openInterface:.

Table 4.1. The Interface-Building Process.

Step	Operation	Hook	Description
1	Prebuild	preBuildWith:	Allows application model to make any changes to the builder prior to handing it the full spec.
2	Build		The builder builds the interface according to the full spec.
3	Postbuild	postBuildWith:	Allows last minute changes to the interface prior to opening.

4.3.1.5 Opening the Window

Once the interface is built, the application model opens the window contained in the builder and then sends postOpenWith: to self. The postOpenWith: method provides a hook for implementing the postopen operation. The **postopen operation** allows the application model to make any final changes to the interface with the window open. There is a distinction between the postbuild operation and the postopen operation. In the postbuild operation, the interface is completely built but exists in memory only, that is, the window is not open and does not reference a host-generated window resource (see Chapter 6, Section 6.1.3.3, for more on what it means for a window to be open). In the postopen operation, the window is open. And finally, the last line in the openInterface: method simply returns the builder.

4.3.1.6 The Building Hooks

There is often a great deal of confusion as to what types of behavior should be included in the prebuild, postbuild, and postopen operations. Table 4.2 is designed to provide some guidelines in this area.

4.3.2 Some Variations

In order to provide flexibility to the concrete application model classes, ApplicationModel provides some variations to the general interface opening process described in Section 4.3.1.

4.3.2.1 open

The open method has both an instance and a class implementation. Each opens the application model with the default specification found in the class method windowSpec. This is the easiest way to open an application model.

Table 4.2. Building Hooks Activities.

Method	Typical implementation
preBuildWith:	Supply builder with resources it will need to build the interface but will not be supplied by the source. Change look policy.
postBuildWith:	Make changes to components such as label changes and visibility. Make changes to the window such a supplying an icon or changing the window label.
postOpenWith:	Anything that involves a graphics context. Send events to the window.

4.3.2.2 openWithInterface:

Each application model can have several different interface specifications. It accomplishes this by having more than one class method that can return a full spec literal array. If you want to open the interface described in one of these alternate specs, use the openWith-Interface: message. The argument for this message is a Symbol that names the class method that returns the desired full spec literal array. The class side version of this method is openWithSpec:, which does the same thing except that it first creates an instance of the application model.

4.3.2.3 allButOpenInterface:

This method is almost identical to openInterface:. It takes a Symbol as an argument and builds the interface described in the class method named by that Symbol. It stops short, however, at actually opening the window. This of course means that the allButOpenInterface: method does not dispatch the postOpenWith: message either. The allButOpenInterface: message is used by objects that want to take control of opening an application model's window.

4.3.2.4 openDialogInterface:

Each application model knows how to open itself as a modal dialog. It does this by handing one of its full specs to an instance of SimpleDialog using itself as the source instead of the SimpleDialog. This behavior of ApplicationModel is covered more thoroughly in Section 4.4.

4.3.3 Closing the Interface

Once an application window is opened, at some point it must be closed. A window can be closed by the user. It can also be closed programmatically either by the application model or by some other object. ApplicationModel provides some nice protocol for handling the window–closing process.

4.3.3.1 Programmatically Closing the Window

To programmatically close a window, send closeRequest to the application model. The closeRequest method, shown below, propagates an update: #closeRequest message to all of the application model's dependents, which is usually just the window.

```
closeRequest
    "Simulate a close event from the host window manager, which
    may cause the application's window(s) to close dependent on
    possible subsequent interaction with the user."

    self changed: #closeRequest
```

4.3.3.2 Notification of a Window Close

Whenever an ApplicationWindow (ApplicationWindow is the kind of window opened by an application model—see Chapter 6) is going to close, it notifies its model, which is the application model that opened it. The window does this by sending the application model the following message.

> noticeOfWindowClose: aWindow.

The default implementation of this method just returns self, but subclasses of Application-Model are free to override this implementation. Thus the application model is notified whenever its window is about to close. This notification happens regardless of the reason for the close. The window could be closed by either the user, the application model, or some other object and the application model is still notified.

4.3.3.3 Validation for Window Close

Whenever an ApplicationWindow is about to close, the window controller (an instance of ApplicationStandardSystemController) first asks the application model that opened the window if it is OK to close. The controller does this by sending the message requestFor-WindowClose to the application model. This message should return true if it is OK to close and false if it is not OK to close. The default implementation for this method is defined in ApplicationModel and is shown below.

```
requestForWindowClose
    "The ApplicationWindow's controller is checking to see if the
    application is in a state such that it can be closed."

    builder == nil ifTrue: [^true].
    ^builder window keyboardProcessor requestForWindowClose
```

This default implementation lets the keyboardProcessor decide if conditions are such that the window can close. Subclasses of ApplicationModel can override this with something more specific to their task.

4.4 Dialogs

Dialogs are an important part of any GUI application. This section covers dialogs as they are implemented in *VisualWorks*. We begin with a discussion of the behavior that distinguishes a dialog from a nonmodal window. Then the discussion shifts to how dialogs are implemented in *VisualWorks*. This is followed by a review of the stock dialogs available and a discussion of how custom dialogs are implemented.

4.4.1 Modality

In *VisualWorks* a dialog is a modal window. A window is **modal** if it receives all user input, remains the active window, and must be closed before any other windows are allowed to receive user input. In *VisualWorks,* a dialog is modal only with respect to other *VisualWorks* windows. Other applications in your window environment can be accessed while a *VisualWorks* dialog is up. When a Smalltalk statement opens a dialog, the statement immediately following is not executed until the dialog is closed.

A dialog's window has an ApplicationDialogController as its controller. An ApplicationDialogController is a kind of ApplicationStandardSystemController (the controller for nonmodal *VisualWorks* windows) with one basic twist—the way it chooses to give up control. Recall from Chapter 1 (Section 1.4) that every controller continually steps through its control loop until such time as the controller is willing to give up control. The test to see if a controller is willing to give up control is the isControlActive message, which returns a boolean. ApplicationDialogController implements the isControlActive method as shown below.

isControlActive
"Answer true as long as the dialog is not finished."

self isFinished ifTrue: [^false].
^true

The isFinished method, shown below, asks the model for its value.

isFinished
"Send the finished selector to the model to determine if the dialog is finished."

^model value

The model variable in this case is the application model running the dialog interface (usually an instance of SimpleDialog) and should respond to the message value by returning a boolean. If the model returns false, then the dialog is not finished and therefore will not give up control and the dialog window stays open. As soon as the model returns true, the dialog is finished and the ApplicationDialogController gives up control, resulting in a closing of the dialog window. This allows the application model running the dialog to decide when the dialog is done. As long as the model returns false, the dialog controller retains complete control and processes all user input. It is in this way that the dialog is able to maintain modality. Disk Example 4.3 covers the topic of dialog modality.

4.4.2 SimpleDialog

Dialogs are implemented by the class SimpleDialog. This name is somewhat misleading since dialogs can be quite perplexing at times. The class SimpleDialog is a subclass of

ApplicationModel. It adds the necessary state and behavior for an application model to operate as a modal dialog.

4.4.2.1 Initializing a Dialog

A SimpleDialog is initialized with the method below.

initialize

```
accept := false asValue.
cancel := false asValue.
close := false asValue.
builder := UIBuilder new.
builder aspectAt: #accept put: accept.
builder aspectAt: #cancel put: cancel.
builder aspectAt: #close put: close.
escapeIsCancel := true
```

A SimpleDialog initializes each of the three instances variables—accept, close, and cancel— as a ValueHolder whose initial value is false. These three variables are also referred to respectively as the accept channel, close channel, and cancel channel. The SimpleDialog then instantiates its builder, and each of the three value models is placed in the builder's bindings. The escapeIsCancel variable is then initialized to true (see Section 4.4.2.7).

4.4.2.2 Opening a Dialog

The method responsible for creating a dialog's interface is the allButOpenFrom: method shown below.

allButOpenFrom: aSpec
    "Do everything short of actually opening the window."

```
preBuildBlock == nil
    ifTrue: [self preBuildWith: builder]
    ifFalse: [preBuildBlock value: self value: builder].
builder source isNil
    ifTrue: [builder source: self].
builder add: aSpec window.
builder add: aSpec component.
self initializeWindowFor: parentView.
self preOpen.
postBuildBlock == nil
    ifTrue: [self postBuildWith: builder]
    ifFalse: [postBuildBlock value: self value: builder]
```

Some of the interface opening behavior is delegated to the preOpen method shown below.

preOpen
    "Do everything short of actually opening the window."

```
builder window model: self.
escapeIsCancel
    ifTrue: [builder keyboardProcessor
        keyboardHook: [:ev :ctrl | self keyboardEvent: ev]].
accept onChangeSend: #close to: self.
cancel onChangeSend: #close to: self.
```

This interface construction process deviates somewhat from that followed by Application-Model>>openInterface: described in Section 4.3.1.1. The main differences are as follows:

⟩ The builder has already been instantiated in the initialize method.

⟩ Blocks can be substituted for the interface opening hooks.

⟩ The keyboard processor can be set to accept an <Esc> key as a close event.

⟩ The dialog registers interest in its accept and cancel variables to dispatch the close message whenever they change value.

4.4.2.3 Interface Building

SimpleDialog has three variables that hold on to blocks: preBuildBlock, postBuildBlock, and postOpenBlock. These blocks can be substituted for their respective interface building hooks preBuildWith:, postBuildWith:, and postOpenWith:. The benefit of this approach over the traditional prebuild, postbuild and postopen methods is that these processes can be implemented on an instance-by-instance basis. Such is the flexibility of blocks.

4.4.2.4 The Postopen Operation

The postopen operation for a dialog presents a little bit of a departure from how the process works in ApplicationModel. Remember that a dialog is modal and as soon as its window is opened, subsequent execution stops until the dialog is closed. This shifts the burden of initiating the postopen operation to the dialog window controller, an ApplicationDialogController. Just before the dialog window controller takes control, it sends itself the message invokePostOpen. This method tells the application model to perform its postopen operation.

4.4.2.5 Closing a Dialog

An instance of SimpleDialog must respond to the value message by returning a boolean. This is the means by which the ApplicationDialogController knows when to close the dialog window. We know that the SimpleDialog is continually asked by the ApplicationDialog-Controller for its value, which should be either true or false. The SimpleDialog responds by returning the value of its close channel. As soon as the close channel is set to true, the dialog is closed on the next pass through the window controller's control loop. The accept and cancel channels, when set to true, trigger a change message, which sets the close channel to true also. The result is that accept, close, and cancel can all be set up as action methods for an action button, and when that button is pushed, the dialog closes.

4.4.2.6 Dialog Return Value

When a dialog closes, it returns the value of its accept channel. That is, all dialogs are opened as a result of sending some opening message to the dialog. The object returned by this opening message is the value of the SimpleDialog's accept channel. If the user pushed a button associated with the accept channel, then the accept channel is set to true and true is returned. If a button associated with either the close or cancel channels was pushed, then the accept channel's value remains false and false is returned. As an illustration, if we were to inspect on the statement

        SimpleDialog openFrom: aFullSpec

then a dialog would open, we would have to satisfy the dialog by pressing a button, and an Inspector would open on the return value, which would be a boolean. If the button's corresponding action method is accept, then true is returned. Otherwise, false is returned. All dialogs, regardless of their nature, return a boolean, and this boolean is the value of the SimpleDialog's accept channel.

4.4.2.7 Escape Is Cancel

If the escapeIsCancel variable is set to true, then a keyboard event that is an <Esc> key will close the dialog. The default is for escapeIsCancel to be set to true so the <Esc> key, by default, will close a dialog.

4.4.3 Stock Dialogs

VisualWorks provides several stock dialogs. A **stock dialog** is a dialog that performs a small service and can be opened with a single line of code. The stock dialogs are implemented by the Dialog class. Each of the examples provided in this discussion of stock dialogs is found in the Disk Example 4.4.

4.4.3.1 Warning Dialogs

A *warning dialog* pops up a dialog with a single message for the user to read. The user must then close the dialog to continue with the application. Warning dialogs are good for notifications, warnings, or error messages. To open a warning dialog, send the message warn: to the class Dialog. The argument is a String indicating the message you want to appear.

        Dialog warn: 'Job has been printed.'

4.4.3.2 Confirm Dialogs

A *confirm dialog* is used to solicit a yes/no response from the user. The dialog has a **Yes** button and a **No** button. A yes response from the user returns true. A no response returns false. The confirm dialog opening message has two basic forms: confirm: and confirm: initialAnswer:

The confirm: message takes a single argument, which is a string as shown below.

    Dialog confirm: 'Work has not been saved. Save now?'

The confirm:initialAnswer: message takes a boolean as the second argument, which is used to determine a default button selection. For instance, the statement below creates a dialog that returns true if the user hits the <Enter> key.

    Dialog confirm: 'Proceed with disk format?' initialAnswer: false

4.4.3.3 Request Dialogs

A *request dialog* asks the user to type in a string. If the user presses the **OK** button, then the string is returned. If the **Cancel** button is pressed, then an empty string is returned regardless of what the user types in.

There are three basic forms of the request dialog opening message.

    Dialog request: 'Enter the city name'

    Dialog request: 'Enter the city name' initialAnswer: 'Dallas'

    Dialog request: 'Enter the city name' initialAnswer: 'Dallas' onCancel: ['No city']

The first form merely asks the user to type in something. The second form provides a default selection. The third form also provides a default selection and in addition provides a default reply should the user hit the cancel button.

In Section 4.4.2.4 it was stated that all dialogs return a boolean and here we have a dialog returning a string. This apparent contradiction is resolved by the fact that it is a Dialog class method that is actually returning the string. The instance of SimpleDialog employed by the Dialog class still returns a boolean as do all instances of SimpleDialog and its subclasses. A Dialog class method instantiates a SimpleDialog and uses it to open an interface. Based on the return value of this dialog, true or false, the class method can decide to return a string, a number, nil, or any other kind of object. The point is that the class method that opens the dialog is in no way restricted to returning a boolean and can return an object more pertinent to the task at hand. This is a very common technique (see Chapter 10, Section 10.2.4.5). An instance method could easily perform the same type of service of course, however, it is most often a class method as in case of the Dialog class.

4.4.3.4 Choose Dialogs

A *choose dialog* presents the user with a set of choices in the form of action buttons, a list, or both. A value is associated with each button/list item. This dialog returns either nil or the value corresponding to the button or list item selected. To have a choose dialog with nothing but buttons for selections, use the form shown in the following example.

```
Dialog
    choose:     'Pick a flavor'
    labels:     #('Chocolate' 'Vanilla' 'Strawberry')
    values:     #(#chocolate #vanilla #strawberry)
    default:    #vanilla
```

To have a dialog with a list of selections, use the form shown in this next example.

```
Dialog
    choose:     'Pick a flavor'
    fromList:   #('Chocolate' 'Vanilla' 'Strawberry' 'Butter Crunch' )
    values:     #(#chocolate #vanilla #strawberry #butterCrunch )
    lines:      3
    cancel:     [nil]
```

To combine both buttons and a list, use the following form.

```
Dialog
    choose:     'Pick a flavor'
    fromList:   #('Chocolate' 'Vanilla' 'Strawberry')
    values:     #(#chocolate #vanilla #strawberry)
    buttons:    #('Butter Crunch' 'Coffee')
    values:     #(#butterCrunch #coffee)
    lines:      3
    cancel:     [nil]
```

4.4.3.5 File Dialogs

Dialog class has a dialog used to acquire legitimate file names. This dialog returns either a string naming the file or an empty string in case the file does not exist or is unavailable for some reason. There are several class messages that can be used to invoke the file name dialog, the most general of which is shown below.

```
requestFileName: message default: default version: versionType ifFail: failBlock
```

The arguments are as follows.

message	A string indicating the message to the user such as 'File name'.
default	A string that is the default file name. This can be a pattern such as '*.st', and only file names that match will be considered legitimate.

versionType   A Symbol, the description of which is
                   best explained in the method com-
                   ments.

failBlock   A Block that takes no arguments and is
                   evaluated in the case of a failure. The
                   default failBlock is to return an empty
                   string.

As an example, the statement below prompts the user for a text file containing Smalltalk source code—a *.st file.

```
Dialog
    requestFileName:    'Smalltalk file name'
    default:            '*.st'
    version:            #mustBeOld
```

If you accept the dialog with the wild card still in the name, then a choose dialog is opened containing all matching files.

4.4.3.6 Client Look and Feel

Each of the stock dialog messages mentioned so far has a variation that opens the dialog with a specific look and feel. To do this, append the for: keyword to the end of the message. For example,

```
Dialog request: 'Enter the file name' initialAnswer: '*.doc' for: aWindow
```

and

```
Dialog
    choose:     'Pick a flavor'
    fromList:   #('Chocolate' 'Vanilla' 'Strawberry' 'Butter Crunch' )
    values:     #(#chocolate #vanilla #strawberry #butterCrunch )
    lines:      3
    cancel:     [nil]
    for:        aWindow.
```

The argument of the for: keyword is a visual part or a window. This argument is to supply the color scheme (look preferences), border types (edge decoration policy), and button types (widget policy) to be used in constructing the dialog.

4.4.4 Custom Dialogs

There are two approaches to creating custom dialogs in *VisualWorks,* and each has its advantages and disadvantages. The first approach is to design a dialog that is a subclass of

SimpleDialog. The second approach is to design an application model (a subclass of ApplicationModel) and tell it to open as a dialog. These two approaches are discussed below and illustrated in Disk Example 4.5.

4.4.4.1 Subclassing SimpleDialog

When you paint a canvas, you have the option of saving that canvas as a subclass of SimpleDialog. The benefit of this approach to creating a dialog is that you can take advantage of the preBuildWith: and postBuildWith: methods. You can also gain access to the running interface by way of the builder. The problem with this approach is that any additional abstract functionality for application models must be implemented twice, once in ApplicationModel or an abstract subclass, and once in SimpleDialog or an abstract subclass (this shortcoming will become more apparent in Chapter 10). Another problem is that you do not have the option of opening a nonmodal interface. SimpleDialog and its subclasses only open modal windows.

4.4.4.2 Subclassing ApplicationModel

Any subclass of ApplicationModel can be opened as a dialog by sending it the message openDialogInterface: aSymbol. The implementation of this method is shown below.

```
openDialogInterface: aSymbol
    "Answer the result of opening a dialog using the named specification.
    A SimpleDialog with the receiver as the source of bindings is
    initialized and used. The SimpleDialog provides bindings for 'accept'
    and 'cancel'"

    ^SimpleDialog new openFor: self interface: aSymbol
```

The problem with this approach is that the builder that constructs the interface belongs to the instance of SimpleDialog and not to your application model, whose builder remains nil. This means that your application model does not have access to the window, keyboard processor, or components during runtime. Nor will the preBuildWith:, postBuildWith:, and postOpenWith: messages be sent to your application model.

4.4.4.3 Close, Cancel, and Accept Actions

Because a SimpleDialog preloads the close, accept, and cancel channels into the builder's bindings, any action method with any of these names will never be executed. This is because any button whose action method is #close, #accept, or #cancel will use the corresponding channel (ValueHolder) for its model instead of a PluggableAdaptor to trigger the intended action method.

4.5 Summary

VisualWorks uses a special kind of model, called an application model, to run a window. An application model delegates much of its responsibilities to other objects. It delegates interface construction to its builder and it delegates model behavior for active components to its aspect models. An application model manages application information only. It lets its aspect models manage the domain information. Such an approach to application model building is referred to as the application model architecture. The abstract behavior for all application models is implemented in the class ApplicationModel.

An application model serves as the source for its builder. It instantiates the builder, provides it with a full spec describing an interface, and provides it with any necessary resources. An application model uses its builder to create its user interface. Each builder can create only one window. The application model provides hooks for prebuild, postbuild, and postopen operations. These operations make last-minute changes to the interface as it is being created and opened.

All dialogs are modal in that they capture all user input until they are closed. Dialog behavior in *VisualWorks* is implemented by SimpleDialog. The Dialog class provides several stock dialogs. A custom dialog can be created as a subclass of either ApplicationModel or SimpleDialog.

CHAPTER 5

Subcanvas Technology

In Chapter 2 we divided all *VisualWorks* components into five categories: active, passive, arbitrary, composite, and subcanvas. Chapter 2 covered the first four of these component categories. This chapter covers the fifth kind of *VisualWorks* component, subcanvas components. Included in this category are the subcanvas component as well as the notebook and the embedded data form components. But more fundamentally, this chapter covers the broader topic of canvases and subcanvases, which is collectively referred to as subcanvas technology.

Subcanvas technology adds a very powerful dimension to *VisualWorks*. It is a paragon of the benefits of Smalltalk and OOP. I use the term **subcanvas technology** to mean the ability to reuse an entire user interface, including all behaviors, as a portion of another user interface. In order to understand subcanvas technology, however, it is necessary to have a sufficient understanding of MVC, *VisualWorks* components, the builder, and application models. In addition, subcanvas technology involves a recursion among many of the ideas discussed so far, making it quite a difficult subject to master. For these reasons, the discussion of subcanvas technology has been deferred until now.

This chapter covers the machinery behind both canvases and subcanvases. It does not cover design strategies for using subcanvases, nor does it provide any suggestions as to when it is appropriate or inappropriate to create a subcanvas. Such decisions, however, do depend on a good command of the material presented in this chapter. The first section of this chapter covers the basic definitions of canvas and subcanvas and the benefits of subcanvasing. The second section discusses the implementation of the subcanvas component. Section 3 covers the process of building a subcanvas. And in Section 4, we look at the notebook and the embedded data form components whose implementations depend very much on subcanvas technology.

5.1 Basic Definition

Before continuing with the discussion on subcanvases, we need to fix a firm definition not only for the term *subcanvas*, but also for the term *canvas*. This section describes these terms using the concepts covered so far in the book.

5.1.1 Types of Canvases

Canvases can be differentiated based on the following three attributes.

- mode of operation
- implementation class
- the position they assume in the visual component tree

A canvas can be used in edit mode or in runtime mode. I use the term edit mode to refer to the canvas painting process and the term runtime mode to refer to a canvas that has been opened to perform its intended function. Canvases can also be distinguished by their implementation classes—SubCanvas, CompositePart, and UIPainterView. Finally, canvases vary in the place they take in the visual structure. Some canvases are the component of a window, while others are the component of another canvas, that is, a subcanvas. Disk Example 5.1 gives concrete examples of the various types of canvases.

5.1.1.1 Canvas

For the purposes of this book, I will use the term **canvas** to refer to a composite whose container is a window and whose components are all *VisualWorks* components bound to a common application model. With this definition, the canvas can be in either runtime mode or edit mode. As an example, when you paint a canvas, you are populating a composite with *VisualWorks* components. In this case the composite is a UIPainterView and it satisfies the definition above. As another example, an ApplicationWindow opened as a runtime interface contains a component that is a composite of *VisualWorks* components. In this case, the composite is a CompositePart, and it too satisfies the definition of canvas given above. In these two examples, the first canvas operates in an edit mode and the second operates in a runtime or execution mode. In both examples, the canvas is the component of a window and contains *VisualWorks* components, which serve a common application model.

Sometimes the term *canvas* is used to refer explicitly to the painting process. For example, the phrase *open a canvas* is often used to mean opening an interface for editing with the Palette, Canvas Tool, etc. It is usually clear from the context how the term is being used.

5.1.1.2 Subcanvas

I will use the term **subcanvas** to indicate a canvas used as the component of another canvas. A subcanvas' container is not a window but another canvas (actually, there are a few wrappers in between). The subcanvas components, however, are all bound to a common application model. A subcanvas is both a *VisualWorks* component as well as the interface for an application model. It is this duality that makes the topic of subcanvas technology somewhat difficult at first.

5.1.1.3 Roles of a Canvas

Any canvas can be used in edit mode or runtime mode. Any canvas can be used as a subcanvas. If a canvas needs to be edited, it is implemented as a UIPainterView. If a canvas is used to provide a runtime window interface, it is implemented as a CompositePart. If a canvas is to be used as a subcanvas component in either edit or runtime mode, then it is implemented as a SubCanvas. In all three cases, we have a composite of *VisualWorks* components all bound to the same application model.

5.1.2 Subcanvas as a Window Interface

A subcanvas starts out as a canvas, that is, the window interface for an application model. It is designed and installed just like any other application model interface. This of course is part of the beauty of subcanvases. Any window interface that can be opened can also be a subcanvas in another window interface. Therefore, an application model can manage either a window or a subcanvas component inside of a window. The two tasks are almost identical. In either case, the application model has its own builder and can access its components during runtime. The application model behaves the same whether it is managing a subcanvas component or an entire window.

5.1.3 Subcanvas as a *VisualWorks* Component

A subcanvas component is just another *VisualWorks* component. It is composed of a spec wrapper, which contains a widget. It is similar to active components in that it requires an aspect model. Like all *VisualWorks* components, it has its own type of spec object. Officially, a **subcanvas component** is a *VisualWorks* component whose widget is an instance of SubCanvas and whose aspect model is an application model.

5.1.3.1 Subcanvas Widget

The widget for a subcanvas component is an instance of SubCanvas. The widget implementation of subcanvas components is discussed in detail in Section 5.2.

5.1.3.2 Subcanvas Aspect Model

A subcanvas component requires an aspect model much like an input field, check box, or any of the other active components. There is a clear distinction, however, in what an aspect model provides to the subcanvas as opposed to what an aspect model provides to an active component. In the case of active components, the widget is a view and the aspect model provides a value model as the model for this widget. In the case of subcanvases, however, the widget is not a view and the aspect model does not provide a value model for the subcanvas widget. Instead, the aspect model is an application model that serves as a source of additional aspect models for the *VisualWorks* components within the subcanvas.

5.1.3.3 Parent Application

Just as an input field gets its aspect model from the application model (via the builder), a subcanvas gets its aspect model from the application model as well. Since the aspect model for the subcanvas is also an application model, we need some terminology to distinguish the two application models. The term **subapplication** refers to the application model managing the subcanvas. The subapplication is also referred to as the *subenvironment*, the *child application*, the *embedded application*, or the *client*. The term **parent application** refers to the application model providing the subapplication as an aspect model. The parent application can also be referred to as the *containing application*—or *top model* in the event that it is the root of an application model tree and has no parent application of its own. For the purposes of this book, I will use the terms *parent application* and *subapplication* (an exception is made in the subcanvas building process where the term *client* is preferred to *subapplication*).

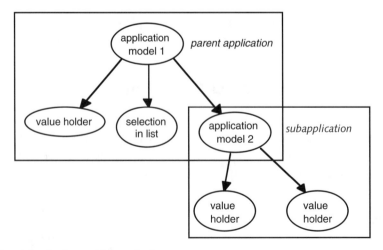

Figure 5.1. Parent Application and Subapplication.

For an example of the relationship between the parent application and subapplication, see Figure 5.1. In this figure, application model 1 has three aspect models: value holder, selection in list, and application model 2. Each of these aspect models supports a component. The value holder aspect model could be the model for a variety of *VisualWorks* components such as a radio button or text editor. The selection in list aspect model most likely supports a list component. The third aspect model, application model 2, is the aspect model for a subcanvas component. Since it too is an application model, it has its own additional aspect models—in this case two ValueHolders. We can say that application model 1 is the parent application of application model 2. And we can say that application model 2 is a subapplication of application model 1.

5.1.3.4 Subcanvas Spec

Like all *VisualWorks* components, a subcanvas has a corresponding component spec, which is implemented by the class SubCanvasSpec. Because of the special nature of subcanvases, a SubCanvasSpec has some very unique behavior. SubCanvasSpec is discussed in detail in Section 5.2.2.

5.1.4 Benefits of Subcanvas Technology

Subcanvas technology gives the developer a great deal of power. The benefits of subcanvasing are listed in Table 5.1.

Table 5.1. Benefits of Subcanvas Technology.

Benefit	Description
Reuse	An interface, and all of its complexity, can be designed once and reused several times.
Consistency	Through subcanvasing, a set of components that appear in several places can always have the same look and behavior.
Customization	A subcanvas can be reviewed as a custom-built component.
Factoring	Subcanvasing allows a large, complex application model to be factored into several smaller, more manageable application models.
Recursion	Any subcanvas can contain other subcanvases.
Maintenance	Any necessary changes are made once in the subcanvas and propagate to all areas where that subcanvas is used.

5.2 Subcanvas Component Implementation

A subcanvas is implemented much like a composite component (see Chapter 2, Section 2.2.6). Both of these are just composites whose component parts are *VisualWorks* components. Both of them require a WidgetStateWrapper to provide the *VisualWorks* widget protocol discussed in Chapter 2, Section 2.1.2. At this point, however, the similarities stop. Disk Example 5.2 gives a demonstration of how a subcanvas component is fundamentally just like any other *VisualWorks* component.

5.2.1 SubCanvas

The widget behavior for a subcanvas component is implemented by SubCanvas, which is a subclass of CompositePart. It adds no state and very little behavior to its superclass.

5.2.1.1 Inherited Behavior
As a kind of CompositePart, a SubCanvas is a container for a collection of components. In the case of SubCanvas, these components are *VisualWorks* components, that is, spec wrappers containing widgets. A CompositePart is not a view so it does not have a model or a controller. It is merely a collection of components positioned within a common bounds.

5.2.1.2 Rebuilding
The only behavior that SubCanvas adds to its superclass is the ability to rebuild itself during runtime. When a SubCanvas rebuilds itself, it empties its components collection and repopulates that collection with all new *VisualWorks* components. The SubCanvas class has three instance methods that do just that.

> client: appModel
>
> client: appModel spec: aSpec
>
> client: appModel spec: aSpec builder: aBuilder

The arguments for these messages are as follows.

appModel	Some application model that serves as the subapplication for the SubCanvas and therefore serves as the source for aspect models, specs, and other resources required to build the new set of *VisualWorks* components.
aSpec	A FullSpec or a Symbol. If it is a FullSpec, it describes the new set of components that

will populate the subcanvas. If it is a Symbol, it names the appModel class method, which returns a literal array for the FullSpec.

aBuilder   The UIBuilder that will be used to build the new set of *VisualWorks* components.

When a subcanvas is rebuilt, its current component collection is emptied and then repopulated with the components described in aSpec. Each time a subcanvas is rebuilt, a new instance of UIBuilder is required. Recall that Chapter 2 stated that each builder builds only one window. A more correct statement is that each builder builds only one canvas, which is used as either a window interface or a subcanvas component. The subcanvas rebuilding process is further discussed in Section 5.3.3.

5.2.2 SubCanvasSpec

A subcanvas is just like any other *VisualWorks* component in that it has its own component spec, SubCanvasSpec, which is a subclass of NamedSpec.

5.2.2.1 Inherited Behavior

Because it is a kind of NamedSpec, a SubCanvasSpec describes a subcanvas component's layout, look preferences, opacity, and ID. It also knows how to create the subcanvas component it describes and how to add that subcanvas component to a builder's interface. A SubCanvasSpec is one of the few component specs that assumes the responsibility of creating the component it describes instead of delegating component construction to the look policy object. This is because a subcanvas component is independent of look policy and the SubCanvasSpec has no incentive to defer to a look policy object to build the component. It should be pointed out, however, that while the subcanvas component is not look policy dependent, its components usually are.

5.2.2.2 Subcanvas Specifications

A SubCanvasSpec, in order to adequately describe a subcanvas, needs to know three things in addition to those mentioned above.

- ▶ the name of the message sent to the parent application in order to acquire the subapplication that will run the subcanvas component

- ▶ the name of the class of application model that builds and runs the subcanvas component

> ◆ the name of the class method that returns a full spec describing the interface to be used to populate the subcanvas component

It should come as no surprise then that SubCanvasSpec defines three instance variables—clientKey, majorKey, and minorKey—one for each of these three pieces of information. The clientKey is a Symbol and is used to acquire the subapplication for the subcanvas from the builder's bindings or from the builder's source. It is the name of an aspect method of the parent application. The majorKey is a Symbol and is the name of the class of the subapplication that operates the subcanvas. The minorKey is a Symbol and is the name of the class method that returns a full spec literal array describing the subcanvas interface.

5.2.2.3 Properties

A SubCanvasSpec also defines certain properties for its component. These properties determine if the subcanvas component will have a menu bar, a horizontal scrollbar, and a vertical scrollbar. The SubCanvasSpec uses its flag variable to keep track of whether or not the component will have these properties.

5.3 Building a Subcanvas

When a runtime interface opens, the window's component is a canvas that is a Composite-Part. This canvas is the container for the *VisualWorks* components comprising the interface. Since the canvas is the component of the window, it is responsible for filling the entire bounds of the window's display surface (see Figure 5.2a and b).

Now suppose we have the same interface, from the same application model, but built inside of another kind of composite, a SubCanvas. And further suppose that this composite is not a window's component but just a widget for a spec wrapper, which itself is one of the components of another canvas. Furthermore, the SubCanvas will have a bounds that is only a portion of the window's total display area. This, in a nutshell, is the concept of a subcanvas (see Figure 5.2c and d).

5.3.1 Building the Subcanvas

Like all *VisualWorks* components, a subcanvas is constructed when a component spec describing the subcanvas is handed to an instance of UIBuilder. This component spec of course is a SubCanvasSpec. Just as with any other component spec, the builder appeals to the spec to construct the object it represents. It does so by sending it the message addTo: self withPolicy: policy

where self is the builder and policy is a look policy object. The SubCanvasSpec implementation of this message is to dispatch the message dispatchTo: policy with: builder to itself. At this point, most component specs appeal to the policy object to actually construct the component because most components have a look policy-dependent appearance. The SubCanvasSpec, however, elects to build the component itself in its dispatchTo: policy with: builder method. It can do this because subcanvas components are not look policy dependent. The *VisualWorks* com-

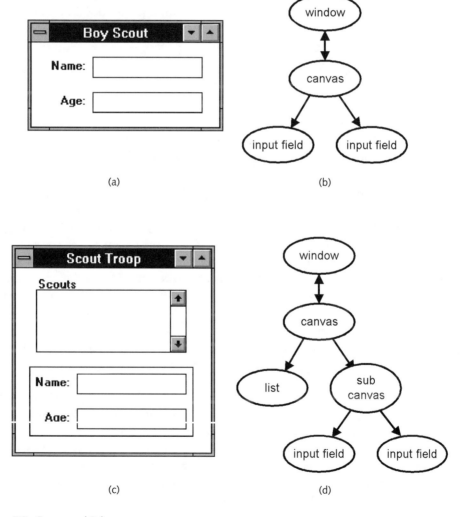

Figure 5.2. Canvas and Subcanvas.

ponents that comprise a subcanvas may be look policy dependent, but the subcanvas itself is not. Therefore, there is no need to have a building method within the look policy object for constructing a subcanvas. The dispatchTo: policy with: builder method implemented in SubCanvas-Spec is very long but the main course of events is as follows.

1. Acquire the full spec describing the internals of the subcanvas from the builder.

2. Acquire the subapplication, which is an application model, responsible for running the subcanvas.

3. Create a subbuilder dedicated exclusively to building the subcanvas interface.

4. Have the subapplication build the interface using the subbuilder.

These four steps are described below and illustrated with concrete examples in Disk Example 5.3.

5.3.1.1 Acquire the Full Spec

A UIBuilder caches any full specs used to construct a subcanvas component in its subCanvas-Specs instance variable, which is an IdentityDictionary. Each key in this IdentityDictionary is a Symbol that is the class name of an application model that will serve as a subapplication for a subcanvas. Such a Symbol is referred to as a major key. The **major key** is a Symbol that is the name of the class of application model that will serve as the subapplication. The value associated with each major key is another IdentityDictionary. Each key in this embedded IdentityDictionary is also a Symbol that is the name of a class method in the subapplication that returns a full spec literal array. Such a Symbol is referred to as a minor key. A **minor key** is a Symbol that is the name of the class method that returns the interface spec describing the subcanvas. The value associated with each minor key is a FullSpec object, which describes a subcanvas interface. Thus it takes a major key and a minor key to access a subcanvas full spec from the builder. The SubCanvasSpec object uses its majorKey and minorKey instance variables to acquire the appropriate full spec cached in the builder.

5.3.1.2 Subapplication

The subapplication is the application model that manages the subcanvas. The subapplication is provided by the parent application as an aspect model. In the context of building subcanvases, the subapplication is referred to as the **client**. The SubCanvasSpec acquires the client from the builder by sending the message clientAt: aSymbol, where aSymbol is the name of the aspect method in the source (parent application) that returns the client. The builder caches the client in its bindings variable along with all the other aspect models such as ValueHolders and SelectionInLists.

5.3.1.3 Create the Subbuilder

Since a subcanvas component is actually an entire interface in and of itself, it is constructed by its own separate builder called a subbuilder. A **subbuilder** is an instance of UIBuilder and is responsible for constructing the interface that makes up a single subcanvas. Even though a subbuilder is an instance of UIBuilder, it does not build a window, only a composite containing *VisualWorks* components. It is the builder's responsibility for creating any required subbuilders. The builder and its subbuilders share the same look policy, window, and keyboard processor.

5.3.1.4 Build the Subcanvas

Since application models know how to construct their own interfaces using a builder, it only makes sense that the client (subapplication) has the ultimate responsibility of creating the interface that makes up the subcanvas component. This is done by sending the following message to the client.

> buildInSubCanvas: spec withBuilder: subBuilder

This method is defined in ApplicationModel so all application models know how to build their interface as a subcanvas. The implementation is shown below.

```
buildInSubCanvas: spec withBuilder: aBuilder
    "This message is sent by the builder when it begins work on a
    SubCanvas."

    builder == nil ifTrue: [builder := aBuilder].
    aBuilder source: self.
    self preBuildWith: aBuilder.
    aBuilder add: spec.
    self postBuildWith: aBuilder.
    ^aBuilder
```

The argument spec is a FullSpec, which contains a description of the *VisualWorks* components that are to populate the subcanvas. The argument subBuilder is an instance of UIBuilder, which is a subbuilder dedicated exclusively to building these very components as described in spec. The application model receiving the message above acts as the source for subBuilder.

5.3.2 Prebuild and Postbuild Operations

Since there is an application model called the subapplication (client) that actually builds and manages a subcanvas, that application model has prebuild and postbuild operations. When the subapplication is asked to provide its interface as a subcanvas, it includes the preBuildWith: and postBuildWith: messages as part of that building process (see buildInSub-Canvas:withBuilder: method above). Since the subapplication is not building a window, only a subcanvas, it does not include a postopen operation.

Because of the recursive nature of subcanvas construction, there can be a bit of confusion as to when the various preBuildWith: and postBuildWith: messages are dispatched. The rules are simple, however. A parent application's prebuild operation will always take place prior to any prebuild operations for its subapplications. A parent application's postbuild operation will always take place after all of its subapplication's postbuild operations have occurred. For example, the order of operations for building the application shown in Figure 5.2c would be as follows.

1. Parent application prebuild.

2. Build list component.

3. Build subcanvas component.

    3.1 Subapplication prebuild.

    3.2 Build first input field.

    3.3 Build second input field.

    3.4 Subapplication postbuild.

4. Parent application postbuild.

5. Parent application postopen.

5.3.3 Sharing the Keyboard Processor

When a subcanvas is built, it has its own builder called a subbuilder. But since the subcanvas shares a window with other components, it must also share the keyboard processor of that window. Understand that the subcanvas is often a logical structure that has meaning for the developer but not necessarily for the user. To the user, the components inside of a subcanvas may appear as just additional components inside the window. Therefore, the components inside a subcanvas should be every bit a part of the window interface as the other components.

There is only one keyboard processor for each window. This means that as the subcanvas is built, its components must register with the keyboard processor for the window in which they appear. When a builder creates a subbuilder, it makes sure that the subbuilder references the same keyboard processor.

5.3.4 Rebuilding the Subcanvas

A subcanvas distinguishes itself from other *VisualWorks* components in that it can rebuild itself during runtime. This is because it has its own builder which can be reinstantiated for each rebuild process. The rebuilding process is nothing more than repopulating the components collection of the SubCanvas object. Do not confuse redrawing with rebuilding. All components can redraw themselves, including subcanvases. When a subcanvas rebuilds itself however, it rips out its existing collection of *VisualWorks* components and replaces them with newly instantiated *VisualWorks* components. The implementation for rebuilding a subcanvas is found in the SubCanvas instance method shown below.

```
client: appModel spec: aSpec builder: aBuilder
    "Will release all existing components underneath the SubCanvas in
    the view structure; the new client will become the source of the new
    builder later."

    | oldContainer spec |
    appModel == nil ifTrue: [^self releaseAllComponents].
    aBuilder window == nil
        ifTrue: [aBuilder setWindow: self topComponent].
    aBuilder keyboardProcessor: aBuilder window keyboardProcessor.
    oldContainer := container.
    self releaseAllComponents.
    aBuilder composite: self.
    spec := aSpec.
    spec isSymbol ifTrue: [spec := appModel class interfaceSpecFor: spec].
    appModel buildInSubCanvas: spec component withBuilder: aBuilder.
    container := oldContainer.
    self isOpen
        ifTrue: [self bounds: self bounds.
            self changedPreferredBounds: nil.
            self invalidate]
```

The arguments for this method are as follows.

appModel
An application model that will act as the source for aBuilder and run the completed subcanvas. It is this application model that will ultimately be responsible for building this subcanvas. This application model is referred to as the subapplication or the client.

aSpec
A FullSpec or Symbol. If it is a FullSpec, then its SpecCollection describes all the components that will populate the subcanvas. If

> it is a Symbol, then it is the name of an appModel class method that returns the literal array representing the FullSpec.
>
> aBuilder   A UIBuilder, referred to as a subbuilder, which will be used by appModel as a builder to construct the interface described by aSpec.

The method above, although quite involved, is basically a five-step process.

1. Release the SubCanvas object's current components.

2. Make sure the builder's current composite is the SubCanvas.

3. Acquire the full spec from the client.

4. Build the new interface, thereby repopulating the SubCanvas object's components collection.

5. If the window is open, then redraw the subcanvas.

One caveat of the rebuilding process is that the tab order is affected. The components of a rebuilt subcanvas will always be at the end of the tab order. See Disk Example 5.4 for an example of the material covered in this section on subcanvas rebuilding.

5.4 Other Subcanvas Components

Included in this chapter on subcanvas technology is a discussion of the notebook component and the embedded data form. The notebook component does not fit our rigid definition of a subcanvas, but its implementation is certainly dependent upon subcanvas technology so it is placed in the general category of subcanvas components. The embedded data form is actually a special kind of subcanvas, so it does fit our rigorous definition of subcanvas component. Both types of components are briefly described in this section.

5.4.1 Notebook Component

The widget for a notebook component is actually a composite, a NoteBookComposite, with four component parts: a VisualBinderComponent, a SubCanvas, a VerticalTabBarView, and a HorizontalTabBarView. Like all active *VisualWorks* components, the notebook component also has an aspect model and a component spec. Each of these parts of the notebook component is described below.

5.4.1.1 NoteBookComposite

A NoteBookComposite is a subclass of CompositePart and the widget for a notebook component. It has four component parts in its components collection: a VisualBinderComponent, a SubCanvas, a VerticalTabBarView, and a HorizontalTabBarView. Actually, the NoteBookComposite object's components are wrappers containing these visual parts, but the NoteBookComposite also maintains direct pointers to these objects with its four instance variables: binder, tabBar, bottomTabBar, and subCanvas.

5.4.1.2 VisualBinderComponent

A VisualBinderComponent is a subclass of SimpleComponent and provides the appearance of several pages to give the illusion of a notebook. The NoteBookComposite directly references its VisualBinderComponent with its binder variable.

5.4.1.3 SubCanvas

A SubCanvas is the main piece of the NoteBookComposite. The rebuilding characteristic of subcanvases is the key to the notebook component's functionality. When the user selects a new tab, the NoteBookComposite merely rebuilds its SubCanvas with the interface associated with that tab. The NoteBookComposite directly references its SubCanvas with its subCanvas instance variable.

5.4.1.4 Tab Bar Views

The NoteBookComposite references two tab bar views: a VerticalTabBarView and a HorizontalTabBarView. Both of these are subclasses of TabBarView, which is a subclass of SelectionView. The tab bar views are responsible for drawing the tabs and detecting a selection of a tab by the user. The NoteBookComposite references both of its tab bar views with its instance variables tabBar and bottomTabBar. The controller for a tab bar view is a TabBarController, and its model is a ValueHolder on a sequenceable collection (e.g., OrderedCollection, SortedCollection, or List), which is maintained by the notebook component's aspect model.

5.4.1.5 Aspect Model

The aspect model for a notebook component is a SelectionInList. Its list holder contains a sequenceable collection of strings or Association objects. This list holder serves as the model for a tab bar view. The key of each Association is a string that serves as the label for a tab. The value of each Association is a Symbol that is the name of a class method returning a full spec literal array describing the interface for the subcanvas.

5.4.1.6 Spec

The spec object for a notebook component is a NoteBookSpec, which is a kind of Widget-Spec. It defines eight instance variables in order to fully describe a notebook component. A notebook component is look policy dependent, so the NoteBookSpec delegates the component construction to the look policy object.

5.4.2 Embedded Data Form

The embedded data form is just a special subcanvas for use in the lens application. The widget is in fact a SubCanvas that holds the embedded portion of a lens application. Its component spec is an EmbeddedDetailSpec, which is a subclass of SubCanvasSpec. An EmbeddedDetailSpec contains the necessary information for generating that portion of a lens application to do with its use of an embedded subapplication. It describes the layout and appearance of the subcanvas holding the embedded subapplication and also the connections between the parent application and the subapplication.

5.5 Summary

A canvas is a composite of *VisualWorks* components, which are all bound to the same application model. A canvas serves as the component for a window. A subcanvas is a special type of canvas, which serves as a component for another canvas. A subcanvas component has an aspect model, which is an application model. A subcanvas application model is referred to as a subapplication to distinguish it from the parent application, which contains the subapplication as an aspect model. A canvas in edit mode is implemented by a UIPainterView. A canvas in runtime mode is implemented by a Composite-Part. A subcanvas in either edit or runtime mode is implemented by a SubCanvas.

A subcanvas component is a spec wrapper whose widget is a SubCanvas. SubCanvas is a subclass of CompositePart. It adds the additional behavior of being able to rebuild its components during runtime. A SubCanvasSpec maintains three pieces of information in order to adequately describe its component: a client key, a major key, and a minor key. The client key is the name of the aspect method that returns the subapplication (also called client). The major key is the name of the class of the client. The minor key is the name of the class method which returns a full spec literal array describing the subcanvas user interface.

When a subcanvas is built, the current builder creates a subbuilder, which references the same keyboard processor. This subbuilder is provided to the subapplication so it can build the interface that populates the subcanvas. Whenever a subcanvas is rebuilt, a new subbuilder is created.

A notebook component is a composite of four objects: a binder, a subcanvas, and two tab bar views. The aspect model for a notebook component is a SelectionInList whose list is a sequenceable collection of strings or Association objects. An embedded data form is just a subcanvas that holds the embedded portion of a lens application.

CHAPTER 6

Windows

It goes without saying that one of the more important elements of a window programming language is the windows themselves. In *VisualWorks*, windows are implemented by the ApplicationWindow class. An ApplicationWindow is a very rich object. It has a total of 30 instance variables, and much of its state and complex behavior is inherited from several superclasses. The ApplicationWindow is also where several other parts of *VisualWorks* all come together. This makes a certain amount of intuitive sense because a well functioning window, or set of related windows, is the ultimate goal of a *VisualWorks* programmer.

The ApplicationWindow is the window for an application model—hence its name. In the vast majority of cases, each application model is equipped to build and run only one ApplicationWindow.

This chapter covers the following topics of ApplicationWindow:

- The hierarchy from which ApplicationWindow is spawned.

- The event-handling mechanism of *VisualWorks*.

- The keyboard-handling mechanism of *VisualWorks*.

- Drawing on the display surface of an ApplicationWindow.

- Scheduling and manipulating an ApplicationWindow.

Much of the information covered in this chapter is quite detailed and probably more than most *VisualWorks* developers really care to know—or need to know for that matter. Nevertheless, there are circumstances where such information can be critical to the success of an application.

6.1 Inherited Behavior

In order to fully understand all the intricacies of an ApplicationWindow, it is first necessary to cover the rich set of state and behavior provided by its superclasses. ApplicationWindow is a member of the DisplaySurface hierarchy shown in Figure 6.1.

The purpose of this section is to provide a feel for where much of the state and behavior of ApplicationWindow originates. For completeness, however, the sections following describe *all* state and behavior of ApplicationWindow, inherited or not. These conflicting goals dictate a certain amount of redundancy of material. Therefore, much of what is covered in this section will be repeated or expanded upon in subsequent sections. Also, several terms are introduced for the first time in this section, but most of the formal definitions are deferred until the later sections.

6.1.1 Graphics Medium

A **graphics medium** represents a blank area of pixels upon which the developer draws. GraphicsMedium is the abstract implementation of the graphics medium concept.

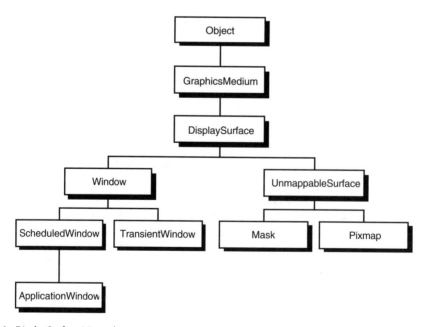

Figure 6.1. DisplaySurface Hierarchy.

It is the superclass for all objects that intend to be the destination of graphics operations. Such objects include windows and print jobs.

6.1.1.1 Graphics Parameters

All graphics mediums must specify certain parameters. The most important of these are listed in Table 6.1.

6.1.1.2 Graphics Device

Many of the parameters listed in Table 6.1 are determined by the graphics device. A **graphics device** is the actual destination of graphics operation such as the screen or a printer. Therefore, the actual color depth and bits per pixel parameters are determined by the graphics device on which you are drawing. For example, your screen may support 256 colors while your printer may be only black and white.

The *VisualWorks* virtual image has an object to represent each graphics device. The abstract implementation for all graphics devices is the GraphicsDevice class. Two examples of its concrete subclasses are Screen and PostScriptPrinter. Each concrete class of graphics device has a single instance, which is accessed by sending the message default to the class. For example, the single instance of Screen is accessed as follows.

> Screen default

Likewise, the single PostScriptPrinter graphics device is accessed as follows.

> PostScriptPrinter default

These two objects represent the current hardware's screen and printer, respectively.

Table 6.1. Graphics Medium Parameters.

Parameter	Description
height	Height in pixels of the area that can be drawn
width	Width in pixels of the area that can be drawn
color depth	Number of colors available for graphics operations
bits per pixel	Number of bits required to describe a pixel
graphics context	The graphics context object that contains parameters for displaying graphics on the graphics medium
graphics device	An object representing the actual destination of the graphics

6.1.1.3 Graphics Context

A **graphics context** is an object that contains parameters that indicate how graphics and text operations will be rendered on the graphics medium. Among these parameters are color, line thickness, and font. The abstract superclass for all graphics context objects is GraphicsContext. Its concrete subclasses specify parameters for specific graphics devices. For example, ScreenGraphicsContext specifies parameters for drawing on a Screen graphics device, and PostScriptGraphicsContext specifies parameters for drawing on a PostScript-Printer graphics device.

Whenever an object wants to draw on a graphics medium, it must first ask the graphics medium for a graphics context object for the corresponding graphics device. This is accomplished by sending the message graphicsContext to the graphics medium. A window responds by returning a new instance of ScreenGraphicsContext, and a print job responds by returning a new instance of PostScriptGraphicsContext. Once an object has acquired a graphics context from the graphics medium, it can then draw with reference to this graphics context and the graphic or text is displayed on the graphics medium (i.e., screen or printer).

6.1.2 Display Surface

A **display surface** is a graphics medium whose graphics operations are screen related (as opposed to printer related). There are two general kinds of display surfaces: windows and unmappable surfaces. An **unmappable surface** contains screenlike graphics but exists only in memory. Any graphics operations applied directly to an unmappable surface are not visible to the user. The image of an unmappable surface can be quickly transferred to the screen, however.

The class DisplaySurface is the abstract implementation of all display surface objects. Among the concrete classes that are subclasses of DisplaySurface are Window, Transient-Window, ScheduledWindow, ApplicationWindow, Mask, and Pixmap (see Fig. 6.1). The common state and behavior for all of these kinds of objects is provided in DisplaySurface. Disk Example 6.1 illustrates some of the topics common to all kinds of DisplaySurface objects.

While this chapter is about ApplicationWindow and its superclasses, much of what is covered in this section also applies to the unmappable surface types Mask and Pixmap. You can see from the hierarchy in Figure 6.1 that Pixmaps and Masks are each a kind of DisplaySurface, so everything mentioned about DisplaySurface applies to Pixmap and Mask as well as the window classes.

6.1.2.1 Graphics Handle

A **graphics handle** is an object that represents a graphics medium provided by the host window environment as a resource. The graphics handle concept is implemented by the class GraphicsHandle. The class DisplaySurface defines an instance variable called handle, which points to an instance of GraphicsHandle. A GraphicsHandle is known to the virtual machine, or VM. Any object with one or more instance variables that are known to the VM should not be made persistent. This includes open windows and any object referencing an open window, either directly or indirectly.

6.1.2.2 Dimension and Drawing Parameters

The DisplaySurface class provides rudimentary state and behavior for describing the graphics medium parameters listed in Table 6.1. In particular, it defines the following instance variables:

height	The height in pixels of the display surface
width	The width in pixels of the display surface
background	The color used to clear the display surface

6.1.2.3 Converting to an Image

Any DisplaySurface can be converted to an image using one of two messages: asImage and completeContentsOfArea: aRectangle. An image is the *VisualWorks* equivalent of a bitmap and is an instance of some subclass of Image (do not confuse the term *image* with the term *virtual image,* which is something else entirely). The message asImage returns the complete contents of the DisplaySurface as an image. The message completeContentsOfArea: aRectangle returns an image representing that portion of the DisplaySurface described by aRectangle.

6.1.2.4 Open

A display surface is considered **open** if it references a graphics handle with its handle instance variable. If this is the case, then the display surface object is associated with a host-provided resource. A display surface is **closed** if it does not reference a graphics handle. These definitions apply to all display surfaces—Mask, Window, ApplicationWindow, etc.

6.1.3 Window

A Window is a kind of DisplaySurface that is scheduled by the host window manager as one of its windows. It defines the basic behavior for all windows. *VisualWorks* does not create windows; it asks the host window environment to provide them. The host window environment also provides decoration for the window and sends events to the window. An instance of Window or one of its subclasses is more or less a *Visual-Works* surrogate for this host-generated resource. Instances of Window can be created and opened, but this is quite rare.

6.1.3.1 Sensor

All execution in *VisualWorks* is ultimately driven by the host window environment. To the host, *VisualWorks* is nothing but the virtual machine running as just another of its many application programs. The host generates events and passes them to the virtual machine, which dispatches them to the virtual image. A Window has an instance variable, sensor, which holds on to a WindowSensor. The WindowSensor processes and stores the events generated by the host window environment. Such events are keyboard events, mouse events, and window-related events. Section 6.2 covers the event dispatching and handling process in its entirety. It is mentioned here only because it is the Window class that first begins to address event processing.

6.1.3.2 Dimensions and Drawing Parameters

The Window class augments the dimension and drawing parameter services provided by its superclass DisplaySurface. In particular, a Window must know where it is on the screen so it keeps track of its own current origin. It must also know where to open initially so it knows its own creation origin as well. An instance of Window keeps these two pieces of information in its inputOrigin and creationOrigin instance variables, respectively.

6.1.3.3 Label and Icon

Window implements the ability to assign a title to the window. This title is referred to as the label, and it is set with the label: accessing message. Window also implements the ability to assign an Icon object to serve as the window icon. The icon is set with the icon: accessing message.

6.1.4 ScheduledWindow

ScheduledWindow is a subclass of Window and adds a great deal of functionality to its superclass. The two primary additions it makes are a controller for processing user input and the necessary machinery for dealing with a visual structure. Some of its other contributions include an association with a model, scheduling protocol, minimum and maximum sizes, and drawing policies and preferences.

6.1.4.1 The Controller

A ScheduledWindow has an instance variable, controller, which holds on to a StandardSystemController. StandardSystemController is a subclass of Controller. A StandardSystemController is responsible for displaying a <window> menu and for locating a view within the window that wants to handle user input-related events such as mouse activity and keystrokes.

All StandardSystemControllers are registered with ScheduledControllers. ScheduledControllers is a global variable (visible throughout the image) and an instance of ControlManager. A ControlManager keeps track of all StandardSystemControllers and knows which one is currently active.

6.1.4.2 Dependency

Since a ScheduledWindow has a controller, it only makes since that it can also have a model. A ScheduledWindow can reference a model with its model instance variable. This allows a ScheduledWindow to register as a dependent of its model and receive updates whenever its model changes. In this respect, a ScheduledWindow behaves as a view for its model.

6.1.4.3 Events

A ScheduledWindow gets events from its window sensor. A ScheduledWindow knows how to process four types of window events: a resize event, a close event, a destroy event, and a mouse double click event. As we will see in Section 6.2, such window-related events are referred to as *meta events.* ScheduledWindow also has a mechanism for passing user-type events—mouse events and keyboard events—down the visual structure to the various components.

6.1.4.4 Dimensions and Drawing Parameters

ScheduledWindow augments the dimension and drawing parameter services of its superclasses. In particular it can fix a minimum and maximum size for its extent. It can also determine the look and feel of buttons, borders, menus, and scroll bars that are drawn on its display surface. Finally, it maintains a full suite of colors, called look preferences, which describe its default color scheme.

6.1.4.5 Scheduling

To schedule a window is to open it up and register its controller with ScheduledControllers. It is this scheduling of a ScheduledWindow's controller with ScheduledControllers that gives ScheduledWindow its name. ScheduledWindow has several scheduling methods for opening windows in a variety of ways. It defines three different types of decoration for the windows it opens.

6.1.4.6 Visual Structure

ScheduledWindow provides the necessary mechanism for maintaining a visual structure (visual component tree) and for redrawing this structure whenever damage is recorded. A ScheduledWindow has an instance variable, component, which holds on to a visual component (see Chapter 1, Section 1.3). This visual component is responsible for filling the entire display surface of the ScheduledWindow. This visual component is usually a composite of other visual components and facilitates message passing between its container (the ScheduledWindow) and its components. Whenever damage is recorded, the Scheduled-Window has its component redraw those areas of the display surface marked as damaged.

[Just a bit of semantics here. It was stated above that the visual component fills the display surface *of* the ScheduledWindow. Actually, the display surface *is* the ScheduledWindow, it just reads better the other way. I will carry this slight inaccuracy throughout the remainder of the book. It is very convenient to refer to the display surface as being *part of* the window.]

6.1.5 Summary

An ApplicationWindow inherits much of its state and behavior from GraphicsMedium, DisplaySurface, Window, and ScheduledWindow. A graphics medium is an object that represents a grid of pixels on which other objects can render graphics and text. A graphics medium has a height and a width and several other drawing parameters governing how graphics will be rendered on it. Very much associated with a graphics medium are two other types of objects: a graphics device and a graphics context. A graphics device is an object representing the actual physical device on which the graphics will eventually be displayed such as the screen or a printer. A graphics context is an object that specifies several parameters indicating how text and graphics will be rendered on the graphics medium. Such parameters include color, line thickness, and font.

A display surface is a graphics medium that is used to render graphics on the screen (as opposed to a printer). DisplaySurface is the abstract superclass for all display surface types. DisplaySurface defines the state and behavior for associating with a host-supplied resource such as a window or a pixmap. It also defines the state and behavior of certain drawing parameters. An unmappable surface is a display surface whose graphics do not appear on the screen, although they can be transferred to the screen very quickly.

A Window is a kind of DisplaySurface that appears on the screen inside of a window decoration provided by the host window environment. A Window is known to the host window environment and can receive events generated by the host window environment. These events are processed and stored by the Window's sensor, which is an instance of WindowSensor. A Window knows its initial and current location on the screen. It also has a label in its title bar and can be collapsed into an iconic representation.

A ScheduledWindow is a kind of Window that adds a great deal of functionality to its superclass. Its primary contributions are a scheduled controller and the ability to redraw itself based on damage events. It also provides linking with a model, more scheduling behavior, a minimum and maximum size restriction, and drawing preferences and policies.

The next section begins the discussion proper of ApplicationWindow. Some of the material just presented may be repeated or expanded upon.

6.2 Processing and Handling Events

The term *event* is often used quite loosely, so I will keep my definition somewhat broad. An **event** is an occurrence such as a keystroke or a mouse button press that invokes some kind of response by an application.

An event object gets passed around and processed quite a bit before it is finally handled. It also assumes up to three different formats along the way. Figure 6.2 illustrates

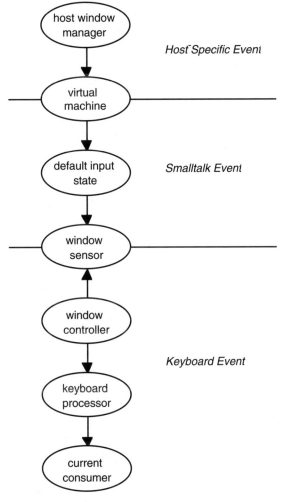

Figure 6.2. Life of a Keyboard Event.

the life and various incarnations of a keyboard-type event and is a good reference for the remainder of this section.

6.2.1 Event Creation and Processing

An event is usually created by the host window environment, although events can also be created by artificial means. This section deals exclusively with events that originate with the host window environment and eventually become some type of event object. An event of this type is born in the host and treks its way from the host window manager, to the virtual machine, and through the image until some object handles it. Before proceeding further, let us pause to define two useful terms for this topic. To **process** an event is to dispatch it to another object, store it, or change it in some way. To **handle** an event is to take some action affecting the application based on the nature and content of the event. Once an event object is handled, it is considered dead and should be available for garbage collection.

6.2.1.1 Host Window Environment

All interface behavior is ultimately driven by the host window environment. Events exist for such things as keyboard input, mouse input, window control, and window damage. Each host window environment has its own particular format for events. That is, a given event, such as a certain keystroke, is represented one way on a *Macintosh,* a different way in *MS Windows,* and yet a third way in *OS/2.*

The host window environment can have several application programs running at once. I use the term *application program* to refer to such things as spreadsheets and word processors running in the host window environment. The *VisualWorks* virtual machine is just such an application program. When the host generates an event, it must determine the application program to which it belongs and send the event to that program. That is, when a user clicks the mouse inside of a spreadsheet, an event is generated by the host window environment and forwarded to the spreadsheet application program for processing. Likewise, when a user clicks the mouse inside of a *VisualWorks* window, a System Browser for example, the host generates an event and forwards it to the *Visual-Works* virtual machine, which then routes it to the System Browser.

6.2.1.2 Virtual Machine

When the virtual machine receives an event from the host window environment, it forwards the event on to the default instance of InputState for further processing and dispatching. Since *VisualWorks* is binary compatible across platforms, events must first be converted from the host-specific format into a common format understood by the

VisualWorks virtual image. An event formated in this way is called a Smalltalk event. A **Smalltalk event** is an Array of 16 elements, which represents a host–generated event. The format for a Smalltalk event is well documented in the class method whatIsAnEvent of the class InputState.

6.2.1.3 Default Input State

There is only one instance of InputState, referred to as the default InputState, and it is known to the VM. The default InputState performs two main functions: it dispatches the incoming events to the target window, and it records the current state of the mouse and keyboard.

A Smalltalk event contains, among other things, information indicating both the target window and the type of event (mouse event, keyboard event, etc.). The target window is the window in which the event occurred. The default InputState determines the type of event and sends the event to the target window's sensor with a method specific to that type of event. For instance, a keyboard event is dispatched to the target window's sensor with the message eventKeyPress: anEvent. A mouse move type of event is dispatched with an eventMouseMoved: anEvent message. In both cases, the argument anEvent is a Smalltalk event (the Array of 16 elements mentioned above).

InputState defines several instance variables, most of which record the current state of the mouse and keyboard. The default InputState always knows the current mouse position and the up/down state of its three buttons. The default InputState also knows the up/down state of certain keyboard keys such as the <Shift> and <Ctrl> keys. Each time the default InputState receives a Smalltalk event concerning a mouse event or keyboard event, it updates the appropriate variables so that its information remains current. The default InputState keeps this information primarily for the benefit of the controllers. The default InputState is also responsible for determining if two successive mouse clicks constitute a double click or just two separate mouse clicks.

6.2.1.4 Window Sensor

An ApplicationWindow has an instance variable called sensor, which holds on to an ApplicationWindowSensor. ApplicationWindowSensor is a subclass of WindowSensor, which was discussed briefly in Section 6.1.3.1. An ApplicationWindowSensor processes the events targeted for its window. An ApplicationWindowSensor does two things with each Smalltalk event it receives. It first converts the Smalltalk event into a more specific type of event object (such as a KeyboardEvent, which is discussed shortly), and then, depending on the type of event, it stores it for later handling by a controller.

Smalltalk events that originate from the host window environment can be divided into four broad categories: keyboard events, mouse events, meta events, and damage events. These four types of events are defined and discussed more thoroughly in Sections 6.2.2 and 6.2.3.

When the host window environment creates an event, it targets that event for a specific window called the target window. The target window is usually the active window. The **active window** is the window that is the current receiver of mouse and keyboard input, and it is usually visually distinguished from the other windows by having a uniquely colored title bar and decoration. The active window is also referred to as the *current window*. An ApplicationWindow has three useful methods for dealing with its active state.

isActive	Return true if the receiver is the active window, return false otherwise
becomeActive	Make the receiver the active window
becomeInactive	Have host window manager make some other window the active window

6.2.1.5 Active Controller

An ApplicationWindow's controller is an ApplicationStandardSystemController, which is a subclass of StandardSystemController (StandardSystemController was covered briefly in Section 6.1.4.1). This controller references the window's sensor, an instance of ApplicationWindowSensor. Any views that reside in the window also have controllers called widget controllers. Each of these widget controllers references an instance of TranslatingSensor, which also references the ApplicationWindowSensor. Therefore, all controllers in a *VisualWorks* window—both the window controller and all the widget controllers—have access to the events stored in that window's ApplicationWindowSensor. So regardless of which controller is active, it always has access to the events stored in the window's sensor.

6.2.2 Event Categories

As mentioned previously, there are four categories of Smalltalk events: keyboard events, mouse events, meta events, and damage events. All of these are dispatched to the target window's sensor for processing. Only three of these, however—keyboard events, meta events, and damage events—are actually processed by the target window's sensor. There, the target window's sensor converts the Smalltalk event, which is an Array, into an object that is more easily processed and handled by a controller or window. The ApplicationWindowSensor then stores these objects for later use by a controller. Smalltalk events that are mouse events, however, are never processed and stored by the window's sensor.

6.2.2.1 Keyboard Events

An ApplicationWindowSensor converts a Smalltalk event representing a keyboard event into an instance of KeyboardEvent. A KeyboardEvent contains the information indicating the key(s) pressed by the user (KeyboardEvent is discussed more thoroughly in Section 6.3). KeyboardEvent objects are queued up by the ApplicationWindowSensor in its keyboard instance variable. The KeyboardEvent objects are requested by the keyboard processor (the keyboard processor is also discussed in Section 6.3), who routes them to the appropriate widget controller.

6.2.2.2 Mouse Events

Smalltalk events that are mouse events are the one type of Smalltalk event that is not processed and stored by the target window's sensor. When the default InputState receives a mouse event, it updates its mouse state instance variables (bitState, x, and y) and then forwards the event to the target window's sensor. The window sensor, however, does not process or store the event. Instead, the sensor takes some kind of appropriate action based on the message sent by the default InputSensor. There are five kinds of mouse events, and for each one the default InputState sends a different message to the target window's sensor. Table 6.2 summarizes these five mouse events and the messages used to notify the window sensor.

The double click event is somewhat of an exception to all of this. The double click event is not manufactured by the host window environment but is created artificially by the default InputState based on the timing of two successive <select> button mouse clicks. If the time interval between the two successive mouse clicks is small enough, the default InputState interprets this as a double click and sends the message eventDoubleClick: anEvent to the window sensor. The window sensor deals with this as a meta event, which is described below.

6.2.2.3 Meta Events

A **meta event** is an event concerning operations on a window such as opening, resizing, and closing. An ApplicationWindowSensor converts a Smalltalk event, which is a meta event, into an Association. The Association's key is a Symbol describing the meta event, and

Table 6.2. Mouse Input Messages.

Description	Message	Action taken
Entered a window	eventEnter:	Make target window the active window
Exited a window	eventExit	Make target window inactive
Button pressed	eventButtonPress:	Determine if double click has occurred, otherwise, short delay
Button released	eventButtonRelease:	Short delay
Moved	eventMouseMoved:	Do nothing

its value is any necessary information pertaining to the event. For example, a close event looks like #close->nil and a resize event looks like #resize->300@250. The Application-WindowSensor queues meta events in its metalnput instance variable. Double click events (described above) are also queued in the metalnput instance variable.

6.2.2.4 Damage Events

The term *damage* applies to an area of the window that needs to be redrawn. Damage events come in from the host window environment as a result of a window having been covered and uncovered by another window or because a window needs to be redrawn for some other reason (damage also occurs because a view has become invalid, but this has nothing to do with the event handling mechanism). The ApplicationWindowSensor converts Smalltalk events, which describe damage events into Rectangles describing the damaged area. It collects these Rectangles in its damage instance variable, which holds on to an Array of these Rectangles.

6.2.3 Handling Mouse and Keyboard Events

Recall that there is only one active controller at a given time. The active controller continually steps through its control loop until it chooses to give up control. In an Application-Window, the active controller is almost always the window controller, an Application-StandardSystemController. The widget controllers assume control only for the fleeting moment required to process mouse input. In a *VisualWorks* window, the window controller handles the keyboard events and the widget controllers process mouse input.

6.2.3.1 ApplicationStandardSystemController

When an ApplicationWindow becomes the active window, it starts up its controller, an ApplicationStandardSystemController. This controller becomes the active controller and, therefore, starts to step through its control loop. In the third step of the control loop, the control activity step, the ApplicationStandardSystemController does the following:

- Checks to see if any of the window's widgets wants to take control and, if so, gives control to that widget's controller

- Checks to see if the window sensor has any keyboard events in its queue and, if so, has the keyboard processor process those keyboard events

The first of these is covered below, and the second is covered in Section 6.3.

6.2.3.2 Widget Controllers

Most widget controllers gain control because a mouse button has been clicked inside the widget's bounds. Most widget controllers maintain control only as long as the mouse is within the widget's bounds and the <select> or <operate> button is down. The exceptions are the button controllers, such as ToggleButtonController, which only check for the <select> button since they do not have <operate> menus. Otherwise, they immediately give control back to the window controller. This is why the window controller is almost always the active controller.

The widget controllers do not handle mouse events but instead ask their sensor for the current mouse state. As an example, suppose the user makes a selection in a list component with a <select> button. Just prior to the button click, the window controller has control and is cycling through its control loop. Each time through the control loop the window controller will see if there is a widget that wants control. The list component widget controller will respond yes during the time that the user is clicking the mouse to make a new selection. Therefore, the window controller gives control to the this widget controller, a SequenceController, making it the active controller. This SequenceController then goes through the motions of updating the view and model as to the new selection. Since the user's mouse click does not last very long, the mouse button is soon up again, and the next time through its control loop the SequenceController gives control back to the window controller. All of this transpires well within a fraction of a second. Also, the Sequence-Controller did not *handle a mouse event*. Instead it performed its actions based on the *current state of the mouse* as recorded in the default InputState.

6.2.3.3 Mouse Information

A widget controller gets mouse information from its sensor, which is a Translating-Sensor, and is only interested in <select> and <operate> button mouse activity (the window controller is interested in <window> button mouse activity in order to operate its <window> menu and it obtains this information from its sensor as well). Table 6.3 lists all the messages a controller can send its sensor to acquire information about the current mouse state.

6.2.3.4 Keyboard Information

While widget controllers do not normally handle keyboard events directly from their sensor (they get them from the keyboard processor instead), they do have occasion to want to know certain things about the current state of the keyboard. For instance, if a widget controller wants to distinguish a <Shift>-<select> from a <select>, then that widget controller must be able to determine if the <Shift> key is down during the

Table 6.3. Mouse State Messages.

Message	Behavior
redButtonPressed	Return true if the \<select\>|\<red\> button is down, false otherwise
yellowButtonPressed	Return true if the \<operate\>|\<yellow\> button is down, false otherwise
blueButtonPressed	Return true if the \<window\>|\<blue\> button is down, false otherwise
noButtonPressed	Return true if no buttons are down, false otherwise
anyButtonPressed	Return true if any button is down, false otherwise
nonBlueButtonPressed	Return true if either the \<select\>|\<red\> or \<operate\>|\<yellow\> button is down, false otherwise
waitButton	Wait until any mouse button is pressed and then return the cursor location
waitClickButton	Wait until any mouse button is pressed and then released and then return the cursor location
waitNoButton	Wait until any mouse button is released and return the cursor location
cursorPoint	Return a Point describing the cursor's current location in local coordinates
cursorPoint: aPoint	Move the cursor to aPoint
globalCursorPoint	Return a Point describing the cursor's current location in screen coordinates
mousePoint	Return a Point describing the mouse's current location in local coordinates
mousePointNext	Return the cursor point if the \<select\>|\<red\>, button is down—return false otherwise

mouse click. For just such cases, a widget controller can solicit its sensor for information about the keyboard.

6.2.4 Handling Meta and Damage Events

Meta events and damage events are handled by the ApplicationWindow. It is given the chance to do so with each pass through the active controller's control loop according to the following three-step process:

1. The active controller yields control to ScheduledControllers.

2. ScheduledControllers tells each of its window controllers to check for events.

Table 6.4. Keyboard Messages.

Message	Behavior
keyboard	Return true if a keyboard event is waiting in the queue, return false otherwise
keyboardEvent	Return the next KeyboardEvent in the queue
keyboardPeek	Return the value of the next KeyboardEvent in the queue, raise notifier if queue is empty
keyboardPressed	Return true if a keyboard key is currently down, false otherwise
altDown	Return true if the <Alt> key is currently down, false otherwise
ctrlDown	Return true if the <Ctrl> key is currently down, false otherwise
shiftDown	Return true if the <Shift> key is currently down, false otherwise
metaDown	Return true if any meta key is down, false otherwise
nextPut: aKeyboardEvent	Place aKeyboardEvent in the keyboard queue

3. Each window controller has its window handle any meta and damage events currently residing in the window sensor.

Each of these three steps is described below.

6.2.4.1 Active Controller

Meta and damage event handling starts with the active controller. Recall from Chapter 1 that the active controller is the controller that is currently stepping through its control loop shown below. The active controller can be either the window controller or one of the widget controllers.

```
controlLoop
    "Sent by Controller|startUp as part of the standard control sequence.
    Controller|controlLoop sends the message Controller|isControlActive to test
    for loop termination. As long as true is returned, the loop continues. When
    false is returned, the loop ends. Each time through the loop, the message
    Controller|controlActivity is sent."

    [self poll.
    self isControlActive]
        whileTrue:
            [self controlActivity]
```

Also recall that this loop has three steps and that the first step, self poll, temporarily yields control to ScheduledControllers. The poll method is shown below.

```
poll
    "Announce that we are iterating through the polling loop. If
    there has been no input for a significant time, wait on a semaphore"

    ScheduledControllers checkForEvents.
    self view == nil "if the top view is closed"
        ifTrue: [ScheduledControllers class closedWindowSignal raiseRequest].
    self sensor pollForActivity
```

The first statement in the poll method asks ScheduledControllers to check for events, and this statement corresponds to step one of the three-step process for handling meta and damage events outlined above.

Notice that the last statement in the poll method asks the controller's sensor to poll for activity. This results in the ApplicationWindowSensor asking the default InputState if it has any waiting Smalltalk events. It is at this point that the default InputState has the opportunity to dispatch to the window sensors any host-generated events—mouse, keyboard, meta, and damage—that have recently arrived from the host window manager.

6.2.4.2 ScheduledControllers

Each time the active controller steps through its control loop, ScheduledControllers receives the message checkForEvents as is shown above in the poll method implementation. Recall that ScheduledControllers is a global variable, the only instance of ControlManager, and is responsible for managing all current window controllers. ControlManager's implementation of checkForEvents is to iterate over its collection of window controllers and send the message checkForEvents to each one. The window controller then forwards the checkForEvents message to its window. This behavior is the second step in the three-step process of handling meta and damage events.

6.2.4.3 ApplicationWindow

It is the ApplicationWindow's checkForEvents method that handles the meta and damage events. The implementation of this method is shown below.

```
checkForEvents
    "Do resizes and closes before damage."

    | damage |
    self sensor hasDamage ifTrue: [damage := self sensor getAndResetDamage].
    [self sensor hasEvents] whileTrue:
        [self processEvent: self sensor nextEvent].
    damage == nil ifFalse: [self displayDamageEvent: damage]
```

In this method, the ApplicationWindow first accesses any damage recorded since the last check for events. Next, it checks its sensor for any meta events, such as closing or resizing events, and handles them (see Section 6.2.4.4). Finally, if damage was recorded, then those damaged parts of the display surface are redrawn (see Section 6.2.4.5). So the checkFor-Events method in ApplicationWindow handles two of the four types of events: the meta events and the damage events. After all of the window controllers known to Scheduled-Controllers have processed all meta and damage events, control is then returned back to the active controller, which resumes with step two of its control loop, that is, testing to see if it wants to maintain control.

It is important to realize that control loop cycles occur with an incredible frequency. Therefore, meta and damage events are handled almost as quickly as they arise. It is also important to realize that the three steps of checking for meta and damage events occur with each control loop cycle and require very little time—virtually no time as far as the user is concerned. While it takes very little time to check for the events, handling them is a different matter and may take a noticeable amount of time from the perspective of the user (one or more seconds). You should also be aware that all of this happens in a single thread of execution, which is to say that the active controller does not resume its control loop until all the damage events and meta events are handled.

6.2.4.4 Handling Meta Events

Meta events are in the form of an Association. Below are a few of the more common meta events understood by an ApplicationWindow.

#expand->nil	Expand icon into full window
#collapse->nil	Collapse window into icon
#bounds->aRectangle	Adjust window's size and location
#exit->nil	Mouse has left the window
#enter->nil	Mouse has entered the window

The ApplicationWindow handles meta events in its processEvent: method. This method determines the type of meta event and dispatches a message corresponding to that type of meta event. A few of these meta event-specific messages are shown below.

extentEvent:	Sent to the ApplicationWindow so that it can resize
downcastEvent: with:from:	Sent to the ApplicationWindow's component, which then propagates it throughout the visual structure

| closeNoTerminate | Sent to the ApplicationWindow's controller so that it can close and unschedule the window |

6.2.4.5 Handling Damage Events

Damage is handled quite automatically, and you rarely need to be concerned with it. The ApplicationWindow merely creates a new ScreenGraphicsContext and passes it down the visual structure so that each of the visual components can display itself. The ScreenGraphicsContext is only defined for the bounds of the damaged area—called the clipping bounds. Only those visual components in the visual structure that intersect this bounding box will receive the displayOn: message (see Section 6.4.5).

6.2.5 Multiwindow Behavior

VisualWorks provides mechanisms for coordinating several windows under the umbrella of a single application. It is this mechanism that allows the act of closing one window to close several others as is the case with the three canvas-painting tools: canvas (UIPainter), Palette, and Canvas Tool.

6.2.5.1 Application

An ApplicationWindow has an instance variable, application, which it uses to reference an application model. Whenever the ApplicationWindow's application variable is set, the ApplicationWindow automatically registers itself as a dependent of that application model. This allows the ApplicationWindow to receive any updates broadcasted by that application model. Several ApplicationWindows can register with the same application model, and each one will reference that same application model with its own application instance variable.

6.2.5.2 Forwarding Window Events

When an ApplicationWindow handles a meta event (a window-related event), it has the option of forwarding that event to its application; however, it will only forward certain events. The types of events it chooses to forward are kept in its instance variable, sendWindowEvents. When an ApplicationWindow decides to forward an event to its application, it sends the message windowEvent: anEvent from: self.

6.2.5.3 Application Model

All application models (i.e., objects that are a kind of ApplicationModel) know how to respond to the message

    windowEvent: anEvent from: anApplicationWindow.

When an application model receives such a message, it broadcasts the message

update: #windowState with: anEvent from: anApplicationWindow

to all of its dependents, each of whom is most likely an ApplicationWindow. The first argument indicates to the receiver that this update concerns its window state. The second argument is the meta event, and the third argument is the originating window. The originating window is the ApplicationWindow that first processed the meta event and decided to forward it to its application.

6.2.5.4 Receiving Window Event Updates

When an ApplicationWindow receives an update message concerning its window state, it does two things. First, it makes sure that it is not the event's originating window. That is, an ApplicationWindow that forwards an event to its application is also a dependent of that application and will receive the event again in the form of an update message from its application (see Section 6.2.5.3). Since it has already processed the event once, it must ignore the update.

If the ApplicationWindow determines that it is not the event's originating window, it must decide to handle the event or not. An ApplicationWindow has an instance variable, receiveWindowEvents, which holds on to a collection of the types of events that the window will handle as an update from its application.

6.2.5.5 Window Event Block

When an ApplicationWindow chooses to handle an event received from its application, it first gives its window event block the opportunity to handle the event. The **window event block** is a block that takes three arguments: the ApplicationWindow, the event, and the originating window. This block must return true if it handles the event, false otherwise. If the window event block is not defined (i.e., the instance variable windowEventBlock points to nil) or if it does not handle the event, then the ApplicationWindow handles the event. An ApplicationWindow references its window event block with its windowEventBlock instance variable.

6.2.5.6 Master, Partner, and Slave

ApplicationWindow defines three types of multiwindow behavior: master, partner, and slave. A **master** is an ApplicationWindow that forwards any close, collapse, or expand events to its application and updates only on expand events dispatched from its application. A master window is usually the main window of the application. Sending the message beMaster will automatically establish an ApplicationWindow as a master window.

A **partner** is an ApplicationWindow that both forwards and updates on close, collapse, and expand events. Partner windows are the primary windows of the application, but they are not as important as the master window. Sending the message bePartner will automatically establish an ApplicationWindow as a partner window.

A **slave** is an ApplicationWindow that forwards an expand event to its application and updates on close, collapse, and expand events. The destiny of a slave window is very much driven by master and partner windows, as slave windows typically play ancillary roles in an application. Sending the message beSlave will automatically establish an ApplicationWindow as a slave window.

The default behavior for ApplicationWindow does not include assigning an application or behaving as a master, partner, or slave window. All of this must be established by the developer on an instance-by-instance basis.

6.2.6 Summary

All events originate with the host window manager, which passes them to the virtual machine. The virtual machine formats each event as an Array called a Smalltalk event and dispatches the event to the default InputState object. This object updates its variables, which monitor the current mouse and keyboard state, and then dispatches the event to the target window's sensor. The window sensor converts the Smalltalk event into a more specific type of object and stores it for later user by a controller.

For convenience, we can place all events into one of four categories: keyboard events, mouse events, meta events, and damage events. The window sensor stores all but the mouse events. *VisualWorks* does not handle mouse events but responds to the current state of the mouse as recorded by the default InputState object. Keyboard events are handled by the window controller and its keyboard processor object. The window controller is almost always the active controller in an ApplicationWindow, and the widget controllers take control only for the amount of time it takes to respond to a mouse button down. The meta events and damage events are handled with each pass through the active controller's control loop. Meta events are events that concern the window such as closing and resizing. Damage events indicate the areas of the window that are in need of being redrawn.

6.3 Keyboard Control

Any good window application needs to coordinate the keyboard activity. It should always know what component is currently receiving keyboard input, and it should allow tabbing from one component to the next. Furthermore, it should allow all operations to be accomplished with keyboard input only (i.e., with out the aid of a mouse). An

ApplicationWindow is fully capable of such behavior. The object responsible for coordinating the keyboard activity is a KeyboardProcessor. The keyboard activity that it coordinates comes in the form of KeyboardEvent objects. Disk Example 6.2 illustrates some of the material covered in this section.

6.3.1 Keyboard Event

Keyboard control is all about managing keyboard events. A **keyboard event** is a keystroke or a combination of keystrokes that the host window environment interprets as a single event. The virtual machine is responsible for packaging the keyboard events provided by the host as Smalltalk events (an Array of 16 elements). An ApplicationWindow-Sensor then converts these Smalltalk events into KeyboardEvent objects and queues them in its keyboard variable (see Figure 6.2).

Smalltalk represents a keyboard event as a KeyboardEvent object. A KeyboardEvent has two instance variables: keyCharacter and metaState. The instance variable keyCharacter is a Character, a Symbol, or an integer. It is a Character if the key pressed by the user can be represented as a Character object. It is a Symbol if it corresponds to one of the special keys such as <F1>, <Home>, or an arrow key. A Symbol object is used because most of the special keys do not have a corresponding Character object representation. The instance variable keyCharacter is an integer for any other key.

Smalltalk refers to the <Shift>, <Alt>, and <Ctrl> keys as meta keys. A **meta key** is a key that does not generate a KeyboardEvent by itself, but only in combination with other keys. For example, pressing <Alt> does not result in a KeyboardEvent. Pressing <Alt>-<H>, however, does result in a KeyboardEvent. Furthermore, this KeyboardEvent is not equivalent to the KeyboardEvent resulting from pressing just <H>. The metaState variable is the difference. It indicates which meta keys were involved in generating the keyboard event.

A KeyboardEvent can be created artificially by sending the instance creation message code:meta: to the KeyboardEvent class. The first argument is the integer value of the key character, and the second argument is an integer representing the combined state of the meta keys.

6.3.2 Keyboard Processor

The **keyboard processor** is responsible for dispatching keyboard events to the component with keyboard focus and for maintaining the tab order of tabable components. The keyboard processor concept is implemented by the class KeyboardProcessor. Each Application-

Window has its own keyboard processor and references it with its keyboardProcessor instance variable.

6.3.2.1 Keyboard Consumers

The keyboard processor keeps track of all keyboard consumers in the window. A **keyboard consumer** is a *VisualWorks* component that handles keyboard events. It is actually the components widget controller that handles the keyboard events. Only one keyboard consumer can handle keyboard events at any given time. The **current consumer** is the widget controller that is the current receiver of keyboard events.

A KeyboardProcessor maintains two references to the current consumer: a direct reference and an indirect reference. The currentConsumer instance variable references the current consumer directly. The currentConsumerChannel instance variable is a ValueHolder whose value is the current consumer. This allows any arbitrary object to register interest in a change of keyboard focus.

6.3.2.2 Focus

The current consumer is said to have **focus** since it is the current recipient of all keyboard activity. The process of replacing the current consumer with another keyboard consumer is called a **focus shift** or a *change of focus*. The KeyboardProcessor has an OrderedCollection of all widgets within the window, which are consumers of keyboard events. It references this collection with its instance variable keyboardConsumers. The ordering of keyboard consumers determines the order of focus shift and is referred to as **tab order** or *tab chain* because focus can change from one consumer to the next based on a <Tab> or <Shift>-<Tab>. It should be emphasized that the collection of keyboard consumers is a collection of *widgets,* but the current consumer is a *widget controller.*

6.3.2.3 Keyboard Hook

In Chapter 2, Section 2.4.2.2, we learned that each widget controller has a keyboard hook, which is a block. The keyboard hook has first option at handling any keyboard events destined for that controller. A KeyboardProcessor has a keyboard hook as well. It gets first option at handling any keyboard event destined for the entire window.

6.3.2.4 Processing a Keyboard Event

If the KeyboardProcessor's keyboard hook does not handle a keyboard event, then the KeyboardProcessor will process the keyboard event in its processKeyboardEvent: method. This method first checks to see if the keyboard event includes a meta key. If so, then the keyboard event may be a short-cut key, but not necessarily. A **short-cut key** is a special keystroke that involves a meta key and invokes an action method or menu selection. A short-cut key is sometimes referred to as a *quick key, access character,* or *accelerator key.* A short-cut key can be handled by one of three objects: the current consumer, the window menu bar, or one of the other keyboard consumers. The current consumer gets first crack at handling a short-cut key, followed by the window menu bar, and then each of the remaining keyboard consumers. As soon as an object handles the short-cut key, all processing stops on that particular keyboard event. If the keyboard event is not a short-cut key (i.e., has no meta key or has a meta key but was not handled by one of the short-cut key–handling objects), then the keyboard event is offered to the current consumer to be handled as a regular keyboard event.

6.3.2.5 Changing Focus

When changing focus, the keyboard processor will send certain messages to both the current and new keyboard consumers. These focus messages are described below and presented in the order in which they are dispatched by the keyboard processor.

requestFocusOut	Ask current consumer if it is willing to give up focus. If it returns false, then abort focus shift.
requestFocusIn	Ask new consumer if it is willing to take focus. If it returns false, then abort focus shift.
deactivate	Notify current consumer that it is no longer the current consumer.
activate	Notify new consumer that it is now the current consumer.

After this has transpired, the KeyboardProcessor updates its currentConsumer and currentConsumerChannel variables.

6.3.2.6 Dispatching Changing Focus Messages

In Chapter 2, Section 2.4.2.3, we learned that each widget controller has a dispatcher object. When a widget controller receives one of the messages listed above, it appeals to its dispatcher object to handle the message. The dispatcher object responds by forwarding a predefined validation or notification message to the application model.

6.3.2.7 Aborting a Focus Shift

The KeyboardProcessor will shift focus only if its focusIsShifting variable is true. Any object can abort a focus shift by sending the message abortFocusShift to the KeyboardProcessor. This method merely sets the focusIsShifting variable to false, preventing any change in focus that may be in progress.

6.3.3 Summary of Handling a Keyboard Event

When a user presses a key on the keyboard, a great deal of activity results. As a summary of processing keyboard events, the steps below outline exactly what transpires. You may want to refer to Figure 6.2 when reading this sequence.

1. User presses a key on the keyboard so the host window environment generates a host-formated event and sends it to the virtual machine.

2. The VM creates a Smalltalk event based on the host-formated event and forwards it to the default InputState.

3. On the next pass through the active controller's control loop, each window sensor is given the opportunity to acquire any events in the default InputState that have arrived since the last pass through the control loop and are targeted for its window.

4. The window sensor receives the Smalltalk event, and if it is a keyboard event, it uses information in the Smalltalk event to manufacture a KeyboardEvent and puts this KeyboardEvent in its keyboard input queue.

5. Each time the window controller steps through its control loop, it asks the window sensor if it has a keyboard event queued up. If it does, the window controller tells the keyboard processor to process the keyboard event.

6. The keyboard processor first acquires the keyboard event from the window controller's sensor. Then it allows its keyboard hook to handle the keyboard event. If there is no keyboard hook or if the keyboard hook decides not to handle the event, then the keyboard processor decides to handle the keyboard event itself.

7. If the keyboard event has a meta key, then it may be fielded by one of the following as a short-cut key: current consumer, window menu, or one of the other consumers. If the keyboard event has no meta key, or has a meta key but is not handled as a short cut key, then the keyboard event is offered to the current consumer as a regular keyboard event.

6.3.4 Summary of Changing Focus

The process of changing focus is very involved, and several things must happen in order for the change to transpire. The following steps outline this process.

1. A change of focus starts when a widget controller sends the message prevField-From: or nextFieldFrom: to the keyboard processor. A widget controller usually does this as a result of handling a <Tab>, <Shift>-<Tab>, or <Enter> keyboard event.

2. The keyboard processor makes sure that the widget controller sending this message is in fact the current consumer, otherwise the change of focus is aborted.

3. The keyboard processor sets its focusIsShifting variable to true and asks the current consumer if it is OK to change focus. The current consumer defers this request to its dispatcher object, which may defer the request to the application model via a validation message. If the request for focus shift is not granted, then the change of focus is aborted.

4. The keyboard processor then checks its focusIsShifting variable to make sure it is OK to change focus. If this variable is false, then the change of focus is aborted. Even though the keyboard processor just set this variable to true in the previous step, it is conceivable that some other object has set it to false by sending the abortFocusShift message to the keyboard processor.

5. Finally, the keyboard processor begins iterating over its collection of keyboard consumers looking for a candidate to become the new current consumer. To qualify, the keyboard consumer must desire focus and respond true to a request to take focus. The keyboard consumer defers this request to its dispatcher, which may defer the request to the application model via a validation message. If the keyboard consumer does not desire to take focus or does not grant the request to take focus, then the keyboard processor continues with the next keyboard consumer in its collection. If the keyboard processor gets around to the original current consumer without finding a qualified candidate to take focus, then the change of focus is aborted.

6.4 Graphics

This section covers some of the special topics of drawing in a window. The topics covered are graphics context, drawing preferences and policies, display surface dimensions, symbolic paint, and repairing damage.

6.4.1 ScreenGraphicsContext

Recall from Section 6.1.1 that an ApplicationWindow is a graphics medium and that any drawing on a graphics medium is actually done indirectly through a graphics context. The kind of graphics context used by all windows is a ScreenGraphicsContext. ScreenGraphicsContext is a subclass of GraphicsContext, where most of its state and behavior is actually defined.

When you want to draw on an ApplicationWindow, ask it for its graphics context by sending it the message graphicsContext. This message returns a new instance of Screen-GraphicsContext on each access as shown below.

> **graphicsContext**
>   "Answer a new graphics context on my surface."
>
>   ^ScreenGraphicsContext on: self

A ScreenGraphicsContext has several instance variables, many of which are known to the virtual machine, disqualifying it and any object that references it as an object available for persistent storage. Among these instance variables is the medium variable, which points back to the graphics medium that created it—in this case, the ApplicationWindow.

Certain other ScreenGraphicsContext instance variables indicate how objects will appear when drawn on the window. These variables are listed in Table 6.5.
Each of the variables listed in Table 6.5 has a get a put selector so its value can be both accessed and changed during the drawing process.

ScreenGraphicsContext has two other variables—fontPolicy and paintPolicy—which affect the values of the font and paint instance variables listed in Table 6.4. The fontPolicy variable holds on to a FontPolicy object and determines how FontDescription objects are matched with the host window environment fonts. The paintPolicy variable holds on to a PaintPolicy object that maps pure color values to actual paint values available from the host window environment. The ScreenGraphicsContext initializes its paint, font, paintPolicy, and fontPolicy variables to those values found in its graphics medium, which in this case is an Application-Window. If you look back at Section 6.1.1, you will find that all objects that are a kind of GraphicsMedium keep default values for paint, font, paint policy, and font policy.

Table 6.5. TScreenGraphicsContext Drawing Parameters.

Variable	Purpose	Initial value
lineWidth	Width of lines	1
capStyle	How end of lines are shaped	1 for butt
joinStyle	How line intersections are shaped	1 for miter
font	Font for drawing strings	Determined by window
paint	Color for rendering colorless objects	Determined by window

6.4.2 Drawing Preferences and Policies

An ApplicationWindow has certain drawing preferences and policies, which determine how things will appear on its display surface. There are four types of drawing preferences and policies: look preferences, paint preferences, widget policy, and edge decoration policy. These topics are covered in Disk Example 6.3.

6.4.2.1 Look Preferences

A **look preferences** is the set of default colors used for drawing primitive geometrics and text in an ApplicationWindow. The notion of a look preferences is implemented by the LookPreferences class. An ApplicationWindow has an instance variable called look-Preferences, which holds on to an instance of LookPreferences. A look preferences defines a preferred color for each of the following color roles: foreground, background, selected foreground, selected background, border, highlight, and shadow. By default, anything drawn in a window uses the window's look preferences as a color scheme.

Each *VisualWorks* component can define its own look preferences to override that of the window. This overriding of look preferences occurs when the SpecWrapper receives the displayOn: message (the actual implementation is WidgetWrapper>>displayOn::).

The lookPreferences variable will be nil unless the developer explicitly defines window colors using the Color Tool. If lookPreferences is nil, then the window defaults to a look preferences defined by the current platform look.

6.4.2.2 Paint Preferences

A LookPreferences object creates a **paint preferences**, which is an object that facilitates the mapping of a symbolic paint to an actual color value. ApplicationWindow defines an instance variable, paintPreferences, to reference this paint preferences object.

6.4.2.3 Widget Policy

The **widget policy** indicates the look and feel of the non-*VisualWorks* buttons in an ApplicationWindow. Such non-*VisualWorks* buttons are implemented by Button and Action-Button. Examples of these buttons are found in the Browser and in the Contact Manager application from Chapter 1.

WidgetPolicy is the abstract superclass for all widget policy objects. It has five concrete subclasses, one for each of the five different window environments emulated by *VisualWorks*. Each ApplicationWindow holds on to an instance of one of these five classes with its widget-Policy instance variable. For example, if an ApplicationWindow wants *MS Windows* looking buttons, then its widgetPolicy variable will hold on to an instance of Win3WidgetPolicy.

The widgetPolicy instance variable is actually populated by the look policy object, which builds the ApplicationWindow. For instance, when a MacLookPolicy object builds a window, it loads an instance of MacWidgetPolicy into the ApplicationWindow. This assures that any non-*VisualWorks* buttons will be consistent with the intended look policy.

6.4.2.4 Border Decoration Policy

A **border decoration policy** indicates how borders, scroll bars, and window menus will appear in the ApplicationWindow. The class BorderDecorationPolicy is the abstract superclass for all border decoration policy objects. It has a concrete subclass for each of the five window environments emulated by *VisualWorks*. An ApplicationWindow has an instance variable, edgeDecorationPolicy, which holds on to an instance of one of these subclasses. For example, if an ApplicationWindow wants its borders and scroll bars to emulate the *Motif* look, then its edgeDecorationPolicy variable will hold on to an instance of MotifBorderDecorationPolicy.

Like the widgetPolicy instance variable mentioned in Section 6.4.2.3, the edgeDecoration-Policy instance variable is actually populated by the look policy object that builds the ApplicationWindow. For instance, when a CUALookPolicy object builds a window, it loads an instance of CUABorderDecorationPolicy into the ApplicationWindow.

6.4.3 Window Dimensions

An ApplicationWindow has dimensions for its display surface height and width. It references these dimensions with its height and width instance variables, respectively. These values are integers that measure height and width in pixels. There are several messages related to an ApplicationWindow's dimensions, and these are listed in Table 6.6.

Table 6.6. Dimension Messages.

Message	Behavior
height	Returns the receiver's height
height:	Sets the receiver's height
width	Returns the receiver's width
width:	Sets the receiver's width
bounds	Returns a Rectangle describing the receiver's bounds
preferredBounds	Returns a Rectangle describing the receiver's preferred bounds
extent	Returns a Point describing the receiver's extent (width by height)
changeExtent: aPoint	Changes the receiver's extent to that described by aPoint

In addition to the messages above, Section 6.5.2 discusses how to set the maximum and minimum values of the window's dimensions.

6.4.4 Drawing with Symbolic Paint

The material that follows assumes that you are already somewhat familiar with Paint and ColorValue and with how colors are rendered in *VisualWorks*. You should also be familiar with LookPreferences and ScreenGraphicsContext discussed earlier in this section. Disk Example 6.4 covers SymbolicPaint and some other aspects of color in Smalltalk.

6.4.4.1 SymbolicPaint

A **symbolic paint** is a way to describe the color of something based on the role of the color instead of the actual color value. Put another way, a symbolic paint maps to a ColorValue specified in a LookPreferences object. For example, instead of deciding to draw something in red or green, you decide to draw it in the background color specified by a LookPreferences object. The class SymbolicPaint is a subclass of Paint and implements this idea of symbolic paint. An instance of SymbolicPaint contains a Symbol, which describes a color role, #backgroundColor, for example. There are 10 different color roles, and these are listed in Table 6.7.

An instance of SymbolicPaint is created by sending the SymbolicPaint class one of its many instance creation messages such as hilite or background. For example, the following

Table 6.7. Symbolic Paint Color Roles.

Symbolic name	Role
#foreground	Color of text and lines of primitive shapes
#background	Color of screen immediately behind text
#selectedForeground	Color of text when text is selected
#selectedBackground	Color of screen immediately behind text when text is selecte
#inactiveForeground	Foreground color when inactive.
#inactiveBackground	Background color when inactive
#inactiveSelectionForeground	Selected foreground color when inactive.
#inactiveSelectionBackground	Selected background color when inactive.
#shadow	For 3D effects—indicates sloping away from light source.
#hilite	For 3D effects—indicates a sloping towards the light source.

statement is used to create an instance of SymbolicPaint, which will render objects in the current foreground color.

>   SymbolicPaint foreground

6.4.4.2 Visual Properties

Part of *VisualWorks* widget protocol (see Chapter 2, Section 2.1.2) includes the visual properties protocol, which includes messages such as backgroundColor, foregroundColor, selectionBackgroundColor, and selectionForegroundColor. Each of these messages returns an instance of SymbolicPaint. Each class that implements the *VisualWorks* widget protocol (e.g., SimpleView and SimpleComponent) defines these methods in the protocol 'visual properties.' As an example, the backgroundColor method is implemented as follows.

>   **backgroundColor**
>
>   ^SymbolicPaint backgroundColor

6.4.4.3 Using a SymbolicPaint

Ordinarily, to draw text or graphics in a specific color, we change the paint attribute of the graphics context object. For example, to draw a red Rectangle, we might write

```
aGraphicsContext paint: ColorValue red.
(0@0 extent: 100@100) displayFilledOn: aGraphicsContext
```

The paint attribute can also be set to a SymbolicPaint. We know that all graphics context objects (including ScreenGraphicsContext objects) contain a LookPreferences object. And we also know that a SymbolicPaint will map to an actual ColorValue held within that Look-Preferences. If the LookPreferences object specifies a background color of red, then the red Rectangle can now be rendered with the following code.

```
aScreenGraphicsContext paint: SymbolicPaint background.
(0@0 extent: 100@100) displayFilledOn: aScreenGraphicsContext
```

VisualWorks widget classes would implement this as follows.

```
aScreenGraphicsContext paint: self backgroundColor.
(0@0 extent: 100@100) displayFilledOn: aScreenGraphicsContext
```

6.4.4.4 Advantages of Symbolic Paints

VisualWorks components should always be drawn using SymbolicPaint objects instead of ColorValue objects. The advantages to this approach are as follows.

- ▸ A component's colors can be easily changed during editing or during runtime without changing the implementation of the display code.

- A component can assume its container's color scheme, which provides a consistent appearance.

- A component can easily modify or override its container's color scheme when necessary.

- Specially manufactured colors such as *hilite* are readily available and always consistent with the current color scheme.

6.4.5 Repairing Damage

An ApplicationWindow is charged with the responsibility of keeping itself visually up to date. It fulfills this responsibility by recording any areas that need to be redrawn—called damage—and then having its component redraw those areas. Much of the material that follows is related to Section 6.2 and also Chapter 1, Section 1.3. Any overlap presented here is necessary for completeness.

6.4.5.1 Recording Damage

There are two reasons why an ApplicationWindow may record damage. First, it may be obscured by another window in which case the host window manager notifies it of the area that needs to be redrawn. Second, a model may change, rendering its view invalid (i.e., the view no longer accurately reflects the information in its model). When a view notifies the ApplicationWindow that it is no longer valid, the ApplicationWindow records the area occupied by that view as damaged. Damage is recorded in the ApplicationWindowSensor as a collection of Rectangles.

6.4.5.2 Initiating the Drawing Process

Each time the active controller passes through its control loop, each open window is given the opportunity to handle any meta events and redraw any damaged areas (see Section 6.2.4). To handle the damage, the ApplicationWindow calculates the smallest Rectangle containing all the damaged Rectangles and considers this to be the damaged area. Then the ApplicationWindow manufactures a ScreenGraphicsContext object that is active only for the pixels within this Rectangle, which is called the clipping bounds. That is, the ScreenGraphicsContext is clipped to include only the damaged area, and any drawing done outside of the damaged area will not be rendered on the window's display surface. The window then tells its component to display itself by sending it the message displayOn: aGraphicsContext.

6.4.5.3 Displaying Components

The ApplicationWindow's component is a composite and that composite responds to the displayOn: message by forwarding the message to each of its component parts whose bounds intersect the ScreenGraphicsContext's clipping bounds. Each of these in turn draws on its allotted portion of the display surface and forwards the displayOn: to any of its own component parts in a recursive fashion. This continues on down to the leaf components in the visual structure.

6.4.5.4 Lazy Repair of Damage

Normally, when damage is recorded by a component, the damage is collected in the ApplicationWindowSensor and repaired when the current controller yields control to ScheduledControllers. Sometimes this can cause quite a delay in visually updating the interface because we have to wait for the active controller to conclude its current control loop cycle. To short-circuit this behavior, ApplicationWindow allows for immediate damage repair of any damage registered by a component in the visual structure. The ApplicationWindow has an instance variable called damageRepairIsLazy. When this variable is set to true, the damage from a component is stored in the sensor as usual and repaired on the next pass through the active controller's control loop. When the variable is false, however, the damage is repaired immediately, bypassing the sensor altogether. The default value for damageRepairIsLazy is true.

6.4.6 Summary

Drawing on an ApplicationWindow is done through a special type of graphics context object, which is an instance of ScreenGraphicsContext. This object maintains certain drawing parameters, which indicate how graphics and text will be rendered in the window. Each time a window needs to be redrawn, it creates a new instance of ScreenGraphicsContext and passes it to its component using the displayOn: message. The component then dispatches the message on down the visual structure so that each component that needs to be redrawn can do so.

The ApplicationWindow decides for itself how buttons and edge decoration such as borders and scroll bars will be rendered on its surface. Button look and feel is determined by the widget policy and edge decoration look and feel is determined by the border decoration policy. An ApplicationWindow has an instance variable for each and these variables, and they are set by the look policy object that built the ApplicationWindow.

VisualWorks components draw themselves using symbolic paints. A symbolic paint describes a color role such as foreground or selection background and maps to an actual color value kept in a look preferences object. A symbolic paint is an instance of Symbolic-

Paint, and a look preferences is an instance of LookPreferences. This approach to drawing in color allows a component to use the window's color scheme or override part or all of that color scheme with its own color choices. It also allows colors to be changed during runtime, and it helps provide a consistent color scheme for the interface.

A window redraws itself because it has been obscured by another window or because one of its views is invalid. The areas that are in need of being redrawn are referred to as window damage. The window sensor records the damaged parts as Rectangles describing the damaged areas. The window gets the chance to redraw these areas each time the active controller steps through its control loop. An ApplicationWindow redraws itself by instantiating a ScreenGraphicsContext object and passing it down the visual structure using the displayOn: aGraphicsContext message.

6.5 Scheduling and Manipulating

An ApplicationWindow can be manipulated by both the user and the application. This section discusses all the operations that can be conducted on an ApplicationWindow as a whole.

6.5.1 Scheduling

As was discussed in Section 6.1.2.4, an ApplicationWindow (or any display surface) is open when its handle variable references a GraphicsHandle object. This means it has a patch into a host-supplied resource and can display itself on the screen. Conversely, an ApplicationWindow is closed when its handle instance variable references nil. This means the ApplicationWindow has no link back to a host-supplied resource and has no representation on the screen.

When an ApplicationWindow is opened, its controller is automatically scheduled with ScheduledControllers. To **schedule** an ApplicationWindow is to open it and register its controller with ScheduledControllers. The following request of ScheduledControllers can be used to find the active, or current, window.

> ScheduledControllers currentController view

There are three parameters that indicate the manner in which an ApplicationWindow can be scheduled: duration, decoration, and bounds.

6.5.1.1 Duration

An ApplicationWindow can be opened in two different ways: transient or persistent. A **transient window** is expected to be closed soon after it is opened. A **persistent win-**

dow is expected to remain open for a considerable amount of time and operate in concert with several other windows. Pop-up menus and dialogs are opened as transient windows, and nonmodal windows are opened as persistent windows. When a transient window is opened, the portion of the screen that it covers is cached in memory so that when the transient window closes, that portion of the screen can be quickly reinstated without having to damage any underlying windows. In *VisualWorks* 2.0, the class TransientWindow handles most requests for transient type windows. This was not the case in *VisualWorks* 1.0, however, where ScheduledWindow and ApplicationWindow handled transient windows.

6.5.1.2 Decoration

Most host window environments provide several options for decorating a window. *VisualWorks,* however, will open a window with only one of three decoration types: normal, dialog, and pop-up. A **normal decoration** is for persistent windows, and it contains full trimmings such as a border, a title bar, and a collapse button. A **dialog decoration** looks the same as a normal decoration, but it does not include any collapse buttons. A **pop-up decoration** type actually provides no decoration at all. These three decoration types are fixed by the virtual machine for each host window environment, and the virtual image has no control over their appearance.

It should be pointed out that the decoration is provided by the host window environment and is not considered part of the display surface. That is, an ApplicationWindow with dimensions 200@200 has a display surface of 200@200, around which the host environment places a decoration. The ApplicationWindow's input origin is the upper lefthand corner of the display surface, not the upper left hand corner of the decoration (see Figure 6.3).

An ApplicationWindow that is opened with normal or dialog decoration can have a label that appears in the ApplicationWindow's title bar. To set the label, send the message label: aString where aString is the intended title for the window.

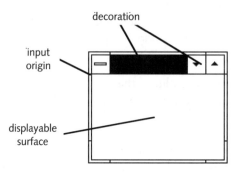

Figure 6.3. Displayable Surface and Decoration.

6.5.1.3 Bounds

The bounds of the window indicates the size and location of the display surface and is expressed as a Rectangle. The bounds can be specified when the window is opened (scheduled). The origin and extent can each be expressed separately, each as a Point.

6.5.1.4 Scheduling Protocol

There are several variations on the opening process. Table 6.8 lists some of the scheduling protocol.

6.5.1.5 Closing and Unscheduling

A window can be closed programmatically, but the message must be sent to the controller so that it is unscheduled from ScheduledControllers. The following statement closes and unschedules a window.

>   window controller closeAndUnschedule

The code above should be used very rarely. A better approach is to send closeRequest to the application model, and the application model will then see to it that the window is closed.

6.5.2 Moving and Resizing

An ApplicationWindow can be moved and resized. Both of these operations can be done either by the user or programmatically. I am including raising and lowering among the

Table 6.8. Scheduling Messages.

Message	Behavior
open	Open the receiver at its inputOrigin and with its minimum size
openDialogIn: aRectangle	Open the receiver with dialog decoration and with location and extent specified by aRectangle
openDisplayAt: aPoint	Open the receiver with minimum size and centered around aPoint
openIn: aRectangle	Open the receiver with regular decoration with the size and location specified by aRectangle
openPopUpIn: aRectangle	Open the receiver with no decoration with location and extent specified by aRectangle
openWithExtent: aPoint	Open the receiver at its inputOrigin and with extent specified by aPoint

Table 6.9. Moving and Resizing Messages.

Message	Behavior
raise	Bring the window to the front of all windows
lower	Place the window behind all other windows
moveTo: originPoint	Move window to screen coordinate aPoint
moveTo: aPoint resize: extentPoint	Move window to aPoint with the new size extentPoint
resizeFromUserWithMinimum: minimumSize manixmum: maximumSize	Allow user to resize window within the specified max and min sizes
minimumSize: aPoint	Set the minimum size of the window to aPoint
maximumSize: aPoint	Set the maximum size of the window to aPoint

moving behaviors. Some of the more useful methods for moving and resizing a window are shown in Table 6.9.

6.5.2.1 Raising and Lowering

To **raise** an ApplicationWindow is to display it as if it were resting on top of all other windows. A raised window automatically becomes the active (current) window. To **lower** an ApplicationWindow is to display it as if it were hiding behind all other widows.

6.5.2.2 Origin

When drawing in an ApplicationWindow, it is convenient to use local coordinates. That is, objects that draw in a window would like to refer to the upper lefthand corner of the window as coordinate 1@1.

In order to accomplish this translation from screen/global coordinates to window/local coordinates, the ApplicationWindow needs to know where on the screen it is located. This information is kept in its instance variable inputOrigin. The inputOrigin variable holds on to a Point, which indicates the current location, in screen/global coordinates, of the Application-Window's origin. A window's origin is the upper lefthand corner of its display surface (see Figure 6.3). Whenever the ApplicationWindow is moved, the inputOrigin variable is updated to the new coordinates of the origin. The ApplicationWindow has another origin–related instance variable called creationOrigin. This instance variable also holds on to a Point and indicates where the ApplicationWindow should appear when it is first opened (i.e., the initial origin). Unlike inputOrigin, the value of creationOrigin remains fixed while the window is open.

6.5.2.3 Moving and Resizing Protocol

To move a window is to change its origin—its inputOrigin variable. From Table 6.9, we can see that to move a window programmatically, we can send it the message moveTo: aPoint. To resize a window is to change its extent—its dimension variables width and height. From Table 6.9, we can see that to resize a window, we can send it the message

> moveTo: aPoint resize: extentPoint

or

> resizeFromUserWithMinimum: minExent maximum: maxExtent

The first message requires a new origin as well. The second message requires a minimum and maximum extent and requires the user's help.

6.5.2.4 Minimum and Maximum Extent

ApplicationWindow has two variables—minimumSize and maximumSize—which constrain the resizing process. Each of these references a Point, which describes the extent of the window. Each of these can be set programmatically with minimumSize: and maximumSize: accessing messages respectively.

6.5.3 Collapsing and Expanding

An ApplicationWindow can be represented as an icon, and that icon can be reinstated as the full window. To **collapse** an ApplicationWindow is to shrink it down to an icon representing the ApplicationWindow. Some may refer to this process as *minimize* or *iconify*. In Smalltalk, however, the proper term is *collapse*. To **expand** a window is to redisplay a collapsed window as a full-sized window, that is, to make an icon become a full window again. The favorite synonym for this is *maximize,* but again, we should stay with the Smalltalk term *expand.*

Table 6.10. Icon Messages.

Message	Behavior
isCollapsed	Returns true if the window is iconized, false if it is not
icon: aMask	Makes aMask be the icon of the window
expand	Makes an icon become a window again
collapse	Has a window shrink itself to an icon
label: aString iconLabel: anIconString	Makes aString the window's label but anIconString the icon's label

Do not confuse collapse and expand with open and close. An ApplicationWindow is considered open when it references a GraphicsHandle that represents a host-generated window. A closed ApplicationWindow does not have a corresponding host window and, therefore, cannot appear anywhere on the screen—collapsed or expanded. If an Application-Window is collapsed or expanded, it is necessarily open! Table 6.10 shows the messages that deal with icons, expanding, and collapsing.

6.6 Summary

An ApplicationWindow is the type of window of choice in *VisualWorks*. It inherits much of its behavior from GraphicsMedium, DisplaySurface, Window, and ScheduledWindow. A graphics medium is an object that is a destination for graphics operations and is implemented by the abstract class GraphicsMedium. A display surface is a graphics medium object that displays graphics and text on the screen as opposed to a printer. The abstract class for all display surfaces is DisplaySurface. A Window is a kind of DisplaySurface that has a sensor, knows its opening and current location, and has some rudimentary scheduling behavior. Pixmaps and Masks are special kinds of display surfaces known as unmappable surfaces. An unmappable surface is a screen-related graphics medium that is not visible on the screen and exists only in memory. A ScheduledWindow is a kind of Window that has a model and a controller. It has a component tree structure, which it keeps fresh by handling damage events. A ScheduledWindow has a rich set of scheduling behaviors and registers itself with ScheduledControllers—a global variable and the only instance of ControlManager.

The events in *VisualWorks* can be conveniently placed into four categories: keyboard, mouse, meta, and damage events. An event is usually created by the host window manager and passed to the virtual machine, which passes it to the default instance of InputState. From here it is acquired by the sensor of the target window for processing and storage by that sensor. The window sensor does not process or store mouse events, only keyboard, meta, and damage events. Mouse events instead are used to update the default InputSensor, which tracks current mouse state as well as some keyboard state. An ApplicationWindow has the option of forwarding any meta events to other windows that share its application. In *VisualWorks*, the window controller handles keyboard events and the widget controllers process mouse input. The window controller handles keyboard events by passing them to its keyboard processor. The keyboard processor knows about the widget controllers that can take focus and tracks the widget controller with current focus. The widget controllers do not *handle mouse events,* but instead *poll for current mouse state.* The window controller is usually the active controller since widget controllers remain active only as long as it takes process mouse input.

Each ApplicationWindow has an instance of KeyboardProcessor, which manages all keyboard events for that window. Each time the window controller steps through its control loop, the keyboard processor is given the opportunity to handle any KeyboardEvent objects queued up in the window's sensor. The keyboard processor keeps track of all components that handle keyboard input. The widget controller belonging to the current recipient of keyboard activity is referred to as the current consumer. The keyboard processor also routes short-cut keys to the appropriate menu or widget controller. Each widget controller has a dispatcher, which can both notify the application model of change of focus and ask the application model to validate a change of focus.

An ApplicationWindow collects damage in its sensor and is given the opportunity to redraw the damaged parts each time the active controller passes through its control loop. When an ApplicationWindow needs to redraw itself, it creates a ScreenGraphicsContext for its display surface. This ScreenGraphicsContext is valid for only the smallest Rectangle that contains all the damaged regions. This rectangle is called the clipping bounds. The ApplicationWindow passes this ScreenGraphicsContext down the visual structure, and each visual component that intersects the clipping bounds redraws itself. All of the components in the window's visual structure render themselves according to the parameters, preferences, and policies contained within this ScreenGraphicsContext, but the components can override some of these such as look preferences and font.

An ApplicationWindow is open when it references a GraphicsHandle, and it is closed when it does not. The GraphicsHandle represents the host-supplied resource, which allows a *VisualWorks* window to actually draw on a host-supplied window. To schedule a window is to open it and register its controller with ScheduledControllers. An Application-Window can be opened with three different styles of decoration: normal, dialog, and pop-up. A window can also be assigned an icon and a label. To collapse a window is to shrink it down to an icon. To expand a window is to reinstate the icon as a full window. A window can be moved both interactively and programmatically. A window can be resized both interactively and programmatically.

CHAPTER 7

Canvas-Painting Tools

As ANY GOOD SMALLTALK developer knows, Smalltalk is written in Smalltalk. Therefore, it should come as no surprise that *VisualWorks* is written in *VisualWorks*. By this I mean that the tools for *VisualWorks*, such as the Image Editor and the Properties Tool, are creations of *VisualWorks* itself. It is this self-generating quality of *VisualWorks* that distinguishes it from most other GUI builders and makes such a powerful development environment.

VisualWorks is not just a tool for building user applications, it is a tool for building tools! This places an incredible amount of power at the hands of the developer. It also gives rise to the notion of a meta-tool. Let us define the term **meta-tool** to be a tool that can create other tools, including itself, as well as modify itself. *VisualWorks* is very much a meta-tool, as is Smalltalk.

The most fundamental tools in *VisualWorks* are what I refer to as the *canvas-painting tools*. These are the three tools that open for a canvas-painting session: a canvas, a Palette, and a Canvas Tool. Not included in this group are such things as the Properties Tool, the Menu Editor, and the Image Editor. I refer to these as support tools, and they are discussed in Chapter 8. The canvas-painting tools allow the developer to visually edit a user interface and generate the specifications for that interface. The canvas-painting tools, like all *VisualWorks* tools, are themselves *VisualWorks* applications. In this chapter we will closely examine the canvas-painting tools and see how they work. I would like to emphasize that this is not a discussion on how to use the tools. You are expected to already know this. Instead we look at these tools just as we might look at any application developed in *VisualWorks*.

There are several reasons why we might invest some time investigating how *VisualWorks* itself is implemented. First, we may have the need to customize or enhance the *VisualWorks* canvas editing process (this is actually done in Chapters 13 and 14). Second, there are several techniques and classes that may improve our own applications. Third, we may want to add new types of *VisualWorks* components to the Palette (this is done in Chapter 12). Finally, we may have the need to implement a graphical application similar to *VisualWorks* canvas editing, and an analysis of the *VisualWorks* tools can provide some insights into the design and implementation of such an application.

In the first section, we will look at these tools just as we would any other *VisualWorks* applications. The next three sections cover the various painting functions: painting the canvas with components, editing the components within the canvas, and other related behavior.

7.1 Canvas-Painting Constructs

In this section we will look at the basic parts of the canvas-painting tools. The canvas-painting tools consist of three applications: the canvas, the Palette, and the Canvas Tool. A UIPainter is an application model that opens and operates the canvas. Likewise, a UIPalette is the application model for the Palette and a UICanvasTool is the application model for the Canvas Tool. There are several other related tools, such as the Properties Tool and the Menu Editor, but these will be discussed in Chapter 8. The canvas window's component is a UIPainterView (wrapped in a GridWrapper), and the UIPainterView's controller is UIPainter-Controller. In this section we will look at each of these five constructs in turn: the UIPainter, the UIPainterView, the UIPainterController, the UIPalette, and the UICanvasTool.

7.1.1 UIPainter

At the heart of the canvas is its application model, a UIPainter. UIPainter is a subclass of ApplicationModel, so a UIPainter is just another *VisualWorks* application model. Like all application models, it has a builder, specs, and resources. It also has a great deal of very special state and behavior. A UIPainter has three main responsibilities:

- To open and operate the canvas window and open the corresponding Palette and Canvas Tool windows

- To create and install the full spec

- To maintain the spec information for the canvas window

While a UIPainter is the application model for the canvas, it is up to the UIPainterController to actually conduct the editing session. UIPainterController is discussed in Section 7.1.3.

The ultimate goal of a canvas-painting session is to install a full spec literal array describing an interface drawn by the developer. Recall from Chapter 3 that a full spec consists of a window spec and a spec collection. The canvas contains the information that will eventually become the spec collection. The window spec is created from information contained within the canvas window and the UIPainter. Disk Example 7.1 covers some of the UIPainter features mentioned in this section.

7.1.1.1 Instance Variables

UIPainter defines nine instance variables (see Table 7.1). These variables are instrumental in helping a developer design and store a full spec.

7.1.1.2 Class Variables

UIPainter defines a single class variable, ControlsOffsets, that references a Dictionary. The keys are Symbols, each naming one of the types of host window environments such as #Macintosh or #Motif. The values are Points that indicate how much of an offset is required when positioning the Canvas Tool window above the canvas window. The differences in offsets account for the different heights of window title bars among the different host environments. For example, a *Motif* host provides windows with rather high, or thick, title bars, while a *Macintosh* host provides windows with rather thin title bars. Since the Canvas Tool window is opened above the canvas, this difference in title bar heights must be taken into account.

Table 7.1. UIPainter Instance Variables.

Variable	Description
targetClass	The class, usually a kind of ApplicationModel, that is to receive the interface spec, installed as a class method. The aspect methods, action methods, and resource methods also destined for the target class are generated by other tools.
targetSelector	A Symbol that is the name of a class method in the target class that will store and return the full spec literal array describing the interface designed by the developer.
acceptedState	An Array that is the full spec literal array describing the interface when last accepted.
windowSpec	A WindowSpec that is the specification for the window that contains the canvas.
minWindowExtent	A Point that describes the current minimum extent of the window being edited.
prefWindowExtent	A Point that describes the current preferred extent of the window being edited.
maxWindowExtent	A Point that describes the current maximum extent of the window being edited.
currentLook	A ValueHolder on a Symbol that indicates the current look of the canvas.
definer	A UIDefiner that is used in code generation.

7.1.1.3 Initialization Behavior

A UIPainter does a fair amount of initialization, but of greatest interest is how it initializes its builder. Two things are unique to a UIPainter's builder. First, a UIPainter is the only application model whose builder operates in edit mode (see Chapter 3). Second, its builder's top composite is not a CompositePart, as it is in runtime mode, but a UIPainterView (see Section 7.2.2). Both of these attributes of the builder are set in the UIPainter instance method initializeBuilder shown below.

> **initializeBuilder**
>
>   self builder: UIBuilder new.
>   builder isEditing: true.
>   builder composite: UIPainterView new.
>   builder composite controller: UIPainterController new.

7.1.1.4 Opening Behavior

There are four ways in which a UIPainter is opened: from the Launcher, from the Resource Finder, from evaluating the comment in an interface specs class method, or spawned from another UIPainter. All but the last of these opening techniques eventually wind their way to the UIPainter instance method openPainterWindows:. It is this method that actually opens the canvas window and dispatches messages to open the two satellite windows: the Palette and the Canvas Tool.

The openPainterWindows: method replaces the canvas window's controller (ordinarily an ApplicationStandardSystemController) with a UIPainterSystemController (a subclass of ApplicationStandardSystemController). The only behavior that UIPainterSystemController adds to its superclass is to make sure the maximum and minimum window extents are enforced when the user tries to resize the canvas window from the <window> menu.

The Palette window is opened in the class method openPaletteFor: mainWindow, and the canvas control window is opened in the instance method openToolsFor: mainWindow. Opening the Palette and Canvas Tool are discussed further in Sections 7.1.4 and 7.1.5, respectively.

7.1.1.5 Menu Actions

Of the several menu selections available in the canvas <operate> menu, UIPainter is responsible for three: **install...**, **edit→accept**, and **edit→cancel**. The UIPainterController is the menu's performer, so it is the first to receive the messages corresponding to these menu selections—doInstall, accept, and cancel, respectively—but it quickly forwards them to its model, a UIPainter.

The controller forwards the doInstall message as an installFor: self message. The UIPainter's implementation of the installFor: aController method is to install the full spec as a literal array in a class method of the target class. The target class and the name of the class method are indicated by the UIPainter's targetClass and targetSelector instance variables.

UIPainter's implementation of accept is to merely store the current full spec, as a literal array, in its acceptedState variable. The cancel message causes the UIPainter to reset the canvas window to its previous state as indicated by the full spec literal array contained in its acceptedState variable.

7.1.1.6 Window Information

As we learned in Chapter 2, all *VisualWorks* components keep a copy of their own spec. This is not the case for ApplicationWindows, however. Therefore, the UIPainter assumes the responsibility of keeping the specs for the canvas window in its windowSpec instance variable. In addition to this, it keeps the window's minimum, preferred, and maximum extents. The UIPainter holds on to these values in its instance variables minWindowExtent, prefWindowExtend, and maxWindowExtent, respectively.

7.1.1.7 The Role of the Builder

Perhaps the most interesting (and most important) facet of a UIPainter is the role of its builder. Of course, its builder constructs and opens the canvas window just like the builder of any application model builds that application model's window. Unlike other application models, however, the UIPainter's builder continues to build the interface the entire time that the canvas window is open. The UIPainter's builder is the mechanism by which the developer adds new components to the canvas. Recall from Chapter 3 that component specs can be added to the builder one at a time, such as

> builder add: aRadioButtonSpec

Also recall that as soon as the builder receives a spec, it immediately constructs the component described by the spec and adds the component to the interface. Now consider a canvas that is being edited. When the developer selects a radio button component in the Palette, a RadioButtonSpec is instantiated. And when the developer clicks the mouse in the canvas, the RadioButtonSpec is added to the builder as in the statement above. It is at this point that the builder builds the new component and adds it to the canvas interface. The process of adding components is further discussed in Section 7.2.1.

7.1.2 UIPainterView

When an application model opens, it opens its canvas window, which is an Application-Window. An ApplicationWindow's component ordinarily is a CompositePart. It is the CompositePart that contains all of the *VisualWorks* components and is the runtime canvas (see Chapter 5, Section 5.1.1.1). The UIPainter, however, replaces this CompositePart with an instance of UIPainterView wrapped by a GridWrapper (see Chapter 8, Section 8.1.3.6, for more on GridWrapper). This instance of UIPainterView is in fact the canvas being painted (see Chapter 5, Section 5.1.1.1). The UIPainter makes this swap in its instance method initializeBuilder. We already know from Section 7.1.1.3 that the UIPainterView is also the builder's initial or top composite.

To look at it another way, each canvas-painting session involves one UIPainterView. It is known to the other players in different ways, however. All at once, this single instance of UIPainterView is

- a dependent of the UIPainter

- the top composite of the UIPainter's builder

- the wrapped component of the canvas window

- the view of the UIPainterController

Disk Example 7.2 covers some of the UIPainterView features mentioned in this section.

7.1.2.1 General Description

UIPainterView is a subclass of CompositeView. Its components collection contains *Visual-Works* components and DragHandle objects. The UIPainterView's main responsibilities are to dynamically add and remove components to provide a means for graphically manipulating its components according to its controller's instructions, and to maintain the specs for the canvas currently being edited. A UIPainterView registers as a dependent of its corresponding UIPainter, which is the UIPainterView's model. The UIPainterView's controller is a UIPainter-Controller (see Section 7.1.3).

7.1.2.2 Adding and Removing Components

A UIPainterView has one method each for adding and removing a component: addCompo-nent: and removeComponent:, respectively. The component is either a *VisualWorks* compo-nent—that is, a SpecWrapper—or a DragHandle (discussed below). In either case the new component is always added at the end of the UIPainterView's components collection. The ordering of the *VisualWorks* components within the UIPainterView's components collection is important, as we will see in Section 7.1.2.4. Whenever a component is added to or removed from the components collection, then the UIPainterView redraws the affected portion of its bounds to visually reflect the change in its contents.

7.1.2.3 Handles

In a canvas, a selected *VisualWorks* component is visually offset from the nonselected *VisualWorks* components in the canvas by handles. A **handle** is a small rectangular visual component that appears in the corner of a *VisualWorks* component's bounds and is used to indicate that that component has been selected. The handles are implemented by the DragHandle class. The handles are actually created by the component's spec object, but it is up to the UIPainterView to display them. DragHandles can be added to and removed from the UIPainterView's components collection using the addComponent: and removeComponent: messages mentioned above. A UIPainterView also has two additional methods for dealing specifically with handles: addHandleCollection: aCollection and removeHandleCollection: aCollection. In both cases, the argument aCollection is an array of DragHandle objects.

7.1.2.4 Component Order

The ordering of the UIPainterView's components is important for two reasons. First, it dictates the order in which the *VisualWorks* components will be drawn in the runtime interface. If the bounds of two components overlap, then the component drawn last will obscure the one drawn previously. Second, the ordering of the components in UIPainterView is used to determine the tab order used by the keyboard processor. The first tabable widget in the UIPainterView's components collection will be the widget that has initial focus when the runtime window is opened. The next tabable widget in the components collection will be the next widget to take focus in the runtime interface, and so on.

These two issues of ordering, display order and tab order, are runtime issues, and therefore we are only interested in the ordering of the SpecWrappers in the UIPainterView's components. The DragHandles can all be at the front of the collection, the back of the collection, or scattered throughout, and this will have no effect on the final display order or the tab order.

UIPainterView has four methods for managing the ordering of its components. These are described in Table 7.2.

Table 7.2. Component-Ordering Methods.

Method	Implementation
toVisualBack: aCollection	Move all the components in aCollection to the front of the components collection
toVisualBackOneNotch: aCollection	Move all the components in aCollection forward one spot in the components collection
toVisualFront: aCollection	Move all the components in aCollection to the end of the components collection
toVisualFrontOneNotch: aCollection	Move all the components in aCollection back one spot in the components collection

7.1.2.5 Moving and Resizing Components

While editing a canvas, any *VisualWorks* component can be moved and most can be resized. While it is the UIPainterController that allows the developer to decide which component to move or resize and by how much to resize it, it is the UIPainterView that actually changes the bounds of the component and redraws it.

7.1.2.6 Maintaining a Specification

The UIPainterView is in fact the canvas being edited (see Chapter 5, Section 5.1.1.1). Each of its components is a *VisualWorks* component or a DragHandle object. Each *VisualWorks* component maintains a description of itself, a component spec, in its SpecWrapper. Therefore, the UIPainterView contains all the specifications necessary for recreating the canvas currently being edited by the developer. Creating the spec collection that describes the canvas is only a matter of iterating over UIPainterView's components collection and extracting the component spec from each component.

7.1.3 UIPainterController

UIPainterController is a paragon of Smalltalk controllers in that it is large, complex, and far outweighs its model and view in terms of state, behavior, and responsibility. It is this controller that actually manages the canvas–painting session. UIPainterController is a subclass of the abstract class ModalController, which implements the modal controller concept. In this section we will look at UIPainterController's along the lines of its instance and class variables and how it processes mouse state, menu selections, and keyboard events. First however, we should look at the modal controller concept. Disk Example 7.3 illustrates some of the UIPainterController features and the modal controller concept covered in this section.

7.1.3.1 Modal Controller

A **modal controller** is a controller that redirects user input to an internally held object called a control mode object. A **control mode object** processes user input for its controller. The modal controller concept is a way to logically factor a controller's behavior among several other objects, thereby lessening the controller's load. It also allows the controller to vary the way it deals with user input according to circumstance. That is, a controller can change from one mode to the next simply by changing its control mode object.

The modal controller concept is implemented in the abstract class ModalController, a subclass of ControllerWithMenu. ModalController defines one instance variable, mode, that is a ValueHolder on a control mode object. This particular implementation of the modal controller concept only deals with mouse state, leaving its controller to field any keyboard activity. For the remainder of the book, the term *modal controller* will refer to the specific implementation specified in ModalController and not just the general modal controller concept defined above.

When a modal controller acquires current mouse state from its sensor, it passes on the information to its control mode object in the form of a pseudomouse event object, which is nothing more than a Point indicating the current mouse position. If the control mode handles the event, it returns nil. If it does not handle the event, then the modal controller proceeds with more conventional mouse handling protocol such as redButtonActivity or yellowButtonActivity.

7.1.3.2 Control Modes

UIPainterController can operate in several different modes. Consequently, there are several different classes of control mode objects. The UIPainterController object changes its mode of operation simply by changing its control mode object from one type to the next. For instance, when a developer is dragging an object in a canvas, the UIPainterController is in a

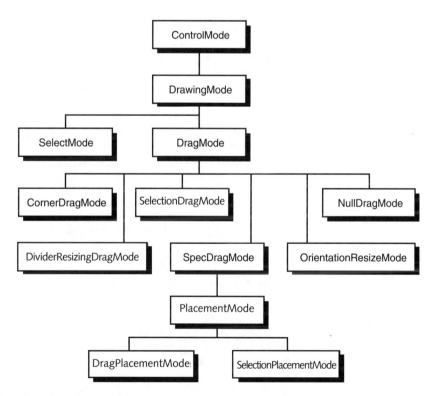

Figure 7.1. Control Mode Hierarchy.

selection drag mode and its control mode object is an instance of SelectionDragMode. As soon as the developer is done dragging and releases the mouse button, the UIPainter-Controller switches to select mode and its control mode object becomes an in instance of SelectMode. It is the current type of control mode object that determines the mode of the UIPainterController—that is, how the UIPainterController will respond to mouse input.

Table 7.3. Control Mode Types.

Class	Description
ControlMode	Abstract super class for all control mode objects.
DrawingMode	Abstract subclass of ControlMode, which adds the capability of drawing rectangles in the canvas. These rectangles are used for making multiple selections.
SelectMode	Concrete subclass of DrawingMode whose instances act as the default control mode object for the UIPainterController. A SelectMode is used for making selections in the canvas.
DragMode	Abstract superclass for all control mode objects that will drag, resize, or drop components in the canvas.
CornerDragMode	Concrete subclass of DragMode whose instances are used to resize a component by dragging one of its corner handles.
DividerResizingDragMode	Concrete subclass of DragMode whose instances are used specifically for resizing a divider component.
NullDragMode	Concrete subclass of DragMode whose instances are used to prevent dragging in the event that the developer has grabbed a nonorigin handle of an unbounded component.
OrientationResizeMode	Concrete subclass of DragMode whose instances are used specifically for dragging a slider component that can change orientation based on the relative sizes of its width and height.
SelectionDragMode	Concrete subclass of DragMode whose instances are used to drag an entire component across the canvas instead of just a handle.
SpecDragMode	Abstract subclass of DragMode and defines behavior for dragging new components which have been selected in the Palette for dropping into the canvas.
PlacementMode	Abstract subclass of SpecDragMode.
DragPlacementMode	Concrete subclass of PlacementMode whose instances are used to begin dragging a new component as soon as the mouse enters the canvas.
SelectPlacementMode	Concrete subclass of PlacementMode whose instances are used to begin dragging new component once the developer has actually clicked the mouse in the canvas.

The hierarchy for the control mode classes is quite deep, as can be seen in Figure 7.1. ControlMode is an abstract class describing basic behavior for all control mode objects. There are four other abstract control mode classes and eight concrete control mode classes. Each of the eight concrete types of control mode objects is used by a UIPainterController for one of four functions: placing a component, selecting a component, moving a component, or resizing a component. UIPainterController is constantly changing its control mode from one type to the next, based on the developer's actions and intentions. All of the control mode classes, both abstract and concrete, are listed in Table 7.3.

7.1.3.3 Instance Variables

UIPainterController defines nine instance variables (Table 7.4) to add to the six it inherits (model, view, sensor, menuHolder, performer, and currentMode).

UIPainterController inherits its currentMode instance variable from its superclass Modal-Controller. This instance variable references the UIPalette class variable CurrentMode, which is a ValueHolder on a control mode object. Therefore, *all* instances of UIPainter-Controller reference this same instance of ValueHolder with their currentMode instance variable. Whenever a developer selects a component from the Palette, the value of this ValueHolder changes. It is in this way that all canvases can respond to the same Palette (see Section 7.2.1.).

Table 7.4. UIPainterController Instance Variables.

Instance variable	Description
showGrid	A ValueHolder on a Symbol that indicates the grid control setting #Off, #On, or #Hidden
gridStep	A ValueHolder containing an integer that describes the number of pixels in the current grid
griddedHorizontally	A ValueHolder on a boolean that indicates if the grid is in effect along the x-axis of the canvas
griddedVertically	A ValueHolder on a boolean that indicates if the grid is in effect along the y-axis of the canvas
fenced	A ValueHolder on a boolean that indicates whether components can be moved beyond the bounds of the canvas or not
primarySelection	A SpecWrapper that is the currently selected component
selections	An Array of any subsequently selected components in a group selection
handles	An OrderedCollection of DragHandle objects that are the handles of the currently selected component(s)
canvasHasChanged	A boolean that indicates if the canvas has changed since the last installation

7.1.3.4 Class Variables

UIPainterController defines nine class variables. These are described in Table 7.5.

7.1.3.5 Mouse Actions

As mentioned in Section 7.1.3.1, all mouse activity is fielded by the control mode object. It is the <select> button activity that is of interest here. The <operate> and <window> buttons retain their standard behavior of invoking the <operate> and <window> menus, respectively. There are four basic functions provided by the red mouse button: placing a new component, selecting a component, moving a component, and resizing a component. Furthermore, there are two ways to make multiple selections. First there is a <Shift>-<select> click action, which allows the developer to select an arbitrary number of secondary components. Second, the developer can draw a rectangle around all components he or she intends to include in the selection.

7.1.3.6 <operate> Menu Actions

Since a UIPainterController is a kind of ControllerWithMenu, it has an <operate> menu. In fact, a UIPainterController has three different versions of its <operate> menu, each held in a different class variable: NoSelectMenu, SingleSelectMenu, and MultiSelectMenu. Which

Table 7.5. UIPainterController Class Variables.

Class variable	Description
KeyboardDispatchTable	A DispatchTable used to interpret keyboard input as edit commands
LastControllerWithSelection	A ValueHolder on a UIPainterController used as a global reference for the canvas currently being edited
MultiSelectMenu	The <operate> menu used when more than one component is selected
NoSelectMenu	The <operate> menu used when no component is selected
SingleSelectMenu	The <operate> menu used when only one component is selected
OperationParameters	A Dictionary that maintains the most recently used settings for the align, distribute, and equalize dialogs
Scrap	A paste buffer used to hold any secondary selections that might have been copied or cut with the primary selection
ScrapPrimary	A paste buffer used to hold the copied or cut component that was the primary selection
StickyMode	A ValueHolder on a boolean indicating if repeat mode is in effect or not

menu is invoked by the <operate> button depends on how many components are in the current selection: zero, exactly one, or more than one. The UIPainterController is the menu performer and so receives any message based on the developer's menu selection.

There are several menu selections among the three menus. Table 7.6 lists all of the possible menu selections and the corresponding messages sent to the UIPainterController.

7.1.3.7 Keyboard Actions

Much of what can be done using the mouse or <operate> menu can also be accomplished with the keyboard. Certain functions are actually easier with the keyboard. The class variable KeyboardDispatchTable is responsible for binding methods to certain keystrokes. The KeyboardDispatchTable is initialized in the initializeDispatchTable class method that binds certain key events to certain action methods listed in Table 7.6.

7.1.4 UIPalette

The Palette is created and opened by an instance of UIPalette. A Palette can be opened from the Launcher, with a canvas, from the canvas <operate> menu, or from the Canvas Tool. The UIPalette class is a subclass of ApplicationModel, so it is just another *VisualWorks* application. A UIPalette's main responsibility is to put all canvas controllers in placement mode (i.e., the mode for adding a new component to the canvas) whenever the developer selects a component from the Palette. What is interesting about Palettes is that each Palette, regardless of how it was opened, operates on any and all currently opened canvases. A UIPalette is also responsible for controlling the sticky attribute for component placement. Disk Example 7.4 illustrates some of the UIPalette features covered in this section.

7.1.4.1 User Interface Description

The Palette interface is shown in Figure 7.2. At the top of the user interface are two buttons for controlling placement behavior—the *select* button and the *sticky* button. For convenience, these two buttons are referred to collectively as the *placement control buttons*. The select button places the canvas in select mode. The sticky button toggles the sticky attribute on and off. The term *sticky* is perhaps a misnomer. When the sticky attribute is on, the UIPainterController continues to add a component of the selected type to the canvas with each <select> button mouse click until such time as the sticky mode attribute is turned off again. A more suitable name for the sticky attribute might be the *repeat* attribute.

Below the placement control buttons are 20 action buttons used for selecting the type of component to be placed in the canvas. For the purpose of this book, these are referred to collectively as the *component selection buttons*. At the bottom of the interface is a read-

Table 7.6. UIPainterController Menu Selections.

Menu Selection	Message
edit→copy	doCopy
edit→cut	doCut
edit→paste	doPaste
edit→accept	accept
edit→cancel→confirm	cancel
edit→spawn	doSpawn
tools→palette	doPalette
tools→canvas control	doCanvasTool
tools→image editor	maskEditor
tools→menu editor	menuEditor
tools→reusable data form components	openReusableComponents
layout→window→fixed size	setAllWindow
layout→window→min size	setWindowMinSize
layout→window→pref size	setWindowPrefSize
layout→window→max size	setWindowMaxSize
layout→window→clear all	setWindowToDefaults
layout→fixed	beFixedKey: nil
layout→relative	beRelative: nil
layout→constrained…	fractionalConstraintDialog
layout→be bounded	doMakeBounded
layout→be unbounded	doMakeUnbounded
arrange→snap to grid	doSnapSelectionToGrid
arrange→group	doGroup
arrange→ungroup	doUngroup
arrange→bring forward	toVisualFrontOne
arrange→bring to front	toVisualFront
arrange→/send backward	toVisualBackOne
arrange→send to back	toVisualBack
arrange→align…	alignDialog
arrange→/distribute…	distributeDialog
arrange→equalize…	equalizeDialog
properties	doDialog
install…	doInstall
define…	doDefine
open…	doOpen

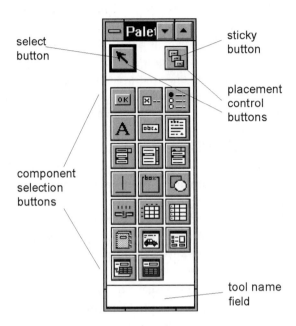

select
button

sticky
button

placement
control
buttons

component
selection
buttons

tool name
field

Figure 7.2. Palette Interface.

only field that displays the type of component currently selected. For the purposes of this book, this field is referred to as the *tool name field*.

7.1.4.2 Instance Variables

UIPalette defines two instance variables: activeSpecs and toolName. The activeSpecs variable is an OrderedCollection of all component spec classes represented in the Palette interface by a component selection button. That is, the activeSpecs collection contains such things as the InputFieldSpec class and the CheckBoxSpec class, and for each class in the collection there is a corresponding component selection button in the Palette's user interface. The activeSpecs collection is initialized in the updateActiveSpecs method.

The toolName variable is a ValueHolder whose value is a string and which serves as the aspect model for the tool name field. The value of toolName is changed each time the developer selects a new component type.

7.1.4.3 Class Variables

UIPalette defines three class variables: ActiveSpecsList, CurrentMode, and PaletteOffsets. ActiveSpecsList keeps an Array of component spec class names (these are Symbols). Each of these component spec classes is represented in the Palette interface by a component selection button. This class variable is used to initialize the activeSpecs instance variable mentioned above. It may appear that the ActiveSpecsList class variable and the activeSpecs instance variable are the same, but there is a real distinction. The ActiveSpecsList class variable contains component spec *class names* such as #TextEditorSpec, and the activeSpecs instance variable contains component spec *classes* such as the TextEditorSpec class.

CurrentMode holds onto a ValueHolder whose value is a control mode object, such as a SelectMode, a SelectPlacementMode, or a DragPlacementMode. This ValueHolder is extremely critical to the entire canvas-painting operation. This very same ValueHolder is also referenced by all instances of UIPainterController. Each instance of UIPainterController has an instance variable, currentMode, which is initialized to reference this UIPalette class variable. When a developer selects a component to be dropped into a canvas, the value of this ValueHolder is changed to a placement mode object, either a SelectPlacementMode or a DragPlacementMode. The process of adding a component and the role played by the UIPalette class variable CurrentMode is covered more thoroughly in Section 7.2.1.

PaletteOffsets is a Dictionary whose keys are host platform names and whose values are Points. Window border thickness varies across host platforms. For example, *Macintosh* windows have thin borders and *Motif* windows have thick borders. When opening a UIPalette next to a canvas, this variation in border thickness must be taken into account. The PaletteOffsets Dictionary associates each host platform with its appropriate adjustment. The information provided by PaletteOffsets is very similar to that provided by the UIPainter class variable ControlsOffsets (see Section 7.1.1.2).

7.1.4.4 Opening a Palette

A Palette can be opened with a canvas, from a Launcher, from the canvas <operate> menu, or from the Canvas Tool. The Launcher opens a Palette from its toolsPalette action method shown below.

> **toolsPalette**
> "Open a new Palette."
>
> UIPalette openPalette

When a Palette is opened either initially with the canvas or subsequently from the canvas <operate> menu or Canvas Tool, the message openPaletteFor: mainWindow is sent to the UIPainter. The argument mainWindow is the ApplicationWindow of the canvas and the Palette is opened to the left of this canvas. The openPaletteFor: method checks to see if a Palette is already opened for this canvas (see the findPalette method below). If this is the case, that Palette is raised or expanded so that it is to the left of the canvas. If there is not a Palette already opened for the UIPainter, then the UIPainter sends the message openPaletteNear: mainWindow to the UIPalette class, which opens the Palette next to the canvas. The UIPainter also makes sure that this Palette is a slave window to the canvas window.

Since the Palette is opened as a slave of the canvas, the ApplicationWindow of the Palette is a dependent of the UIPainter. So when the UIPainter wants to see if it already has a Palette open that is just hidden or collapsed, it checks its dependents collection. The UIPainter does this in its instance method findPalette shown below.

findPalette

```
^self dependents
    detect:
        [:dpndnt |
        ((dpndnt isKindOf: ApplicationWindow) and:
            [dpndnt model isKindOf: UIPalette])]
    ifNone: nil
```

7.1.4.5 The Prebuild Operation

The interface described in UIPalette class>>windowSpec contains only the placement control buttons (select and sticky), the tool name field, and an empty composite. It does not contain any of the component selection buttons! In addition to this, UIPalette does not have action methods defined for either the placement control buttons or the component selection buttons. All of these things are taken care of in the prebuild and postbuild operations.

In its prebuild operation, UIPalette populates its builder's bindings with models for its select and sticky buttons. The model for the select button is a PluggableAdaptor whose responsibility it is to put all instances of UIPainterController in select mode whenever the select button is pressed. It does this by placing a SelectMode object in the UIPalette class variable CurrentMode, which is a ValueHolder. Recall that all instances of UIPainterController reference this very same instance of ValueHolder with their currentMode instance variable. The model for the sticky button is UIPainterController's class variable StickyMode, which is a ValueHolder on a boolean. Since this is a class variable, the sticky button on *each* Palette controls the sticky behavior of *all* canvases. It is interesting to note that each instance of UIPalette references (indirectly) a UIPainterController class variable, StickyMode, and each instance of UIPainterController references a UIPalette class variable, CurrentMode.

7.1.4.6 The Postbuild Operation

The postbuild operation for a UIPalette is very involved. The UIPalette accesses the interface's empty composite, whose component ID is #iconView, and makes this the builder's current composite. This ensures that any component specs added to the builder will populate this particular composite. UIPalette then iterates over its activeSpecs variable, which is an Ordered-Collection of component spec classes, and for each class in the collection it does the following.

- Creates an action button spec describing the action button that will represent that component spec in the Palette

- Acquires an image from the component spec class and places this image in its builder's visuals cache to serve as the label for the action button

- Constructs a PluggableAdaptor and places it in the builder's bindings cache to serve as the model for the action button

- Creates a layout for the action button spec so that the button will appear in one of three columns

- Adds the action button spec to the builder, thereby adding the action button to the Palette's interface

At this point the Palette user interface is complete and can be opened. This dynamic construction of the component selection buttons allows the Palette to be customized merely by editing the ActiveSpecsList class variable.

7.1.5 UICanvasTool

The Canvas Tool provides all the functionality of the canvas <operate> menu, plus it is responsible for setting the grid, fencing, and look policy parameters for the canvas. The Canvas Tool is implemented by UICanvasTool, which is a subclass of UIPainterWatcher (see Chapter 8, Section 8.1.1). The Canvas Tool interface is shown in Figure 7.3.
    Disk Example 7.4 illustrates some of the UICanvasTool concepts covered in this section.

7.1.5.1 User Interface Description

The Canvas Tool has a main menu, which mirrors that of the canvas <operate> menu very closely. It adds two main selections, however: **Grid** and **Look**. The **Grid** selection displays a submenu that allows the developer to control the gridding in the canvas. The **Look** menu selection displays a submenu that allows the developer to set the look policy

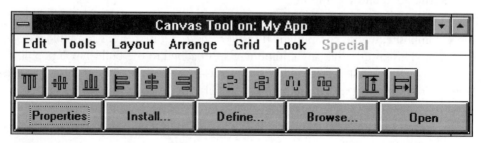

Figure 7.3. Canvas Tool Interface.

of the canvas. In addition, the Canvas Tool interface provides buttons for easy access to certain canvas control operations such as arranging components, installing the canvas, and opening a Properties Tool.

7.1.5.2 Instance Variables

UICanvasTool defines five instance variables, which are listed in Table 7.7.

7.1.5.3 Opening a Canvas Tool

A Canvas Tool can be opened from the Launcher, with a canvas, or from the canvas <operate> menu. The Launcher opens a Canvas Tool from its toolsCanvas action method shown below.

> **toolsCanvasTool**
>   "Open Canvas Tool."
>
>   UICanvasTool new openInterface: #windowSpecTight

When a Canvas Tool is opened either initially with the canvas or subsequently from the canvas <operate> menu, the message openToolsFor: mainWindow is sent to the UI-Painter, where mainWindow is the canvas ApplicationWindow. The openToolsFor: method checks to see if there is a Canvas Tool already opened for this canvas (see the findControls method below). If this is the case, that Canvas Tool is raised or expanded such that it is just above the canvas. If there is not a Canvas Tool already opened, then the UIPainter sends the message openToolsNear: mainWindow to self, which opens the Canvas Tool above the canvas. The UIPainter also makes sure that the Canvas Tool window is one of its slave windows.

Since the Canvas Tool is opened as a slave of the canvas, the ApplicationWindow of the Canvas Tool is a dependent of the UIPainter. So when the UIPainter wants to see if it already

Table 7.7. UICanvasTool Instance Variables.

Variable	Description
menuBar	A Menu that is the main menu for the window.
controller	A UIPainterController that is the controller for the corresponding canvas.
arrangeMode	A ValueHolder on a Symbol. Currently, this value is initialized to #first and never changed.
constValue	A ValueHolder on an Integer. Currently, this value is initialized to 25 and never changed.
statusBarText	A ValueHolder on a string, which is the window label of the corresponding canvas.

has a Canvas Tool open that is just hidden or collapsed, it checks its dependents collection. The UIPainter does this in its instance method findControls shown below.

findControls

```
^self dependents
    detect:
        [:dpndnt |
        ((dpndnt isKindOf: ApplicationWindow) and:
            [dpndnt model isKindOf: UICanvasTool])]
    ifNone: nil
```

7.1.5.4 Menu Items and Action Button

The menu items and action buttons provide the same functionality as that provided by the canvas <operate> menu. The exceptions are the **Grid** and **Look** menu items (see Section 7.1.5.6). In either case, the corresponding action messages are initially fielded by the UICanvasTool. Since the UICanvasTool references the UIPainterController with its controller instance variable, the UICanvasTool merely forwards the action message on to the UIPainterController.

7.1.5.5 Current Controller

Unfortunately, it is not quite that easy. Before the UICanvasTool can forward the message to the UIPainterController, it must make sure that it is referencing a UIPainterController and that it has the correct instance. It does this in the controllerDo: instance method. The argument is a block that contains the code to forward the action message onto the controller, and this block takes a single argument—the controller of interest. The controllerDo: method makes sure the correct UIPainterController is referenced and then evaluates the block with this particular controller as the single argument.

7.1.5.6 Grid and Look Menu Selections

The **Grid** and **Look** menu selections are used to actually populate instance variables in the UIPainterController. These variables are: showGrid, gridStep, griddedHorizontally, griddedVertically, fenced, and currentLook. In this respect, the UICanvasTool is an editor for its corresponding UIPainterController.

7.1.5.7 Updating on Current Selection

The UICanvasTool is notified each time the selection changes in the canvas. It is notified by receiving the message reloadSelectionInformation. It inherits this ability from its superclass UIPainterWatcher (see Chapter 8, Section 8.1.1). Based on the current selection, the UICanvasTool will disable/enable the arrange buttons and certain menu items. It also makes sure that the controller is still there (i.e., the canvas is still open). If it is not, everything is disabled except for the **Properties** button.

7.2 Painting a Canvas

Since *VisualWorks* is a GUI builder, one of its most obvious features is building a GUI! In short, this involves opening a canvas, editing that canvas, and installing the canvas as an interface for some application model. In *VisualWorks*, this process is often referred to as *painting a canvas*. This section covers the mechanics of painting a canvas as a whole, which includes

- adding components
- selecting components
- cutting, copying, and pasting components
- grouping components
- ordering components

Editing the individual components themselves as well as editing the window's attributes is covered in Section 7.3.

7.2.1 Adding a Component

In order to add a component to a canvas, the developer selects a component type by pressing its corresponding component selection button in the Palette. Then he moves the mouse over to the canvas and drops the component in the canvas. It is important to realize that when the developer is adding a component to the canvas, he is adding a genuine instance of a *VisualWorks* component and not just some mock representation.

We have already seen that adding a new component to the canvas is nothing more than adding a component spec to the UIPainter's builder (see Section 7.1.1.7). Furthermore, when the developer selects a component in the Palette, he is actually selecting a component spec. When he clicks the mouse inside the canvas, he is telling the UIPainterController to add the component spec to the builder. The builder then builds the component and adds it to the interface. All the topics covered in this section are further illustrated in Disk Example 7.5.

7.2.1.1 Selecting a Component

The process of adding a component begins when the developer selects a component represented in the Palette. When the developer presses a component selection button in the Palette (see Figure 7.1), that action button view sends value: true to its model. The model is a PluggableAdaptor whose model is UIPalette's class variable CurrentMode. This class variable is a ValueHolder on a control mode object. When the PluggableAdaptor receives the message value: true, it evaluates its put block. This block in turn sends the following message to its model, the CurrentMode ValueHolder.

> value: (self placementFeelFor: aSpecClassName)

The code segment (self placementFeelFor: aSpecClassName) returns a placement mode object referencing the component spec class whose name is aSpecClassName. The placement mode object is either a DragPlacementMode or SelectPlacementMode depending on the current user settings (see Chapter 8, Section 8.3.3 for more on user settings). As an example, if the developer presses the component selection button for a list component, the argument aSpecClassName will be #SequenceViewSpec and (self placementFeelFor: aSpecClassName) will evaluate a placement mode object, which references the SequenceViewSpec class.

7.2.1.2 Spec Generation Blocks

Each of the concrete component spec classes is responsible for returning a block called a spec generation block. A **spec generation block** is used to instantiate a component spec for the purpose of creating the component that the developer intends to drop into the canvas. This block is accessed from the component spec class using the specGenerationBlock class message. A spec generation block takes two arguments: a UIPainterController and a Point. The Point represents the mouse position within the canvas where the component is to be placed, that is, where the developer clicked the mouse to drop the component. When a spec generation block is evaluated, it returns an instance of a component spec with default characteristics and a layout that is a function of the Point argument. Since the Point represents where inside the canvas the developer clicked the mouse, we want the component to show up at that location.

7.2.1.3 Entering the Canvas

After the user has pressed a Palette's component selection button, he will move the mouse over to the canvas window. As soon as the UIPainterController becomes the current controller, it sends the message

> mouseEnteredAt: aPoint inController: self

to its control mode. At this point, the control mode is one of the placement mode objects— either a DragPlacementMode or a SelectPlacementMode. If the control mode is a SelectPlacementMode, nothing happens when UIPainterController becomes the current controller. If the control mode is a DragPlacementMode, however, the component spec is created from the spec generation block and added to the builder of the canvas window using the same add: message used to add components to a runtime interface (see Section 7.1.1.7). The builder in turn builds the corresponding component from the component spec and adds the component to the UIPainterView. The UIPainterView then has the new component draw itself in the canvas window. As the mouse moves within the canvas, a drag mode is used to change the bounds of the component such that the component appears to follow the cursor.

7.2.1.4 Dropping the Component

When the user presses the <select> mouse button, the controller sends the following message to its control mode.

> redDownAt: aPoint inController: self

If the control mode object is a DragPlacementMode object, then the component, which has been following the mouse cursor up to this point, comes to rest at that location. If the control mode object is a SelectPlacementMode, then the spec is added to the canvas's builder at that time, which builds the corresponding component and adds it to the UIPainterView. In both cases, the procedure of adding a *VisualWorks* component is complete and the control mode is changed back to a SelectMode object, which is the default control mode. Again, it should be emphasized that any change of control mode affects all instances of UIPainterController by virtue of the fact that they all reference the same ValueHolder for their control mode—the UIPalette class variable, CurrentMode.

7.2.2 Making a Selection

Before anything can be done to a component, it has to be selected. Some canvas-editing operations, such as grouping and aligning, require more than one component to be selected. Also, for certain operations requiring a multiple selection, it is necessary that one of the selections be distinguished as the primary selection. A **primary selection** is a single component among a group of selected components that is used as a frame of reference for certain group operations such as aligning and equalizing.

All selecting and unselecting is done by a SelectMode object. A SelectMode object is the default control mode object for the UIPainterControllers. All UIPainterControllers are in select mode whenever the value of the ValueHolder in the UIPalette class variable CurrentMode is a SelectMode object. The topic of selecting components covered in this section is also illustrated with some concrete examples in Disk Example 7.6.

7.2.2.1 Types of Selections

There are three types of selections: a single selection, a multiple selection with a primary selection, and a multiple selection without a primary (for now, a *no selection* is not considered as a kind of selection). Each of these is discussed in turn below. All selected components, including any primary selection, are held in the UIPainterController's selections instance variable. If there is a primary selection, it is additionally referenced by the primary-Selection instance variable.

7.2.2.2 Single Selection

A single selection consists of exactly one selected component. A single selection is made in one of three ways. First, when a component is first added to the canvas, by means of a Palette selection or a paste operation, it becomes the single selection automatically. Second, a <select> mouse button click on a component already in the canvas will make that component the single selection. Third, a <Tab> or <Shift>-<Tab> will transfer a single selection from the currently selected component to the next component in the tab order. When a single selection is made, any current selection, single or multiple, is automatically unselected.

All selections, including single selections, are made by a SelectMode object. When a SelectMode object determines a component should be selected, it sends the select: message to the UIPainterController with the component to be selected as the argument. Once a single selection is made, the UIPainterController instance variable primarySelection references that component and the selections variable references a collection with that component as its only element.

Selection status can be transferred from one component to the next using the <Tab> key and <Shift>-<Tab> key combination. These keys will unselect the current selection and select the next (previous) component in the tab order. These keys do nothing when there is a multiple selection. The tab order is dictated by the ordering of the components in the UIPainterView's components collection. When the UIPainterController fetches a <Tab> event from its sensor, it sends the action message selectNextElement to self (the UIPainter-Controller class variable KeyboardDispatchTable binds the tab event to the selectNextElement action message). It is this method that unselects the current single selection, and selects the next component in the UIPainterView's components collection. In a similar fashion, the <Shift>-<Tab> event results in a selectPrevElement action message.

7.2.2.3 Multiple Selection with Primary

A multiple selection with a primary selection consists of two or more selected components, one of which has been marked as the primary selection. The primary selection is always the first component selected. The components selected in addition to the primary selection are referred to as *additional selections*. The additional selections are added with a <Shift>-<select> mouse click or a <Shift>-<select> mouse drag. The handles of additional selections are distinguished from handles of the primary selection by white dots at their center.

Like all selections, additional selections are made by a SelectMode object. It does this by sending the message additionalSelections: aCollection to the UIPainterController where the argument aCollection is a collection of components to be added as additional selections. A UIPainterController references the primary selection with its primarySelection instance variable, and it references all selections, including the primary, with its selections variable. It is the selections instance variable that is updated when additional selections are made, while the primarySelection variable remains unchanged.

7.2.2.4 Multiple Selection Without a Primary

A multiple selection without a primary selection is made by drawing a rectangle around all the components to be included in the selection. This is true even if there is already one or more selected components. With this technique, there is no way to distinguish one of the components as the primary. To make a multiple selection without a primary, the SelectMode object uses a default Screen service for drawing a rectangle in the canvas. It then determines which components fall entirely inside the bounds of this rectangle. All those that qualify are placed in a collection, which is sent to the UIPainterController as the argument in the message selectionList:. This collection becomes the new selections collection. If there is only one element in the collection, then it is also made the primary selection. Otherwise, there is no primary selection and primarySelection instance variable references nil.

7.2.2.5 Unselecting

Just as important as selecting components is unselecting them. There are three ways to unselect a component:

- Unselect all components in the selection.

- Unselect one component in the selection.

- Select a currently unselected component, which automatically unselects all of the components in the current selection.

Unselecting the components using the mouse is the responsibility of a SelectMode object. Unselecting as a result of a <Tab> or <Shift>-<Tab> event is strictly the responsiblity of the UIPainterController, and no control mode object is involved.

To unselect all the components in the current selection, the developer clicks the <select> mouse button outside of the bounds of any components, in which case the SelectMode object sends the message removeSelections to the UIPainterController. To unselect a single component from a multiple selection, the developer performs a <Shift>-<select> mouse click inside the bounds of that component, in which case the SelectMode sends the message removeSelection: aComponent to the UIPainterController. When the developer selects a currently unselected component, the SelectMode sends the message removeSelections-InController:, which unselects any currently selected components. Also, when the developer hits the <Tab> key or <Shift>-<Tab> key combination, the message selectNextElement (selectPrevElement) is sent to the UIPainterController, which unselects any current selections.

7.2.3 Cut, Copy, and Paste

Canvas painting is much like text editing. Just as with text, a selected portion of the canvas interface can be cut or copied and then pasted. Also as with text editing, selections can be cut or copied from one canvas and pasted to another. Cutting, copying, and pasting components are illustrated in Disk Example 7.7.

7.2.3.1 Paste Buffer

The canvas paste buffer consists of two UIPainterController class variables: ScrapPrimary and Scrap. Each of these is a SpecCollection object. There are three points of interest about the canvas paste buffer. First, the fact that class variables are used allows components to be cut or copied from one canvas and pasted to another. This is because all UIPainterController objects have access to the same class variables (this same technique is used by ParagraphEditor for working with text).

The second point of interest is that the paste buffer consists of two variables and not just one. This is necessary because a UIPainterController can distinguish between a primary selection and additional selections. This distinction should not be lost in the processes of cutting, copying, and pasting. Therefore, the ScrapPrimary variable holds the primary selection and the Scrap variable holds the additional selections. Notice that this differs from how the corresponding instance variables distinguish the primary from the additional selections. The instance variable selections references *all* selections including the primary. The corresponding class variable, Scrap, references *only* additional selections and does not reference the primary selection.

The third point of interest is that it is not the components that are copied to the paste buffer, but their spec objects. Component specs provide a convenient means for copying components that are currently embedded in an interface. Instead of having to release a component's widget from its model, uncouple the component from the visual structure, and do any other special procedures for copying, we can simply copy the component's spec, which is a rather simple object to copy. After all, the component's spec describes the component and can be used to recreate multiple copies of the component, so why not copy the spec to the paste buffer in lieu of the component itself? So, instead of copying components to the paste buffer, we are actually copying component descriptions, or component specs, to the paste buffer. The Scrap and ScrapPrimary class variables both reference SpecCollection objects to hold these component specs.

7.2.3.2 Cut

A selected component or set of components can be cut from the canvas by selecting **edit→cut** from the <operate> menu or by pressing one of the keys bound to the action method cutKey:. The result is that the action message doCut is sent to the UIPainter-Controller. The doCut method does the following.

1. Acquires the collection of selected components

2. Notifies the controller that the canvas has changed

3. Places the copies of the component specs of the selected components into the paste buffer

4. Removes any of the selected components that happen to be named components from the builder's collection of named components

5. Empties the selections instance variable since the selected components are now removed from the canvas

6. Removes the components from the UIPainterView and releases the components from any models

After doCut is finished, the components are no longer a part of the canvas, but copies of their specs reside in the paste buffer.

7.2.3.3 Copy

A selected component or set of components can be copied from the canvas to the paste buffer without being removed from the canvas. This is done by selecting **edit→copy** from the canvas <operate> menu or by pressing one of the keys bound to the copyKey: action method. The result is that the action message doCopy is sent to the UIPainterController. This does nothing more than put copies of the selected components specs in the paste buffer. No changes are made to the canvas.

7.2.3.4 Paste

When one or more component specs are in the paste buffer, they are available for pasting into a canvas. When the developer selects **edit→paste** from the <operate> menu or presses one of the keys bound to the pasteKey: action method, the doPaste message is sent to the UIPainterController. The doPaste method adds the SpecCollections in the paste buffer to the builder. By adding the component specs to the builder, new instances of the components are automatically created, added to the UIPainterView, and drawn on the screen. The do-Paste method also selects these components and updates the UIPainterController instance variables selections and primarySelection.

7.2.4 Grouping Components

Grouping occurs when the developer elects to manipulate the current selection of components as a single component. A group is actually a *VisualWorks* component called a composite component and has its own component spec. The composite component is the only *VisualWorks* component that is not available from the Palette. Instead, it is manufactured in the canvas based on the current set of selected components. This composite manufacturing process is referred to as *grouping*. Once a composite component has been manufactured, it can be selected, manipulated, and edited just like any other *VisualWorks* component. Disk Example 7.8 gives some concrete examples of the topics covered in this section.

7.2.4.1 Composite Component

When the developer selects **arrange→group** from the canvas <operate> menu or presses the <Esc> <g> key sequence, the message doGroup is sent to the UIPainterController. The doGroup method does nothing more than forward the message doEmbed. The doEmbed method does the following.

1. Makes sure there is more than one currently selected component, makes a copy of this collection of components, and unselects these components

2. Starts a new composite in the canvas window's builder

3. Iterates through the collection of selected components, adding each component to the new composite and removing it from the UIPainterView

4. Creates a CompositeSpec corresponding to the new composite component and adds it to the canvas's builder

5. Makes the new composite component the current selection

7.2.4.2 Ungrouping Components

A group of components that have been grouped into a composite component can also be ungrouped. That is, the composite is decomposed into its original components, and these components become the currently selected components. When the developer selects **arrange→ungroup** from the canvas <operate> menu or presses the <Esc> <u> key sequence, the message doUngroup is sent to the UIPainterController. The doUngroup method merely forwards the message doExtract. The doExtract method does the following.

1. Captures the list of components in the current selection, loads these components into the sels temporary variable, and then unselects them

2. Iterates over the sels collection to determine which elements are composites and which ones are not, collects the composites in the temporary variable composite-Selections, and collects the simple components in the temporary variable new-Selections

3. Iterates of over the composite selections and decomposes each one, and then for each constituent component, calculates its layout, adds it to the UIPainterView, and adds it to the temporary variable newSelections

4. Makes the temporary variable newSelections the current set of selections

There are three interesting things about the ungrouping behavior. First, ungrouping works for multiple selections. It even works if some of the components in the selection are not composite components (e.g., action buttons and input fields). Consider a multiple selection where some of the selected components are composite components and some are not. The ungrouping behavior will decompose each of the composites, completely ignoring the remaining components. The second item of interest about ungrouping is that the doExtract method is also the method used to decompose a subcanvas into its constituent parts using the <Shift> key and **arrange→ungroup** menu selection in combination. And finally, the ungrouping behavior is not recursive. That is, if a composite component contains other composite components among its constituent parts, then these contained composite components will *not* be decomposed as well.

7.2.5 Ordering Components

There are four operations a developer can perform to change the ordering of the components. By ordering of the components, I mean the order in which they appear in the UIPainterView's components collection. This ordering affects both the order in which the components display themselves in the window and the order in which tabable components take focus (see Chapter 6, Section 6.3).

The four operations affecting the ordering of components include moving the selected component(s) forward one spot, back one spot, to the front of the collection, or to the back of the collection. The UIPainterController has a method for each of these cases, and these methods are invoked by a selection from the canvas <operate> menu (see Table 7.6). Each method is implemented in much the same way. The controller records that the canvas has changed, hides the handles, tells its view, the UIPainterView, to do the reordering, and then shows the handles again. The real work is done in the UIPainterView. It is responsible for actually reordering its components collection and then redrawing the effected components in the canvas (see Section 7.1.2.4).

7.3 Editing Components and the Window

This section focuses on the editing activities, which apply to a either a component selected in the canvas or to the window when no component is selected. In this section we will look at

- how properties are set for a component

- setting a component's layout

- generating and browsing code

- setting a component's color attributes

- editing the window's properties

7.3.1 Properties

The properties of a component are all of the attributes of the component described by the component spec. This can include a variety of things depending on the type of component. Among the more common attributes are such things as aspect method, menu method, ID, label, color (look preferences), and layout. Each of these attributes is stored in the component spec. Not included in this definition of properties are such things as the component's actual menu or any images used by the component. Menus and images are not included in the component spec but are provided by a source object as resources. The component spec does need to know the method name, however, used to look up such resources.

The component properties are edited by the Properties Tool, which is implemented by UIPropertiesTool (discussed in depth in Chapter 8, Section 8.2.1). The developer opens a Properties Tool from either the canvas <operate> menu (UIPainterController>>doProperties) or from the Canvas Tool's **Properties** button (UICanvasTool>>openPropertyTool).

The important thing to remember is that when the developer sets the properties for a component, he is actually editing a copy of that component's spec object. After all, generating specs is the purpose of a canvas–editing session, not generating components. If the developer accepts his changes, a new component is created from this edited copy of the original component spec, and this new component replaces the current component in the canvas. So the developer is not actually editing a component, but replacing it with a newer version based on an edited copy of the orginal component's spec object. The notion of the Properties Tool editing component specs is illustrated in Disk Example 7.9.

7.3.2 Layout and Position

A very important attribute for every component is its layout. This determines where in the window the component appears and how much real estate it consumes. This section reviews the concepts of bounds and layout and covers all the ways that a component's bounds can be changed. See Disk Example 7.10 for some concrete examples of the topics covered in this section.

7.3.2.1 Component Bounds and Layout

It is necessary that you understand the distinction between bounds and layout. A *bounds* is the particular real estate a component occupies in its window and is always expressed as a Rectangle. A *layout* is an object that determines how a component's bounds is to be calculated. A layout can be either a Point, a Rectangle, a LayoutOrigin, an AlignmentOrigin, or a LayoutFrame. A component's bounds is a function of its layout and perhaps some other attributes such as its container's bounds. A component's layout is recorded in its component spec.

7.3.2.2 Bounded and Unbounded Layout

A component's layout can be either bounded or unbounded. A *bounded component* has an origin and definite dimensions given the current dimensions of the window (or container). A typical example of a bounded component is an input field whose dimensions are either fixed (e.g., 20 pixels high and 100 pixels wide) or are a function of its container's bounds (e.g., 20 pixels high and half as wide as its container). In either case, given the dimensions of the container, the input field's dimensions are fixed. An *un-*

bounded component has an origin, but its dimensions are unknown because they depend on several parameters that remain unknown until runtime. In addition, these dimensions do not depend at all on the window's (or container's) dimensions. A good example of an unbounded component is a label whose origin is known but whose dimensions depend on such things as the number of characters in the label and the particular font used to display the label. The dimensions of a component are more properly referred to as the *extent*.

The type of bounds can be changed for the selected component(s) by selecting **layout→be bounded** or **layout→be unbounded** from the canvas <operate> menu. Each of these results in a message being sent to the UIPainterController—doMakeBounded or doMakeUnbounded, respectively. Both of these methods have the same implementation. They remove the currently selected components from the canvas. Then they iterate over these components changing the layout to the indicated type (bounded or unbounded). Finally, they add the changed components back to the canvas as new components.

7.3.2.3 Relative or Fixed Layout

A layout can be relative or fixed. A *relative layout* is some function of the container's bounds and is expressed by a LayoutOrigin, an AlignmentOrigin, or a LayoutFrame. To make a component's layout relative, the developer selects **layout→relative** from the <operate> menu. This results in the message beRelativeKey: being sent to the UIPainterController. The argument for this message is ignored by the method. The implementation of the beRelativeKey: method is to send beRelativeIn: aBounds to each of the components in the current selection. Each of the components is a SpecWrapper, of course, and aBounds is a Rectangle describing the size of the container. The SpecWrapper implementation of beRelativeIn: aBounds, shown below, changes the spec's layout to be a relative layout and then changes the component's layout, which causes a visual update of that component.

> **beRelativeIn: containingBounds**
>
>   spec beRelativeFor: self bounds containedBy: containingBounds.
>   component layout: spec layout

A *fixed layout* is independent of the container's bounding box and is either a Point or a Rectangle. To make a component's layout fixed, the developer selects **layout→fixed** from the <operate> menu. This results in the message beFixedKey: being sent to the UIPainterController. As with beRelativeKey:, the argument is ignored. The implementation of the beFixedKey: method is to send beFixedIn: aBounds to each of the components in the current selection. The SpecWrapper implementation of beFixedIn: aBounds, shown below, changes the spec's layout to be a fixed layout, and then changes the component's layout, which causes a visual update of that component.

beFixedIn: containingBounds

> spec beFixedFor: self bounds containedBy: containingBounds.
> component layout: nil

7.3.2.4 Handles

Whenever a selected component is moved or resized, its handles are hidden first. After the component is moved or resized, the handles are redrawn. These operations are done with the UIPainterController methods hideHandles and showHandles. The handles are hidden by removing them altogether from the UIPainterView's components collection. They are shown again by adding them back to the components collection. Regardless of whether the handles are currently in the UIPainterView's components collection or not, the UIPainterController always references them with its handles instance variable.

7.3.2.5 Moving and Resizing with the Mouse

The most obvious way to move or resize a component is with the mouse. The developer moves a component by dragging it with the mouse. Dragging involves holding the <select> button down and moving the mouse. This functionality is provided by a SelectionDragMode object. That is, the UIPainterController's control mode object is a SelectionDragMode for dragging behavior.

The developer can also use the mouse to resize the currently selected component. The developer does so by dragging on one of its four handles. In general, this type of dragging is handled by a CornerDragMode object; there are two special cases, however: the slider and divider components. A slider component is resized using an OrientationResizeMode object. This type of mode object guarantees that the slider will always be oriented such that its sliding motion occurs along the major axis. Resizing a divider component requires a DividerResizingDragMode object. Dividers are special because they only have two handles, not four like the other types of components, and can only be resized along their major axis.

7.3.2.6 Moving and Resizing with the Keyboard

A developer has the option of moving and resizing the selected component with the keyboard—or more specifically, the arrow keys. Each arrow key will move the currently selected component one grid in that particular direction. When the meta keys <Shift> and <Ctrl> are used in conjunction with the arrow keys, a single side of a component can be moved by one grid.

When the UIPainterController acquires a keyboard event from its sensor that involves an arrow key, it dispatches one of four messages based on the exact arrow key. These messages are listed in Table 7.8.

Table 7.8. UIPainterController Arrow Key Control.

Message	Behavior
bumpDownKey: ignored	Move the selected component down one grid. If <Shift> is down, then move the top border only. If <Ctrl> is down, then move the bottom border only.
bumpLeftKey: ignored	Move the selected component left one grid. If <Shift> is down, then move the right border only. If <Ctrl> is down, then move the left border only.
bumpRightKey: ignored	Move the selected component right one grid. If <Shift> is down, then move the left border only. If <Ctrl> is down, then move the right border only.
bumpUpKey: ignored	Move the selected component up one grid. If <Shift> is down, then move the top border only. If <Ctrl> is down, then move the bottom border only.

These actions are not restricted to just a single selection but will apply to all components in the current selection.

7.3.2.7 Moving and Resizing with a Dialog

The developer can invoke a dialog to edit a component's layout by selecting **layout→ constrained...** from the <operate> menu. There are two versions of this dialog: one for bounded layouts and one for unbounded layouts. The UIPainterController class method layoutFrameDialog returns a full spec literal array describing the interface for the bounded layout dialog. This dialog edits a LayoutFrame object to be the component's layout. The class method placementFrameDialog returns a full spec literal array describing the interface for the unbounded layout dialog. This dialog edits an AlignmentOrigin object to be the component's layout.

The appropriate dialog is opened when the developer selects **layout→constrained...** from the canvas <operate> menu. This sends the fractionalConstraintDialog message to the UIPainterController. This method determines the selected component's layout to be either bounded or unbounded and forwards the appropriate message. If the component's layout is bounded, then the message

fractionalConstraintDialogForRectangular: sel frame: frame

is sent, and if the layout is unbounded then the message

fractionalConstraintDialogForOriginal: sel frame: frame

is sent. Each of these creates one of the two dialogs mentioned above from the appropriate full spec literal array. In both cases, the dialog edits the layout object, and if the developer selects the **OK** button, then the selected component's layout is replaced with the edited layout and the component is redrawn.

Table 7.9. Group Layout Methods.

Menu selection	Special key	Action method	Interface method
arrange/align…	\<Esc> \<a>	alignDialog	alignDialogSpec
arrange/distribute…	\<Esc> \<d>	distributeDialog	distributeDialogSpec
arrange/equalize…	\<Esc> \<e>	equalizeDialog	equalizeDialogSpec

7.3.2.8 Arranging

Certain types of postioning operations apply only to groups of components. These positioning operations are referred to as *arranging* the components. The three arranging operations are align, distribute, and equalize. Each of these can be performed by the Canvas Tool, a dialog, or a special key. The dialogs can be invoked by an \<operate> menu item or a special key (see Table 7.9). UIPainterController class has the full specs for each of these dialogs and it has an instance method dedicated to opening each.

7.3.2.9 Gridded Position

The grid is very crucial to the positioning of components. It determines the granularity of movement. The UIPainterController has four variables that determine the grid. These four variables are changed by various selections from the Canvas Tool menu. The showGrid variable is a ValueHolder whose value is a Symbol and indicates whether the grid is on or off. The gridStep variable is a ValueHolder whose value is an Integer that determines the size of the grid in pixels. The variables griddedHorizontally and griddedVertically are each a ValueHolder on a boolean and indicate the axes to which gridding is applied. Turning off the grid is the same as having a grid of one pixel, so we can assume that there is always grid. The grid affects only the editable canvas; it does not apply during runtime.

If a component is currently not positioned according to the grid, the developer can either drag its handles until it snaps to the grid or select **layout→grid snap** from the \<operate> menu. As a result of this menu selection, the doSnapSelectionToGrid message is sent to the UIPainterController. This method positions the component according to the closest grid coordinates.

7.3.3 Generating and Browsing Code

VisualWorks does a limited amount of code generation. For components, this amounts to adding instance variables to the target class and compiling aspect methods and resource methods (for menus and images). The UIDefiner generates the aspect methods and action methods and adds the corresponding instance variables. The Menu Editor and Image

Editor generate the resource methods. While painting a canvas, the developer can browse the existing application model code.

7.3.3.1 Code Generation

Code generation for a component's aspect methods is the responsibility of the definer. The definer is an instance of UIDefiner, and the UIPainter references it with its definer instance variable. In order to generate code for the currently selected component(s), the developer selects **define...** from the canvas <operate> menu. This results in the message doDefine being dispatched to the UIPainterController. The doDefine method merely tells the UIPainter's definer to upgrade the source code in the target class. The UIPainter's definer is an instance of UIDefiner. The UIDefiner class is discussed in detail in Chapter 8, Section 8.1.2.

7.3.3.2 Browse Method

In order to browse the method(s) of the currently selected component(s), the developer selects **browse...** from the canvas <operate> menu, which sends the message doBrowse to the UIPainterController. The doBrowse method checks to make sure that there is a target class and that each of the selected components has an aspect method in that class. If this is the case, then each component's model is collected in a Set called models. In edit mode, a component's model is represented by a Symbol, which is the name of an aspect method in the target class. If each component's model has a corresponding method in the target class, then a Method Browser is opened on all of these methods.

7.3.4 Color

Color is a very important attribute of a component. Recall that a *VisualWorks* component has the option of maintaining its own color scheme, which is a LookPreferences object. This object defines colors for background, foreground, selected background, and selected foreground. The selected component's look preferences can be set only from the Color slice of the Properties Tool. This portion of the Properties Tool is implemented by ColorToolModel, which is an application model used as a subcanvas of the Properties Tool. The ColorToolModel is discussed in detail in Chapter 8. A ColorToolModel edits a copy of the selected component's LookPreferences object. In fact, it is convenient to think of the ColorToolModel as a LookPreferences editor. If the developer accepts the changes in the ColorToolModel, then the edited copy is sent back to the selected component, a SpecWrapper, with the lookPreferences: message. When a SpecWrapper receives the lookPreferences: message, it

- updates its WidgetState with the new LookPreferences

- invalidates itself so it will be redrawn in the new colors

- updates its component spec with a copy of the LookPreferences

7.3.5 Window

The window is not a *VisualWorks* component, but it is similar to a component in that the developer sets its properties just as if it were a component. Unlike the components, the window does not have a SpecWrapper containing its corresponding spec. Instead, the window's spec is kept by the UIPainter.

The window has its own set of properties. These properties are displayed by the Properties Tool whenever there are not any selected components. The developer has the option of defining the window's minimum, maximum, and preferred extent. These are set by resizing the canvas window and selecting the appropriate selection from the <operate> menu or the Canvas Tool menu. The window's creation origin is whatever the current origin of the canvas window happens to be at the time of installation. The developer can also set the window's look preferences by using the Color slice of the Properties Tool.

7.4 Other Painting Functions

There are several painting functions not covered so far, such as spawning a copy of the canvas, opening other tools, installing the canvas, and opening the runtime interface.

7.4.1 Spawning

Spawning is the process of one canvas opening another canvas with a copy of its own interface. A canvas can be spawned by selecting the canvas <operate> menu selection **edit→spawn**. This results in the message doSpawn being sent to the UIPainterController. The doSpawn method does the following.

1. Creates a new instance of UIPainter

2. Populates the new UIPainter's targetClass, targetSelector, and acceptedState instance variables with those of the current UIPainter

3. Creates a full spec from the current canvas

4. Populates the new UIPainter's windowSpec variable and builds the new canvas

5. Replaces the canvas window's controller with a new instance of UIPainterSystem-Controller

6. Populates the new UIPainter's three window extent variables with the corresponding values in the current UIPainter

7. Makes the new UIPainter the application of the new canvas window

8. Opens the new canvas along with a Palette and a Canvas Tool (user settings permitting)

7.4.2 Menu and Image Editors

There are two additional tools that complement the canvas painting tools. These are the Image Editor and Menu Editor. Each of these tools will be discussed in detail in Chapter 8. The Menu Editor and Image Editor are mentioned here only with respect to how they are launched from the Launcher, the canvas, and the Canvas Tool.

7.4.2.1 Opening from the Launcher

Both tools are opened from the Launcher by selecting the **Tools→Menu Editor** and **Tools→Image Editor**, respectively. These menu selections invoke action methods, which simply send the open message to their respective classes, UIMenuEditor and UIMaskEditor.

7.4.2.2 Opening from the Canvas

The canvas <operate> menu opens these tools with the **tools→menu editor** and **tools→image editor** selections, respectively. These invoke the corresponding UIPainterController action methods menuEditor and maskEditor. These methods will open the corresponding tool on the selected component should it currently have a menu/image to edit. Otherwise, the tools are opened blank.

7.4.2.3 Opening from the Canvas Tool

The Canvas Tool opens the Menu Editor with its **Tools→Menu Editor** menu selection and the Image Editor with its **Tools→Image Editor** menu selection. Each of these invokes an action message, which defers execution to the UIPainterController with the appropriate message—menuEditor and imageEditor, respectively.

7.4.2.4 Tool Operation

The Menu Editor and Image Editor are like the Properties Tool in that they can operate on the current selection of any open canvas (provided that component can take a menu/image). They can read in a copy of the current menu/image of the component and edit it or they can start a new menu/image. They can then apply the edited copy back to the component by installing it as a resource in the target class. Both tools can also operate independently of any canvas–painting session.

7.4.3 Installation

Installation starts with an **install** selection from the canvas <operate> menu or by pressing the **Install...** button in the Canvas Tool. In either case, the message doInstall is sent to the UIPainterController, who merely forwards the message installFor: self to its model, the UI-Painter. The UIPainter method installFor: aController is shown below.

installFor: aController

```
"make sure anything unaccepted is applied by the PropertiesTool"
aController broadcastPendingSelectionChange.
(self targetTrouble or:
    [(UIPainter preferencesFor: #avoidInstallationDialog) not or:
        [ScheduledControllers activeController sensor shiftDown]])
ifTrue:
    [self runInstallationDialog isNil
        ifTrue: [^nil]].
self installInSystem.
aController canvasHasChanged: false
```

7.4.3.1 Conditions for Installation

The first statement in the method above makes sure that any changes in the Properties Tool are applied before installation. The second statement runs the installation dialog if any one of the following conditions is true.

- There is no target class or selector.

- The developer has not set the preference to skip the installation dialog.

- The shift key is down.

The interesting thing about the installation dialog is that it is defined in the UIFinderVW2 class. The installation dialog is responsible for making sure that the UIPainter has a target class and selector in which to place the literal spec for the canvas.

7.4.3.2 Installing the FullSpec

If all conditions are OK for an installation, then the third statement in the installFor: method dispatches the installInSystem message. This is the method that actually performs the installation. Its implementation is shown below.

installInSystem

```
FullSpec
    store: self makeFullSpec
    toClass: self targetClass class
    methodName: self targetSelector.
Transcript cr; show: self trgetClass name, '>',self targetSelector, ' defined'.
UIFinderVW2 installed: (Array with: self targetClass name with: self targetSelector).
self accept
```

This method makes a full spec by sending makeFullSpec to self (the UIPainter) and passing the return value as an argument, along with the target class and selector, to the FullSpec class. It is the FullSpec class that is actually responsible for converting the full spec to a literal array and compiling the target method. Next, the method above sends notification of the change in the system to the System Transcript. The UIFinderVW2 is also updated and the current state of the canvas is accepted.

7.4.3.3 Creating the FullSpec

The last interesting aspect of the installation process is how the full spec is created. It starts in the makeFullSpec method, which is implemented in UIPainter as shown below.

makeFullSpec

```
| spec |
spec := FullSpec new.
spec window: self makeWindowSpec.
spec component: self makeSpecCollection.
^spec
```

Recall that a full spec is just a combination of a window spec and a spec collection. Therefore, the makeFullSpec factors out its responsibilities among two more methods, makeWindowSpec and makeSpecCollection. The makeWindowSpec method edits the UIPainter's windowSpec instance variable with information in the canvas window and with the UIPainter's maxWindowExtent, minWindowExtent, and prefWindowExtent instance variables. The makeSpecCollection method makes a SpecCollection by passing the collection of *Visual-Works* components in the UIPainterView's components collection to an instance of Spec-Collection, which iterates over this collection extracting the component spec from each spec wrapper. Disk Example 7.2 shows how easy it is to make a SpecCollection from a UIPainterView's collection of components.

7.4.4 Opening

The runtime interface is opened by selecting the canvas <operate> menu selection **open**. This dispatches the doOpen message to the UIPainterController. It is the doOpen method that opens the runtime interface. This method does the following.

1. Makes sure there is a target class and selector (if not, prompts user to define them)

2. Checks to see that the canvas does not have any unsaved changes (if so, prompts user to install)

3. Sends the openOn: aTarget withSpec: aSelector message to the target class where aTarget is an instance of the target class and aSelector is the target selector naming the interface spec method

7.5 Summary

The canvas painting tools are at the center of *VisualWorks* functionality and like all other *VisualWorks* tools, they are themselves *VisualWorks* applications. Just like its native language of Smalltalk, *VisualWorks* exhibits a self-generating quality. The canvas painting tools consist of five major constructs: a UIPainter, a UIPainterView, a UIPainterController, a UIPalette, and a UICanvasTool. The UIPainter is an application model and is in charge of the canvas-editing session. The UIPainterView is the component of the canvas window and manages the *VisualWorks* components as well as the drag handles. The UIPainterController actually runs the canvas-editing session and triggers various painting action methods based on mouse, keyboard, and menu input. The UIPainterController delegates the handling of mouse input to a control mode object. The Palette is opened and operated by an instance of UIPalette. It is responsible for putting all UIPainterController's in placement mode—the mode for adding a new component to a canvas. The Canvas Tool is opened and operated by an instance of UICanvasTool. It mirrors the functionality of the canvas <operate> menu and allows setting of the grid properties and look policy. The objective of editing a canvas is not to produce an interface, but to produce a full spec describing an interface.

To add a component to a canvas, a component spec class is selected by pressing the corresponding button in the Palette. The component spec class creates an instance of itself using a spec generation block, and this component spec is added to the UIPainter's builder. The builder then builds the component described by the component spec and adds it to the canvas interface. Selecting and unselecting are performed primarily with mouse input and are the responsibility of a SelectMode object. Selected components can be cut, copied, and pasted using either the menu items or the keyboard. The paste buffer consists of two class variables so that selections can be cut or copied from one canvas and pasted to another. The paste buffer actually contains component specs and not components. Grouping selected components involves removing them as components, adding them to a CompositePart, and adding the CompositePart as a new component. Changing the ordering of the components is primarily the responsibility of the UIPainterView, which knows how to reorganize the components in its components collection.

The selected component's properties are edited from a Properties Tool, which is opened by an instance of UIPropertiesTool. A component's layout/position is changed in several ways. The Properties Tool has a subcanvas run by an instance of PositionToolModel, which allows the user to edit a component's layout. Dialogs can be launched to edit the layout as well. Mouse input is handled by a SpecDragMode to move or resize a component. Keyboard events involving arrow keys trigger messages in the UIPainterController, which move or resize the components as well. Selections from the <operate> menu or the Canvas Tool menu change the kind of layout of a component or cause the UIPainterController to position the component according to the closest grid settings. Code generation for the components is primarily the responsibility of a UIDefiner contained within the UIPainter. The Properties Tool has a subcanvas operated by an instance of ColorToolModel, which allows the developer to edit a component's color (or LookPreferences). The properties of the window can be edited just like the properties of a component.

The remaining functions of the canvas-painting tools are spawning a canvas, opening other tools, installing the canvas, and opening the runtime interface. Spawning is handled by the UIPainterController. A Menu Editor and an Image Editor can be opened to provide menu and image resources for the components and the window. These are implemented by the UIMenuEditor and UIMaskEditor, respectively. These two tools can be opened from the Launcher, the Resource Finder, the canvas <operate> menu, or the Canvas Tool. Installing a canvas is the responsibility of the UIPainter. This action can be invoked by either the canvas <operate> menu or the Canvas Tool. The FullSpec is actually installed in the target by the FullSpec class. Opening the runtime interface is the responsibility of the UIPainterController.

8

Support Tools

THERE ARE SEVERAL other tools in *VisualWorks* besides the canvas painting tools discussed in Chapter 7. One category of tools, which includes such tools as the Properties Tool and Menu Editor, directly supports the canvas-painting process. I refer to these as *painter watchers* because they are constantly aware of the current selection in the current canvas. Another category of tools, such as the Resource Finder and Settings Tool, has a more ancillary role—supporting the overall effort of application development. There is even a category of tools, such as the System Browser and Workspace, that predates *VisualWorks* altogether and provides the most fundamental support for any Smalltalk development. In this chapter, however, we will only look at the first two categories—those tools that were developed by *VisualWorks* for *VisualWorks*. First, however, we will take a look at some special classes that support tool building in *VisualWorks*. This will be followed by a discussion of the various painter watcher tools that support the canvas-painting process. Finally, we will look at the remaining *VisualWorks* tools: the Settings Tool, the Launcher, the Resource Finder, and the Help Browser. The motivation for such an in-depth study of these tools is similar to that provided at the beginning of Chapter 7. We may want to extend these tools or create new ones (this is done in Chapters 13 and 14). There is also much to learn from the implementation of these tools, and such knowledge can help us in developing other applications.

8.1 Support Classes

There are several support classes that make the *VisualWorks* tools possible. Many of these, such as UIPainterController and UIPainterView, have already been discussed in considerable detail (see Chapter 7). This section is dedicated to the remaining tool support classes. First we will discuss the UIPainterWatcher class, which is the superclass of all tools that need to interact with the current canvas. Next we will look at the UIDefiner, which supports a UIPainter with its ability to generate code. Finally, we will look at some of the more specific support classes used in the implementation of some of the other tools.

8.1.1 UIPainterWatcher

Several of the *VisualWorks* tools are interested in the current selection of the current canvas. Included in this list are the Properties Tool, Canvas Tool, Menu Editor, and Image Editor. These types of tools are called painter watchers because they are sensitive to any change of selection in any open canvas. Each time a selection is changed in any canvas, each of these tools will update to reflect the properties of the new selection. Since there is a shared behavior among these tools, they are all subclasses of the abstract class UIPainter-Watcher. Therefore, a **painter watcher** is a *VisualWorks* tool that is interested in the current selection of the current canvas and whose application model is a subclass of UIPainterWatcher. Very much related to UIPainterWatcher are SpecModel and IntegratedSpec-Model, which are abstract classes describing special types of subapplications appearing in *VisualWorks* tools.

8.1.1.1 Referencing Current UIPainterController

UIPainterWatcher defines an instance variable called selectionHolder. This variable is initialized to reference the UIPainterController class variable LastControllerWithSelection, which is a ValueHolder on a UIPainterController. That is, all painter watchers reference this same instance of ValueHolder with their selectionHolder variable. For example, if you have a Menu Editor, a Properties Tool, and an Image Editor open at the same time, each references this same ValueHolder with its selectionHolder instance variable. Each time any UIPainterController changes its selection or becomes the active controller, it registers itself as the value of this ValueHolder. In this way, each painter watcher has access to the current UIPainterController.

8.1.1.2 Notification of UIPainterController Activity

Since all painter watchers reference the same ValueHolder (see Section 8.1.1.1), they can each register as a dependent of that ValueHolder and be immediately notified each time its value changes. That is, each time any instance of UIPainterController changes its selection and makes itself the value of that ValueHolder, all painter watchers that are dependents of the ValueHolder are immediately notified with an update message. The UIPainterWatcher method watchPainter registers the painter watcher as a dependent of this ValueHolder variable, and the method dontWatchPainter removes the dependency.

8.1.1.3 Updating on a Change of UIPainterController

Each time a UIPainterController makes a change of selection in its canvas, each dependent painter watcher is notified by receiving an update:with:from: message from its selection-Holder variable (which, of course, is really the UIPainterController class variable Last-ControllerWithSelection). UIPainterWatcher's implementation of

> update: anAspectSymbol with: aParameter from: anObject

is to make sure the receiver's window is available to be visually updated and then to send reloadSelectionInformation to self (in this context, self is the concrete painter watcher instance such as a UIMenuEditor or a UIPropertiesTool). The method reloadSelectionInformation is the hook that all subclasses of UIPainterWatcher implement to update themselves because a change of selection has just occurred in a canvas. Therefore, each time a change of selection occurs in any canvas, reloadSelectionInformation is sent to each painter watcher that is a registered dependent of the LastControllerWithSelection ValueHolder. Those painter watchers that are not dependents of LastControllerWithSelection will not receive this message and, therefore, will not be notified of the change in selection.

8.1.1.4 Interface Control Protocol

UIPainterWatcher provides some nice facilities for its subclasses to manage the components in their interface. These are methods that make it easy to display, hide, enable, and disable components. These methods are referred to as *interface control protocol* since they facilitate manipulating the user interface. Table 8.1 lists these messages and describes their behavior (in Chapter 10 we will further explore the idea of interface control protocol).

Table 8.1. UIPainterWatcher Interface Protocol.

Message	Behavior
disableApply	Disable the component whose ID is #applyButton
disableRead	Disable the component whose ID is #readButton
enableApply	Enable the component whose ID is #applyButton
enableRead	Enable the component whose ID is #readButton
disableGroup: idList	Disable the components whose IDs are in the collection idList
enableGroup: idList	Enable the components whose IDs are elements in the collection idList
vanishGroup: idList	Make invisible the components whose IDs are elements in the collection idList
reappearGroup: idList	Make visible the components whose IDs are elements in the collection idList

8.1.1.5 Subclassing UIPainterWatcher

A painter watcher tool is an instance of a concrete subclass of UIPainterWatcher. Such concrete subclasses include UIMenuEditor and UIPropertiesTool, among others. Each concrete subclass of UIPainterWatcher will want to override the reloadSelectionInformation method to do whatever is necessary to update its particular user interface based on the new canvas selection. Any painter watcher tool can always reference the current UIPainter-Controller by way of its selectionHolder instance variable. Invariably, the current UIPainter-Controller contains information, such as the current selection, required by a painter watcher in order to do its job. Each concrete subclass should also know certain message protocol for communicating with the components in the canvas. Examples of such protocol are lookPreferences: for changing the component's color and beRelativeIn: for changing the components layout type.

8.1.1.6 SpecModel

SpecModel is an abstract subclass of ApplicationModel. It provides state and behavior for its subclasses, which are used as subapplications for subcanvases appearing in other tools. These subapplications are used for editing some portion of a component's (or the window's) spec properties and are referred to as *spec models*.

SpecModel defines one instance variable, specChannel, which is a ValueHolder. The value of specChannel is the current selection in the current canvas. A spec model registers as a dependent of this instance variable so that it can be notified whenever the current selection of the current canvas has changed. Upon this notification, the spec model can update its interface.

The behavior of a spec model is very similar to that of a painter watcher. The difference is that a painter watcher is notified of a change in component selection directly by the UIPainterController class (see Section 8.1.1.1). A spec model, however, is notified by its parent application, which directly changes the value of the spec model's specChannel variable. The parent application is always a painter watcher, so when the parent application is notified of a change of selection in a canvas, it then notifies its subapplication, which is a spec model.

8.1.1.7 IntegratedSpecModel

IntegratedSpecModel is an abstract subclass of SpecModel. It describes spec models that will be used specifically by a UIPropertiesTool to operate subcanvases, which edit a subset of component spec information called a slice (see Section 8.2.1). It adds the ability to read and apply spec information for the current selection. It has four concrete subclasses, each of which is a subapplication for a subcanvases in the Properties Tool. These subclasses are ColorToolModel, PositionToolModel, DataSetCallbacksSpecModel, and DataSetSpecColumnModel.

8.1.2 UIDefiner

The Define Dialog (see Figure 8.1) provides the facility for adding instance variables, aspect methods, and action methods to the UIPainter's target class. Recall from Chapter 7 that the target class is the class of application model for whom the UIPainter is painting an interface. The Define Dialog is opened by an instance of UIDefiner. The UIDefiner actually has two main responsibilities: opening the Define Dialog and compiling the methods for the aspects selected by the developer.

Each UIPainter has its own UIDefiner, which it references with its definer variable. It is the UIPainterController that tells the UIDefiner to open its Define Dialog. The UIPainterController does so each time the developer selects **define...** in the canvas <operate> menu.

8.1.2.1 Instance Variables

UIDefiner is a subclass of Object and defines three instance variables, described below.

aClass   A Smalltalk class, usually a subclass of
ApplicationModel, which is the target class
for the code generation.

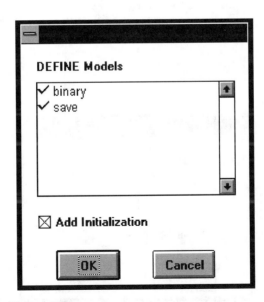

Figure 8.1. Regular Define Dialog Interface.

initializeModels   A ValueHolder on a boolean, which indicates if the compiled methods should include lazy initialization. This ValueHolder also serves as the aspect model for the **Add Initialization** check box in the UIDefiner's dialog interface.

excludedBindings   An IdentityDictionary whose keys are Symbols and whose values are aspect models. Each Symbol is the name of a component's aspect method, and each value is the default aspect model associated with that component. This dictionary includes all aspect methods which should *not* be generated.

8.1.2.2 User Interface

UIDefiner defines the specification for two dialog boxes: the *regular* Define Dialog and the *small* Define Dialog. The regular Define Dialog is used when there is more than one method to compile. The interface for the regular Define Dialog is defined in the UIDefiner's class method defineDialogSpec and is shown in Figure 8.1.

    The small Define Dialog is used when there is exactly one method to generate. The interface for the small Define Dialog is defined in the UIDefiner's class method smallDefineDialogSpec and is shown in Figure 8.2.

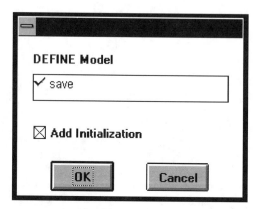

Figure 8.2. Simple Define Dialog Interface.

Both of these dialogs are opened from the UIDefiner instance method

openDefinitionDialogOn: models selecting: modelsToDefine

This method returns a collection of Symbols, which are the names of the aspects and actions the user has selected for code generation. The method returns nil if the developer cancels.

8.1.2.3 The Code-Generation Process

The following is a three-step summary of how the UIDefiner generates methods and defines instance variables.

1. The process starts when the user selects **define...** in the canvas <operate> menu, which results in the message interactivelyUpgradeDefns:for: being sent to the UI-Painter's definer, which is a UIDefiner.

2. The interactivelyUpgradeDefns:for: method is quite long, but its main responsibility is to pop up a dialog asking the user to select the methods that need to be defined. The dialog also allows the user to turn off the lazy initialization for the aspect methods.

3. The method writeDefinitions: bindings for: aController is actually responsible for generating the methods and defining the necessary variables. It creates a string of Smalltalk code in the same format as a file-out. This string is then filed-in to compile the code into the image.

8.1.3 Other Support Classes

There are several special classes of objects that make the functionality of the tools possible. The more predominant of these are ColorBitView, ColorBitEditor, ColoredArea, ColoredArea-Controller, DirectBitView, and GridWrapper. It is a good idea to know about these classes for two reasons. First, you may have need to change the tools that employ these classes. Second, you may want to reuse these classes in other projects, and knowing that they exist and what they can do will prevent you from having to reinvent them.

8.1.3.1 ColorBitView

A ColorBitView is used by a UIMaskEditor to allow a developer to display a magnified version of an image. This image serves as the model for the ColorBitView. A ColorBitView is gridded to indicate the actual pixels of the enlarged image. ColorBitView uses a ColorBitEditor as its controller so that the user can edit the image (see Section 8.1.3.2). A ColorBitView inherits all of its state and behavior from its superclass BitView.

BitView defines four instance variables: pixmap, policy, scale, and gridding. The pixmap variable is a Pixmap that is a magnified rendering of the model. The policy variable is an OrderedDither and determines how colors should be rendered. The scale variable is a Point and determines the magnification of the model used to create pixmap. The gridding variable is also a Point and indicates the grid size.

When a ColorBitView receives an image as its new model, that image is rendered on pixmap and magnified by the amount indicated in scale. The displayOn: method merely transfers pixmap to the graphics context.

A ColorBitView receives the update message update: aSymbol with: aParameter from its model. The argument aParameter is a Rectangle, which describes those pixels of the model that have changed and need to be redrawn. This information is used to update pixmap, which is then redisplayed on the screen. Disk Example 8.1 covers the ColorBitView and its related classes ColorBitEditor and DirectBitView.

8.1.3.2 ColorBitEditor

ColorBitEditor is the controller for a ColorBitView (see Section 8.1.3.2), and its model is an image. ColorBitEditor inherits most of its state and behavior from its superclass BitEditor.

ColorBitEditor defines a single instance variable, currentColor, which contains an integer. This integer is the index of a color in the image's palette. Whenever the developer clicks the <select>|<red> mouse button inside the ColorBitView, the ColorBitEditor receives the redButtonActivity message (this is a basic behavior inherited from ControllerWithMenu). This method merely dispatches the message colorPoint. The colorPoint method determines the mouse position and uses the view's scale to map this position to a pixel in the model, which is an image. It then changes the value of that pixel in the model to the integer held in its currentColor instance variable. Since the model changed, it updates the view so the developer sees the change as well. Disk Example 8.1 covers the ColorBitEditor and its related classes ColorBitView and DirectBitView.

For ColorBitView and ColorBitEditor, the model is an image. If you browse the hierarchy of Image, you will notice that Model is not included among its superclasses. This means that any dependents (i.e., the ColorBitView) are kept in the DependentsField class variable of Object and must be explicitly released. This is a good example of an object, which is not a kind of Model, acting as a model (see Chapter 1, Section 1.2).

8.1.3.3 ColoredArea

A ColoredArea is a view that fills its bounds with a single color. Its model is a ValueHolder on a ColorValue, and its default controller is a NoController. ColoredArea is used exclusively by ColorToolModel, although it certainly could be used in other areas as well.

ColoredArea defines two additional instance variables: select and wasSelected. The select variable is a ValueHolder on the ColorValue, which determines the color being displayed.

The wasSelected variable is a boolean and indicates whether the ColoredArea should display itself with a thick border or not. A ColoredArea registers as a dependent of both its select variable and its model and redraws itself based on updates sent from either. However, it only renders itself in the color contained by its select variable.

ColoredArea, as it is defined, differs from the traditional role of a view in two ways. First, its default controller is a NoController that does not handle input from the mouse or keyboard. When its controller is changed to a ColoredAreaController, however, it can be used interactively with the user. Second, a ColoredArea does not represent information in its model and changes in its model's value will not cause the ColoredArea to redraw itself in that new color. A change in the color value of its select variable will, however. Typically, a group of ColoredArea objects will depend on of the same model. Each of the colored areas will have a different color, and the model represents the selected color. The ColoredArea and its related class ColoredAreaController are covered in Disk Example 8.2.

8.1.3.4 ColoredAreaController

As mentioned above, a ColoredAreaController can be installed as the controller for a Colored-Area. A ColoredAreaController is a kind of SelectController. It is used to detect a <select> button down while the mouse is within its view's bounds. When this occurs, it updates its model with the value of its view's select variable. The ColoredAreaController and its related class ColoredArea are covered in Disk Example 8.2.

8.1.3.5 DirectBitView

DirectBitView is a subclass of View. A DirectBitView displays the contents of its model, which is a kind of Image. It is used by the UIMaskEditor to provide the developer with a current view of the image he or she is editing. It does not have a default controller and does not process any user input. It receives updates from its model and responds by rendering its model (an image) on its graphics context. Disk Example 8.1 covers the DirectBitView and its related classes ColorBitView and ColorBitEditor.

8.1.3.6 GridWrapper

GridWrapper provides a canvas with a visual representation of its grid used for positioning components. A GridWrapper is the component of the canvas ApplicationWindow and the wrapper for the UIPainterView (see Chapter 7, Section 7.1.2). It defines three instance variables: showGrid, grid, and gridPaint. The showGrid variable references the corresponding UIPainterController's showGrid variable, which is a ValueHolder whose value is either #On, #Off, or #Hidden. The grid instance variable is set to reference the UIPainterController's grid-Step variable, which is a ValueHolder on an integer. This integer indicates the size, in pixels, of the grid. The gridPaint instance variable indicates the color of the grid lines.

The displayOn: aGraphicsContext method will draw the grid only if the value of show-Grid is #On and the value of grid is greater than one. If both of these conditions hold, then the displayGridOn: aGraphicsContext is sent. It is the method displayGridOn: aGraphicsContext that actually draws the grid.

8.2 Painter Watchers

As mentioned in Section 8.1.1, a painter watcher is a tool that is interested in the current selection of the current canvas. The painter watcher tools are instances of concrete subclasses of UIPainterWatcher. There are four such classes, one for each type of painter watcher tool: UIPropertiesTool, UIMenuEditor, UIMaskEditor, and UICanvasTool. The latter, UICanvasTool, was covered in Chapter 7, Section 7.1.5.

The painter watchers directly support the canvas-painting process. A painter watcher is notified of any change of selection in any canvas. It is expected to update itself based

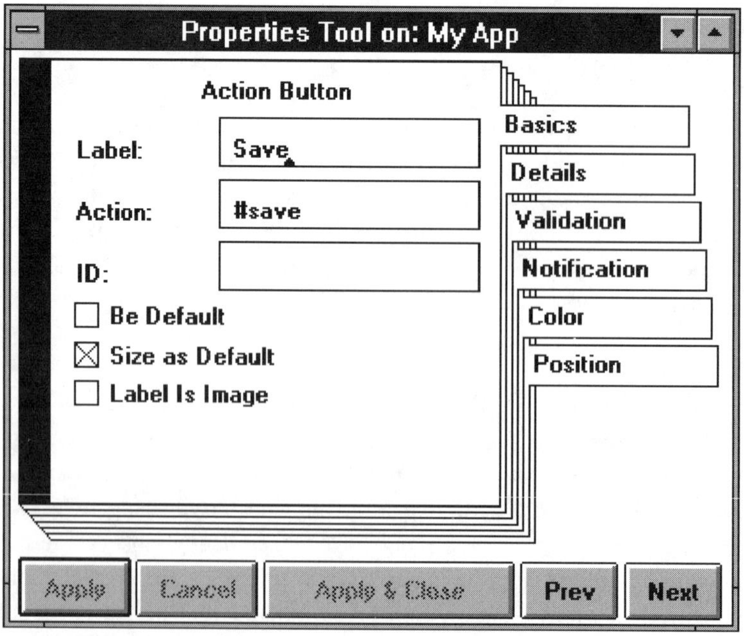

Figure 8.3. Properties Tool Interface.

on this selection. Like a UIPainter, the painter watcher tools are just *VisualWorks* applications built by *VisualWorks* (the meta-tool concept).

In this section we will take a brief look at the implementations of the three remaining painter watchers: Properties Tool, Menu Editor, and Image Editor. In addition, we will cover the Color Tool and Position Tool, which are not painter watchers themselves, but are integral parts of the Properties Tool.

8.2.1 Properties Tool

The Properties Tool is the means by which the developer edits the attributes of a component (or window) and is by far the most important of all the painter watchers. This usage of the term *properties* applies to all of those attributes of a component or window described by its spec. In fact, the Properties Tool is a component spec (window spec) editor.

The Properties Tool is a painter watcher, so it is aware of the current selection in the current canvas. Each time a new selection is made in a canvas (any canvas), every open Properties Tool updates itself with the spec values that correspond to the new selection. The Properties Tool is implemented by the class UIPropertiesTool, which is a subclass of UIPainterWatcher.

The Properties Tool consists of several subcanvases, each one editing a subset of the component's attributes. Each subset of attributes is referred to as a *slice*. (The slice concept is further discussed in Section 8.2.1.2.) The Properties Tool can use either a notebook component or a menu button to select which subcanvas will be displayed. Figure 8.3 shows the notebook version, which is the default. This particular version of the interface consists of a notebook component and five action buttons.

8.2.1.1 Instance Variables

UIPropertiesTool defines 17 instance variables, shown in Table 8.2.

Table 8.2. UIPropertiesTool Instance Variables.

Variable	Description
selection	An Array that includes all components—that is, SpecWrappers—that comprise the current selection in the current canvas.
selectionKind	A Symbol that is either #single, #multi, #window, or #none and indicates if one component is selected, many components are selected, or if no components are selected, in which case the window is the selection.
controller	A reference to the current UIPainterController operating the canvas in which the most recent selection was made.

currentSpecCopy	A copy of the spec object describing the currently selected component in the current canvas, i.e., the same component held by the SpecWrapper referenced by selection variable above. This spec object is what is to be edited by the Properties Tool.
currentSpecBindings	An IdentityDictionary that contains the bindings for the current subcanvas. The keys are Symbols naming the aspect models of the widgets in the subcanvas, and the values are AspectAdaptors which operate on currentSpecCopy, their subject, and are the models for the widgets in the subcanvas.
specChannel	A ValueHolder whose value is currentSpecCopy and serves as the subject channel for the AspectAdaptors in currentSpecBindings.
subBuilder	The UIBuilder used to rebuild the subcanvas each time a new selection is made in the canvas or a new slice of information is selected in the Properties Tool.
lock	A boolean used to indicate if the newly selected component is of the same type as that of the previously selected component. If it is the same type, then the subcanvas does not have to be rebuilt, merely re-populated with the new information.
slice	A ValueHolder on a Symbol. This serves as the model for the slices menu in the event that the menu option is used to select the slice. The value of this ValueHolder indicates which subcanvas to use.
lastSlice	A Symbol that is the name of the previous slice displayed by the UIPropertiesTool. This is used to make sure the interface is not needlessly redrawn when the new slice and previous slice are the same.
slicesMenu	A ValueHolder on a Menu. The Menu contains all the slices available for the current selection and is expected to be replaced with each new selection.
sliceInfo	An IdentityDictionary whose keys are slice names for the current selection and whose values are Arrays. The first element in each Array is the same as the key and the remaining elements indicate the source and location for that particular slice's subcanvas.
client	The client variable references the application model which runs the current subcanvas. It is either self (i.e. the UIPropertiesTool) or a spec model such as a PositionToolModel or a ColorToolModel.
statusBarText	A ValueHolder on a string. This string is the window label of the canvas being edited. UIPropertiesTool uses this string in constructing its own window label.
list	A SelectionInList that serves as the model for the note book component when that interface option is used. It has a List of Symbols that name the slices available for the current selection.
sliceChanging	A boolean set to true while a new subcanvas is being built. This prevents any multiple updates of the interface. Used only for the menu version of the interface.
sliceTabChanging	A boolean set to true while a new subcanvas is being built. This prevents any multiple updates of the interface. Used only for the notebook version of the interface.

8.2.1.2 Editing by the Slice

A **slice** is a subset of spec properties for the current selection. Associated with each slice is a subcanvas. This subcanvas is used to edit the set of properties represented by the corresponding slice. The six basic slices are shown in Table 8.3.

Not all component specs have all six slices. Some components even have a unique type of slice. Of the six slices in Table 8.3, only the first two will vary from one type of spec to the next. The remaining four are standard across all components that use them. For the window, only the Basics, Details, Color, and Position slices apply.

8.2.1.3 Spec Class Responsibility

Each spec class is responsible for supplying the list of slices required to edit its instances. The spec class is also responsible for providing the FullSpec objects describing both the Basics slice subcanvas and the Details slice subcanvas. The spec class also provides the mechanism for binding the components in these two subcanvases to their appropriate attributes in the spec object being edited. These bindings are AspectAdaptors, and the subject is the component spec (window spec) being edited. See Chapter 12, Section 12.1.2, for more on the role of the spec class in properties editing.

When a single component or the window is selected, then the UIPropertiesTool is updated for editing that component's spec object. It is the spec object's class that returns the slices list and interface descriptions for each slice. When more than one component is selected, however, there is potentially more than one type of component and therefore more than one source for the slices. In such a case, a MultiSpec is used instead of a component spec class. A MultiSpec is a spec object that describes the common attributes of several components. It allows the common properties of a group of components to be set

Table 8.3. Basic Slices.

Name	Description
Basics	Most fundamental properties such as label and aspect method
Details	Visual appearance and special behavior such as border, font, read only, and tabability
Validation	Messages to be sent to application requesting permission for a change of value, change of focus, or double click
Notification	Messages to be sent to application due to a change of value, focus, or double click
Color	LookPreferences of the component or window
Position	Layout of the component

at the same time. The MultiSpec class provides the slices list and interface descriptions for multiple selections.

8.2.1.4 Updating on a Change of Selection

A UIPropertiesTool is a painter watcher and therefore receives a reloadSelectionInformation whenever a new selection is made in the current canvas or when another canvas becomes the current canvas. The reloadSelectionInformation method as implemented in UIProperties-Tool does the following.

- Acquires the current UIPainterController from its selectionHolder variable

- Acquires the current selection within that controller

- Sets the currentSpecCopy and selectionKind instance variables based on the selection and its type

- Acquires the slices for the new selection and builds a menu

- Builds a subcanvas associated with current slice

8.2.1.5 Selecting a New Slice

When the menu interface is used, the developer selects a slice by making a selection in the pull-down menu. This changes the value of the slice channel that dispatches the setSpecChannel change message. This method uses the new value of the slice channel to acquire the corresponding interface spec from the class of the current component spec and rebuilds the subcanvas with that interface. When the notebook interface is used, the developer selects a slice by selecting a page in the notebook. The notebook takes care of swapping in the proper canvas.

8.2.1.6 Editing the Spec

At this point we have a copy of the spec of the currently selected component (or window, or a MultiSpec). This spec object is referenced by the currentSpecCopy instance variable. The widgets in the subcanvas effect changes in this spec object since their models are AspectAdaptors whose subject is this spec object. As soon as the first change is made to currentSpecCopy, the **Apply** and **Cancel** buttons are enabled and the **Prev** and **Next** buttons are disabled. This is possible because UIPropertiesTool has implemented the aspectFor: method so that each AspectAdaptor is fitted with two blocks as dependents. When the widget changes and sends the message value: to its AspectAdaptor, the AspectAdaptor evaluates these two blocks, which turn the appropriate buttons on and off.

8.2.1.7 Applying the Changes

When the developer presses the **Apply** button, the apply method is executed. There are several lines of code in this method, but the code of interest is the part shown below.

```
selection :=
    controller replaceElement: sel
    basedOnSpec: currentSpecCopy copy.
controller select: selection.
```

The code tells the UIPainterController to replace the currently selected component with the component described by currentSpecCopy. A copy of currentSpecCopy is actually used in case further spec editing is conducted. The selection is then reselected causing any other painter watchers to be updated appropriately.

8.2.1.8 Next and Previous Selections

The Properties Tool has the ability to index to the next or previous component in the current canvas. This allows the developer to sequentially edit several components without leaving the Properties Tool. The **Prev** button triggers the selectPrev method, and the **Next** button triggers the selectNext method. While both of these methods have several lines of code, most of this code is defensive programming. It is the last line in each case that is of interest. For the selectPrev method, this line reads

```
controller selectPrevElement
```

and for selectNext method, the last line reads

```
controller selectNextElement.
```

In each case, this line of code merely tells the current UIPainterController to select the previous or next component. Nothing more is necessary. The UIPropertiesTool will update automatically by virtue of the fact that it is a painter watcher and updates on any change of selection in any canvas. The **Prev** and **Next** buttons are only enabled if the currentSpec-Copy has not been changed or after changes have been applied.

8.2.2 PositionToolModel

The Position Tool is used by the Properties Tool to edit the Position slice of a component. It is a nonmodal version of the layout dialog boxes opened by the UIPainterController. It offers two advantages over the dialog version, however. First, it can toggle a component's layout between bounded and unbounded. Second, with the press of a button, it can clear all offset fields or clear the offset and proportion fields for a given side of the layout.

The Position Tool is implemented by PositionToolModel, which is a subclass of Integrated-SpecModel. As a subclass of IntegratedSpecModel, a PositionToolModel knows how to work within a UIPropertiesTool. It expects to be notified by the UIPropertiesTool whenever a new selection is made in a canvas or whenever the developer is trying to apply or cancel changes. The user interface for the Position Tool is shown in Figure 8.4.

8.2.2.1 Instance Variables

PositionToolModel defines 18 instance variables. These can be divided into two broad categories: those that apply to the tool at large and those that apply specifically to the layout parameters. Two instance variables apply to the tool in general: selectionType and tracking. The selectionType instance variable is a Symbol that indicates the type of layout for the current selection. Its possible values are #unknown, #frame, #original, and #na. The tracking instance variable is a boolean that is true while the information for the new selection is being loaded and false otherwise.

There are 16 variables that apply specifically to the layout parameters left, top, right, and bottom. For each of these layout parameters, there are three variables: a *fraction* variable, an *offset* variable, and a *slide* variable. The fraction variable is a ValueHolder with a string and serves as the aspect model for the corresponding fraction input field. The offset

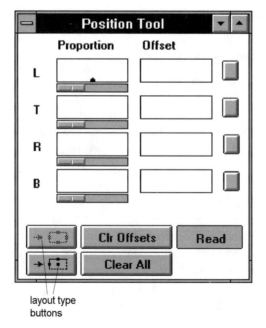

Figure 8.4. Position Tool Interface.

variable is also a ValueHolder with a string and serves as the aspect model for the corresponding offset input field. The slide variable is a TypeConverter and serves as the aspect model for the corresponding slider. There are four additional variables for aligning an unbounded component. There is an *alignment* and *alignment slide* variable for both the x and y coordinates.

8.2.2.2 Loading the Layout

Each time the UIPropertiesTool receives a reloadSelectionInformation message, it forwards the message on to the PositionToolModel so it can update as well. The PositionToolModel implementation of reloadSelectionInformation does the following.

- ▶ Sets the tracking variable to true and asks the UIPropertiesTool for the type of the current selection.

- ▶ If there is no selection, then the selection type is set to #na, buttons are disabled, and tracking is set back to false.

- ▶ If the selection is a multi-selection, then the selection type is set to #na and the appropriate buttons are enabled .

- ▶ Otherwise, the selection type is set and either the components for editing a bounded layout are made visible or the components for editing an unbounded layout are made visible.

8.2.2.3 Editing the Layout

The layout information, though numerical in nature, is captured as strings. Each time an input field is changed, the readMode variable is set to a value of false (the readMode instance variable definition is inherited from the superclass IntegratedSpecModel). All layout fields can be emptied from a variety of buttons. Each input field is emptied by sending the value: String new message to the corresponding aspect model.

8.2.2.4 Changing the Layout Type

The Properties Tool can toggle a component's layout type between bounded and unbounded. There are two action buttons in the interface that allow the developer to change the layout type. In Figure 8.4, these action buttons are referred to as the layout-type buttons. Each button has a corresponding action method, makeBounded and makeUnbounded, which is responsible for this feature. Since the UIPainterController already knows how to change a component's layout type, the implementation of these methods is to merely send the appropriate message, doMakeBounded or doMakeUnbounded, to the current UIPainterController. The PositionToolModel then reloads the information for the current selection, which is now of a different layout type, by sending itself the reloadSelectionInformation message. As an example, PositionToolModel's makeBounded action method is shown below.

makeBounded

```
| controller |
(controller := selectionHolder value) isNil ifTrue: [^self].
controller doMakeBounded.
self reloadSelectionInformation
```

8.2.2.5 Applying the Layout

When the developer wants to apply the layout described in the layout fields, he or she presses the **Apply** button, which triggers the apply action message in the UIPropertiesTool. The UIPropertiesTool then dispatches the message preapply to the PositionToolModel. The PositionToolModel implementation of the preapply method does the following.

- Checks to make sure there is a selection in the current canvas and, if not, then returns

- Acquires a collection of all components in the selection

- Determines the new layout for each component in this collection as described by the layout fields

- Validates each component's new layout and returns if one of them is degenerate (e.g., if the right border is postioned to the left of the left border)

- Iterates through the collection and sets each component's layout to be its new layout

- Redraws the canvas window to reflect these changes and resets the readMode variable to true

8.2.3 ColorToolModel

The Color Tool is used by the Properties Tool to edit the look preferences slice of a component (or window). The Color Tool is the only means by which a developer can set a component's color scheme (except for programmatically, of course). A component's colors are held in its look preferences. The component's spec, since it is required to recreate the component, also keeps a copy of the look preferences. The mission of a Color Tool is to read and edit the look preferences of the currently selected component(s) and to apply the edited look preferences back to the selected component(s). The Color Tool is actually a LookPreferences editor.

The Color Tool is implemented by the class ColorToolModel, which is a subclass of IntegratedSpecModel. As a subclass of IntegratedSpecModel, a ColorToolModel knows how to work within a UIPropertiesTool. It relies on the UIPropertiesTool to know when a new selection is made in a canvas and when the developer is trying to apply or cancel changes. The Color Tool user interface is shown in Figure 8.5.

8.2.3.1 Instance Variables

The ColorToolModel class defines five instance variables, which are described in Table 8.4.

The basic behavior is to first set the color value held by colorValue and displayed in the master color patch, and then to set one or more of the look preferences color patches to this same color. The color of the master patch can be set via the color cube, HSB sliders, the named colors menu, or one of the look preferences color patches.

The color of a look preferences color patch can be set by a <select> button click within its bounds. The first click will make its color the same as that of the master color patch. The next click will give it a nil color value, and it will appear transparent.

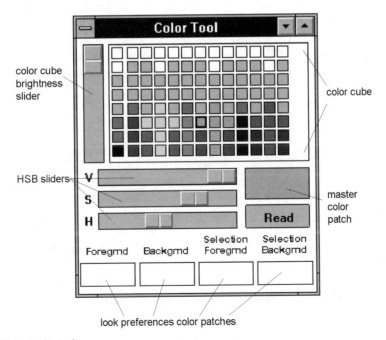

Figure 8.5. Color Tool Interface.

Table 8.4. ColorToolModel Instance Variables.

Variable	Description
cubesBrightness	A ValueHolder on a ColorValue that controls the brightness dimension for the color cube and serves as the model for the cube's brightness slider.
cubeColors	An OrderedCollection of ValueHolders, each with a value that is a ColorValue. Each of these colors is displayed as a cell in the color cube.
colorValue	A ValueHolder on a ColorValue that represents the master color. The master color patch is used to change the value of the look preferences color patches.
colorName	ValueHolder on a string that is the name of the color selected from the named colors menu.
lookPreferences	The LookPreferences object being edited by the tool.

8.2.3.2 Building the Interface

The interface of the Color Tool is defined in ColorToolModel class>>propSpec and consists of several parts (see Figure 8.5). Let's review these for purposes of naming consistency. Most of the window is consumed by the *color cube*. This is the grid of color patches. The axes of this grid control the hue and saturation dimensions of color. The color cube is referred to as a cube because the slider to the left controls a third dimension—brightness. This slider is referred to as the *color cube brightness slider.* Below the color cube are the *master color patch* and the *HSB sliders*. The four *look preference color patches* are shown along the bottom.

The Color Tool's interface presents a few interesting twists. First, there is the color cube, which is actually not a cube but a grid of colors and a slider. Then there are the color patches. The color patches are the small rectangular regions that visually indicate a color value. Finally, there is a triplet of sliders determining and indicating HSB for the current color selection.

The color cube is implemented as a composite, which is populated with 104 components during the build process. This happens in the setupVisuals method. These components are instances of ColoredArea (see Section 8.1.3.3 for more on ColoredArea). Each ColoredArea has the same model, colorValue, which is a ValueHolder. When a ColoredArea detects a <select> button hit, it changes the model's value to its own color. Thus, color-Value keeps track of the current color selection within the color cube. The color values are calculated from a formula that guarantees a representative distribution of the colors available on the current platform.

Included as part of the color cube is the brightness slider, which runs along the left side of the color cube. The model behind this slider is the cubesBrightness instance variable, and a change in its value forwards the change message changedCubesBrightness. The changed-CubesBrightness method iterates over the cubeColors collection, changing the brightness value of each color.

A look preferences color patch actually consists of an action button superimposed on a region. The action button triggers an action method, which changes that color patch's corresponding color in the lookPreferences instance variable to the color indicated by the master patch and redraws its region in the new color. If the color patch's color is already the same as the master patch, then it is set to nil and the region is drawn as transparent. The action buttons are themselves transparent because they have no border (see Chapter 2, Section 2.2.2.1, and Chapter 9, Section 9.5.1.5).

The master color patch consists of a composite superimposed on yet another transparent action button. The composite has a single component, a ColoredArea, whose model is colorValue.

The last interesting part of the interface are three sliders, which can set the master color using a combination of hue, saturation, and brightness (HSB). These sliders are also updated on a change of colorValue. Each time colorValue is changed, the message changed-Color is dispatched. This message updates the visibility of the HSB sliders based on the new color's saturation and brightness values. Each slider has as its model a PluggableAdaptor, which extracts just that component of colorValue in which the slider is interested. For example, the hue slider only looks at the hue component of the color value in colorValue. If the brightness is zero, both the saturation and hue sliders are made invisible. If the saturation is zero, just the hue slider is made invisible.

8.2.3.3 Editing Component Look Preferences

All of the Color Tool machinery discussed so far exists to edit a LookPreferences object. The look preferences is originally acquired from the current selection in the current canvas.

Since ColorToolModel is a subclass of IntegratedSpecModel, it is notified of any change of selection in any canvas by its UIPropertiesTool. The UIPropertiesTool does this by forwarding the reloadSelectionInformation message. The ColorToolModel implementation of reload-SelectionInformation makes sure the new selection is not the same as the previous selection and updates itself based on the new selection's look preferences. If there is no current selection, then the window's look preferences are used.

8.2.3.4 Applying the Look Preferences

When the developer wants to apply the colors described in the Color Tool, he presses the **Apply** button, which executes the apply action method in the UIPropertiesTool. The UI-

PropertiesTool then dispatches the message preapply to the ColorToolModel. The ColorToolModel implementation of the preapply method sets the look preferences of the currently selected component(s) to the look preferences in the ColorToolModel. If there are no currently selected components, then the window's look preferences are updated. Setting a component's (or window's) look preferences causes an automatic redraw, so the change is automatically reflected in the canvas. The preapply method also notifies the UIPainterController that its canvas has been changed and sets the value of readMode to true (the readMode instance variable definition is inherited from the superclass IntegratedSpecModel).

8.2.4 Menu Editor

The Menu Editor allows the developer to create a menu for a component or the window. The menu can be built and tested within the edit session. The menu is then stored as a literal array in a class method of the target class. The Menu Editor is implemented by UIMenuEditor, which is a subclass of UIPainterWatcher.

8.2.4.1 Instance Variables

UIMenuEditor defines six instance variables and no class variables. The instance variables are listed in Table 8.5.

Table 8.5. UIMenuEditor Instance Variables.

Variable	Description
targetClass	The class in which the menu is to be installed as a resource.
targetSelector	A Symbol that is the name of the class method which will define the menu.
menu	The actual Menu object built by the developer. It is also the value of menuBar.
menuBar	A ValueHolder used as a channel for the menu instance variable. Serves as the source of the menu for both the window and the menu button.
menuString	A ValueHolder on a string that serves as the model for the text component where the developer defines the menu.
modified	A boolean that indicates whether the developer has made a change or not.

8.2.4.2 Interface

UIMenuEditor defines its interface in its class method windowSpec. This interface consists of a text view, five action buttons, and a menu button. In addition to the menu button, the Menu Editor window has a menu bar. The menu bar and the menu button get their menu from the same source, the menuBar instance variable. The text view has its own <operate> menu, which it acquires from the class method fieldMenu. This menu facilitates the developer's efforts to describe the menu under construction.

8.2.4.3 Interface Opening

The Menu Editor can be opened from the Launcher, the canvas <operate> menu, the Canvas Tool, the Resource Finder, or by evaluating a resource class method's comment. If there is no specified target class and target selector, then the Menu Editor is opened as follows.

        UIMenuEditor open

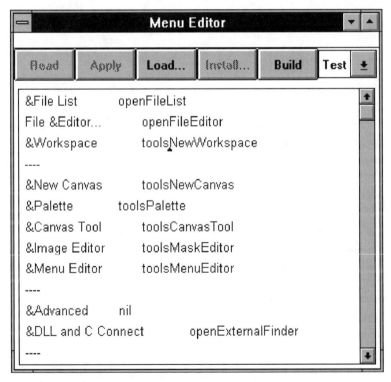

Figure 8.6. Menu Editor Interface.

If there is a target class and target selector, however, the Menu Editor is opened as shown below.

> UIMenuEditor new openOnClass: self andSelector: #resourceSelector

In this context, self is an application model class and #resourceSelector is a class method that returns an instance of Menu.

8.2.4.4 Updating on a New Canvas Selection

As a painter watcher, a UIMenuEditor receives the message reloadSelectionInformation whenever a new selection is made in a canvas or a new canvas becomes the current canvas. This method is responsible for enabling and disabling the **Apply** and **Read** buttons based on the current conditions of the canvas and the Menu Editor. If there is no current UIPainterController or if the current UIPainterController has a multiple selection, then both buttons are disabled and nothing more is done. Otherwise, the **Apply** button is enabled provided that the following conditions are true.

- The current selection (single component or window) can support a menu

- There is a Menu object in the menu instance variable

- In the case of the window, the Menu Editor's menu is of a full hierarchical structure

The **Read** button is enabled provided the current selection has a menu.

Even if the current selection has a menu, the Menu Editor does not automatically read in the menu for editing. The menu must be explicitly read in by pressing the **Read** button. Contrast this with the Properties Tool, Position Tool, and Color Tool, which automatically read in those attributes of the current selection that they are responsible for editing on each change of selection.

8.2.4.5 Building the Menu

Once the developer has described the menu in the text view, he or she builds the menu by pressing the **Build** action button. This forwards the build action message to the UIMenuEditor. The build method does the following:

1. Accepts the contents of the text view

2. Checks to see if the contents of the text view is an empty string and backs out of the menu-building process if the string is empty

3. Has the createMenu method build a Menu object from the string and loads this Menu into the menu instance variable

4. Loads this new Menu into the menuBar ValueHolder, which updates both the menu button and the window menu on the Menu Editor's interface so that the developer can test the new menu

5. Disables the **Build** button, enables the **Install** button, and enables **Apply** button provided the current selection in the current canvas can support a menu

The createMenu method mentioned in step 3 assumes the initial responsibility of building the Menu object, but the methods that actually do the work are makeMenuFromString:, bustUpLineFrom:, and createMenuAt:startingAt:in:.

8.2.4.6 Installing the Menu

A Menu can be installed as a static resource in an application model class (actually any class). The installation process creates a class method that contains the Menu as a literal array. The name of the target class and the target selector are contained in the UIMenuEditor's targetClass and targetSelector instance variables. The install method is responsible for the installation process and it does the following.

1. Makes sure it is OK to proceed with an installation. This includes making sure there is a target class and target selector.

2. Sends the message runInstallationDialog, which pops up a dialog prompting the developer to enter or verify the target class and target selector.

3. Sends the message installInSystem, which creates the class method and compiles it into the system.

8.2.5 Image Editor

The Image Editor allows the developer to create and edit color images of up to 16 colors. Such an image is installed in the application model class as a static resource in a class method. The image itself is represented in a store string format. The Image Editor is implemented by UIMaskEditor, which is a subclass of UIPainterWatcher.

8.2.5.1 Instance and Class Variables

UIMaskEditor defines 10 instance variables and one class variable. The instance variables are listed in Table 8.6.

UIMaskEditor defines a single class variable, PasteBuffer, which acts as the paste buffer for parts of the image that are cut or copied by the developer. By having the paste buffer

Table 8.6. UIMaskEditor Instance Variables.

Variable	Description
magnifiedBitView	A ColorBitView that is the part of the interface that the developer edits interactively.
directBitView	A DirectBitView that displays the real-sized image the developer is editing.
acceptedState	A copy of the image last time it was accepted, applied, installed, etc. Replaces current image when developer cancels last changes.
targetClass	The class on which the image will be installed as a resource.
targetSelector	The name of the class method that will contain the image as a resource for the target class.
modified	A boolean indicating whether the image has been edited since being loaded, read, applied, or installed.
menuBar	A Menu that is the window's main menu.
storeMask	A ValueHolder with a boolean that indicates whether the developer wants to install the image such that it represents a Mask.
useCachedImage	A ValueHolder with a boolean that indicates whether the developer wants to install the image as a CachedImage.
doTheCurrentColor	A ValueHolder on an empty string. Serves as the dummy model for the input field that is used to indicate the current color selection.

as a class variable, the developer can cut or copy from one Image Editor and paste to another.

8.2.5.2 Interface

UIMaskEditor describes its interface in its class method windowSpec. This interface spec describes a window with a window menu, several action buttons, and two arbitrary components: one for the color bit view and editor, and one for the direct bit view (see Figure 8.7). The color bit view and the direct bit view share a model, which is the image being edited. There are 16 action buttons used as color selectors and an input field used as the current color indicator field.

The menu is described in the class resource method maskEditorMenu. Both of the menu items **Image→Store Mask** and **Image→Cache** have a ValueHolder as a model to track whether that menu item is checked or not. These models are the instance variables storeMask and useCachedImage, respectively.

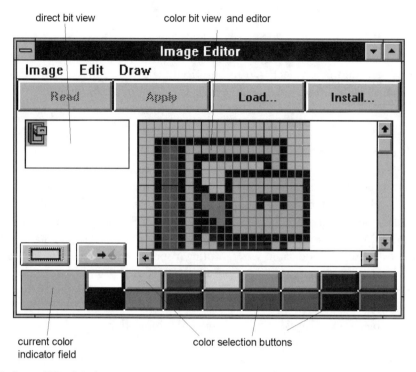

direct bit view   color bit view and editor

current color
indicator field

color selection buttons

Figure 8.7. Image Editor Interface.

8.2.5.3 Updating on New Canvas Selection

A UIMaskEditor receives the message reloadSelectionInformation whenever a new selection is made in a canvas or a new canvas becomes the current canvas. This method is responsible for enabling and disabling the **Apply** and **Read** buttons based on the current conditions of the canvas. If there is no current UIPainterController or if the current UIPainterController has a multiple selection, then both buttons are disabled and nothing more is done. Otherwise, the **Apply** button is enabled provided that the current selection can have a label (which means it can take an image). The **Read** button is enabled provided that the current selection already has a label that is an image.

If the current selection has an image for a label, the Image Editor does not automatically read in the image for editing. The image must be explicitly read by pressing the **Read** button. The Image Editor is like the Menu Editor in this regard and unlike the Properties Tool, which reads in the information automatically.

8.2.5.4 Selecting a Color

The Image Editor has 16 action buttons, which are used to make a color selection. In Figure 8.7 these are referred to as *color selection buttons*. Each of these action buttons has a different background color. Each action button also has its own action method but the implementation is the same. Take, for example, the doCyan action method below.

doCyan
    self setColorFor: #cyanButton

The implementation is to dispatch the setColorFor: aSymbol message where aSymbol is the ID of the corresponding action button component. The setColorFor: method accesses the action button component using the ID, reads that component's background color, and updates the color bit editor and the current color indicator field. The color bit editor is a ColorBitEditor (see Section 8.1.3.2) and it keeps track of the integer index that represents the current color selection in the image's palette (typically the image has a palette of 16 colors and each color is associated with an integer index of 0 to 15).

The *current color indicator field* is an input field that is used to indicate the current color selection. Each time a new color is selected, the background color of this input field is changed to the new current color. The aspect model for this field is doTheCurrentColor instance variable, however, it is never used since the input field is read only and it is used strictly to display the current color selection and not to receive user input.

The palette of 16 colors represented by the color selection buttons can be edited by opening UIMaskEditor in edit mode (i.e., opening a canvas on UIMaskEditor class>>window-Spec). All that is required is that one change the background color of the action buttons used to select the current color and install the canvas. The changes take effect upon opening a new Image Editor.

8.2.5.5 Draw and Edit Features

The Image Editor has nine draw and edit features to help the developer in the image design: clip, cut, copy, paste, fill current color, change a color to the current color, maski-fy, accept, and cancel. Each of these has a menu item and a corresponding action method implemented in UIMaskEditor. A few have action buttons as well.

8.2.5.6 Getting an Image

There are three ways to acquire an image for editing: load one from a class, read one from a canvas component, or capture one from the screen. Each of these corresponds to an action method implemented in UIMaskEditor—load, read, and grab respectively.

8.2.5.7 Image Storage Options

There are two options in storing an image. The first is to store the image as either a color or a black-and-white image representing a Mask (in *VisualWorks* 1.0 only the Mask option was available, hence the class name UIMaskEditor). The instance variable storeMask, which is a ValueHolder, keeps track of this attribute. If the value of storeMask is true, then the image is converted to a Depth1Image with a monocolored palette, which is used to represent a Mask. All white pixels of the original image are interpreted as transparent, and all remaining pixels of the original image are interpreted as opaque. The storeMask value is set by the **Image→Store B&W Mask** menu selection.

The second option allows the developer to store the image as a CachedImage. The instance variable useCachedImage, which is a ValueHolder, keeps track of this attribute. When the value of useCachedImage is true, the image is stored as a CachedImage, otherwise it is stored as an image. A CachedImage optimizes the speed with which an image is rendered on the screen. The useCacheImage variable is set by the **Image→Store Cached Image** menu item.

8.2.5.8 Installing the Image

There are two ways to save an image that has been edited: apply it to the current component or install it in a class. The apply process includes the install process. The installation process starts with the install action method. This method first runs the installation dialog if either the target class or target selector has not been defined or if the developer has not specified a preference for avoiding the installation dialog. It then sends the installInSystem message, which does the real installation. The installInSystem method does the following.

1. Acquires the image from the color bit view and if the developer has specified that the image is to be stored as a Mask, converts the image such that it can represent a Mask

2. Creates a write stream on a string and puts on that stream the target selector name and a method comment, which, when evaluated as Smalltalk code, will open the Image Editor on this method's image

3. Puts either the literal representation of the image on the stream or the literal representation of a CachedImage containing the image on the stream

4. Compiles the contents of the stream into the image, notifies the system transcript, accepts the image, and sets the modified variable to false

The apply method does the following:

1. Acquires target class and selector from the UIPainter of the current canvas

2. Installs the image to this target class and selector as described above

3. Edits the spec so that the component will use the image stored in the target class/selector as its label

4. Replaces the current selection with a component created from the edited spec, thereby giving the effect of redrawing the selection with the image as its label

8.3 Other Support Tools

This section covers the class of tools that are implemented as *VisualWorks* applications but do not directly support the canvas-painting process. These tools are the Settings Tool, the Launcher, the Resource Finder, and the Help Browser.

8.3.1 Settings Tool

The Settings Tool has two main responsibilities: it maintains a globally accessible list of user preferences and it provides a user interface for editing these user preferences. The other tools in *VisualWorks* depend a great deal on these user preferences. The user preferences include such things as the default system text style, the default look policy, and whether or not a Palette should be opened with a canvas. The Settings Tool is implemented by the class UISettings, which is a subclass of ApplicationModel.

In this section on the Settings Tool, we will look at the following.

▸ UISettings implementation with respect to the instance and class variables

▸ The user interface

▸ Single instance behavior

▸ User preferences accessing protocol

▸ Legacy user preferences protocol

See Disk Example 8.3 for some concrete examples on how the setting tool works.

8.3.1.1 Instance and Class Variables

UISettings defines three class variables, described below.

Development
SpecList

An Array of Associations. This class variable
references the UISettings class methods that
define interfaces for editing the development environment.

RuntimeSpecList

An Array of Associations. This class variable
references the UISettings class methods that
define interfaces for editing the runtime
environment.

UserPreferences

A Dictionary whose keys are Symbols and
values are value models—BlockClosure, ValueHolder, and PluggableAdaptor types—that
contain the user preferences. This Dictionary serves as the repository for all user
preferences systemwide.

UISettings defines a single instance variable, list, which is a SelectionInList. This SelectionInList
can be initialized to operate on either DevelopmentSpecList or RuntimeSpecList. The default
is DevelopmentSpecList, which is a superset of RuntimeSpecList. The runtime list includes
such things as default text size and the preferred look and feel style. The development list
adds to this such things as default canvas grid size. The default preference for which list
is used is kept, of course, in UserPreferences.

8.3.1.2 User Interface

The user interface for the Settings Tool consists of a notebook component (see Figure
8.8). The UISettings class protocol 'interface specs' contains all of the methods defining the
subcanvases used as the pages in the notebook component. The bindings for the components in these subcanvases come from the class variable UserPreferences. UserPreferences is a
Dictionary whose keys are Symbols and whose values are ValueHolder, PluggableAdaptor, and
BlockClosure objects. These objects not only maintain the current user preferences, but also
act as the aspect models for the components in the Settings Tool user interface. For example, from the Settings Tool, the developer can set the default grid size for all canvases
by changing the value of an input field. In UserPreferences, there is a key, #initialGridSize,
whose associated value is a ValueHolder, which holds on to this initial grid size and serves
as the aspect model for that input field.

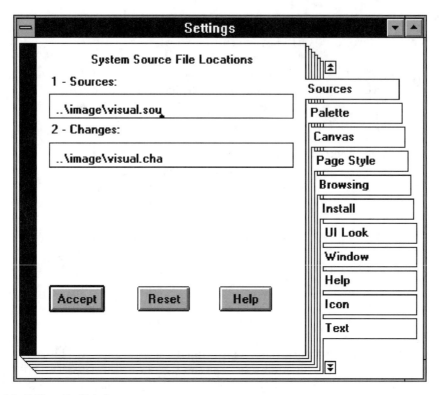

Figure 8.8. Settings Tool Interface.

When a UISettings is opened, the entire contents of UserPreferences is placed in the builder's bindings as part of the prebuild operation. Each component in the Settings Tool can then bind with its aspect model during the building process.

8.3.1.3 Single Instance Behavior

The opening mechanism for UISettings is such that only one instance of UISettings will ever be opened at a time. This behavior is implemented in the UISettings class method open shown below.

```
open
    | settingsView |
    settingsView := nil.
    UISettings allInstances size = 0 ifFalse: [ScheduledControllers scheduledControllers do: [:
c | Object errorSignal handle: [:ex | ex return]
        do: [(c model isKindOf: self)
```

```
                     ifTrue: [settingsView := c view]]]].
        settingsView isNil
          ifTrue: [Cursor execute showWhile: [super open]]
          ifFalse: [settingsView isCollapsed
                 ifTrue: [settingsView expand]
                 ifFalse: [settingsView raise]]
```

When the open message is sent to the UISettings class, it checks ScheduledControllers to see if there might already be an open instance of itself. If so, the window for this instance is expanded or raised such that it becomes the active window. Otherwise, a new instance is created and opened in the normal fashion.

8.3.1.4 User Preferences Accessing Protocol

UISettings contains all the user preferences in its UserPreferences class variable. Several tools and other objects in *VisualWorks* depend on these user preferences. For example, when a Canvas Tool is opened, its grid size, grid status, fencing, and look preferences are all initialized according to the preferences contained in the UISettings class. Any object in the image can access or change any of these preferences.

A user preference is accessed by sending the preferencesFor: aSymbol message to the UISettings class. The argument aSymbol is the key identifying the value model that holds on to the preference. The return value is the preference value itself and not the value model. That is, the statement

```
     UISettings preferenceFor: #initialGridSize
```

returns the integer that is the initial grid size, and not the value model containing that integer. The message preferenceModelFor: aSymbol, however, will return the value model. You can change the preference by changing the value of this value model. For example, the following statement will change the default grid size to 10 pixels.

```
     (UISettings preferenceModelFor: #initialGridSize) value: 10
```

Finally, the message

```
     preferenceModelFor: aSymbol put: aValueModel
```

will replace the value model associated with aSymbol. This will also disassociate any component in the open UISettings user interface that is currently bound to the value model being replaced.

8.3.1.5 Legacy Protocol

In *VisualWorks* 1.0, the UISettings class did not exist and the UIPainter class acted as the repository of the user preferences. Therefore, in version 1.0, all requests for preferences were directed at UIPainter. There are many objects in version 2.0 that still request preferences from the UIPainter class. The current UIPainter implementation of the class method preferencesFor:, however, is merely to forward the request on to UISettings as shown below.

preferenceFor: aSubject

> ^UISettings preferenceFor: aSubject

8.3.2 Launcher

The Launcher is the gateway into the rest of *VisualWorks* and is also referred to as the *VisualWorks* Main Window. It consists of the environment's main menu, a speed button bar, and a text view that operates as a system transcript. The Launcher is nothing more than a way to open the other tools, either by selecting a menu item, pushing an action button, or using a short-cut key.

The Launcher is implemented by VisualLauncher, which is a subclass of Application-Model. It defines more than 100 instance and class methods, but the vast majority of these are action methods and resource methods for the menu and action buttons. VisualLauncher defines three instance variables: menuBar, oldHeight, and textCollector. The menuBar variable references the menu so that the menu can be accessed and changed during runtime. The textCollector variable is initialized to be the global variable Transcript and serves as the model of the text view so the text view can operate as a system transcript. When the user unchecks the menu item **Tools→System Transcript**, the current height of the text view must be captured so that when the text view is reinstated it will have the same height. This height is recorded in the oldHeight instance variable.

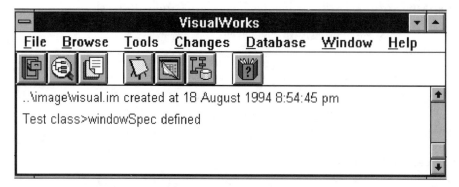

Figure 8.9. Launcher Interface.

8.3.3 Resource Finder

The Resource Finder is an organizational tool for *VisualWorks* development. It provides easy access to all of the resources found in the system. Counted among these resources are interface specs for canvases, images, menus, data models, and queries. It is easy to think of the Resource Finder as a special browser for such resources and the classes that contain them. In addition to these responsibilities, the finder supports the UIPainter, Menu Editor, and Image Editor with installation dialogs. It can also launch several other tools, such as the canvas-painting tools and an Image Editor. Finally, each time the resource-creating tools such as a canvas and the Menu Editor create, edit, or visit a resource, they are required to notify the Resource Finder so that it can keep a current account of the resource bearing classes. The Resource Finder is implemented by the class UIFinderVW2.

In this section on the Resource Finder, we will look at each of the following.

- The basic implementation with respect to interface, instance variables, and class variables

- The class filtering mechanism

- Operations performed on the selected class

- Operations performed on the selected resource

- How other tools update the Resource Finder

8.3.3.1 Implementation

UIFinderVW2 is a subclass of ApplicationModel, which defines 14 instance variables and 10 class variables (see Tables 8.7 and 8.8). In addition, it defines its main interface as well as 6 dialog interfaces. The main interface, defined in the class method windowSpec and illustrated in Figure 8.10, consists of a window menu, two lists, and five action buttons. The first list is the class name list and displays a certain subset of Smalltalk classes. The second list is the selector list and it displays all selectors of the selected class that return resources.

8.3.3.2 Filtering

A UIFinderVW2 can filter the list of resource-bearing classes. This filtering is performed by the seven action methods, whose names all start with show, as in showAllClasses or show-RecentlyVistedClasses. Each of these methods does the following:

Table 8.7. UIFinderVW2 Instance Variables.

Variable	Description
classNameList	A SelectionInList that holds the filtered list of class names. Serves as the aspect model for the class names list.
selectorList	A SelectionInList that holds the names of the resource-defining methods of the currently selected class. Serves as the aspect model for selector list.
iconList	A List of Associations whose keys are the selector names currently in the selector list and whose values are Symbols that indicate the corresponding icon to use in the selector list.
filter	A Symbol indicating the kind of filtering used to populate classNamesList.
menuBar	A Menu that serves as the window menu for the finder.
addWhat	Currently not used.
partSortType	A ValueHolder on a Symbol. The Symbol indicates how selectors are to be sorted in the list—#byName or #byType.
updateTrigger	Currently not used.
lastCategory	A Symbol naming the most recent category of classes displayed.
classListMenuForNoSelection	A Menu used as the <operate> menu for the class names list when no class is selected.
classListMenuWithSelection	A Menu used as the <operate> menu for the class names list when a class is selected.
menuBarMenuWithNoCanvasSelected	A Menu used as the window menu bar when a class is selected but no selector is selected.
menuBarMenuWithNoSelection	A Menu used as the window menu bar when no class is selected.
menuBarMenuWithSelection	A Menu used as the window menu bar when a class and a corresponding selector are selected.

1. Sets the filter variable to the name of the appropriate filtering method—#show-SystemClasses, for example

2. Changes the label above the class list appropriately—'System Classes', for example

3. Gives the classNameList variable a new collection to display in the class list component based on the new filter

Table 8.8. UIFinderVW2 Class Variables.

Variable	Description
CanvasIcon	An OpaqueImage used to prefix canvas resources in the selector list
ImageIcon	An OpaqueImage used to prefix image resources in the selector list
MenuIcon	An OpaqueImage used to prefix menu resources in the selector list
ModelIcon	An OpaqueImage used to prefix data models in the selector list
QueryIcon	An OpaqueImage used to prefix query resources in the selector list
RecentlyVisitedClasses	An OrderedCollection listing the last 10 classes visited
SelListMenuForNoSelection	A Menu used by the canvas list when no canvas is selected
SelListMenuWithSelection	A Menu used by the canvas list when a canvas is selected
SpecBearingClasses	A Set of all classes known to have instance or class methods that return a resource
SpecBearingCategories	A Set of all Symbols naming all class categories that contain resource bearing classes

8.3.3.3 Operations on the Selected Class

There are seven operations that can be conducted on the selected class (including adding a new class, which does not require a class to be selected). These operations are available from the main menu, the class list <operate> menu, the action buttons, or short-cut keys. These operations and a description of their implementations are listed in Table 8.9.

8.3.3.4 Operations on the Selected Resource

There are eight operations UIFinderVW2 can perform on the selected resource (including adding a resource which does not require a resource, to be selected). These operations are available from the main menu, the canvas list <operate> menu, the action buttons, or short-cut keys. Table 8.10 lists the corresponding action methods and describes their implementation.

8.3.3.5 Updating the Resource Finder

Each of the tools in *VisualWorks* is required to notify the UIFinderVW2 class of any action taken on a resource. These actions include visiting a resource-bearing class, adding a new

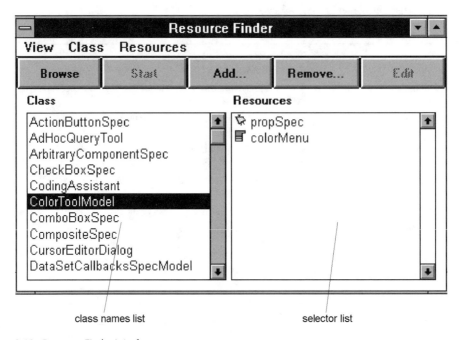

Figure 8.10. Resource Finder Interface.

resource, editing a resource, or removing a resource. This allows the Resource Finder to stay current with the resources available in the virtual image.

The UIFinderVW2 class keeps a list of all resource-bearing classes in its class variable SpecBearingClasses (the name is a legacy from *VisualWorks* 1.0, which only tracked interface specs). It also keeps a list of all class categories that contain resource-bearing classes in their SpecBearingCategories class variable. A third class variable, RecentlyVisitedClasses, keeps a list of the 10 most recently visited resource-bearing classes. Each time a *VisualWorks* tool interacts with a resource, it notifies the UIFinderVW2 by sending it a statistics message. All the statistics methods are implemented in the UIFinderVW2 class protocol 'statistics.' The implementation of each of these methods is to update the appropriate class variable and notify any open Resource Finder tools so that they can visually update themselves if necessary.

Strangely enough, each instance of UIFinderVW2 that is opened registers itself as a dependent of its class, UIFinderVW2. So when UIFinderVW2 needs to notify all instances of a change in the resources, it broadcasts an update to its dependents. This is a most unique feature—a class whose instances are also its dependents!

Table 8.9. Operations on the Selected Class.

Action method	Description of implementation
addClass	Bring up the class installation dialogs and open a canvas on the new class.
fileOutClass	Make sure class still exists, prompt the user for the file name, and file out class source code to this file.
renameClass	Make sure the class still exists, prompt the user for a new name, make sure the new name is valid, reuse code in Browser to perform the renaming process, and select the new class name in the class list.
browse	Make sure the class still exists, register the class as being visited, and open the preferred browser on the class.
removeClass	Make sure the class still exists and have the removeClass: method remove the class. The removeClass: method prompts the user to verify removal, and removes the class from the Smalltalk, SpecBearingClasses, and RecentlyVisitedClasses dictionaries.
startApplication	Make sure the class still exists, make sure the class is visually startable, register the class as being visited, and open the class interface.
showDatabaseApplication Structure	Open a LensApplicationStructureView as a slave of the Resource Finder window and have it operate on the selected class.

Table 8.10. Operations on the Selected Resource.

Action method	Description of implementation
addCanvas	Make sure the selected class still exists and open a canvas for this class and an unspecified target selector
addDataModel	Make sure the selected class still exists and open the data modeler on this class and an unspecified target selector
addIcon	Make sure the selected class still exists and open the Image Editor on this class and an unspecified target selector
addMenu	Make sure the selected class still exists and open the Menu Editor on this class and an unspecified target selector
addQuery	Make sure the selected class still exists and open the query editor on this class and an unspecified spec
browseSenders	Make sure the selected class still exists and that it still implements the current selector as a resource method and then open a Method Browser on all senders of this method
removeCanvas	Make sure the selected class still exists and make sure that it still defines the current selector as a resource method, then prompt user for confirmation, and remove the method from class
edit	Make sure the selected class still exists and make sure that it still defines the current selector as a resource method, and open the appropriate tool on the current class and selector

8.3.4 Help Browser

The Help Browser is an online hypertext help facility. It allows the user to set bookmarks, view a list of recently visited topics, search for topics, and jump to related topics. This help system adopts the metaphor of a library. The library is composed of books, the books are composed of chapters, and the chapters are composed of pages. This forms a hierarchical structure of information with the library as the root node and the pages as the leaf nodes. The help information is kept in boss files. The Help Browser provides a good example of how a single application model can run several window interfaces.

The approach to discussing this rather complex tool is to first talk about the several domain objects that make up the library (see Chapter 11 for more on domain objects in general). Next we will look at some of the support help objects. Then we will look at the class which implements the tool, HelpBrowser, and discuss its interface and instance variables. Finally, we will look at how each of its main features are implemented.

8.3.4.1 Domain Objects

The Help Browser is a marvelous example of an application that segregates its domain information from the rest of the application (Chapter 11 deals exclusively with segregating the domain from the application). The Help Browser has several domain objects, which it uses to hold the information it displays. These domain objects are called help elements, and they are the books, chapters, and pages containing the help information.

Table 8.11. Concrete Help Element Classes.

Class	Description
HelpBook	Represents a book in the library. A HelpBook knows the name of the file that contains it. Its contents is an OrderedCollection of HelpProxy objects representing HelpChapters. *VisualWorks* ships with three books.
HelpChapter	Represents a set of related help pages. A HelpChapter's contents variable is an OrderedCollection of HelpProxy objects containing HelpPages. HelpChapters are referenced by their containing HelpBooks.
HelpExample	Contains a snippet of Smalltalk code to be evaluated by the user/developer. Its instances are pre-set to either **do it**, **print it**, or **inspect**.
HelpLibrary	Represents a library. Its contents variable is an OrderedCollection of HelpProxy objects containing HelpBooks. *VisualWorks* ships with one library.
HelpPage	Represents a page in a chapter. A HelpPage's contents is just text. It also has a collection of HelpExample objects and a collection of HelpSeeAlso objects.

Each of the different types of help elements has its own concrete class. Each concrete domain class is a subclass of the abstract class HelpElement. HelpElement is a subclass of Object and defines two variables: contents and title. The contents variable contains the help information. The actual type of help information it references varies by subclass. The title variable is a string or text for the title of that information.

There are six concrete subclasses of HelpElement, which together make up all of the different types of help elements used in the Help Browser. These are described in Table 8.11.

8.3.4.2 Support Help Classes

There are some additional help objects that support the overall effort of the online help system. These are listed in Table 8.12.

8.3.4.3 Help Browser Interface

The Help Browser is implemented by the HelpBrowser class, which is a subclass of Application-Model. Its interface is described in the class method windowSpec and is illustrated in Figure 8.11. The interface consists of a main menu, five action buttons, a composite of two action buttons for indexing the page, a container field for indicating the current help element's container element, a page number field, a title field, and a list and text editor superimposed on each other for displaying the current help element's contents.

Besides the main user interface, HelpBrowser defines four other user interfaces, which are used as satellite windows for various purposes. The class methods defining these user interfaces and their corresponding functions are listed below.

aboutHelpSpec	Describes the About Help Window interface
finderSpec	Describes the Search Window interface
historySpec	Describes the History Window interface
seeAlsoSpec	Describes the See Also Window interface

Table 8.12. Support Help Classes.

Class	Description
HelpAccessor	Provides random access file support for the HelpProxy objects.
HelpProxy	A HelpProxy is a wrapper for a help element. It provides efficient storage and access for the help elements that are stored in a boss file.
HelpSeeAlso	Represents a pointer to a HelpPage that is related to the current HelpPage. The pointing mechanism is actually the titles of the book, chapter, and page of the related HelpPage.

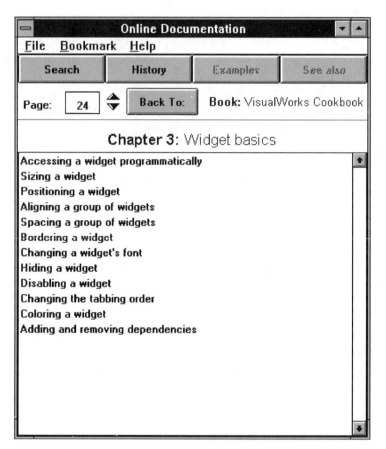

Figure 8.11. Help Browser Interface.

In addition, there is an ancillary tool specifically designed to browse example text, which supports a given help topic. This is the Examples Browser, and it is implemented by the class ExamplesBrowser, which is a subclass of ApplicationModel.

8.3.4.4 HelpBrowser Instance and Class Variables

HelpBrowser defines 22 instance variables. These are listed and described in Table 8.13.

In addition, HelpBrowser has two class variables: DefaultDir and SearchDefaults. DefaultDir is a string that is the default path name of the help files. SearchDefaults is an Array that caches default search parameters.

Table 8.13. HelpBrowser Instance Variables.

Variable	Description
pageNumber	A ValueHolder on an integer—serves as the aspect model for the page number indicator field
text	A ValueHolder on a text and serves the aspect model for the text component that displays the help information
element	A ValueHolder on the current help element
selectionInList	A SelectionInList containing the current help elements of contained help elements
history	A SelectionInList containing a collection of all recently visited help elements
bookmarks	A SelectionInList containing bookmark help elements
searchScope	A ValueHolder on a Symbol. The Symbol indicates the granularity of the search—books, chapters, etc.
ignoreCase	A ValueHolder on a boolean; indicates whether the search includes matching on case or not
useWildCards	A ValueHolder on a boolean; indicates whether search includes wild cards
searchString	A ValueHolder on a string; the string is used as the match value in a search
finderBuilder	The UIBuilder that builds the find dialog for searching for references
searchStatus	ValueHolder on an integer; acts as the model for the status meter used when conducting a search
cancelSearch	A ValueHolder on a boolean; used to indicate if the user is canceling a search in progress
library	A HelpLibrary that is the current library
menuBar	A Menu that is the Help Browser window menu
aboutHelpText	A ValueHolder on a string and serves as the aspect model for the help on help text
helpDir	A String naming the path that contains the help files
pathnames	A Set of strings that are the names of the paths used by the HelpAccessor to access help files
book	Reference to current HelpBook
chapter	Reference to current HelpChapter
page	Reference to current HelpPage
container	Reference to help the element that contains the current element

8.3.4.5 Bookmark

A bookmark is set by selecting the menu option **Bookmark→Insert**, which triggers the insertBookmark action method. This method adds the current help element to the bookmarks instance variable, which is a SelectionInList. This SelectionInList is emptied by selecting the menu option **Bookmark→Remove...**, which triggers the clearBookmarks action method. This method merely empties the bookmarks SelectionInList collection. A bookmark is selected by selecting the **Bookmark→Bookmarks** menu option and then selecting one of the bookmarks in the submenu. When a bookmark is selected, the change message bookmark-Selected is forwarded to the HelpBrowser. This method makes the selected bookmark the current help element.

8.3.4.6 Search

A search is initiated by pressing the **Search** button, which triggers the openFinder action method. If the Search Window is already open, this method does nothing, otherwise it opens the Search Window. The interface for the Search Window is specified in the class method finderSpec. The instance variable finderBuilder is the builder for this interface, and this builder's source is the HelpBrowser. This is necessary because the aspect models and action methods for the Search Window all come from the HelpBrowser. These aspect models are the instance variables searchString, searchScope, ignoreCase, and useWildCards. The action methods are search and interruptSearch. The HelpBrowser cannot use its builder instance variable for the purpose of building the finder dialog because that particular instance of UIBuilder was used to build the main interface described in windowSpec.

The search method dispatches a more specific search message, such as searchCurrent-Page, based on the search scope (value of searchScope). Each specific search method conducts its search within a Promise object. A Promise object calculates a value using a process running in parallel with the current thread of execution. The HelpBrowser continually polls the Promise object to see if it is finished processing. Each time the Promise object says it is not finished conducting the search, the HelpBrowser then checks to see if the user is trying to press the **Cancel** button in the Search Window. If so, control is temporarily given to that button so it can set the value of cancelSearch to true.

8.3.4.7 History

The History Window is opened by pressing the **History** button, which triggers the open-History action method. This method opens the interface described in the class method historySpec. A temporary builder is instantiated to build this interface (i.e., the HelpBrowser cannot use its builder instance variable because it was used to build the main interface described in windowSpec). This temporary builder references the HelpBrowser as its source because it uses the history instance variable as an aspect model for the History Window's list component.

The history instance variable is a SelectionInList that contains a collection of recently visited help elements. Whenever a selection is made in the Help Browser's list view, that selection is appended to the collection of recently visited help elements. When the user selects one of the help elements in the History Window, then the change message historyItemSelected is dispatched, which makes that help element the current selection in the Help Browser.

8.3.4.8 Examples Browser

The **Examples** button is enabled if the current help page has examples, otherwise it is disabled. A HelpPage references any examples it may have with its examples instance variable. Pressing the **Examples** button triggers the openExamples action method. This method instantiates an ExamplesBrowser. This instance of ExamplesBrowser is handed the current help page and told to open relative to the Help Browser.

ExamplesBrowser is a subclass of ApplicationModel and displays a HelpPage's examples. The user can take one of six actions on the example by pressing the appropriate action button. Each of these action buttons has a corresponding action method.

Each example is an instance of HelpExample, which is a subclass of HelpElement. A HelpExample's contents is the text of the example. The HelpExample class defines an instance variable, evaluationStyle, which is either #printIt, #doIt, or #inspect. This variable indicates what type of evaluation can be performed on the example. All examples can be spawned into an independent window or printed.

8.3.4.9 See Also

The See Also Window is opened by pressing the **See also** button, which triggers the openSeeAlso action method. This method opens the interface described in the seeAlsoSpec class method. A temporary builder is instantiated to build this interface. The HelpBrowser cannot use its builder instance variable because it was used to build the main interface described in windowSpec. This temporary builder references the HelpBrowser as its source because it accesses the aspect model for the list component in the See Also Window from the HelpBrowser.

The seeAlso method is the aspect method that returns a SelectionInList whose collection is the current help element's seeAlso instance variable. The elements in this collection are HelpSeeAlso objects. A HelpSeeAlso object contains the titles of the book, chapter, and page of a related HelpPage. When the user selects one of the help elements in the see also window, the change message seeAlsoSelected is dispatched, which makes that help element the current selection in the Help Browser.

8.3.4.10 Back To

The user can return to the most recently visited help element by pressing the **Back To:** button, which dispatches the prevLevel action message. This method makes the current help element's container the new current help element. The variables element, container, library, book, chapter, and page are updated appropriately.

8.4 Summary

There are several classes that facilitate tool implementation in *VisualWorks*. Preeminent among these is UIPainterWatcher. UIPainterWatcher is a subclass of ApplicationModel and the superclass of all painter watcher tools. UIPainterWatcher gives all of its subclasses, known collectively as painter watchers, the ability to track the current selection in the current canvas. Very much related to UIPainterWatcher are the classes SpecModel and IntegratedSpec-Model, which describe subapplication behavior for *VisualWorks* tools. Another important supporting class is UIDefiner, which is responsible for the Define Dialog used to compile aspect methods and action methods and add instance variables to the target class. Some of the other support classes are ColorBitView, ColorBitEditor, ColoredArea, ColoredAreaController, DirectBitView, and GridWrapper.

There are four painter watchers in *VisualWorks*. These tools are all subclasses of UI-PainterWatcher and directly support the canvas–painting process. The four painter watchers are Properties Tool, Menu Editor, Image Editor, and Canvas Tool. The Properties Tool and Canvas Tool operate only when a canvas is opened. The Image Editor and Menu Editor can also operate stand alone and, like a canvas (UIPainter), can install resource methods in a target class. All of these tools are interested in the current selection of the current canvas. They are also interested whenever there is a change of selection or a change of current canvas.

There are four additional *VisualWorks* tools that indirectly support the GUI-building process. These are the Settings Tool, the Launcher, the Resource Finder, and the Help Browser. The Settings Tool not only allows the developer to set user preferences, but also acts as the global repository for these user preferences. The Launcher, also known as the *VisualWorks* Main Window, is just a collection of action methods accessed by various buttons and menu selections. The Launcher gives access to the rest of the *VisualWorks* environment. The Resource Finder acts as a special browser for application model classes and provides installation facilities for the other tools. The Help Browser is an online help facility. It operates on the metaphor of a library that forms a hierarchical representation of the help information. The library contains books, which contain chapters, which contain pages. The Help Browser provides several facilities for navigating the library, including a history of visited help elements, bookmarks, and a search facility.

VisualWorks Practice

PART II IS meant to demonstrate the value of having the thorough understanding of *VisualWorks* concepts provided in Part I. However, it is not necessary that you cover Part I in order to benefit from Part II. There is no specific order to the material in Part II except for Chapters 10 and 11, which should be taken in sequence.

Chapter 9 is a collage of tips, tricks, and miscellany, which is of interest to most *VisualWorks* developers. Chapter 9 depends on the material covered in Chapters 1, 2, 5, and 6 of Part I.

Chapters 10 and 11 are by far the most important chapters in the book. If you do nothing else, study these two chapters, for they provide a solid foundation for successful application development in *VisualWorks*. Chapter 10 covers the idea of creating abstract subclasses of **ApplicationModel** to facilitate application development. Chapter 11 talks about segregating application and domain information by introducing domain objects, which are the keepers of domain information, and domain adaptors, which provide the user interface for the domain objects. These chapters depend on the material covered in Chapters 1, 2, 3, 4, and 5 of Part I.

Chapter 12 is a thorough description of what it takes to add new customized *Visual-Works* components. A tutorial walks you through the process of actually adding a new component. There is also a discussion of using arbitrary components as an alternative. This chapter depends primarily on the material covered in Chapters 1, 2, and 3 of Part I.

Chapters 13, 14, and 15 are about enhancing the *VisualWorks* environment. Chapter 13 is a set of small tutorials, which add some nice functionality to the canvas–editing tools of *VisualWorks*. Chapter 14 is a single large tutorial, which greatly enhances the Image Editor tool. Chapter 15 discusses some additional tools, which are available on the accompanying disk. These chapters depend primarily on Chapters 7 and 8 and to a lesser extent on the other chapters of Part I.

CHAPTER 9

Tips and Tricks

As a developer of software, you are probably constantly asked by your manager or client, *Can you make the application...?* Or perhaps, *Can we have a component which...?* With Smalltalk, the answer is almost always *yes*. But this is a loaded question. The question should not be *What can be done?* but instead *What can be done within five minutes?* as opposed to *What can be done within five weeks?* The difference is usually a matter of reuse verses rolling your own. This chapter answers the question *What can be done within five minutes?* In other words, what does *VisualWorks* provide the developer that can be done with just a few lines of code?

This chapter extrapolates from the information in Part I to provide several *Visual-Works* tips and tricks that require very little effort. Most of the examples are just a few lines of code in a Workspace or a method. The value comes in just knowing that they are available and can be obtained for a very inexpensive price. One of the important edicts of Smalltalk is reuse. In order to reuse, however, you must know what is already provided. This chapter is a tour of many (certainly by no means all) of the things *VisualWorks* has to offer with minimal effort on the part of the developer. None of the tips and tricks require tampering with the existing *VisualWorks* classes or creating any new tools or widgets.

This chapter also provides some additional fundamentals about *VisualWorks* not covered in Part I. In particular, the topics of component layout, menus, text, fonts, and cursors are discussed with a certain amount of rigor, and several new terms are defined.

It is important that you not depend exclusively on this book or the *VisualWorks* manuals to provide all of your tips, tricks, and techniques. You should continually explore the system and experiment to discover your own approaches and solutions to problems. This chapter is merely a means to getting started.

9.1 Components in General

In this section we will talk about those things that apply to all (or at least most) *VisualWorks* components. A *VisualWorks* component is a SpecWrapper containing a widget. A widget is a visual part that gives the component its unique appearance and behavior. Components can be accessed from the builder during runtime only if they have a name or ID that is a Symbol. This ID is set in the Properties Tool during canvas painting. The technique for accessing the component is shown in the example below.

```
comp := self builder componentAt: #notesText.
```

In this example, self is the application model and #notesText is the unique ID for some component. The componentAt: message returns a SpecWrapper, which is the *VisualWorks* component. For the remainder of this chapter, the variable comp will be used to refer to a *VisualWorks* component. The widget can be accessed from the component as shown below.

```
widget := comp widget
```

Most of the communication between the application and the component should occur with the SpecWrapper and not the widget. This is highly recommended since the SpecWrapper protocol is less likely to change from version to version than are the internal implementation details of the widget. However, some of the more interesting tricks deal directly with the widget, so it becomes very tempting to ignore this guideline.

9.1.1 Component Layout

To position a component within an interface is to give it a layout. A **layout** is an object that determines the exact real estate a component will occupy inside a window (or container). There are three attributes associated with a component's layout, which are subject to change: bounds, fixed vs. relative, and bounded vs. unbounded. In addition to this, a component is positioned inside of its container, and therefore the layout describes the component's position in terms of the container's coordinate system. Each of these topics about a component's position and layout are discussed below, and examples are provided in Disk Example 9.1.

9.1.1.1 Bounds

A component's **bounds** is a Rectangle that describes the exact area of the window or container occupied by that component. Since the bounds is a Rectangle, it can also be described by two Point objects: the origin and the extent. The **origin** is the location of the upper lefthand corner of the Rectangle. The **extent** is the width and height of the Rectangle, usually expressed in Point notation like width@height. All dimensions are in pixels. Do not confuse bounds and layout. The bounds is a Rectangle describing the area currently occupied by a component. The layout is some object used to determine that Rectangle.

VisualWorks provides two easy methods for changing a component's location during runtime: moveBy: aPoint and moveTo: aPoint. The moveBy: aPoint message moves the component by the amount specified by aPoint. The moveTo: aPoint message moves the component's origin to aPoint, which is specified in its container's coordinate system. Moving a component to the right by 15 pixels would look something like the following

```
comp moveBy: 15@0.
```

To move the component so that its origin is at its container's coordinate 30@25, do the following

```
comp moveTo: 30@25.
```

Changing a component's bounds involves sending it the message

```
newBounds: aRectangle
```

where aRectangle describes the area where you would like the component to reside. There is no explicit way to change a component's extent, so we must revert to changing its bounds to a new bounds with the same origin. This may require some Rectangle and Point arithmetic. A first attempt to increase the component's extent by 10 pixels in both the x and y directions while leaving the component at its current origin would look something like the following.

```
| origin extent |
origin := comp bounds origin.
extent := comp bounds extent + 10@10.
comp newBounds: (origin extent: extent)
```

A more sophisticated implementation of the above example might look like the following.

```
comp newBounds: (comp bounds insetBy: (0@0 extent: 10@10))
```

9.1.1.2 Fixed Layout vs. Relative Layout

When a component has a **fixed layout**, its bounds does not change with the container's extent. That is, as the window is resized, the component maintains its same size and location. When a component has a **relative layout**, its bounds is some function of the container's size (or extent). That is, as the window is resized, the component's size and location will change accordingly. A fixed layout is a Point or Rectangle, and a relative layout is a LayoutOrigin, an AlignmentOrigin, or a LayoutFrame.

The fixed/relative attribute of a component's layout is determined while editing the canvas; however, it can be changed during runtime. The fixed/relative attribute of a component can be set during runtime with the beFixedIn: and beRelativeIn: messages, respectively. In each case, the argument should be the bounds of the component's container, which is usually the window's component, but not necessarily (see Section 9.1.1.4). So to change a fixed layout to a relative layout during runtime, a message such as the one below might be used.

```
comp beRelativeIn: comp container bounds
```

9.1.1.3 Bounded Layout vs. Unbounded Layout

A **bounded layout** occurs when a component's extent is determined by the layout object. An **unbounded layout** leaves the determination of the component's extent up to the component itself. For example, buttons and text editors are usually positioned as bounded components. Their exact dimensions are either fixed or calculated as some fraction of the container's dimensions. Labels and check boxes, on the other hand, are usually positioned as unbounded components. Their exact extent depends on such things as the number of characters in the label and the font selection.

The bounded/unbounded attribute of a component's layout is determined while editing the canvas; however, it can be changed during runtime. The bounded/unbounded attribute can be set during runtime as follows.

```
comp newLayout: aLayout.
```

If aLayout is a LayoutFrame or a Rectangle, then the resulting layout is bounded. If aLayout is a LayoutOrigin, an AlignmentOrigin, or a Point, then the resulting layout is unbounded. You must be sure to invalidate any affected regions of the window in the event that there is a change of bounds. This can be tricky because if the bounds shrinks, then the invalid area is the old bounds, and if the bounds grows, then the invalid area is the new bounds. Covering both cases might look like the following.

```
| oldBounds |
oldBounds := comp bounds.
comp newLayout: newBounds.
comp invalidate: (comp bounds merge: oldBounds)
```

9.1.1.4 Container's Coordinate System

A component is positioned within its container's coordinate system (ignoring any intermediate wrappers). The container is usually the CompositePart that is the window's component, and it shares the window's coordinate system. Sometimes the container is a another component, such as a composite component or a subcanvas, and has its own local coordinate system. In such cases, the layout determines the component's position using the containing component's coordinate system and not the window's coordinate system.

9.1.2 Active Components

The next few items apply exclusively to the active components. Recall that an active component is a *VisualWorks* component whose widget is a view. Input fields and lists are active components; labels and regions are not. Each of the following topics on active components is also covered in Disk Example 9.2.

9.1.2.1 MVC

The widget for an active component is a view that, of course, has a model and a controller. All three parts of the widget—model, view, and, controller—are easily accessible. The widget is the view, so the widget message returns the view. To access the model and controller, send model and controller to the view, respectively. This is summarized in Table 9.1.

In the case of the combo box component, the widget for the active component is not a view but a composite of views, and Table 9.1 does not apply. The combo box widget is a ComboBoxView, which is a subclass of CompositePart. It has two views: the input field and the action button. The input field is the view of interest, and it is accessed as follows.

```
comp widget editor
```

It has a model and controller, which are accessed in the usual ways.

9.1.2.2 Replacing the Widget Controller

You can change a widget's controller during runtime as shown below.

```
comp widget controller: aNewController
```

You must be very careful, however, because a widget controller is linked to several other objects, and some or all of these links should be addressed when swapping controllers. In the statement above, the widget and its model will be automatically linked to the new controller. The following objects, however, will not.

- menu and menu holder
- menu performer
- keyboard processor
- dispatcher

Table 9.1. Accessing an Active Widget's MVC Parts.

Smalltalk statement	Return value
comp widget	widget/view
comp widget controller	widget/view's controller
comp widget model	widget/view's model

If both controllers are a kind of ControllerWithMenu, then you will want to make sure that
the menu and performer are passed along as shown in the following code.

```
((oldController isKindOf: ControllerWithMenu) and: [
(newController isKindOf: ControllerWithMenu]) ifTrue: [
    newController menuHolder: oldController menuHolder.
    oldController performer == oldController
        ifFalse: [newController performer: oldController performer]].
```

To make sure the new controller references the keyboard processor, you will want to add
the following.

```
((newController respondsTo: #keyboardProcessor:) and: [
oldController respondsTo: #keyboardProcessor]) ifTrue: [
newController keyboardProcessor: oldController keyboardProcessor.
```

To make sure the new controller will dispatch the appropriate notification and validation
messages, you may want to include the following code.

```
(newController respondsTo: #setDispatcher:)
    ifTrue: newController setDispatcher: oldController dispatcher.
```

9.1.2.3 Keyboard Focus

Most active components can process keyboard events, and therefore they can take key-
board focus and participate in the tab order (menu buttons and sliders are the exceptions).
To cause an active component to take focus out of turn, send it the message takeKeyboard-
Focus. If a component is disabled or invisible, it cannot take focus.

To prevent a current change of focus from proceeding, send abortFocusShift to the
keyboard processor.

```
self builder keyboardProcessor abortFocusShift
```

This only aborts the shift brought about by keyboard activity. The mouse can always
change focus directly.

9.1.2.4 Keyboard Hook

Any active component that can take focus can also have a keyboard hook. Recall from
Chapter 2, Section 2.4.2.2, that a keyboard hook is a block that expects two arguments—
the KeyboardEvent and the widget controller—and gets first crack at handling any Key-
boardEvents targeted for the component. If the block evaluates to nil, then the KeyboardE-
vent is considered to have been handled and requires no further processing. Otherwise,
the KeyboardEvent is passed to the widget controller for handling in the usual manner.

By default, a widget controller's keyboard hook is nil. To set a widget controller's
keyboard hook, send it the message keyboardHook: as shown below.

```
comp widget controller keyboardHook: aBlock
```

9.1.2.5 Menu

Most active components can have an <operate> menu. This menu is kept by the widget controller and is provided either by the application model or by the widget controller class. The application model can provide the menu as either a static resource (unchanging during runtime) or a dynamic resource (changes or is replaced during runtime). A static menu is provided by an application model class method. A dynamic menu resides inside of a Value-Holder (i.e., a channel), which is provided by an application model instance method. The example below shows an application model instance method that provides an edit menu with the intention that this menu will change or be replaced during runtime.

```
editOptions
    ^editOptions isNil
        ifTrue: [editOptions := self class editOptionsMenu asValue].
        ifFalse: [editOptions]
```

If the widget controller has a menu, then it has a menu performer. In Chapter 1 we learned that the performer is the object that fields the menu action message. The following is an example of how to change the performer during runtime.

```
comp widget controller performer: aPerformer
```

Some components provide their own default menus. In such cases the widget controller is the performer and handles all menu messages. In the event that the application model provides a menu to the component, then the application model is the performer and handles the menu messages.

Menus in general are covered in depth in Section 9.7, and <operate> menus specifically for text components are covered in Section 9.4.1.7.

9.1.2.6 Model

The model for a widget is always a value model—usually a ValueHolder, a PluggableAdaptor, or an AspectAdaptor. Table 9.2 lists the protocol that applies to these widget models.

As a tip, do not overload your value models with change messages. Try to limit your value models to one interested object and one change message. Also try to avoid the construct of retracting interest, changing the value model, and then reinstating interest. The reason for these suggestions is that change messages often may affect other value models, causing a cascading effect that is often too unwieldy to manage. Furthermore, there is no reason for the same interested object to register more than once with the same value model, using a different change message each time. As an example, the following code

```
self name onChangeSend: #updateBox to: self.
self name onChangeSend: #redrawPatch to: self
```

should never occur. Either the two change methods should be combined into one method or the implementation of one should include invoking the other.

Table 9.2. Widget Model Protocol

Message	Description
value	Returns value of model
value:	Sets value of model and updates dependents
setValue:	Sets value of model but does not update dependents
onChange:Send:	Registers interest in value model
retractInterestsFor:	Removes a specific object's interest in a value model

By limiting your value models to just one or two interested objects and just one change message per interested object, your code will be much cleaner, more easily maintained, and easier to understand. Registering interest in value models is a very powerful feature of *VisualWorks* but, when abused, can result in code that is unmanageable and unpredictable.

9.1.2.7 Notification and Validation Protocol

Those active components that can process keyboard events have the option of notifying the application model when they

- acquire focus
- give up focus
- change value
- receive a double click event

Similarly, these components can request validation from the application model for doing these same four operations. This notification and validation protocol allows the application model to decide what happens in such cases.

9.1.2.8 Change Message Versus Notification of Change

You should be aware that there is a real difference between a notification of change message established using the Properties Tool and a change message established by registering interest in the corresponding value model. They may appear to be the same, but they are not! They are implemented differently and they behave differently. The notification message is dispatched only when the user causes a change via the user interface component. The change message is dispatched, however, upon any change of the value model, whether it be from the user or programmatically (see Disk Example 9.2).

The notification and request protocol is usually determined during the editing of the canvas, but it can be changed any time, as in the example below.

```
disp := comp widget controller getDispatcher.
disp doubleClickSelector: #openDialog
```

The code above accesses the widget controller's dispatcher, which is a UIDispatcher, and changes the message used to notify the application model that the component is about to take focus. When comp receives a double click event, the dispatcher will send the message openDialog to the current receiver of notification and request messages. By default, this receiver is the application model. This can be changed, however, by creating a Message-Channel as shown below.

```
msgChannel := MessageChannel new
        receiver: someOtherObj
        selector: #openValve.
disp := comp widget controller getDispatcher.
disp focusIn: msgChannel
```

The code above edits the component's dispatcher such that when comp takes focus, the message openValve is sent to the someOtherObj object.

9.1.3 Other Component Attributes

Some of the other attributes that apply to most components are color, label, opacity, visibility, and availability. These general component attributes are discussed below, and examples are given in Disk Example 9.3.

9.1.3.1 Color

To change a component's color is to change its LookPreferences. While painting a canvas, a component's LookPreferences can be edited using the Properties Tool's Color interface, also known as the Color Tool. The LookPreferences can also be changed during runtime. The first attempt at doing this might look like the following.

```
comp lookPreferences
    backgroundColor: ColorValue blue;
    foregroundColor: ColorValue yellow
```

There are two things wrong with this approach. First, certain put messages, such as back-groundColor: and selectionForegroundColor:, return a mutated copy of the receiver but have no effect on the receiver itself. The appropriate put messages in this case would be setBack-groundColor: and setForegroundColor:. Second, the component is never notified of this change in its look preferences and therefore does not redraw itself in the new color scheme.

The proper technique is to first make allowances for either editing the original Look-Preferences or a copy. Second, after all color roles have been changed, set the component's look preferences with the appropriately edited LookPreferences object using the lookPreferences: message. The advantage of having to set the component's look preferences using the lookPreferences: message is that the component is aware of when its colors are being changed and can immediately update itself visually. An example of changing a component's background to blue and its foreground color to yellow is shown below.

```
| lookPref |
lookPref := comp lookPref foregroundColor: ColorValue yellow.
lookPref := lookPref backgroundColor: ColorValue blue.
comp lookPreferences: lookPref
```

9.1.3.2 Label

Many components have a label, which is usually a Label object but in general can be any visual component. The message label: aLabel replaces the Label object held by a component with another Label object. The message labelString: aString changes the Label object's string directly. Both of these messages cause the component to redraw itself to reflect these changes in the window. The following example will change the string displayed by a component's label.

```
comp labelString: 'Save As...'
```

The message is sent to the SpecWrapper, which simply forwards the message to its widget, which actually contains the label. You can also replace the Label object with another Label object or some other visual component such as an image. The following code replaces a component's label with an image.

```
comp label: anImage
```

For more on labels, see Section 9.2.1.

9.1.3.3 Opacity

When a component's background color is different from its container's background color, then the component will fill its bounds with its own background color whenever it is asked to redraw itself. If the background colors are the same, however, there is no need to do so. This gives the component a transparent appearance because any components drawn previously within its bounds will show through. To prevent this, a component can become opaque, in which case it always draws its background and covers anything else drawn previously within its bounds.

Normally opacity is set in the Properties Tool during canvas painting. To make a component opaque during runtime, send it the message isOpaque: true as shown below.

> comp isOpaque: true

To make the component transparent again, send it the message isOpaque: false.

> comp isOpaque: false

In both cases, the component is immediately redrawn to reflect the changes in its state.

9.1.3.4 Visibility

Any component can be made invisible, and an invisible component can be made visible again. To make a component invisible, send it the message beInvisible:

> comp beInvisible

To make it visible again, send beVisible:

> comp beVisible

In both cases, the component is immediately redrawn to reflect the changes in its state. An invisible component cannot take keyboard focus.

9.1.3.5 Availability

Each component can be disabled such that it is drawn in a gray hue. In addition, active components will not take focus or respond to user input when disabled. A disabled active component indicates to the user that it is unavailable for use. It also indicates to the user that the component is not just read only but can become enabled again under the correct circumstances. While passive components can be disabled, the semantic is somewhat meaningless.

A component is disabled by sending the component (not the widget) the message disable as shown below.

> comp disable

Likewise, a component can become enabled again by sending it the message enable:

> comp enable

9.2 Component Borders and Labels

Much of a component's look policy appearance has to do with its border and label. You are not confined however to the look policy's interpretation of how a given component should appear. *Motif* should not have a monopoly on 3D borders! This section shows you several runtime alternatives to the standard options available in the Properties Tool.

9.2.1 Labels

Labels are used quite extensively in *VisualWorks*, however, you are not at all restricted to the options available during canvas painting. There are several label tricks and tips to enhance the visual appearance of your applications. Any *VisualWorks* component's label can be changed or edited on a dynamic basis (while the application is running). Disk Example 9.4 provides examples for all the label tips and techniques discussed below.

9.2.1.1 Label

The Label object is used by several widgets including the PassiveLabel discussed shortly. A Label is a visual component and therefore knows how to display itself on a graphics context. It holds onto a text object, a TextAttributes, a width, and an offset or left margin. The text of a Label is a Text object. It is easy to change the text of a label. You also have the option of formating the text. The code below changes a Label to have an italic text, rendered using the #large character set.

```
someLabelObject
    text: ('Open File' asText emphasizeAllWith: #( large italic));
```

You can create a new Label with one of four instance creation methods.

```
with: aText
with: aText attributes: aTextAttributes
with: aText attributes: aTextAttributes offset: anInteger
with: aText offset: anInteger
```

9.2.1.2 LabelAndIcon

A variation of Label is its subclass LabelAndIcon. It is common in graphical user interfaces to see a label prefixed by a small icon or bitmap. In *VisualWorks*, this feature is provided by LabelAndIcon. A LabelAndIcon is created in the same way as a Label (see Section 9.2.1.1). In addition, you supply an image using the icon: anImage message. It is your responsibility to ensure that the extent of the image is consistent with the size of the text. Typically an image with extent 16@16 pixels is appropriate. Also, you can specify the distance between the image and the text measured in pixels. This is called the *gap* and is set using the gap: anInteger message, where anInteger is the number of pixels separating the image and the text. The default value of the gap is 4 pixels, which is usually adequate. A typical LabelAndIcon creation is shown below.

```
(LabelAndIcon with: 'Help')
    icon: anImage;
    gap: 6
```

A LabelAndIcon can be used quite effectively with lists, tables, and action buttons. A Label-AndIcon can be used in place of any *VisualWorks* component's label as shown below.

```
comp label: aLabelAndIcon
```

9.2.1.3 VisualBlock

A VisualBlock is like a generic visual component. It supports all the corresponding visual component protocol. A VisualBlock is generic because its drawing behavior is specified on a per instance basis using a block. The block takes two arguments: a graphics context and a Rectangle describing the bounds. The code within the block draws on the graphics context just like any other visual component. VisualBlocks provide a means for creating simple visual components without having to create a new class. The example below creates a VisualBlock that draws a small, red Rectangle with thick borders.

```
VisualBlock with: [:gc :rect |
    gc lineWidth: 3.
    gc paint: ColorValue red.
    (0@0 extent: 30@30 displayOn: gc]
```

Since a VisualBlock is a visual component, it can be used in place of a Label object as a component's label. The example below replaces a component's label with a VisualBlock.

```
comp label: aVisualBlock
```

9.2.1.4 Image

An image is a visual component and can also be used for a component's label as is shown below.

```
comp label: anImage
```

Images are covered more fully in Section 9.9.1.

9.2.1.5 PassiveLabel

A PassiveLabel is the widget for the label component. It is a subclass of SimpleComponent and holds onto a visual component, called its label, and a TextAttributes. It also has a left margin that specifies the distance in pixels between its left border and the beginning of the label. Typically, the label is a Label object, but this is not necessary. You can use any visual component as the label. For example, changing the PassiveLabel object's label to a LabelAndIcon would look like

```
comp widget label: aLabelAndIcon.
```

Or you can use an image as the label.

> comp widget label: anImage

Another idea is to use a VisualBlock to actually draw something dynamically for the label.

> comp widget label: aVisualBlock

If the label is a Label object or any other object that responds to textStyle:, you can also change the PassiveLabel's text attributes.

> comp widget textStyle: aTextAttributes

Be careful with this last one. When you change the text attributes of a PassiveLabel, it forwards the message to its label. It is your responsibility to make sure that the label object responds to the message textStyle:. Label, LabelAndIcon, and AlignmentLabel objects respond to textStyle:, and images, Mask objects, Pixmap objects, and VisualBlock objects do not.

9.2.2 Borders

VisualWorks provides four different kinds of borders: simple, normal, etched, and beveled. Usually the look policy dictates which one is used, but you can easily override this during the postopen operation or even change it during runtime. Disk Example 9.5 illustrates the information about component borders described below.

9.2.2.1 A Component's Border

Several components contain borders. Table 9.3 lists these components and how to access their borders.

It is never a good idea to begin editing a component's default border. The reason is that most default borders are class variables. Changing a default border means changing the same instance of a border shared by many other views in *VisualWorks*. This can have adverse effects on not only your application, but any application running in the same virtual image. Instead, make a copy of the current border and then edit the copy. The two

Table 9.3. Accessing a Component's Border.

Components	Accessing border
Slider and Input Field	comp component border
Group Box	comp widget border
Combo Box	(comp widget components at: 1) border
List, Table, Arbitrary Component, Subcanvas, Composite, Text Editor	(comp decorator components at: 1) border

examples below change the border for an input field. This first example copies the current border and replaces the current border with the edited copy.

```
| borderCopy |
borderCopy := comp component border copy.
comp component border: borderCopy
```

This next one just replaces the current border with a new border.

```
comp component border: SimpleBorder new
```

Any time you replace or change a component's border, send the invalidate message to the component so that the change is reflected on the screen.

9.2.2.2 SimpleBorder

A SimpleBorder has two attributes, width and color, both of which can be changed at any time and both of which affect all four sides of the border. The example below changes a SimpleBorder object's color.

```
simpleBorder setBorderColor: ColorValue red
```

The next example changes its width or thickness to three pixels.

```
simpleBorder setBorderWidth: 3
```

A new SimpleBorder is created as follows.

```
SimpleBorder new
```

9.2.2.3 Border

A Border, sometimes called a normal border, is similar to a SimpleBorder except that the color and thickness of each side can be changed independently. The four sides are known as top, bottom, left, and right. The example below changes the left side's thickness to 2 pixels.

```
border setLeftWidth: 2
```

The next example changes the top side's color to blue.

```
border setTopColor: ColorValue blue
```

A Border is initialized with all sides set to a thickness of zero. Therefore, it is best to create a Border using the with: creation message to initialize all the sides to a nonzero thickness as is shown below.

```
Border with: 1
```

9.2.2.4 EtchedBorder

EtchedBorder objects have color components, but it is best left to the border to determine these colors based on the current look preferences. This leaves only the thickness as a variable parameter, but any value other than 1 or 2 yields a very ugly visual effect. Therefore, you can change an EtchedBorder object's thickness from 1 to 2—any more, and you risk losing the etched effect.

> etchedBorder setBorderWidth: 2

To create a new EtchedBorder, just send the message new to the class and everything will be initialized appropriately.

> EtchedBorder new

9.2.2.5 BeveledBorder

A BeveledBorder is like an EtchedBorder in that its colors should be determined internally. Unlike the EtchedBorder, however, its thickness can vary widely. The example below changes a BeveledBorder object's thickness to 4 pixels.

> beveledBorder setBorderWidth: 4

Furthermore, a BeveledBorder can appear inset or raised by sending it the inset or raised message, respectively. The default is to appear raised. To create a new BeveledBorder, just send the message new to the class.

> BeveledBorder new

9.3 Selection Components

List and table components provide a very flexible means for displaying a collection of objects and allowing the user to make a selection. List components are one-dimensional and operate on a collection whose elements are indexed by an integer. Table components are two-dimensional and operate on collections whose elements are indexed by a Point. Lists can operate in single selection or multiselection mode. Tables can operate with cell selection, row selection, or column selection. Most of this section concerns list components, but much of what can be done with a list component can also be done with a table component.

9.3.1 The List Component Collection

A list component displays a collection and allows the user to select elements of that collection. There are certain things you should know about a list component's collection. These are discussed below and supported by examples in Disk Example 9.6.

9.3.1.1 Kinds of Collections

The SelectionInList will only operate on sequenceable collections. This is because a Selection-InList tracks the current selection by its index, not by referencing the object directly. Sequenceable type collections include OrderedCollection, List, SortedCollection, and Array, among others. Nonsequenceable collection types include Set, Bag, and Dictionary, among others.

9.3.1.2 What Can Go in the Collection?

It is important to remember that the objects in the collection can be of any type and we are not restricted to just using textual type objects such as strings and text. Every object—whether it is an image, a geometric, or even a *VisualWorks* tool such as a UIMaskEditor—knows how to represent itself as a string because all objects respond to printString. Furthermore, since Smalltalk is typeless, we can have a heterogeneity of objects in the same collection and the list widget will perform admirably.

9.3.1.3 Beware of the Dependency

You should know that the collection that is displayed by a list component incurs a dependent. The collection contained by the SelectionInList is also known to the widget, a Sequence-View. The SequenceView registers itself as a dependent of the collection. The reason is that if the collection object is a List, it can notify the SequenceView of a change of its contents and the SequenceView will initiate a visual update to reflect the change. However, even if the collection is not a List, the dependency is established. In such a case, we are setting up a dependency on something which is ill equipped to behave as a model (i.e., is not a kind of Model), and this can have adverse ramifications if improperly handled (see Chapter 1, Section 1.2.4.8).

9.3.1.4 List

The List class was created specifically for operating in tandem with a SelectionInList. A List object behaves as a model whose one aspect of information is a collection. Whenever an element is added or removed, the List notifies its dependents of this change. Since the SequenceView is a dependent, it redraws itself to reflect this change in the collection. This is not so for other sequenceable collection types such as OrderedCollection and Sorted-Collection. Although these other collection types do acquire the SequenceView as a dependent, their class definition does not include model type behavior so they are ill equipped to know about any internal changes and broadcast updates. Any changes to these collections will not automatically update the list component. In such cases, the burden is on the developer to invalidate the list component. This will cause the list component to redraw itself based on the new information in the collection maintained by the SelectionInList.

9.3.2 Displaying the Items in the List

There are several ways to display objects in a list. They can appear as strings, formated text, or visual components. Furthermore, each object can have a different appearance for different list components. Below are several approaches to displaying objects in a list. These are also covered in Disk Example 9.7.

9.3.2.1 displayString Method

By default, a SequenceView tries to display the elements in its collection as text. It sends the message displayString to each element in order to obtain a Text object or a string to represent that element. Each object in Smalltalk knows how to respond to the displayString message. This is because the displayString method is implemented in the Object class as shown below.

> **displayString**
> "Allows any Object to be used as the basis for a Label, although the purpose of displayString is to provide something more suitable than printString, primarily for use in SequenceViews."
>
> ^self printString

The result is that the SequenceView, by default, represents each element with its print string.

9.3.2.2 printString Method

Every object in Smalltalk knows how to respond to printString. The default behavior is for the object to return a string describing its type such as 'a BoundedWrapper' or 'a TextEditor-Spec'. It is the printOn: method that is the method actually responsible for constructing the string returned by printString. If you want to change the way an object displays itself as a string, edit the printOn: aStream method. As an example, the printOn: method for a fictional Person class is shown below.

> **printOn: aStream**
>
> aStream
>   nextPutAll: 'Person named ';
>   nextPutAll: self first;
>   space;
>   nextPutAll: self middle;
>   space;
>   nextPutAll: self last

With this implementation, instead of returning 'a Person', the printString message returns something much more meaningful, such as 'Person named Brian R. Jones'. It is strongly recommended that you define a printOn: method for each kind of object you create. Even if this kind of object never appears in a list component, the dividends will pay off enormously in debugging and inspecting because it is the printString message that displays an object in a Debugger or Inspector. It is also recommended that you include the object type somewhere in the print string as was done in the example above.

9.3.2.3 Implementing displayString

Suppose we now want to display the elements in our list in a manner other than that provided by the printString method. To do this, we can implement the displayString method. Using the Person example from above, suppose we desire to list the Person objects with last name first. To do this we could implement the displayString method for the Person class as shown below.

> **displayString**
> "Return the full name, last name first."
>
> ^self lastName , ', ' , self firstName , ' ' , self middleName

9.3.2.4 Arbitrary Display String Selector

Sometimes it is convenient to have objects displayed one way in one list component and a different way in another list component. In such cases, you have the option of telling the SequenceView which selector to use to retrieve a printable representation of the objects. Do this by sending the SequenceView the message

> displayStringSelector: aSymbol

where aSymbol is a message selector understood by each of the objects in the collection. For example, if the objects in the collection are line items in an invoice and each one returns a string when sent the message nameAndQuantityString, then the postbuild operation that opens an application on an invoice might include a line like the following.

> comp widget displayStringSelector: #nameAndQuantityString

This flexibility allows objects of the same type to appear differently in different list components or in different situations. The nameAndQuantityString method defined in the line item object's class might look something like the following.

> **nameAndQuantityString**
>
> ^self name , ' ' , self quantity printString

9.3.2.5 Formated Text

The display string selector does not necessarily have to return a string. It can also return formated text, that is, a Text object. This allows you to have certain items in the collection appear italicized, or bold, or even in a different character size or font. To use the invoice line item example above, if the line item object wants to appear bold, it might implement a method called nameAndQuantityBold, as shown below, and have the SequenceView use this as the display selector.

nameAndQuantityBold

^(self name , ' ' , self quantity printString) asText allBold

To take it a step further, the display string method might be called nameAndQuantityText and return bold text if the line item is over some amount, say $100.00, and normal text if it is not. This gives the user an easy visual indication as to what are the high dollar items in the invoice. Such a display string might look like the following.

nameAndQuantityText

```
^self amount > 100.0
    ifTrue: [self nameAndQuantityBold]
    ifFalse: [self nameAndQuantityNormal]
```

9.3.2.6 Graphical Representation

The objects in a list component do not have to display themselves in a textual manner at all. The objects can be displayed as any arbitrary visual component, although this does require some setup. Graphical display of the objects in the list requires defining the SequenceView's visual blocks. Recall from Chapter 2 that a SequenceView holds on to two blocks: visualBlock and selectedVisualBlock. These blocks determine how the items in the list are represented visually (including both text and graphics representations). Each block takes two arguments: the SequenceView itself and the index of the selection currently being drawn. The blocks are set by sending the messages visualBlock: and selectedVisualBlock: to the list widget. This procedure should be performed in a postbuild operation.

As an example, suppose the list collection contains ColorValue objects. We could display the name of each color, but for better visual effect, we could also display the actual color, which is done by the example below.

postBuildWith: aBuilder

```
comp widget
    visualBlock: [:view :index | | vb |
        vb := VisualBlock
                block: [:aGC :bounds |
                    aGC paint: (view sequence at: index).
                    aGC displayRectangle: bounds]
        BoundedWrapper on: vb].

    selectedVisualBlock: [:view :index | | rw vb |
        vb := VisualBlock
                block: [:aGC :bounds |
                    aGC paint: (view sequence at: index).
```

```
        aGC displayRectangle: bounds]
    rw := ReversingWrapper on: vb.
    rw reverse setValue: true.
    BoundedWrapper on: rw].
```

LabelAndIcon objects, VisualBlock objects, and ReversingWrapper objects are very instrumental in defining a list widget's visual blocks. A SequenceView's visual blocks can be set at any time during the life of the list component, and they will take effect immediately upon the next display. Do not confuse the term *visual block* with the VisualBlock class (see Section 9.2.1.3)—they are related but not the same thing. The term *visual block* in this context refers to a block object referenced by the SequenceView. VisualBlock is a class and a subclass of VisualComponent. It is sometimes the case, as in the example above, that an instance of VisualBlock is used in the definition of a SequenceView's visual block.

9.3.2.7 Columnar Information—Fixed Font

Another trick is to display the object in a columnated format. To do this, set the font attribute of the list component to be a fixed font using the Properties Tool. Next, the display string method must be clever enough to count columns and pad with spaces where necessary. To proceed with the line item example, a columnated display string might be implemented like the following.

```
nameAndQuantityString
    "Place the name starting in column 1 and the quantity
    starting in column 21."

    | stream |
    stream := WriteStream on: Sting new) nextPutAll: self name.
    self name size + 1 to: 20 do: [stream nextPut: Character space].
    stream nextPutAll: self quantity printString.
    ^stream contents
```

In Chapter 11, we will abstract this implementation so that display string methods can provide columnated information with very little effort.

9.3.2.8 Columnar Information—Variable Font

Columnar information is more difficult when the font of choice is a variable font. In this case, the start of the next column must be indicated in pixels and the item must be displayed on a graphics context using a VisualBlock. This requires that the SequenceView visual blocks be set in a postbuild operation as was done in Section 9.3.2.6. Below is an example of just such an implementation.

```
postBuildWith: aBuilder

    | listView |
    listView := (aBuilder componentAt: #lineItems) widget.
```

```
listView visualBlock: [:sv :index | | lineItem vb |
    lineItem := sv at: index.
    vb := VisualBlock block: [:gc :bnds |
        gc displayString: linItem name at: 5@16.
        gc displayString: lineItem quantity at: 150@16].
    BoundedWrapper on: vb].
listView selectedVisualBlock: [:sv :index | | lineItem vb rv |
    lineItem := sv at: index.
    vb := VisualBlock block: [:gc :bnds |
        gc displayString: linItem name at: 5@16.
        gc displayString: lineItem quantity at: 150@16].
    rv := ReversingWrapper on: vb.
    rv reversing: true.
    BoundedWrapper on: rv].
```

9.3.2.9 Grid Spacing

It is often necessary to change the height, in pixels, of the selections in the list. This height is called the *grid,* or *linegrid,* and its value is initialized to be just high enough to accommodate the default text. If, however, you intend to represent the items graphically, then you may want to change the grid size. For example, the following code changes the grid size to 35 pixels.

```
comp widget lineGrid: 35
```

9.3.2.10 Selection Styles

By default, a single selection list widget displays its selection with the selection background color. A multiselection list widget displays its selections with check marks. Actually, both a single or multiselection list can represent its selections in one of three ways: normal (which is a highlighted background), checked, or with strike out. To achieve this behavior you can send one of the following three messages to a list widget in the postbuild operation: normalSelection, checkedSelection, strokedSelection. So, to have a multiselection list use highlighted selections instead of check marks, send normalSelection to the Multi-SequenceView in a postbuild operation as shown below.

postBuildWth: aBuilder

    (aBuilder componentAt: #namesList) widget normalSelection

9.3.3 Displaying Items in a Table Component

Much of what can be done to lists can also be done to tables. Tables are just two-dimensional lists. Below are a few suggestions, which are also illustrated in Disk Example 9.8.

9.3.3.1 Visual Blocks

Tables have visual blocks just like lists do (see Section 9.3.2.6). The only difference is that instead of receiving an integer index as an argument, the table's visual blocks receive a Point index. This makes perfect sense considering a table's two-dimensional structure.

A nice way to display a color palette is to use a table and redefine the GeneralSelection-TableView's visual blocks to fill the cell with a color from the palette. This is done in Chapter 14, Section 14.2.1.

9.3.3.2 Formated Text

Table components use display string selectors to display the objects in the table structure. This can greatly enhance the appearance of the tabular information in the component.

9.4 Text Editors and Input Fields

Although *VisualWorks* is about graphical interfaces, the reality is that most of the information in an application is in the form of text. There is a great deal that can be done with the text-related components of *VisualWorks*. The majority of the tips and tricks in this section are provided courtesy of ParagraphEditor. It will serve you well to study this class as much as possible. ParagraphEditor and its subclasses that are used in the text components were covered in Chapter 2, Section 2.4.5. It is also helpful to know about Text, Composed-Text, TextAttributes, VariableSizeTextAttributes, and CharacterAttributes (some of these are covered in Section 9.11).

9.4.1 Text Widgets in General

The set of tips and tricks in this section apply equally to text editors, input fields, and combo boxes since these three components are so closely related. For brevity I will use the term *text widget* to represent the widgets of such components. As always, comp refers to the component that is a SpecWrapper returned when the message componentAt: aSymbol is sent to the builder as shown below.

```
comp := self builder componentAt: #streetAddress
```

The text widget for text editors and input fields is acquired by sending the widget message to the component.

```
comp widget
```

For combo boxes, the text widget is acquired as below.

```
comp widget editor
```

All those things common to text editors, input fields, and combo boxes are covered in this section as well as in Disk Example 9.9 and are discussed below.

9.4.1.1 Accessing the Text

All text widgets are a kind of ComposedTextView. As the name suggests, a ComposedTextView is a view for a ComposedText object. A ComposedText object contains a Text object plus additional information for displaying the Text object in a view. Among this additional information is a TextAttributes object. The Text of a text widget can be accessed by sending the message displayContents to the widget to get the ComposedText and then sending the message text to the ComposedText to get the actual Text object.

```
comp widget displayContents text
```

This is the value that will be sent to the model on an accept action. The Text object can also be acquired from the controller as shown below.

```
comp widget controller text
```

9.4.1.2 Adding Emphasis

The term **emphasis** applies to the font used to display the characters in a text. Emphasis values are Symbols that describe the emphasis such as #italic, #bold, and #serif. To arbitrarily add emphasis to the text during runtime, access the text as above, add the emphasis, and then invalidate the widget. The example below underlines the first 10 characters in a text widget.

```
comp widget displayContext text
    emphasizeFrom: 1
    to: 10
    with: #underline.
comp invalidate
```

The following makes only the selected text italic.

```
cntl := comp widget controller.
(text := cntl text)
    addEmphasis: #(italic)
    removeEmphasis: Array new
    duplicate: false.
cntl replaceSelectionWith: text
```

9.4.1.3 The Paste Buffer

All text widgets in *VisualWorks* share the same paste buffer. It is located in a class variable in ParagraphEditor. To access the contents of the paste buffer, send the message current-

Selection to the ParagraphEditor class. To replace the contents in the paste buffer, send currentSelection: aText, where aText is the text you are placing in the paste buffer. A copy of whatever is contained in the paste buffer can be pasted into any text widget in *VisualWorks*.

9.4.1.4 Menu Actions

All of the actions provided in the text widget's <operate> menu can also be initiated programmatically from within your application. These are listed in Table 9.4.

It is interesting to note that again, align, changeTextStyle, and toggleWordWrap are currently not used anywhere in *VisualWorks!* To use any of the messages in Table 9.4, just send the message to the text widget's controller. For example, to cut the currently selected text in a text widget, do the following.

```
comp widget controller cut
```

Table 9.4. Text Widget Menu Actions.

Message	Behavior
accept	Accept a change in text
again	Repeat the last operation
align	Cycle through the various paragraph justifications
cancel	Restore text to previously accepted state
changeTextStyle	Pop up a menu allowing user to select a new text style such as default or system
copySelection	Copy current selection to the paste buffer
cut	Cut current selection to the paste buffer
doIt	Evaluate the current selection as Smalltalk code
find	Open find dialog so user can search body of text for a match
hardcopy	Send text to printer
inspectIt	Inspect on current selection
paste	Paste current contents of paste buffer into text widget
printIt	Apply a doIt and insert the result as text
replace	Open find/replace dialog so user can replace text
toggleWordWrap	Toggle between wrapping lines and wrapping only with carriage returns
undo	Reset the state of the text widget to previous cut or paste edit operation

9.4.1.5 Justification

Unknown to many is how to change the justification attribute of a text widget. The alignment variable in a TextAttributes is what indicates the justification of a text widget. The alignment variable can take on a value of 0, 1, 2, or 3, where

0	left justification
1	center
2	right justification
3	full justification

To change a text widget's justification to full justification for example, do the following.

```
comp widget displayContents setAlignment: 2.
comp widget resetSelections.
comp invalidate
```

It is necessary to reset the text widget's selections and invalidate so that the change is displayed visually and correctly.

9.4.1.6 Text Style

A widget's text style is a TextAttributes object, and it indicates how all of the text in the text widget will appear. It includes a CharacterAttributes, which indicates the base font used for the characters in the text. The CharacterAttributes also includes variations of this font for the various emphases such as bold and italic. *VisualWorks* ships with nine TextAttributes such as #default, #system, and #fixed. To change a text widget's text style to #large, for example, do the following.

```
comp widget
    textStyle: (TextAttributes styleNamed: #large);
    resetSelections;
    invalidate
```

9.4.1.7 Text Widget Menus

By default, *VisualWorks* text widgets have an <operate> menu, which is defined by Paragraph-Editor and maintained in the class variable TextEditorYellowButtonMenu. This menu provides all the essential menu items for text editing such as find, replace, cut, copy, etc. Paragraph-Editor defines another menu in its CodeYellowButtonMenu class variable. This menu is a superset of the TextEditorYellowButtonMenu and adds the source code manipulation menu items such as inspect and do it. The TextEditorYellowButtonMenu can be replaced by the CodeYellowButtonMenu if you would like to provide source code control with your text widget. The switch can be made in a postbuild operation by sending the *initializeMenuFor-*

Text message to the text widget's controller. To do this, include a line of code in a post-BuildWith: method such as the one shown below.

```
comp widget controller initializeMenuForText
```

You also have the option of using a completely arbitrary menu for the text widget. Such a menu is provided by the application model as a resource. This menu can be created using the Menu Editor, a MenuBuilder, or a Menu creation method. The performer for this menu is the application model itself. However, when a text widget controller handles a menu selection, it first looks to see if it can handle the selection internally before passing it on to the performer. Therefore, menu selections such as **cut** and **paste** are always handled by the text widget controller no matter who the performer may be. This makes it very convenient to create custom menus that include both text editing and application model processing. It also makes it necessary to become familiar with the text widget controller menu actions listed in Table 9.4 so that your application model does not define menu action methods that conflict with those that will be intercepted by the text widget controller. For example, a text widget controller will never dispatch a cut or paste message to an application model even though the application model is the performer and has the cut or paste method defined. The reason is that the text widget controller recognizes these particular messages (and all others in Table 9.4) and will handle them itself.

9.4.1.8 Continuous Accept

Ordinarily the text widget's model is not updated until there is a change of focus. A text widget can be set to update the model on each keystroke. This is accomplished by setting the text widget controller's continuousAccept variable to true.

```
comp widget controller continuousAccept: true
```

9.4.2 Text Editors

While much of what is covered in this section can also apply to input fields and combo boxes, most of the particular behaviors mentioned are usually reserved for text editors. For example, input fields, combo boxes, and text editors can all conduct searches for substrings. This is due to their common ancestry in both the view and controller hierarchies. However, as a practical matter, this does not make much sense where input fields are concerned. Users very rarely, if ever, need to search an input field for a substring. All the tricks and tips about text editors are illustrated in Disk Example 9.10.

9.4.2.1 Word Wrapping

Unknown to many is that word wrapping in a text editor can be toggled on or off. The action method toggleWordWrap defined in the text widget controller provides this behavior. An example is shown below.

```
comp widget controller toggleWordWrap
```

Repeat this message to toggle word wrapping back on again.

9.4.2.2 Selected Text

The text widget controller keeps track of a current selection, which is some substring of its text. The current selection can appear highlighted to indicate to the user what text is selected. It is not required, however, that the selection be highlighted. Many times it is helpful to access the currently selected text. To do this, use the following code.

```
comp widget controller selection
```

If the selection is highlighted, you can unhighlight it with

```
comp widget controller unselect
```

Unfortunately, the semantics are misleading in this case because the code above does not really unselect anything, it merely turns off the highlighting. The text widget controller still has the selection marked. This allows us to redisplay the highlight as shown.

```
comp widget controller select
```

Again, the actual selection did not change, the code above merely allows the user to view the selection.

9.4.2.3 Making a Selection

The **type in point** is the insertion point in the text editor where the next character will appear. It is usually marked by a small triangle at the base of the current line of text. To search for a string in the text from the current type in point, use the following.

```
comp widget controller find: 'test string'.
```

To search from the beginning of the text, regardless of the type in point, use the alternate form shown below.

```
comp widget controller find: 'test string' startingAt: 1
```

Each of these statements returns a boolean indicating whether the string was found or not. If the string was found, then it becomes the new selection and can become highlighted with a select message. For this reason, it is best to unselect (that is, unhighlight) the current selection, if any, before conducting any searches, otherwise it will give a false visual indication to the user by remaining highlighted even if the new selection becomes highlighted as well. If the substring is not found in the search, the previous selection remains the current selection and can be rehighlighted.

9.4.2.4 Replacing the Selection

The currently selected text can be easily replaced with any other arbitrary text. An example is shown below.

```
comp widget controller
    replaceSelectionWith: 'hey diddle diddle' asText
    saveSelectionForUndo: true
```

The second argument determines if the previous selection will be copied to the paste buffer or not. If you do not plan to copy it to the paste buffer, you can use the shorter version shown below.

```
comp widget controller
    replaceSelectionWith: 'hey diddle diddle' asText
```

9.4.2.5 Margin, Tab Stops, and Line Height

The information for margins, tab stops, and line height is held in the TextAttributes. The TextAttributes is contained in a ComposedText object, which is held by the text editor widget. The TextAttributes keeps two lefthand margins: one for the first line in the paragraph and one for each subsequent line. The margin for the first line in the paragraph is called the **first indent**, and the margin for the remaining lines is called the **second indent**. The right margin for a paragraph of text is called the **right indent**. Each of the margins is measured in pixels.

The **tab stops** are the pixel positions in a line of text that will be arrived at through a sequence of tab events. These tab stops are integer values held in an array, called the **tabs array**. The tabs array can also be an Interval object, which is more efficient if all the tab stops are at regular intervals.

The **line height** is the distance, in pixels, between consecutive lines of text measured from the top of the first line to the top of the second. In *VisualWorks*, this is also called the *line grid*.

Changing any one of these attributes requires changing the text editor's text attributes. The following code changes the left margins, tab stops, and line height for a text editor. It is rare that you would want to change all of these attributes at the same time. It is done so here only for the purpose of illustration. Once the TextAttributes has been changed, reset the widget's selections and invalidate the component so that it will redraw itself using these new parameters.

```
comp widget displayContents textStyle .
    firstIndent: 10;
    secondIndent: 10;
```

```
        tabsArray: (10 to: 1000 by: 10)
          gridLine: 20.
    comp widget resetSelections.
    comp invalidate
```

9.4.3 Input Fields

There are several things that can be done to enhance the behavior of input fields. This also applies to combo box input fields, which vary only slightly from input fields in how they behave. All of the suggestions included in this section are also illustrated in Disk Example 9.11.

9.4.3.1 Removing the Menu

It can be argued quite effectively that an input field does not require a menu at all. The easiest way to assure that no menu is employed is to define the widget controller's menu holder as a ValueHolder on nil. This can be done in a postbuild operation and should look something like the following.

```
        comp widget controller menuHolder: nil asValue
```

9.4.3.2 When Not to Use Continuous Accept

A good tip is to not use continuous accept with input fields that edit numbers or dates. The reason is that the numbers and dates cannot be accepted successfully unless all required characters are present. For example, a user that tries to type in the float value 12.34 will have trouble on the third key stroke because the string '12.' will be passed to the InputFieldView, which will be unable to convert it to a number and will therefore flash the input field component.

9.4.3.3 Displaying Nontext Objects

Any object can be displayed in an input field as long as it responds to the message asText by returning a text or string object. However, it is necessary that the field be in read-only mode, lest it try to update an object that is not textual in nature. As an example, suppose we have a User class whose instances represent the set of users who can access an application. A User object might have several attributes such as name, password, and access rights. We might have occasion to display a User in an input field such as a current user field. In order to do so, it is only necessary that the User class have an instance method, asText, which returns a text object or string. It might be as simple as the following.

asText

```
    ^self printString
```

9.5 Buttons

Buttons give the user control over the interface. There are several things that can be done with these components. In this section, we will first look at what can be done with action buttons and then we will look at radio buttons and check boxes as a group.

9.5.1 Action Buttons

Do not think you are confined to look policy for how your buttons appear and behave. Do not think you must always implement an action method for an action button. There are several things that can be done with action buttons that go well beyond the default behavior. These things are described below and illustrated in Disk Example 9.12.

9.5.1.1 Changing the Label

Action buttons have a label attribute, which is a Label object by default. Section 9.2.1 provides several ideas as to what can be done to labeled components. These include replacing the text and text attributes in the Label object and replacing the Label object itself with a LabelAndIcon, an image, a VisualBlock or some other visual component. Refer to Section 9.2 for more on these techniques.

9.5.1.2 Arbitrary Action Blocks

In Chapter 4, Section 4.2.2, we learned that an *action block* is a block that, when evaluated, dispatches an action message to an application model. The action block is manufactured by the application model. We can easily override this to define our own arbitrary action block. This eliminates the need to define a corresponding action method. To do this, place a zero argument block in the builder's bindings, keyed to the action button's action name. This should be done in a prebuild operation so that the block is available during interface construction when the action button is built and connected to its model. This technique allows you to tie any arbitrary code to the press of an action button. For example, suppose we want a button to open a System Browser. If the button's action has been defined to be #openBrowser, then we could implement a prebuild statement such as

```
aBuilder actionAt: #openBrowser put: [Browser open].
```

This makes a corresponding openBrowser action method unnecessary.

9.5.1.3 Toggle Behavior

To get an action button to act as a toggle, do not define an action method, but instead, define an aspect method that returns a value model (e.g., a ValueHolder) whose value is a boolean. This value model acts as the model for the button widget in lieu of a PluggableAdaptor. The button is down when the model is true and up when the model is false. Whenever the button is pressed, the model's value is toggled to the opposite state, which causes the button to visually toggle as well. Also, the model can be set programmatically and the button will automatically respond to reflect the change in value. This is the very same behavior exhibited by a check box component. As an example of how this might be used, suppose we have an application that has an aspect called pumpIsOn, which is a ValueHolder on a boolean. An action button can be used to not only operate the pump, but also indicate whether the pump has been turned on or off by some other means.

9.5.1.4 Touch Pad

All of the look policies have action buttons, which give a 3D visual impression of being pushed in. Sometimes it is nice to have a button that is flat and only temporarily changes colors when it is pressed. This kind of action button is called a *touch pad*. Touch pads are used by the ColorToolModel.

   Touch pads are easy to set up. In the Properties Tool, unselect the border attribute. Then choose appropriate background and selection background colors—something different from that of the button's container. It is usually nice to give the button some kind of visual boundary, so divider lines or a group box might be a nice touch.

9.5.1.5 Invisible Button

Sometimes it is nice to have the button be completely invisible. This is used when some other object will provide visual indication of the button but the button is still needed to capture the user's mouse input and forward the action message. An example of this is provided in the Color Tool (see Chapter 8, Section 8.2.4). To provide an invisible button, define no look preferences and unselect the border attribute. Also, you must turn off the selection highlighting. When a button is pressed or selected, it is highlighted regardless of the color chosen for the selection background attribute. To disable this selection highlighting effect, send the message hiliteSelection: false to the action button widget in a post-build operation as demonstrated below.

```
comp widget hiliteSelection: false
```

At this point, the button will dispatch its action message whenever the user clicks the <select> mouse button within its bounds, but the user will have no visual indication that a button is there or that it has been pressed.

9.5.2 Check Boxes and Radio Buttons

All of the tips and tricks discussed below, except for the fourth one, apply to both radio buttons and check boxes. The widgets for these buttons—CheckButtonView and RadioButtonView—are almost identical and the widget controller is the same—ToggleButtonController. The only real difference between the two is their model and how the view is initialized. The tips and tricks for check boxes and radio buttons are discussed below and illustrated in Disk Example 9.13.

9.5.2.1 Changing the Label

Like all labeled components, you can change or replace the label in a check box or radio button. The various techniques and gimmicks employed for doing so are discussed in Section 9.2.1.

9.5.2.2 Arbitrary Visual Images

In *VisualWorks* 1.0, the images used to indicate on/off state in a check box or radio button could be set arbitrarily during runtime for any given instance. Unfortunately, in *Visual-Works* 2.0, this is no longer the case. Now all check box and radio button images are hard-coded into class variables, which means any changes are at the class level and not the instance level. Furthermore, these class variables are fixed during initialization and do not have put accessors, so they are not available for editing. To regain the ability to use arbitrary images in check boxes and radio buttons would require rewriting the classes that implement them, including all the concrete, look policy specific classes.

9.5.2.3 Labels on Lefthand Side

Radio buttons and check boxes automatically place the label to the right of the visual. While there is no option for placing the label on the left (or any other orientation for that matter), it is very easy to construct this effect using a label component in addition to the visual pair button. Simply set the button's label to a blank and create a passive label lined up to the left of the image. It is best to turn off the tabbing, otherwise the rectangle used to indicate keyboard focus will form around the empty label on the left when the button takes focus. The same applies of course for placing the label above or below the button.

9.5.2.4 Radio Buttons and Smalltalk Code

A radio button usually sets the value of its model to a Symbol. There is a good reason for doing so. Symbols are recognized by Smalltalk as elements of the language. They can be used as class names or message selectors. By choosing your radio button values carefully, you can play off of this fact and instill a great deal of power into your radio buttons. Instead of having your radio buttons select some arbitrary Symbol, your radio buttons can select a class name or a message selector to be used by some part of the application.

9.6 Composite and Arbitrary Components

The addition of composite components and arbitrary components can provide a great deal of pizzazz and flexibility to your applications. Some tips and tricks for these three types of components are described below.

9.6.1 Composite Components

One of the benefits of composites is that they can provide a great deal of interface while taking up a very limited amount of real estate on the screen. By giving the composite component scroll bars, we create a viewport into another interface. Another benefit is that they can group two or more components to facilitate layout.

Composite components can be built during the canvas-painting process or during runtime when the application is opening. Each of these is discussed below and illustrated in Disk Example 9.14.

9.6.1.1 Edit Mode Construction

While in edit mode (the canvas-painting process), composites are constructed using the **arrange→group** selection in the canvas <operate> menu. Once a composite is created, its bounds can be reduced and the user can still scroll for all of its contents. The group of components in the composite can also be positioned as a single component.

9.6.1.2 Runtime Mode Construction

The problem with constructing composites during the canvas-painting process is that we are required to know ahead of time how many components will be included in the composite. If this determination cannot be made until runtime, then we need a new strategy. Fortunately, composites can be created and populated with components during runtime.

The procedure takes place in a postbuild operation, and it is a three-step process. The first step is to tell the builder to start a new composite by sending it the message new-Composite as shown below.

aBuilder startNewComposite.

Step 2 is to add component specs describing the components that are to inhabit the composite.

aBuilder add: anInputFieldSpec.
aBuilder add: aTextEditorSpec.

The third step is to tell the builder that the composite is finished and give the composite a layout and properties. An example is shown below.

endCompositeLayout: aLayout properties: anArray

The argument aLayout is the composite's layout object, and anArray is an array of Symbols representing unary messages understood by CompositeSpec and describing the decoration properties for the composite. Table 9.5 gives is a list of available decoration properties messages.

The full example below is a postbuild operation, which creates a composite containing a label and an input field. The layouts of the label and input field are relative to the composite's bounds. The composite is also given a border.

postBuildWith: aBuilder

```
| layout model |
aBuilder newComposite.
aBuilder add: (LabelSpec label: 'Name:' layout: 10@10).
layout := 70@10 extent: 150@20.
model := 'Your Name' asValue
aBuilder add: (InputFieldSpec model: model layout: layout).
aBuilder
    endCompositeLayout: (50@50 extent: 200@50)
    properties: #(bordered)
```

Table 9.5. Composite Component Decoration Properties.

Symbol name	Description
#bordered	include a border
#horizontalScrollBar	include a horizontal scroll bar
#noHorizontalScrollBar	do not include a horizontal scroll bar
#notBordered	do not include a border
#noVerticalScrollBar	do not include a vertical scroll bar
#verticalScrollBar	include a vertical scroll bar

Building composites during runtime requires some familiarity with creating component specs on the fly and adding them to a UIBuilder as is done in Chapter 3.

9.6.2 Arbitrary Components

An arbitrary component (or view holder) takes any visual part as its widget—even a non-*VisualWorks* visual part. By non-*VisualWorks* visual part, I mean a visual part designed prior to *VisualWorks* and/or a visual part that does not conform to any of the *VisualWorks* widget protocol described in Chapter 2, Section 2.1.2. Using this technique, entire applications written outside of the scope of *VisualWorks* can be added to a *VisualWorks* window.

Arbitrary components are very easy to set up. All that is required is that the resource method responsible for providing the widget ensure that it is properly initialized. For example, if the widget is a view, it must be connected to its model. The application model provides the widget as a dynamic resource and usually references the widget with an instance variable. If the widget is a view, the application model may reference the model in addition to, or instead of, the widget.

Disk Example 9.15 illustrates the flexibility of arbitrary components by placing both a rather simple arbitrary component and an entire System Browser inside of a *VisualWorks* window along with other *VisualWorks* components. Using arbitrary components is a great way to augment the set of *VisualWorks* components without having to also create a new spec class, a properties box interface, a spec generation block, and a new button for the Palette (these topics are discussed in Chapter 12, which covers the process of adding a first-class *VisualWorks* component).

9.7 Menus

Menus are a very integral part of an application interface, and many *VisualWorks* components (the window too) have menus. Menus in *VisualWorks* are instances of the Menu class. The menu items are instances of MenuItem. With these two classes, the developer has a great deal of flexibility in designing and managing an application's menus. In this section, we will cover creating menus, the menu button component, dynamic menus, menu attributes, and menu item attributes.

9.7.1 Creating Menus

There are three ways to create a menu in *VisualWorks*. The traditional way is to create an instance of Menu using the protocol of the Menu class's forerunner PopUpMenu. The PopUpMenu class has several instance creation methods, and these are included in the Menu class for backward compatibility. This technique of creating a menu can be somewhat awkward and is no longer in vogue. You should be familiar with it, however, since there is a substantial amount of legacy code that creates menus in just such a manner. The second way to build a menu is to use MenuBuilder, which is a great improvement over the instance creation protocol of Menu and PopUpMenu. It distributes the menu-building process over several messages instead of running it all into a single instance creation message. The MenuBuilder approach is much more intuitive for the task. The third way to build a menu is the best of all—use the Menu Editor! That's what its there for, to make your life simpler.

Each of these techniques is described below, and the example in each case is the same—an instance of Menu that is a simple accept/undo/copy/cut/paste type of text-editing menu. Each of these examples is also provided in Disk Example 9.16.

9.7.1.1 Menu Instance Creation

A menu can be built by sending instance creation messages to the Menu class directly as is shown below.

```
Menu
    labelArray:      #('accept' 'undo' 'cut' 'copy' 'paste')
    lines:           #(2)
    values:          #(accept undo cut copySelection paste)
```

The advantage of this technique is that it supports the traditional menu creation protocol used in previous version of *VisualWorks*. The instance of Menu can also be sent additional messages to further define the menu. The disadvantages of this technique are that the menu creation is somewhat cumbersome and it is not completely backward compatible with *VisualWorks* 1.0, which used the PopUpMenu class instead of the Menu class.

9.7.1.2 Menu Builder

A good way to build menus programmatically is to use a MenuBuilder. The MenuBuilder class provides the means to easily and logically create a menu programmatically. The developer just sends messages to an instance of MenuBuilder as is shown below.

```
MenuBuilder new
    add: 'accept'->#accept;
    add: 'undo'->#undo;
    line;
    add: 'cut'->#cut;
    add: 'copy'->#copySelection;
    add: 'paste'->#paste;
    menu
```

The advantages of this technique are that it allows a menu to be built naturally, one item at a time, and that it is completely backward compatible with *VisualWorks* 1.0. The disadvantages are that it does not support the following menu features: disabling, icons, indicator items, and short–cut keys.

9.7.1.3 Menu Editor

The easiest way to create a menu is to use the Menu Editor. The Menu Editor compiles a resource method whose source code for our example menu would look like the following.

```
<resource: #menu>
^#(#Menu #(
    #(#MenuItem
        #label: 'accept' )
    #(#MenuItem
        #label: 'undo' )
    #(#MenuItem
        #label: 'cut' )
    #(#MenuItem
        #label: 'copy' )
    #(#MenuItem
        #label: 'paste' ) ) #(2 3 ) #(#accept #undo #cut #copy #paste ) ) decodeAsLiter-
alArray
```

The main advantage of this technique is that it is easy and requires no knowledge of special menu defining protocol as do the other two techniques. The disadvantages are that it is not backwards compatible with *VisualWorks* 1.0 and does not support the following menu features: disabling, icons, and indicator items.

9.7.2 Menu Button Component

Menu buttons are somewhat of a special case of *VisualWorks* components. This section covers some things you should know about the menu button component. These are also illustrated in Disk Example 9.17.

9.7.2.1 No Keyboard Operations

The menu button component is one of the two types of active components (the other being the slider component) that do not handle keyboard input and cannot take keyboard focus. Since the menu button cannot take focus, it does not send or receive validation and notification messages either.

9.7.2.2 Label

By setting a menu button's label, you remove the possibility of having the current selection appear in the component. That is, the label is written on the component in lieu of the current selection. Not only that, but the menu button's aspect model is initialized to nil, and a label may mislead the user into thinking that something is selected. So be careful when labeling a menu button.

9.7.2.3 Menu Values

By default, the menu button's menu returns Symbols. Using the menu builder, however, you can have it return any kind of object. For example, the following code builds a menu that lists some cursors used in *VisualWorks* and returns an opaque image representing each cursor when selected.

```
MenuBuilder
    add: 'execute'->Cursor execute asOpaqueImage;
    add: 'normal'>Cursor normal asOpaqueImage;
    add: 'read'->Cursor read asOpaqueImage;
    menu
```

9.7.3 Dynamic Menus and Menu Attributes

A dynamic menu is a menu that can be edited or replaced during runtime. The various techniques for manipulating menus during runtime are discussed below and illustrated in Disk Example 9.18.

9.7.3.1 Making a Menu Dynamic

To make a menu dynamic, have the application model supply it as a dynamic resource. In order to do this, the application model should supply not the menu but a ValueHolder whose value is the menu. The application model can also allocate an instance variable to constantly maintain a reference to this ValueHolder so that it is always accessible, but this is not necessary. Two versions of the same dynamic resource menu method are shown below.

myDynamicMenu

^self class myMenu asValue

myDynamicMenu

```
^myDynamicMenu isNil
    ifTrue: [myDynamicMenu := self class myMenu asValue]
    ifFalse: [myDynamicMenu]
```

In the first version above, no instance variable is required and the ValueHolder is accessed from the builder's bindings using the menu ID. In the second version above, the Value-Holder is referenced directly by an instance variable. In either case, the menu is accessible during runtime.

9.7.3.2 Accessing Menu Items and Submenus

The most common way to access a menu item from the menu is to send the message menuItemLabeled: aString to the menu where aString is the label of the menu item. The example below accesses the **File** menu item from a menu.

menu menuItemLabeled: 'File'

This statement returns an instance of MenuItem (see Section 9.7.4 for more on MenuItem). A menu item can also be accessed by its integer index or by its value as is done in the examples below, respectively.

menu menuItemAt: anInteger

menu menuItemWithValue: anObject

If the menu item has a submenu, then this submenu is accessed by sending the submenu message to the menu item as is shown below.

(menu menuItemLabeled: 'File') submenu

This statement returns an instance of Menu, and we can now access any of its menu items and begin a recursive process.

9.7.3.3 Replacing a Menu

In order to replace a menu dynamically, simply send the value: message to the ValueHolder containing the dynamic menu as is shown below.

self myDynamicMenu value: aNewMenu

Next time the menu is accessed, aNewMenu will be used instead of the previous menu. This can be done at any time while the application is running.

9.7.3.4 Removing a Menu Item

A menu item can be removed from a menu during runtime by using the removeItem: message as shown below.

```
menuItem := menu menuItemLabeled: 'accept'.
menu removeItem: menuItem
```

The next time this menu is displayed, the **accept** selection will not appear. This type of operation can be done at any time while the application is running.

9.7.3.5 Adding a Menu Item

A menu item can be added to a menu during runtime by using the addItemLabel:value: message as shown below.

```
menu addItemLabel: 'undo' value: #undo
```

On the next access of the menu, the **undo** selection will be available. Menu items can be added when the menu is first built, as part of the postbuild operation, or at any time while the application is running.

When a menu item is added to a menu, it appears at the bottom of the list of selections.

9.7.3.6 Hiding a Menu Item

A menu item can be hidden from the user, but it is still part of the menu. This is similar in spirit to how a *VisualWorks* component is hidden, but it is still part of the interface. To hide a menu's menu item, send it the message hideItem: aMenuItem as is shown below.

```
menu hideItem: (menu itemLabeled: 'paste')
```

This example makes the **paste** operation unavailable until the following statement causes the item to reappear again.

```
menu unhideItem: (menu itemLabeled: 'paste')
```

A menu item can be hidden at any time while the application is running. Hiding a menu item is much preferred to removing it if you plan on making it available again. The reason is that a removed item will lose its place in the order since items are always added at the end.

9.7.3.7 Menu Background Color

To change the background color for a menu, send it the backgroundColor: message with a ColorValue as the argument as is shown below.

```
menu backgroundColor: ColorValue cyan
```

The next time the menu is accessed, its background will be cyan. This can be done when the menu is first built, in the postbuild operation, or at any time while the application is running.

9.7.4 Menu Item Attributes

There are several options for menu items in *VisualWorks*. These are described below and further illustrated in Disk Example 9.19.

9.7.4.1 Disabling a Menu Item

A menu item can be disabled such that it appears in the menu but cannot be selected. To do this, merely send the message disable to the menu item. To enable it again, send the message enable. This is very similar to disabled/enabled state of a *VisualWorks* component. It is also similar to hiding a menu item as discussed in Section 9.7.3.6. When hiding a menu item, that item is completely unavailable. When disabling a menu item, however, you are telling the user that the menu item is only temporarily unavailable and that it could be available again under different circumstances.

9.7.4.2 Icons

A menu selection can be prefixed by a small icon or image. This is a very common semantic in graphical user interfaces. To give a menu item an icon, send it the labelImage: message, where the argument is the image. For most purposes, the image should have an extent of 16@16. This size best fits the default text in the most menus.

  Actually, this icon can be any visual component and is not restricted to being an image. A VisualBlock, for example, would work just as well. In addition, the label need not be included, and the entire menu item can be represented by this visual component.

9.7.4.3 Indicator Menu Item

Menu items can be used to indicate an on/off condition. This type of behavior is very similar to that of a check box. Such menu items are called *indicator* menu items. To set up an indicator menu item, initialize the menu item with a beOn or beOff message as shown below.

```
menuItem beOn
```

To change the menu item's state during runtime, send it the same messages, beOn and beOff. To check to see if an indicator menu item is currently on or off, send the message isOn or isOff, respectively.

  A menu item used as an indicator can also be associated with a value model that holds a boolean. The menu item is linked with such a value model using the indication: message shown below.

> menuItem indication: valueModel

This allows the state of the menu item to be controlled by the value model. Likewise, the value model always indicates the current state of the menu item.

9.7.4.4 Short-Cut Keys

A menu item can be set up so that the user can select it with a *short-cut key* (see Chapter 6, Section 6.3.2.1). To do so, send the message shortCutKeyCharacter: aCharacter to the menu item as is shown below.

> menuItem shortCutKeyCharacter: $C

This statement allows the menu item to be selected when the user presses the <Ctrl> or <Alt> key in combination with the <C> key. The short-cut key should be established when the menu is built, either with the Menu Editor or programmatically as shown above. It can also be established in the postbuild operation or at any time while the application is running, but this is typically not something done programmatically.

When using the Menu Editor, the short-cut key is added at then end of a line and enclosed in curly brackets as is shown below.

> Close   close   {C}

This will create a menu item that looks like

> Close   Alt+C

and that triggers the close method when the user presses <Alt>-<C>. A short-cut key is also known as a *hot key* or an *accelerator key*.

9.7.4.5 Access Characters

For the *MS Windows* and *CUA-OS/2* look policies, the menus can have access characters. Access characters are very similar to short cut keys. An **access character** is a character in the menu item label that is underlined as is shown in the example menu item label below.

> <u>F</u>ile

When an access character is pressed in combination with the <Alt> key (the <Ctrl> does not work with access characters), the corresponding menu item is selected. The access character is usually set in the Menu Editor by prefixing the character with the $& character. To give a menu item an access character programmatically, you must tell the menu item the position of the access character in the menu item label as is shown below.

> menuItem accessCharacterPosition: 1

This example makes the first character in the label the access character. This type of operation is usually done when the menu is first built, but it can also be done programmatically. An access character is also known as a *mnemonic.*

9.7.4.6 Menu Item Foreground Color

The foreground color in which a menu item is rendered is changed by sending the color: message as shown below.

> menuItem color: ColorValue red

This can be done when the menu is first built, in a postbuild operation, or at any time while the application is running. The next time the menu item appears, it will be rendered in red letters.

9.8 Windows

An application model's window can always be accessed by sending the message window to the builder as shown below.

> self builder window

This window is an instance of ApplicationWindow, which was covered in detail in Chapter 6. You may want to review that chapter, especially Section 6.5.

In the window examples below, sometimes we will access the window from the builder and sometimes we will assume we already have a window. Disk Example 9.20 gives concrete examples of the material covered in this section.

9.8.1 The Window Icon

There are three things you want to know about where window icons are concerned: setting the icon, iconizing or collapsing a window, and expanding a collapsed window. You may also be interested in setting the label length for icon's label.

9.8.1.1 Setting a Window's Icon

To set a window's icon, you must first create an Icon object from an image as shown below.

> Icon image: anImage

The image should have an extent of 32@32 and a single color palette. To set the window's icon, send it the icon: message. This is usually done in the postbuild operation. The statement might look something like the following.

aBuilder window icon: (Icon image: self class iconImage)

More than likely, the image will designed using the Image Editor.

9.8.1.2 Collapsing and Expanding a Window

As was explained in Chapter 6, a *collapsed* window is represented by an icon and an *expanded* window is represented as a full window (not collapsed). To programmatically collapse a window into its icon representation, send the collapse message to the window as shown below.

self builder window collapse

To expand the window again, send the expand message.

self builder window expand

9.8.1.3 Icon Label Length

The length of the icon label can be changed, but the change affects all instances. The change of label length is made by sending the message maxIconLabelLength: anInteger to the Window class or any of its subclasses as is shown below.

ApplicationWindow maxIconLabelLength: 40

The effect is global to all windows because the maximum icon label length is stored in a class variable defined in Window. Therefore, even though the message in the example above is sent to a subclass of Window, all instances of Window, Scheduled-Window, and ApplicationWindow are affected. The icon label length can also be set from the Settings Tool.

9.8.2 Scheduling a Window

Scheduling a window means opening it up and scheduling its controller with Scheduled-Controllers—the global instance of ControlManager. What follows are some tips and tricks concerning scheduling windows.

9.8.2.1 Window-Scheduling Protocol

There are three parameters that can vary when opening a window: origin, extent, and type. There are several scheduling methods that cover the various permutations of these parameters. For the most part, you will not want to specify the type of the window, opting for the default of #normal. Table 9.6 shows the more frequently used scheduling messages.

Table 9.6. Window-Scheduling Protocol.

Message	Behavior
open	Open the window at its self-determined bounds
openDisplayAt: aPoint	Open the window with its origin at aPoint
openIn: aRectangle	Open the window with bounds described by aRectangle
openIn: Rectangle fromUser	Open the window with the bounds described by the user
openAroundCursorWithExtent: aPoint	Open the window with extent of aPoint and centered around the cursor

9.8.2.2 UIBuilder-Scheduling Protocol

The builder also has its own scheduling protocol so that we can send scheduling messages to the builder without having to first access its window. An example of this is shown below.

> self builder openAt: 20@20

This is convenient when creating additional windows for an application model using temporary builders (i.e., not the builder referenced by the application model's builder instance variable).

9.8.2.3 Prompt User

The default opening behavior for all windows can be set to either prompting the user for a Rectangle in which to place the window or opening the window directly in its predefined bounds. This default behavior is set by sending the promptForOpen: aBoolean message to ScheduledWindow or any of its subclasses. To set the default opening behavior such that the user decides the window's initial size and location, use the following statement.

> ApplicationWindow promptForOpen: true

Even though the message in the example above is sent to ApplicationWindow, all instances of ScheduledWindow are affected as well (this includes system tools such as System Browsers and Inspectors). This is because the decision to prompt the user is determined by a class variable defined by ScheduledWindow. This default behavior is overridden by several of the scheduling messages such as the two below.

> openAt: aPoint

> openWithRectangleFromUser.

The default opening behavior for windows can also be set from the settings tool.

9.8.2.4 Active Window

Recall that the active window (or current window) is the window currently receiving the user input and is usually distinguished from other windows by a uniquely colored title bar. The active window can be ascertained programmatically from the global variable Scheduled-Controllers

    ScheduledControllers activeController view

or from the Window class or any of its subclasses

    Window currentWindow.

To make any window the active window, send it the becomeActive message. To make the active window yield to another window, send it the becomeInactive message.

9.8.2.5 Stuck Dialogs

During dialog development, a dialog can become stuck to the screen. (That is, they cannot be closed by any obvious means.) This usually happens because an error occurred during the execution of the dialog and a notifier was raised but the developer did not proceed with the thread of execution that opened the dialog. To remove the unwanted dialog, evaluate the following statement in a Workspace.

    DialogControllers allInstancesDo: [:each | each closeAndUnschedule]

9.8.3 Other Window Tips

Several other things can be done to a window during runtime, such as moving, resizing, and changing the label.

9.8.3.1 Moving

A window's bounds, which includes its origin and extent, can be changed at any time. The *origin* is the location of the window's upper left hand corner in screen coordinates. The *extent* is the actual dimensions of the window in pixels. To move a window, send it the message moveTo: aPoint, and it will relocate such that its new origin is at aPoint.

9.8.3.2 Resizing

To resize a window, use the moveTo:resize: message as demonstrated below.

    window moveTo: window globalOrigin resize: 200@350

The statement above changes the window's extent without changing its origin.

9.8.3.3 Raising and Lowering

As was explained in Chapter 6, a raised window rests on top of all other windows and is the active window. A lowered window appears as if it is behind all other windows. To programmatically raise a window, send it the raise message. Likewise, to lower a window, send it the lower message.

9.8.3.4 Changing the Label

To change the label of a window, send it the label: message as shown below.

```
window label: 'New Document'
```

Of course, to do this within an application model, the statement would look more like the following.

```
self builder window label: 'New Document'
```

9.9 Images, Masks, and Pixmaps

This section gives a very brief overview of images, Masks, and Pixmaps and provides some suggestions on how these objects might be used in a *VisualWorks* application. Chapter 6, Section 6.1 might be a good review for this section. Images, Masks, and Pixmaps are also covered in Disk Example 9.21.

9.9.1 Images

An *image* is the Smalltalk equivalent of a bitmap, and it is an instance of some subclass of Image. It describes a rectangular area of pixels, and each pixel has a color. An image has a palette, which describes the range of colors available to describe each pixel.

Unlike a Mask or a Pixmap, an image is not a graphics medium and is not associated with a host-supplied resource. Therefore it cannot produce a graphics context object and cannot be the destination of graphics-related operations. An image is merely a holder of information describing the colors of a grid of pixels.

Most images are created with the Image Editor, but they can also be created programmatically. The Image Editor will create images with up to 16 colors (depth of 4).

9.9.1.1 Store String

Like all objects, images can be stored in a literal format as Smalltalk source code. That is, an image can write itself out as a string, which when compiled as Smalltalk source code instantiates a copy of the original image. As was mentioned in Chapter 3, such a string is referred to as a store string. This is a very convenient way to make images persistent. To ascertain the store string for an image, simply send it the message store-String. This will return a string that, when compiled as Smalltalk code, will create a copy of the original image.

9.9.1.2 OpaqueImage

Normally, an image rendered on a target display surface overwrites all pixels within its bounds. Now consider that most images represent a figure drawn on a background. If the image's background color does not match that of the target display surface, the result is a somewhat awkward visual effect. What we would like to do is transfer just the pixels of the intended figure and not the background pixels. This can be accomplished using an OpaqueImage. An OpaqueImage holds on to an image and a Mask. The Mask is used to indicate which pixels of the image are transferred to the target surface. An OpaqueImage is created by sending the figure:shape: message the OpaqueImage class as illustrated below.

```
om := OpaqueImage figure: anImage shape: aMask
```

9.9.2 Masks

A Mask is like a window or Pixmap in that it represents a display surface provided by the host. It is unlike a window or Pixmap, however, in that it does not describe pixel color, but instead describes pixel opaqueness. In *VisualWorks*, this opaqueness attribute is referred to as *coverage*. Currently, a pixel can be either completely transparent (a coverage value of 0) or completely opaque (a coverage value of 1). Masks are used by OpaqueImages, Cursors, and Icons to transfer only certain pixels of an image on to a display surface.

9.9.3 Pixmaps

A Pixmap is just like a window except that it never appears on the screen and it never becomes damaged. Pixmaps are convenient for off-screen drawing, communicating with the window manager's clipboard, and creating images programmatically.

9.9.3.1 Off-Screen Drawing

A Pixmap can generate a ScreenGraphicsContext just like a window. You draw on this Screen-GraphicsContext just as you would any other. When you are done, the contents of the Pixmap can be transferred to a window's display surface for visual display. This technique makes it handy to create a complex picture off screen and then transfer the finished image to the screen all at once. Using this technique reduces the total amount of time required to render the final picture on the screen since drawing off screen is much faster than drawing directly on the screen. It also makes for a very clean visual update.

A Pixmap is created by sending the instance creation message extent: aPoint to the Pixmap class. The argument aPoint indicates the extent (or dimension) of the Pixmap. For example, the following code creates a Pixmap that is 30 pixels wide and 50 pixels high.

```
Pixmap extent: 30@50
```

Once you have created a Pixmap, you can draw on its display surface just as if it were a window. The example below creates a Pixmap, writes a string on it, and frames the string with a red box.

```
| pixmap gc |
pixmap := Pixmap extent: 100@100.
gc := pixmap graphics context.
gc displayString: 'VisualWorks' at: 10@30.
gc paint: ColorValue red.
gc dsplayRectangle: 5@5 extent: 100@40.
```

9.9.3.2 Displaying on the Screen

To get the Pixmap to show up on the screen, you must transfer its contents to a window. Fortunately, a Pixmap knows how to render itself on another display surface. Therefore, to display a Pixmap object's contents in a window, send it the message

```
displayOn: aGraphicsContext
```

where aGraphicsContext is the window's ScreenGraphicsContext object.

9.9.3.3 Host Clipboard

A Pixmap can copy from and paste to the window manager's clipboard. The following code creates a Pixmap holding a copy of the contents of the clipboard.

```
Pixmap fromClipboard
```

The next statement copies the contents of a Pixmap to the clipboard.

```
aPixmap toClipboard
```

9.9.3.4 Creating an Image

Since Pixmap is a subclass of DisplaySurface, it knows how to return an image representation of its display surface or any portion of its display surface. The asImage message returns an image representing the entire extent of the Pixmap. The asImage: aRectangle returns an image created from only the part of the Pixmap described by aRectangle.

This technique can be used to programmatically instantiate images. Simply create the Pixmap, draw on it as any other display surface, and then ask it for its image representation.

9.10 Cursors and the Screen

Proper use of cursors and certain screen effects can add a tremendous flair to your applications. In this section we will investigate some tips and tricks in this area.

9.10.1 Cursors

VisualWorks ships with over two dozen cursors ready to be used, or you can create your own as described in Section 9.10.1.1. In either event, there are certain times in an application when it is either convenient, colorful, or crucial to change the cursor. The current cursor can be changed on a temporary basis or a more permanent one. Cursors are implemented by the Cursor class. Proper use of cursors can give your application the professional touch. The cursor techniques described below are also illustrated in Disk Example 9.22.

9.10.1.1 Creating a Cursor

There are three steps involved in creating a Cursor.

1. Create an image of extent 16@16 using the Image Editor and edit the resulting source code such that its palette is as follows.

   (MonoMappedPalette whiteBlack)

   Call this the *color image.*

2. Create a second image of extent 16@16 using the Image Editor. Call this the *coverage image.*

3. Use the creation message image:mask:hotSpot:name: to create a new Cursor.

Cursors in *VisualWorks* have an extent of 16@16, so both images must have this extent. Cursors are also black and white only. The first image, the color image, represents all parts of the cursor that will appear black. The second image, the coverage image, represents all parts of the cursor that will mask out the screen background. Any pixels that are masked out but not defined by the color image will appear white.

In the method generated by the Image Editor for the color image, it is necessary to edit the source code to get the appropriate palette. Change the palette: argument from

        CoveragePalette monoMaskPalette

to

        MonoMappedPalette whiteBlack.

Once you have both images available, create the cursor as shown below.

        Cursor
            image: colorImage
            mask:coverageImage
            hotSpot:7@7
            name:'My Cursor'

The **hot spot** is used to indicate the cursor's exact location, and its value can range from 1@1 to 16@16. The cursor's name is of no significance.

While this three-step process is somewhat involved, Chapter 15 introduces a tool that allows a developer to more easily draw the cursor, see the work in progress, and install the cursor in a repository for future use.

9.10.1.2 Permanent Change of Cursor

To change the cursor for a long duration, send the message currentCursor: aCursor to the Cursor class, where aCursor is an instance of Cursor. For example, to change the cursor to the hour glass (formally known as the wait cursor), use the following.

        Cursor currentCursor: Cursor wait

The new cursor will remain the current cursor until explicitly replaced by another cursor. To change the cursor back to the usual pointer type cursor (formally known as the normal cursor), use the following.

        Cursor currentCursor: Cursor normal

Controllers will often use a permanent change of cursor to indicate a change of mode of operation. For instance, the select mode for a certain kind of controller might use the normal (pointer) cursor and the draw mode might use a pencil looking cursor.

9.10.1.3 Temporary Change of Cursor

Sometimes it is necessary to change the cursor just for the duration of a specific event such as the execution of a message or block. To do this, send the showWhile: aBlock message to a cursor where aBlock is any zero argument block. That cursor will temporarily replace the current cursor for the duration of the execution of the block and then reinstate the original cursor once the block execution is complete. For example, you may want to show the reading glasses cursor while a file is being read as is shown below.

```
Cursor read showWhile: [self readFile]
```

9.10.1.4 Accessing the Cursor Image

A cursor's image can be obtained as an OpaqueImage by sending the message asOpaque-Image to the instance of Cursor as shown below.

```
Cursor execute asOpaqueImage
```

9.10.2 Screen Operations

There is only one instance of the Screen class called the default Screen. It is accessed by sending the default message to the Screen class (this is similar to the default InputState). Proper use of the default Screen object can provide some professional effects. It is this object that allows a user to draw rectangles and other shapes with the mouse. The default Screen also provides the dragging of images and some very useful system information. In order to maximize the potential of these techniques, it helps to be well versed in the geometry classes such as Point, Rectangle, Circle, PolyLine, and LineSegment. In particular, you will want to review Point and Rectangle arithmetic. The default Screen operations are illustrated in Disk Example 9.23.

9.10.2.1 Displaying Shapes

The default Screen has two methods for displaying shapes on the screen. The message for the simpler of the two is shown below.

```
Screen default
    displayShape:     aShape
    at:               aPoint
    forMilliseconds:  anInteger.
```

The second one is a slight variation.

```
Screen default
    displayShape:     aShape
```

```
lineWidth:        aLineWidth
at:               aPoint
forMilliseconds:  someTime.
```

The arguments are described below.

aShape   Either an array of Points or any object that
                can display itself on a Mask and under-
                stands the message bounds. The shape will
                only show up in monochrome.

aLineWidth   An integer describing the line width, in
                pixels, to be used in rendering the shape.

aPoint   An instance of Point and a global reference
                for rendering the shape. The Point objects
                referenced in the shape are relative to this
                Point.

someTime   An integer describing the number of mil-
                liseconds to display the shape. For rubber-
                banding (discussed shortly), a value of 50
                or 100 is typical.

An example displaying a triangle of thickness two for a full second would look like the following.

```
| triangle |
triangle := Array with: 5@5 with: 100@100 with: 100@30 with: 5@5.
Screen default
    displayShape:     triangle
    lineWidth:        2
    at:               0@0
    forMilliseconds:  1000.
```

9.10.2.2 Rubberbanding

Very seldom are the messages above used by themselves. Most often they are used in a technique called rubberbanding. **Rubberbanding** is the rapid redrawing of shape whose dimension are constantly changing due to a cursor drag. The visual effect is such that it appears as if the user is stretching a rubber band on the screen. A similar technique is used by the UIPainterController to allow the user to drag a rectangle over several components for a simultaneous selection. It is important to point out that this drawing is done directly on the screen and has nothing to do with a window, the window's visual structure, or its graphics context.

Controllers are usually the objects responsible for rubberbanding. A controller method that allows the user to dynamically draw a line on the controller's view might look like the following.

getLineFromUser

```
| line initialPoint |
initialPoint := self sensor cursorPoint.
line:= Array with: initialPoint with: initialPoint.
Cursor crossHair showWhile: [[self sensor redButtonPressed]
    whileTrue: [
        Screen default
            displayShape: line
            at: self sensor globalOrigin
            forMilliseconds: 50.
        self viewHasCursor
            ifTrue: [line at: 2 put:self sensor cursorPoint]
            ifFalse: [nil]]]
```

The variable initialPoint is the cursor's initial location and acts as the anchor for the line. The line variable is an array with its first and last points initialized to the anchor point initialPoint. Next we change the cursor to a cross hair for the duration of the dragging motion. While the <select> button is pressed, the while true block is evaluated. Each evaluation of this block draws the line on the screen for 50 milliseconds and then checks to see if the cursor is still within bounds of the view. If it is, the line is recalculated according to the new cursor point. As soon as the user releases the <select> button, the loop is broken. There is an almost infinite number of variations on this basic theme.

9.10.2.3 Dragging Shapes

The default Screen also offers dragging capabilities. There are several ways to approach dragging and this is but one.

```
Cursor hand showWhile:
    [Screen default
        dragShape: aShape
        offset: 16@16
        gridPhase: 1@1
        gridSpacing: 1@1
        boundedBy: nil
        whileButton:0
        isDown: false]
```

The example above will change the cursor to a hand and drag aShape around the screen as long as the <select> button is up. Once the user presses the <select> button, the cursor changes back and aShape disappears.

Table 9.7. Default Screen Information.

Message	Return value
availableFonts	A collection of available fonts as FontDescription objects.
resolution	A Point describing the measure of a square inch in pixels. This is very useful for WYSIWYG type applications.
platformName	A string naming the current platform such as 'MS-Windows' or 'Macintosh.'
colorBitsPerPixel	An integer describing the number of pixels used to indicate color. This tells you how many colors the current system will support.
bounds	A Rectangle describing the size, in pixels, of the screen. The origin is 0@0 and the extent gives the actual size of the screen.
colorPalette	The palette used to render colors on windows and Pixmap objects.

9.10.2.4 System Information

The default Screen is also a source of useful information as is shown in Table 9.7.

9.11 Fonts

ParcPlace has done an excellent job of porting their product to all the popular platforms, however, there is still one facet of the porting issue that rears its ugly head—fonts. The wide variety of fonts and how they are handled by the different platforms has forced certain compromises. This is the primary reason why the *VisualWorks* image ships with such a limited *out of the box* font capability. However, the authors of *VisualWorks* have given you many powerful tools for dealing with fonts on your own. If you plan to port to several platforms or if you would like to go beyond the minimal fonts available within the image as shipped, then you must learn about fonts in *VisualWorks*.

9.11.1 Some Background

Even though this is a chapter of tips and tricks, the topic of fonts requires some explanation up front before we indulge in their use.

9.11.1.1 Describing a Font

Since *VisualWorks* ports to so many different platforms, it is difficult to say what fonts will be available. For the most part, it is just a guessing game. This explains why *VisualWorks* ships with such a limited set of available fonts. Fortunately the authors of *VisualWorks* developed the FontDescription object. A FontDescription is aptly named in that it describes the desired attributes of a font but does not itself represent or reference a host-supplied font. When an actual font resource is needed from the host environment, a lookup is initiated to find the host font that best matches the information contained within the FontDescription.

Acquiring the proper font from the host can take a fair amount of time—up to a few seconds. This is just enough time to give concern to the user. Therefore, the virtual image will cache fonts that have already been acquired so that the next lookup will appear instantaneous to the user. As a tip, you may want to find all your fonts as part of the initialization of your application so that they are readily available when needed.

9.11.1.2 Font Matching

A FontPolicy object is the agent responsible for conducting the lookup procedure that matches a FontDescription to an actual platform font resource. The default Screen and all graphics context objects hold on to the default FontPolicy. To have a FontPolicy object find a platform-specific font based on a FontDescription, we send it the findFont: aFontDescription message. It returns an instance of one of four subclasses of DeviceFont used for screen graphics: MSWindowsFont, MacFont, OS2Font, or XFont. I will refer to any instance of one of these four classes as a device font. A **device font** is a surrogate for an actual platform font resource that can be rendered on a graphics context. For the most part, FontPolicy and device font objects operate behind the scenes. Your main interest as a developer is to create FontDescription objects and let *VisualWorks* do the rest.

9.11.1.3 Text and Character Attributes

Unfortunately, the story of fonts does not stop with FontDescription. This is because a Text object is rendered as a ComposedText object, which uses a TextAttributes object to describe how the text should appear. Among other things, a TextAttributes references a Character-Attributes object. A CharacterAttributes object contains a FontDescription and a dictionary of variations of that same basic FontDescription. The FontDescription will describe a base font such as a Courier or an Arial, and the variations will apply bold, italics, or some other type of emphasis to this base font.

9.11.1.4 Adding New Fonts

The appearance of your application can be greatly enhanced by the addition of fonts. Fonts are actually added to the image by creating new CharacterAttributes and TextAttributes objects. This process is outlined below and further illustrated in Disk Example 9.24. Also, in Chapter 15 a tool is introduced that automates this process.

9.11.1.5 Creating a Font Description

In this example, we will create a FontDescription for a Times font. We choose a Times because it is available on most platforms.

```
fontDesc := FontDescription new
        pixelSize:     16;
        family:        'times'
```

To get an idea of how the current platform will match against this font description, you may inspect on the following.

```
Screen default defaultFontPolicy findFont: fontDesc
```

Trying to match fonts based on family or name can be a real crap shoot if you do not know ahead of time the particular platform on which your application may eventually run. A Times font is a fair bet, however, since most platforms support this kind of font. Each of the concrete device font classes—MSWindowsFont, MacFont, OS2Font, and XFont—has one or more class variables describing the family of fonts *VisualWorks* expects to find for its corresponding platform. The general wisdom, though, is to use attributes other than font family and font name in describing a font. At this point we have a FontDescription that can be used for setting the font attribute of a graphics context object. This is just fine for specialized display of text in a view; however, most font work is directly related to rendering text in some kind of text component—such as an input field or text editor—which requires a few more steps.

9.11.1.6 Creating a CharacterAttributes

To define a CharacterAttributes using the FontDescription above, you might do something like the following.

```
(charAtt := CharacterAttributes new setDefaultQuery: fontDesc)
        at: #bold      put: [:fd | fd boldness: 0.7];
        at: #italic    put: [:fd | fd italic: true];
        at: #underline put: [:fd | fd underline: true]
```

If you create a new CharacterAttributes, you may want to consider defining the following emphases as a minimum: #large, #small, #bold, #italic, #underline, #serif, and #sansserif (the example above does not define all of these). The reason for this is that the ParagraphEditor, the controller behind all text operations, expects to have these attributes available in its edit sessions. The instance creation method newWithDefaultAttributes will return an instance of CharacterAttributes with all the necessary emphases defined. Instances of Character-

Attributes can be cached in the CharacterAttributes class so that they are always available, but this is not necessary.

9.11.1.7 Creating a TextAttributes

To create a new TextAttributes based on the CharacterAttributes above would look something like the following.

```
(textAtt := TextAttributes characterAttributes: charAtt)
    lineGrid:    20
    baseline:    16
```

To store this new TextAttributes for later use, add it to the TextAttributes class variable Text-Styles as shown below.

```
TextAttributes styleNamed: #times put: textAtt.
```

By doing this, the new TextAttributes will automatically become available in the Properties Tool for components that use text. The drop menu used to select a component's font in Properties Tool is populated primarily by the contents of TextStyles.

9.12 Summary

This chapter introduced a variety of tips a tricks to augment your application development and depended heavily on the information covered in Part I. It also provided some new information about the fundamentals of *VisualWorks* and introduced several new terms. This new information was primarily in the areas of text, fonts, cursors, layout, and menus.

There are several things that apply to components in general, such as layout and color. Certain operations, such as keyboard control and model accessing, apply only to active components. Several things can be done with a component's border and label. There are also several techniques that can be applied specifically to lists, tables, buttons, and text components. Building arbitrary components and composites can also add a great deal of flexibility to your applications. It is important to know how to get the most out of windows and menus. Knowledge of images, pixmaps, masks, cursors, the default Screen, and fonts can also add a great deal to your applications.

You should always be willing to explore *VisualWorks* to find out for yourself just how much is really available. The term *reuse* implies knowing what is there to reuse. The *ParcPlace* literature or other books such as this one will never give you the complete picture. Ultimately, it is up to you to populate your own bag of tricks, tips, and techniques.

CHAPTER 10

Extending the Application Model

THIS CHAPTER ADDRESSES some of the issues concerning application models and application development. The authors of *VisualWorks* have given you a wonderful class in ApplicationModel on which you can base your own applications. However, as with all Smalltalk products, the door has been left wide open for modifications and improvements. Several more levels of abstract application model classes can be developed to facilitate application development. Extending ApplicationModel by subclassing can be either an enhancement to overall application development or an implementation of all common behavior for a specific application.

Consider that a well-designed application will have windows that have a consistent look, feel, and behavior. That is, if a gray background indicates a read-only status in one window, then it should indicate a read-only status in all windows across the application. For a large application, all of the common and consistent behaviors and user interface features should be generalized and placed in an abstract application model class, which serves as the superclass for all application models in the application. If done properly, the concrete application model classes should consist of methods that average just a few lines of source code.

In the first section of this chapter, we will subclass ApplicationModel to create a new, abstract, application model class, ExtendedApplicationModel. As its name suggests, this class enhances the services provided by ApplicationModel by adding some new features and reinforcing a few current ones. Since ApplicationModel already has a subclass for dialog development, SimpleDialog, the second section of this chapter is dedicated to creating the class ExtendedSimpleDialog to complement ExtendedApplicationModel. In Chapter 11 we will create yet another abstract application model class, which is a subclass of ExtendedApplicationModel and which provides a full segregation between application and domain information.

The purpose of this chapter is really twofold. The first, which is of more immediate concern, is to add a rich set of features for application model development. The second, which is of a more fundamental nature, is to get you started with the idea of developing abstract application model classes in general.

10.1 ExtendedApplicationModel

In this section, we will extend the class ApplicationModel to make application development even easier than it already is. This extension is a subclass of ApplicationModel and is called ExtendedApplicationModel. Its concrete subclasses will have access to features currently not available in ApplicationModel but of tremendous utility to application model building. The features of ExtendedApplicationModel fall into five categories: interface control protocol, aspect support protocol, parent application access, single instance operation, and interface opening protocol. Each of these is described in this section. Several other features could be added—help facilities and menu bar facilities, just to name two. In fact, you may want to augment ExtendedApplicationModel with some ideas of your own or create yet another abstract application model class.

It is important to realize that one of the constraints in designing ExtendedApplicationModel is that subclasses can be implemented just as if they were immediate subclasses of ApplicationModel. That is, ExtendedApplicationModel should not override any of the behavior provided by ApplicationModel but instead should be a superset of ApplicationModel behavior. The acid test for conforming to such a constraint is that any subclass of ApplicationModel can be made a subclass of ExtendedApplicationModel without having to reimplement any methods. The value of such a constraint is that ExtendedApplicationModel can become the default superclass for all applications models without any loss of generality, and all consistency is maintained with the original intent of *VisualWorks*.

10.1.1 Interface Control Protocol

Interface control protocol is a set of methods that facilitates control over user interface components—*VisualWorks* components, windows, menu bars, keyboard hooks, etc.—during runtime. These methods offer the developer the following benefits.

- Elegance and readability of code

- Brevity of code

- Encapsulation of functionality

- Code reuse and development efficiency

- Flexibility of interface management

- Safe component access

Disk Example 10.1 demonstrates the utility of interface control protocol in developing application models.

10.1.1.1 Elegance and Readability

After you have written a few meaningful applications in *VisualWorks*, you may begin to notice a certain repetition of code where component control is concerned. For example, suppose we want a method that is responsible for disabling three components whose IDs are #name, #address, and #phone. The implementation for such a method might look like the following.

```
(self builder componentAt: #name) disable.
(self builder componentAt: #address) disable.
(self builder componentAt: #phone) disable.
```

At first glance, one notices that this code is not very readable. A statement such as *self builder component at … disable* does not fit very well with our common vernacular. To a second party reviewing this code, it is not readily apparent what is going on. Smalltalk code should be concise and readable. Also, notice how much redundancy is involved. There is no excuse for this in Smalltalk, which leads us to the next implementation. Most veteran Smalltalk developers would implement our example method as follows.

```
#(name address phone) do: [:each |
    (self builder componentAt: each) disable]
```

This is an improvement, but we are still not quite there. This second implementation is more elegant and removes the redundancy but is even less readable than the first. In English, what we are trying to do is *disable #name, #address,* and *#phone.* Is there any reason why we cannot write the method just this way? Certainly not! Application models that are subclasses of ExtendedApplicationModel implement such a method as follows.

```
self disable: #(name address phone)
```

This third implementation is short, concise, and readable. In the time it takes to read this very short line, we know exactly what is taking place. Application models that are subclasses of ExtendedApplicationModel are able to control their components and other parts of the user interface in just such a fashion using the interface control protocol. Most of the interface control protocol consists of nothing more than simple attempts at reducing the amount of code that needs to be written and making that code more readable.

10.1.1.2 Brevity

Certain component operations require a long succession of messages. For instance, to obtain the controller of the widget of an active component, we normally write

```
(self builder componentAt: #shipDate) widget controller
```

We know that component access goes through the builder, that #shipDate is the ID of a component, and that the component has a widget. This renders the tokens builder, componentAt:, and widget mostly superfluous. The parentheses certainly add nothing to the readability of the statement. This statement should be written as follows.

```
self controllerFor: #shipDate
```

As another example of the brevity provided by interface control protocol, setting a widget controller's keyboard hook is usually written

```
(self componentAt: #totalAmount) widget controller
    keyboardHook: aBlock
```

but with the ExtendedApplicationModel, it is written as

```
self setKeyboardHookFor: #totalAmount to: aBlock
```

Again it should be emphasized that not only are the implementations that use interface control protocol much shorter, but they are also much more readable.

10.1.1.3 Encapsulation, Reuse, and Development Efficiency

Several things can be done to the user interface during runtime (see Chapter 9 for more on this topic). Many times, however, we are not quite sure if we remember just how to do it. A very good example is changing one of the colors of a component's look preferences during runtime. This is not a straightforward task. Not only does it involve several lines of code, but there are some subtleties involved as well. The first of these subtleties concerns sending a put method, such as backgroundColor:, to a LookPreferences object. Ordinarily we would expect this to change the backgroundColor instance variable of the receiver. LookPreferences defines certain put methods, however, that return an edited copy, and the receiver remains unchanged. There are, however, other put methods, such as setBackgroundColor:, which operate directly on the receiver. The second subtlety is that editing a component's look preferences does not cause the change to be updated immediately. Only if you give a component a new look preferences using the lookPreferences: message will it redraw itself in its new colors. These are both very important points, and not knowing them can cause hours of frustration for the developer trying to change the color of a component during runtime.

If we wanted to change the foreground color of a component whose ID is #notes, we would write something like the following.

```
| lp comp |
comp := self builder componentAt: #notes.
lp := comp lookPreferences.
lp setForegroundColor: ColorValue red.
comp lookPreferences: lp
```

This is quite a bit of code and not at all readable. Of course, the acid test of readability is to state in English exactly what we are trying to accomplish. In this case, the English version reads *change the foreground color of component #notes to the color red*. The Extended-ApplicationModel offers an interface control message, which allows us to write the code in just such a way.

```
self
    change:       #foregroundColor
    ofComponent:  #notes
    to:           ColorValue red
```

Notice that we also gain in readability. For someone reviewing the code, it is immediately obvious what this statement does.

10.1.1.4 Flexibility

Many of the interface control messages that take a component ID as an argument can also take an Array of component IDs. For instance, we can disable a single component with

```
self disable: #name.
```

Or, with the same message, we can disable an arbitrary number of components such as

```
self disable: #(name rank serialNumber).
```

As another example of flexibility, in the color-changing component service mentioned above, the color argument can be either some kind of Paint object or a Symbol identifying one of the named ColorValues such as #navy or #lightGray.

10.1.1.5 Safe Component Lookup

The interface control protocol is robust enough to ignore any errant component IDs—those which do not identify a component. The component lookup is conducted such that component IDs not found in the builder's named components collection are ignored. Other errors could be trapped as well, but currently, only component lookup errors are trapped. Errant component IDs is by far the most prevalent type of error, and therefore should be given due attention.

10.1.1.6 The Available Interface Control Methods

Currently, the interface control protocol consists of 20 methods, which are listed in Table 10.1. Disk Example 10.1 demonstrates the utility of some of these methods.

10.1.2 Aspect Support Protocol

When designing an application model that manages several components, the instance variable list tends to become somewhat overloaded. Traditionally, good Smalltalk style frowns on class definitions with excessive amounts of instance variables. Such a symptom can be indicative of

- ◆ lack of factoring in the hierarchy

- ◆ lack of support and collaborator object types

- ◆ unnecessary instance variables

In general, an excess of instance variables usually indicates that the class is assuming too much responsibility and that some of this responsibility should be defined in one or more superclasses or delegated to collaborator objects. In the case of application model development, however, these two options do not really apply. This leaves only one avenue of reducing our number of instance variables—removing those that are unnecessary. Well, the aspect instance variables are unnecessary! The reason for this is that a UIBuilder caches these objects in its bindings variable. This means that the application model maintains redundant references to its aspect models. The application model can always reference its aspect models via its builder, so why keep them as instance variables? ExtendedApplicationModel uses this information to provide aspect models for the components without having to load up on aspect instance variables. Disk Example 10.2 illustrates the value of the aspect support protocol.

10.1.2.1 Brief Description

Typically, an aspect method returns some type of value model or some other type of aspect model such as a SelectionInList. For example, in a traditional application model, a method for the #documentName aspect might look like the following

```
documentName

    ^documentName isNil
        ifTrue: [documentName := String new asValue]
        ifFalse: [documentName]
```

Table 10.1. Interface Control Protocol.

Message	Behavior
abortFocusShift	Prevents a shift of focus from taking place
change: aSymbol ofComponent: aSymoblOrArray to: aSymbolOrColor	Change the color role aSymbol of the component(s) identified by aSymbolOrArray to the color indicated by aSymbolOrColor
component: aSymbol	Return the component (SpecWrapper) whose ID is aSymbol
controllerFor: aSymbol	Return the controller for the widget identified by aSymbol
disable: aSymbolOrArray	Disable the component(s) identified by aSymbolOrArray
enable: aSymbolOrArray	Enable the component(s) identified by aSymbolOrArray
enable: aSymbolOrArray1 disable: aSymbolOrArray2 onCondition: aBoolean	If aBoolean is true, enable the components identified by aSymbolOrArray1 and make disable identified by aSymbolOrArray2; if aBoolean is false, do the exact opposite
enable: aSymbolOrArray onCondition: aBoolean	If aBoolean is true, enable the components identified by aSymbolOrArray; if aBoolean is false, disable them
invalidate: aSymbolOrArray	Redraw the component(s) identified by aSymbolOrArray
makeInvisible: aSymbolOrArray	Make invisible the component(s) identified by aSymbolOrArray
makeReadOnly: aSymbolOrArray	Make the component(s) identified by aSymbolOrArray read only
makeVisible: aSymbolOrArray	Make visible again the component(s) identified by aSymbolOrArray
makeVisible: aSymbolOrArray1 invisible: aSymbolOrArray2 onCondition: aBoolean	If aBoolean is true, make the components identified by aSymbolOrArray1 visible and make those identified by aSymbolOrArray2 invisible; if aBoolean is false, do the exact opposite
makeVisible: aSymbolOrArray onCondition: aBoolean	If aBoolean is true, make the component(s) identified by aSymbolOrArray visible; if aBoolean is false, make them invisible
menuBarMenu	Return the Menu used by the menu bar; return nil if there is no menu bar
redrawSelectionInList: aSymbol	Redraw the currently selected item in the list component whose ID is aSymbol
redrawElement: anObject inList:aSymbol	Redraw the element anObject in the list component whose ID is aSymbol
setKeyboardHookFor: aSymbol tTo: aBlock	Set the keyboard hook of the widget whose component ID is aSymbol to aBlock
setKeyboardHookForWindowTo: aBlock	Set the keyboard hook of the window to aBlock
widget: aSymbol	Return the widget identified by aSymbol
window	Return the builder's window

This approach requires the allocation of an instance variable—documentName. In an extended application model, the method can also be written as

documentName

^self valueHolderFor: #documentName initialValue: String new

This second implementation does not require an instance variable. As long as the aspect model is accessed using the accessing message (a practice strongly encouraged), the correct value will be returned and the application model will behave just as if the implementation was that of the first type. Also, notice how much more readable it is than the first implementation.

10.1.2.2 Aspect Support for ValueHolder

The two aspect support methods for ValueHolders are

valueHolderFor: aSymbol initialValue: anObject

and

valueHolderFor: aSymbol initialValue: anObject changeMessage: aSymbolOrArray

The arguments are described as follows.

aSymbol	A Symbol that is the name of the method using the service.
anObject	The initial value of the ValueHolder.
aSymbolOrArray	A Symbol or an Array. If it is a Symbol, it is the name of a message to be sent to the application model on a change of value of the ValueHolder. If it is an Array, the first argument is the change message and the second argument is the interested object and receiver of the change message.

10.1.2.3 Registering Interest

One of the benefits of the aspect support messages is that they allow the developer to register interest in the change of value of the aspect model (see Section 10.2.2.2). This single feature has three benefits.

- The amount of code that must be written is reduced.

- The code is much more readable.

▶ Everything about the aspect model—type, initial value, and change notification—is indicated in a single statement.

The argument for registering interest in an aspect model can be a Symbol or an array. If the argument is a Symbol, then the Symbol is the name of the change message and the interested object (receiver of the change message) is understood to be the application model. This is the case the vast majority of the time. For the few exceptions where the interested object is not the application model, then the argument can be a two-element Array. In this case, the first element is a Symbol and the name of the change message and the second element is the interested object.

10.1.2.4 Aspect Support for SelectionInList

There are two forms of the aspect service for SelectionInList:

    selectionInListFor: aSymbol collection: anObject

and

    selectionInListFor: aSymbol collection: anObject collectionChange: aSymbolOrArray1
    selectionChange: aSymbolOrArray2

The arguments are defined as follows.

aSymbol	A Symbol that is the name of the aspect and of the method.
anObject	This can be nil, a collection, or a Symbol. If it is nil, an empty SelectionInList is created. If it is a collection, the SelectionInList is initialized with the collection. If it is a Symbol, then it is interpreted as a message sent to the application model to retrieve the list, which is then used to initialize the SelectionInList.
aSymbolOrArray1	A Symbol or an Array. If it is a Symbol, then it is the message sent to the application model on a change of the list. If it is an Array, the first argument is the change message and the second argument is the interested object and receiver of the change message.

aSymbolOrArray2	A Symbol or an Array. If it is a Symbol, then it is the message sent to the application model on a change of the list. If it is an Array, the first argument is the change message and the second argument is the interested object and receiver of the change message.

A similar aspect service is available for multiple selection lists.

10.1.2.5 Aspect Support for Subapplications

When the component is a subcanvas, then the aspect model is another application model and a subapplication to the receiver. The aspect support method in this case is

> subApplicationFor: aSymbol model: aModel

The arguments are as follows.

aSymbol	A Symbol that is the name of the aspect and of the method
aModel	A subclass of ApplicationModel or an instance of such a class

Also, if the argument aModel is itself an extended application model, then it will automatically receive a reference to its parent application. The parent application properties of ExtendedApplicationModel are covered in Section 10.1.3.

10.1.2.6 How It Works

All of the aspect support methods use the same approach. For our illustration, we will use the method

> valueHolderFor: aSymbol
> initialValue: anObject
> changeMessage: aSymbolOrArray.

Whenever someone sends a message to access an aspect, that method's implementation uses an aspect support message. For instance, an application model with a productID aspect might have an aspect method that looks like the following.

productID

```
^self
    valueHolderFor:       #productID
    initialValue:         String new
    changeMessage:        #changedProductID
```

The ExtendedApplicationModel implementation of the aspect support method is shown below (comments omitted).

valueHolderFor: aSymbol initialValue: anObject changeMessage: aSymbolOrArray

```
^(self builderHasModel: aSymbol)
    ifFalse:    [self registerInterestIn: (ValueHolder with: anObject)
using: aSymbolOrArray]
    ifTrue:     [self builder aspectAt: aSymbol]
```

The implementation of the method above first checks to see if the builder already has the aspect model in its bindings. If so, the method accesses it from the builder and returns it (ifTrue: clause). If not, then the method creates the ValueHolder with the initial value of anObject and uses the information in aSymbolOrArray to register interest in the ValueHolder. Then the method returns this new ValueHolder (ifFalse: clause). The interest in the ValueHolder is registered by sending the message registerInterestIn: aValueHolder using: aSymbolOrArray. The implementation for this method is shown below (comments omitted).

registerInterestIn: aValueModel using: aSymbolOrArray

```
aSymbolOrArray isNil ifTrue: [^aValueModel].
(aSymbolOrArray isKindOf: Array)
    ifTrue: [aValueModel
            onChangeSend: (aSymbolOrArray at: 1)
            to: (aSymbolOrArray at: 2)]
    ifFalse: [aValueModel onChangeSend: aSymbolOrArray to: self].
^aValueModel
```

If aSymbolOrArray is a Symbol, then it is understood that the interested object is the application model itself. If aSymbolOrArray is an Array, then its first element is expected to be a Symbol naming the change message, and its second element is expected to be the interested object, that is, the receiver of the change message.

10.1.2.7 Costs and Benefits

In order to use the aspect support protocol, we must abandon the code generation provided by *VisualWorks* or rework it so that it can also generate aspect methods that use aspect support protocol. Also, using aspect support protocol makes any aspect model public because all methods in Smalltalk are public. If a completely private aspect model is desired, you must abandon the aspect support protocol and declare an instance variable that does not have an accessing method. Another caveat is that the first access of the aspect model must be by the builder because the builder will cache the aspect model in its bindings collection so that it is available for subsequent access. Any access of the aspect model prior to interface construction will result in an instance of the aspect model that is different from the instance actually cached by the builder and bound to the component. This could be remedied in the implementation of the aspect model services, of course, but since this is such a rare case, there has been no real need to do so. In addition, the aspect support protocol does not support aspect methods for table components. Due to the complexity and variation in such aspect methods, the necessary number of permutations in support protocol is potentially quite large. This makes it difficult to generalize support for such aspect methods.

There is no functional benefit in using aspect model services at this stage (in Chapter 11 they will provide a very useful functional value), however, they do augment an application model implementation in the following ways.

- They reduce amount of instance variables in the class definition.

- They force the discipline of referencing aspects by their accessing messages.

- They make for much more readable and descriptive code.

- They provide a single source for all information—type, initial value, and change notification—concerning an aspect model.

10.1.3 Parent Application Reference

Quite often when an application model or dialog is launched from another application model, the new application model will want to reference its progenitor. Also, it is quite convenient for an application model running a subcanvas to reference the parent application model. For these reasons, ExtendedApplicationModel defines an instance variable, parentApplication, which allows an application model to reference the parent application model that launched it or that contains it as a subapplication. Disk Example 10.3 illustrates some of the possibilities of having a reference to the parent application.

10.1.4 Single Instance

Sometimes it is convenient to guarantee that only one instance of an application model will ever exist. For extended application models, this can be accomplished by sending the message openSingleInstance to the application model class. For example, if the application model class SessionLog is a subclass of ExtendedApplicationModel, then the following interface opening message will guarantee that only one such application will ever be opened.

```
SessionLog openSingleInstance
```

If the window is already open, then it is brought to the front of all windows and made the active window. If the window is collapsed, then it is expanded. If the window is not currently open, then a new one is created and opened. The single instance behavior provided by ExtendedApplicationModel is just a generalization of a similar behavior, which is already implemented in UIPainter for the Palette and Canvas Tool. Disk Example 10.4 gives an example of using the single instance feature of ExtendedApplicationModel.

10.1.5 Interface Opening Protocol

ExtendedApplicationModel includes several changes and additions to the interface opening methods provided in ApplicationModel. The intention is to provide more flexibility, functionality, and a consistency in the interface opening protocol.

10.1.5.1 Specific Interface

By default, the interface defined in the class method windowSpec is opened whenever the open message is sent to either the class or instance of the extended application model. If a particular interface is required—one defined in some other class method—then the message openInterface: aSymbol is sent to either the class or instance where aSymbol is the name of the class method, which returns the literal array spec defining the interface. There is nothing new here, of course, since all of this is inherited from ApplicationModel.

10.1.5.2 Single Instance

To open the extended application model's single instance, send the message openSingleInstance to your extended application model class. To specify a particular interface, send the message openSingleInstanceInterface: aSymbol. Opening the single instance will guarantee that the same instance is opened each and every time. The single instance opening protocol is implemented on the class side only.

10.1.5.3 Opening at a Location

To open an ExtendedApplicationModel at a certain location on the screen, send the message openAt: aLocation. If aLocation is a Point, then it indicates the intended opening origin of the window. If it is a Symbol, then it can be #centerOfWindow, #centerOfScreen, or #centeredAroundCursor. Each of these opens the window in the manner described by the Symbol. The argument aLocation can also be a Rectangle, which specifies the window's extent as well as its origin.

10.1.5.4 Parent Application

To open an extended application model such that it references a parent application, send the message openFrom: aParentApp to the class or instance where the argument aParentApp is the parent application model. Some other permutations are

> openInterface: aSymbol from: aParentApp
>
> openSingleInstanceFrom: aParentApp
>
> openSingleInstanceInterface: aSymbol from: aParentApp

10.1.5.5 Opening as a Dialog

To open an extended application model as a dialog, send the message openAsDialog to the class or instance. Some other permutations are

> openAsDialogInterface: aSymbol
>
> openAsDialogInterface: aSymbol at: aLocation
>
> openAsDialogFrom: aParentApp
>
> openAsDialogFrom: aParentApp at: aLocation
>
> openAsDialogInterface: aSymbol from: aParentApp
>
> openAsDialogInterface: aSymbol from: aParentApp at: aLocation

10.1.5.6 Naming Convention

You may have noticed a consistency in the naming convention of the messages above. The window can be opened normally (that is, a modal window), as a single instance, or as a dialog. These three have the following options:

> open{Interface: aSymbol}{From: aParentApp}{At: aLocation}
>
> openSingleInstance{Interface: aSymbol}{At: aLocation}
>
> openAsDialog{Interface: aSymbol}{From: aParentApp}{At: aLocation}

The bracketed elements are optional. The From: and At: options sometimes appear as key words, in which cases they are not capitalized, as is the case below.

> openInterface: aSymbol at: aLocation

And sometimes they are just part of a key word and therefore appear capitalized.

> openAt: aLocation

10.1.6 Adding ExtendedApplicationModel to *VisualWorks*

To make ExtendedApplicationModel available from the canvas install dialog, open the interface in LensApplicationCreationDialog class>>windowSpec for editing. Now add a radio button just to the right of the **Application** radio button (increase the height if necessary). Give this new radio button the following properties.

Label	Extended
Aspect	#'spec appType'
Select	#ExtendedApplicationModel

Install this canvas. Now when you create a new application model class from the canvas, you have the option of making it a subclass of ExtendedApplicationModel.

10.2 Enhanced Dialog Development

Developing good dialogs can be quite intimidating, even for well-seasoned *VisualWorks* developers. Ideally, custom dialog development should be easy and straightforward. Unfortunately, this is often not the case. With the explanations and enhancements provided in this section, however, custom dialog development becomes everything it should be.

In this section we will first look at some issues concerning custom dialog development. This includes the basic role of dialogs in the application, questions of development, and some basic guidelines for custom dialog development. Then we will extend SimpleDialog with a subclass, ExtendedSimpleDialog, as a companion to ExtendedApplication-Model. The intention is to have ExtendedSimpleDialog address some of these issues and make custom dialog development easy, straightforward, and flexible.

10.2.1 Basic Role of Dialogs

Dialogs are used to perform certain functions. We know that they are modal and therefore have an ephemeral existence. Dialogs are used typically to

- notify user of an error or provide a simple message

- acquire permission or simple information from user

- perform application specific services

- add and edit objects in the application

The first two purposes are handled quite nicely the by stock dialogs provided by the Dialog class (see Chapter 4, Section 4.4.3). While there is some room for improvement, for the most part, the stock dialogs provide a great service for the meager price of a single line of code. It is the third and fourth items that cause grief among *VisualWorks* programmers. These are the dialogs that are written by the developer to perform application specific tasks.

10.2.2 Questions About Dialog Development

Below are some questions that confront most *VisualWorks* developers pertaining to dialog development. See if any of these are familiar to you.

- When should a dialog be used in an application?

- When is it necessary to build a custom dialog instead of using a stock dialog?

- Should custom dialog classes be subclasses of ApplicationModel or SimpleDialog?

- Why is it that an application model opened as a dialog cannot access its components at runtime?

- Why is it that an application model opened as a dialog will not execute preBuildWith: and postBuildWith: methods?

- Why is it that accept and cancel action methods are never executed?

- What should a custom dialog return: an edited object, nil, a boolean?

- Should a dialog ever edit an object directly, or just a copy of the object?

- How can a dialog be opened at a specific location?

The answers to all of these questions are found in the remainder of this section.

10.2.3 ExtendedSimpleDialog

Chapter 4, Section 4.4.4, covered the problems with developing custom dialogs as subclasses of either ApplicationModel or SimpleDialog. To rectify these problems, the class ExtendedSimpleDialog has been developed to work in conjunction with Extended-ApplicationModel. Application models intended to be dialogs should be subclasses of ExtendedApplicationModel—do not bother with either ApplicationModel or SimpleDialog. Create dialogs as subclasses of ExtendedApplicationModel and keep life simple. By designing your dialogs as subclasses of ExtendedApplicationModel, you gain the following functionality.

- All interface components can be accessed via the builder.

- Prebuild and postbuild methods are executed automatically without having to define pre- and postbuild blocks.

- Implementations for accept and cancel action methods will be executed whenever the corresponding action button is pressed.

- All functionality in ExtendedApplicationModel is available for implementing the behavior of the dialog.

- A single application model can be opened as either modal window or a non-modal window.

Disk Example 10.5 gives some examples of dialogs developed as subclasses of Extended-ApplicationModel. The remainder of this section covers the benefits of ExtendedSimple-Dialog.

10.2.3.1 Accessing the Interface

The problem with opening a subclass of ApplicationModel as a dialog is that it is an instance of SimpleDialog that actually builds the user interface. This means that the dialog client application's builder is nil and therefore the dialog client application cannot access its own components during runtime. To rectify this, ExtendedSimpleDialog makes sure that the builder is also referenced by the dialog client application.

10.2.3.2 Pre- and Postbuild Operations

A second problem with opening a subclass of ApplicationModel as a dialog is that the dialog client application's pre- and postbuild operations never occur. It is the SimpleDialog's pre- and postbuild operations that are executed. To overcome this, ExtendedSimpleDialog has changed the allButOpenInterface: method to make sure it is the builder's source that receives the pre- and postbuild messages and not the ExtendedSimpleDialog. The builder's source is the dialog client application, which is the subclass of ExtendedApplicationModel designed to be the dialog.

10.2.3.3 Accept and Cancel Actions

Another problem with all dialogs is that the **OK** and **Cancel** action buttons cannot trigger corresponding accept and cancel action methods. This can be overcome by redefining these aspects in the builder's bindings. The initialize method in SimpleDialog defines the

#accept and #close aspects as ValueHolders on a boolean. With these aspects, any imple-
mentation of the action methods accept and cancel cannot be executed. ExtendedSimple-
Dialog redefines the #accept and #cancel aspects in its own initialize method, shown below,
to include the appropriate action messages.

initialize

```
"Initialize such that the source can implement #accept and #cancel which are
triggered whenever that button is pressed but prior to the actual closing."
super initialize.
self builder
    aspectAt: #accept
    put: [self builder source accept. self accept value: true].
self builder
    aspectAt: #cancel
    put: [self builder source cancel. self cancel value: true]
```

Now, whenever an **Accept** button is pressed, a corresponding accept method in the client
application model is executed first, then the accept channel is set to true, which results in
closing the dialog.

10.2.3.4 ExtendedApplicationModel Functionality

A problem with implementing a dialog as a subclass of SimpleDialog is that all the functionality provided by abstract subclasses of ApplicationModel, such as ExtendedApplication-
Model, are not available for the implementation. This is quite a sacrifice considering all
of the benefits to application model development ExtendedApplicationModel has to offer.
By making the dialog class a subclass of ExtendedApplicationModel, we can use the interface control protocol, aspect support protocol, and interface opening protocol provided
by ExtendedApplicationModel.

10.2.3.5 Opening Modal or Nonmodal

Another of the problems with subclassing SimpleDialog is that the window is necessarily
modal. There is no option for opening a nonmodal version. Any subclass of Extended-
ApplicationModel can be opened in either a modal or a nonmodal fashion.

10.2.4 Dialogs as Object Editors

Many of the dialogs you create will be used to edit an object of some type. In this vein
we can see dialogs as object editors. Object editors allow the user to edit an object, such
as an Address object, and accept the changes or cancel to roll back to the previous state of
the object. Since the object editors are dialogs, the user must conclude the object–edit-

ing session before moving on to anything else. A very good example of this is the dialog opened from a canvas <operate> menu selection **layout→constrained...**. This dialog edits a copy of the layout object belonging to the current canvas selection. The user can edit this copy and accept the changes or cancel, and no changes will be applied.

A good way to approach object editing is to

1. Copy the object to be edited.

2. Open a dialog on the copy.

3. If the dialog returns nil, do nothing. If the dialog returns the copy, then replace original with copy.

For example, we might design a dialog that edits a ColorValue object. Let's call this the ColorValueDialog, and of course, it will be a subclass of ExtendedApplicationModel. We could create a class method called edit: whose implementation is shown below.

```
edit: aColorValue
    "Open a dialog on aColorValue and return the edited
    ColorValue or nil."

    | inst |
    ^(inst := self new color: aColorValue) openAsDialog
        ifTrue: [inst color]
        ifFalse: [nil]
```

Remember, it is the responsibility of the requesting object to provide the copy of the object to be edited. This allows our method to operate directly on the argument aColor-Value. First, we create an instance of our dialog and pass it the argument aColorValue. Presumably, it initializes certain instance variables based on this argument—perhaps RGB values. Then we open the instance as a dialog and wait for its return value, which is a boolean. If the dialog returns true, then the edit: method returns the edited ColorValue object. If the dialog returns false, then the edit: method returns nil. Based on this return value, the requesting object can take the appropriate action. See Disk Example 10.6. for some concrete examples of dialog editors.

10.3 Summary

In this chapter, we extended the functionality of abstract application models by creating the ExtendedApplicationModel class. The ExtendedApplicationModel class is an abstract subclass of ApplicationModel, and it provides five additional types of functionality: interface control protocol, aspect support protocol, single instance operation, parent application reference, and a rich set of interface opening protocol. The interface control protocol is a set of messages that allows the developer to exercise a great deal of control over the runtime interface using short, elegant, and readable statements. The aspect support methods remove the need for instance variables for the aspect models and provide all initialization and registration of interest in a single line of code. Single instance operation is a way to guarantee that only one instance of the application exists. The parent application reference is a reference to the application model that launched the current application model or that contains the current application model as a subapplication. The interface opening protocol offers a consistent convention for opening an application model in a variety of ways.

Dialogs are application models that open a modal window. There are four basic purposes for dialogs: displaying simple messages, acquiring simple information, providing specific application services, and editing objects. There are a few drawbacks to the current implementation of dialogs in *VisualWorks*. Dialogs that are subclasses of SimpleDialog cannot benefit from the powerful features provided in ExtendedApplicationModel, nor can they implement the accept and cancel methods Dialogs that are a subclass of ApplicationModel cannot access components during runtime or implement pre- and postbuild methods. For these reasons, the ExtendedSimpleDialog class was created to complement the ExtendedApplicationModel class and facilitate rich dialog functionality. A dialog should be designed as a subclass of ExtendedApplicationModel. This provides the following benefits: pre- and postbuild implementations, accept and cancel action method implementation, runtime component access, choice between modal and nonmodal window, and all the additional features of ExtendedApplicationModel.

CHAPTER 11

Segregating the Domain

O NE OF THE objectives of the ever-evolving MVC architecture is the segregation of application and domain information. The application information includes such things as menus, error messages, help information, icons, labels, and even dependency relationships—anything necessary to make the visual interface function appropriately. The domain information is the information germane to the task at hand, such as maintaining personnel records or running a factory, and includes such information as names, dates, addresses, financial reports, production schedules, etc. Under the current application model architecture, the domain information is scattered throughout the application. This chapter addresses the issue of segregating the domain information from the rest of the application model. This is absolutely essential if we are to build distributed, production worthy, client/server applications with a persistent store. This is because it is the domain information that persists in a database while the application information resides entirely in the client. Therefore, it is necessary that we be able to identify that which is domain information and that which is application information and keep the two completely segregated.

Whereas Chapter 10 enhanced application model development, this chapter proposes to extend the application architecture itself. In the first part of this chapter, we will discuss the reasons for wanting to segregate the domain information from the application. Next, we will develop a framework for the objects that will be used to reference the domain information—called domain objects. Finally, we will create a new application model architecture, which allows an application model and its interface to operate on domain objects.

Keep in mind that while segregating the application and domain is essential, the actual approach may vary, and this chapter offers just one such approach. While the proposed architecture may not suit all of your particular needs, it is founded on some very fundamental principles and covers issues relevant to all types of application development. Furthermore, this architecture has gone through several cycles of rework and has much to recommend it.

11.1 Why Segregate the Domain?

The complete segregation of domain information from the application model becomes essential when an application of any merit is intended. This is especially true in a client server architecture where the application resides on a client machine but the data or domain information is kept somewhere else. The reasons for such a strict segregation of application and domain information constitute the body of this section.

11.1.1 Persistence

The application information typically resides on the client machine and has no need to persist outside of the image. For all but the most trivial applications, however, the domain information must persist in a database. A Smalltalk virtual image, regardless of the client machine's available resources, soon becomes inadequate as a persistent store for domain information. Furthermore, a virtual image does not offer traditional database facilities such as concurrency control, security, locking, transactions, rollbacks, recovery, and multiuser access. Therefore, the domain information should reside in some kind of persistent store where it can be managed by a database management system and be available to several client machines.

11.1.2 Domain Cohesion

The problem with making domain information persist under the current application architecture is that it is so scattered throughout the application model. It is contained in various ValueHolders, SelectionInLists, and even within additional, embedded application models (subapplications) in the case of subcanvases or satellite windows. In fact, an application model, by design, is nothing more than a loose confederation of independent models, each operating on its own piece of domain information. As an illustration, suppose we have an application for maintaining employee information for a very large corporation. Such an application could be filled with all sorts of domain information about each employee—name, Social Security number (ssn), salary, supervisor, address, date of birth, etc. Each time we want to store the information for a single employee, we have to traverse all the input fields, lists, text editors, and subcanvases, collecting all the relevant domain information for that employee, and ship it all to the database. In the event that we want to fetch the information for a given employee from the database for viewing or editing, we have to access several pieces of information and target each one for its particular aspect model. It would be nice if we had a single handle, or reference point, for all of this information. We would like to bundle all the relevant domain information into a single cohesive object—perhaps something like an Employee object that contains all the domain information for a single employee of the company. Ideally, we would like to hand this single domain object to the database for storing or hand it to an application model for viewing and editing.

11.1.3 Application Information

One might argue that if the application model references all of the pertinent domain information, why not just have it persist in the database? While this is true enough and quite appealing at first, upon closer scrutiny we can see that this idea has two serious flaws. First, application information usually does not need to persist in a database. We do not need a copy of the same menu to accompany each Employee object (see Section 11.1.2) stored in the database. Second, the domain information is very loosely affiliated within the application model. There are too many intermediaries from one piece of domain information the next. Primarily, these intermediaries are the value models, aspect models, and application models that contain the domain information.

It is conceivable that certain types of application information might be so large that it is inconvenient or impossible to burden each client machine with a copy. A mature help environment is a good example. Such cases require a change in perspective. The help facility becomes an application in and of itself, and its domain information is the text and bitmaps that comprise the help information. What actually constitutes domain information and what constitutes application information can sometimes be a gray area. It is essential, however, that the design process clearly resolve what is part of the application and what is part of the domain. For example, error codes might be part of the application in one project and part of the domain in another. In either case however, it must be resolved one way or another before implementation.

11.1.4 Dependents

Another problem in trying to store the application model in the database is that the application model has dependents and references other models, each with its own dependents. We do not want to store anything in the database that has dependents! This is a cardinal rule of persistent objects. The reasons for this are as follows.

*OR AN
INTERNAL
VIEW*

- Dependents exist only for purposes of the user interface and therefore constitute application information.

- Dependents do not describe domain information. An object does not care how many dependents it has, who its dependents are, or what they are. This relationship has no translation into the domain and, therefore, does not constitute domain information.

- Dependents exist solely to provide a means of communication during interface operation; therefore, they would have no meaning to a persistent object.

- Dependents have a way of compounding the relationships among objects such that a single application model can end up referencing a sizable portion of the virtual image.

- Dependents inevitably reference objects that are known to the virtual machine. Another cardinal rule for persistent storage is to never make an object persistent if it is referenced by the virtual machine. Such references are specific to the client machine and have no meaning in a persistent media; they cannot be accurately reconstituted when the persistent object is fetched from the database.

For these reasons it is best to leave models and any other objects with dependencies out of the database.

11.1.5 Analysis and Design

Describing the application strictly in terms of the domain information facilitates the analysis and design processes and removes any unnecessary details of interface development. In fact, a good design should exclude application-specific information as much as possible and concentrate strictly on the domain. Such a design is largely independent of the actual application development and can even be independent of the language of implementation. Domain objects are the fruits of a good design; application models are the results of development.

11.1.6 Summary

Before we embark on the work required for adequately segregating the domain information from the application, it is important that you understand exactly why we want to do this. The main reasons for segregating the domain information from the application are summarized below.

- Domain information usually resides in a database, while application information should stay in the client machine's virtual image.

- Domain information should be bundled into convenient container objects that are relevant to the problem domain.

- Domain information should be clear of any dependent objects and should be completely independent of the virtual machine.

- Domain information represents the problem space, and design issues should relate as much as possible to the domain information and exclude as much as possible the application information.

11.2 Domain Objects

In the previous section we talked about the need to bundle domain information into cohesive objects relevant to the problem space. A typical example would be an Address object that references four pieces of domain information: the street, city, state, and zip. More than likely, these four pieces of information would be strings. In the previous section we talked about an Employee object that contained all kinds of information relevant to an employee. Such information probably includes various strings, numbers, and booleans. Since all employees have an address, it is also very likely that an Employee object also contains an Address object. Objects such as an Address and an Employee are referred to as domain objects. A **domain object** is a logical container of purely domain information, usually represents a logical entity in the problem domain space, and is void of any dependents or model behavior. In this section, we will discuss the general definition of a domain object and create the class DomainObject—an abstract superclass for domain objects.

It should be pointed out that this particular implementation is but one approach to segregating the application and domain. While this implementation of DomainObject may not apply to all applications, it does incorporate the most fundamental features of domain objects. What is more important, however, is that you appreciate the general approach. That is, all domain objects for a particular application should have a common abstract superclass for describing common state and behaviors. In fact, most implementations include a hierarchy of abstract classes of domain objects. In this chapter, however, we will stay with a single abstract superclass, DomainObject.

11.2.1 General Characteristics

For the reasons mentioned in Section 11.1, the DomainObject class has been created to provide the common characteristics of all domain objects. Its superclass is Object. All domain information in an application should reside in a subclass of DomainObject or some similar class.

Some may refer to a domain object as a *domain model*. This is true to the extent that these objects are modeling the domain problem space. However, the term *model,* as used in Smalltalk, strongly implies an object that has dependents, and it has already been pointed out that domain objects should not have dependents. Therefore, this book prefers the term *domain object* to the term *domain model*.

It is appropriate to use the term *domain model* to describe all the domain object types and the relationships among their instances, which collectively describe the domain space. In other words, all the domain objects that make up an airline reservation system and the ways in which they interact can be referred to as the airline reservation domain model. For this chapter, we will be looking at just a few types of domain objects, and the term *domain model* will not be used.

11.2.1.1 What Domain Objects Should Not Do

It is very important that our domain objects avoid model type behavior at all cost. They should not deal in any way with user interface issues, and they should have no dependents. In general, domain objects should not

- contain models such as ValueHolders or SelectionInLists
- have dependents
- deal with interface issues
- contain nondomain information
- perform application-type functions

11.2.1.2 What Domain Objects Should Do

It is necessary that domain objects know how to do certain things. In general, domain objects should know how to

- recognize which references indicate aggregation and which ones indicate association
- copy themselves completely and correctly
- maintain business logic

- compare themselves to other domain objects of the same type

- facilitate other objects that choose to print or display them

- conduct tests on their domain information

There are other categories of behaviors that domain objects can assume. Appendix B covers domain objects that know when they have been edited. Appendix C talks about domain object differencing and how this can be used in a change management application.

11.2.1.3 Communicating with the Domain Object

As a developer, you should refrain from sending messages directly to the domain object. Communication with the domain object should be restricted to the application model, and ultimately the user, as much as is possible. Remember, the domain object exists as a way to logically bundle certain domain information into a single cohesive object and to model the domain space. Sometimes, however, it is necessary to directly manipulate the domain object. In such cases, it is your responsibility as the developer to assure that any visual updates are initiated because there is no dependency mechanism to do it for you.

11.2.2 Domain Object Structure

The objects referenced by a domain object's instance variables can be divided into four groups: atomic objects, mutable objects, collections of atomic objects, and collections of mutable objects. Each of these presents its own set of unique problems. The first two express a one to one relationship between the domain object and the object it is referencing. The second two express a one to many relationship between the domain object and the elements in the collection. Disk Example 11.1 covers the material presented in this section.

11.2.2.1 Atomic Objects

Some domain object instance variables reference objects that should not be edited directly but instead should be replaced with another object of a similar type. Such objects are referred to as atomic objects or literal objects. **Atomic objects** are objects that are perceived to be the smallest units of information from which the domain space can be described, and they should not be edited but replaced by another atomic object. If you look at a domain object as a tree structure, then the atomic objects are the leaf nodes of that tree. Usually counted among the atomic object types are the standard data types such as strings, integers, floats, dates, and booleans. The classification of atomic objects can be quite arbitrary, however.

There are typically two accessing methods associated with each atomic object: the accessor and the mutator methods. An **accessor method** simply returns the atomic object, and the **mutator method** replaces the current atomic object with a new one. Sometimes these two methods are referred to as the *get* and *put* methods. The accessor and mutator terms, however, provide a better fit for our discussion. An accessor message *accesses* information contained within the domain object, and a mutator message *mutates* or changes the domain object. In the case of instance variables that reference atomic objects, this change is an atomic replacement.

Suppose we have a FullName domain object. If the FullName class defines an instance variable called last, which is meant to be a string, then its accessor method might look like

last

    ^last

and its mutator method might look like

last: aString

    last := aString.

The definition for atomic object given above mentioned that these objects are perceived to be the smallest units of information, but this is often just a matter of perspective. Dates and strings are examples of objects that are usually considered to be atomic but can quite easily be edited directly. It is the responsibility of the developer to assure that a domain object's atomic information is never edited, only replaced. For example, while strings are considered to be atomic, they are also collections and can be edited. As an illustration consider changing the first name of a FullName object from 'Rob' to 'Bob'. The approach that should be taken is shown below.

    fullName first: 'Bob'

In this example, an accessor is used to replace the 'Rob' string with the 'Bob' string. However, it is also possible to do the following.

    fullName first at: 1 put: $B

In this second example, the string referenced by the FullName object's first instance variable is actually edited instead of being replaced by a different string. It is incumbent upon the developer not to engage in such heresy.

Atomic objects can also be other domain objects that are referenced by association. Such domain objects are never edited directly but merely replaced by another instance. See Section 11.2.2.6 for more on this topic.

11.2.2.2 Mutable Objects

Mutable objects are objects referenced by the domain object, which can be edited directly. Such objects are other domain objects, which are referenced as part of the original domain object's aggregation. That is, a domain object can be an aggregate composition of other domain objects (see Section 11.2.2.6 for a formal definition of aggregation). For instance, an Employee object might contain a WorkHistory object, an Address object, and a FullName object—each being another type of domain object and part of the Employee object's aggregation. This means that these objects are directly editable (see Section 11.1.2.6). In such a case, the Employee class will define the instance variables address, workHistory, and fullName, and define accessing methods such as those shown below for the fullName instance variable.

fullName

```
fullName isNil
    ifTrue: [fullName := FullName new]
    ifFalse: [fullName]
```

and

fullName: aFullName

```
fullName := aFullName
```

It is necessary to make sure that the instance variables that reference other domain objects are properly initialized, either in the accessor method (as is done in the example above) or in an initialize method.

11.2.2.3 Collections

A domain object can contain a collection of other objects. In this way, domain objects can express a one-to-many relationship with other objects. These collections for the most part are loosely typed, that is, all of the elements in the collection are usually all of the same type or very similar type of object.

The collection's accessing method should also initialize the collection if necessary (or it should already have been done in an initialize method). Suppose we have a Company domain object that maintains a collection of vendors in its vendors instance variable. The vendors accessing method might look like the following.

vendors

```
^vendors isNil
    ifTrue: [vendors := OrderedCollection new]
    ifFalse: [vendors]
```

A collection can have a mutating method in the sense that the entire collection is replaced with another collection as shown below.

vendors: aCollection

> vendors := aCollection

The domain object can also provide specific accessing methods for the elements in the collection. A typical collection element accessing method might be

vendorWithName: aString

> ^self vendors detect: [:each | each name = aString] ifNone: [nil]

Be careful when expressing one-to-many relationships. A designer might say that one student object references many course objects. This type of one-to-many relationship is a fiction, however, and you should recognize it as such. The reality is that a student object references a collection object, which references many course objects. The actual implementation of a one to many relationship in Smalltalk introduces a level of indirection imposed by the collection object. This indirection is in no way trivial and should be taken into account during implementation and, if possible, even during design. Failure to account for this indirection can have an adverse impact upon the success of the implementation.

11.2.2.4 Collections of Atomic Objects

The elements in the collection can be atomic objects or mutable objects. In the event that the elements in the collection are all of an atomic nature, there are really just two editing operations that can occur: add an element or remove an element. Suppose the vendor objects in the vendor collection are meant to be atomic. That is, they are meant to be added or removed from the collection, but not edited directly. In such a case, the vendor collection element accessing methods might be

addVendor: aVendor

> self vendors add: aVendor

and

removeVendor: aVendor

> self vendors remove: aVendor ifAbsent: nil

Such collection element accessing and mutating methods are very beneficial because they allow the domain object to know when its collection is being modified. (See Appendix B for a discussion on domain objects that know when they have been edited.)

11.2.2.5 Collections of Mutable Objects

In the event that the elements in the collection are other mutable domain objects, then each element is directly editable. Such a collection and its elements constitute part of the domain object's aggregation. With these types of collections, not only can elements be added and removed, but the elements can also be accessed and edited directly as is shown below.

```
vendor := company vendorWithName: 'ACME'.
vendor contact: 'Franklin Black'
```

In the code above, a vendor object is accessed from a collection of vendor objects. Then this vendor object is edited by changing its contact.

11.2.2.6 Aggregation vs. Association

As was mentioned earlier, sometimes a domain object references other domain objects because it is *made up of* or *composed of* these other domain objects. This concept of composition is referred to as an aggregation. An **aggregation** is a reference to another domain object and specifies composition. As an illustration, consider the Employee object that has served us well in several of the preceding sections. An Employee object, for example, could be an aggregation of an Address object, a WorkHistory object, a FullName object, and perhaps other domain objects as well. That is, an Employee object is composed of these other domain objects, and each instance of Employee has its own unique instances of these other object types.

There are times, however, when one domain object maintains a reference to another domain object for reasons of illustrating a relationship. In such cases, the perception is that the first domain object *knows about* the second but does not *contain* it per se as part of its aggregation. This is what is referred to as an association. An **association** is a reference to an object but does not indicate composition. For example, an Employee object may reference a Company object as its employer and reference a second Employee object as its supervisor. We would never consider an Employee to be composed of a Company or composed of other Employees, yet it is necessary to maintain the reference for purposes of indicating the employer and supervisor relationships. When an Employee object changes supervisors, it merely breaks the reference to the Employee that is currently associated as its supervisor and references a new Employee object instead.

Unfortunately, there is no real distinction between an aggregation reference and an association reference in Smalltalk because they are implemented the same way (with instance variables), and it is only a matter of perspective that draws the distinction. When one object references another, it is not always apparent if the first object is composed of the second object or if it is just trying to illustrate an association with the second object. Therefore, it is up to the designer of the domain object, and the developer who uses the domain object, to know when an instance variable is used to indicate an aggregation relationship or an association relationship. This distinction will have profound effects on checks for a dirty state (see Appendix B), persistent storage, copying (Section 11.2.3), and domain object differencing (see Appendix C).

11.2.3 Copying Domain Objects

It is very important that domain objects know how to copy themselves such that the copy and the original do not share any information they are not meant to share. There is nothing more frustrating than editing what you suppose to be a copy only to find out that the original has changed as well! Unfortunately, there are far too many seasoned Smalltalk developers who still do not appreciate all the finer points of copying objects. Therefore this section starts with a brief overview/review of some of the general issues of copying objects in Smalltalk. This is followed by a discussion of copying domain objects in particular. Disk Example 11.2 provides concrete examples of copying domain objects.

11.2.3.1 Copying Objects in Smalltalk

All objects know how to copy themselves because the copy method is defined in Object; its implementation is shown below.

```
copy
    " Answer another instance just like the receiver.
    Subclasses normally override the postCopy
    message, but some objects that should not be
    copied override copy. "

    ^self shallowCopy postCopy
```

The copy method, by default, only makes a shallow copy because the postCopy method, by default, simply returns the receiver. A **shallow copy** is just a new object header (the header is an 8-byte data structure) and a new set of handles to the same objects referenced by the original object (each handle is a 4-byte data structure). In Figure 11.1a address 1 references three strings in memory. In Figure 11.1b the object address 2 is a shallow copy of address 1 and references these same exact strings. While address 1 and address 2 are distinct objects, their instance variables reference the same objects.

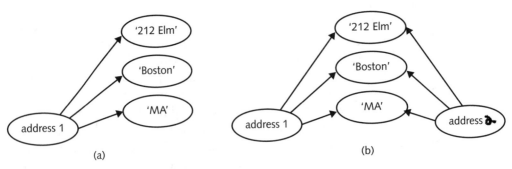

(a)   (b)

Figure 11.1. Shallow Copy of a Simple Object.

Shallow copies are dangerous especially where more complex objects are concerned. In Figure 11.2a we have an Employee object, employee 1, which references an Address object. (For the purposes of this illustration, we are ignoring any of an Employee object's instance variables previously discussed and concentrating exclusively on its reference to an Address object.) In Figure 11.2b we have a shallow copy as well, employee 2. Now suppose we edit the address of the copy as follows:

employee2 address city: 'Atlanta'

This leaves us with the situation in Figure 11.2c. By changing the address of employee 2, we have also inadvertently changed the address of employee 1!

11.2.3.2 Postcopy

For most domain objects, a shallow copy falls far short of the mark. Fortunately the copy method also initiates a postcopy operation. A **postcopy** includes any additional copying that might need to be conducted beyond the shallow copy. A postcopy is implemented in the postCopy method. Each object that wants to copy to a deeper level than a shallow copy should implement a postCopy method. Each type of domain object that defines

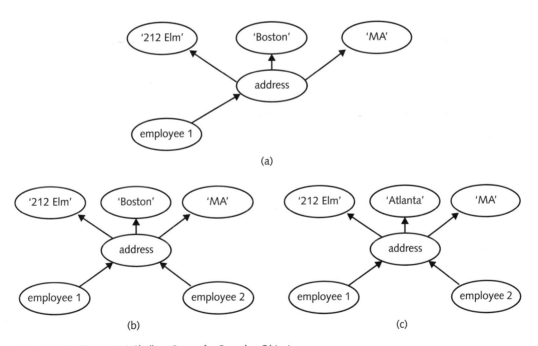

Figure 11.2. Figure 11.2 Shallow Copy of a Complex Object.

instance variables should also implement its own postCopy method to define what its copies are to look like. A postCopy method should almost always begin with super post-Copy. This ensures that the any instance variables defined by the superclasses are also copied appropriately. An implementation of postCopy should result in a full copy. **A full copy** is a copy that can be edited without adversely impacting the original object.

To rectify the Employee copying problem illustrated in Figure 11.2, we would implement the postCopy method for the Employee class as follows.

postCopy

```
super postCopy.
address := address copy.
```

This assures us that the object referenced by the address instance variable is copied as well, resulting in Figure 11.3. Now we can change the street address of employee 2 and employee 1 will still be safe on Elm Street (see Section 11.2.4.3).

Look again at the copy method shown below.

copy

```
" Answer another instance just like the receiver.
Subclasses normally override the postCopy
message, but some objects that should not be
copied override copy. "
```

^self shallowCopy postCopy

The shallowCopy message is sent to the original object, self. This message returns a new instance, however, so the postCopy message is sent to the new instance, that is, the copy. The shallow copy is performed by the original object and the postcopy is performed by the new instance. Once the original object has performed the shallow copy and created the new instance, it is finished copying. It is then up to the new instance to continue the copying process in its postCopy method.

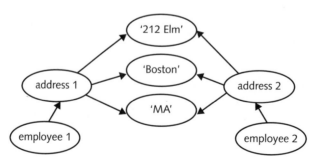

Figure 11.3. Full Copy of a Complex Object.

11.2.3.3 Copying Atomic Instance Variables

Copying atomic objects is the easiest part of the copying process because nothing more needs to be done than the shallow copy. This is because atomic information is swapped and not edited, so it is quite all right if the copy and the original share the same atomic objects initially. In the example in Figure 11.3, even though address 1 and its copy, address 2, still reference the same three strings, we can change the street of address 1 without affecting address 2. This is because the strings themselves are not edited, but simply replaced with other strings. If we change the street address of employee 2 to '4001 Pine', then address 2 will now reference the '4001 Pine' string but address 1 will still reference the '212 Elm' string (see Figure 11.4).

11.2.3.4 Copying Mutable Instance Variables

Instance variables that reference domain objects as a matter of aggregation need to be copied in the postCopy method. Fortunately, since these are domain objects and already know how to copy themselves fully, each one only requires a simple copy statement. Suppose that we try to copy a Factory object that holds on to a Schedule object with an instance variable called schedule. The Factory class postCopy method should include a statement like the following.

      schedule := schedule copy.

This assures us that the original Factory object and the copy are not sharing the same Schedule object. And in a recursive fashion, it is then up to the Schedule class to implement a postCopy that makes sure that an original and its copy are appropriately distinct objects.

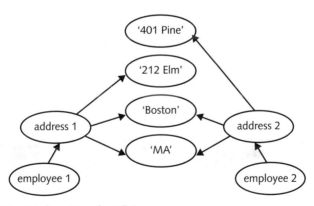

Figure 11.4. Editing Atomic Information of a Full Copy.

Instance variables that reference domain objects as a matter of association do not need to be copied at all. Since the associated object is not considered to be part of the domain object, it should not be copied. This means that both the copy and the original are associated with the same object, which is as it should be. This ensures that the integrity of the association is maintained.

11.2.3.5 Copying Collection Instance Variables

Copying collections presents somewhat of a puzzler. To effectively copy a collection, you must not only copy the collection, but also copy each element it contains. For copying collections, DomainObject has a private method, copyCollecton: aCollection, where aCollection is the original and the method returns a full copy. To adequately copy a collection variable, fileNames, for instance, the postCopy method should include a statement such as the following.

         fileNames := self copyCollection: fileNames.

11.2.3.6 Domain Object Copying Guidelines

Each domain object class that defines instance variables should also implement its own postCopy method to define what its copies are to look like. A postCopy method should almost always begin with the super postCopy statement. This assures us that any instance variables defined by the superclasses are also copied appropriately. An implementation of postCopy should result in a full copy.

In implementing a domain object's postCopy method, you must be sensitive to the type of reference made by each of the domain object's instance variables. For copying domain objects, the following guidelines apply based on the type of object referenced by each instance variable.

- Atomic objects need not be copied since they will be replaced anyway.

- Mutable objects should be copied.

- Collections of atomic objects should be copied, but their elements need not be copied.

- Collections of mutable objects should be copied, and their elements should be copied as well.

For the last guideline above, the DomainObject class provides a private method called copyCollection:, which takes an original collection as an argument and returns a copy of that collection whose elements are copies of the original's elements.

11.2.4 Comparing and Testing

Domain objects need to know how to compare themselves to other domain objects. Mostly this is for the benefit of certain collection operations such as sorting, detecting, and tests for uniqueness. Domain objects should also know how to conduct tests on their domain information. Disk Example 11.3 covers comparing behavior, and Disk Example 11.4 covers testing behavior.

11.2.4.1 Equals

Each domain object should be able to determine if it is equal to another domain object of the same type. The exact determination of equality is strictly up to the design requirements. For instance, in one design, a Person class might implement the method = as

> = **aPerson**
>
>   ^self name = aPerson name

and another design might use

> = **aPerson**
>
>   ^self ssn = aPerson ssn

In the first case, the designers determined that two people are the same if their names are the same. In the second case, the designers feel that two people are the same if their Social Security numbers are a match.

The equals operator = should not be confused with the identity operator ==. The = operator compares the attributes of two distinct objects of the same type. If the attributes match, then the = message returns true. The == operator tests to see if two variables reference the same object. If they do, the == message returns true.

11.2.4.2 Less Than or Equals

Very often domain objects are presented in a sorted collection. The default behavior for a SortedCollection is to rank its elements using a less than or equals comparison. This makes it convenient to implement a <= instance method in each domain object class. Usually, a <= method compares on the same parameters as the = method, but not always. Using the Person example from above, Person objects might be ranked alphabetically such as

> <= **aPerson**
>
>   ^self name <= aPerson name

11.2.4.3 Sort Blocks

In the event that you do not want to rank a collection according to <=, you can also define sort blocks to determine ranking. A sort block takes two arguments, which represent two consecutive elements in the collection. The sort block's implementation describes the relationship that must hold between any two consecutive elements. The default descending ranking looks like

> [:e1 :e2 | e1 <= e2].

An ascending sort block looks like

> [:1 :e3 | e1 >= e2].

A sort block access method for ranking Person objects by ssn would look like

> **descedingSSN**
>
> ^[:e1 :e2 | e1 ssn <= e2 ssn].

and a sort block access method for ranking by name would look like

> **alphabeticalByName**
>
> ^[:e1 :e2 | e1 name <= e2 name].

Sort blocks allow the same type of domain object to have different types of ranking within different SortedCollections.

11.2.4.4 Testing

A domain object should be able to perform any necessary tests on its domain information. For example, we might implement our Employee class so that employee objects respond to messages such as isManager, hasSeniority, and hasSkill: aSkill.

A very common test among domain objects is a test for completeness. It may be the case that a domain object must have certain attributes set in order to be considered complete. A domain object that represents an application for employment is a good example. An applicant domain object should be populated with all the essential information such as name, ssn, and previous experience before it is considered complete. Therefore, the applicant domain object should respond to a message such as isComplete.

Another common test is a test for type. For instance, the DomainObject class can implement isAddress to always return false, and the Address class can implement it to always return true. This makes the isAddress message the test to ascertain if a domain object is an Address or not.

11.2.5 Printing and Displaying

Domain objects should not be responsible for displaying themselves on a graphics medium. They can make it easier, however, for other objects that wish to display them. Domain objects should provide several mechanisms for representing themselves as strings, text, and even visual components. It may be argued that this type of behavior is inappropriate for a domain object because it tends to cross the boundary into application information. While this is true, these types of behaviors are very convenient for application development, and as long as the domain object does not include application state (i.e., instance variables that reference application specific objects such as models and menus), then there is no real harm done. Disk Example 11.5 covers the printing and display features of domain objects.

11.2.5.1 Print Methods

Every Smalltalk object knows how to respond to the message printString by returning a string that describes itself. The default implementation provided in Object is to just return the object's type such as 'an ApplicationModel' or 'a PluggableAdaptor'. The printString message is what is used to describe an object in the programming tools such as the Inspector and the Debugger. For the purposes of debugging, it would be nice if the printString message returned something a little more descriptive than just the type. For this reason, it is advantageous to customize the printString behavior for your object types. The printString method, however, is not responsible for building the string. This is done in the printOn: aStream method. It is this method you want to override for your domain objects. For example, by default a Person object will return 'a Person' as its print string. We might want to override the printOn: aStream method to return something like

> 'Person - Jones, William Robert'.

To do this, we would implement the printOn: aStream method as

printOn: aStream

```
aStream
    nextPutAll: 'Person - '
    nextPutAll: self lastName;
    nextPutAll: ', ';
    nextPutAll: self firstName;
    space;
    nextPutAll: self middleName
```

11.2.5.2 Display Methods

The display methods are similar to the printString method in that they return a string or text representing the receiver. The display methods are used primarily by list and table components. An object can have several different display methods. The default display method is displayString. See Chapter 9, Section 9.4, for more on display methods.

11.2.5.3 Visual Blocks

Visual blocks are used exclusively by lists, tables, and notebooks. Do not confuse these visual blocks with the VisualBlock class. They are related but not the same thing. A visual block is a block that describes how an object should be drawn in a list, table, or notebook tab, and it takes two arguments—the widget (a SequenceView for list and a GeneralSelectionTableView for a table) and the index of the element. A visual block should evaluate to an object that understands visual component protocol. A VisualBlock, on the other hand, is a visual component whose drawing behavior is described by a block that it references with its block instance variable. For more on visual blocks and VisualBlock, see Chapter 9, Section 9.4.

11.2.5.4 asText Method

Sometimes it is convenient to display a domain object in a read-only input field. Any object that responds to asText by returning a string or text can be displayed in an input field. Therefore, DomainAdaptor implements the asText method to return the print string as a text object. This means that all domain objects can be displayed in a read-only input field. Subclasses can override this behavior if necessary.

11.3 Domain Adaptor

Now that we have a domain object, we would like to build an application model to provide a user interface for allowing the user to view and edit the domain object. This object will be a special kind of application model, which we will call a domain adaptor. Let's define a **domain adaptor** as an application model that knows how to provide model behavior and a user interface for a domain object. It is convenient to think of a domain adaptor as a domain object editor. This section is dedicated to designing the DomainAdaptor class, which will serve as the abstract superclass of all domain adaptors.

11.3.1 Desired Characteristics

There are certain characteristics and behaviors we would like for our domain adaptors. Remember that what we are after is an easy and elegant way to have a purely application type object—the domain adaptor—provide a user interface for a purely domain type object—the domain object. We would also like the design and construction of such domain adaptors to be easy and intuitive for the developer.

11.3.1.1 One Domain Object per Domain Adaptor

For each type of domain object we would like to build at least one special type of domain adaptor. Each domain adaptor, however, will operate on only one type of domain object. So for an Address domain object we might build a domain adaptor class called AddressUI, which is designed specifically for viewing and editing a single Address object. This convention of naming the domain adaptor class by using the domain object class name with a 'UI' appended at the end is very convenient and intuitive and emphasizes the one-to-one relationship between domain adaptor classes and domain object classes. This convention will be used throughout the remainder of this chapter.

11.3.1.2 Domain Object Accessing

While a domain adaptor's window is open, we should be able to easily swap domain objects in and out and have the entire interface update accordingly. This means that we need accessor methods for accessing a domain adaptor's domain object. For this purpose we will use the messages domain and domain:.

As an example of the intended behavior, we would like to create an instance of a domain adaptor

    addressDA := AddressUI new.

then hand that domain adaptor an instance of its corresponding domain object.

    addressDA domain: Address new

Then we would like to open the interface,

    addressDA open

have the user edit the interface, and then acquire the edited domain object from the domain adaptor.

    addressDA domain

We can then place this domain object in a database, use it as an aggregate for a larger domain object such as an Employee object, or perform some other operation. Also, while the interface is still running, we would like hand it another instance of Address

```
newAddress := Address street: 'Elm' city: 'Houston' state: 'TX'.
addressDA domain: newAddress
```

and have the interface update automatically with the information in the new domain object.

11.3.1.3 Value Model Protocol

It is easy to see the parallel between domain adaptors and ValueHolder objects. A Value-Holder provides model behavior for an object that is not a model such as a string, number, or boolean. This allows such an object to be viewed and edited in a user interface component such as an input field or check box. The domain adaptor is providing the very same service for a domain object only on a larger scale. Recall that the domain objects are designed specifically to omit any model behaviors. The domain adaptor is providing the necessary application model behavior so that the domain object can be viewed and edited by a user interface. Therefore, for purposes of idiomatic consistency, the domain adaptor's domain object should be accessed using value model protocol in addition to the domain/domain: protocol mentioned above. This effort to conform to value model protocol will continue throughout the development of the domain adaptor architecture, and as you will see later, it will pay tremendous dividends. To generalize, all domain information—strings, numbers, booleans, collections, and other domain objects—should be accessed from their models using value model protocol.

11.3.1.4 Default Domain Object

Since each domain adaptor will be designed for a specific class of domain object, it should be clever enough to create a new instance of this class in the event that an instance is not provided. For the example given in Section 11.3.1.2, the statement

```
addressDA domain: Address new
```

would be unnecessary. An AddressUI domain adaptor should be prepared to instantiate an Address object if one is not provided using domain: or value:.

11.3.1.5 Adapting the Domain Information

We want to be able to design each domain adaptor such that it can display and edit any aspect of information in the domain object regardless of the type of information—simple atomic information, collections, or other domain objects. This means that as the user edits the user interface, he or she is actually editing and populating the domain object. This trick of adapting the domain information to various interface components is not an easy one, and much of this section on domain adaptors is dedicated to just this endeavor.

11.3.1.6 Parallel Structure

We know that domain objects are often composed of other domain objects (or maintain associative references to other domain objects). An Employee object can contain an Address object, for example. This allows us to build very rich structures of domain information. Such are the benefits of object–oriented technology. This complexity of domain information can pose quite a problem, however, when trying to create a corresponding user interface. The approach we would like to take, which will simplify matters, is to have the domain adaptor structure run in parallel with the domain object structure. For example, we can design an AddressUI as the domain adaptor for viewing and editing an Address domain object. Now consider an Employee domain object which includes an Address object as part of its aggregation. When we design the EmployeeUI domain adaptor, we already have an AddressUI for editing the Address portion of the Employee domain object so we will reuse the AddressUI in the EmployeeUI. The AddressUI can appear as a sub-canvas, or it can be spawned as a child window.

11.3.1.7 Managing the User Interface

We would like to be able to design our domain adaptors so that they can easily manage a user interface. We would also like the implementation of the methods to be concise and readable. Furthermore, we would like have domain adaptors that can be easily opened as a modal dialogs. It is a very common semantic to have a dialog open up on a copy of a domain object and return either the edited copy or nil. The process of developing domain adaptor classes with complex user interfaces should be made as easy and straightforward as possible. Therefore, the abstract class DomainAdaptor should provide a wealth of abstract behavior and support methods.

11.3.2 The DomainAdaptor Class

Let's start the design of the DomainAdaptor class by addressing its basic mechanisms for dealing with a domain object. We will let the desired features and behaviors mentioned in Section 11.3.1 drive this design. The fundamental relationship between the domain adaptor and its domain object described in this section is also illustrated in Disk Example 11.6.

11.3.2.1 Subclass of ExtendedApplicationModel

In Section 1.3.1.7, it was stated that we want our domain adaptors to have complex interface behaviors, but at the same time we want the implementation of such domain adaptors to be concise, readable, and easy to construct. Therefore, we will make DomainAdaptor a subclass of ExtendedApplicationModel.

11.3.2.2 Domain Class

It was stated in Section 11.3.1.1 that each domain adaptor class is developed for a single type of domain object. Furthermore, the domain adaptor should be able to instantiate such a domain object if one is not explicitly provided (Section 11.3.1.4). Therefore, each concrete domain adaptor class should implement the method domainClass, which merely returns the class of domain object for which the domain adaptor was designed. For example, AddressUI would have the following implementation.

> **domainClass**
> "The receiver views and edits Address objects."
>
> ^Address

The DomainAdaptor class has the following abstract implementation.

> **domainClass**
> "Each concrete subclass must override this method and declare the type of
> domain object on which it operates."
>
> ^self subclassResponsibility

11.3.2.3 Domain Channel

The domain object will be referenced via a ValueHolder called the **domain channel**. The DomainAdaptor class defines an instance variable, domainChannel, for referencing this ValueHolder. The reason for placing the domain object in a ValueHolder instead of referencing it directly will become more apparent when we begin adapting the information in the domain object to the various parts of the user interface. By placing the domain object in a ValueHolder, the various interface components can be notified of when the domain object is replaced, and therefore they can redraw themselves according to the information in the new domain object.

11.3.2.4 Domain Accessing

The DomainAdaptor class defines the following domain-accessing methods.

> **domainChannel**
> "Return the receiver's domain channel. Instantiate it with a fresh
> domain object if necessary."
>
> ^domainChannel isNil
>   ifTrue: [domainChannel := self domainClass new asValue]
>   ifFalse: [domainChannel]

> **value**
> "Return the receiver's domain object."
>
> ^self domainChannel value

value: aDomainObject
　　"Replace the receiver's current domain object with aDomainObject.
　　If the argument is nil, instantiate a fresh domain object."

　　self preDomainChange.
　　domainIsChanging := true.
　　aDomainObject isNil
　　　　ifTrue:[self domainChannel value: self domainClass new]
　　　　ifFalse:[self domainChannel value: aDomainObject].
　　domainIsChanging := false.
　　self postDomainChange

domain
　　"Return the receiver's domain object."

　　^self value

domain: aDomainObject
　　"Replace the receiver's current domain object with aDomainObject."

　　self value: aDomainObject

With this protocol, you can access or replace a domain adaptor's domain object. If nil is used as the argument for value: or domain:, then the domain adaptor will replace the current domain object with a new instance of the domain class. The domain channel can also be accessed in the event that some outside object wants to register interest in the domain adaptor's change of domain.

11.3.2.5 Notification of a Domain Change

The DomainAdaptor class provides two hooks for subclasses to gain access to the domain-changing process. The preDomainChange message is dispatched just prior to replacing the domain object. The postDomainChange message is dispatched immediately after the domain object has been replaced by a new domain object.

11.3.2.6 Testing for a Domain Change

When implementing concrete domain adaptor classes, it may become necessary to distinguish between those changes that occur as a result of the user editing the interface and those changes that occur as a result of a change in the domain object. Therefore, the value: method shown in Section 11.3.2.4 sets the domainIsChanging variable to true prior to replacing the domain object and sets it to false after the swap of domain objects has occurred. This allows domain adaptor subclasses to send the test message domainIsChanging to self to see if the domain object is currently being replaced.

11.3.3 Adapting the Domain Information to the User Interface

Now that we have established the relationship between the domain adaptor and the domain object, we need a way to populate the user interface with the information held within the domain object. Furthermore, we want any changes the user makes in the interface to directly affect the domain object. It is convenient to think of the domain adaptor as the editor for the domain object.

11.3.3.1 Aspect Support Protocol

What we are after is a set of aspect support methods, much like those defined in ExtendedApplicationModel, that will allow us to easily set up special aspect models for binding the various aspects of domain information to the user interface components. For example, we would like a message that automatically binds an input field to a string held by the domain object. We would like another message that binds a list component to a collection held by the domain object. And if the domain object contains other domain objects, then we would like an aspect message that binds a subcanvas to that contained domain object.

11.3.3.2 Change Messages

The aspect support protocol should allow us to conveniently set up any necessary change messages. This is similar to the aspect support protocol of ExtendedApplicationModel. This allows us to set up the aspect model and any corresponding change messages in a single, concise, and readable method.

11.3.3.3 No Instance Variables

Continuing with the example set by ExtendedApplicationModel, there is no reason to allocate instance variables for each of our aspect models. Domain adaptors should use the builder's bindings to maintain the references to the aspect models.

DomainAdaptor should provide aspect support protocol for defining the aspect methods in the subclasses. Sections 11.3.3, 11.3.4, and 11.3.5 cover the development of such protocol.

11.3.4 Adapting the Simple Aspects

Recall that a domain object can reference all kinds of objects. For now we are only interested in the simple aspects of information. I use the term *simple aspects* to refer to such things as strings, text, dates, booleans, and numbers. These simple aspects are atomic references in that they are not edited directly but instead are replaced. Not included in this set of simple aspects are collections of other objects or references to other domain objects.

These simple aspects are usually displayed and edited by interface components such as input fields, drop down menus, text editors, radio buttons, and check boxes. Disk Example 11.7 shows how to adapt the simple aspects of a domain object to a user interface using the technique discussed below.

11.3.4.1 AspectAdaptor

VisualWorks already has a mechanism for binding simple aspects of a domain object— the AspectAdaptor. Recall from Chapter 2, Section 2.3.3, that an AspectAdaptor is a value model whose value actually belongs to another object called the subject. In this case the subject is the domain object. Furthermore, the subject is usually referenced by a ValueHolder called the subject channel. Yes, the subject channel in this case is the domain channel. It appears as if we are all set up to begin using AspectAdaptors to bind interface components to corresponding simple aspects of domain information.

11.3.4.2 Aspect Support Protocol

The DomainAdaptor class provides aspect support protocol for automatically setting up an AspectAdaptor and registering interest in its change of value. The messages that do this are

aspectAdaptorFor:	aSymbol
aspectAdaptorFor:	aSymbol changeMessage: aSymbolOrArray
aspectAdaptorFor: accessWith: changeMessage:	aSymbol anAccessorOrArray aSymbolOrArray
aspectAdaptorFor: accessWith: pathToTarget: changeMessage:	aSymbol anAccessorOrArray anArray aSymbolOrArray

The arguments are as follows.

aSymbol	A Symbol that is the name of the aspect model as defined in the Properties Tool. It is also the default for the accessor and mutator methods for accessing the simple aspect from the domain object.
aSymbolOrArray	A Symbol or an Array. If it is a Symbol, it is the name of a message to be sent to the application model on a change of value of the AspectAdaptor. If it is an Array, the

first argument is the change message and
the second argument is the interested object and receiver of the change message.

anAccessorOrArray   A Symbol or an Array. If it is a Symbol, then
it is the name of the accessor and mutator
methods for accessing the simple aspect
from the domain. If it is an Array, then
the first element is the accessor and the
second element is the mutator.

anArray   The path used to access the target in the event
that the domain object is not the target.

11.3.4.3 Example Aspect Method

As an example, consider an AddressUI domain adaptor that is designed to edit an Address
object. The AddressUI class will want to define an aspect method so that an input field
can edit the street name of the Address object. The default implementation for such a
method as defined by a UIDefiner looks like the following.

```
street
    "This method was generated by UIDefiner. Any edits made here
    may be lost whenever methods are automatically defined. The
    initialization provided below may have been preempted by an
    initialize method."

    ^street isNil
      ifTrue:
          [street := String new asValue]
      ifFalse:
          [street]
```

The problems with this implementation are as follows.

- The string that is to be the street name is not accessed from or put into the
  domain object.

- An instance variable must be allocated to reference the aspect model.

- There is no easy support for including a change message.

- The code is not very readable, especially if the code for establishing a change
  message is included.

The AddressUI class should implement this aspect method using the aspect support protocol defined in DomainAdaptor as is shown below.

street

        ^self aspectAdaptorFor: #street changeMessage: #streetChanged

This implementation mitigates the four concerns listed above. Whenever the user edits the input field, the street instance variable of the Address domain object is automatically updated and the change message streetChanged is dispatched to the domain adaptor.

Disk Example 11.7 gives more concrete examples of binding a domain object's simple aspects to a user interface managed by a domain adaptor.

11.3.5 Adapting a Collection

In addition to simple aspects of information, a domain object can reference a collection of objects. Such a collection usually translates visually into a list component. What we need now is a way to display a domain object's collection in a list component. Disk Example 11.8 provides examples of the information presented in this section on adapting a domain object's collection.

11.3.5.1 SelectionInList

VisualWorks does have a means for adapting a list component to a collection that resides inside a domain object. This is provided in the SelectionInList instance creation method adapt:aspect:list:selection:. This method employs AspectAdaptor objects instead of ValueHolder objects to serve as the listHolder and selectionIndexHolder instance variables. This implementation, however, does not quite fit our purposes for the following reasons.

- It requires that the domain object also track the current selection. This behavior is really an application responsibility and not a domain responsibility.

- The collection in the domain object incurs a dependency, which is a violation of our rules about domain objects.

- The domain information, which is the collection, is accessed using list and list:, which is not value model protocol.

- Some domain objects are designed such that elements are added to and removed from the collection by sending messages to the domain object (see Section 11.2.2.4). SelectionInList has no facility for dealing with this type of collection element accessing.

- If the collection is not a List object (domain objects should never use List objects because they are models), then a change in the collection is not immediately updated in the list component.

11.3.5.2 CollectionAdaptor

What we would like is a collection adaptor object that solves all of the problems listed above. We will define the class CollectionAdaptor to implement this collection adaptor behavior. CollectionAdaptor is a subclass of SelectionInList and therefore provides all of its superclass's features. In addition, it provides the following.

- The collection is accessed using value model protocol.

- There are several element-accessing methods, and these guarantee that if the collection is changed, the list component will be visually updated as well.

- If the domain object has its own element-accessing methods, then these can be employed by the collection adaptor instead of accessing the elements directly from the collection.

- The domain object's collection does not incur a dependent as is the case with the superclass SelectionInList.

- The domain object's collection can be transformed and or sorted by specifically defined blocks.

11.3.5.3 Aspect Support Protocol

The DomainAdaptor class provides aspect support protocol, which, in a single statement, connects the CollectionAdaptor to the proper variable in the domain object, initializes any features and options, and sets up any change messages for a change in selection. These aspect support messages are listed below.

collectionAdaptorFor:	aSymbol
collectionAdaptorFor:	aSymbol
	changeMessage: aSymbolOrArray
collectionAdaptorFor:	aSymbol
addSelector:	anAddSelector
removeSelector:	aRemoveSelector
collectionAdaptorFor:	aSymbol
changeMessage:	aSymbolOrArray
addSelector:	anAddSelector
removeSelector:	aRemoveSelector

The arguments are as follows.

aSymbol	A Symbol that is the name of the aspect model as defined in the Properties Tool. It is also the message sent to the domain object to access the collection.

aSymbolOrArray	A Symbol or an Array. If it is a Symbol, it is the name of a message to be sent to the application model on a change of selection. If it is an Array, the first argument is the change message and the second argument is the interested object and receiver of the change message.
anAddSelector	The message sent to the domain object to add an element to the collection.
aRemoveSelector	The message sent to the domain object to remove an element from the collection.

11.3.5.4 Example Aspect Method

Suppose we have an Employee domain object that references a collection of skills. To display this collection in a list component, the EmployeeUI domain adaptor will want to implement an aspect method such as the following.

skills

```
^self
    collectionAdaptorFor: #skills
    changeMessage: #skillSelelctionChanged
```

This method also makes sure that the message skillSelectionChanged is dispatched to the domain adaptor each time the user makes a new selection in the list. See Disk Example 11.8 for more concrete examples of binding a domain object's collections to list components in an interface managed by a domain adaptor.

11.3.6 Adapting a Reference to Another Domain Object

As pointed out in Section 11.3.1.6, a domain object can reference other domain objects. So now we need a class that adapts a contained domain object to the interface. As you may have guessed, the adaptor will be the domain adaptor designed for that domain object and the interface component will be a subcanvas. Disk Example 11.9 gives some examples of binding referenced domain objects to subcanvas components.

11.3.6.1 DomainAdaptor

Like any other type of application model, a domain adaptor can run a window as well as a subcanvas component. For example, we have an AddressUI as the domain adaptor for an Address domain object. Now suppose we want to design an EmployeeUI as the domain adaptor for an Employee domain object. We would use an AspectAdaptor to adapt the Employee object's ssn attribute, which is a string, and this would appear in an input field. We would use a CollectionAdaptor for any collections the Employee domain object has which need to appear in list components. And we would use an AddressUI to adapt the Employee object's address attribute, which is an Address object, and the interface component would be a subcanvas. In all three cases—string, collection, and domain object—we use value model protocol to access the domain information from the adaptor.

11.3.6.2 Aspect Support Protocol

The DomainAdaptor class defines aspect support protocol, which, in a single statement, determines the type of domain adaptor and connects it to the proper domain object in the parent domain object. These aspect support messages are listed below.

> domainAdaptorFor: aSymbol
> model: aDomainAdaptorOrClass

> domainAdaptorFor: aSymbol
> model: aDomainAdaptorOrClass
> accessWith: anAccessorOrSelector

The arguments are described below.

aSymbol	A Symbol that is the name of the aspect model as defined in the Properties Tool. It is also the default access selector for accessing the domain object from the parent domain object.
aDomainAdaptor OrClass	An instance or class of the domain adaptor to be used to adapt the domain object and run the subcanvas.
anAccessSelector	The access selector for accessing the domain object from the a parent domain object in the event that the accessor is something other than aSymbol.

Notice that there are no change messages. While the subcanvas is used to edit the domain object, it does not replace the domain object. That is, the subcanvas does not send value: to its adaptor, and so we have no reason to register interest. This is unlike the input fields and check boxes, which do replace the domain information by sending value: to their adaptors.

Since DomainAdaptor is a subclass of ExtendedApplicationModel, all domain adaptors can maintain a reference to their parent application model. Therefore, these aspect support methods automatically make sure that the subdomain adaptor references the parent domain adaptor.

11.3.6.3 Example Aspect Method

In our EmployeeUI example, the EmployeeUI class will define an aspect method for a sub-canvas to display the Employee domain object's address attribute—which, of course is an Address object. Such an aspect method might look like the following.

> **address**
>
>> ^self domainAdaptorFor: #address model: AddressUI

11.3.7 Domain Adaptor Architecture

The approach to segregating the application and domain information using domain objects and domain adaptors is what I refer to as the **domain adaptor architecture**. Formally defined, the domain adaptor architecture is an extension of the application model architecture that allows a certain kind of application model, called a domain adaptor, to provide user viewing and editing of a purely domain object.

In Chapter 4, Figure 4.1 showed the basic object diagram for an application model. Figure 11.5 shows an object diagram that illustrates the enhancements made by the domain adaptor architecture.

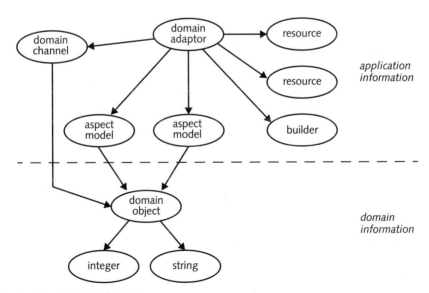

Figure 11.5. Domain Adaptor Architecture.

Table 11.1. Adaptors for the Domain Object.

Domain information	Adaptor	Component
String, Number, Date	AspectAdaptor	Input Field
Text	AspectAdaptor	Text Editor
Symbol	AspectAdaptor	Radio Button
Boolean	AspectAdaptor	Check Box
OrderedCollection SortedCollection	CollectionAdaptor	List
DomainObject	DomainAdaptor	Subcanvas or Window

Table 11.1 summarizes the domain information a domain object can contain, the adaptor used to bind it to an interface component, and the typical kinds of interface components used to display that information.

11.3.8 Simple Example

Consider again the Address domain object. Let's formally define some instance variables for this class of object.

Variable	Type
street	String
city	String
state	String
zip	String

We could define a domain adaptor, a subclass of DomainAdaptor called AddressUI (Address User Interface), to view and edit such an object. This domain adaptor's interface might look like that of Figure 11.6.

The AddressUI class would need to define the following aspect methods to bind its domain object's information to the input fields in the interface.

street

    ^self aspectAdaptorFor: #street

city

    ^self aspectAdaptorFor: #city

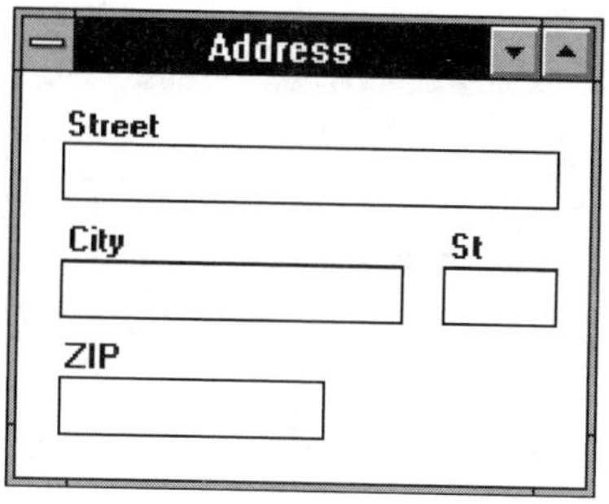

Figure 11.6. AddressUI.

state

^self aspectAdaptorFor: #state

zip

^self aspectAdaptorFor: #zip

Now consider an Applicant domain object which has the following instance variables.

Variable	Type
name	String
ssn	String
references	Collection of Strings
address	Address

Thus an Applicant object is composed of two strings, a collection, and an Address object. That is, an Applicant object contains an Address object as part of its state.

To view and edit an Applicant object, we create another subclass of DomainAdaptor called ApplicantUI (Applicant User Interface), whose interface is shown in Figure 11.7.

Notice that the ApplicantUI interface contains the AddressUI interface as a subcanvas in just the same way that the Applicant domain object contains and Address domain object. The ApplicantUI class would have to define the following aspect methods in order to bind the components in its interface to the information contained within its domain object.

name

^self aspectAdaptorFor: #name

ssn

^self aspectAdaptorFor: #ssn

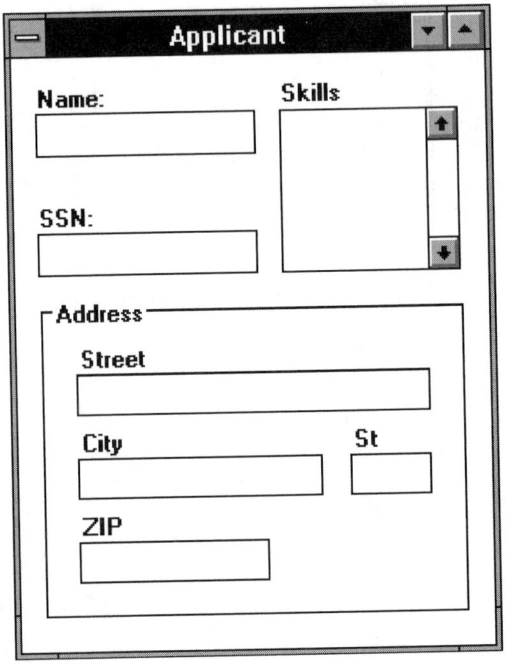

Figure 11.7. ApplicantUI.

references

> ^self collectionAdaptorFor: #references

address

> ^self domainAdaptorFor: #address model: AddressUI

Disk Examples 11.10 and 11.11 provide more involved examples of the domain adaptor architecture.

11.3.9 Guidelines

Here are a few guidelines for developing applications with the domain adaptor architecture. Since all rules are meant to be broken, then these guidelines are certainly fair game. Bear in mind, however, that these guidelines are not offered frivolously. They have evolved through several painful experiences and have served their purpose well since the introduction of *VisualWorks* 1.0.

11.3.9.1 Parallel Structures

Each type of domain object should have at least one corresponding type of domain adaptor—perhaps more. Each time a domain object contains another domain object, its domain adaptor should use the contained domain object's domain adaptor as a subapplication. The layout of the domain objects should drive the layout of the domain adaptors. While in actuality it is an iterative process, and application model development can influence domain development, in each iteration the domain considerations come first. After all, the domain objects are the abstract representation of the problem domain.

11.3.9.2 Editing the Domain Object

You should directly manipulate the domain object as little as possible, as this is the user's job. The main purpose of the domain object is to provide a common link among all the domain information contained in the application and to model the domain problem space. It is not meant to be an object that is constantly manipulated by agents other than the user interface. All programmatic editing of the domain should go through the adaptors as much as possible. In this way, any changes to the domain are automatically displayed visually. Remember, the domain objects are not models and do not broadcast updates when they are changed. It is the responsibility of the developer to make sure that the domain adaptor is notified of any direct manipulations of its domain object in case the domain adaptor needs to update its interface.

11.3.9.3 Collections

Collections and lists are ubiquitous in application development, however, they are often the source of much frustration. One problem is that the one-to-many relationship expressed so elegantly in all the design methodologies is a fiction. In reality it is a one-to-one-to-many relationship. This added piece of indirection imposed by the collection object can wreak havoc during development time if not properly taken into account.

The CollectionAdaptor makes it easy to bind a list component to the collection held by a domain object. It also provides

- value model protocol compliance

- visual updates on a change of the collection adaptor

- domain collections free of dependents

- an adaptor for collections

- transformation and sorting of the domain object's collection

- use of domain object accessors for collection elements

11.3.9.4 Dialogs

When dialogs are used to edit domain information, they should be implemented as domain adaptors. Furthermore, they should always operate on a copy of the domain object so that the user has the option to cancel out of the dialog and roll back any changes. The dialog should return the edited copy in the case of an accept or nil in the case of a cancel.

11.3.9.5 Abstract Classes

Before embarking on a major application, create one or more abstract subclasses of both DomainAdaptor and DomainObject to serve as the superclasses of all your application's domain adaptors and domain objects. The reason is that, invariably, each application has its own particular look, feel, behavior, architecture, and standards. Most of this commonality can be loaded into these abstract classes. In fact, a well-designed application with strict adherence to standards, coupled with the appropriate abstract classes that implement those standards, should yield concrete classes which average just a few lines of code per method.

11.4 Summary

In the current application model architecture, the domain information is just an unorganized set of objects scattered throughout the application. In order to develop production-worthy client/server applications, we need a way to organize and reference the domain information independently of the application. This facilitates persistent storage and analysis and design of the problem domain. The approach taken in this chapter to segregating the domain from the application is called the domain adaptor architecture, and its two main constructs are the domain objects and the domain adaptors.

The objects that reference and manage domain information are called domain objects. Domain objects should not exhibit model behavior or contain objects that are models. They should not perform application-type functions or contain application information. The domain objects should be able to copy themselves, compare themselves to other domain objects, facilitate their being displayed by other objects, and conduct meaningful tests on their domain information. Domain objects contain four types of objects: atomic objects, mutable objects, collections of atomic objects, and collections of mutable objects. An atomic object is any object that is not to be edited directly but replaced by another atomic object. Typical atomic objects are strings, numbers, and dates, however, domain objects themselves can also be considered atomic. A mutable object is another domain object that can be edited directly and constitutes part of the original domain object's aggregation. Domain objects can use collections to express one-to-many relationships. The collections can contain atomic objects or mutable objects. Domain objects can reference other domain objects as part of their aggregation. Domain objects can also reference other domain objects as an association. The difference between association and aggregation is a matter of perspective because they are implemented the same in Smalltalk. The DomainObject class was created to describe the abstract behavior for all domain objects.

A domain adaptor is an application model that provides the user interface for a domain object. It is similar to a ValueHolder in that it provides application model behavior for a purely domain type object. The DomainAdaptor class is the abstract implementation of the domain adaptor concept. The DomainAdaptor class defines the state and behavior for managing a domain object. Each type of domain adaptor is developed specifically for a single type of domain object. The DomainAdaptor class provides aspect support protocol for creating the adaptors for the three types of information contained in the domain object: atomic, collection, and domain object. AspectAdaptors are used for the atomic objects such as strings, numbers, dates, and text. CollectionAdaptors are used for the collections. DomainAdaptors are used for the contained domain objects. There is a strong parallel between the structure of a domain object and the structure of its corresponding domain adaptor.

CHAPTER 12

Building New Components

VISUAL WORKS HAS SEVERAL components with which a developer can build an interface. Most of these components are very standard and found in almost any graphical development environment. Most applications can be built entirely with just these components. Sometimes, however, this set of components is not enough. Fortunately, new components can be added to *VisualWorks*. Adding a new component is somewhat involved, but the benefits make it well worth the effort.

Adding new components is a testimony to *VisualWorks*'s ability to adapt and evolve to new situations. The authors of *VisualWorks* had neither the time nor the precognition to include all of the components that may be required by any given application. They did, however, have the foresight to provide the developer with the ability to add new components as the need arises. A new *VisualWorks* component can be specific to a particular application, type of application, or industry, or it can be as general as the standard *VisualWorks* components and apply to almost all applications.

In this chapter we will discuss what it takes to add a new component to *Visual-Works*. This is followed by a tutorial that walks you through the process of adding a new component. Two additional new components, available as file-ins on the distribution disk, are also discussed at a somewhat more general level. Finally, we will look at the alternative to adding a new component—using an arbitrary component.

For the purposes of this chapter, as well as the remaining chapters of this book, it is important that you shift your perspective as to who is the developer and who is the user. Until now, the user was usually the person using the application designed and built using *VisualWorks*. In this chapter, as well as the subsequent chapters, another *VisualWorks* developer is now the user. For the remainder of this book, the term *developer* will be used to refer to the person using the *VisualWorks* component or tool that you are building.

12.1 Requirements for Adding a New Component

Adding a new component to *VisualWorks* is quite involved, but in general, there are three basic steps.

1. Build the new widget class and any necessary supporting classes such as a new controller class or a new aspect model class.

2. Build a corresponding component spec class, which describes the new component, provides an interface for editing instances of the component spec class, and provides other necessary class and instance protocol required by the *VisualWorks* tools.

3. Add the necessary behavior to UILookPolicy for constructing the component from specifications and edit UIPalette so that the new component is available to the developer during canvas painting.

Each of these steps is described in this section.

12.1.1 Building the Widget

Recall from Chapter 2 that a *VisualWorks* component is a SpecWrapper and its widget is a visual part. Building a new widget is no trivial task and requires a thorough knowledge of MVC, the visual structure of a window, and *VisualWorks* widget and controller protocols (see Chapters 1, 2, and 6). This section covers only the basic approach to widget development and offers a few tips and suggestions.

A new type of widget can usually fit into one of three broad categories: those for new passive components, those for new active components, and those that are a subclass of a current concrete widget class. Certain characteristics are common to all of these, and certain other characteristics are unique to each.

There may be more than one type of widget for a given component. The best example of this is the list component. When a list component operates with a single selection, its widget is a SequenceView. When it operates with multiple selections, its widget is a MultiSelectionSequenceView. A single component may also have different widget types for the different look policies. A good example of this is the slider component. The Default, *OS/2*, and *Motif* look policy slider widgets are implemented by SliderView, and the *Macintosh* and *MS Windows* look policy slider widgets are implemented by MacSliderView and Win3SliderView, respectively.

In this discussion of widget building, we will first address those things common to all widgets. Then we will take a look at each of the three categories given above: new passive widgets, new active widgets, and subclasses of current concrete widgets. Brief discussions of model and controller development are included as well.

12.1.1.1 All Widgets

All new components need a widget class. Recall that the widget is a visual part and that a visual part is anything that is a subclass of VisualPart. All new widgets should implement the method displayOn:. The displayOn: method is responsible for drawing the widget in the window. The displayOn: method should almost always start with the statement

> self displayBackgroundIfNeededOn: aGaphicsContext

which draws the widget's background in the event that the component is opaque or has an assigned background color. The drawing process should, whenever possible, use the look preferences for rendering colors. That is, instead of using a statement such as

> aGraphicsContext paint: ColorValue black

use the following.

> aGraphicsContext paint: self foregroundColor

12.1.1.2 Passive Component Widgets

The widget class for a passive component should be a subclass of SimpleComponent. SimpleComponent is a subclass of VisualPart and provides the *VisualWorks* widget protocol (see Chapter 2, Section 2.1.3). This includes such things as visual properties, enabling, and tests for visibility.

12.1.1.3 Active Component Widgets

The widget class for most new active components will be a subclass of SimpleView. SimpleView is a subclass of View and provides the *VisualWorks* widget protocol (see Chapter 2, Section 2.1.3). This includes such things as visual properties, enabling, and tests for visibility. The new widget class may require a new kind of model, aspect model, or controller as well.

12.1.1.4 Extended Component Widgets

If the new component is merely an extension of an existing component, then the widget will be a subclass of the current component's widget class. In such cases, all that is required is that you override or add the appropriate state and behavior for the subclass. An example might be a highly specialized button that you would like to add to *Visual-*

Works as a new component. More than likely the widget class would be a subclass of one of the existing button widget classes such as LabeledButtonView or PushButtonView.

12.1.1.5 Building a New Model

Widgets for active components are views and therefore require a model. All such widgets have a value model for their model. While it is not required that your widget use a value model, it is consistent with *VisualWorks* idiom.

In addition to the actual model for the widget, there can also be a new kind of aspect model. Recall from Chapter 2 that a component's aspect model may or may not be the widget's actual model. For example, a list component has a SelectionInList for its aspect model. The list component's widget is a SequenceView, which requires a model. The SequenceView's model is not the SelectionInList, however, but a ValueHolder contained by the SelectionInList. In very much the same way, a new aspect model type can be created for a new component and such an aspect model would contain the widget's model.

12.1.1.6 Controller Class

Widgets for active components may require a new controller class. There are two sets of issues involved with *VisualWorks* widget controllers. The first set is common to all Smalltalk controllers and includes such things as the control loop, control activity, and the input sensor. These topics are covered in Chapter 1, Section 1.4. Another set of issues are specific to *VisualWorks* widget controllers and includes such things as a dispatcher, keyboard hook, keyboard processor, and taking focus. These are covered in Chapter 2, Section 2.4. Since it is the widget controller that integrates a component with the rest of an interface, it is very important that the new type of widget controller be *VisualWorks* compliant and provide the necessary protocol and behavior expected by all *VisualWorks* widget controllers.

12.1.2 Building the Component Spec

Each new component should have its own component spec class. If the new component is a pie chart component, then the widget class could be called PieChartView, and the corresponding component spec class could be called PieChartSpec. A PieChartSpec would be used to describe the particulars of a pie chart component.

There are nine steps to building the component spec class:

1. Choosing a superclass

2. Adding component description protocol

3. Defining the default model (active components only)

4. Adding component construction behavior

5. Building the spec-editing interface

6. Adding the interface bindings

7. Creating the spec generation block

8. Creating the Palette icons

9. Adding other spec class protocol

Each of these steps is discussed below.

12.1.2.1 Choosing a Superclass

The superclass of your new component spec class will depend on the type of component you are building. If you are creating a new passive component, you will want to subclass from NamedSpec. If you are creating a new active component, then you will want to subclass WidgetSpec, MenuComponentSpec, or ButtonSpec. If you are extending a current component, then you will want to subclass that component's spec class. See Chapter 2, Section 2.5, for more on the existing component spec classes.

12.1.2.2 Adding Component Description Protocol

A component spec is nothing more than a description of a component. The component spec object's **component description protocol** is the set of instance methods that provides access to that description. The component description protocol includes an accessor and mutator method for each attribute of the component described by the spec object. Some of the more common attributes include look preferences, layout, model, and tabability. These attributes and their component description protocol will already be provided by your component spec class's superclass. Your new component spec class however, will add its own unique attributes and therefore implement its own component description protocol for these attributes.

For each attribute you add to your new component spec class, an instance variable must be defined. This instance variable is then used to reference some object that describes an attribute of the component. This object can be as simple as a string, Symbol, or boolean or as complex as a layout object or look preferences object. Each descriptive attribute requires an accessor and a mutator. Furthermore, the accessor may include a default value. For example, if our new component has a border thickness attribute, then the new component spec class definition should include an instance variable such as borderThickness. The component spec class should also include component description protocol methods such as the following.

borderThickness

```
^borderThickness isNil
    ifTrue: [2]
    ifFalse: [borderThickness]
```

borderThickness: anInteger

```
borderThickness := anInteger
```

The get method returns a default border thickness of 2 pixels.

12.1.2.3 Defining the Default Model

New active components require a default model to be defined. The default model serves three purposes.

- It serves as the model for the component in a canvas being edited.
- It serves as the model for the component in the runtime interface when no model is specified.
- It describes the model used by the UIDefiner to generate an aspect method.

The component spec is expected to provide the default model with the instance method defaultModel. If your new component expects to have as its model a ValueHolder that contains an integer, then the corresponding component spec class should implement an instance method something like the following.

defaultModel

```
^0 asValue
```

12.1.2.4 Adding Component Construction Behavior

Recall that a UIBuilder is not so much a builder as it is a contractor who subcontracts the interface building work to other objects such as component specs and look policies. When a UIBuilder receives a component spec, it turns to that spec and makes the following request.

> *Create the component you describe, make sure it is compliant with my look policy, and add it to the interface I am building.*

The builder does this by sending the message addTo: self withPolicy: policy to the component spec. The argument self is the UIBuilder, and the argument policy is a look policy object such as a MacLookPolicy or a Win3LookPolicy. A component spec's implementation of this method is inherited from the superclass UISpecification and is shown below.

addTo: builder withPolicy: policy

> self dispatchTo: policy with: builder.
> self finalizeComponentIn: builder

This method sends the message dispatchTo: aBuilder with: aPolicy to the component spec (in this context, self is the component spec). It is in the implementation of dispatchTo: with: that a component spec is supposed to create the component it describes. But since almost all of the *VisualWorks* components are look policy dependent (a few exceptions), the component spec usually passes this responsibility onto the look policy object. Therefore, each new component spec class should have its own implementation of dispatchTo:with:, which consists of a single statement. This statement is a unique message sent to the look policy object requesting that it build the component. The look policy object will then create the new component according to spec and policy. As an example, suppose we have created a WordProcessorView widget and a corresponding WordProcessorSpec, then the WordProcessorSpec class should implement a method such as the one shown below.

dispatchTo: aBuilder with: aPolicy

> aPolicy wordProcessor: self into: aBuilder

This requires that UILookPolicy implement the method wordProcessor:into:. Component construction by UILookPolicy is discussed in Section 12.1.3. Right now, we are only interested in the component spec's role in component construction.

Other instance methods can be added to the component spec class. The most notable is the defaultFlags method. The defaultFlags method describes the default settings for the flag instance variable. The defaultFlags method will determine if the newly created component will have the following features by default: menu, border, vertical scroll bar, and horizontal scroll bar.

12.1.2.5 Building the Spec Editing Interface

When a developer adds a component to a canvas, he or she expects to be able to edit the various attributes of that component from the Properties Tool. Actually, the developer edits not the component but a copy of the component spec. It is the responsibility of the component spec class to provide the necessary user interface to the Properties Tool for such editing. Recall from Chapter 8, Section 8.2.1, that the Properties Tool edits a component spec by the slice. A slice is a subset of a component spec's attributes, and it is edited using an interface defined in that component spec's class. There are generally just two slice interfaces that a component spec may define: Basics and Details. Each of these is defined in a class method under the protocol 'interface specs.' These class methods are basicsEditSpec and detailsEditSpec. It is not necessary that the component spec define both of these slice interfaces or that it adopt these names necessarily.

The Basics slice usually edits the most critical information of the component spec such as aspect name, menu name, and ID. The Details slice usually edits the secondary characteristics of the component spec such as font, opacity, and tabability.

12.1.2.6 Adding the Interface Bindings

Since these slice interfaces are used to edit the component spec object, AspectAdaptors must be used to bind the components in the slice interface to the appropriate instance variables in the component spec object. This is done in the component spec class method

    addBindingsTo: env for: inst channel: aChannel.

The arguments in this method are as follows.

env	The bindings variable of the UIBuilder building the slice interspace. As the method name above suggests, the intention is to add to (or populate) this builder's bindings so that the fields, radio buttons, etc., in the slice interface will have aspect models.
inst	The component spec that is being edited and that will serve as the subject of the AspectAdaptors.
aChannel	A ValueHolder whose value is inst. This ValueHolder serves as the subject channel for the AspectAdaptors.

For each attribute you add to your component spec class, a statement should be added to this method that creates an AspectAdaptor for that attribute and places the AspectAdaptor in the bindings of the UIBuilder building the slice interface. As an example, we will use the border thickness attribute added to our fictitious component in Section 12.1.2.2. To allow a developer to set the border thickness from the Properties Tool, our new component spec should implement the following class method.

addBindingsTo: env for: inst channel: aChannel

```
super addBindingsTo: env for: inst channel: aChannel.
env at: #borderThickness put: (self adapt: inst forAspect: #borderThickness channel:
aChannel).
```

The first statement is necessary so that all the attributes defined in the superclasses can also be edited by the Properties Tool.

12.1.2.7 Creating the Spec Generation Block

When a developer adds your new component to his canvas, he expects to see some type of default, visual representation of it. For instance, whenever you add an input field into a canvas, you see an empty field, with a border, and sized to 100@20. This description of how a component first looks when added to a canvas comes from its spec generation block. A spec generation block was defined in Chapter 7 as a block that takes a UI-PainterController and a Point as arguments and evaluates to a component spec object. The UIPainterController is the controller running the canvas in which the developer is trying to drop your component. The Point is the location where the developer clicked the mouse to drop the component. From this information, the spec generation block should create an instance of the component spec with the appropriate layout and any other pertinent information. For the most part, layout is all that is required. The other information for the component spec will be supplied by the developer in the Properties Tool. The spec generation block is defined in the class method specGenerationBlock. Continuing with the WordProcessorSpec example from Section 12.1.2.4, the spec-GenerationBlock method for WordProcessorSpec might look something like the following

specGenerationBlock

```
^[:ctrl :point | WordProcessorSpec
        layout: ((ctrl gridPoint: point) extent: 100@100)]
```

The block above evaluates to an instance of WordProcessorSpec whose layout is a Rectangle. The Rectangle's origin is the canvas grid point closest to the location of the developer's mouse click (i.e., snapping to the grid), and the extent is a default 100@100.

12.1.2.8 Creating the Palette Icons

Each *VisualWorks* component is represented in the Palette by an action button whose label is an image uniquely representing the component. Each component spec class is responsible for providing its own unique icon image to the instance of UIPalette when it builds its interface (see Chapter 7, Section 7.1.4.5). Each component spec class is expected to define two class methods: paletteIcon and paletteMonoIcon. Both of these class methods belong to the class protocol 'resources,' and each returns an image with extent of 26@26. The palettelcon method typically returns a color image. The paletteMonolcon method necessarily returns a Depth1Image, which uses a MonoMappedPalette for its palette. It is up to the UIPalette to select either the color or mono image based on what is currently supported by the user's hardware. Both images can be created by an Image Editor. You should realize that the image includes the look of the button. That is, the border, background, and 3D effect of the button are part of the image. This will become more clear in the tutorial in Section 12.2.

12.1.2.9 Adding Other Spec Class Protocol

There are a few other class methods that are required of the component spec class. These are listed below.

componentName	Returns a string identifying the name of the component begin edited such as 'List' or 'Input Field'. This method is used by the Palette and Properties Tool.
placementExtent-Block	Returns a block that evaluates to a Point describing the component's default extent. Used by the placement mode objects when dropping a new component into a canvas.
slices	Returns an Array of Arrays. Each subArray describes the name of a slice and the interface for the slice. The implementation inherited from WidgetSpec is usually appropriate.

12.1.3 Editing UILookPolicy and UIPalette

The third step in adding a new component to *VisualWorks* requires adding the necessary look policy behavior and editing UIPalette to make the component available to the developer from a Palette. There are three types of additions to the look policy.

1. A component-building method

2. Implementation methods

3. Look policy-specific methods

The first item is required, and the last two are added as needed. All three items, along with the necessary change to UIPalette, are discussed below.

12.1.3.1 Adding a Component-Building Method

Each new component that is look policy specific (as most are) should have its own component-building method in UILookPolicy. This is the method that builds the component according to the description provided by the component spec and applies it to the user interface being constructed by the builder. Each building method is required to do the following.

- Create the new component

- Provide a wrapper for the component

- Position the component in the builder's interface

Depending on the type of component and the options specified in the component spec, the building method may also do the following.

- Connect the widget to a model

- Install a new controller

- Install a menu and menu a performer

- Add a border

- Add a label

- Add scroll bars

- Connect the component to the keyboard processor

- Provide any other component specific options

12.1.3.2 Adding Implementation Methods

An implementation method is a UILookPolicy instance method that simply returns an object or type of object to be used in the construction of a component. An implementation method can return a widget, a visual component, a controller, a wrapper, a border, or a class for one of these. For a new component, you should probably add an implementation method for your new widget class—especially if the widget type depends on the look policy. For the word processor component from the previous section, the widget class implementation method would look like the following.

wordProcessorClass

    ^WordProcessorView

For borders and wrappers, you can (and probably should) use the defaults provided by the look policy object. For controllers, use implementation methods only for look policy-specific controllers. That is, you may have a different controller class for one or more of the look policies making an implementation method necessary for each of these.

12.1.3.3 Adding Look Policy-Specific Methods

Most of a component's compliance with a particular look policy comes from the border, scroll bars, and look preferences. This makes it unnecessary in most cases to create look policy-specific subclasses of a new component. In some cases, however, it is necessary to build one or more look policy-specific types of a new widget. If this is the case, then the various look policy classes such as MacLookPolicy and CUALookPolicy will need to be edited as well.

12.2 Tutorial for Adding a Percent Bar Component

In this section, we will actually go through the process of adding a new component. Our new component is called a percent bar. It displays a fraction of some whole using a colored bar (see Figure 12.1).

The percent bar component has several options. It can be oriented horizontally or vertically. It can have a border or no border. The bar on the inside can also have one of three borders or no border. Finally, the percent bar can be labeled with the current per-

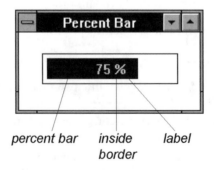

Figure 12.1. Percent Bar Component.

centage if so desired. The percent bar is an active component, so it requires an aspect model. The aspect model is a value model whose value is between 0.0 and 1.0. As with all components, a developer should be able to do the following.

1. Select a percent bar component from the Palette

2. Edit the component properties using a Properties Tool

3. Use the Define Dialog to auto generate a stub aspect method

This section adds the percent bar component to *VisualWorks* using the three-step process described in Section 12.1. First we will build the widget. Then we will create a component spec class to describe the component. Next, we will edit UIPalette and UILookPolicy as is appropriate. Finally, we will test the new component.

This tutorial is designed to illustrate all the steps involved in adding a new component to *VisualWorks*. In order to keep focus on this process, the component itself is kept as simple as possible without loss of generality. The entire source code for this tutorial is available in the file c12_3.st.

12.2.1 Building the Widget

Let's call the class implementing the percent bar's widget PercentBarView. The percent bar component will connect to an aspect model, which will contain the current percent or decimal fraction (a value between 0 and 1) displayed by the view. Since our widget is a view, we will choose SimpleView to be the superclass. SimpleView is the superclass for most *VisualWorks* widgets that are views. SimpleView is a subclass of View and adds all of the necessary state and behavior required of a *VisualWorks* widget (see Chapter 2, Section 2.1.2). So to get started with building the widget, create the class category 'SDGVW-New Components' and define the following class in that category.

```
SimpleView subclass: #PercentBarView
    instanceVariableNames: ''
    classVariableNames: ''
    poolDictionaries: ''
    category: 'SDGVW-New Components'
```

12.2.1.1 Standard View Protocol

As a view, our widget should implement certain view protocol such as preferredBounds, displayOn:, and defaultControllerClass. The PercentBarView will draw itself according to its bounds and will not have a preferred bounds. The PercentBarView will not have a controller so it will not implement defaultControllerClass. A controller can be added at any time in the future with very little trouble (this is done in Section 12.3.3). This leaves only the displayOn: method. For now the displayOn: method should look like the following.

> **displayOn: aGraphicsContext**
>   "Draw the receiver using aGraphicsContext."
>
>   self displayBackgroundIfNeededOn: aGraphicsContext.

Add the instance protocol 'displaying' to PercentBarView and add the instance method above to that protocol. The displayBackgroundIfNeededOn: method is already implemented in the superclass SimpleView. It fills the bounds of the widget in the current background color if the background color is something other than the default or if the component is meant to be opaque.

12.2.1.2 Accessing the Model's Value

We expect the model's value to be between 0.0 and 1.0, but there is no guarantee of this so we need a safe way to access the model's value. Add the instance protocol 'private,' and then add the following instance method to that protocol.

> **modelValue**
>   "Safely access the model's value."
>
> | val |
>   (val := self model value) isNil ifTrue: [^0.0].
>   val <= 1.0 ifFalse: [^1.0]
>   ^val < 0 ifTrue: [0.0] ifFalse: [val]

This protects us from a nil or a number which is out of range. It does not protect us, however, in the event that the model's value is some other type of object such as a string.

12.2.1.3 Adding Instance Variables

The look of the percent bar is going to depend on the desired orientation and whether or not there is an interior border. It will also depend on the inset value, which is the space between the outside border and the inside border. Therefore, it is necessary to add the following instance variables to the current class definition: inside Border, orientation, and inset. Edit the class definition so that it reads as shown below and accept the changes.

> SimpleView subclass: #PercentBarView
>   instanceVariableNames: 'insideBorder orientation inset'
>   classVariableNames: ''

```
poolDictionaries: ''
category: 'SDGVW-New Components'
```

These variables also need some accessing methods. Add the instance protocol 'accessing,' and then add the following instance methods to that protocol.

inset
"The inset is initialized to a 4 pixel gutter."

```
^inset isNil
    ifTrue: [inset := 4@4]
    ifFalse: [inset]
```

inset: aPoint
"On a change of inset, redraw."

```
inset := aPoint.
self invalidate
```

insideBorder

```
^insideBorder
```

insideBorder: aBorder

```
insideBorder := aBorder
```

orientation
"The default orientation is horizontal."

```
^orientation isNil
    ifTrue: [orientation := #horizontal]
    ifFalse: [orientation]
```

orientation: aSymbol

```
orientation := aSymbol
```

12.2.1.4 Displaying the Bar

Now we need a way to display the bar. The bar is nothing more than a Rectangle whose dimensions are determined by the model's value and the widget's bounds. Its final look depends on the selection background color, orientation, inset, and inside border. In the protocol 'private,' add the following instance method.

displayBarOn: aGraphicsContext
"Draw the bar according to the desired orientation and in the

selection background color. Draw the interior border if there is one."

```
| rect |
rect := self bounds insetBy: self inset.
self orientation == #horizontal
    ifTrue: [rect right: rect width * self modelValue]
    ifFalse: [rect top: (rect top + (rect height * (1.0 - self modelValue)))].
aGraphicsContext paint: self selectionBackgroundColor.
rect displayFilledOn: aGraphicsContext.
self insideBorder isNil ifTrue: [^nil].
self insideBorder displayOn: aGraphicsContext forDisplayBox: rect
```

Now edit the displayOn: method so that it includes the displayBarOn: message.

displayOn: aGraphicsContext
"Draw the receiver using aGraphicsContext."

```
self displayBackgroundIfNeededOn: aGraphicsContext.
self displayBarOn: aGraphicsContext.
```

12.2.1.5 Displaying the Label

Displaying the label is an option so we need to add the instance variable isLabeled. Edit the class definition so that it reads as follows and accept the changes.

```
SimpleView subclass: #PercentBarView
    instanceVariableNames: 'insideBorder orientation inset isLabeled'
    classVariableNames: ''
    poolDictionaries: ''
    category: 'SDGVW-New Components'
```

Now add the following accessing methods for this new variable in the instance protocol 'accessing.'

isLabeled
"By default, the bar is not labeled."

```
^isLabeled isNil
    ifTrue: [isLabeled := false]
    ifFalse: [isLabeled]
```

isLabeled: aBoolean

```
isLabeled := aBoolean
```

Now add to the instance protocol 'private' the following private method, which centers the label in the widget's bounds and renders it in the current foreground color.

displayLabelAround: aPoint on: aGraphicsContext
"Draw the label centered around aPoint."

```
| string x y |
string := (self modelValue * 100) asInteger printString , ' %'.
aGraphicsContext paint: self foregroundColor.
x := aPoint x - ((aGraphicsContext widthOfString: string) // 2).
y := aPoint y + 6.
aGraphicsContext displayString: string at: x@y
```

Finally, edit the displayOn: method so that it draws the label if necessary.

displayOn: aGraphicsContext
"Draw the receiver using aGraphicsContext."

self displayBackgroundIfNeededOn: aGraphicsContext.
self displayBarOn: aGraphicsContext.
self isLabeled ifTrue: [self displayLabelAround: self bounds center on: aGraphicsContext]

12.2.1.6 Adding the Class Comment

Add the comment below, which describes the widget to other developers.

This class describes a *VisualWorks* widget which can display a fractional amount as a percent bar.

Instance Variables

insideBorder	<Symbol>	Name of border class for the percent bar
orientation	<Symbol>	#horizontal or #vertical
inset	<Integer>	indicates width between outside and inside borders
isLabeled	<Boolean>	indicates whether the label is to be displayed

This concludes the widget-building process. We now have a well-documented widget class. This class has 4 instance variables and 12 instance methods averaging a little over three lines of code per method.

12.2.2 Building the Component Spec

Now that we have a widget to give the component a visual appearance, we need a component spec to describe the component. Section 12.1.2 listed nine things that must be done to build a new component spec class. For convenience, these are recreated below.

1. Choosing a superclass

2. Adding component description protocol

3. Defining the default model (active components only)

4. Adding component construction behavior

5. Building the spec-editing interface

6. Adding the interface bindings

7. Creating the spec generation block

8. Creating the Palette icons

9. Adding other spec class protocol

The first four items pertain to the instance definition of the component spec class, and the last five pertain to the class definition. Each of these steps is described below for our new component.

12.2.2.1 Choosing a Superclass

Since our new component will require an aspect model, we will choose WidgetSpec to be the superclass for our new component spec class. WidgetSpec is the abstract superclass of all component specs that describe components that have models associated with them. We will call our new component spec class PercentBarSpec. Therefore, add the following class definition to the category 'SDGVW–New Components.'

```
WidgetSpec subclass: #PercentBarSpec
    instanceVariableNames: ''
    classVariableNames: ''
    poolDictionaries: ''
    category: 'SDGVW-New Components'
```

12.2.2.2 Adding Component Description Protocol

Much of the component description protocol for PercentBarSpec is inherited. By subclassing WidgetSpec, we inherit the ability to name the component's aspect method, set the component's look preferences (or colors), assign a border, and determine the opacity. Three characteristics about a percent bar are unique, however, and therefore the corresponding attributes are not inherited. These unique features are listed below.

1. A percent bar can be oriented along either the horizontal or vertical axis.

2. A percent bar can include a label indicating the percent represented by the colored bar.

3. A percent bar can have one of three inside borders or no inside border.

The attributes for such features must be handled exclusively by PercentBarSpec if we are to adequately describe a percent bar component. Therefore, edit the class definition so that it reads as shown below and accept the changes.

```
WidgetSpec subclass: #PercentBarSpec
    instanceVariableNames: 'orientation isLabeled insideBorder'
    classVariableNames: ''
    poolDictionaries: ''
    category: 'SDGVW-New Components'
```

Now we need to add the accessors for these attributes. Each one requires a get and put method (accessor and mutator). Also, each accessor method includes a lazy initialization for the default value of the attribute. Add the instance protocol 'accessing' to Percent-BarSpec and add the following instance methods to that protocol.

insideBorder

```
^insideBorder isNil
    ifTrue: [#none]
    ifFalse: [insideBorder]
```

insideBorder: aBorder

```
insideBorder := aBorder
```

isLabeled

```
^isLabeled isNil
    ifTrue: [false]
    ifFalse: [isLabeled]
```

isLabeled: aBoolean

```
isLabeled := aBoolean
```

orientation

```
^orientation isNil
    ifTrue: [#horizontal]
    ifFalse: [orientation]
```

orientation: aSymbol

```
orientation := aSymbol
```

12.2.2.3 Defining the Default Model

The default model for a percent component is a ValueHolder that has a value between 0.0 and 1.0. We will initialize our default model to 0.0. It is a copy of this model that will be used by the Define Dialog when the developer auto generates a stub method for a percent bar component's aspect method. Add the instance protocol 'private' and add to it the following method.

> **defaultModel**
> "The default model for a percent bar component is a
> ValueHolder initialized to 0.0."
>
> ^ValueHolder with: 0.0

12.2.2.4 Adding Component Construction Behavior

Since our new component is look policy dependent, the component spec will not assume responsibility for constructing the component but instead pass this responsibility on to the look policy object. It will do this by sending a message to the look policy object that is specific to building a percent bar component.

Add the instance protocol 'building' to PercentBarSpec and add to it the following method. When you try to accept the new method, the compiler will raise a dialog box notifying you that it does not recognize the message percentBar:into:. Simply choose the **proceed** button to accept the method anyway.

> **dispatchTo: policy with: builder**
> "Since percent bar components are look policy dependent,
> pass component building responsibility onto the look policy object."
>
> policy percentBar: self into: builder

The reason the dialog was raised is that UILookPolicy does not yet implement such a method as percentBar:into:. This is a method we will add later on in Section 12.2.3.2.

We need two more methods to finish the instance definition of our new component spec class. First we need to define the defaultFlags method, which sets the default values for the boolean attributes for bordering, menu, and scroll bars. We will set the default flags of the component spec class so that the component has a border by default but no menu or scroll bars. Add the following instance method in the 'private' protocol.

> **defaultFlags**
> "A percent bar will have a border by default but not menu
> or scroll bars."
>
> ^2r1000

Also, the insideBorder instance variable is used to reference the name of the class of inside border preferred by the developer. For convenience, we will add a private method that returns the actual class for the current value of insideBorder. In the 'private' protocol, add the following instance method.

insideBorderClass
"Return the class of the border named by insideBorder."

^Smalltalk at: self insideBorder

Up to this point you have been dealing with the instance side of the definition of Percent-BarSpec. The remaining work will be done on the class side so make sure you toggle your System Browser over to the class side before proceeding.

12.2.2.5 Building the Spec-Editing Interface

Our new component spec class requires two interface specifications for editing one of its instances via the Properties Tool. These interface specifications will be kept in two class methods: basicsEditSpec and detailsEditSpec. The basicsEditSpec and detailsEditSpec can both be created from existing versions of these interface specs defined by other concrete component spec classes such as TextEditorSpec and ActionButtonSpec. In fact, this is strongly suggested because the canvas will already have the proper dimensions for fitting into the Properties Tool as a subcanvas and certain parts of the interface can be reused.

To create the basicsEditSpec class method, open a canvas on the interface spec defined in TextEditorSpec class>>basicsEditSpec (you can do this by evaluating that method's comment). Next, remove the **Menu:** field and its corresponding label. Next, move the **ID:** field and corresponding label to where they are just below the **Aspect:** field. Finally, edit the label at the top of the canvas to read 'Percent Bar'. The interface should now look like the one in Figure 12.2. Install this canvas as PercentBarSpec class>>basicsEditSpec and you are done with the basicsEditSpec (make sure you change the class name in the installation dialog!).

To create the detailsEditSpec, open a canvas on the interface spec defined in TextEditorSpec class>>detailsEditSpec (you can do this by evaluating that method's comment). Next, edit the interface so that it looks like Figure 12.3. The **Initially Disabled** and **Initially Invisible** check boxes should be reused, and the remaining component should be added.

Give the new radio buttons and check boxes the properties described in Table 12.1. Now install this canvas as PercentBarSpec class>>detailsEditSpec. If you had any trouble with creating these two interfaces, file in the file c12_1.st.

12.2.2.6 Adding the Interface Bindings

Now that we have defined an interface for editing an instance of our new component spec class, we need to provide AspectAdaptors that bind the fields and buttons in the interface to the appropriate attribute in the component spec being edited. Most of the bindings are inherited from the superclass. We only need to provide bindings for the three attributes defined by our new component spec class, namely, the instance variables

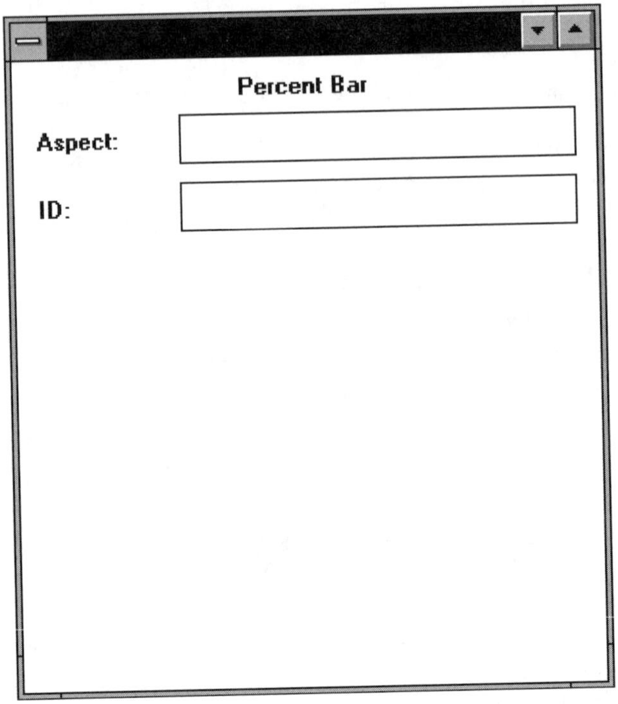

Figure 12.2. Basics Slice Interface.

orientation, isLabeled, and insideBorder. So add the class protocol 'private-interface build-ing' and add to it the following class method.

addBindingsTo: env for: inst channel: aChannel
   "Add bindings for all attributes defined in the superclass plus
   the three attributes defined by this class."

   super addBindingsTo: env for: inst channel: aChannel.
   env at: #insideBorder put: (self adapt: inst forAspect: #insideBorder channel: aChannel).
   env at: #isLabeled put: (self adapt: inst forAspect: #isLabeled channel: aChannel).
   env at: #orientation put: (self adapt: inst forAspect: #orientation channel: aChannel)

12.2.2.7 Creating the Spec Generation Block

Each concrete component spec class needs a spec generation block to create the com-ponent spec instances with the appropriate initial values. These initial values determine how the component will appear to the developer when first dropped into the canvas. In the class protocol 'private-interface building,' add the following class method.

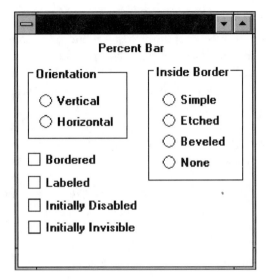

Figure 12.3. Details Slice Interface.

specGenerationBlock
"Return a block which when evaluated with a UIPainterController
and a Point as arguments will return an instance of this class."

^[:ctrlr :point |
    self layout: ((ctrlr gridPoint: point)
                extent: (ctrlr currentMode value class
                        placementExtentFor: self
                        inBuilder: ctrlr builder))]

Table 12.1. Details Slice Interface Component Properties.

Label	Aspect	Select
Vertical	#orientation	#vertical
Horizontal	#orientation	#horizontal
Bordered	#hasBorder	
Labeled	#isLabeled	
Simple	#insideBorder	#SimpleBorder
Etched	#insideBorder	#EtchedBorder
Beveled	#insideBorder	#BeveledBorder
None	#insideBorder	#none

12.2.2.8 Creating the Palette Icons

Each concrete component spec class needs to implement two class methods for returning a color and mono image to represent the component in a Palette. These two methods are paletteIcon and paletteMonoIcon, respectively, and they are class methods in the
'resources' class protocol. Both images have the extent of 26@26. You can design your
own images or use the ones provided in the file **c12_2.st**.

A few tips about designing your own image icons for the Palette buttons. The image includes the appearance of the button. To verify this, open an Image Editor on any
of the existing Palette icon images such as TextEditorSpec class>>paletteIcon (you can do
this buy evaluating the method's comment). For this reason, it is best to use a current
component spec class's Palette icon images as a the starting point for any new Palette
icon images. To do this, open an Image Editor on the current component spec's Palette
icon image. Edit this image, but save it under the name of the new component spec
class. Also, the Palette icon images for each component spec class are cached in the palette-
Icon class variable. Therefore, if you edit a component spec's Palette icon image, you
must send the message flushIcons to the component spec class in order for the new icon
image to be used in the next Palette to be opened. Otherwise, the image in the cache is
used and not the new version you just edited.

12.2.2.9 Additional Component Spec Class Protocol

There are three final class methods needed for PercentBarSpec: componentName, slices, and
placementExtentBlock. The componentName method merely returns the name of the component and is used by the Palette. The slice method tells the UIPalette which slices are
required to edit an instance of the component spec. Our component will not need the
notification and request slices since it does not have a controller (a controller is added in
Section 12.3.3). The spec generation block requires another method, placementExtent-
Block, to evaluate successfully. The placementExtentBlock method returns the initial extent
of the component being added to the canvas. Add the following class methods in the
class protocol 'private-interface building.'

```
componentName
    "Identification of component"

    ^'Percent Bar'


slices
    "Return the slice interfaces used by specs of this type."

    ^#((Basics basicsEditSpec)
       (Details detailsEditSpec)
```

      (Color propSpec ColorToolModel)
      (Position propSpec PositionToolModel))

placementExtentBlock
    "A percent bar will be dropped into the canvas with the
    initial extent of 100 by 20."

    ^[:bldr | 100 @ 20]

As a final touch, add the following class comment.

A PercentBarSpec describes a percent bar component.

Instance Variables

orientation	<Symbol>	indicates the orientation
isLabeled	<Boolean.	indicates if there is a label
insideBorder	<Symbol>	name of border type

This concludes the implementation of PercentBarSpec. This class has three instance variables. It has 10 instance methods, which average a little over one and a half lines of code per method. It also has 8 class methods, 4 of which are resource methods and the other 4 of which average less than three lines of code per method.

12.2.3 Editing UIPalette and UILookPolicy

The third step in adding a new component involves editing the class UILookPolicy, and perhaps its subclasses, and making a small change to the class UIPalette.

12.2.3.1 Adding the Implementation Method

UILookPolicy has certain methods, called implementation methods, which return either a class or an instance of a class used in constructing the component. We need an implementation method that returns the widget class for the percent bar component. In the protocol 'implementation classes' add the following instance method to UILookPolicy.

percentBarClass
    ^PercentBarView

12.2.3.2 Adding the Building Method

Each component that is look policy dependent requires a building method in UILook-Policy. In Chapter 3, Section 3.6.5.1 covers the basic steps in how a UILookPolicy component-building method builds a component from a component spec. Our method will follow these same basic steps, which are provided below.

1. Instantiate the model if necessary.

2. Instantiate the widget and connect to model, if any.

3. Instantiate the controller and connect to widget if necessary.

4. Set any component specific attributes.

5. Instantiate decoration object if necessary.

6. Apply layout.

In the instance protocol 'building,' add the following instance method to UILookPolicy.

percentBar: spec into: builder

```
| component model |
model := spec modelInBuilder: builder.
component := self percentBarClass new model: model.
component orientation: spec orientation.
spec insideBorder == #none
    ifFalse: [component insideBorder: spec insideBorderClass new].
component isLabeled: spec isLabeled.
builder component: component.
spec decorationType == #bordered
    ifTrue: [
        builder wrapWith: self borderedWrapperClass new.
        builder wrapper inset: 0.
        builder wrapper border: self inputFieldBorder]
    ifFalse: [builder wrapWith: self boundedWrapperClass new].
builder applyLayout: spec layout.
builder wrapWith: (self simpleWidgetWrapperOn: builder spec: spec)
```

Notice that this method makes use of the percentBarClass method from Section 12.2.3.1. Some of the other implementation methods used in the method above are bordered-WrapperClass, boundedWrapperClass, and inputFieldBorder. These implementation methods are already defined by UILookPolicy and are available for our use.

12.2.3.3 Adding It to the Palette

Now we need to add our component to the Palette. The UIPalette class is designed so that all we have to do is add our component spec class name to the class method standardSpecsForPalette and reinitialize the class. A caveat here is that #LinkedDetailSpec and #EmbeddedDetailSpec are not already in the list and must also be added before reinitializing. For each subsequent component added, however, you only need to add that component's spec class name. Therefore, edit the standardSpecsForPalette method to read as follows.

standardSpecsForPalette
```
^#(#ActionButtonSpec #CheckBoxSpec #RadioButtonSpec #LabelSpec #InputFieldSpec
#TextEditorSpec #MenuButtonSpec #SequenceViewSpec #ComboBoxSpec
#DividerSpec #GroupBoxSpec #RegionSpec #SliderSpec #TableViewSpec
#DataSetSpec #NoteBookSpec #ArbitraryComponentSpec #SubCanvasSpec
#LinkedDetailSpec #EmbeddedDetailSpec #PercentBarSpec)
```

The only change made in the method above was to add #LinkedDetailSpec and #Embedded-DetailSpec and the name of our new component spec class, #PercentBarSpec, to the end of the Array. Now evaluate the code below in a Workspace, or in UIPalette class method initialize, highlight the comment, and evaluate it.

```
UIPalette initialize
```

Now each subsequent Palette you open will include a button for adding percent bar components to a canvas.

12.2.4   Testing the Percent Bar Component

Now we will test our new component. We expect the percent bar component to behave just as if it were included in *VisualWorks* right out of the box. If your percent bar component proves to be unsuccessful, then you can file it in from **c12_3.st**. You must, however, edit UIPalette class>>standardSpecsForPalette by adding #PercentBarSpec to the array and reinitializing UIPalette (see Section 12.2.3.3).

12.2.4.1 Adding a Percent Bar Component

First, open a blank canvas. Notice that the Palette includes a new button at the bottom. This is the button for adding a percent bar component. Press this button to add a percent bar component and drop the component into the canvas. Verify that you can resize and drag the component. Now select **properties** from the canvas <operate> menu and verify that the Properties Tool contains the interface for our component's spec developed in Section 12.2.2. Give the percent bar component an aspect and ID of #fraction. Now install this canvas as ExamplePercentBar in the category 'SDGVW-New Components'.

12.2.4.2 Auto-Generating the Aspect Method

Since our component takes an aspect, we should be able to auto-generate the aspect method. With the percent bar component selected, choose **define...** from the canvas <operate> menu and define the fraction aspect method. Browse this method to verify that it was in fact created and created correctly. Now open the application to make sure the percent bar works in runtime. The percent bar will not display a bar at this point because the value in its model is zero.

12.2.4.3 Operating the Percent Bar

In a Workspace, evaluate the following code (add AM as a global if necessary).

```
AM := ExamplePercentBar new.
AM open
```

This will create an instance of ExamplePercentBar, AM, and open it. Now evaluate the following code, which changes the value of the percent bar component's aspect model.

```
AM fraction value: 0.45
```

Notice that the component updates with a colored bar. Try a few more values and then close this instance of the application.

12.2.4.4 Editing the Properties

In the canvas that is editing ExamplePercentBar, select the percent bar component and open the Properties Tool (if it is not already open). Give your percent bar component an inside border and select the labeling option. Also change the selection background color and foreground color. The selection background color is the color of the percent bar. The foreground color is the color of the label. Install ExamplePercentBar again and evaluate the following code:

```
AM open
```

You should now see the see the percent bar with an inside border, a colored bar, and a label indicating the percent represented by the colored bar.

12.3 Some Additional Custom Components

Two additional new components are available for study, review, and use in your applications. These two components were developed just like the percent bar—according to the guidelines laid down in Section 12.1. Also, an enhanced percent bar component is provided.

12.3.1 Clock Component

The clock component displays the time in hours/minutes/seconds. It does so in a digital fashion. A clock component can display the time in a variety of styles. The clock

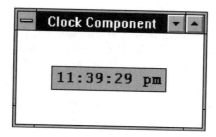

Figure 12.4. Clock Component.

component is shown in Figure 12.4. To add the clock component to *VisualWorks*, file in c12_4.st.

You must also edit UIPalette class>>standardSpecsForPalette by adding #ClockSpec to the array and reinitializing UIPalette (see Section12.2.3.3).

12.3.2 Ruler Component

The ruler component displays a ruler in either a horizontal or a vertical orientation and is shown in Figure 12.5. It can measure pixels, centimeters, or inches. The gradations can be labeled or unlabeled. The ruler component is a passive component, so it does not have a model. To add the ruler component to *VisualWorks*, file in c12_5.st.

You must also edit UIPalette class>>standardSpecsForPalette by adding #RulerSpec to the array and reinitializing UIPalette (see Section12.2.3.3).

12.3.3 Enhanced Percent Bar Component

The percent bar component as developed in Section 12.2 was simplified for purposes of illustration. It was necessary that the percent bar component be only complex enough

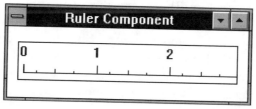

Figure 12.5. Ruler Component.

to sufficiently illustrate all the steps required in building a new component. It was equally important, however, that it not be so complex that these lessons were lost in the intricacies of the component itself. Now I will introduce some additional functionality that, under different circumstances, probably would have been included in the initial implementation. To include this functionality in your percent bar, file in **c12_6.st**.

It was mentioned in Section 12.2.1.1 that it would be easy to add a controller to the widget at some later time. This is just what has been done. The user can now grab the edge of the color bar and slide it backwards and forwards to change the percent value. The percent bar component can take focus, and the user can also use the arrow keys to bump the color bar higher or lower. The percent bar can still be operated without a controller by checking the **Read Only** check box in the Properties Tool. The controller is fully *VisualWorks* compliant in that it has a keyboard hook and registers with the keyboard processor.

12.4 Arbitrary Component Option

The benefit of developing a new *VisualWorks* component is that you can add functionality and flexibility to *VisualWorks* componentry that is not already provided. There is an alternative to achieving this very same benefit—using an arbitrary component. In this chapter on adding components to *VisualWorks*, it is necessary that we address this alternative.

12.4.1 Adding an Arbitrary Component

Adding an arbitrary component to a canvas was covered in Chapters 2 and 9, but for the purpose of our discussion, I will review it here. An arbitrary component is a *Visual-Works* component whose widget is any visual part and not necessarily one designed for *VisualWorks*. It does not have to conform to *VisualWorks* widget protocol, in fact, it can be a visual part that predates *VisualWorks* altogether. This is because a WidgetStateWrapper wraps the widget and the WidgetStateWrapper does conform to widget protocol.

The widget for an arbitrary component is provided by the application model in an instance resource method. The instance resource method is responsible for instantiating the widget and connecting it to any model it might require. This means of course that there is no corresponding aspect method for the model (there can be a method, however, that returns the model used by the widget).

12.4.2 Comparison and Contrast

There are several things to consider when weighing the options of creating a new *Visual-Works* component versus using an arbitrary component. Below are the advantages and disadvantages of each.

12.4.2.1 Advantages of New Component

The following are some of the advantages of building a first-class *VisualWorks* component.

- It conforms to *VisualWorks* idiom.
- There is better encapsulation, in that the developer is not required to know much about its internal implementation.
- Most attributes of component are editable from the Properties Tool.
- There is reuse, in that once the component is built, anyone can use it easily.

12.4.2.2 Disadvantages of New Component

The following are some of the disadvantages to building a first class *VisualWorks* component.

- The new widget and controller classes should conform to *VisualWorks* widget protocol and *VisualWorks* controller protocol, respectively.
- The widget should be restricted to using a value model as its model.
- It must implement a complementary component spec class.
- It requires editing system classes such as UILookPolicy and UIPalette.
- The process is long and involves many particulars, such as creating the spec-editing interface and creating an image to represent the component in the Palette.

12.4.2.3 Advantages of Arbitrary Component

The following are some of the advantages of using an arbitrary component.

- It provides backward compatibility to pre-*VisualWorks* interface components.
- The widget's model does not have to be a value model.

▶ It does not require a corresponding spec class or any editing of other *VisualWorks* classes such as UILookPolicy.

▶ It does not require a thorough understanding of *VisualWorks*.

12.4.2.4 Disadvantages of Arbitrary Component

The following are some of the disadvantages of using an arbitrary component.

▶ It falls outside of *VisualWorks* idiom, in that the model is not provided by an aspect method and placed in builder's bindings.

▶ Widget is not created by a component spec or look policy but by an application model resource instance method.

▶ There is limited look policy representation.

▶ It usually does not know about the keyboard processor and cannot participate in the tab order.

12.4.3 Guidelines for Choosing Between an Arbitrary Component and a New *VisualWorks* Component

In general, if you are intending to use a component several times and in several different applications, or if you intend other developers to use the component, then it is appropriate to invest the time and energy in building a first class *VisualWorks* component. If the component is a special one-time use or if the widget is already built without *Visual-Works* widget protocol, then it is appropriate to use an arbitrary component.

12.4.3.1 Guidelines for *VisualWorks* Component

In order to make the commitment to building a first class *VisualWorks* component accessible from the Palette, you should consider the following.

▶ The component is general enough that many other developers will use it quite often and benefit from it through reuse.

▶ The widget class and any accompanying classes have not been designed and built yet and therefore could be tailored to the *VisualWorks* idiom (i.e., value model protocol, *VisualWorks* widget protocol, *VisualWorks* controller protocol).

▶ There is already a very similar widget class from which you can subclass.

12.4.3.2 Guidelines for Arbitrary Component

The following are good reasons for using an arbitrary component.

- The widget classes already exist and are not *VisualWorks* compliant.

- The model is very complicated and does not conform to value model protocol.

- The component is very application specific and not likely to be used by many other developers.

12.5 Summary

In this chapter we learned how to add a new component to *VisualWorks*. There are three basic steps: building the widget class and associated classes, building the complementary component spec class, and editing UILookPolicy and UIPalette.

Building the widget requires picking an appropriate superclass and also building any necessary controllers and models as well. If the new component is a passive component, then SimpleComponent is a good choice. If the new component is active, the SimpleView is a good choice. The widget's model should be a value model to maintain compliance with *VisualWorks* idiom. The aspect model class, however, does not have to be a value model. Any new controllers should be compliant with the *VisualWorks* control mechanism.

Building the component's corresponding spec class involves nine steps. Several instance and class methods must be added to a new component spec class. The instance methods are mostly the component description protocol that provide accessors the attributes that describe the component. The class methods include the interface mechanisms for editing an instance of the component spec, methods expected by UIPalette for adding the component to a Palette, and methods used by the drag and drop process of adding a component to a canvas.

To complete the addition of a new component, you must edit UILookPolicy and UIPalette. UILookPolicy must be edited in the event that the component is look policy dependent (which is usually the case). Sometimes it is even necessary to edit UILookPolicy subclasses. UIPalette must be edited so that the new component is available from the Palette.

This chapter offered a tutorial for adding a new component, a percent bar component, to *VisualWorks*. Two additional components, a clock component and a ruler component, were also provided for study and use. In addition, an enhancement to the percent bar component was added.

Finally, this chapter weighed the benefits of adding a *VisualWorks* component with respect to the option of using an arbitrary component. Adding a *VisualWorks* component requires quite a bit of work, but it is very reusable and consistent with *VisualWorks* as a whole. Using an arbitrary component is more of a quick fix or one-time use and can be quite unconventional with respect to the *VisualWorks* approach to application development.

CHAPTER 13

Canvas Editing Enhancements

VISUAL WORKS PROVIDES A very rich set of tools for developing graphical user interfaces. It cannot, however, provide every feature desired by every developer. Fortunately, the *VisualWorks* environment is open and each developer can tailor it to his or her own needs—provided of course that the developer understands the mechanics of *Visual-Works*. In this chapter, we will build upon the material presented in previous chapters to enhance the graphical development environment.

In the previous chapter, we made some minor modifications to the system classes UILookPolicy and UIPalette. (I am using the term *system* classes to refer to all of the classes included with the *VisualWorks* virtual image.) In this chapter and the one following, we will make somewhat more significant changes to several system classes. There are two schools of thought on such matters. One adheres to the notion that the system classes should be altered as little as possible, if at all. The second takes the position that *Visual-Works* (actually Smalltalk) is an open system and should be adjusted by the developer to suit his or her own needs whenever necessary. Both sides have valid points to make, and while there are reasonable people in both camps, the premise of this book requires that you belong to the second!

In this chapter, the following enhancements are added to the canvas-editing process.

- The pasting feature for the canvas is enhanced to provide the option of pasting to the cursor position or to the component's original bounds as is done currently.

- A menu option is added to the canvas <operate> menu to set a component's colors directly through the menu.

- The Position slice of the Properties Tool is enhanced to provide buttons for easily applying certain types of layouts.

- A dialog is added for setting the canvas window's bounds.

13.1 Paste to Cursor

Currently, when a developer pastes a selection into the canvas from the paste buffer, the components in the selection appear at their established bounds automatically. Sometimes this can cause some confusion. If the components are cut or copied from the bottom right corner of a large canvas and then pasted into a smaller canvas, they will not appear in the smaller canvas. The developer then must increase the size of this canvas and drag the components to their intended position. It would be nice if the developer had the option of using the mouse to drop the copied components into the canvas at any arbitrary location. This section offers a lesson on adding this very functionality. We will refer to this piece of functionality as *pasting to cursor*.

This section depends on a good understanding of the UIPainterController class, so you may want to review Sections 7.1.3 and 7.2.3. You should also know about using menus as pop-up menus and about component layout.

13.1.1 General Description

The paste-to-cursor option is a menu item added to the canvas <operate> menu, which allows the developer to paste components in the paste buffer to a location determined by a <select> button click. This paste functionality does not replace the original paste functionality, but complements it. Therefore, a new menu item is added to the canvas <operate> menu called **paste to cursor**, and the existing paste menu item is relabeled to read **paste to layout**.

This section requires that you make some modifications to the UIPainterController class. The changes will be an edit of a class method and the addition of four instance methods. When changing an existing system class, making additions is somewhat innocuous. Editing an existing method is where you must be careful.

13.1.2 Editing the Menu

To start with, we need to edit the canvas <operate> menu. Recall that there are three versions of this menu, each of which is held in a UIPainterController class variable—Multi-SelectMenu, NoSelectMenu, SingleSelectMenu. Actually, these are just edited versions of the same menu defined in UIPainterController class>>canvasMenu. Since all three versions are to have the new paste feature, we want to edit the menu defined in canvasMenu. So open a Menu Editor on the menu defined in canvasMenu—a class method in the 'resources' protocol (you can do this easily by evaluating the method's comment). Edit the part that reads

```
edit   nil
    copy              doCopy
    cut               doCut
    paste             doPaste
    ---
```

to read

```
edit   nil
    copy              doCopy
    cut               doCut
    paste to layout   doPaste
    paste to cursor   doPasteToCursor
    ----
```

and then build and install the menu. In order for this change to take effect, you must reinitialize the class because you have redefined the menu in canvasMenu, but the three class variables mentioned above are still holding onto their modified versions of the old definition. To reinitialize the class, evaluate the following in a Workspace.

```
UIPainterController initialize
```

13.1.3 Adding the Private Methods

Obviously we need an action method to correspond to the new menu item. First, however, we need some private methods to support the action method. We need a method that waits for a <select> button mouse click and returns the difference between the point of the cursor and the origin of the upper left most component in the selection. This will result in a Point that indicates how much each component should be moved from its current bounds to its new location dictated by the cursor. This method will be called getScrapDeltaPoint. We also need a private method to determine the component with the origin closest to 0@0. This will allow us to make sure the upper leftmost component is pasted to the cursor and all other components in the paste buffer are pasted relative to it. This method will be called getTopOriginIn: aCollection, where aCollection is a collection of component specs constituting the paste buffer. So add the following instance methods to the 'private' protocol in UIPainterController (make sure your System Browser is on the instance side).

```
getTopOriginIn: aCollection
    "Return the top (smallest) origin of all the layouts of the component
```

specs in aCollection. If the layout is not a Point or Rectangle, it is
assumed to be some type of relative layout object and its origin must
be computed based on the canvas' bounds."

```
^aCollection inject: 1000@1000 into: [:min :each | | origin |
    (each layout isKindOf: Point)
            ifTrue: [origin := each layout].
    (each layout isKindOf: Rectangle)
            ifTrue: [origin := each layout origin].
    (each layout isKindOf: LayoutOrigin)
        ifTrue: [origin := (each layout leftRelativeTo: self view bounds) @
                (each layout topRelativeTo: self view bounds)].
    origin min: min]
```

getScrapDeltaPoint
"Return a point which is the difference between the next cursor
down point and the origin of the first component in the paste buffer.
Return nil if not red button."

```
| primaryPoint scrap |
scrap := ScrapPrimary isNil
            ifTrue: [Scrap collection]
            ifFalse: [ScrapPrimary collection , Scrap collection].
primaryPoint := self getTopOriginIn: scrap.
self sensor waitButton.
self sensor redButtonPressed ifFalse: [^nil].
^self sensor cursorPoint - primaryPoint
```

Now we need a method that copies a collection of component specs in the paste buffer
and moves the layout of all the specs in this collection by the amount of the delta point
calculated in the method above and returns the collection. We need to make copies because we do not want to alter the component specs that actually reside in the paste buffer. We also need to convert any relative layout objects to bounded layout objects. The
method that implements this is the moveScrap:by: method shown below (the term *scrap*
refers to a SpecCollection object residing in the paste buffer). Add this instance method to
the 'private' protocol of UIPainterController.

moveScrap: scrap by: aPoint
"Copy the collection in the SpecCollection scrap, and move
each of the elements by aPoint. Relative layouts become fixed."

```
| specs |
specs := OrderedCollection new.
scrap collection do: [:each | | newSpec newLayout rect |
    newSpec := each copy.
    newLayout:= newSpec layout copy.
    rect := self view bounds.
    (newLayout isKindOf: LayoutFrame)
```

```
        ifTrue: [newLayout := (newLayout rectangleRelativeTo: rect preferred: nil].
    (newLayout isKindOf: LayoutOrigin)
        ifTrue: [newLayout := (newLayout leftRelativeTo: rect)@(newLayout
            topRelativeTo: rect)].
    (newLayout isKindOf: Point)
        ifTrue: [newLayout := newLayout + aPoint].
    (newLayout isKindOf: Rectangle)
        ifTrue: [newLayout := newLayout moveBy: aPoint].
    newSpec layout: newLayout.
    specs add: newSpec].
^specs asArray
```

13.1.4 Adding the Action Method

Finally, we want to add the UIPainterController action method dispatched by the **edit→ paste to cursor** menu selection. This is the doPasteToCursor method. Add the instance method as shown below to the 'commands' protocol in UIPainterController. This method was patterned after the doPaste method, which is the action method for the normal paste procedure. It may be helpful to start with a copy of doPaste.

```
doPasteToCursor
    "Paste the contents of the paste buffer according to
    where the developer clicks the red mouse button."

    | deltaPoint |
    Scrap == nil ifTrue: [^nil].
    self quietlyNoteChangeToCanvas.
    self broadcastPendingSelectionChange.
    (deltaPoint := self getScrapDeltaPoint) isNil ifTrue: [^nil].
    ScrapPrimary isNil
        ifTrue:
            [self selectionList: (self builder addCollection: (self moveScrap: Scrap by:
    deltaPoint))]
        ifFalse:
            [self select: (self builder addCollection: (self moveScrap: ScrapPrimary by:
    deltaPoint)) first.
            self appendSelections:
                (self builder addCollection: (self moveScrap: Scrap by: deltaPoint))]
```

Now your paste to cursor functionality is ready to be tested. Any time you select **edit→ paste to cursor**, nothing happens until you press the <select> mouse button in the canvas. A copy of the components described in the paste buffer is then pasted in with the upper leftmost origin coinciding with the location of the mouse click. The **edit→paste to layout** pastes the components in the usual fashion. If your pasting function does not work, then you can file in **c13_1.st**, which contains all the changes provided in this section. This file-in redefines the canvas <operate> menu so any previous changes to this menu will be lost. You still need to reinitialize the UIPainterController class to have the file-in take effect. You may consider editing UICanvasTool so that its menu has the paste-to-cursor option as well. This is left as an exercise.

13.2 Color Menu

Currently a component's color is set exclusively from the Color slice of the Properties Tool. The interface that edits this slice is herein referred to as the Color Tool. The Color Tool is a very flexible and powerful tool. It provides the developer with several means for defining the four color types of a component: background, foreground, selection background, and selection foreground. Actually, the Color Tool is a LookPreferences editor since it edits the component's LookPreferences object. Sometimes, however, the Color Tool is overkill for quickly defining a component's color attribute. It requires that the developer leave the canvas and select the Color slice of the Properties Tool, select the color, and then apply it. It would be nice to have the option of setting colors directly from the canvas <operate> menu in a very simple and efficient manner. The purpose of this section is to provide just such an option.

This section depends on a good understanding of *VisualWorks* menus (see Chapter 9, Section 9.7), the UIPainterController class (see Chapter 7, Section 7.1.3), and setting a component's color attributes, or LookPreferences (see Chapter 9, Section 9.1.3.1).

13.2.1 General Description

We will refer to this addition to the graphical editing environment as the *color menu*. The color menu is an option in the canvas <operate> menu that allows the developer to change the look preference colors of the current selection using a menu of 16 colors.

The color menu is accessed by first selecting the **color** menu item in the canvas <operate> menu as is shown if Figure 13.1. Selecting this menu item displays a submenu of four additional menu selections: **background**, **foreground**, **sel background**, and **sel foreground**. By selecting any of these, a version of the color menu is displayed as a submenu. The color menu has 16 selections. The items in the color menu do not have text labels but colored rectangles, each displaying a different color. By selecting **color→foreground**, for example, and then selecting a colored rectangle in the color menu, the developer sets the foreground color of the selected components to the color of the

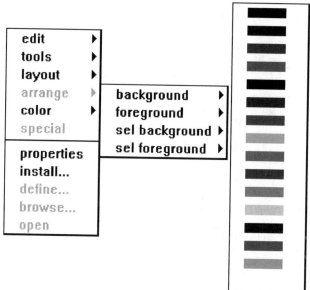

Figure 13.1. Color Menu.

colored rectangle. So there are actually four versions of the color menu—one for each of the four color attributes of a component's look preferences.

This section is divided into two parts. The first part involves adding and editing class methods to UIPainterController for the purpose of adding the color menu to the canvas <operate> menu. The second part involves adding several instance methods to UIPainterController that support the new menu options.

13.2.2 Building the Menu

The first thing we must do is edit the canvas <operate> menu to include the four variations of the color menu. All of the methods in this section are class methods, so make sure you toggle your System Browser to the class side.

13.2.2.1 Defining the Colors

We need a class method that returns a collection of 16 ColorValues. This will be the palette of colors from which the developer chooses. In the class protocol 'private,' add the following class method to UIPainterController. The implementation presented below is recommended for color monitors with 256 or more colors.

colors
    "Return a collection of sixteen color values."

    "self initialize"

    ^OrderedCollection new
        add: ColorValue black;
        add: ColorValue gray;
        add: ColorValue veryLightGray;
        add: ColorValue white;
        add: ColorValue yellow;
        add: ColorValue brown;
        add: ColorValue blue;
        add: ColorValue navy;
        add: ColorValue lightCyan;
        add: ColorValue darkCyan;
        add: ColorValue magenta;
        add: ColorValue darkMagenta;
        add: ColorValue orange;
        add: ColorValue red;
        add: ColorValue green;
        add: ColorValue olive;
        yourself

If you only have a 16-color monitor, you may try using the following alternative implementation.

colors
    "Return a collection of sixteen color values."

    "self initialize"

    ^OrderedCollection new
        add: ColorValue black;
        add: (ColorValue brightness: 0.8);
        add: ColorValue gray;
        add: ColorValue white;
        add: (ColorValue red: 0.502014 green: 0.0 blue: 0.0);
        add: (ColorValue red: 0.0 green: 0.502014 blue: 0.0);
        add: (ColorValue red: 0.502014 green: 0.502014 blue: 0.0);
        add: (ColorValue red: 0.0 green: 0.0 blue: 0.502014);
        add: (ColorValue red: 0.502014 green: 0.0 blue: 0.502014);
        add: (ColorValue red: 0.0 green: 0.502014 blue: 0.502014);
        add: ColorValue red;
        add: ColorValue green;
        add: ColorValue yellow;
        add: ColorValue blue;
        add: ColorValue magenta;
        add: ColorValue cyan;
        yourself

For black-and-white monitors that only display shades of gray, try the following implementation.

colors
> "Return a collection of sixteen color values."

> "self initialize"

> ^(0 to: 15) collect: [:each |
>   ColorValue brightness: each / 15]

You can edit the color collection at any time and you are in no way restricted to sixteen colors, but each time you edit the method, you must reinitialize the UIPainterController class for the changes to take effect (see Section 13.2.2.6).

13.2.2.2 Editing the Canvas Menu

Now we must edit the canvas <operate> menu so that it has a **color** selection that, when selected, pops up a submenu with four selections: **background, foreground, sel background**, and **sel foreground**. Recall that there are three versions of the canvas <operate> menu, each held in a UIPainterController class variable: MultiSelectMenu, NoSelectMenu, and SingleSelectMenu. Actually, these are just edited versions of the same menu defined in UIPainterController class>>canvasMenu. Since all three versions are to have the color menu feature, we want to edit the menu defined in the class resource method canvasMenu. So open a Menu Editor on the menu defined in canvasMenu—a class method in the 're-sources' protocol (you can do this easily by evaluating the method's comment). Edit the part that reads

```
        ----
    align...        alignDialog
    distribute...   distributeDialog
    equalize...     equalizeDialog
  special    nil
```

so that it reads

```
        ----
    align...        alignDialog
    distribute...   distributeDialog
    equalize...     equalizeDialog
  color      nil
    background
    foreground
    sel background
    sel foreground
  special    nil
```

and then build and install the menu.

13.2.2.3 Building the Color Menu

Now we need to build the color menu, which displays the colors in the color collection described in Section 13.2.2.1. Actually, we need four versions of this menu—one for each of the four color parameters. That is, one version of the color menu will be used for setting the foreground color and another will be used for setting the background color, etc. The value of each menu item in the color menu is a block that is evaluated when the corresponding menu item is selected. Each block takes a single argument, which is the UIPainterController. Each block is defined to dispatch a message to the controller with the corresponding ColorValue as a parameter. The message is defined by a selector, and a different selector is used for each of the four versions of the menu. In other words, the selector is #background: for the version of the color menu which sets the background color and #foreground: for the version that sets the foreground color. The selector is passed in as an argument to the method, which constructs the color menus. Add the following class method to the 'private' protocol.

colorMenuFor: aSelector
"Construct and return a menu of 16 colors."

```
| pm menu |
menu := Menu new.
pm := Pixmap extent: 40@10.
self colors do: [:each | | gc item |
    gc := pm graphicsContext.
    gc paint: each.
    gc displayRectangle: (0@0 extent: 40@10).
    item := MenuItem labeled: nil.
    item labelImage: pm asImage.
    menu addItem: item value: [:ctrl | ctrl perform: aSelector with: each]].
^menu
```

13.2.2.4 Building the Resource Menus

Now we need to add four class methods in the 'resources' protocol that actually build the four versions of the color menu using the method defined in Section 13.2.2.3. Add the following class methods to this protocol.

backgroundColorMenu
"Return a color menu for setting the background color of a component."

^self colorMenuFor: #background:

foregroundColorMenu
"Return a color menu for setting the foreground color of a component."

^self colorMenuFor: #foreground:

selectionBackgroundColorMenu
"Return a color menu for setting the
selection background color of a component."

^self colorMenuFor: #selectionBackground:

selectionForegroundColorMenu
"Return a color menu for setting the
selection foreground color of a component."

^self colorMenuFor: #selectionForeground:

13.2.2.5 Editing the <operate> Menus

Now we need a way to add these menus to each of the three versions of the canvas
<operate> menu. In the class protocol 'class initialization,' add the following two class
methods to UIPainterController.

initializeForColor: aMenu
"Add the four versions of the color menu to aMenu."

```
((aMenu menuItemLabeled: 'color') submenu menuItemLabeled: 'foreground')
    submenu: self foregroundColorMenu.
((aMenu menuItemLabeled: 'color') submenu menuItemLabeled: 'background')
    submenu: self backgroundColorMenu.
((aMenu menuItemLabeled: 'color') submenu menuItemLabeled: 'sel foreground')
    submenu: self selectionForegroundColorMenu.
((aMenu menuItemLabeled: 'color') submenu menuItemLabeled: 'sel background')
    submenu: self selectionBackgroundColorMenu.
```

initializeForColor
"Give the color menu option to each of the
three versions of the operate menu."

```
self initializeForColor: MultiSelectMenu.
self initializeForColor: SingleSelectMenu.
self initializeForColor: NoSelectMenu
```

13.2.2.6 Initializing the UIPainterController Class

Finally, we need to reinitialize the class so that the three versions of the <operate>
menu are updated with the color menu. In the class protocol 'class initialization,' add
the following statement to the end of the initialize method.

```
self initializeForColor
```

In a Workspace, evaluate the code below, which reinitializes the class.

```
UIPainterController initialize
```

Each canvas <operate> menu you bring up now will include the **color** menu selection. Each time you edit the colors method, you must reinitialize the class in order for the changes to take effect. You can test the menu at this point, but do not select a color or you will raise a notifier.

13.2.3 Adding the Instance Methods

The menu options we added in Section 13.2.2 send messages to the UIPainterController, but the corresponding methods have yet to be defined. In this section, we will define these action methods and their supporting private methods. All of the methods in this section are instance methods of UIPainterController, so make sure you toggle your System Browser to the instance side.

13.2.3.1 Private Method

The action methods defined in Section 13.2.3.2 all do the same thing, so their behavior has been abstracted into a private method. Each of these action methods affects one of the color attributes (e.g., background, foreground) of all the components in the current selection. If no components are selected, the color change applies to the window. Add the instance method below to the instance protocol 'private' in UIPainterController.

```
lpSelector: aSelector color: aColorValue
    "Set the color attribute specified by aSelector to the
    color aColorValue for the current selection."

    | collection lp |
    collection := OrderedCollection new.
    self primarySelection notNil ifTrue: [collection add: self primarySelection].
    self selections notNil ifTrue: [collection addAll: self selections].
    collection isEmpty
        ifTrue: [ | window |
            window := self sensor window.
            lp := window lookPreferences.
            lp isNil ifTrue: [lp := window defaultLookPreferencesCopy].
            lp := lp perform: aSelector with: aColorValue.
            window lookPreferences: lp.
            ^model windowSpec colors: lp].
    collection do: [:each |
        lp := each getLookPreferences.
        lp isNil ifTrue: [lp := LookPreferences new].
        lp := lp perform: aSelector with: aColorValue.
        each lookPreferences: lp]
```

13.2.3.2 Action Methods

There are really four versions of the color menu, one for each of the color attributes background, foreground, selection background, and selection foreground. Associated with each of these four versions of the color menu is a corresponding action method: background:, foreground:, selectionBackground:, and selectionForeground:. Each selection within a given version of the color menu sends the same message to the UIPainterController. The only difference is the ColorValue, which is the argument in the message. Take, for example, the version of the color menu used for defining the background color. All selections in this menu send background: aColorValue to the UIPainterController. The argument aColorValue, however, varies among the different menu selections, since each menu selection represents a different color. In the instance protocol 'commands,' add the following four instance methods.

> **background: aColorValue**
> "Change the background color of the current
> selection to aColorValue."
>
> self lpSelector: #backgroundColor: color: aColorValue

> **foreground: aColorValue**
> "Change the foreground color of the current
> selection to aColorValue."
>
> self lpSelector: #foregroundColor: color: aColorValue

> **selectionBackground: aColorValue**
> "Change the selection background color of the current
> selection to aColorValue."
>
> self lpSelector: #selectionBackgroundColor: color: aColorValue

> **selectionForeground: aColorValue**
> "Change the selection foreground color of the current
> selection to aColorValue."
>
> self lpSelector: #selectionForegroundColor: color: aColorValue

Now your color menu is ready to be tested. Open a new canvas and add an action button. Bring up the <operate> menu and select **color→background** and a color selection in the color menu. The background of the button should immediately change to the color you selected. Test this functionality for the other three color attributes and for multiple selections and no selection. If for some reason your color menu does not work correctly, the code for this enhancement is available in file **c13_2.st**. This file-in redefines the canvas <operate> menu, so any previous changes to this menu will be lost. You still need to reinitialize the UIPainterController class to have the file-in take effect.

You may consider editing UICanvasTool so that its menu has color menu functionality as well. This is left as an exercise. Another good idea would be to create a tool for editing the color menu. As it is, changing the colors in the color menu requires editing the method UIPainterController class>>colors class method (see Section 13.2.2.1) and reinitializing the class.

13.3 Position Buttons

The interface for the Position slice of the Properties Tool, herein referred to as the Position Tool, is very flexible in that it allows a developer to position any component as a function of its container's bounds. As the container stretches and grows, the component can stretch and grow—and in very specific ways. When we edit a component's layout, we are actually editing its layout object, which can be either a LayoutFrame, a LayoutOrigin, an AlignmentOrigin, a Rectangle, or a Point. A layout object is very much like a formula whose input variable is the containing bounds and whose output is the component's bounds. Once a component knows its containing bounds, it can calculate its own bounds using the formula specified in its layout object. Unfortunately, however, like many formulas, a layout object can be quite terse. The developer is required to do a certain amount of arithmetic in defining a component's layout. The LayoutFrame in particular uses a total of eight parameters set by the developer in determining a layout. Suppose for example, we want to add three buttons to the bottom of a canvas we are editing. If we want the buttons to remain a fixed distance from the bottom of the window no matter how the user stretches the window, then we must know the height of the button and the distance from the bot-

Table 13.1. Position Tool Actions.

Action name	Description
Fix Left to Left	Tie the component's left border a fixed distance from the window's left border
Fix Left to Right	Tie the component's left border a fixed distance from the window's right border
Fix Right to Right	Tie the component's right border a fixed distance from the window's right border
Fix Right to Left	Tie the component's right border a fixed distance from the window's left border
Fix Top to Top	Tie the component's top border a fixed distance from the window's top border
Fix Top to Bottom	Tie the component's top border a fixed distance from the window's bottom border
Fix Bottom to Bottom	Tie the component's bottom border a fixed distance from the window's bottom border
Fix Bottom to Top	Tie the component's bottom border a fixed distance from the window's top border
Relative Vertical	Fix the button's height but let its vertical position be relative to the height of the window
Relative Horizontal	Fix the button's width but let its horizontal position be relative to the width of the window

tom of the window and we must set the bottom relative, bottom offset, top relative, and top offset parameters of the layout frame for each of the buttons. This can be somewhat tedious and requires a little bit of arithmetic on behalf of the developer. The purpose of this section is to provide an easier way for doing just this type of operation.

This section depends on a good understanding of PositionToolModel (see Chapter 8, Section 8.2.2) and component layout (see Chapter 9, Section 9.1.1).

13.3.1 General Description

What we need are some action buttons for defining specific layout parameters for the currently selected component. For example, it would be nice to have a button that ties the component's bottom border a fixed distance from the bottom of the window. Table 13.1 lists 10 such actions, which make the Position Tool much easier to use.

It would also be nice to provide an intuitive visual label for these buttons instead of trying to describe their behavior with a text label. This leads to the interface shown in Figure 13.2.

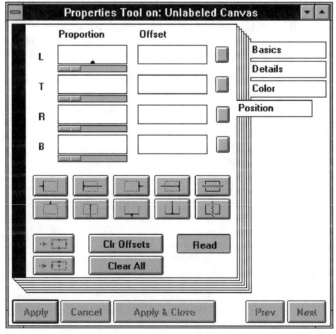

Figure 13.2. New Position Tool Interface.

In this section, you will edit the interface of PositionToolModel by adding several action buttons. You will then add several instance methods to PositionToolModel—both private and action methods.

13.3.2 Editing the Interface

Open the interface defined in PositionToolModel class>>propSpec for editing (you can do this by evaluating the method comment). To change this interface so that it looks like Figure 13.2, we need to lengthen the canvas, add 10 action buttons, and assign the properties to each action button. These three steps are described below.

13.3.2.1 Lengthening the Canvas

Stretch the canvas height so that it will accommodate two additional rows of buttons—about 100 additional pixels. You may have to adjust this height as you proceed with the rest of the tutorial. The exact dimensions of the interface will be determined by the Properties Tool when it loads the Position Tool as a subcanvas.

13.3.2.2 Adding the Buttons

Add five action buttons to the canvas to comprise the first row as shown in Figure 13.2. Give the first action button on the left the following layout parameters.

	Proportion	Offset
L	0	7
T	0	185
R	0.2	1
B	0	213

Give the four remaining buttons from left to right the following layouts.

	Proportion	Offset
L	0.2	5
T	0	185
R	0.4	-1
B	0	213

	Proportion	Offset
L	0.4	3
T	0	185
R	0.6	-3
B	0213	

	Proportion	Offset
L	0.6	1
T	0	185
R	0.8	-5
B	0	213

	Proportion	Offset
L	0.8	-1
T	0	185
R	1	-7
B	0	213

Now copy this first row and paste the copy below to create the second row. The images for the button labels are provided in the file **c13_3.st**. File in this file before proceeding.

13.3.2.3 Assigning Properties

Each button should have the **Label is Image** check box checked. Each button should also have the label, action, and ID attributes set. The first button in the first row has the following attributes.

Label	#fixLeftToLeftImage
Action	#fixLeftToLeft
ID#fix	LeftToLeft
ID	#FixLeftToLeft

Notice that the action and the ID are the same and that the label is also the same except for having 'Image' appended at the end. Proceeding from left to right, the remaining four buttons on the top row are as follows.

- #fixRightToLeft
- #fixRightToRight
- #fixLeftToRight
- #relativeHorizontal

The buttons on the second row from left to right are as follows.

- #fixTopToTop
- #fixBottomToTop
- #fixBottomToBottom
- #fixTopToBottom
- #relativeVertical

Fill out the appropriate properties for each of the buttons and install the canvas.

13.3.3 Adding the Methods

Each of the action buttons requires an action method. In addition to this, we need some private methods to disable and enable the buttons when appropriate. Make sure your System Browser is on the instance side.

13.3.3.1 Action Methods

Each of the 10 action buttons has a corresponding action method, and each of these action methods has the same fundamental implementation.

1. Get the component's bounds and, if necessary, the window's bounds.

2. Set the necessary layout frame fields.

3. Set the Position Tool to apply mode.

Add the instance protocol 'actions–auto layout' to PositionToolModel, and add to this protocol the following instance methods.

fixBottomToBottom

```
| box outsideBox |
propertiesTool selection size = 1 ifFalse: [^nil].
box := propertiesTool selection first bounds.
```

```
outsideBox := propertiesTool controller view bounds.
self bottomFraction value: '1'.
self bottomOffset value: (box corner y - outsideBox height) printString.
self readMode value: false
```

fixBottomToTop

```
| box |
propertiesTool selection size = 1 ifFalse: [^nil].
box := propertiesTool selection first bounds.
self bottomFraction value: '0'.
self bottomOffset value: box corner y printString.
self readMode value: false
```

fixLeftToLeft

```
| box |
propertiesTool selection size = 1 ifFalse: [^nil].
box := propertiesTool selection first bounds.
self leftFraction value: '0'.
self leftOffset value: box origin x printString.
self readMode value: false
```

fixLeftToRight

```
| box outsideBox |
propertiesTool selection size = 1 ifFalse: [^nil].
box := propertiesTool selection first bounds.
outsideBox := propertiesTool controller view bounds.
self leftFraction value: '1'.
self leftOffset value: (box origin x - outsideBox width) printString.
self readMode value: false
```

fixRightToLeft

```
| box |
propertiesTool selection size = 1 ifFalse: [^nil].
box := propertiesTool selection first bounds.
self rightFraction value: '0'.
self rightOffset value: box corner x printString.
self readMode value: false
```

fixRightToRight

```
| box outsideBox |
propertiesTool selection size = 1 ifFalse: [^nil].
box := propertiesTool selection first bounds.
outsideBox := propertiesTool controller view bounds.
```

```
self rightFraction value: '1'.
self rightOffset value: (box corner x - outsideBox width) printString.
self readMode value: false
```

fixTopToBottom

```
| box outsideBox |
propertiesTool selection size = 1 ifFalse: [^nil].
box := propertiesTool selection first bounds.
outsideBox := propertiesTool controller view bounds.
self topFraction value: '1'.
self topOffset value: (box origin y - outsideBox height) printString.
self readMode value: false
```

fixTopToTop

```
| box |
propertiesTool selection size = 1 ifFalse: [^nil].
box := propertiesTool selection first bounds.
self topFraction value: '0'.
self topOffset value: box origin y printString.
self readMode value: false
```

relativeHorizontal

```
| box outsideBox fraction |
propertiesTool selection size = 1 ifFalse: [^nil].
box := propertiesTool selection first bounds.
outsideBox := propertiesTool controller view bounds.
fraction := (box center x / outsideBox center x) asFloat printString.
self rightFraction value: fraction.
self leftFraction value: fraction.
self rightOffset width: (box // 2) printString.
self leftOffset width: (box // 2) negated printString.
self readMode value: false
```

relativeVertical

```
| box outsideBox fraction |
propertiesTool selection size = 1 ifFalse: [^nil].
box := propertiesTool selection first bounds.
outsideBox := propertiesTool controller view bounds.
fraction := (box center y / outsideBox center y) asFloat printString.
self topFraction value: fraction.
self bottomFraction value: fraction.
self topOffset height: (box height // 2) negated printString.
self bottomOffset height: (box height // 2) printString.
self readMode value: false
```

13.3.3.2 Private Methods

The buttons should only be available when there is a single component selected, otherwise they should be disabled. In addition, an unbounded component should only have certain of these buttons enabled, leaving those that do not apply to a LayoutOrigin or an AlignmentOrigin as disabled. Fortunately, PositionToolModel already has private methods explicitly for enabling and disabling those components that apply to bounded components and those that apply to unbounded components. We can use this knowledge to obtain the intended behavior and still minimize the intrusion upon the existing methods. First we need to add two private methods. The first returns a collection of all position button IDs. The second returns only those IDs that apply to unbounded components. In the 'private' protocol, add the following two instance methods.

> **positionButtons**
> "Return the list of ID's for all the position buttons."
>
> ^#(fixLeftToLeft fixLeftToRight fixRightToRight fixRightToLeft fixTopToTop fixTopToBottom fixBottomToBottom fixBottomToTop relativeHorizontal relativeVertical)

> **positionButtonsUnbounded**
> "Return the list of ID's for the position buttons which pertain only to the unbounded components."
>
> ^#(fixLeftToLeft fixLeftToRight fixTopToTop fixTopToBottom)

Now edit the following existing instance methods in the 'private' protocol so that they read as shown below.

> **hideBoundedItems**
> self vanishGroup: #(#GroupBounded) , self positionButtons

> **hideUnboundedItems**
> self vanishGroup: #(#GroupUnbounded) , self positionButtonsUnbounded

> **showBoundedItems**
> self reappearGroup: #(#GroupBounded) , self positionButtons

> **showMutualItems**
> self reappearGroup: #(#GroupMutual) , self positionButtons

> **showUnboundedItems**
> self reappearGroup: #(#GroupUnbounded) , self positionButtonsUnbounded

This completes the position buttons addition to the Position Tool. All of the code added in this section is also available in the file **c13_4.st**.

Test this new functionality with a canvas and a Properties Tool. Experiment with the various buttons to see what effect they have on the component's layout. In each case, you must resize the canvas to witness the effect.

13.4 Window Layout Dialog

Currently the window can only be sized and positioned with the mouse. While in general the mouse is easier and more intuitive than a keyboard for such an operation, in this particular case, it lacks the capability to operate at the pixel level of granularity. That is, sizing a window to exact dimensions with a mouse can be quite difficult and require several attempts. Even if the mouse could operate effectively at the pixel level, *VisualWorks* provides no indication of the window's dimensions (some specific platforms do, however). Therefore, the developer would have no idea of when he or she has achieved the desired dimensions. There is one alternative to this, of course—editing the literal array spec. There is certainly nothing wrong with editing the literal array spec from time to time. Frequent visits to the literal array spec, however, more than likely indicate that there is some missing functionality in the *VisualWorks* suite of tools. The whole point of *VisualWorks* is to be able to draw interfaces and not to have to code them! Unfortunately, the only means currently available for accurately setting a window's size and location is in the literal array spec. Therefore, there is a gap to fill in the functional features provided by the *VisualWorks* interface editing tools. In this section, we will fill this gap.

13.4.1 General Description

For the sake of consistency, the desired layout features for the window should be located on the Position Tool (and its dialog compliment). In general, when there is no currently selected component(s), the window is considered to be selected. In such a case, we would expect the Position Tool to operate on the window. This is precisely how other tools, such as the Color Tool and other slices within the Properties Tool, operate. But there are several reasons for not incorporating window-positioning features in the Position Tool. First, the Position Tool deals exclusively with LayoutFrame, LayoutOrigin, and AlignmentOrigin objects, none of which applies to a window. Contrast this with the Color Tool, which is always editing a LookPreferences object, regardless of whether the selection is one component, several components, or the window. The second (and most practical) reason for not including these features on the Position Tool is the amount of work required to do so. The Position Tool is already the most complicated tool except for the canvas itself (UIPainter, UIPainterView, and UIPainterController). Therefore, we will implement the window layout features as a dialog accessed from the canvas <operate> menu. We will call this dialog the Window Layout Dialog.

To start the Window Layout Dialog, define the following class in the 'UIPainter-Support' class category.

```
ExtendedApplicationModel subclass: #UIWindowLayout
    instanceVariableNames: 'painterController '
    classVariableNames: ''
    poolDictionaries: ''
    category: 'UIPainter-Support'
```

The painterController instance variable will reference the UIPainterController, which opens the Window Layout Dialog. This UIPainterController will provide the access to the canvas window itself, which is what we want to edit. It will also allow us to clear any current restriction on the window's bounds simply by sending it the message setWindowToDefaults.

13.4.2 Building the Interface

The interface for UIWindowLayout is shown in Figure 13.3. The dialog will open with the four input fields displaying the window's current origin and extent. The user can

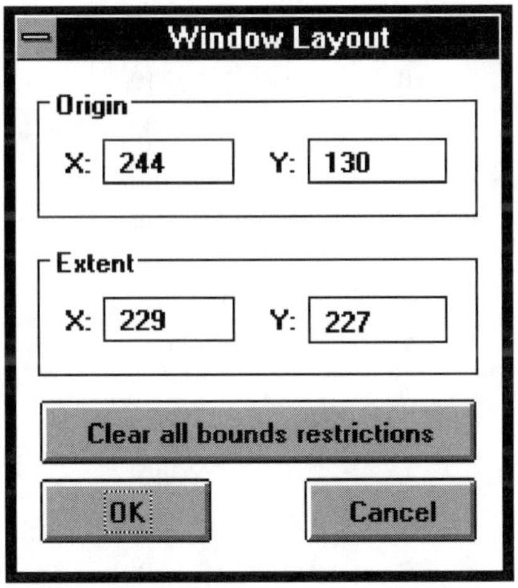

Figure 13.3. Window Layout Dialog Interface.

then edit these parameters. The origin values should be bounded by the current screen's coordinate system, and the extent values should be bounded by any maximum and minimum extent already set by the developer. The **Clear all bounds restrictions** button will clear any of these restrictions and is equivalent to selecting **layout→window→clear all** in the canvas <operate> menu. If the user selects **OK**, then the canvas window is adjusted to the new values in the fields. The **Cancel** button closes the dialog without any changes.

13.4.2.1 Creating the Canvas Window

Open a new canvas, label the window 'Window Layout', and immediately install the canvas as UIWindowLayout class>>windowSpec. The window's extent should be about 220 by 225. If our tool was completed already, we could use it for setting these dimensions exactly. The last thing we will do in this section is set the exact size of the Window Layout Dialog using the Window Layout Dialog. Purposefully make sure that for now the extent is larger than 220 by 225. You can do this by editing the literal array spec in the windowSpec method.

13.4.2.2 Adding the Buttons

Add the **Clear all bounds restrictions** button and give the following properties and layout.

Label	Clear all bounds restrictions
Action	#clearBoundsRestrictions

	Proportion	Offset
L	0	10
T	0	150
R	0	210
B	0	180

Now add the **OK** button with the following properties and layout.

Label	OK
Action	#accept

	Proportion	Offset
L	0	10
T	0	185
R	0	90
B	0	215

Finally, add the **Cancel** button with the following properties and layout.

Label	Cancel
Action	#cancel

	Proportion	Offset
L	0	130
T	0	185
R	0	210
B	0	215

13.4.2.3 Adding the Origin Fields

Add the origin x field with the properties and layout shown below.

Aspect	#originX
Type	Number

	Proportion	Offset
L	0	40
T	0	35
R	0	100
B	0	60

Now add the origin y field with the following properties and layout.

Aspect	#originY
Type	Number

	Proportion	Offset
L	0	135
T	0	35
R	0	195
B	0	60

Now add the labels **X:** and **Y:** to each of these fields, respectively. Use your own judgment to position them appropriately. Finally, add the group box with the label **Origin** and the following layout.

	Proportion	Offset
L	0	10
T	0	10
R	0	210
B	0	70

13.4.2.4 Adding the Extent Fields

Add the extent x field with the following properties and layout.

Aspect	#extentX
Type	Number

	Proportion	Offset
L	0	40
T	0	105
R	0	100
B	0	130

Now add the extent y field with the following properties and layout.

Aspect	#extentY
Type	Number

	Proportion	Offset
L	0	135
T	0	105
R	0	195
B	0	130

Now add the labels **X:** and **Y:** to each of these fields, respectively. Use your own judg-ment to position them appropriately. Finally, add the group box with the label **Extent** and the following layout.

	Proportion	Offset
L	0	10
T	0	80
R	0	210
B	0	140

Install and close the canvas.

13.4.3 Adding the Methods

Now we will add the methods. There are accessing methods for accessing the UIPainter-Controller as well as for accessing the canvas window. There are four aspect methods, one for each of the four fields. Each aspect method has a corresponding change method, which checks to see that the value entered by the developer is within current bounds restrictions and within the current screen coordinates. There are two private methods for calculating a new origin and extent for the window. There is an action method for accepting the changes and calculating the new window bounds. There is also an action method for clearing any current bounds restrictions previously set by the developer in the canvas <operate> menu.

13.4.3.1 Accessing Methods

Make sure your System Browser is on the instance side. Now add the instance protocol 'accessing' to the UIWindowLayout class. Add to this protocol the following instance methods for accessing the UIPainterController and the canvas window.

painterController

> ^painterController

painterController: aUIPainterController

> painterController := aUIPainterController.

window
"Provide an easy access to the canvas window."

[^self painterController model builder window]

13.4.3.2 Aspect Methods

Since UIWindowLayout is a subclass of ExtendedApplicationModel, we can implement the aspect methods using the aspect support protocol provided by ExtendedApplicationModel. Add the instance protocol 'aspects,' and add to it the following aspect methods.

extentX

> ^self
> valueHolderFor: #extentX
> initialValue: self window extent x
> changeMessage: #extentXChanged

extentY

```
^self
    valueHolderFor: #extentY
    initialValue: self window extent y
    changeMessage: #extentYChanged
```

originX

```
^self
    valueHolderFor: #originX
    initialValue: self window globalOrigin x
    changeMessage: #originXChanged
```

originY

```
^self
    valueHolderFor: #originY
    initialValue: self window globalOrigin y
    changeMessage: #originYChanged
```

13.4.3.3 Change Methods

It is important that the developer not be able to set the window's origin outside of the bounds of the screen. It is also important that he or she cannot set the window's extent outside any maximum and minimum currently in effect. For this reason, we need a change message for each of the input field aspects that guarantees a valid value. Add the instance protocol 'change methods,' and add to it the following instance methods.

```
extentXChanged
    "Make sure the window's width is within restrictions
    set by developer."

    | x min max |
    x := self extentX value.
    max := self painterController model maxWindowExtent.
    (max notNil and: [x > max x]) ifTrue: [^self extentX value: max x].
    min := self painterController model minWindowExtent.
    (min notNil and: [x < min x]) ifTrue: [self extentX value: min x].
```

```
extentYChanged
    "Make sure the window's height is within restrictions
    set by developer."

    | y min max |
    y := self extentY value.
    max := self painterController model maxWindowExtent.
```

```
(max notNil and: [y > max y]) ifTrue: [^self extentY value: max y].
min := self painterController model minWindowExtent.
(min notNil and: [y < min y]) ifTrue: [self extentY value: min y].
```

originXChanged
"Make sure originX is within the screen's bounds."

```
| x max |
x := self originX value.
max := Screen default bounds extent x -50.
x > max ifTrue: [self originX value: max]
```

originYChanged
"Make sure originY is within the screen's bounds."

```
| y max |
y := self originY value.
max := Screen default bounds extent y -50.
y > max ifTrue: [self originY value: max]
```

13.4.3.4 Action and Private Methods

One of the action methods depends on two private methods, so we should add them first. Add the instance protocol 'private,' and add to it the following instance methods.

windowExtent
"Return the window's extent as described in the extent fields."

```
^self extentX value @ self extentY value
```

windowOrigin
"Return the window's origin as described in the origin fields."

```
^self originX value @ self originY value
```

Since UIWindowLayout is a subclass of ExtendedApplicationModel, we can implement an accept method. Add the instance protocol 'actions,' and add to it the following instance methods.

accept
"Set the bounds of the canvas window according to the values in the fields."

```
self window moveTo: self windowOrigin resize: self windowExtent
```

clearBoundsRestrictions
"Clear all current restrictions on the window's bounds"

```
self painterController setWindowToDefaults
```

13.4.3.5 Interface Opening Method

We would like to be able to open the Window Layout Dialog simply by sending a message to the UIWindowLayout class with a UIPainterController as an argument. Toggle your System Browser over to the class side. Now add the class protocol 'interface opening,' and add to it the following class method.

> **openOn: aUIPainterController**
> "Open a window layout dialog for the window being edited by aUIPainterController."
>
> self new painterController: aUIPainterController; openAsDialog

13.4.4 Adding It to *VisualWorks*

Now we need to provide a means for invoking a Window Layout Dialog from the canvas <operate> menu. Recall from Chapter 7 that there are actually three versions of the canvas <operate> menu, but the one menu on which they are all based is defined in UIPainterController class>>canvasMenu. Open a Menu Editor on this menu (you can do so by evaluating the method comment). Find the part that reads

```
window          nil
----
    fixed size    setAllWindowInfo
    ----
    min size      setWindowMinSize
    pref size     setWindowPrefSize
    max size      setWindowMaxSize
    ----
    clear all     setWindowToDefaults
```

and edit it to read

```
window          nil
----
    fixed size    setAllWindowInfo
    ----
    min size      setWindowMinSize
    pref size     setWindowPrefSize
    max size      setWindowMaxSize
    ----
    clear all     setWindowToDefaults
    ----
    settings...   setWindowLayout
```

then build and install the menu. To make these changes take effect, evaluate the following code.

UIPainterController initialize

Now whenever the developer selects **layout→window→settings...** in the canvas <oper-ate> menu, the message setWindowLayout is dispatched to the UIPainterController. There-fore, we need to add this action message to UIPainterController. Select UIPainterController in your System Browser and add the following instance method to the instance protocol 'commands.'

> **setWindowLayout**
> "Open the UIWindowLayout dialog on the receiver."
>
> UIWindowLayout openOn: self

Below we will test the Window Layout Dialog by the editing the Window Layout Dia-log interface itself.

13.4.5 Meta Tool Example

In building the interface in Section 13.4.2.1, we wanted to have the extent of our Win-dow Layout Dialog to be exactly 220 by 225 but we lacked the tool (because we were just starting to build it). Well, now we have a tool to do just that—the Window Layout Dialog itself. This is a very good example of the meta tool concept discussed in the in-troduction to Chapter 7.

Open a canvas on the UIWindowLayout interface. Using the canvas <operate> menu, select **layout→window→settings...**, which brings up the Window Layout Dialog. You should now have two window layout dialogs: one in edit mode and one in runtime mode. The runtime mode interface is operating on the edit mode interface. In the runtime interface (i.e., the dialog), set the extent to **220@225** and accept. Install the can-vas. We are now done with the Window Layout Dialog. If for any reason your Window Layout Dialog does not work, you can file in the file **c13_5.st**, which contains all the source code for UIWindowLayout. This file-in redefines the canvas <operate> menu, so any previous changes to this menu will be lost. You still need to reinitialize the UIPainter-Controller class to have the file-in take effect.

13.5 Summary

In this chapter, we enhanced the canvas-editing environment of *VisualWorks* in four ways. We added a paste-to-cursor function, which gives the developer the option of dropping components in the paste buffer using the cursor. Next we added a color menu to the <operate> menu, which allows a developer to easily change a component's color attributes. Then we added some buttons to the Position Tool to facilitate component layout. Finally, we added a dialog for editing a canvas window's bounds. The premise of this chapter is that *VisualWorks* is an open environment and that the developer can augment that environment to suit his or her own needs.

CHAPTER 14

Enhanced Image Editor

In the last chapter, we extended *VisualWorks* functionality by directly editing some of the *VisualWorks* system classes and adding a new class (UIWindowLayout). In this chapter we will subclass a current tool to create a new tool with enhanced functionality. The advantage to creating a subclass instead of directly editing UIMaskEditor is that system classes remain unaffected by our additions.

VisualWorks comes with an image-editing tool, the Image Editor, implemented by the class UIMaskEditor. This is a very convenient tool for editing images of a single black color or up to 16 colors. It is well integrated into the *VisualWorks* application development system since it will create and edit images for both an open canvas or any arbitrary class. Like everything else in *VisualWorks*, however, the Image Editor can be enhanced significantly with several new features and capabilities, which are listed below.

‣ Centering the displayed image

‣ Saving the image as an OpaqueImage

‣ Setting the extent of the image

‣ Alternate color selection for the <operate> button

‣ Additional editing operations

‣ Image Repository for storing images

‣ Editable palette and palette repository

In this chapter, we will subclass UIMaskEditor in order to add these features and capabilities. We will call this new tool the Enhanced Image Editor. After you have completed this chapter, or even if you stop at some point prior to finishing, you can still use UIMaskEditor as it was intended to be used.

481

Chapter 8, Section 8.2.5, covered the operation of the UIMaskEditor. It might be a good idea to review this portion of Chapter 8 before proceeding, but it is not necessary.

This chapter provides step-by-step instruction on how to add the various pieces of the Enhanced Image Editor and its related tools to your virtual image. There is a great deal of code involved—a total of 10 classes and well over 100 methods. Beware that the order in which these classes and methods are added to the system is not the same as the order in which they were originally designed and implemented. The development of such a tool is an evolutionary process involving several iterations of changes and edits. It would be nice if this chapter included the design process and all the relevant decisions and changes made along the way, however, this would be very difficult indeed to present as well as to follow. Instead, this chapter uses a bottom–up approach to constructing the completed tool. This allows the final version of each piece to be added in its entirety and tested before moving on to the next piece. What is lacking in this approach is any insights into how such a tool is designed and implemented from scratch. Also, very little explanation of the implementation is provided. Instead, it is your responsibility to read the comments and browse the code in order to figure out for yourself how things work. Finally, this tutorial is quite long and involved, and all of the code is provided as a set of file-ins should you elect not to type in the code yourself.

14.1 Basic Description

The Enhanced Image Editor tool actually consists of four different tools: the Enhanced Image Editor, the Palette Editor, the Palette Repository, and the Image Repository. The Enhanced Image Editor is the main tool that draws and saves the image. The Palette Editor is a dialog box that edits the palette defining the colors used in the image. The Palette Repository provides a maintainable list of palettes, which can be loaded into the Enhanced Image Editor as the current palette. The Image Repository provides a persistent and maintainable list of images, which can be referenced by any object in the virtual image or copied and edited by the Enhanced Image Editor to create a new image.

14.1.1 Enhanced Image Editor

The Enhanced Image Editor allows the developer to create 16 color images and apply them to an application model or save them in the Image Repository. Like the current Image Editor, it has a grid on which the developer draws a magnified image, a display

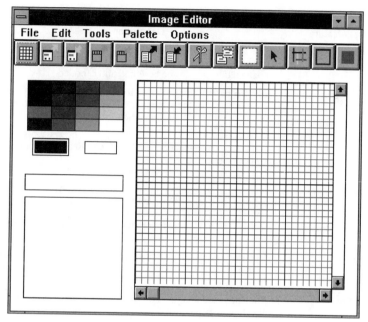

Figure 14.1. Enhanced Image Editor Interface.

that renders the image in its actual size, and a palette of 16 colors. Unlike the current Image Editor, however, its palette is editable and several other features have been added or augmented. The Enhanced Image Editor is shown Figure 14.1

The Enhanced Image Editor has several features, which are listed in Table 14.1.

14.1.2 Palette Applications

There are four places a color palette appears in the Enhanced Image Editor and its support tools: the Enhanced Image Editor, the Palette Editor, the Palette Repository, and the Color Selector Dialog used in creating an OpaqueImage.

14.1.2.1 Palette on Enhanced Image Editor

The palette on the Enhanced Image Editor represents the palette of the image currently being edited. Below the palette are two boxes. The left box indicates the color of the <select> mouse button, and the right box indicates the color of the <operate> mouse button. The color of each of these boxes can be changed by selecting it with the mouse and then selecting a color from the palette.

Table 14.1. Enhanced Image Editor Features.

Main feature	Description
Editing	Like the current Image Editor, the Enhanced Image Editor allows the developer to cut, copy, and paste portions of the image. Edits can also be accepted and canceled.
Drawing Tools	Like the current Image Editor, the Enhanced Image Editor can copy portions of the screen for editing as an image and draw rectangles. In addition, the Enhanced Image Editor can draw lines and rectangular borders.
Palette	A palette can be loaded from the Palette Repository or edited by the Palette Editor. The palette describes a current color for both the <select> and <operate> mouse buttons.
Acquiring Images	Images can be acquired in five ways: a new image can be created, an image can be loaded from an application model, an image can be read from a canvas, an image can be grabbed from the screen, or an image can be copied from the Image Repository.
Saving Format	Like the current Image Editor, the Enhanced Image Editor can save an image as a CachedImage. In addition, the Enhanced Image Editor can save it as an OpaqueImage.
Speed Buttons	The Enhanced Image Editor offers several features at the touch of a speed button.
Saving Images	Images can be saved in three ways: an Image can be applied to a canvas, installed in an application model, or saved to the Image Repository.

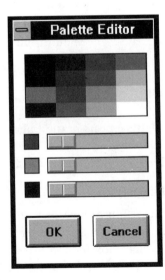

Figure 14.2. Palette Editor Interface.

14.1.2.2 Palette Editor

The Palette Editor is a dialog that edits a MappedPalette object (see Figure 14.2). It displays a palette and three sliders for editing the selected color within the palette. It has an **OK** and a **Cancel** button for accepting or canceling the changes. It is used both by the Enhanced Image Editor for editing the current palette and by the Palette Repository for editing and adding new palettes.

14.1.2.3 Palette Repository

The Palette Repository maintains a persistent set of MappedPalette objects and displays them in a window for selecting, adding, editing, or removing (see Figure 14.3). It can be opened either as a dialog or as a nonmodal window.

14.1.2.4 Color Selector Dialog

The Color Selector Dialog is a dialog used to select the color that is to become transparent when creating an OpaqueImage (see Figure 14.4). The dialog displays the current image object's palette. The developer selects a color to become transparent and selects the **OK** button.

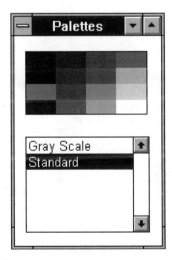

Figure 14.3. Palette Repository Interface.

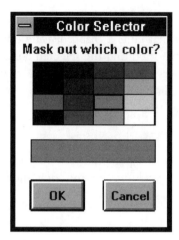

Figure 14.4. Color Selector Dialog Interface.

14.1.3 Image Repository

The Image Repository provides a means of storing images for common access. These images can be accessed directly by applications or copied by the Enhanced Image Editor to be used for creating new images. Each image in the repository has a unique name. The Image Repository displays the list of image names in a window (see Figure 14.5).

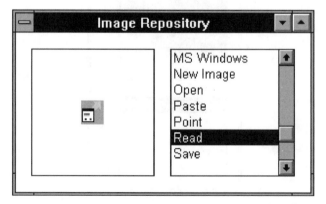

Figure 14.5. Image Repository Interface.

14.1.4 Summary

This concludes the description of the Enhanced Image Editor and its support tools. You will now begin the process of adding this tool to your virtual image. This process is divided into four parts: palette applications, support classes, Image Repository, and the Enhanced Image Editor.

14.2 Palette Applications

The current Image Editor has a 16 color palette for creating images. This size of palette gives the developer a good variety of colors but is still small enough to manage. The palette for the current Image Editor is editable by opening a canvas on its interface spec and then editing the background look preferences of the color buttons used to represent the palette. While this is a terribly clever example of reuse, the tool should have a smoother, more professional approach to palette management. In this section, we create some fundamental palette tools that will be used by the Enhanced Image Editor.

In the Enhanced Image Editor and its ancillary tools, a palette appears in four places: in the Enhanced Image Editor as a subcanvas, in the Palette Editor, in the Palette Repository, and in the Color Selector Dialog used to select a transparent color for creating an OpaqueImage. We will refer to each of these as a *palette application*. The source code for this section is available in its entirety in file **c14_1.st** should you choose not to enter the code yourself as presented here.

14.2.1 UIPaletteApplication

The UIPaletteApplication class is the abstract superclass for all of the palette applications. It defines the basic palette appearance and behavior. All palettes are instances of Mapped-Palette and have 16 entries. A palette is displayed as a 4-by-4 grid, with each cell being 32 by 16 pixels. Each of the cells represents one of the colors in the palette, and the developer should be able to select any one of the 16 colors or cells. The implementation we will use for this grid is a table component. Remember that the table component is really nothing more than a two-dimensional pick list. Furthermore, we know we can draw inside the cells by using the table's visual blocks. This allows us to fill the cell with a color instead of text.

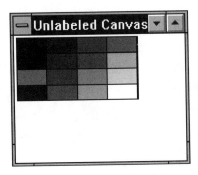

Figure 14.6. UIPaletteApplication Interface.

In this section, you will build the UIPaletteApplication class. When you are done, you will have an interface that looks like Figure 14.6.

Start the UIPaletteApplication class by first opening a System Browser, then adding the class category 'SDGVW-Palette Applications,' and then defining the class shown below.

```
ExtendedApplicationModel subclass: #UIPaletteApplication
    instanceVariableNames: 'palette paletteInterface paletteTable '
    classVariableNames: ''
    poolDictionaries: ''
    category: 'SDGVW-Palette Applications'
```

Now add the associated class comment as shown below.

UIPaletteApplication is an abstract superclass for several other palette applications. It provides the common feature of a table whose structure is a 4 X 4 grid representing a color palette.

Instance Variables

paletteTable	<SelectionInTable>	Used to map a cell index into the palette
paletteInterface	<TableInterface>	the table interface
palette	<MappedPalette>	a 16 color palette represented by the table

14.2.1.1 Drawing the Interface

Open a blank canvas and place a single table component in it. The size and label of the window are not important, since this class is abstract and its interface will never actually be used other than for testing purposes. Give the table component the following properties and layout.

	Proportion	Offset

Aspect	#paletteInterface
ID	#paletteInterface
Scrollbars	None
Grid Lines	Horizontal and Vertical
Can Tab	No

	Proportion	Offset
L	0	0
T	0	0
R	0	128
B	0	66

Install the canvas as UIPaletteApplication class>>windowSpec. Close this canvas and the Properties Tool.

14.2.1.2 Initialize and Accessing Methods

With your System Browser set on the instance side, add the instance protocol 'aspects' to UIPaletteApplication and add the following two instance methods to that protocol.

paletteTable

```
^paletteTable
```

paletteInterface

```
^paletteInterface
```

Add the instance protocol 'initialize-release,' and add to it the following instance methods.

setupChangeMessages

```
"A hook for subclasses to register interest in a change in the table selection."
```

initialize
```
"Initialize the palette table to be 4X4."

| list |
super initialize.
list := TwoDList columns: 4 rows: 4.
paletteTable := SelectionInTable with: list.
paletteInterface := TableInterface new selectionInTable: paletteTable.
self setupChangeMessages
```

Next, file in the file **c14_2.st**, which adds the class method defaultPalette to UIPalette-Application. This class method returns a default instance of MappedPalette, which we will use for testing purposes.

Add the instance protocol 'accessing,' and add the following four instance methods to that protocol.

currentColorIndex
> "Return 0 for the first color and 15 for the last color. This is how the colors are indexed in the palette."

> | aPoint |
> aPoint := self paletteTable selectionIndex.
> aPoint = Point zero ifTrue: [aPoint := 1@1].
> ^aPoint x - 1 + (aPoint y - 1 * 4).

currentSelectionIndex
> "Return 1 for the first color and 16 for the last color. This is how the selections are indexed in the table."

> | aPoint |
> aPoint := self paletteTable selectionIndex.
> aPoint = Point zero ifTrue: [aPoint := 1@1].
> ^aPoint x + (aPoint y - 1 * 4).

palette
> "Initialize the palette to the class's default palette."

> ^palette isNil
>   ifTrue: [palette := self class defaultPalette]
>   ifFalse: [palette]

palette: aPalette

> palette := aPalette

14.2.1.3 Private and Interface Opening Methods

The interface opening procedure relies on two private methods: paletteTableVisualBlock and postBuildPaletteTableWith:. Add the instance protocol 'private,' and add to it the paletteTableVisualBlock method as shown below.

paletteTableVisualBlock
> "Return a block which will serve as the visual block for the palette table. The block should fill the cell with a color in the palette."

> ^[:v :index | | color |

```
color := self palette at: index x -1 + (index y - 1 * 4).
BoundedWrapper on: (VisualBlock
                block:    [:aGC :bounds |
                          aGC paint: color.
                          aGC displayRectangle: bounds]
                extent:   20@20)]
```

This method defines a block that will fill each cell with the color of the palette that cell is to represent. This block will serve as the table component's visual block as shown below in the postBuildPaletteTableWith: method. Add this method to the 'private' protocol as well.

postBuildTableWith: aBuilder
  "Set up the table widget so that it displays the colors in the current palette"

  | tableView |
  tableView := self widget: #paletteInterface.
  tableView visualBlock: self paletteTableVisualBlock.
  tableView lineGrid: [16].

Finally, add the 'interface opening' protocol and add the following instance method to it.

postBuildWith: aBuilder
  "Prepare the palette table by setting its visual block."

  self postBuildTableWith: aBuilder

14.2.1.4 Testing

This application is now complete and can be tested for functionality. In a Workspace, create and open an instance of UIPaletteApplication by evaluating the code below. You may need to declare AM as a global variable if it is not one already.

  (AM := UIPaletteApplication new) open

The window should look something like Figure 14.6. Try selecting various colors in the table component. Now print the first two statements below and inspect the third to ascertain information about the palette.

  AM currentColorIndex

  AM currentSelectionIndex

  AM palette

Notice that the current color index is one less than the current selection index. This is because palettes start with index 0 and table components start with index 1.

14.2.2 UIColorPalette

In this section you will build the UIColorPalette class, which defines the subapplication to run as a subcanvas in the Enhanced Image Editor. When you are done, you will have an interface that looks like Figure 14.7.

As you can see from Figure 14.7, the UIColorPalette interface has a palette (table component) and two regions. Associated with each region is an invisible action button. A group box is used to indicate which of the regions is currently of interest to the palette. To get started, define the UIColorPalette class as shown below in the class category 'SDGVW-Palette Applications.'

```
UIPaletteApplication subclass: #UIColorPalette
    instanceVariableNames: 'paletteName button leftColorIndex rightColorIndex '
    classVariableNames: ''
    poolDictionaries: ''
    category: 'SDGVW-Palette Applications'
```

Add the class comment as shown below.

The interface for a UIColorPalette serves as a subcanvas for the EnhancedImageEditor. It consists of a palette table which it inherits from its superclass UIPaletteApplication. It also consists of two buttons which indicate a chosen color.

Instance Variables

paletteName	\<String\>	name, if any, of current palette
button	\<Symbol\>	name of current button - #left or #right
leftColorIndex	\<Integer\>	index of left color in palette
rightColorIndex	\<Integer\>	index of right color in palette

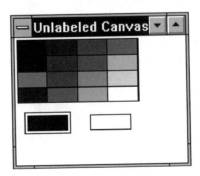

Figure 14.7. UIColorPalette Interface.

14.2.2.1 Drawing the Interface

This interface is a bit tricky. Open up a canvas on UIPalettteApplication class>>windowSpec, the interface you just completed in Section 14.2.1 (you may already have it open). Now install this canvas as UIColorPalette class>>windowSpec (make sure you change the class name in the Install Dialog to UIColorPalette).

Add two region components, rectangular in shape and with thin borders. The first region's ID is #left, and its layout is shown below.

	Proportion	Offset
L	0	12
T	0	78
R	0	54
B	0	94

The second region's ID is #right, and its layout is shown below.

	Proportion	Offset
L	0	77
T	0	78
R	0	119
B	0	94

Next, add two action button components, neither of which has a border or a label. Be careful here because action buttons without borders seem to disappear on the canvas! The first button has an action method named #left, and its layout is the same as the #left region component described above. The second action button has an action method named #right, and its layout is the same as the #right region component above. Neither button should have an ID.

Finally add a group box component whose ID is #frame and layout is described below.

	Proportion	Offset
L	0	9
T	0	75
R	0	57
B	0	97

The window label is unimportant since this interface will be used as a subcanvas. Also, the window dimensions should be large enough to show the palette and other components in their entirety. Install this canvas again as UIColorPalette class>>windowSpec. Close the canvas and Properties Tool.

14.2.2.2 Initialize and Accessing Methods

In your System Browser, add the instance protocol 'initialize-release' to UIColorPalette, and add the following instance method to this protocol.

> **setupChangeMessages**
> "The palette should send the message updateColors
> when its selection changes."
>
> paletteTable selectionIndexHolder onChangeSend: #updateColors to: self.
> paletteName := 'DefaultPalette'

Now add the instance protocol 'accessing,' and add the following instance methods to this protocol.

> **application**
> "Return the application which is the application model for the window."
>
> ^self builder window application

> **button**
> "Initialize with the left button."
>
> ^button isNil
>   ifTrue: [button := #left]
>   ifFalse: [button]

> **leftColorIndex**
> "Initialize the left button to the first color in the palette."
>
> ^leftColorIndex isNil
>   ifTrue: [leftColorIndex := 0]
>   ifFalse: [leftColorIndex]

> **paletteName**
>
> ^paletteName

> **paletteName: aString**
>
> paletteName := aString

rightColorIndex
"Initialize the right button to the last color in the palette."

^rightColorIndex isNil
    ifTrue: [rightColorIndex := 15]
    ifFalse: [rightColorIndex]

14.2.2.3 Building the Palette Repository

In order to go any further with UIColorPalette, we must start the PaletteRepository class because some of the methods in UIColorPalette reference the PaletteRepository class. At this point we will only define the class and add the class methods that allow it to behave as a repository for persistent palettes. The interface and instance methods will be added in Section 14.2.4.

Add the following class to the 'Palette Applications' method.

```
UIPaletteApplication subclass: #PaletteRepository
    instanceVariableNames: 'paletteNames '
    classVariableNames: 'DefaultPalette NilPalette Palettes '
    poolDictionaries: ''
    category: 'SDGVW-Palette Applications'
```

Next, file in the file **c14_3.st**, which adds the class method initializePalettes to the class PaletteRepository. This method initializes the Palettes class variable and populates it with two entries of MappedPalette.

Now toggle your System Browser to the class side and add the following class methods to the 'initialize class' protocol.

initializeNilPalette
"The NilPalette is not in the palettes repository because it is never meant to be used as a palette. It is for representing that no palette is selected in a pick list and it is used as a starting point in creating a new palette."

"PaletteRepository initializeNilPalette"

| color index |
index := PaletteRepository defaultPalette
        indexOfPaintNearest: (ColorValue brightness: 0.8).
color := PaletteRepository defaultPalette at: index.
NilPalette := MappedPalette withColors: [| c |
        c := OrderedCollection new.
        0 to: 15 do: [:i | c add: color].
        c] value.

initialize
"Initialize the palettes."

"self initialize"

```
self initializePalettes.
self initializeNilPalette.
```

The NilPalette is a MappedPalette whose colors are all of the same shade of gray. Its use will become apparent shortly. Now that we have the proper initialization, add the class protocol 'accessing palettes,' and add the following class methods to that protocol.

palettes
```
"Return the palettes dictionary."

Palettes isNil ifTrue: [self initializePalettes].
^Palettes
```

standardPalette
```
"The 'Standard' palette contains 16 colors spanning the entire color
spectrum and it is expected that any color platform of depth 4 or more
should be able to match it"

^self palettes at: 'Standard'
```

grayScalePalette
```
"The 'Gray Scale' palette contains 16 various shades of gray
from black to white"

^self palettes at: 'Gray Scale'
```

nilPalette
```
"Return the nil palette whose colors are all light gray"

NilPalette isNil ifTrue: [self initializeNilPalette].
^NilPalette
```

paletteNames
```
"Return a list of all the palette names."

^self palettes keys
```

paletteNamed: aString
```
"Return the palette whose name is aString. Return the
default palette if no palette has this name."

^self palettes at: aString ifAbsent: [self defaultPalette]
```

nameOfPalette: aPalette
```
"Return name of aPalette or nil if aPalette not found"
```

> ^self palettes keyAtValue: aPalette ifAbsent: [nil]

We now have a fully functioning persistent store for our palettes, which is preloaded with two palettes: the standard palette and the gray scale palette. Any object can access the palettes in the Palette Repository by sending the appropriate message to the class PaletteRepository. Now we can proceed with UIColorPalette. Select the UIColorPalette class again in your System Browser and toggle back over to the instance side.

14.2.2.4 Action, Change, and Interface Opening Methods

There is an action method for each of the two invisible buttons on the interface. Add the instance protocol 'actions,' and add the following two instance methods to this protocol.

```
left
    "Set the current button to be the left button and move the
    group box over to visually indicate this."

    button := #left.
    (self component: #frame) moveTo: 9@75.
```

```
right
    "Set the current button to be the right button and move the
    group box over to visually indicate this."

    button := #right.
    (self component: #frame) moveTo: 74@75.
```

Add the instance protocol 'change methods,' and add the next three instance methods to this protocol.

```
changeToPaletteNamed: aString
    "If aString equals the current paletteName, then do nothing. Otherwise,
    change to a palette which is stored in the PaletteRepository repository
    which goes by the name aString"

    palette := PaletteRepository paletteNamed: aString.
    self paletteName: aString.
    self invalidate: #paletteInterface
```

```
updateColors
    "The user has selected a new color in the palette table. Make the
    current button this color and update its index."

    self change: #backgroundColor of: self button to: (self palette at: self currentColorIndex).
    self button = #left
        ifTrue: [leftColorIndex := self currentColorIndex.]
        ifFalse: [rightColorIndex := self currentColorIndex]
```

changeToPalette: aPalette
> "If aPalette equals the current palette, then do nothing. If aPalette equals a palette stored in the PaletteRepository repository, then switch to that palette, otherwise, use aPalette and set paletteName to an empty string"

> | aName |
> aPalette = self palette ifTrue: [^nil].
> (aName := PaletteRepository nameOfPalette: aPalette) isNil
>   ifTrue: [
>   self palette: aPalette.
>   self paletteName: ''.
>   (self builder componentAt: #paletteInterface) invalidate]
>   ifFalse: [self changeToPaletteNamed: aName]

Finally, add the instance protocol 'interface opening,' and add the following instance method to this protocol.

postBuildWith: aBuilder
> "Initialize all components."

> self postBuildTableWith: aBuilder.
> self change: #backgroundColor of: #left to: (self palette at: self leftColorIndex).
> self change: #backgroundColor of: #right to: (self palette at: self rightColorIndex).
> self paletteTable selectionIndexHolder value: 0

14.2.2.5 Testing

The UIColorPalette is now complete and ready for testing. Remember, this application is meant to be used as a subcanvas, but since all canvases can be either subcanvases or windows, we will test it as a window. Open the UIColorPalette by evaluating the code below. You may need to declare AM as a global variable if it is not one already.

> (AM := UIColorPalette new) open

You should be able to select colors within the palette. As you do so, notice that the bottom left region updates to the color of the new selection. Also notice that the group box is currently around this region. Now click the right region. The group box should now be around this region. Select colors again in the palette and notice that the current selection now updates the right region. Print each of the following to see what is returned.

> AM leftColorIndex

> AM rightColorIndex

14.2.3 Palette Editor

A Palette Editor allows the developer to edit the colors within a palette. It consists of a palette and three sliders indicating RGB (red/green/blue) values (see Figure 14.2). The developer selects a color in the palette and changes its color by sliding the RGB sliders. The Palette Editor is implemented by the class UIPaletteEditor. The UIPaletteEditor is opened only in a modal fashion, that is, as a dialog. To get started with the UIPaletteEditor, define the following class in the class category 'SDGVW-Palette Applications.'

```
UIPaletteApplication subclass: #UIPaletteEditor
    instanceVariableNames: 'colors'
    classVariableNames: ''
    poolDictionaries: ''
    category: 'SDGVW-Palette Applications'
```

Add the following class comment.

A UIPaletteEditor is a dialog which allows the user to edit a 16 color palette. The user selects one of the cells in a table which is displaying the palette and adjusts the RGB sliders to alter the color in that cell. If the user selects OK, then a new palette is created and returned. Cancel returns nil.

Instance Variables

colors   <OrderedCollection>   of ColorValues

14.2.3.1 Drawing the Interface

Figure 14.2 shows the completed interface. Start a new canvas and set the window's dimensions to 160@236 and set its label to 'Palette Editor'. You can set the window dimensions by either editing the full spec literal array or by using the Window Layout Dialog developed in Chapter 13, Section 13.4. Now add a table component with the properties and layout shown below.

Aspect	#paletteInterface
ID	#paletteInterface
Scrollbars	None
Grid Lines	Horizontal and Vertical
Can Tab	No

	Proportion	Offset
L	0	16
T	0	24
R	0	144
B	0	90

Now add three region components, whose IDs are #red, #green, and #blue, and whose layouts are as follows.

	#red		#green		#blue	
	Prop	**Offset**	**Prop**	**Offset**	**Prop**	**Offset**
L	0	16	0	16	0	16
T	0	106	0	130	0	154
R	0	32	0	32	0	32
B	0	122	0	146	0	170

Next add three slider components, whose aspects are #red, #green, and #blue, and whose IDs are #redSlider, #greenSlider, and #blueSlider, respectively. Give these sliders the following layouts.

	#red		#green		#blue	
	Prop	**Offset**	**Prop**	**Offset**	**Prop**	**Offset**
L	0	40	0	40	0	40
T	0	106	0	130	0	154
R	0	144	0	144	0	144
B	0	122	0	146	0	170

Finally add two action button components. The first button's label is 'OK', its action method is named #accept, and its layout is as shown below.

	Proportion	Offset
L	0	16
T	0	188
R	0	74
B	0	220

The second button's label is 'Cancel', its action method is named #cancel, and its layout is as shown below.

	Proportion	Offset
L	0	86
T	0	188
R	0	144
B	0	220

Install this canvas as UIPaletteEditor class>>windowSpec. Close the canvas and Properties Tool.

14.2.3.2 Initialize and Accessing Methods

Make sure that your System Browser is on the instance side and that the class UIPalette-Editor is selected. Now add the instance protocol 'initialize-release,' and add the following instance method to that protocol.

> **setupChangeMessages**
>
> paletteTable selectionIndexHolder onChangeSend: #changeSliderValues to: self.

Now add the instance protocol 'accessing,' and add the following instance methods to that protocol.

> **colorsOfPalette: aPalette**
> "Create an OrderedCollection of ColorValues from the colors in aPalette"
>
> colors := OrderedCollection new.
> 0 to: 15 do: [:i | colors add: (aPalette at: i) copy]

> **colors**
> "Return an ordered collection of colors which will be used to
> create a MappedPallete."
>
> colors isNil ifTrue: [self colorsOfPalette: PaletteRepository defaultPalette].
> ^colors

palette
     "Return a palette based on the current colors."

     ^MappedPalette withColors: self colors

14.2.3.3 Aspect, Change, and Private Methods

Each of the slider components needs an aspect method. Add the instance protocol 'aspects,' and add the following three aspect methods to that protocol.

red

     ^self
         valueHolderFor: #red
         initialValue: 0
         changeMessage: #changeCurrentColor

green

     ^self
         valueHolderFor: #green
         initialValue: 0
         changeMessage: #changeCurrentColor

blue

     ^self
         valueHolderFor: #blue
         initialValue: 0
         changeMessage: #changeCurrentColor

Whenever any of these values changes, the message changeCurrentColor is dispatched, which calculates the new color based on the values of the three sliders. This new color is then used to replace the color currently selected in the palette. Also, whenever a new selection is made in the table, the message changeSliderValues is dispatched, which updates the sliders to reflect the RGB (red/green/blue) values of this new color selection. Add the instance protocol 'change methods,' and add the following two instance methods to that protocol.

changeCurrentColor
     "Make sure there is a current selection in the table. Then
     calculate the new color based on the RGB values and put it
     in the colors list. Finally, tell the palette to redraw itself."

     | color |
     self currentSelectionIndex = 0 ifTrue: [^nil].
     color := ColorValue

```
            red:      self red value
            green:    self green value
            blue:     self blue value.
    self colors at: self currentSelectionIndex put: color.
    (self widget: #paletteInterface)
        updateAt: self paletteTable selectionIndex
```

changeSliderValues
"A new color has been selected in the table so update
the slider widgets to the RGB values of this new color."

```
| color |
self currentSelectionIndex = 0
    ifTrue: [color := ColorValue black]
    ifFalse: [color := self colors at: self currentSelectionIndex].
#( #red #green #blue) do: [:val |
        (self perform: val)
            retractInterestsFor: self;
            value: (color perform: val);
            onChangeSend: #changeCurrentColor to: self]
```

Now add the instance protocol 'private,' and add the following two instance methods to that protocol.

postBuildSliderLabelsWith: aBuilder
"Set the colors of the regions used to label each of the sliders with the primary
color it controls"

```
#( red green blue) do: [:color |
    self change: #backgroundColor of: color to: color]
```

selectedColor
"Return the selected color based on the current selection index or if no
color is selected, then return the defualt background color."

```
^self currentSelectionIndex = 0
    ifTrue: [nil]
    ifFalse: [self colors at: self currentSelectionIndex]
```

14.2.3.4 Interface Opening Methods

There are two interface opening methods: one instance method and one class method. Add the instance protocol 'interface opening,' and add to it the following method.

postBuildWith: aBuilder
"Perform a postBuild on the table view and the slider labels"

```
super postBuildWith: aBuilder.
self postBuildSliderLabelsWith: aBuilder
```

The second interface opening method is a class method, so make sure you toggle your System Browser over to the class side. Now add the class protocol 'interface opening,' and add to it the following class method.

```
edit: aPalette
    "Open a Palette Editor dialog which edits aPalette and returns
    an edited palette or nil."

    "UIPaletteEditor edit: PaletteRepository defaultPalette"

    | inst |
    inst := self new colorsOfPalette: aPalette.
    ^inst openAsDialog
        ifTrue: [inst palette]
        ifFalse: [nil]
```

14.2.3.5 Testing

The Palette Editor is now complete and is ready for testing. In a Workspace, inspect the following line of code. This code acquires a palette from the Palette Repository, copies that palette, and then opens the Palette Editor on that copy for editing.

```
UIPaletteEditor edit: PaletteRepository defaultPalette copy
```

Notice that if you close the dialog with **OK**, then the edited palette is returned. If you **Cancel**, however, nil is returned.

14.2.4 PaletteRepository

The Palette Repository provides persistence for reusable palettes and also provides an interface so the developer can select a palette and maintain the list of available palettes. The Palette Repository is implemented by the class PaletteRepository. This class was begun in Section 14.2.2.3. In this section, we will complete the PaletteRepository class. Select this class in your System Browser and make sure you are on the instance side.

14.2.4.1 Class Comment

While this class was defined and started in Section 14.2.2.3, now would be a good time to add the following class comment.

> The PaletteRepository class is the keeper of all the palettes available to the image editor. The PaletteRepository also has a dialog interface for selecting a palette and a window interface for updating the palette list.
>
> Instance Variables

paletteNames <SortedCollection> of Strings which are the palette names

Class Variables

    NilPalette <MappedPalette> of all gray colors and represents 'no palette'

    Palettes <Dictionary> keys are Strings and values are MappedPalettes

    DefaultPalette <MappedPalette> the default palette

14.2.4.2 Drawing the Interface

Figure 14.3 shows the completed interface. Start a new canvas and make sure the window has the dimensions of 160@216 and a label of 'Palettes'. You can set the window dimensions by either editing the full spec literal array or using the Window Layout Dialog developed in Chapter 13, Section 13.4. Now add a table component and a list component. The properties and layout for the table component are shown below.

Aspect	#paletteInterface
ID	#paletteInterface
Scrollbars	None
Grid Lines	Horizontal and Vertical
Can Tab	No

	Proportion	**Offset**
L	0	16
T	0	16
R	0	144
B	0	82

The list component has the following properties and layout.

Aspect	#paletteNames
Menu	#menu

	Proportion	**Offset**
L	0	16
T	0	104
R	0	144
B	0	200

Install this canvas as PaletteRepository class>>windowSpec. Now, using the Menu Editor, build a menu with the following selections and values.

Selection	Value
add	#add
edit	#edit
remove	#remove

Build and install this menu as PaletteRepository class>>menu. Close the canvas, Menu Editor, and Properties Tool.

14.2.4.3 Accessing and Aspect Methods

Add the instance protocol 'accessing' and add to it the following instance method (make sure your System Browser is on the instance side now).

```
palette
    "Return the currently selected palette or the NilPalette."

    ^self paletteNames selection isNil
        ifTrue: [self class nilPalette]
        ifFalse: [self class paletteNamed: self paletteNames selection]
```

Now add the instance protocol 'aspects,' and add the following instance method to it.

```
paletteNames
    "When the palette selection changes, the palette view must be updated."

    ^paletteNames isNil
        ifTrue: [
            paletteNames := SelectionInList new.
            paletteNames list: self class paletteNames asSortedCollection.
            paletteNames selectionIndexHolder
                onChangeSend: #paletteChanged to: self.
            paletteNames]
        ifFalse: [paletteNames]
```

This method provides the aspect model for the list component. It contains the list of names of all the available palettes. Add the instance protocol 'change methods,' and add the following instance method to it.

```
paletteChanged

    self invalidate: #paletteInterface
```

14.2.4.4 Action Methods

The Palette Repository has the ability to add, edit, and remove palettes, and there is an action method associated with each of these operations. First add the instance protocol 'actions,' and then add the following action methods to it.

add
"Add a new palette to the Palette Repository."

```
| paletteName newPalette |
(paletteName := Dialog request: 'Name of new palette') = '' ifTrue: [^nil].
(self class paletteNames includes: paletteName) ifTrue: [
      (Dialog confirm: paletteName , ' is already in the repository!
Replace?') ifFalse: [^nil]].
   newPalette := self class nilPalette copy.
   (newPalette := UIPaletteEditor edit: newPalette) isNil ifTrue: [^nil].
   self class palettes at: paletteName put: newPalette.
   self paletteNames list: self class paletteNames asSortedCollection.
   self palette: newPalette.
   self paletteNames selection: paletteName
```

edit
"Edit the current palette in the repository."

```
| name reply |
(name := self paletteNames selection) isNil ifTrue: [^nil].
(#('Standard' 'Gray Scale') includes: name)
      ifTrue: [^Dialog warn: 'Should not edit the ' , name , ' palette '].
reply := UIPaletteEditor edit: (self class paletteNamed: name) copy.
reply isNil ifTrue: [^nil].
self class palettes at: name put: reply.
self paletteNames list: self class paletteNames asSortedCollection.
self palette: reply.
self paletteNames selection: name
```

remove
"Remove the current palette from the repository."

```
| name |
(name := self paletteNames selection) isNil ifTrue: [^nil].
(#('Standard' 'Gray Scale') includes: name)
      ifTrue: [^Dialog warn: 'Should not remove palette ' , name].
(Dialog confirm: 'Remove ' , name , ' Palette?') ifFalse: [^nil].
self class palettes removeKey: name.
self paletteNames list: self class paletteNames asSortedCollection.
```

14.2.4.5 Interface Opening Methods

Add the instance protocol 'interface opening,' and add the following method to it.

> **postBuildWith: aBuilder**
> "Disable the palette table."
>
> super postBuildWith: aBuilder.
> self disable: #paletteInterface

14.2.4.6 Making It Modal

The Palette Repository can be opened as a modal dialog. To add this functionality, first create a version of the windowSpec interface called dialogSpec. This interface looks the same as the one contained in windowSpec, but it has an **OK** and **Cancel** button at the bottom. The action method for the **OK** button is named #accept, and the action method for the **Cancel** button is named #cancel. Add these two buttons and install this canvas as Palette-Repository class>>dialogSpec. You can position the buttons and resize the window as is appropriate.

Now toggle your System Browser over to the class side, add the 'interface opening' protocol, and add the following class method to it.

> **openAsDialog**
> "Open the Palette Repository as a dialog and return a palette or nil."
>
> | inst |
> ^((inst := self new) openAsDialogInterface: #dialogSpec)
>   ifTrue: [inst paletteNames selection]
>   ifFalse: [nil]

14.2.4.7 Testing

The Palette Repository is now complete and ready for testing. In a Workspace, inspect on the following code, which opens the Palette Repository as a dialog.

> PaletteRepository openAsDialog

The result should be either a string or nil.

14.2.5 Color Selector Dialog

The Color Selector Dialog is used to allow the developer to pick a color in a palette. The selected color is then made the transparent color in creating an OpaqueImage. The Color Selector Dialog is implemented by the UIColorSelector class. In this section, we will build the UIColorSelector class. Start the UIColorSelector class by defining it as shown below in the class category 'SDGVW-Palette Applications.'

```
UIPaletteEditor subclass: #UIColorSelector
    instanceVariableNames: ''
    classVariableNames: ''
    poolDictionaries: ''
    category: 'SDGVW-Palette Applications'
```

Notice that UIColorSelector is a subclass of UIPaletteEditor. Now add the class comment as shown below.

A UIColorSelector is a dialog which displays a 16 color palette and allows the user to pick a color. If the user presses OK, then that color's index is returned. Otherwise, nil is returned.

14.2.5.1 Drawing the Interface

Figure 14.4 shows the completed interface. Start a new canvas and set the window's dimensions to 160@192, and set its label to 'Color Selector'. You can set the window dimensions by either editing the full spec literal array or by using the Window Layout Dialog developed in Chapter 13, Section 13.4. Now add a table component whose properties and layout are as follows.

Aspect	#paletteInterface
ID	#paletteInterface
Scrollbars	None
Grid Lines	Horizontal and Vertical
Can Tab	No

	Proportion	Offset
L	0	16
T	0	24
R	0	144
B	0	96

Above the table component, center a label that reads 'Mask out color?' Next, add a region component whose ID is #selectedColor and whose layout is as shown below.

	Proportion	Offset
L	0	16
T	0	104
R	0	144
B	0	128

Now add two action buttons. The first button's label is 'OK', its action method is named #accept, and its layout is as shown below.

	Proportion	Offset
L	0	16
T	0	149
R	0	74
B	0	179

The second button's label is 'Cancel', its action method is named #cancel, and its layout is as shown below.

	Proportion	Offset
L	0	86
T	0	149
R	0	144
B	0	179

Install this canvas as UIColorSelector class>>windowSpec. Close the canvas and Properties Tool.

14.2.5.2 Initialize and Change Methods

Make sure your System Browser is on the instance side, and add the instance protocol 'initialize-release' to the UIColorSelector class. Now add the following instance method to this protocol.

setupChangeMessages

```
self paletteTable selectionIndexHolder
    onChangeSend:   #colorSelectionChanged
    to:             self
```

Now add the instance protocol 'change methods,' and add the following instance method to it.

> **colorSelectionChanged**
> "Disable/enable the OK button based on if there is a color selected or not. Change the selected color indicator to the currently selected color in the palette table."
>
> ```
> self currentSelectionIndex = 0
>     ifTrue: [self disable: #ok]
>     ifFalse: [self enable: #ok].
> self change: #backgroundColor of: #selectedColor to: self selectedColor
> ```

14.2.5.3 Interface Opening Methods

The first interface opening method is an instance method. Add the instance protocol 'interface opening,' and add to it the following method.

> **postBuildWith: aBuilder**
> "Give the palette table its color visual block and make sure the OK button is disabled if nothing is selected."
>
> ```
> self postBuildTableWith: aBuilder.
> self colorSelectionChanged
> ```

The second interface opening method is a class method, so toggle your System Browser over to the class side. Add the class protocol 'interface opening,' and add to it the following class method.

> **selectColorIndexFrom: aPalette**
> "Open as a dialog and return the index of the selected color or nil."
>
> "self selectColorIndexFrom: PaletteRepository defaultPalette"
>
> ```
> | inst dlg |
> inst := self new initialize.
> inst colorsOfPalette: aPalette.
> dlg := SimpleDialog new.
> inst builder: dlg builder.
> dlg postBuildBlock: [:d :b | inst postBuildWith: b].
> ^(dlg openFor: inst interface: #windowSpec)
>     ifTrue: [inst currentSelectionIndex - 1]
>     ifFalse: [nil].
> ```

14.2.5.4 Testing

The UIColorSelector is now complete and can ready for testing. In a Workspace, inspect the following line of code.

UIColorSelector selectColorIndexFrom: PaletteRepository defaultPalette

The return value is either an integer in the case in which the **OK** button was pressed or nil in the case in which the **Cancel** button was pressed.

14.2.6 Summary

All of the palette applications are now complete. You should be familiar with the purpose of each one. Also, make sure each palette application is working properly because the remaining sections rely on these classes. If you have any doubts about your work in this chapter or if there are any problems that you cannot rectify, then file in the file c14_1.st and you will be ready to move on to the next section.

14.3 Support Tools

In Chapter 8 we discussed certain types of objects used to support the current Image Editor. These are DirectBitView, ColorBitView, and ColorBitEditor. Unfortunately, these do not provide the functionality required by the Enhanced Image Editor, so we will have to create our own versions of these classes to provide that additional functionality. We will also add some necessary functionality to OpaqueImage and Image. The source code for this section is available in its entirety in file **c14_4.st** should you choose not to enter the code yourself as presented in this section.

14.3.1 CenteredDirectBitView

In the current Image Editor, the image under construction appears in a DirectBitView. Unfortunately, it is flush against the upper lefthand corner of the DirectBitView. A Centered-DirectBitView is nothing more than a DirectBitView that centers the image within its bounds. This is not necessary to the functionality of the Enhanced Image Editor, of course, but it is a small price to pay for a more professional appearance.

In a System Browser, add the class category 'SDGVW-Enhanced Image Editor,' and then define the CenteredDirectBitView class as shown below in this class category.

```
DirectBitView subclass: #CenteredDirectBitView
    instanceVariableNames: ''
    classVariableNames: ''
```

```
poolDictionaries: ''
category: 'SDGVW-Enhanced Image Editor'
```

Also add the class comment shown below.

A CenteredDirectBitView is a DirectBitView which centers the Image within its bounds.

Add the instance protocol 'updating,' and add the following instance method to it (make sure your System Browser is on the instance side).

update: aSymbol with: aRect

```
aSymbol = #invalidate ifTrue:
    [| pixel transRect aGC |
    transRect := aRect translatedBy: (self bounds extent - model extent) // 2.
    aGC := self graphicsContext.
    aRect left to: aRect right - 1 do:
        [:x |
        aRect top to: aRect bottom - 1 do:
            [:y |
            pixel := model atPoint: x @ y.
            aGC paint: (model palette at: pixel).
            aGC displayRectangle: transRect. ]]]
```

Now add the instance protocol 'displaying,' and add to it the instance method below.

displayOn: aGraphicsContext
```
"Center the image in the receiver's bounds."

| aPoint |
aPoint := (self bounds extent - model extent) // 2.
model notNil ifTrue: [model displayOn: aGraphicsContext at: aPoint ]
```

This completes the CenteredDirectBitView.

14.3.2 EnhancedColorBitEditor

The EnhancedColorBitEditor differs from the ColorBitEditor in that it can draw lines and rectangles and assigns a color for both the <select> and the <operate> buttons. In the class category 'SDGVW–Enhanced Image Editor,' define the EnhancedColorBitEditor class as shown below. Notice that EnhancedColorBitEditor is not a subclass of ColorBitEditor but a subclass of BitEditor.

```
BitEditor subclass: #EnhancedColorBitEditor
    instanceVariableNames: 'tool colorAccessor '
    classVariableNames: ''
```

```
poolDictionaries: ''
category: 'SDGVW-Enhanced Image Editor'
```

Also add the class comment shown below.

An EnhancedColorBitEditor knows how to draw lines and rectangles in an EnhancedColorBitView. It also accesses the index of the current color from its application. A EnhancedColorBitEditor is used by an EnhancedImageEditor.

With the UIMaskEditor and ColorBitEditor, too much controller operation is handled by the application. An EnhancedColorBitEditor assumes all traditional controller activity such as fielding mouse input.

The modal controller concept is employed where the mode is referred to as the tool. A red button or yellow button will respond differently based on the setting of the tool (or mode).

Instance Variables

tool   <Symbol>   name of current tool method

colorAccessor <Symbol>   PRIVATE: name of current color accessor

14.3.2.1 Accessing and Control Methods

Make sure your System Browser is on the instance side. Now add the instance protocol 'accessing,' and add to it the following instance methods.

colorIndex
```
"Return either the left color index or the right color index."

^view application perform: colorAccessor
```

tool
```
"The default tool is the #point tool which merely changes the current
grid to the current color."

^tool isNil
    ifTrue: [tool := #point]
    ifFalse: [tool]
```

tool: aSymbol
```
tool := aSymbol
```

Add the instance protocol 'basic control sequence,' and add to it the following instance methods.

controlInitialize

"All tools except the point get a cross hairs cursor."

self tool ~= #point ifTrue: [Cursor crossHair show]

controlTerminate
"Return the cursor to normal in case it happens
to be something else."

Cursor normal show

Add the instance protocol 'control defaults,' and add to it the following instance methods.

redButtonActivity
"When the red button is pressed, perform with whatever tool as selected
in the application. Then return to the point tool and a normal cursor."

colorAccessor := #leftColorIndex.
self perform: self tool.
self tool: #point.
Cursor normal show.

yellowButtonActivity
"When the yellow button is pressed, color the point with the applications
rightColorIndex."

colorAccessor := #rightColorIndex.
self perform: self tool.
self tool: #point.
Cursor normal show.

14.3.2.2 Private Methods

There are three private methods that support the tool methods. Add the instance protocol 'private,' and add these three instance methods to it.

drawLineFrom: aStartPoint to: anEndPoint
"Draw the line (aStartPoint, anEndPoint) in the model in the current color
and redraw the model in both views."

| color image |
color := self colorIndex.
image := model.
aStartPoint x < anEndPoint x
    ifTrue: [aStartPoint x to: anEndPoint x do: [:x |
        image atPoint: x @ aStartPoint y put: color]]
    ifFalse: [aStartPoint y to: anEndPoint y do: [:y |
        image atPoint: aStartPoint x @ y put: color]].
model

```
changed: #invalidate
    with: (Rectangle origin: aStartPoint corner: anEndPoint + 1).
self imageHasChanged: true
```

endPointFrom: aStartPoint and: aPrimePoint
"Return a point which either forms a horizontal or vertical line with aStartPoint
based on the value of aPrimePoint. "

```
^(aPrimePoint x - aStartPoint x) abs > (aPrimePoint y - aStartPoint y) abs
    ifTrue: [aPrimePoint x @ aStartPoint y]
    ifFalse: [aStartPoint x @ aPrimePoint y]
```

When you try to accept this next method, you will receive a warning that lastPoint has
not been assigned a value yet. Simply select the **proceed** button.

pointWithColorIndex: anInteger
"Change a single pixel to the application's current color."

```
| point lastPoint |
point := sensor cursorPoint // view scale.
(model containsPoint: point) ifFalse: [^self].
[self sensor anyButtonPressed]
    whileTrue:
        [((model containsPoint: point) and: [lastPoint ~= point] )
            ifTrue:
                [model atPoint: point put: anInteger.
                model changed: #invalidate with: (point extent: 1@1).
                lastPoint := point].
        point := sensor cursorPoint // view scale].
self imageHasChanged: true
```

14.3.2.3 Tool Methods

Do not worry if you cannot understand the following methods right away, for they can
be very confusing. These methods provide the necessary behavior for drawing lines and
rectangles in the bit view. So naturally they involve quite a bit of Point and Rectangle
arithmetic. In the current Image Editor these types of operations are implemented in
the application model, but they are really the bit editor's responsibility.

Add the instance protocol 'tools,' and add to it the following instance methods.
With the first method below, you will receive a warning about the ifFalse: [nil] construct.
Simply select the **proceed** button. Due to the length of these methods, they are also pro-
vided as a file-in, c14_5.st.

line
"The line tool allows the user to draw a horizontal or vertical line."

```
| startPoint array |
Cursor crossHair
```

```
        showWhile: [startPoint := self sensor waitButton // diviser].
    array := Array with: startPoint with: startPoint.
    Cursor crossHair showWhile: [[self sensor anyButtonPressed]
        whileTrue: [ | point |
            Screen default
                displayShape: array
                at:         self sensor globalOrigin
                forMilliseconds: 100.
            point := self endPointFrom: startPoint and: sensor cursorPoint.
            (self viewHasCursor)
                ifTrue: [array at: 2 put: point]
                ifFalse: [nil]]].
    array := array collect: [:each | each // view scale].
    self
        drawLineFrom: ((array at: 1) min: (array at: 2))
        to:         ((array at: 1) max: (array at: 2)).
```

point
"Change a single pixel to the application's current left color."

```
self pointWithColorIndex: self colorIndex.
```

rectangle
"Allow the user to draw a rectangle in the current color."

```
| r image worker |
r := Rectangle
        fromUser: view scale
        phase: self sensor globalOrigin.
r extent = (8@8) ifTrue: [^self].
r := r translatedBy: self sensor globalOrigin negated.
r := r scaledBy: 1 / view scale.
image := model.
worker := Image
            extent: 1@1
            depth: image depth
            bitsPerPixel: image bitsPerPixel
            palette: image palette.
worker atPoint: 0@0 put: self colorIndex.
image tile: r from: 0@0 in: worker rule: RasterOp over.
view model: image; invalidateRectangle: (r scaledBy: view scale).
view application directBitView model: image; invalidate
```

rectangularBorder
"Allow the user to draw a rectangular border in the current color."

```
| r image aPoint color |
color := self colorIndex.
r := Rectangle
        fromUser: view scale
        phase: self sensor globalOrigin.
```

```
r extent = (8@8) ifTrue: [^self].
r := r translatedBy: self sensor globalOrigin negated.
r := r scaledBy: 1 / view scale.
image := model.
aPoint := r origin copy.
[aPoint x < r corner x] whileTrue: [
    image atPoint: aPoint put: color. aPoint x: aPoint x + 1].
aPoint x: aPoint x - 1.
[aPoint y < r corner y] whileTrue: [
    image atPoint: aPoint put: color. aPoint y: aPoint y + 1].
aPoint y: aPoint y -1.
[aPoint x > r origin x] whileTrue: [
    image atPoint: aPoint put: color. aPoint x: aPoint x - 1].
[aPoint y > r origin y] whileTrue: [
    image atPoint: aPoint put: color. aPoint y: aPoint y - 1].
view model: image; invalidateRectangle: (r scaledBy: view scale).
view application directBitView model: image; invalidate
```

This completes the ColorBitEditor.

14.3.3 EnhancedColorBitView

An EnhancedColorBitView is a kind of BitView that knows how to work with an Enhanced-
ColorBitEditor as its controller. In the class category 'SDGVW-Enhanced Image Editor,'
define the EnhancedColorBitView class as below. Notice that EnhancedColorBitView is a subclass of BitView and not a subclass of ColorBitView.

```
BitView subclass: #EnhancedColorBitView
    instanceVariableNames: ''
    classVariableNames: ''
    poolDictionaries: ''
    category: 'SDGVW-Enhanced Image Editor'
```

Add the class comment shown below.

> A ColorBitView is a BitView which knows how to work with a ColorBitEditor. It also
> facilitates message passing between the controller and the application.

Add the instance protocol 'accessing,' and add to it the following instance methods
(make sure your System Browser is on the instance side).

```
application
    "Return the receiver's application model which is the application
    for the window."

    ^self topComponent application
```

tool: aSymbol
"Make easy access to the controller's tool."

self controller tool: aSymbol

Add the instance protocol 'controller accessing,' and add to it the following instance method.

defaultControllerClass

^EnhancedColorBitEditor

This completes the EnhancedColorBitView. To test the functionality of ColorBitView, ColorBitEditor, and EnhancedDirectBitView, file in the file **c14_6.st** and evaluate the following code in a Workspace.

ImageEditorTestCanvas open

In the window, you should be able to use both the <select> and <operate> buttons to draw in the bit editor. You should also notice that the image you draw is centered in the direct bit view.

14.3.4 Additions to OpaqueImage and Image

The current Image Editor edits objects that are a kind of Image. That is, they are of the type Depth1Image, Depth2Image, or Depth4Image, depending on how many colors are used. The Enhanced Image Editor provides the option, however, of storing the image as an OpaqueImage. Therefore, we need a convenient way to transform an image into an OpaqueImage. Since this conversion would be useful for other applications as well, we will implement it as a service of OpaqueImage class and Image.

14.3.4.1 OpaqueImage

An OpaqueImage is an object that renders an image on a display surface, but it only renders certain pixels of that image, leaving the other pixels to appear as if they were transparent. It is implemented by referencing an image called the *figure* and a mono masked image called the *shape*. The figure is the image we wish to have rendered on the display surface, and the shape describes which pixels of the figure will actually be displayed and which will not.

Converting an image to an OpaqueImage should be a service provided by the OpaqueImage class as an instance creation message. Currently, OpaqueImage only has one instance creation method:

> figure: figure shape: shape

The two arguments are, of course, the two images—the figure and the shape. What would be convenient for our purpose (and several other purposes as well) is to have the second instance creation method shown below. Add this method to the class side of OpaqueImage under the protocol 'instance creation' (make sure your System Browser is on the instance side).

```
figure: anImage maskOut: aColorValueOrInteger
    "Create an instance of receiver based on anImage and a mask which
    masks out any occurances of aColorValueOrInteger in anImage."

    | shape colorIndex row |
    colorIndex := aColorValueOrInteger isInteger
                ifTrue: [aColorValueOrInteger]
                ifFalse: [anImage palette indexOf: aColorValueOrInteger].
    shape := Image extent: anImage extent depth: 1 palette: CoveragePalette
        monoMaskPalette.
    0 to: self height - 1 do:
        [:i |
        row := anImage rowAt: i.
        row := row collect: [:p | p = colorIndex ifTrue: [0] ifFalse: [1]].
        shape rowAt: i putAll: row].
    ^self figure: anImage shape: shape
```

In this method, the figure is provided as an argument as before, but the shape is defined by all the pixels in the figure that are of a certain color. All of the pixels with this color are those that we would like to be transparent. This color is described by the second argument and can be either a ColorValue or the integer index of the color in the figure image's palette. This instance creation method will build a shape image based on the occurrences of this color in the figure image.

14.3.4.2 Image

Since many objects know how to convert themselves to objects of a similar type, it would be nice if an image could convert itself to an OpaqueImage simply by sending it a message with a single argument that indicates the transparent color. In the Image class, define the following instance method under the protocol of 'converting' (make sure your System Browser is on the instance side).

```
maskOut: aColorValueOrInteger
    "Return an OpaqueImage based on the receiver and masking
    out any occurances of aColorValueOrInteger."

    ^OpaqueImage figure: self maskOut: aColorValueOrInteger
```

14.4 Image Repository

It would be nice to have a means for storing common images for use by all applications. We shall refer to this warehouse of images as the Image Repository. Furthermore, new images can be created by copying and editing the images currently in the Image Repository and then saving them back under a different name. The Image Repository not only provides a mechanism for storing and retrieving images, it also provides a user interface to facilitate the access of these images. The Image Repository is implemented by the class ImageRepository. The source code for this section is available in its entirety in file **c14_7.st** should you choose not to enter the code yourself as presented in this section.

14.4.1 Building the Repository

The Image Repository is both a repository and user interface to that repository. We will first implement the repository functionality. The images are maintained in a class variable, and all accessing protocol is through the class ImageRepository. The class variable, called Images, is a Dictionary, and every image will be identified by a unique name. This ImageRepository class will also provide both a modal and a nonmodal user interface for accessing the repository. Start the Image Repository by defining the class shown below in the class category 'SDGVW-Enhanced Image Editor.'

```
ExtendedApplicationModel subclass: #ImageRepository
    instanceVariableNames: 'imageNames imageView '
    classVariableNames: 'Images '
    poolDictionaries: ''
    category: 'SDGVW-Enhanced Image Editor'
```

Add the class comments shown below.

```
The ImageRepository provides a storage mechanism for maintaining a dynamic list of
images. It also provides a user interface for maintaining this list.

Instance Variables
    imageNames    <SelectionInList>        list of image names
    imageView     <CenteredDIrectBitView>  view for displaying selected image
```

14.4.1.1 Class Initialization

First we will initialize the class variable Images to be a Dictionary and load it with some initial images. This will be done in a class method called initialize. To add this class method to ImageRepository, file in the file **c14_8.st**. Now make sure you initialize this class by evaluating the following code in a Workspace (or even in the System Browser).

> ImageRepository initialize.

This ensures that the class variable Images is created and populated with some initial images.

14.4.1.2 Accessing Protocol

Now we need some class methods that allow us to access the images maintained in the Images variable. Add the class protocol 'accessing,' and add to it the following class methods (make sure you are on the class side of the System Browser).

> **imageNamed: aString**
> "Return the image in the repository corresponding to key name aString.
> If not found, return a default image."
>
> ^(Images at: aString ifAbsent: [self nilImage]) copy

> **includesImageNamed: aString**
> "Return true if there is an Image named aString.
> Return false otherwise."
>
> ^Images includesKey: aString

> **nameOfImage: anImage**
> "Return the name of the Image, anImage."
>
> ^Images keyAtValue: anImage ifAbsent: [String new]

> **nilImage**
> "Return an Image which is nothing more than a gray rectangle."
>
> | pixmap gc |
> pixmap := Pixmap extent: 32@32.
> gc := pixmap graphicsContext.
> gc paint: ColorValue veryLightGray.
> gc displayRectangle: (0@0 extent: 32@32).
> ^pixmap asImage

We now have a persistent store for any images we create.

14.4.2 Building the User Interface

Now we need a user interface that provides easy access to the Image Repository. Toggle your System Browser over to the instance side for the next several methods.

14.4.2.1 Drawing the Interface

Start a new canvas and set the window's dimension's to 304@160 and set its label to read 'Image Repository'. You can set the window dimensions by either editing the full spec literal array or by using the Window Layout Dialog developed in Chapter 13, Section 13.4. To this canvas add an arbitrary component (view holder) whose view method is named #imageView and whose layout is as follows.

	Proportion	Offset
L	0	16
T	0	16
R	0	144
B	0	144

Next add a list component whose aspect is #imageNames and whose menu method is name #imagesMenu. The layout of this list component is as follows.

	Proportion	Offset
L	0	160
T	0	16
R	0	288
B	0	144

Install this canvas as ImageRepository class>>windowSpec.

Now define a menu with the following labels and values, and install it as Image-Repository class>>imagesMenu.

Labels	Values
edit	edit
remove	remove
rename	rename

Close the canvas, Menu Editor, and Properties Tool.

14.4.2.2 Aspect and Resource Methods

Add the instance protocol 'aspects' and add to it the following instance method (make sure you are now on the instance side of the System Browser).

imageNames
"Create a SelectionInList object consisting of the names of
the images in the repository."

^self selectionInListFor: #imageNames
    collection: Images keys asSortedCollection
    selectionChange: #changeImage

Now add the 'resources' instance protocol, and add the following instance method to
this protocol.

imageView
"Return a CenteredDirectBitView to display the currently
selected Image."

^imageView isNil
    ifTrue: [imageView := CenteredDirectBitView model: self class nilImage]
    ifFalse: [imageView]

14.4.2.3 Action and Change Methods

There are three action methods for the images menu, so add the 'actions' instance protocol and add to it the following instance methods. The first method will warn you that
EnhancedImageEditor is not yet defined. Simply select the **undeclared** button.

edit
"Open a EnhancedImageEditor on the currently selected image."

self imageNames selection isNil ifTrue: [^nil].
EnhancedImageEditor edit: (self class images at: self imageNames selection)

remove
"Remove the current image"

| name |
(name := self imageNames selection) isNil ifTrue: [^nil].
(Dialog confirm: 'Remove "' , name , '" Image?
(All references will be outdated!)') ifFalse: [^nil].
Images removeKey: name.
self imageNames list: self class images keys asSortedCollection.

rename
"Rename the current image"

| oldName newName image |
(oldName := self imageNames selection) isNil ifTrue: [^nil].
(newName := Dialog request: 'Rename Image?
(All references will be outdated!)' initialAnswer: oldName).

```
(newName = '' or: [newName = oldName]) ifTrue: [^nil].
image := Images at: oldName.
self class images at: newName put: image.
self imageNames list: Images keys asSortedCollection.
self imageNames selection: newName
```

Now add the instance protocol 'change methods,' and add to it the following instance method.

changeImage
"The user has selected an image name. Display the corresponding image in the image view."

```
| image |
image := self class imageNamed: self imageNames selection.
imageView model: image; invalidate.
```

14.4.2.4 Making it Modal

To make the Image Repository interface modal, create a new canvas from the one described in windowSpec and lengthen the window to accommodate two action buttons at the bottom. The first button has a label of 'OK' and an aspect method named accept. Its layout is shown below.

	Proportion	Offset
L	0	63
T	0	160
R	0	127
B	0	196

The second action button's label is 'Cancel', and its aspect method is cancel. Its layout is shown below.

	Proportion	Offset
L	0	178
T	0	160
R	0	240
B	0	196

Install this canvas as ImageRepository class>>dialogSpec. Finally, add the class protocol 'interface opening,' and add the following class method to this protocol (make sure your System Browser is on the class side for this one). Close the canvas and Properties Tool.

openAsDialog
  "Open Image Repository as a dialog, return nil or an image."

  | inst |
  ^((inst := self new) openDialogInterface: #dialogSpec)
      ifTrue: [inst imageNames selection]
      ifFalse: [nil]

14.4.3 Testing

The ImageRepository is now almost complete and ready for testing. We will be adding
the remaining functionality in Section 14.5. In a Workspace, evaluate the following code.

    ImageRepository open

Select a few of the names in the list to see the corresponding image. Do not try the **edit**
menu selection in the pop-up menu as this sends messages to the EnhancedImageEditor
class, which has not been defined yet. Also, do not remove any images because we will
use them later. Close this window and then try the following, which opens the dialog
version.

    ImageRepository openAsDialog

If your code does not work correctly and seems beyond repair, then file in the file
c14_7.st, which contains all the code for ImageRepository. It is important that your Image-
Repository work correctly before proceeding to the next section.

14.5 Enhanced Image Editor

This is where all the pieces built so far finally come together. Since the Enhanced Image
Editor is very similar to the current Image Editor, we will make EnhancedImageEditor a
subclass of UIMaskEditor. This is an arguable call since much of what UIMaskEditor has to
offer is ignored or overridden. The source code for this section is available in its entirety in
file **c14_9.st** should you choose not to enter the code yourself as presented in this section.

To get started, define the following class in the class category 'SDGVW-Enhanced
Image Editor.'

    UIMaskEditor subclass: #EnhancedImageEditor
        instanceVariableNames: 'paletteInterface useOpaqueImage imageName '
        classVariableNames: ''

poolDictionaries: ''
category: 'SDGVW-Enhanced Image Editor'

Now add the class comments shown below.

An EnhancedlImageEditor is similar to a UIMaskEditor. The images can be stored as images or opaque images. The palette can be edited or a new palette can be selected from the Palette Repository. The images can be saved to or retrieved from the Image Repository. There is a color assigned to the <select>|<red> and <operate>|<yellow> mouse buttons. The extent of the image can be set explicitly.

Instance Methods

paletteInterface <UIColorPalette>sub application for palette

useOpaqueImage <ValueHolder>on a Boolean for opaque option

imageName<ValueHolder>on a String for image name

14.5.1 Starting the Interface

In this section, we will start the user interface with the three main components: the bit editor, the direct bit view, and the palette. Then we will add the initialization, accessing, and aspect methods that support these components.

14.5.1.1 Drawing the Interface

Start a new canvas and give the window the dimensions of 448@360 and a label that reads 'Image Editor'. First add a subcanvas component with the following properties and layout.

Name	#paletteInterface
Class	#UIColorPalette
Canvas	#windowSpec
Bordered	No

	Proportion	Offset
L	0	16
T	0	48
R	0	152
B	0	152

Next add an arbitrary component (view holder) that is bordered, and give it a method name and ID of #directBitView and the following layout.

	Proportion	Offset
L	0	16
T	1	-144
R	0	144
B	1	-16

Now add another arbitrary component (view holder) with the following properties and layout.

View:	#magnifiedBitView
ID:	#magnifiedBitView
Scroll Bars	Horizontal and Vertical
Bordered	Yes

	Proportion	Offset
L	0	160
T	0	48
R	1	-16
B	1	-16

Install this interface as EnhancedImageEditor class>>windowSpec. Close the canvas and Properties Tool.

14.5.1.2 Initialize and Private Methods

The EnhancedImageEditor, like its superclass, has a rather long initialize method. First add the instance protocol 'private,' and add to it the method below, which is referenced by the initialize method.

```
newImage
    "Return a blank image"

    | image index buffer |
    image := Image extent: 32@32 depth: 4 palette: self palette.
    index := image palette indexOfPaintNearest: ColorValue white.
    buffer := Array new: image width.
    1 to: buffer size do: [:colIndex | buffer at: colIndex put: index].
    0 to: image height -1 do: [:rowIndex | image rowAt: rowIndex putAll: buffer].
    ^image
```

Now add the instance protocol 'initialize-release,' and add the following instance method to that protocol.

initialize

"Initialize the holder of the current painter controller, the image, the two arbitrary views, and the option variables."

```
| image |
selectionHolder := UIPainterController lastControllerWithSelectionChannel.
image := self newImage.
acceptedState := image copy.
magnifiedBitView := EnhancedColorBitView model: image.
magnifiedBitView scale: 8 @ 8.
directBitView := CenteredDirectBitView model: image.
magnifiedBitView changedPreferredBounds: nil.
useCachedImage := ValueHolder with: true.
useOpaqueImage := ValueHolder with: false.
Screen default colorDepth == 1
    ifTrue: [storeMask := ValueHolder with: true]
    ifFalse: [storeMask := ValueHolder with: false].
modified := false
```

14.5.1.3 Accessing Methods

Add the instance protocol 'accessing,' and add the following instance methods to that protocol.

palette

"Return the current palette of the palette interface."

```
^self paletteInterface palette
```

leftColorIndex

"Return the left color index of the palette interface."

```
^self paletteInterface leftColorIndex
```

rightColorIndex

"Return the right color index of the palette interface."

```
^self paletteInterface rightColorIndex
```

14.5.1.4 Aspect Methods

Now add the instance protocol 'aspects,' and add to it the following instance method.

paletteInterface

```
^paletteInterface isNil
```

```
ifTrue: [paletteInterface := UIColorPalette new]
ifFalse: [paletteInterface]
```

14.5.1.5 Private Methods

It is necessary at this time to add four private methods, but only as stubs. Later these four methods will be removed in favor of the superclass implementation. We override them here only for development purposes. The reason is that these methods control the **Read** and **Apply** buttons, but since our interface does not yet have these buttons (they will be added in Section 14.5.7), a notifier will be raised during intermediate testing. In the protocol 'private,' add the following instance methods.

```
disableApply
    "For now, do nothing."


disableRead
    "For now, do nothing.'


enableApply
    "For now do nothing.'


enableRead
    "For now do noting.'
```

At this point, you can test the functionality of EnhancedImageEditor by evaluating the code below.

```
EnhancedImageEditor open
```

You should be able to draw in the bit editor and select colors from the palette.

14.5.2 Options and Editing Tools

In this section we will add

- a field naming the image

- the window menu

- methods for the editing tools

- methods for the options

14.5.2.1 Drawing the Interface

Open a canvas on the interface defined in EnhancedImageEditor class>>windowSpec, and add a read-only field whose aspect and ID are both #imageName and whose layout is shown below.

	Proportion	Offset
L	0	16
T	1	-177
R	0	144
B	1	-152

Give the window a menu named #imageEditorMenu. The window menu can be filed in from the file **c14_10.st**. Install and close the canvas and close the Properties Tool.

14.5.2.2 Aspect Methods

We need an aspect method for the image name field, so in the 'aspects' protocol, add the following method (you can also autogenerate this method from the canvas).

imageName

```
^imageName isNil
    ifTrue: [imageName := String new asValue]
    ifFalse: [imageName]
```

14.5.2.3 Options Methods

The Enhanced Image Editor adds the option to install an image as an OpaqueImage. Add the instance protocol 'actions-options,' and add to it the following instance method.

toggleUseOpaque

```
useOpaqueImage value: useOpaqueImage value not
```

The method above is an action method, which corresponds to the menu selection **Options→ Store Opaque Image**.

14.5.2.4 Tool Methods

The tool methods are very simple since all the real work is done in the EnhancedColorBit-Editor, which is as it should be. Add the instance protocol 'actions-tools,' and add to it the following methods.

line

    self magnifiedBitView tool: #line

point

    self magnifiedBitView tool: #point

rectangle

    self magnifiedBitView tool: #rectangle

rectangularBorder

    self magnifiedBitView tool: #rectangularBorder

Now open the Enhanced Image Editor again to test its new functionality. In particular, try turning the OpaqueImage option on and off, and try using each of the drawing tools.

14.5.3 Palette Functionality

In this section we will add the functionality for replacing and editing the palette. First add the following instance methods in the 'private' protocol.

```
reset
    "Reset all the parameters for a new, or newly saved image."

    self accept.
    self magnifiedBitView controller imageHasChanged: false.
    self modified: false


loadImage: anImage
    "Have receiver operate on anImage."

    Cursor execute showWhile: [
        self paletteInterface changeToPalette: anImage palette.
        magnifiedBitView model: anImage; changedPreferredBounds: nil; invalidate.
        directBitView model: anImage; changedPreferredBounds: nil; invalidate].
    self reset
```

Now add the instance protocol 'actions-palette,' and add the following instance methods to that protocol.

editPalette
    "Allow user to edit the palette or create a new palette."

    | reply image |
    reply := UIPaletteEditor edit: self palette copy.
    reply isNil ifTrue: [^nil].
    self paletteInterface changeToPalette: reply.
    image := magnifiedBitView model copy.
    image palette: self palette copy.
    self loadImage: image

loadPalette
    "Load a palette contained in the Palette Repository"

    | reply image |
    (reply := PaletteRepository openAsDialog) isNil ifTrue: [^nil].
    self paletteInterface changeToPaletteNamed: reply.
    image := magnifiedBitView model copy.
    image palette: self palette copy.
    self loadImage: image

paletteTool
    "Open the PaletteRepository tool."

    PaletteRepository open

Open the EnhancedImageEditor to test the palette functionality. In particular, try editing the current palette and loading a new palette. Try doing both with an image in progress to see how a change of palette affects the image's appearance.

14.5.4 Saving an Image

In this section we will add the methods necessary for storing and applying the image.

14.5.4.1 Private Methods

First we need a private method that takes the current image and converts it to its final form, which could be either a Depth4Image or an OpaqueImage. We also need to override the superclass's version of installInSystem since we are installing both images and OpaqueImage objects. In the 'private' protocol, add the following instance methods.

finalImage
    "Return an image or an OpaqueImage."

```
| image reply |
image := magnifiedBitView model copy.
storeMask value ifTrue: [^image := self generateMask].
useOpaqueImage value ifFalse: [^image].
reply := UIColorSelector selectColorIndexFrom: self palette.
reply isNil ifTrue: [^nil].
^image maskOut: reply
```

installInSystem
   "This is an edited version of the super implementation."

```
| class image stream |
(image := self finalImage) isNil ifTrue: [^nil].
class := self targetClass class.
stream := WriteStream on: (String new: 64).
stream nextPutAll: self targetSelector; cr.
"Put in a nice comment for re-opening the mask maker."
stream tab;
    nextPutAll: '"EnhancedImageEditor new openOnClass: self andSelector: #';
    nextPutAll: self targetSelector; nextPut: $"; cr;
    crtab; nextPutAll: '<resource: #image>';
    crtab; nextPut: $^.
(useCachedImage value and: [useOpaqueImage value not])
    ifTrue: [stream nextPutAll: 'CachedImage on: '].
stream nextPutAll: image minimalStorageString.
class compile: stream contents classified: #'resources'.
Transcript cr; show: class name, '>', self targetSelector, ' defined'.
class removeSelector: #markedAsSystemClass.
UIFinderVW2 installed: (Array with: self targetClass name with: self targetSelector).
self reset
```

14.5.4.2 Action Methods

Add the instance protocol 'actions–image,' and add to it the following instance methods.

images
   "Open the repository of images."

```
ImageRepository openSingleInstance
```

save
   "Save a copy of the current image to the ImageRepository. If the image has
   not yet been named, then the user must supply a name. If the user supplies
   a new name or a name other than the one already held in imageName, then
   check to see if an image already has that name and warn the user if this is the
   case and allow him to back out of the save or continue."

```
| reply |
reply := Dialog request: 'Name of Image' initialAnswer: self imageName value.
```

```
reply = String new ifTrue: [^nil].
reply = self imageName
    ifFalse: [
        (ImageRepository includesImageNamed: reply)
            ifTrue: [(Dialog confirm: reply,' is already in list!
Replace?') ifFalse: [^nil]].
        self imageName value: reply].
ImageRepository images at: reply put: self finalImage.
self reset
```

Open the EnhancedImageEditor again and you should be able to save images to the repository, apply them to an application model, or install them in a canvas.

14.5.5 Acquiring an Image

There are several ways in which an image can be acquired for editing.

- Start a new image.

- Read an image from a canvas.

- Grab a section of the screen.

- Load an image from an application model's resource method.

- Open an image from the images repository.

In this section we will add the methods that allow us to do these very things.

14.5.5.1 Private Methods

When getting an image from an outside source, that image can actually be a kind of Image, an OpaqueImage, or even a CachedImage. Therefore we need a method to make the necessary conversion to a Depth4Image object. In the 'private' protocol, add the following two instance methods.

```
convertToImage: anImage
    "anImage can be OpaqueImage, CachedImage, or image. Return
    the underlying image or nil if it is none of the above."

    | image |
    image := anImage.
    image class == CachedImage
        ifTrue: [
            useCachedImage value: true.
```

```
        image := anImage image].
image class == OpaqueImage
    ifTrue: [
        useOpaqueImage value: true.
        image := image figure].
(image isKindOf: Image) ifFalse: [^nil].
(storeMask value: image paintBasis == CoverageValue) value
    ifTrue: [
        image palette: MonoMappedPalette whiteBlack.
        self paletteInterface changeToPaletteNamed: 'Standard'].
^image
    convertToPalette: self palette
    bitsPerPixel: 4
    renderedBy: NearestPaint new
    paintTransfer: nil
```

14.5.5.2 Action Methods

Now we need an action method for each of the various ways an image can be loaded for editing. In the 'actions–image' protocol, add the following instance methods.

```
grab
    "Grab an arbitrary image and convert it to the currentPalette."

    | rect image |
    self changeRequest ifFalse: [^self].
    rect := self rectangleFromUserLimitedTo: 128@128.
    (rect height == 0 or: [rect width == 0 or: [rect extent = (1@1)]]) ifTrue: [^self].
    image := Screen default completeContentsOfArea: rect.
    self loadImage: (image convertToPalette: self palette).
    self imageName value: 'Grabbed Image' copy
```

```
load
    "Load an image from an ApplictionModel class protocol 'resources' "

    | image result |
    self changeRequest ifFalse: [^self].
    result := UIFinderVW2
        openSourceDialogForClass: self targetClass
        andCategory: #resources.
    result isNil ifTrue: [^self].
    self targetClass: (result at: 1).
    self targetSelector: (result at: 2).
    self messageNotUnderstoodSignal
        handle:
            [:ex |
            ex parameter selector == self targetSelector
                ifTrue: [ex return]
                ifFalse: [ex reject]]
```

```
          from: self targetClass
          do: [image := self targetClass perform: self targetSelector].
      (image := self convertToImage: image) isNil
          ifTrue: [^Dialog warn: 'The method did not return an image' for: builder window].
      self loadImage: image.
      UIFinderVW2 visited: (Array with: self targetClass name with: self targetSelector).
      self reset
```

openImage
   "Load an image from the Image Repository."

```
   | reply image |
   reply := ImageRepository openAsDialog.
   reply isNil ifTrue: [^nil].
   self changeRequest ifFalse: [^self].
   self imageName value: reply.
   image := ImageRepository imageNamed: reply.
   self loadImage: (self convertToImage: image)
```

read
   "Load the image associated with the current widgit on the current canvas."

```
   | controller spec image |
   self changeRequest ifFalse: [^self].
   controller := selectionHolder value.
   spec := controller selections first spec.
   image := controller builder visualAt: spec getLabel asSymbol.
   image := self convertToImage: image.
   image isNil ifTrue: [^self].
   self loadImage: image.
   self targetClass: controller model targetClass.
   self targetSelector: (spec label isNil
               ifTrue: [nil]
               ifFalse: [spec label asSymbol]).
   self imageName value: self targetSelector
```

new
   "Start a new image."

```
   (self modified or: [self magnifiedBitView controller updateRequest not])
       ifTrue: [(Dialog confirm: 'The image has been altered, but not installed.
Do you wish to discard the changes?') ifFalse: [^nil]].
   self imageName value: String new.
   self loadImage: self newImage
```

Open the EnhancedImageEditor and you should be able to load images in a variety of ways.

14.5.6 Adding Extent Control

The current Image Editor allows the developer to resize the image with the mouse. While this is very flexible, it can sometimes be cumbersome, especially if you want a very specific size. Therefore, the Enhanced Image Editor allows the developer to either set some predefined extents or to open a dialog and set an arbitrary extent.

14.5.6.1 Private Protocol

First we need a private method that changes the extent of the image. Add the following instance method to the 'private' protocol.

```
newSize: aRectangle
    "Change the extent of the image to that of aRectangle."

    | newMap model |
    model := magnifiedBitView model.
    newMap := Image
            extent: aRectangle extent
            depth: model depth
            bitsPerPixel: model bitsPerPixel
            palette: model palette.
    Cursor execute showWhile:
        [newMap
            copy: (Rectangle origin: 0 @ 0 corner: aRectangle extent)
            from: aRectangle origin
            in: model
            rule: RasterOp paint.
        magnifiedBitView model: newMap; changedPreferredBounds:nil; invalidate.
        directBitView model: newMap; changedPreferredBounds: nil; invalidate].
    self modified: true
```

14.5.6.2 Fixed Dimension Methods

The Enhanced Image Editor allows the developer to set four different fixed extents (dimensions) for the image. Each of these has a menu selection and an action method. Add the instance protocol 'actions–dimensions,' and add to it the following instance methods.

```
make16
    "Give image a 16@16 extent."

    self newSize: (0@0 extent: 16@16)
```

```
make26
    "Give image a 26@26 extent. This is included because
    it is the dimension of the palette buttons."
```

self newSize: (0@0 extent: 26@26)

make32
"Give image a 32@32 extent."

self newSize: (0@0 extent: 32@32)

make64
"Give image a 64@64 extent."

self newSize: (0@0 extent: 64@64)

14.5.6.3 Arbitrary Dimension Dialog

We also need to provide the developer with a means for setting an arbitrary dimension. This requires a dialog interface and a method for launching the dialog. Start a new canvas and give the window the dimensions of 235@122. Now add a label component with the label 'Enter New Image Size' and center this label at the top of the window (see Figure 14.8).

Add the two input fields and accompanying labels. You can position these components yourself according to Figure 14.8 or use the following layouts.

	Proportion	Offset
L	0	35
T	0	35
R	0	98
B	0	60

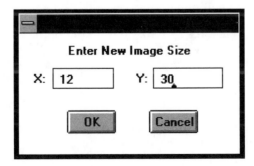

Figure 14.8. Extent Dialog Interface.

	Proportion	Offset
L	0	138
T	0	35
R	0	210
B	0	60

Give the input field on the left the following properties.

Aspect	#x
Menu	
ID	#x
Type	Number
Format	0

Give the input field on the right the following properties.

Aspect	#y
Menu	
ID	#y
Type	Number
Format	0

Now add the two action buttons. You can position these yourself according to Figure 14.8 or use the following layouts.

	Proportion	Offset
L	0	49
T	0	77
R	0	101
B	0	102

	Proportion	Offset
L	0	133
T	0	77
R	0	185
B	0	102

Give the button on the left the following properties.

Label	OK
Action	#accept
ID	#ok

Give the button on the right the following properties.

Label	Cancel
Action	#cancel
ID	#cancel

Now install this canvas as EnhancedImageEditor class>>extentDialog. Close the canvas and Properties Tool.

14.5.6.4 Arbitrary Dimension Method

Now we need an action method that opens the extent dialog and changes the extent of the image based on what the developer enters. Add the following instance method to the 'actions-dimensions' protocol.

```
defineExtent
    "Open a dialog prompting the user to resize the image."

    | x y dlg reply |
    dlg := SimpleDialog new.
    dlg builder bindings
        at: #x put: (x := 0 asValue);
        at: #y put: (y := 0 asValue).
    reply := dlg openFor: self interface: #extentDialog.
    reply isNil ifTrue: [^nil].
    (x value > 0 and: [x value < 129 and: [y value > 0 and: [y value < 129]]])
        ifFalse: [^Dialog warn: 'Invalid Range'].
    self newSize: (0@0 extent: x value @ y value)
```

14.5.6.5 Resize Method

The Enhanced Image Editor has its own implementation of the clip method. Add the following instance method to the 'actions-dimensions' protocol.

```
clip

    | ctrlr r |
    ctrlr := magnifiedBitView controller.
    r := Rectangle fromUser: magnifiedBitView scale phase: ctrlr sensor globalOrigin.
    r extent = (8@8) ifTrue: [^self].
```

```
r := r translatedBy: ctrlr sensor globalOrigin negated.
r := r scaledBy: 1 / magnifiedBitView scale.
self newSize: r
```

We now have the ability to set the extent of the image from the menu. Open the Enhanced Image Editor again and test this new functionality.

14.5.7 Adding Speed Buttons

In this section we will add buttons along the top of the window that allow easy access to certain menu selections. We will call these buttons *speed buttons*. Each button will have an image as its label, and each image will be an intuitive iconic representation of what the button does. To apply these images, we will be using the partially completed Enhanced Image Editor. That is, the Enhanced Image Editor will help build itself. This is a terrific example of the meta-tool concept.

14.5.7.1 Adding the Buttons

Open a canvas on the EnhancedImageEditor interface. Along the top of the window, just below the menu, place 14 action button components, each of which is 32@32 in dimension. Make sure the buttons are not sized as the default. It will be very helpful if you set the grid to 8 pixels. Starting from the left, give each button the action method and ID indicated below.

	Action	ID
1	#new	
2	#read	#readButton
3	#apply	#applyButton
4	#load	
5	#install	
6	#openImage	
7	#save	
8	#cut	
9	#copy	
10	#paste	
11	#point	
12	#line	
13	#rectangularBorder	
14	#rectangle	

Install the canvas. Included in the list of buttons above are the #read and #apply buttons. Now that these are part of the interface again, remove the following methods from the 'private' protocol.

enableRead

enableApply

disableRead

disableApply

Now open the Enhanced Image Editor for use as a tool keeping the canvas open as well. To do this, evaluate the code below.

EnhancedImageEditor open

14.5.7.2 Adding the Images

At this point you should have two EnhancedImageEditor applications open. One is in run-time mode and is functioning just like any other *VisualWorks* tool. The other is in edit mode and is being edited just like any other canvas. In the edit mode EnhancedImageEditor, select the first button on the left. In the runtime EnhancedImageEditor, select the **Image→Open** menu option and the Image Repository dialog will pop up. Select the image named 'New Image' and press the **OK** button. This image should now appear in your runtime Enhanced Image Editor. If the menu item **Options→Store Opaque Image** is not checked, select this item so that it is checked. Finally, select the menu option **Image →Apply**, which will pop up the install dialog. Install this OpaqueImage in EnhancedImage-Editor as #newImage. Before the image is installed, the Color Selector Dialog will pop up, prompting you to select a color to be the transparent color. Select the light gray color and press the **OK** button. At this point, the image should appear in the far left button in the edit mode EnhancedImageEditor. Repeat this procedure for the remaining 13 buttons according to the table below.

	Image Name	Resource Method
1	New Image	#newImage
2	Read	#readImage
3	Apply	#applyImage
4	Load	#loadImage
5	Install	#installImage
6	Open	#openImage

7	Save	#saveImage
8	Cut	#cutImage
9	Copy	#copyImage
10	Paste	#pasteImage
11	Point	#pointImage
12	Line	#lineImage
13	Square	#squareImage
14	Solid Square	#solidSquareImage

When you are done, install the canvas.

14.5.8 Interface Opening Protocol

There are three ways to open the Enhanced Image Editor: without an initial image, with an initial image, and with an initial image originating from an application model resource method. The first case is taken care of with the open message. Since the open method is inherited, there is nothing for us to do here. The second case occurs when the edit: anImage message is sent to the class EnhancedImageEditor. Therefore, toggle your System Browser to the class side, add the 'interface opening' protocol, and add to it the following class method.

```
edit: anImage
    "Open the Enhanced Image Editor on anImage."

    anImage palette depth > 4
        ifTrue: [^Dialog warn: 'Image is not of depth 4 or less'].
    self new loadImage: anImage; openInterface: #windowSpec
```

To properly open the Enhanced Image Editor on an image originating from an application model resource method, we must override the instance method openOnClass:and-Selector:. So toggle the System Browser back to the instance side, and add the following method to the 'private' protocol.

```
openOnClass: aClass andSelector: aSelector
    "This is a modification of the super implementation."

    | image |
    (aSelector isNil or: [aSelector numArgs > 0]) ifTrue: [^nil].
    self targetClass: aClass.
```

```
self targetSelector: aSelector.
image := aClass perform: aSelector.
(image := self convertToImage: image) isNil ifTrue: [^nil].
magnifiedBitView model: image; changedPreferredBounds: nil; invalidate.
directBitView model: image; changedPreferredBounds: nil; invalidate.
UIFinderVW2 visited: (Array with: aClass name with: aSelector).
self reset.
self openInterface: #windowSpec
```

You have now completed the Enhanced Image Editor and its accompanying tools. Make sure that it is fully functional. If you have any bugs that you cannot resolve, file in the file **c14_9.st**, which contains all the code presented in this section.

14.5.9 Adding It to *VisualWorks*

Now that the Enhanced Image Editor is completed and functioning properly, it is time to add it to the *VisualWorks* suite of tools. There are two options here: you can replace the current Image Editor or just add the Enhanced Image Editor so that both are available. For maximum flexibility, we will take the latter approach.

14.5.9.1 Launcher Menu

To make the Enhanced Image Editor available from the Launcher menu, use the Menu Editor to edit the menu defined in VisualLauncher class>>toolsMenu. In the Menu Editor, find the part that reads

```
----
&New Canvas          toolsNewCanvas
&Palette             toolsPalette
&Canvas Tool         toolsCanvasTool
&Image Editor        toolsMaskEditor
&Menu Editor         toolsMenuEditor
----
```

and edit it so that it reads

```
----
&New Canvas              toolsNewCanvas
&Palette                 toolsPalette
&Canvas Tool             toolsCanvasTool
&Image Editor            toolsMaskEditor
&Enhanced Image Editor   toolsEnhancedImageEditor
&Menu Editor             toolsMenuEditor
----
```

then build and install the menu. Now add the instance method below in the 'actions' protocol of VisualLauncher.

> **toolsEnhancedImageEditor**
>   "Open the Enhanced Image Editor."
>
> EnhancedImageEditor open

For these changes to take effect, you will have to open another Launcher. To do so, evaluate the code below.

> VisualLauncher open

14.5.9.2 Canvas Menu

To make the Enhanced Image Editor available from the canvas <operate> menu, you must open a Menu Editor on the menu defined in UIPainterController class>>canvasMenu. In the Menu Editor, find the section that reads

```
----
image editor          maskEditor
menu editor           menuEditor
----
```

and edit it so that it reads

```
----
image editor          maskEditor
enhanced image editor enhancedImageEditor
menu editor           menuEditor
----
```

then build and install the menu. Now in the UIPainterController instance protocol 'commands', add the following method.

> **enhancedImageEditor**
>   "Open mask editor."
>
> model targetClass == nil
>   ifTrue: [EnhancedImageEditor open]
>   ifFalse: [EnhancedImageEditor new openOnClass: model targetClass andSelector: nil]

To have this change take effect, reinitialize the class by evaluating the code below.

> UIPainterController initialize

14.6 Summary

The Enhanced Image Editor is a nice addition to the suite of *VisualWorks* tools, but it is by no means the last word on bit map editing. There are several ways in which it can be further enhanced. It could be made to accommodate any size palette recognized by Smalltalk such as 8-bit and 24-bit palettes. Dithering could be introduced so that hardware with only a 4-bit-deep screen could edit images 8 or 24 bits deep. More drawing tools such as circles and ovals could be implemented. Images could be installed in applications using a direct reference to the image name in the repository instead of having to create the image each time the interface is opened. It would also be nice if we could install images directly to the canvas from the Image Repository without having to first load them into the Enhanced Image Editor. And finally, we should have an actual drag and drop implementation for applying images. This would allow the developer to select an image in the images repository and drag it over to any component in any canvas and have it be automatically applied. You may consider pursuing some of these additional enhancements on your own.

CHAPTER 15

Additional Tools

In this chapter several new tools are introduced. Unlike the previous two chapters, however, this chapter does not contain tutorials for adding the tools to your virtual image. The source code is available on the accompanying distribution disk along with exercises to test their functionality. The implementation of each tool is briefly described, similar in fashion to how the tools in Chapter 8 were described. Unlike the tools in Chapter 8, however, you are not already familiar with the tools in this chapter. Therefore, a brief description of each tool's functionality is provided as well.

The tools introduced in this chapter are the Cursor Editor, the File Dialog, the Image Browser, a suite of font tools, the Full Inspector, and the Disk Browser. It is intended that this chapter not only provide some new features and tools for the *VisualWorks* environment, but that it also do the following:

- Demonstrate the mutability of the *VisualWorks* environment (i.e., the meta tool concept)

- Provide additional examples of tool building, application development, and good Smalltalk code

- Exploit the material covered in the previous parts of this book

- Provide practice for reading and following someone else's source code—an absolutely essential Smalltalk skill

- Provide support classes that may be used in additional tools and applications or extended for greater functionality

This chapter provides the following for each new tool introduced.

- What purpose the tool is serving

- Brief description of the tool, how to file it into the virtual image, and how to open and use it
- A general discussion of its implementation
- If appropriate, how to integrate the tool into *VisualWorks* so that it is readily available

15.1 Cursor Editor

In Chapter 9 we saw how we can make Cursors from two images. This is a somewhat awkward approach, however. Each image is made independently, and the final product is not revealed until the Cursor object is actually created and used. Furthermore, the traditional approach to adding a new cursor to the Smalltalk virtual image is to give the Cursor class an additional class variable and class method for accessing the new cursor.

Now that we have created an image-editing system (Chapter 14), it is easy to construct a cursor editor tool that will make creating and editing a cursor a very simple and intuitive process. Furthermore, a more elegant method of persistent storage is required. For these reasons, the Cursor Editor and the corresponding cursor repository have been developed.

15.1.1 Basic Description

The Cursor Editor is a tool specifically for creating and editing cursors. It is similar to the Image Editor except that its bit view is restricted to 16@16, which is the size of cursors in *ParcPlace\Smalltalk*. It has a direct image view of the cursor as it is being edited, so you can see the end product as you go along. The Cursor Editor also acts as a cursor repository by storing all cursors. The Cursor Editor is implemented by the class CursorTool, and its interface is shown in Figure 15.1.

To open the Cursor Editor, first make sure that you have filed in the file c15_1.st. Then in a Workspace, evaluate the code

        CursorEditor open.

15.1.2 Implementation

Three classes have been developed to implement the Cursor Editor and repository. Each of these is discussed below.

15.1.2.1 CursorBitEditor

The Cursor Editor requires its own special subclass of BitEditor called CursorBitEditor. Like the BitEditor, a CursorBitEditor uses a <select> button down to toggle a pixel between black and white. A CursorBitEditor has the added behavior that the <operate> button will turn the pixel gray. A gray pixel in this case represents a transparent pixel.

15.1.2.2 CursorEditor

The Cursor Editor tool is implemented by CursorEditor. The only available action is to save the cursor in the repository by pressing the **Save** button. Also, in order to make the Cursor Editor work, methods must be added to the class Cursor for accessing its image, mask, and hotSpot instance variables.

The repository functions of the Cursor Editor are very similar to those of the image repository from Chapter 14. Cursors are accessed from the cursor repository based on their name. For instance, a cursor named 'arrow' is accessed as follows.

    CursorEditor name: 'arrow'

This instance of Cursor can then be used like any other Cursor, such as

    (CursorEditor name: 'arrow') showWhile: [...]

In addition, certain class method protocol has been added to facilitate the use of the cursors stored in the repository. For example, the line above can also be written as

    CursorEditor show: 'arrow' while: [...]

The repository itself is actually a class variable in CursorEditor. It is initialized with a copy of all the system cursors that ship with the virtual image.

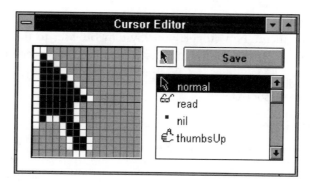

Figure 15.1. Cursor Editor Interface.

15.1.2.3 CursorEditorDialog

The Cursor Editor Dialog is a dialog that is used to acquire the name and hot spot of a cursor that is to be saved. The *hot spot* is the point on the cursor used to determine the cursor's exact location on the screen. The Cursor Editor Dialog is implemented by the class CursorEditorDialog.

15.1.3 Adding It to *VisualWorks*

To make the Cursor Editor and its corresponding cursor repository readily available in the *VisualWorks* development environment, they must be added to the Launcher menu. There is no need to make this tool available from the canvas <operate> menu or Resource Finder since it is not instrumental in painting canvases.

Use the Menu Editor to edit the menu in VisualLauncher class>>toolsMenu. Edit the section of the menu that reads

```
----
&New Canvas      toolsNewCanvas
&Palette         toolsPalette
&Canvas Tool     toolsCanvasTool
&Image Editor    toolsMaskEditor
&Menu Editor     toolsMenuEditor
----
```

so that it reads as follows.

```
----
&New Canvas      toolsNewCanvas
&Palette         toolsPalette
&Canvas Tool     toolsCanvasTool
&Image Editor    toolsMaskEditor
&Menu Editor     toolsMenuEditor
C&ursor Editor   toolsCursorEditor
----
```

Build and install the menu. Now toggle your System Browser to the instance side and, in the protocol 'actions,' add the following instance method to VisualLauncher.

```
toolsCursorEditor
    "Open the Cursor Editor"

    CursorEditor open
```

To have these changes take effect, open a new Launcher.

15.2 *MS Windows* **File Dialog**

Currently *VisualWorks* provides a stock dialog for prompting the user for a file name. The user types in the file name along with its path and selects the **OK** button. The return value is guaranteed to be a legitimate file name or nil. This stock dialog is implemented by the class Dialog (see Chapter 4, Section 4.4.3.5). While this is sufficient for acquiring a valid file name, today's user expects a flexible yet easy way to navigate a disk for the purpose of selecting a file. For this reason, a facsimile of the *MS Windows* file Dialog has been developed, implemented by MSWindowsFileDialog. Since it is implemented in *VisualWorks*, it is available to all platforms supported by *VisualWorks*. Furthermore, it is not restricted to the look policy for which it was originally intended. That is, the *MS Windows* File Dialog can be drawn in a *Motif* look, a *Macintosh* look, etc. To add this dialog to your system, file in the file **c15_2.st**.

The *MS Windows* File Dialog can be opened by evaluating the code below.

```
MSWindowsFileDialog open
```

This will return a valid file or nil.

Of particular interest in the implementation is the way the visual blocks are set up for the directories list. The directories are indented up to the current directory, but the directories within the current directory are not indented in the list. Therefore, an MSWindowsFileDialog keeps these in two separate collections even though they appear in the same list.

15.3 **Image Browser**

All the other tools in this chapter were developed to enhance current *VisualWorks* functionality. The Image Browser, however, was developed to enhance one of the tools we added in a previous chapter. In Chapter 14 we built the Image Repository to hold the images created using the Enhanced Image Editor. The Image Repository has an interface that allows the developer to view the available images and select one for editing. There are two shortcomings to this current interface. First, it only shows one image at a time. Second, an image must be loaded into an Enhanced Image Editor before it can be applied to a component in a canvas. The Image Browser was developed to overcome these two deficiencies.

15.3.1 Brief Description

The Image Browser provides a way to look at several images at one time and select one of these images for the purpose of editing it or applying it to a component in a canvas. The Image Browser only displays images of the same dimension. It has a bank of radio buttons for selecting the current dimension. The Image Browser is implemented by the class ImageRepositoryBrowser, and its interface is shown in Figure 15.2.

To open the Image Browser, first make sure that you have filed in the file **c15_3.st**. Next, evaluate the following code in a Workspace.

      ImageRepositoryBrowser open

Notice that you can stretch the window and the images will be repositioned within the new dimensions of the Image Browser. While the Image Browser has some advantages over the image repository interface, it does not indicate the image names.

15.3.2 Implementation

The Image Browser is implemented by the four classes ImageRepositoryBrowser, Visual-ComponentWrapper, VisualComponentBrowserView, and VisualComponentBrowserController. The last three are support classes developed specifically for the Image Browser. These three classes and ImageRepositoryBrowser are discussed below.

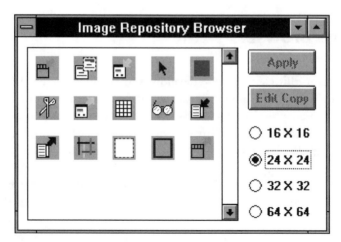

Figure 15.2. ImageRepositoryBrowser Interface.

15.3.2.1 Support Classes

A VisualComponentWrapper wraps an arbitrary visual component (in this case images) and provides the following services: it tracks the component's bounds within a larger view, it tests to see if the component's bounds contains a Point, and it displays the component only if its bounds intersect with the graphics context's clipping bounds. A Visual-ComponentBrowserView displays a collection of VisualComponentWrapper objects in a gridded fashion. It maintains the component collection, the grid size, and the currently selected component. It has a VisualComponentBrowserController for its controller. This type of controller is a subclass of SelectController and merely notifies the view of the location of a mouse click. It is then up to the view to determine what component, if any, owns that point, deselect any current selection, and select the new component.

15.3.2.2 ImageRepositoryBrowser

The ImageRepositoryBrowser is a subclass of UIPainterWatcher. This is because it has the capability of applying an image to the current selection in the current canvas. The image display and selection is handled by its image browser view. The radio buttons are tied to the size aspect variable, and when its value changes, images of the new size are collected from the repository and handed to the image browser view for display. When the **Extent...** button is pressed, a list of all unique extents is displayed in a dialog and you can select the extent you want.

The methods for supporting the **Apply** action button were copied from UIMaskEditor and slightly modified. These methods are apply, installInSystem, reloadSelectionInformation, runInstallationDialogFor:, targetTrouble, targetClass, targetClass:, targetSelector, and targetSelector:.

15.3.3 Adding It to *VisualWorks*

To make the Image Browser readily available in the *VisualWorks* development environment, it can be added to the Launcher menu and/or canvas <operate> menu.

15.3.3.1 Launcher Menu

Use the Menu Editor to edit the menu in VisualLauncher class>>toolsMenu. Edit the section of the menu that reads

```
    ----
    &New Canvas       toolsNewCanvas
    &Palette          toolsPalette
    &Canvas Tool      toolsCanvasTool
    &Image Editor     toolsMaskEditor
    &Menu Editor      toolsMenuEditor
```

```
C&ursor Editor     toolsCursorEditor
----
```

so that it reads

```
----
&New Canvas     toolsNewCanvas
&Palette        toolsPalette
&Canvas Tool    toolsCanvasTool
&Image Editor   toolsMaskEditor
&Menu Editor    toolsMenuEditor
C&ursor Editor  toolsCursorEditor
&Browse Images  toolsBrowseImages
----
```

and then build and install the menu. The example above assumes you have added the Cursor Editor from Section 15.1. Now toggle your browser to the instance side and in the protocol 'actions,' add the following instance method to VisualLauncher.

toolsBrowseImages
   "Open the Image Browser."

   ImageRepositoryBrowser open

To have these changes take effect, open a new Launcher.

15.3.3.2 Canvas <operate> Menu

To make the Image Browser available from the canvas <operate> menu, we must edit the menu in UIPainterController class>>canvasMenu using a Menu Editor. In the Menu Editor, find the part that reads

```
tools    nil
    palette               doPalette
    canvas tool           doCanvasTool
    ----
    image editor          maskEditor
    menu editor           menuEditor
    ----
    reusable data form components   openReusableComponents
```

and edit it so that it reads

```
tools    nil
    palette               doPalette
    canvas tool           doCanvasTool
    ----
    image editor     maskEditor
```

menu editor   menuEditor
----
reusable data form components   openReusableComponents
----
browse images   browseImages

and build and install the menu. Now toggle your System Browser over to the instance side and add the following instance method to the 'commands' protocol in UIPainterController.

browseImages
   "Browse images in repository."

   ImageRepositoryBrowser open

To make these changes take effect, evaluate the following code.

   UIPainterController initialize

15.4 Font Tools

VisualWorks provides wonderful font matching capabilities in order to maintain platform independence. In Chapter 9, Section 9.12 we saw how a FontDescription is defined and then how this FontDescription is used to create a CharacterAttributes and a TextAttributes. This text attributes can then be added to the repository of all available TextAttributes which is kept in the TextAttributes class. It is the TextAttributes objects kept in this repository which are available to the developer from a Properties Tool. The one problem with this scheme is that all the work must be done programmatically. It is very easy however to use *VisualWorks* to build a user interface to help the developer in this font creation process. This is the idea behind the font tools.

The font tools consist of four tools which work in cooperation to add new font and text selections to the *VisualWorks* environment. The primary tool is referred to as the Font Tool and it allows the developer to describe a font. Or to look at it another way, the Font Tool is a FontDescription editor.

From the Font Tool the developer can launch a dialog listing all the fonts available on the current platform. The developer can also launch a window which allows him to browse all of the current TextAttributes. Once the developer has described his font, he can install it. From the install dialog, the developer assigns a TextAttributes name, emphasis, line grid, and base line. This creates a new TextAttributes and adds it to the repository of TextAttributes.

To add the font tools to your system, first file in the file **c15_4.st**. To open the Font Tool, evaluate the following code in a Workspace.

```
UIFontTool open
```

The code above launches the main Font Tool, which can then launch the remaining Font Tools.

15.4.1 Font Tool

The Font Tool is implemented by UIFontTool, which is a subclass of ExtendedApplication-Model. The Font Tool interface is shown in Figure 15.3.

15.4.1.1 Defining the Font

The interface has two fields and five check boxes, which are used for defining the attributes of a FontDescription object. Each of these forwards the same change message, match, which creates a new FontDescription and updates a ValueHolder holding on to the current font. The two input fields each have two corresponding action buttons, which index the value of the field up or down.

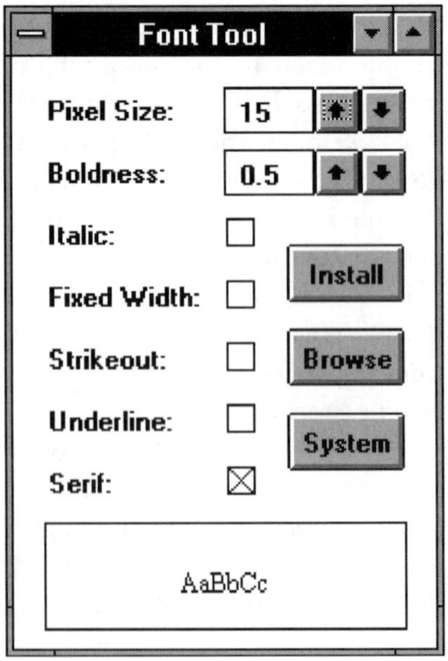

Figure 15.3. Font Tool Interface.

15.4.1.2 Displaying the Font

The current font is displayed in a special type of object called a FontDisplay. FontDisplay is a subclass of VisualPart. A FontDisplay centers a default string in its bounds and renders the string in the font specified.

15.4.1.3 Spawning Other Tools

The Font Tool has three action buttons that open other tools. The **System** button opens the System Fonts Dialog, which lists the fonts available on the current hardware. The **Browse** button opens the Attributes Browser, which is a window for browsing the current set of TextAttributes. The **Install** button opens the Text Attributes Installation Dialog, which is a dialog for defining and installing a TextAttributes. Each of these is described in turn below.

15.4.2 System Fonts Dialog

The System Fonts Dialog displays a list of all fonts available on the current hardware. The System Fonts Dialog is implemented by the UISystemFonts class, and its interface is shown in Figure 15.4. The collection of available fonts is generated by the private method systemFonts, which accesses all system fonts, selects those with a nonzero pixel size, and sorts

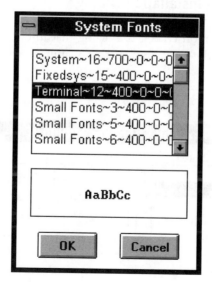

Figure 15.4. System Fonts Dialog Interface.

them by name. The list aspect model has a change message, changedFont, which places the new selection in the font display. Therefore, when a new font is selected in the list, a visual representation of that font is displayed in the font display. The changedFont method also enables or disables the **OK** button based on if there is a selection in the list or not.

The System Fonts Dialog is opened by sending the open message to the UISystem-Fonts class. The open method returns either a FontDescription or nil depending on if the user pressed the **OK** button or the **Cancel** button.

15.4.3 Attributes Browser

The Font Attributes Browser displays the currently available set of TextAttributes (see Figure 15.5). It is implemented by the class UIAttributesBrowser. The Text Attributes Browser allows the developer to see what kind of text attributes are currently available in the virtual image. The TextAttributes list is initialized with

> TextAttributes styles asSortedCollection

A change of selection dispatches the message changedTA, which updates the text editor displaying text rendered in the current TextAttributes.

15.4.4 Text Attributes Installation Dialog

The Text Attributes Installation Dialog is a dialog that installs a new TextAttributes based on the font described in the Font Tool. It first manufactures a CharacterAttributes with

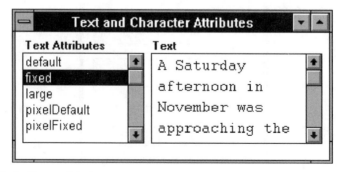

Figure 15.5. Attributes Browser Interface.

the font described in the Font Tool as the default font. It also creates the basic emphasis for this font such as bold and underline. The Text Attributes Installation Dialog uses this CharacterAttributes as the basis for a new TextAttributes. The developer is expected to supply a name, line grid, and base line. The Text Attributes Installation Dialog is implemented by UITextAttributes, and its interface is shown in Figure 15.6.

15.4.4.1 Input Fields

There are three input fields in the Text Attributes Installation Dialog. The first of these input fields obtains the name of the new TextAttributes. This input field forwards the change message changedTextAttributes, which enables/disables the **Install** button based on whether the field is empty or not. The other two input fields are for the line grid and baseline. Each of these has two action buttons associated with it. These action buttons index the value of the input field.

15.4.4.2 Installation

The **Install** action button invokes the install action method. This method installs the TextAttributes, notifies the user, and closes the dialog.

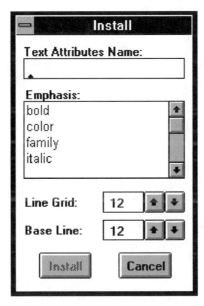

Figure 15.6. Text Attributes Installation Dialog Interface.

15.4.5 Adding It to VisualWorks

Since the font tools do not play a direct role in canvas painting, they should only be added to the Launcher menu. Use the Menu Editor to edit the menu in VisualLauncher class>>toolsMenu. Edit the section of the menu that reads

```
    ----
    &New Canvas      toolsNewCanvas
    &Palette         toolsPalette
    &Canvas Tool     toolsCanvasTool
    &Image Editor    toolsMaskEditor
    &Menu Editor     toolsMenuEditor
    C&ursor Editor   toolsCursorEditor
    &Browse Images   toolsBrowseImages
    ----
```

so that it reads

```
    ----
    &New Canvas      toolsNewCanvas
    &Palette         toolsPalette
    &Canvas Tool     toolsCanvasTool
    &Image Editor    toolsMaskEditor
    &Menu Editor     toolsMenuEditor
    C&ursor Editor   toolsCursorEditor
    &Font Tool       toolsFontTool
    &Browse Images   toolsBrowseImages
    ----
```

and then build and install the menu. The menu text above assumes you have already added the Cursor Editor and Image Browser. Now toggle your System Browser over to the instance side and in the protocol 'actions,' add the following instance methods to VisualLauncher.

```
    toolsFontTool
        "Open the Font Tool"

        UIFontTool open
```

These changes take effect upon opening a new Launcher.

15.5 Hierarchy Tools

Trees and hierarchies play a major role in the computer sciences. This is especially so in object–oriented languages such as Smalltalk. Both object state and object type can be expressed with these types of structures. In addition, most standard file structures are also hierarchical in nature.

There are many different ways for expressing a hierarchy, each with its own advantages and disadvantages. One common technique is to display the hierarchy as an outline in a list component. This section introduces some tools that use list components to walk down a tree, or hierarchy, one path at a time. The list components are arranged left to right; the list on the far left represents the root node and the items in the list are its child nodes (see Figure 15.7). Child nodes that branch to other nodes are displayed with a small triangular pointer at the far right of that list item. If one of these branching nodes is selected, then another list pops up to the right representing that node and listing its child nodes.

For lack of a better term, the tools that bear this behavior are referred to as the *hierarchy tools*. There are two support classes that encapsulate and abstract this tree-walking behavior: HierarchicalListComposite and HierarchyHolder. These two classes are then used to build the Full Inspector. All the code for this section is available in the file **c15_5.st**.

15.5.1 Support Classes

The two classes HierarchicalListComposite and HierarchyHolder define the view and model for a tree or hierarchical structure. Together they provide a row of list components where each list component represents a node in the traversed path.

15.5.1.1 HierarchyHolder

HierarchyHolder is the model for a hierarchical structure, and it is a subclass of Model. It contains the root object, the current node object, and blocks that support the branching process. Table 15.1 describes each of the instance variables.

The following is a brief synopsis of walking a tree structure.

Table 15.1. HierarchyHolder Instance Variables.

Variable	Description
root	A reference to the root object
selectionChannel	A ValueHolder that holds the current node object
branchTestBlock	A block that tests whether a node is a branch or leaf node
collectionAccessorBlock	A block that returns a collection representing a node's children
nextNodeBlock	A block that returns the next node based on the selection in a list

1. The hierarchy holder is handed a root object, and it becomes the value of the selection channel (the selectionChannel instance variable).

2. The root object is passed to the collection accessor block as its only argument, and the block returns a collection of objects representing the root object's children. The elements in the collection may actually be the child nodes or other objects, such as strings, which merely represent the nodes.

3. An element in this collection is selected and passed to the nextNodeBlock as its only argument and the block returns the child node represented by that element in the collection. By default, this block does nothing more than return the argument assuming that the element in the collection is the node.

4. This node then becomes the value of the selection channel and the process starts over.

15.5.1.2 HierarchicalListComposite

HierarchicalListComposite is a subclass of DependentComposite and serves as the view for a HierarchyHolder. It has several interesting implementation features. It maintains a reference to the builder of the window it inhabits. It builds list components on the fly by handing list component specs to this builder. It also removes these lists from its components collection when necessary. The developer can also specify visual blocks to be used by the lists for displaying the child nodes. Table 15.2 describes the instance variables for a HierarchicalListComposite.

15.5.2 Full Inspector

When inspecting a complex object, such as an ApplicationWindow, you may end up opening several Inspectors before getting to the part of the object that is of interest. All of these

Table 15.2. HierarchicalListComposite Instance Variables.

Variable	Description
builder	A reference to the builder that built the window
visualComponentBlock	A block that describes how items should appear in the list
titleBlock	A block that describes how lists should be titled
includeTitle	A boolean that indicates whether titles will be included with the lists

Inspectors can become quite troublesome to manage. Also, it can become confusing as to the exact sequence of Inspectors that arrived at the current Inspector. Finally, once you are done inspecting, you have all of those Inspector windows to close. Because of this awkwardness in the current inspection mechanism, the Full Inspector was developed.

15.5.2.1 Brief Description

The Full Inspector uses the hierarchy tool classes to walk down the various branches of an object. The root node is the object being inspected. Leaf nodes are objects such as integers, booleans, and characters. All other objects that have named or indexed instance variables are branching nodes. Each list indicates the names or indices of the selection in the previous list. The text component of the Full Inspector shows the current selection's print string as is done in the standard Inspector.

A standard Inspector can be brought up at any time on the current selection.

15.5.2.2 Implementation

The Full Inspector is implemented by the class FullInspector (see Figure 15.7) which is a subclass of ExtendedApplicationModel. It initializes its hierarchy holder and hierarchy list composite to walk an object's structure. It is necessary to add the methods isBranchNode and slots to certain system classes such as Object, Boolean, and Dictionary in order for the

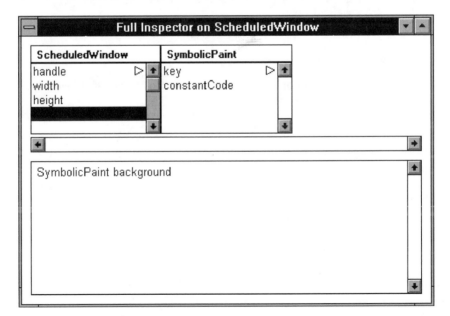

Figure 15.7. Full Inspector Interface.

Full Inspector to function properly. These messages facilitate the branch test and collection accessor blocks.

15.5.2.3 Adding It to VisualWorks

The intention here is to add the Full Inspector but not necessarily replace the standard Inspector. Make sure you have filed in **c15_5.st**. Next we must add the following instance method to the class Object in the protocol 'user interface.'

```
fullInspect
    "Open the full Inspector on the receiver."

    FullInspector openOn: self
```

This ensures that each object in the system can be inspected in a Full Inspector simply by sending it the message fullInspect. Next we should edit the definition of the <operate> menu defined in ParagraphEditor. Toggle your System Browser over to the class side, and in the class method initialize, edit the lines that read

```
CodeYellowMenuButton :=
    Menu
        labelList: ParagraphEditor editGroupLabels, #(('do it' 'print it' 'inspect') ('accept'
            'cancel') ('hardcopy'))
        values: ParagraphEditor editGroupSelectors, #(#doIt #printIt #inspectIt #accept
            #cancel #hardcopy).
```

to read

```
CodeYellowButtonMenu :=
    Menu
        labelList: ParagraphEditor editGroupLabels, #(('do it' 'print it' 'inspect' 'full inspect')
            ('accept' 'cancel') ('hardcopy'))
        values: ParagraphEditor editGroupSelectors, #(#doIt #printIt #inspectIt #fullInspectIt
            #accept #cancel #hardcopy).
```

and accept the changes. Finally, add the following instance method to ParagraphEditor in the protocol 'menu messages.'

```
fullInspectIt
    "Evaluate the current text selection as an expression and
    fully inspect the result"

    self class compilationErrorSignal
        handle: [:ex | ex returnWith: nil]
        do: [self evaluateSelection fullInspect]
```

To make these changes take effect, evaluate the following code in a Workspace.

```
ParagraphEditor initialize
```

15.6 Disk Browser

A large part of application development in Smalltalk is to first develop a prototype to learn what you can about the application. The next step is to *throw away* that prototype and start over. This is very difficult for most developers to do, and understandably so. Many times the prototype includes several good tidbits of code that should not have to be rewritten or should at least provide some insights as to how it might be better implemented. Therefore, most developers file out the prototype code prior to starting over so that it can be referenced later or even reused. There are other reasons why developers keep filed-out code on a disk. For instance, developers file out classes and categories that are currently not being used to keep from bloating the virtual image. Another good reason to have file-outs is to maintain a history of current work—that is, a versioning process.

There are currently two ways to view the code that resides on a disk file; unfortunately, both have some limitations or adverse effects. First, a developer can file in the file and browse the code using a browser such as the System Browser. But what is filed in may conflict with or override code currently in the virtual image. This leads to the second approach, which is to view the file in a File List tool. This presents the code in a terse and linear fashion. In this format, the code is very difficult to read and navigate. The Disk Browser was developed to solve this dilemma.

15.6.1 Brief Description

The Disk Browser presents the information in a file-out as it would appear in a System Browser. It does so, however, without actually compiling code into the virtual image. The Disk Browser looks just like the System Browser except that the category list is replaced by a list of files (see Figure 15.8). As the developer selects a file in this list, the classes contained in that file are available for viewing just as if they were in a Browser. It should be emphasized that these classes are *not* Smalltalk classes in the virtual image. The developer can, however, compile these classes into the virtual image with a simple menu command. The code in the file-out can be loaded into the virtual image in the following granularities.

- Entire file
- Entire class
- Class comments
- Class definition
- Method protocol
- Single method

The Disk Browser is implemented by the DiskBrowser class, and its interface is shown in Figure 15.8.

To run the Disk Browser, first make sure you have filed in the file **c15_6.st**. Now in a Workspace, evaluate the code DiskBrowser open. Enter a relative or absolute directory in the field at the top, and all the ***.st** files in that directory will populate what is normally the category view. From there you can navigate the Disk Browser just as if it were a System Browser. The Disk Browser is *read-only* of course, so you cannot edit anything. Furthermore, since this code is not actually in the hierarchy, it will not be included in any searches for references, senders, implementors, etc. The main purpose of the Disk Browser is to be able to view the source code on a disk in a useful and familiar fashion and to have the option of loading that source code into the virtual image.

15.6.2 Implementation

The Disk Browser differs from the other tools in this chapter in that it has certain domain objects on which it operates. These domain objects are called *surrogate meta objects,* and they hold on to the meta data describing the classes and methods in the file-out.

15.6.2.1 Surrogate Classes and Methods

In order to browse classes and methods without bringing them into the virtual image, we need certain types of objects to hold the class and method meta data, that is, the

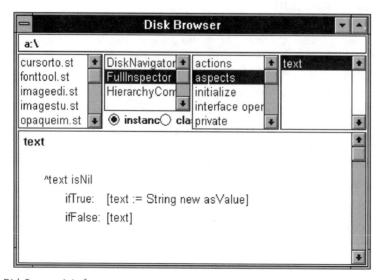

Figure 15.8. Disk Browser Interface.

Table 15.3. SurrogateClass Instance Variables.

Variable	Description
name	A string that is the name of the class
definition	A string that is the definition of the class
comment	A string that is the class comments
instanceMethods	A collection of SurrogateMethod objects that constitute the instance methods
classMethods	A collection of SurrogateMethod objects that constitute the class methods
classInstVars	A string that lists the class instance variables

source code for the class such as the class definition, comments, and method definitions. Two types of objects serve this purpose: SurrogateClass and SurrogateMethod. Basically, SurrogateClass and SurrogateMethod objects are containers of meta data (i.e., Smalltalk source code). The instance variables for SurrogateClass are listed in Table 15.3, and those for SurrogateMethod are listed in Table 15.4.

In addition to being containers of meta data, the surrogate objects also have two special behaviors. First, they can populate themselves based on a read stream which has been opened on a file out. Second, they can compile their meta data into the virtual image.

15.6.2.2 The Browser

The actual Disk Browser is implemented by the class DiskBrowser. This is an interesting implementation, because it is a *VisualWorks* application that somewhat mirrors the Browser—a traditional MVC application. The implementation itself is very simple. A change in the directory field causes an update in the files list. Any change of selection in any list causes updates in all the lists to the right of it just as it does in a System Browser.

Table 15.4. SurrogateMethod Instance Variables.

Variable	Description
name	A string that is the method signature
protocol	A string that is the name of the protocol to which the method belongs
isMeta	A boolean that indicates whether the method is a class method or instance method
className	A Symbol that is the name of the class to which the method belongs
sourceCode	A string that is the source code for the method

The four list components and the text component each has an <operate> menu, which allows the developer to compile into the virtual image the source code represented by that component. The action methods triggered by these menu selections merely forward the responsibility for compiling the code on to the surrogate objects, which know how to compile their meta data into the virtual image. When a file is selected, a stream is opened on that file and the class SurrogateClass creates a collection of instances of itself based on the contents of that stream. This collection is then used to populate the class list and the subsequent list components and text component.

15.6.3 Adding It to *VisualWorks*

Since the Disk Browser does not play a direct role in canvas painting, it should only be added to the Launcher menu. Use the Menu Editor to edit the menu in VisualLauncher class>>browseMenu. Edit this menu so that it reads as follows.

&All Classes	browseAllClasses
&Disk	browseDisk
Class &Named...	browseClassNamed
&Resources	browseApplications

&References To...	browseSendersOf
&Implementors Of...	browseImplementorsOf

then build and install the menu. Now toggle your Browser over to the instance side and in the protocol 'actions' add the following instance method to VisualLauncher.

browseDisk
    "Open the Disk Browser"

    DiskBrowser open

These changes take effect upon opening a new Launcher.

15.7 Summary

In this chapter, we added several tools to the *VisualWorks* environment. It is this kind of malleability and extendibility of *VisualWorks* that puts it in a class of its own. The purpose of this chapter was to provide some extra functionality for the *VisualWorks* environment and to provide additional examples of tool building and application development. This chapter refers to a great deal of source code that you can use, extend, and borrow—and from which you can also learn. This chapter added a total of six new tools. The Cursor Editor allows a developer to easily create and store his or her own cursors. The MS File Dialog allows an easy, intuitive way to select a file. The Image Browser is an enhancement of the Image Repository and allows the developer to install images directly onto a canvas. The suite of font tools allow the developer to browse system fonts and create new font descriptions and text attributes. The hierarchy tools display a hierarchy as a succession of list boxes. The Full Inspector is a hierarchy tool that allows the developer to fully inspect an object within a single window. The Disk Browser allows a developer to view file-outs as if they were in a browser.

Accompanying Disk and the Examples Browser

THIS BOOK COMES with an accompanying disk. This disk contains Smalltalk source code and a bos file containing the examples referenced in the chapters. The examples are viewed by a special browser called the Examples Browser.

A.1 Licensing Agreement

The source code and examples on this disk are licensed to only one developer per copy of this book. The licensed developer is free to integrate any of the source code into his or her own applications and distribute those applications in a closed, runtime image. The licensed developer may not reproduce or distribute the source code or the examples, in either their current form or any modified form.

A.2 Disk Contents

Table A.1 lists the files that are on the accompanying disk.

Table A.1. Disk Files.

File name	Contents
install.st	Installation file that files in the rest of the code
examples.bos	Contains all exercises for Examples Browser
examples.st	Source code for Examples Browser
c1.st	Chapter 1 disk example classes

c1a.st	Chapter 1 classes entered by reader
c2.st	Chapter 2 disk example classes
c3.st	Chapter 3 disk example classes
c4.st	Chapter 4 disk example classes
c5.st	Chapter 5 disk example classes
c6c7c8.st	Chapters 6, 7, and 8 disk example classes
c9.st	Chapter 9 disk example classes
c10.st	Chapter 10 disk example classes
c11.st	Chapter 11 disk example classes
appfrwks.st	Application Frameworks classes covered in Chapters 10 and 11
c12_1.st	Interface specs for percent bar component tutorial
c12_2.st	Icons used in percent bar component tutorial
c12_3.st	Source code for percent bar component tutorial
c12_4.st	Source code for clock component
c12_5.st	Source code for ruler component
c12_6.st	Source code for enhanced percent bar component
c13_1.st	Source code for paste to cursor functionality
c13_2.st	Source code for color menu
c13_3.st	Images for the position buttons added to the Position Tool
c13_4.st	Source code for position buttons added to the Position Tool
c13_5.st	Source code for Window Layout Dialog
c14_1.st	Complete source code for all of the palette application of Section 14.2
c14_2.st	Method UIPaletteApplication class>>defaultPalette
c14_3.st	Method PaletteRepository class>>initializePalettes
c14_4.st	Source code for Enhanced Image Editor support classes
c14_5.st	Tool methods for EnhancedColorBitEditor
c14_6.st	ImageEditorTestCanvas class used for testing the support classes
c14_7.st	Source code for Image Repository
c14-8.st	Method ImageRepository class>>initialize
c14_9.st	Source code for the EnhancedImageEditor class
c14_10.st	Menu defined in EnhancedImageEditor class>>imageEditorMenu
c15_1.st	Source code for Cursor Editor
c15_2.st	Source code for File Dialog
c15_3.st	Source code for Image Browser
c15_4.st	Source code for the font tools

c15_5.st	Source code for the hierarchy tools
c15_6.st	Source code for Disk Browser
a.st	Appendices classes
ab.st	Class changes for Appendix B
ac.st	Class changes for Appendix C

A.3   Installation

The Examples Browser and supporting example classes should be filed in before work-ing the examples. Not all of the files listed above are filed into the image in this opera-tion and are used for some later reference. There may be some conflict in names between the classes in the file-ins and classes you may have already added to your virtual image. Therefore, you may want to use a new virtual image.

UNIX Installation

1. The disk is a DOS-formatted disk, so you must have a 3½" disk drive that reads the DOS format, or you must be networked to such a machine. Furthermore, you should use ftp or a DOS to UNIX utility to translate all of the *.st files to the UNIX text format. Do not translate the **examples.bos** file however—this should be a binary transfer. The text translation on the *.st files is recommend-ed so that the source code will appear correctly in the browsers.

2. In the directory that contains your virtual image, create a subdirectory called **sdgvw.**

3. Copy or ftp the entire contents of the disk to the **sdgvw** directory.

4. In *VisualWorks,* open a File List on **install.st** and file it in. This will file in all of the necessary files for working the disk examples. You may want to take a snap-shot of your virtual image once this is completed.

Windows and OS/2 Installation

1. In the directory that contains your virtual image, create a subdirectory called **sdgvw.**

2. Copy the entire contents of the disk to the directory **sdgvw.**

3. In *VisualWorks,* open a File List on **install.st** and file it in. This will file in all of the necessary files for working the disk examples. You may want to take a snapshot of your virtual image once this is completed.

Macintosh Installation

1. The disk is a DOS-formatted disk, so you must have a 3 1/2" disk drive that reads the DOS format, or you must be networked to such a machine. Furthermore, you should use a utility to translate all of the ***.st** files to the Macintosh text format. Do not translate the **examples.bos** file however—this should be a binary transfer. The text translation on the ***.st** files is recommended so that the source code will appear correctly in the browsers.

2. In the folder that contains your virtual image, create a new folder called **sdgvw.**

3. Copy the entire contents of the disk to the new folder.

4. In *VisualWorks,* open a File List on **install.st** and file it in. This will file in all of the necessry files for working the disk examples. You may want to take a snapshot of your virtual image once this is completed.

A.4   Examples Browser

The disk examples referenced in this book are contained in a special browser called the Examples Browser, shown in Figure A.1.

The list on the left is a list of all chapters that reference disk examples. If you select a chapter, the list on the right is populated with all the disk examples for that chapter. If you select a disk example, that example appears in the text editor.

The intention of the Examples Browser is to allow you to work an example without having to type in much code. The emphasis is on understanding the concepts at

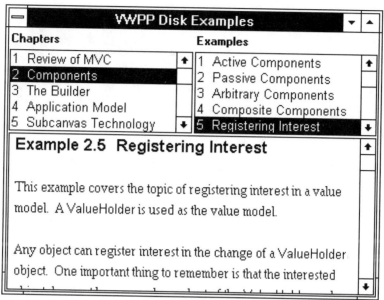

Figure A.1. Examples Browser.

hand, not on sharpening your typing skills. Most of the time, you just read the text and inspect on, or evaluate, the code.

To open the Examples Browser, evaluate the following code in a Workspace.

```
SDGVWExamplesUI open
```

To make a hard copy of a disk example, select the **hardcopy** item in the text editor's <operate> menu. Such a hard copy is meant for the convenience of the licensed developer and not to be reproduced or distributed.

The text editor is not read only so you can change the text of a disk example. The original set of examples can be reread from the bos file, however, by selecting the **refresh** item in the text editor's <operate> menu.

Domain Object Dirty State

I̶T IS OFTEN convenient to have domain objects that are responsible for knowing when they have changed. A domain object that has been changed is said to be **dirty**. When the changes of a dirty object have been accepted, that domain object is said to become **clean**. To add this behavior to domain objects, the abstract class StateDomainObject has been developed as a subclass of DomainObject. The information in this appendix is illustrated with examples in Disk Example B.1.

B.1   Dirty State

The StateDomainObject class defines an instance variable called isDirty. This is a boolean used to indicate if the domain object has been changed in some way. Many object-oriented database management systems (OODBMS) provide a similar service, but we should make no assumptions about the type of persistent store that may be used by an application. Furthermore, the implementation described below allows a domain object to be particularly clever about what actually constitutes a dirty state, while most OODBMSs have a rather simplistic view of this concept.

When a domain object is instantiated, the isDirty variable should be set to false. Whenever a mutating message is sent to the domain object, the isDirty variable should be set to true. When a dirty domain object is accepted (i.e., the user elects to save any changes), the isDirty variable is set to false and the domain object is said to become clean. Only clean domain objects should be made persistent, and domain objects fetched from a database should already be in a clean state.

B.2   Mutators

Since a domain object can be changed by way of its mutator-accessing methods, the implementation of these methods should include setting the isDirty variable to true. For instance, the mutator method for a variable called effectiveDate might look like the following.

effectiveDate: aDate

```
effectiveDate := aDate.
self becomeDirty
```

The implementations of the becomeDirty and becomeClean methods as implemented in StateDomainObject are shown below.

becomeDirty

```
isDirty := true
```

becomeClean

```
isDirty := false
```

B.3   Collection Mutators

Keeping track of when a domain object's collection has been changed can be tricky. One approach is to create mutators for the elements in the collection such that the collection is never edited directly but only by sending the appropriate collection mutator message to the domain object. This allows the domain object to know when one of its collections has been changed. To illustrate, suppose a domain object has a collection of file names called fileNames. The accessor for this collection might look like

fileNames

```
^fileNames isNil
    ifTrue: [fileNames := OrderedCollection new]
    ifFalse: [fileNames]
```

We could also have collection-mutating methods such as

addFileName: aString

```
self fileNames add: aString.
self becomeDirty
```

and

removeFileName: aString

> self fileNames remove: aString.
> self becomeDirty

If, however, the domain object is edited in the following manner

domainObject fileNames at: 2 put: 'temp.prt'

then the domain object will never know that its internal state has been changed. If you are disciplined enough to edit the domain object's collection using only the domain object's collection-mutating methods, then the domain object will always know when its collection has been changed. The problem is that it is too easy to cheat. That is, we can access the domain object's collection and edit it directly, as in the example above, and the domain object will never know about it. One alternative is to use a DomainCollection as the collection object (see below).

B.4   DomainCollection

DomainCollection is a subclass of StateDomainObject, and it manages one piece of information: a collection. A DomainCollection can respond to the standard collection protocol. However, any mutating messages such as add:, remove:, and at:put: will set the isDirty variable to true. Since the domain collection is a state domain object, it knows if it is clean or dirty and responds to the appropriate protocol. DomainCollection also defines its own copying protocol.

B.5   Test for Dirty State

The implementation of the method isDirty is not just a simple return of the isDirty instance variable, and each type of state domain object should have its own implementation of isDirty. This is how the dirty status implementation of a state domain object differs from that of most OODBMSs. The variable isDirty is set only when a mutating message is sent to the domain object. If a domain object contains another domain object or a collection of domain objects, then these too can become dirty without the knowledge of the containing domain object. Therefore, a domain object must not only check its own isDirty variable, but it must also check any of its aggregated domain objects to see if they are dirty as well. This type of checking should continue recursively on down to the leaf nodes of the domain object structure.

As an illustration, let's use the Employee object, which, for the purposes of this example, is an aggregation only of an Address object and a WorkHistory object. The Employee class will implement the isDirty method in a manner similar to the following.

isDirty
```
"The receiver is dirty if its isDirty variable is true or
if its address or work history is dirty."

^isDirty or: [self address isDirty or: [self workHistory isDirty]]
```

The corresponding Address object and WorkHistory object each have their own implementation of isDirty, which guarantees that anything within their aggregation is also checked for a dirty state. In this way, the entire transitive closure of the Employee object is checked for a dirty state and not just the immediate instance variables.

B.6   Guidelines

Here are some simple guidelines for developing state domain objects that know when they have become dirty.

1. Mutating methods should set the instance variable and then tell the domain object to become dirty.

2. The domain object class should favor collection-mutating methods for adding and removing elements from its collections.

3. Each state domain object class should implement isDirty to check its own isDirty variable plus test all aggregate domain objects to see if they are dirty.

4. A policy should be used to determine if copies are automatically clean or if they just copy the original's isDirty attribute.

5. Dirty objects that have been accepted and stored in a database should be made clean by sending them the message becomeClean.

6. Objects fetched from a database should always be clean.

7. Each state domain object class should implement becomeClean to set its own isDirty variable to true plus have any of its aggregate domain objects become clean as well.

Domain Object Differencing

DOMAIN OBJECT DIFFERENCING is the notion of determining the difference between a domain object and an edited copy of that domain object and storing these differences in a single object called a delta object. The delta object can then be used some time later to mutate the original to where it is equivalent in every respect to the copy. Such a technique can be used as the basis for a change-management system or an object version process. This idea of domain object differencing is described and developed below and illustrated with examples in Disk Example C.1.

C.1   General Description

A **delta object** is the collection of differences between an initial version of a domain object and an edited copy, or final version, of that domain object. That is, a delta object is the result of finding the *difference* between these two domain objects. The delta object can then be stored in a persistent media to be used at some later time to mutate the initial version into an exact replica of the final version. That is, the delta object is *added back* to the initial domain object, thereby producing an exact equivalent of the final domain object.

The difference between the two domain objects might be deeply nested within their internal structure and the delta object will still operate correctly. Since this is rather special behavior, delta objects only operate on special kinds of domain objects called **mutable domain objects**.

Since a delta object is the *difference* between two domain objects, which can be added back at some later time, the arithmetic operators - and + have been adopted as the binary messages used to manipulate mutable domain objects and their corresponding delta objects. The minus operator is the binary message sent to the final domain object

with the initial domain object as the argument. The - method then returns a delta object that fully records the differences between the two. Suppose M_i is a mutable domain
object and M_f is an edited copy of M_i. The delta between the two is calculated using the
following Smalltalk statement.

delta := M_f - M_i

Once the delta object is created, it can be stored in a persistent media. The delta object
can be added back to M_i to mutate it into an exact replica of M_f. To add back the delta,
the addition operator + is sent as a message to the initial mutable domain object with
the delta object as the argument. The result is that the initial mutable domain object M_i
is mutated to be identical in every way to the final mutable domain object M_f. Using
the example from above, this would be

M'_f := M_i + delta.

Here, M'_f is the same object as M_i only certain of its attributes have been changed as is
dictated by delta. These changes now make M'_f identical in every way to M_f. That is to
say, the following statements hold true.

M'_f = M_f

M'_f == M_i

M_f = M_i + delta.

The delta is not restricted to mutating the initial into an equivalent of the final. The
same delta object can mutate the final into an equivalent of the initial. That is, if

delta := M_f - M_i

then

M'_i := M_f - delta

so that

M'_i = M_i

and

M'_i == M_f.

Now suppose we have the following scenario.

M_1 is an edited copy of M_i and $delta_1 := M_1 - M_i$

M_2 is an edited copy of M_1 and $delta_2 := M_2 - M_1$

M_3 is an edited copy of M_2 and $delta_3 := M_3 - M_2$

M_4 is an edited copy of M_3 and $delta_4 := M_4 - M_3$

We now have an initial object, M_i, and four versions of that object. We also have the measured difference between any two successive versions captured in a delta object. We know that

$$M_1 := M_i + delta_1$$

and

$$M_2 := M_1 + delta_2.$$

We can apply rules of arithmetic by substituting for M_1 to get

$$M_2 := M_i + delta_1 + delta_2.$$

This can be extended to

$$M_4 = M_i + delta_1 + delta_2 + delta_3 + delta_4.$$

Going backwards we have

$$M_i = M_4 - delta_4 - delta_3 - delta_2 - delta_1.$$

As long as we have any one version, the delta objects can be used to recreate all of the remaining versions. The implementation details that provide the object differencing functionality are described below.

C.2   Mutable Domain Objects

Only certain kinds of domain objects can be affected by delta objects. These are called *mutable domain objects*. The class MutableDomainObject is the abstract superclass of all domain objects that can be differenced and mutated by a delta object. In particular, MutableDomainObject defines two methods for this purpose: the - and + operators.

Consider that each mutable domain object will reference only one of three types of objects that can participate in the differencing process.

1. Atomic objects that are noncollection, noneditable objects such as dates, strings, and other domain objects referenced by association

2. Other mutable domain objects

3. A collection whose elements are either all of type 1 or all of type 2

Mutable domain objects can certainly reference other objects, including nonmutable domain objects, which are not intended to participate in the differencing/mutating process.

In order for the object differencing mechanism to succeed, each concrete implementation of MutableDomainObject is expected to implement the following four methods as needed.

replaceableSlots	Return an array of the accessor names accessing objects of type 1 that are available to participate in the differencing process.
mutableSlots	Return and array of the accessor names accessing objects of type 2 that are available to participate in the differencing process.
collectionsOf ReplaceableElements	Return an array of the accessor names accessing collections that have elements of type 1 and are available to participate in the differencing process.
collectionsOf MutableElements	Return an array of the accessor names accessing collections that have elements of type 2 and are available to participate in the differencing process.

In addition, subclasses of MutableDomainObject should follow a certain convention for naming accessors and mutators. That is, the mutator method name should be the same as the accessor method name with a colon appended at the end. For consistency, the accessor name should be the same as the instance variable it returns, but this is not necessary. It is necessary, however, that the accessor and mutator method names differ by only the colon.

C.3   Delta Operations

Each object in Smalltalk contains slots, or instance variables, which are used to reference other objects. Consider that each slot in a mutable domain object can reference one of two categories of objects:

1. Noncollection objects such as booleans, strings, dates, and other domain objects

2. Collection objects such as OrderedCollection objects

In the first case, the slot is representing a one-to-one relationship. The objects referenced by these kinds of slots correspond to object types 1 and 2 described in Section C.2. In the second case, the slot is representing a one-to-many relationship by way of a collection. The objects referenced by these kinds of slots correspond to object type 3 described in Section C.2.

A **delta operation** is the act of changing a single attribute of a mutable domain object. In the first of the two cases mentioned above—the noncollection objects—two different delta operations can take place.

1. *Slot replacement*—replace the object referenced by the slot

2. *Slot mutation*—mutate the object referenced by the slot

In the second type of slot reference—collection objects—three different delta operations can take place.

1. *Collection element addition*—add a new element to the collection

2. *Collection element removal*—remove an existing element from the collection

3. *Collection element mutation*—mutate an existing element in the collection

This gives us five types of delta operations:

1. Slot replacement

2. Slot mutation

3. Collection element addition

4. Collection element removal

5. Collection element mutation

Items 2 and 5 above are of special interest because they begin a recursion process. First it must be said that the mutated object in both cases is assumed to be another mutable domain object. The mutation that occurs is just another delta object being applied to the mutable domain object referenced by the slot or contained by the collection. This recursion continues down to the leaf nodes of the original mutable domain object's structure. In this way, all differences between two mutable domain objects of the same type can be recorded as nothing more than a collection of delta operations.

C.4   Delta Classes

There is a different type of object for each of the five delta operations described above. A domain object delta is nothing more than a collection of these delta operation objects. The DomainObjectDelta class is the concrete implementation of the delta object concept, and a delta object is an instance of this class. DomainObjectDelta defines a single variable, operations, which is a collection of delta operation objects.

The delta operation classes are shown in the hierarchy in Figure C.1. These classes are further described below.

DeltaOperation (DomainObject): The abstract superclass for all objects that perform some type of delta operation. DeltaOperation defines one variable, aspect, which references a Symbol. This Symbol is the accessor for a particular aspect of the domain object's information.

SlotOperation (DeltaOperation): The abstract superclass for all objects that perform some type of slot operation.

SlotMutation (SlotOperation): The concrete class that describes which objects mutate a slot that references a contained domain object. SlotMutation defines one instance variable, delta, which is an instance of DomainObjectDelta. This DomainObjectDelta is used to mutate the contained domain object at this particular slot.

SlotReplacement (SlotOperation): The concrete class that describes which objects replace an object referenced by a slot. SlotReplacement defines two instance variables—newValue and oldValue—each of which references any type of object. The newValue vari-

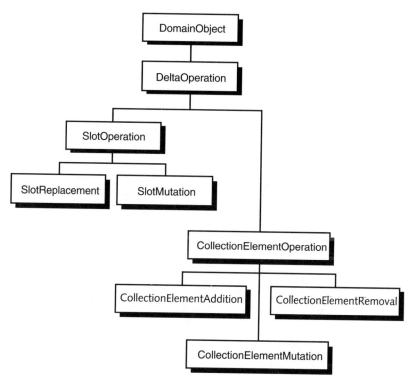

Figure C.1. Delta Operation Class Hierarchy.

able is the intended new value of the slot. The variable oldValue is the value being re-placed.

CollectionElementOperation (DeltaOperation): The abstract superclass for all objects that perform some type of collection element operation. The collection is accessed using the aspect variable. It is assumed that the collection responds to add: and remove:. Other than this, there is no restriction on the type of collection. CollectionElementOperation defines one instance variable, element, which can be any object. The element variable is the object being added, replaced, or mutated.

CollectionElementAddition (CollectionElementOperation): The concrete class that de-scribes which objects add an element to a collection referenced by a slot.

CollectionElementMutation (CollectionElementOperation): The concrete class that describes which objects mutate an element in collection referenced by a slot. CollectionElementMutation defines the instance variable delta that is a DomainObjectDelta. This DomainObjectDelta is used to mutate the element accessed with the element variable.

Be sure to work Disk Example C.1, which gives concrete examples of the domain object differencing technique.

GLOSSARY OF TERMS

abstract class a class that is not intended to have instances but describes the state and behavior common to its subclasses.

access character similar to a short-cut key. It allows a user to select a menu item with a keyboard character and actually pulls down any intermediate menus. It only applies to *MS Windows* and *OS/2* look policies. Also known as a *mnemonic*.

accessor method see *get method*.

accessing protocol the set of methods that access and replace instance variables.

action block a block that, when evaluated, dispatches an action message to an application model. An action block is placed inside of a PluggableAdaptor, which then serves as the model for an action button widget.

action button a *VisualWorks* component that looks like a push button. When the user presses this push button with a mouse, some corresponding action is triggered in the application.

action method the method that is executed as a result of a user pressing an action button. An *action message* is dispatched to execute an action method.

active component 1. a *VisualWorks* component that interacts with the user and whose widget is a view with a model and a controller. **2.** a visual component that references its container.

active controller the controller that is currently stepping through its control loop and is said to have control in that it is the current processor of user input.

active window the window that is the current recipient of user input and is usually distinguished from the remaining windows by a differently colored title bar. Also know as *current window.*

adaptor an aspect model whose domain information belongs to another object, usually a purely domain type object. The most common adaptor type is the AspectAdaptor.

aggregation a reference one object has to another, which specifies composition or ownership; that is, the first object logically contains the second object. This term particularly applies to domain objects but can apply to other objects as well.

application 1. one or more windows that work in a coordinated or related effort to provide a service to the end user. **2.** the application model that coordinates one or more windows and is referenced by each of these window's application instance variable.

application model 1. a model that is composed of one or more aspect models, manages at least one window (or canvas) and its components, and employs a builder to build its interface. **2.** an instance of a subclass of ApplicationModel

application model architecture the architecture used by *VisualWorks* for developing user applications. This architecture centers around the application model, which manages application information only.

application information the information that pertains specifically to running the application such as aspect models, menus, labels, error messages, icons, interface builders, and interface descriptions.

arbitrary component a *VisualWorks* component whose widget is any visual part—even one designed prior to the introduction of *VisualWorks*—and/or does not respond to *Visual-Works* widget protocol. Also known as *view holder*.

aspect an identifiable subset of the domain information, usually referenced by an instance variable. The name of an aspect is expressed as a Symbol such as #address, #workSchedule, and #effectiveDate.

aspect model a model that manages a single aspect of information for an application model and is usually associated with a single interface component such as a list, input field, or check box.

association a reference one object has for another that does not specify composition or ownership. That is, the first object knows about the second but does not logically contain it. This term particularly applies to domain objects but can apply to other objects as well.

atomic object an object that is not meant to be directly edited only replaced by another object. Typical atomic objects are strings, numbers, and dates. Domain objects referenced by association can be considered atomic as well.

behavior 1. the functionality of an object, what it does. **2.** an object's methods as defined in its class or any of its superclasses.

bitmap a grid of colors where each cell represents a pixel on the screen. In *Parc-Place\Smalltalk*, a bitmap is implemented by Image and its subclasses.

border decoration policy determines how borders and scroll bars should appear in a window and helps determine the look policy.

bounded layout a component layout that constrains the component's x and y dimensions in some way, either by a fixed number of pixels or by some fraction of the container's size.

bounding box see *bounds*.

bounds a Rectangle that determines the actual real estate consumed by an interface component or window.

builder an instance of UIBuilder that builds an interface for a client, based on a specification, using building materials from its source, and according to a look policy.

canvas 1. any composite of *VisualWorks* components that are all bound to the same application model. **2.** a *VisualWorks* interface opened for editing by the painting tools.

change message the message to be sent to an interested object whenever a certain value model changes value.

changed/update mechanism the behavior that allows a model to broadcast a notification of change to its collection of dependents.

changing protocol the set of messages a model sends to itself in order to trigger the changed/update mechanism. These messages are changed, changed:, and changed:with:.

channel a value model used as a constant reference point for a changing value. Provides the benefit that only the value model needs to be changed and that any references to the value model remain fixed.

check box a *VisualWorks* active component that allows the user to toggle a true/false condition.

child application an application model that is either spawned by a parent application model to run a child window or serves as the subapplication for a subcanvas.

child window a window that is opened from another window and usually plays some kind of support role. The child window is usually a slave to the parent window. Also known as a *satellite window*.

class 1. an object that describes a set of objects that have common state and behavior. **2.** an object that can have instances.

classical MVC architecture the approach to application development used prior to *Visual-Works* that used large monolithic models with several dependents. Such models managed both application and domain information and built their user interfaces with source code existing in class methods.

clean the state of a domain object that indicates that it has not been changed.

client the object that instantiates a builder for the purposes of building an interface—usually an application model.

client key a Symbol that belongs to a SubCanvasSpec and is used to look up the subapplication in a builder.

clipping bounds the active bounds of a graphics context object indicating the area on which graphics operations will be successful. Any attempts to draw outside of the clipping bounds will not be successful.

closed when a window or any other display surface is no longer affiliated with a host resource and therefore cannot appear on the screen or receive graphics operations.

collapse to shrink a window down to its icon representation.

combo box a *VisualWorks* active component that combines a list, an action button, and an input field. The input field allows a user to enter arbitrary text, and the list allows the user to fill the input field with a selection from a predefined set of values. The list remains hidden until the user presses the button which then displays the list.

component(s) 1. in traditional MVC, any visual component. **2.** in *VisualWorks*, specifically a SpecWrapper containing a widget.

component-building method a method defined in a look policy class 'building' protocol that actually instantiates a *VisualWorks* component and sets its attributes according to a component spec.

component description protocol the set of messages sent to a component spec object to acquire, or set, its description of a *VisualWorks* component. This protocol includes such messages as name, model, isOpaque, and colors.

component ID a Symbol used to uniquely identify a *VisualWorks* component within a given user interface. Also known as *component name*.

component name see *component ID.*

component spec a spec object that describes the properties and attributes of a *VisualWorks* component.

composite a visual part that contains several other visual components as its component parts. This allows a grouping effect for visual components within a window.

composite component a *VisualWorks* component that is actually a composite of other *VisualWorks* components. It is distinguished from other *VisualWorks* components in that it is not available from the Palette but created by grouping one or more selected components in a canvas.

composite view a composite that has its own model and controller for the purposes of allowing the user to manipulate the various component parts. UIPainterView is a good example of a composite view.

concrete class a class that is intended to have instances as opposed to an abstract class, which does not have instances.

construction variables the instance variables defined in UIBuilder that facilitate the component construction process.

container a visual part that contains one or more other visual components. Two broad categories of containers are wrappers and composites. A window is also the container of a visual component.

containing application see *parent application.*

control to be the current recipient of user input. The current controller is said to have control.

control activity the third step of the control loop, it is the controller's opportunity to process user input.

control loop a loop defined in Controller>>controlLoop and executed by the current controller. Each pass through the loop consists of a three-step process: temporarily give control to the window controller, test for the condition of maintaining control, and execute any specific control activity.

control mode an object that can serve as the current mode of a modal controller. There is a different type of control mode object for each different mode of operation (selecting, dragging, stretching, etc.).

controller the part of the MVC triad that is concerned with interacting with the user and processing user input.

copy the reproduction of an object. There are two steps to the copy process: shallow copy and postcopy. There are three main types of resulting copies: shallow copy, deep copy, and full copy.

current consumer a widget controller marked by the window's keyboard processor to be the current recipient of any keyboard events.

current window see *active window.*

damage the area of a window in need of being redrawn. Damage occurs usually because a view no longer accurately reflects the information in its model or because the window has been obscured by another window.

damage event an event passed in by the host window manager that notifies a window that part or all of its display surface needs to be redrawn.

data set a *VisualWorks* component that is a grid of smaller components such as input fields, menu buttons, and check boxes.

decoration 1. a window's border, title bar, and control buttons provided by the host window manager. **2.** the trimmings supplied to a component such as border and scroll bar.

deep copy a copy of an object in which the copy and the original share no information.

dependent any object that depends on information in a model in order to perform its duties. Such an object is added to that model's collection of dependents and has a reference back to the model. Whenever an aspect of information changes within the model, the dependent is notified with an update message as to the nature of the change. It is then up to the dependent to determine if it should take action. Most dependents are views, windows, DependencyTransfer objects, and other models.

dependents collection a collection of objects that depend on a single model. When the model changes in any way, it broadcasts an update message to each of these dependents.

device font an object that maps to a host-supplied font.

dialog 1. a modal window usually used to display a message or acquire simple information from the user. **2.** an application model whose window is opened as a modal window.

dialog client application an application model that is asked to open as a dialog but uses an instance of SimpleDialog for opening its interface and establishing the modal behavior.

dialog decoration window decoration that includes a frame and title bar but does not include maximize and collapse buttons.

direct redraw a technique of redrawing a view that bypasses the view invalidation and window damage recording process. Instead, the view accesses the window's graphics context directly and draws itself.

dirty the state of a domain object that indicates that it has been changed in some way.

disable to redraw a component in a gray hue and remove its ability to interact with the user. This semantic is different from read-only. It conveys to the user that the component is currently unavailable but could become available again under different circumstances.

dispatcher an instance of UIDispatcher that determines what notification and validation messages, if any, should be sent to the application model in the event of a change of focus, change of value, or double-click. Each widget controller has its own dispatcher.

display surface a graphics medium that is the destination for screen-related graphics as opposed to printer graphics.

divider a *VisualWorks* passive component that is nothing more than a line used to divide groups of other interface components.

domain adaptor an application model that is a kind of DomainAdaptor and developed specifically to be the interface for a certain type of domain object. The DomainAdaptor class is a special abstract subclass of ApplicationModel.

domain adaptor architecture an extension to application model architecture that allows a developer to build one or more domain object classes and then develop the corresponding application models (called domain adaptors) to act as the user interfaces for those types of domain objects.

domain information the information that pertains to the problem space and exists independently of the issues of user interface and application development. For an inventory application, domain information might include such things as part numbers, quantities on hand, and shipping lead times.

domain model 1. the entire set of domain object types used to model a given domain space. **2.** an object that contains domain information. Also known as *domain object*.

domain object an object that contains only domain information, does not contain application information, and does not have any dependents.

drop-down menu one of the three types of menus, it appears just below a menu button or menu bar and displays its items in a vertical fashion.

dynamic resource a resource provided by an application model instance method with the expectation that it will be manipulated during runtime.

edit mode when a *VisualWorks* user interface is open for editing by the *VisualWorks* painting tools.

emphasis a modification to a font such as applying italics or underlining.

enable to make a disabled component available to the user again.

event an occurrence of some type that triggers a response by the application. Events originate with the host window manager, often as a result of some user action such as mouse or keyboard activity.

expand to take a window from its iconic representation to its full window representation.

extent the x and y pixel dimensions of a bounds or Rectangle expressed as a Point. The term is used quite frequently with positioning components within a window (or other container), positioning windows on the screen, and in drawing objects on a graphics context.

first indent the left margin of the first line of a paragraph of text.

fixed layout a component layout that determines a component's location and dimensions to be some fixed number of pixels.

focus the status of a *VisualWorks* component in which it is the current recipient of keyboard events. The component with keyboard focus usually has some kind of visual distinction, such as an outline.

full copy a copy of an object in which the original and the copy do not share any critical or potentially editable information but can in fact share some information such as atomic objects or domain objects referenced by association.

full spec an instance of FullSpec and a full description of a user interface composed of a window spec and a spec collection.

garbage the set of objects no longer accessible by the root object (the Smalltalk dictionary) and therefore of no use to the Smalltalk environment.

garbage collector the object responsible for making sure that the memory allocated to garbage objects is released and available for further use.

get method the method that returns the value of an instance variable. Often such methods also initialize the variable or alter its value in some way. Also known as *accessor method*.

graphics context an object that describes the drawing parameters of a graphics device such as a screen or printer. These drawing parameters include such things as font, color, and line thickness.

graphics device an object representing the actual device, such as the screen or printer, that will display the results of a graphics operation.

graphics handle the attribute of a graphics medium that references a host-supplied resource. When this attribute references such a host resource, the graphics medium is said to be open. When the graphics handle is nil, the graphics medium is said to be closed.

graphics medium a grid of pixels that is the destination for graphics operations. Such a grid of pixels is usually a portion of the screen or a portion of a printable page.

grid 1. the height, measured in pixels, of a single selection in a list component. **2.** the overlay for a canvas that establishes the granularity by which components are positioned within that canvas.

group box a *VisualWorks* passive component that displays itself as a box—with or without a label. It is hollow in nature in that a point within its interior is not considered part of the group box; only points that are actually on the line or label are considered part of the box.

handle a small black square that appears in the corners of a selected component to indicate that that component is currently selected. The handle also provides the developer with the means to distinguish between an intended drag operation and an intended resize operation. In *VisualWorks*, handles are implemented by the DragHandle class.

handle an event to respond to an event such that the event is no longer required and can be marked as garbage.

hook 1. a method defined in a superclass with the expectation that the subclasses may reimplement the method. The intention is to grant the subclasses access into a thread of execution defined in the superclass. **2.** a block defined in a class with the expectation that the instances may redefine the block. The intention is to grant the instances access into a thread of execution defined in the class.

host the hardware platform, operating system, and windowing system running the *VisualWorks* image. Also loosely referred to as *host platform, host window environment,* and *host window manager,* although technically these terms can be distinguished from one another.

hot spot the one pixel on a cursor that is used to determine the cursor's exact location on the screen.

icon 1. a bitmap which, in most window environments, is used to represent a collapsed or minimized window. **2.** an instance of Icon.

image an instance of a subclass of Image used as a bitmap in *ParcPlace\Smalltalk.*

implementation method a method defined in a look policy class that returns either a type or instance of some object used in constructing a *VisualWorks* component.

indicator menu item a menu item that can be checked or unchecked by the user to represent a boolean condition. Such a menu item can also be associated with a value model that maintains the item's current boolean state.

input field a *VisualWorks* active component that allows a user to enter a single line of data such as a string, number, or date.

instance an object whose state and behavior is described in its class.

interested object an object that registers interest in the value of a value model and expects to receive a specific change message whenever the value changes.

interface spec see *full spec.*

invalid the state of a view that is in need of being redrawn because it no longer accurately reflects the information in its model or its visual representation has become damaged in some way.

keyboard consumer any *VisualWorks* active component that can handle keyboard events and take focus. The only active components that do not handle keyboard events are menu buttons and sliders.

keyboard event an instance of KeyboardEvent, it represents a keyboard key press.

keyboard focus see *focus.*

keyboard hook an optional block defined for a keyboard processor or a widget that gets first crack at handling any keyboard events destined for the corresponding window or component, respectively.

keyboard processor an instance of KeyboardProcessor that manages the distribution of keyboard events for a single window. It is also responsible for managing the set of keyboard consumers and determining which one is the current keyboard consumer.

label 1. a *VisualWorks* passive component that displays a label or any visual component. **2.** the title of a window that appears in the window's title bar.

layout an object used to position a component within its container, which is usually a window or composite. The types of layout object are Point, Rectangle, LayoutOrigin, LayoutFrame, and AlignmentOrigin.

lazy dependency a boolean attribute of an AspectAdaptor that determines if the AspectAdaptor should forward updates from its subject to its dependents.

lazy initialization when one or more of an object's instance variables are not initialized in an initialization method, but instead are initialized in the accessing method when accessed for the first time.

lazy instantiation see *lazy initialization*.

line height the height, measured in pixels, of a single line of text. Also known as *line grid*.

list a *VisualWorks* active component that displays a sequenceable collection of objects in a scrolling list from which the user can select some subset.

literal a piece of source code converted immediately into an object by the compiler. This includes strings, numbers, booleans, dates, and arrays.

literal array an array whose elements are all literal objects. Such arrays are used by *VisualWorks* to store interface-related objects as the source code of a method.

look policy an instance of some subclass of UILookPolicy used to determine the platform-specific look and feel of a user interface.

look preferences an instance of LookPreferences used to describe the color scheme of a window or interface component.

lower to place a window behind all other windows.

major key a Symbol attribute of a subcanvas spec that names the class of application model that will serve as the subapplication for a subcanvas component.

master window a window that, when it collapses, expands, or closes, causes any corresponding partner or slave windows to collapse, expand, or close as well. A master window has complete control over its partner and slave windows and is itself not controlled by any other windows.

menu a user interface device that prompts the user with several selections. The three basic types of menus are pop-up menu, drop-down menu, and menu bar. In *VisualWorks*, menu behavior is described by an instance of Menu.

menu bar one of the three types of menus, it is permanently displayed at the top of a window and its selections are aligned horizontally.

menu button a *VisualWorks* active component that by default displays itself as a button but, when pressed, displays a menu as either a pop-up or drop-down. The menu selection is used to set the value of a value model.

menu item an instance of Menu, it is an object that describes the selection of a menu including the label and what action is to be taken when that selection is made.

message a request sent to an object to have it execute one of its methods.

message selector a Symbol that is the name of a message or method. It is used to select which method will be executed as a result of a message send.

meta going beyond or transcending. This modifier is used quite a bit in Smalltalk terminology, but it is not always used consistently or correctly.

meta class the class of a class object, it is written as the class name followed by the qualifying term *class*. Since each class object is unique, it is also the only member of its meta class. Each meta class is also an object and an instance of MetaClass. For example, the class Model is the only instance of its meta class Model class, and Model class is an instance of MetaClass.

meta data data used to describe other data. A class is often considered meta data because it is the description of an object.

meta event an event that concerns a window operation and is usually expressed as an Association.

meta key a keyboard key that by itself does not create a keyboard event. Such keys include the <Shift> key and the <Ctrl> key.

meta tool a tool for building other tools including itself. Both *VisualWorks* and Smalltalk are meta tools.

method 1. the description of the behavior that is to transpire as a result of sending a message to an object. **2.** similar to a function or subroutine in other programming languages.

minor key a Symbol attribute of a subcanvas spec that names the class method that describes the interface to be used as the subcanvas component.

modal the characteristic of a window such that it handles all user input and blocks all other windows from receiving input until it is closed.

modal controller a controller that uses a control mode object to determine how user input will be handled in a given situation. The modal controller has a different type of control mode object for each mode of operation (selecting, dragging, stretching, etc.). UIPainterController is a paragon of modal controllers.

model part of the MVC triad, it is an object that manages information and usually has one or more objects that depend on that information to perform their functions. Whenever the model changes an aspect of its information, it can notify all of these dependent objects of the change by broadcasting an update message.

mouse event an event passed in from the host window manager as a result of the user manipulating the mouse—either moving it or pressing one of the buttons. In *ParcPlace\Smalltalk*, mouse events are not handled by the controllers as are keyboard events. Instead, mouse events are used to monitor the current state of the mouse.

mutator method see *put method*.

MVC model-view-controller, an approach to application development that divides the application into the information of interest (model), the visual representation of that information (view), and the handling of user input (controller).

named component a *VisualWorks* component that is uniquely identified within a window or subcanvas by a developer-assigned Symbol. This Symbol is referred to as the *component name* or *component ID*.

normal decoration window decoration that includes a frame, title bar, and all the necessary control buttons for manipulating the window. Normal decoration is used for non-modal application windows.

notebook a *VisualWorks* active component that emulates a notebook with page tabs where each page is implemented as a subcanvas.

notification message a predetermined message sent by a dispatcher to the application model notifying the application model of a change of focus, change of value, or double click.

object 1. an instance of a class. **2.** the fundamental building block of an object-oriented programming language. **3.** the binding of data and behavior into a single cohesive unit.

object engine see *virtual machine*.

open when a window or any other display surface is associated with a host resource and can therefore appear on the screen and perform graphics operations.

<operate> the middle button of a three-button mouse, usually used for displaying the <operate> menu. Also known as the *<yellow>* button.

<operate> menu a pop-up menu displayed when the user presses the <operate> mouse button. The menu items are context sensitive in that each component within the window can have its own version of this menu.

origin the upper lefthand corner of a Rectangle object.

painter watcher any of the *VisualWorks* tools interested in the current selection of the current canvas. All such tools inherit the necessary state and behavior from the abstract class UIPainterWatcher.

parent application an application model that contains other application models as subapplications or child applications.

parent window a window that spawns other windows as its children to perform related functions. A parent window is usually a master window.

partner window a window that, when it collapses, expands, or closes, causes any corresponding partner or slave windows to collapse, expand, or close as well. A partner window can control a partner or slave window but is itself controlled by a master window or another partner window.

passive component 1. a *VisualWorks* component that does not interact with the user and whose widget is not a view. **2.** a visual component that does not specify a container.

performer an attribute of the controller, it is the object that fields the message selectors from an <operate> menu. The performer is initialized to be the controller, however, it is often reassigned to be a model.

persistent window a window that is expected to be open for comparatively long time.

pop-up menu one of the three types of menus, it pops up centered around the cursor and displays menu items in a vertical column. The <operate> menu and <window> menu are both pop-up menus.

pop-up decoration window decoration that does not include any frame or title bar, i.e., pop-up decoration is no decoration. Pop-up decoration is used for pop-up and drop-down menus.

postbuild operation the behavior of an application model that immediately follows the builder's construction of the interface but precedes the actual opening of the window. It is the application model's opportunity to make any last-minute manipulations of the user interface.

postcopy the copying activity that takes place after a shallow copy and determines the actual depth of the copy process.

postopen operation the behavior of an application model that immediately follows the opening of the window. Application models that open windows have postopen operations, application models that construct subcanvases, however, do not.

prebuild operation the behavior of an application model that immediately precedes the builder's construction of the interface. It is the application model's opportunity to modify the builder before it constructs the user interface.

preferred bounds the bounds, or real estate, that a visual component would like to have within its window or container.

primary selection in a canvas, the one component of several selected components that provides a frame of reference for certain canvas-editing operations such as aligning and sizing.

process an event to convert an event from one type to another (such as a Smalltalk event into a KeyboardEvent), to store or queue an event, or to dispatch it to some other object.

print string a string used to represent an object—especially in the Debugger and Inspector. Each object's print string is accessed by sending printString to the object.

protocol 1. a group of messages or methods that can be logically grouped into a category. **2.** the group of methods organized under the same method category within a class description.

put method a single keyword method that reassigns an instance variable to the value of the argument. Sometimes the argument is changed before the actual assignment (e.g., converting a number argument to a float). Also know as *mutator method*.

radio button a *VisualWorks* active component that allows a user to make a single selection out of many labeled selections. Unlike other components, a radio button necessarily works in conjunction with other radio buttons in a set in order to assure that only one of the set is selected at any given time.

raise to make a window rest on top of all other windows and become the active window.

refresh to redraw all or part of a window.

region a *VisualWorks* passive component that appears as a rectangle or an oval and has a border and a colored background.

register as a dependent to become a dependent of a model in order to respond to update messages broadcasted by that model when it changes.

register interest to create a DependencyTransformer that will register as a dependent of a value model and send a predetermined message to an interested object whenever the value model changes value.

relative layout a component layout that determines a component's location and/or dimensions to be some fraction of the container's dimensions.

resource 1. an object that is necessary for building a user interface according to specifications. Resources include such things as menus, icons, labels, aspect models, and widgets for arbitrary components. Resources can be either static or dynamic. **2.** an object supplied by the host window environment such as a font or graphics medium.

right indent the righthand margin, measured in pixels, of a paragraph of text.

root object the Smalltalk dictionary that acts as the single access point to all other objects in the virtual image. Any object not accessible from the root object is available for garbage collection.

rubberbanding the technique of continually drawing an outline whose dimensions are determined by the movement of the mouse. The visual effect is to give the appearance that the user is stretching a rubber band.

runtime mode when a *VisualWorks* interface is opened for its intended use in an application as opposed to being opened for visual editing.

satellite window see *child window.*

schedule to open a window and register its controller with ScheduledControllers.

second indent the lefthand margin, measured in pixels, of each line of text in a paragraph except for the first.

<select> the left button of a three-button mouse. This button is typically used to make selections, hence its name. Also known as the *<red>* button.

<select> menu a pop-up menu displayed when the user presses the <select> mouse button. <select> menus are quite rare, since the <select> button is used primarily for such things as selecting and dragging.

selector see *message selector.*

sensor an attribute of a controller, it gives the controller access to mouse and keyboard input.

shallow copy 1. a copy of an object that shares all of its information with the original, that is, the instance variables of the original and the instance variables of the copy reference the same objects. **2.** the first part of the copy process in which the copy is actually instantiated. At this point the copy consists only of an object header and a new set of instance variables, but the objects referenced by these instance variables are the same as those referenced by the original object.

shifting focus when the keyboard processor takes focus away from the current keyboard consumer and gives focus to the next keyboard consumer in the tab order. Also called *changing focus.*

short-cut key a keyboard key that triggers a menu item action. Also called *hot key* or *accelerator key.*

slave window a window that closes, expands, and collapses according to the whims of a partner or master window.

slider a *VisualWorks* active component that allows the user to set some fraction of an interval by sliding a scroll like handle along a single axis.

slice a subset of a component spec's attributes that are displayed and edited in a single page of the Properties Tool.

Smalltalk event an array of 16 elements used to represent a host-formatted event in the virtual image.

source the object that supplies a builder with the necessary resources for building an interface according to spec. A source is always an application model, because the Application-Model class defines the necessary resource accessing protocol used by the builder.

spawn to open a canvas-editing session that is an exact copy of the current canvas-editing session with respect to components in the canvas, target, selector, and grid settings.

spec an object that is used to describe some piece of a user interface, such as a window, input field, or check box. All specs share the abstract superclass UISpecification. All spec objects have a literal array representation, and such literal arrays can be used to create a copy of the original spec object.

spec generation block a block that evaluates to an instance of a component spec and is used to determine how a component will first appear when dropped into a canvas by a developer.

spec object see *spec.*

spec collection an instance of SpecCollection and a collection of one or more component specs. It is used to describe all of the components that will inhabit a window or subcanvas.

spec wrapper a *VisualWorks* component and an instance of SpecWrapper.

state 1. the data associated with an object. **2.** the instance variables of an object.

static resource a resource that is not expected to change during runtime. Such resources are usually provided by an application model class method but can be provided by an instance method. The method typically creates a new instance of the static resource with each access.

stock dialog any one of several predefined dialogs opened by sending a single message to the class Dialog.

store string a string that represents an object such that when the string is compiled as Smalltalk code, a copy of the object is instantiated.

subapplication the application model that manages a subcanvas. Also known as *subenvironment.*

subbuilder an instance of UIBuilder that builds all of the components defined in a subcanvas. The subbuilder's source is the subapplication running the subcanvas. The subbuilder shares the builder's look policy, keyboard processor, and window.

subcanvas a *VisualWorks* user interface defined by an application model and used as a *VisualWorks* component. The application model serves as the aspect model for such a component.

subcanvas technology the feature of *VisualWorks* that allows an entire window interface, including all behaviors, to be reused as the component of another window interface.

subenvironment see *subapplication*.

subject the object that contains the value for a value model. For an AspectAdaptor object, the subject is any arbitrary object and the value is accessed with specific access selectors. For a BufferedValueHolder object, the subject is necessarily another value model and the value is accessed using value model protocol.

subject channel a value model that contains the subject for an AspectAdaptor.

submenu a menu displayed as a result of selecting an item in another menu.

subspec a spec object that is actually an attribute of another spec object. Normally a spec object's attributes are literal objects, such as a strings, numbers, Symbols, and booleans. The subspec allows a more complex structure.

symbolic paint an instance of SymbolicPaint used to map a color role such as background or foreground to an actual color value such as blue or gray. This mapping is determined by the current look preferences. All components display themselves using symbolic paints. This guarantees that the foreground parts will be drawn in the current foreground color, the background parts will be drawn in the current background color, etc.

tab chain see *tab order*.

tab order the order in which components take focus in a window as a result of tab events. Also known as *tab chain*.

table a *VisualWorks* active component that displays a two-dimensional pick list in tabular format and allows the user to select a row, column, or cell.

target the object that contains the value of interest to an AspectAdaptor. By default the target is the subject. The target could be contained by the subject, however, in which case the aspect adaptor needs to know how to traverse the subject's object structure in order to obtain the target.

target window the window that is the destination of an event passed in by the window manager.

text an instance of Text that consists of a string and a formating object indicating the font, emphasis, etc., of how that string is to be displayed.

text editor a *VisualWorks* active component that allows the user to enter an arbitrary amount of formated text and operates much like a simple word processor.

text widget any of the widgets that display and edit text, such as input fields, combo boxes, and text editors.

top component the root node in a visual component tree, which is always a window.

top model a parent application model, which itself does not have a parent and serves as the root in a network of application models.

traditional application development the approach to application development used prior to *VisualWorks* that employed the classical MVC architecture.

transient window a window that is expected to have a very short duration on the screen. Usually used for pop-up menus.

trigger channel an attribute of a BufferedValueHolder. If the value of this attribute becomes true, then the information in the buffer is forwarded to the subject. If it becomes false, then the information is flushed from the buffer.

type-in point the point at which characters are added to a line of text. It is usually marked with a small triangle, square, or line.

unbounded layout a component layout that does not constrain the component's x and y dimensions in any way and whose dimensions are set according to the requirements of the component.

unmappable surface any display surface that does screenlike graphics (as opposed to printer graphics) but exists only in memory and is never displayed directly on the screen. Mask objects and Pixmap objects are the two most common unmappable surfaces.

update protocol the update messages update:, update:with:, and update:with:from:, which a model broadcasts to all of its dependents whenever it wants to notify them of an internal change.

validation message a predetermined message sent by a dispatcher object to the application model requesting a change of focus, change of value, or double click. The return value is a boolean used to grant or refuse the request.

value model a model whose primary aspect of information is called its value and which responds to value model protocol. A value model is often used to provide model behavior for a nonmodel type of object. Another use is to provide a channel for a value. The class ValueHolder provides the purest implementation of the value model concept.

value model protocol the messages value and value:. This has become the standard means of communication in *VisualWorks*, especially communication with models.

view 1. a part of the MVC triad, it is the overall visual presentation of a model's information. **2.** a kind of visual part, which has both a model and a controller and provides a visual interpretation for a model. Such view behavior is defined in the abstract class View.

view/controller pair a view and a controller that work in tandem to provide the complete user interface for a model.

view holder see *arbitrary component*.

virtual image the set of all objects that constitute the Smalltalk environment. The virtual image exists as a file between Smalltalk sessions and is loaded into the host machine's memory whenever the virtual machine is executed. The virtual image is binary compatible across all platforms running *ParcPlace\Smalltalk*.

virtual machine the executable program that runs in the host environment and combines with the virtual image to constitute the Smalltalk environment. The virtual machine is not binary compatible across platforms, and it is compiled in the host's native machine language. Also known as the *object engine*.

visual block a block that evaluates to a visual component. Visual blocks are used primarily by list and table components to give a graphical representation to the elements they display.

visual component any object that can display itself on a window's display surface and responds to visual component protocol. VisualComponent is the abstract superclass for all visual component objects.

visual component protocol the set of messages all visual components respond to including displayOn: and preferredBounds. This protocol is defined in the abstract class VisualComponent.

visual component tree see *visual structure*.

visual part a kind of visual component that knows about its container. This behavior is defined in the abstract class VisualPart.

visual properties protocol the set of messages that concern a window's or visual component's color scheme (look preferences).

visual structure the network of interconnected visual components responsible for filling the display surface of a window. Also known as *visual component tree*.

VisualWorks component 1. the fundamental building block of a *VisualWorks* interface including such things as input fields, action buttons, and lists. **2.** an instance of SpecWrapper.

VisualWorks component protocol the set of messages that all *VisualWorks* components understand, such as moveTo:, label:, and disable. Most of this protocol is defined in SpecWrapper and its superclass WidgetWrapper.

widget a visual part contained by a SpecWrapper, it is the widget that gives a *VisualWorks* component its visual appearance.

widget controller the controller of a view that serves as the widget for a *VisualWorks* component. Some examples are TriggerButtonController and SequenceController.

widget policy an object governing how non-*VisualWorks* buttons will be drawn in a window.

widget protocol the set of methods that widgets understand (not all widgets respond to the entire set of widget protocol).

widget state an instance of WidgetState, it is an object used to describe the current state of a widget such as its color scheme, if it is disabled, and if it has a border.

window 1. the fundamental interface of a windowing environment. **2.** an instance of ScheduledWindow or ApplicationWindow.

<window> the right button of a three-button mouse. It is usually used to pop up a menu pertaining to window operations—hence its name. Also known as the *<blue>* button.

window event block a block defined by an ApplicationWindow that gets first crack at handling any meta events targeted for that window.

<window> menu a pop-up menu displayed when the user presses the <window> mouse button. The menu items pertain to window operations such as closing, resizing, and collapsing.

window spec a spec object that describes the attributes of a window. Such attributes include color, size, and label.

wrapper a visual part that contains another visual component. The wrapper provides certain services to the underlying component, such as translation of coordinates and scrolling. A *VisualWorks* component is actually a wrapper—an instance of SpecWrapper.